D1713432

HANDBOOK OF LOGIC IN COMPUTER SCIENCE

Editors

S. Abramsky, Dov M. Gabbay, and T. S. E. Maibaum

HANDBOOKS OF LOGIC IN COMPUTER SCIENCE
and
ARTIFICIAL INTELLIGENCE AND LOGIC PROGRAMMING

Executive Editor
Dov M. Gabbay

Administrator
Jane Spurr

Handbook of Logic in Computer Science

Volume 1 Background: Mathematical structures
Volume 2 Background: Computational structures
Volume 3 Semantic structures
Volume 4 Semantic modelling
Volume 5 Theoretical methods in specification and verification
Volume 6 Logical methods in computer science

Handbook of Logic in Artificial Intelligence and Logic Programming

Volume 1 Logical foundations
Volume 2 Deduction methodologies
Volume 3 Nonmonotonic reasoning and uncertain reasoning
Volume 4 Epistemic and temporal reasoning
Volume 5 Logic programming

Handbook of Logic in Computer Science

Volume 2

Background: Computational Structures

Edited by

S. ABRAMSKY
Professor of Computing Science

DOV M. GABBAY
Professor of Computing Science

and

T. S. E. MAIBAUM
Professor of Foundations of Software Engineering

Imperial College of Science, Technology and Medicine
London

Volume Co-ordinator

DOV M. GABBAY

CLARENDON PRESS · OXFORD
1992

Oxford University Press, Walton Street, Oxford OX2 6DP
Oxford New York Toronto
Delhi Bombay Calcutta Madras Karachi
Petaling Jaya Singapore Hong Kong Tokyo
Nairobi Dar es Salaam Cape Town
Melbourne Auckland
and associated companies in
Berlin Ibadan

Oxford is a trade mark of Oxford University Press

Published in the United States
by Oxford University Press, New York

A catalogue record for this book is available from the British Library

Library of Congress Cataloging in Publication Data
Handbook of logic in computer science / edited by S. Abramsky, Dov M. Gabbay, and T. S. E. Maibaum.
v. 2
Contents: — v. 2. Background, computational structures.
1. Computer science. 2. Logic, Symbolic and mathematical.
I. Abramsky, S. II. Gabbay, Dov M., 1945– . III. Maibaum, Thomas S. E., 1947– . QA76.H2785 1992 92–510

ISBN 0–19–853761–1

Typeset by the authors
using TEX
Printed and bound in
Great Britain by Biddles Ltd.,
Guildford and Kings Lynn

Preface

We are happy to present the first volumes of the *Handbook of Logic in Computer Science.* Logic is now widely recognized to be one of the foundational disciplines of computing and has found applications in virtually all aspects of the subject, from software engineering and hardware to programming language and artificial intelligence. There is a growing need for an in-depth survey of the application of logic in computer science and AI. The *Handbook of Logic in Computer Science* and its companion, the *Handbook of Logic in Artificial Intelligence and Logic Programming* have been created in response to this need.

We see the creation of the Handbook as a combination of authoritative exposition, comprehensive survey, and fundamental research exploring the underlying unifying themes in the various areas. The intended audience is graduate students and researchers in the areas of computing and logic, as well as other people interested in the subject. We assume as background some mathematical sophistication. Much of the material will also be of interest to logicians and mathematicians.

The tables of contents of the volumes were finalized after extensive discussions between handbook authors and second readers. The first two volumes present the background logic and mathematics extensively used in computer science. The point of view is application oriented. The other four volumes present major areas in which the methods are used. These include Volume 3 — Semantic Structures; Volume 4 — Semantic Modelling; Volume 5 — Specification and Verification; and Volume 6 — Logical Methods.

The chapters, which in many cases are of monographic length and scope, are written with emphasis on possible unifying themes. The chapters have an overview, introduction, and a main body. A final part is dedicated to more specialized topics.

Chapters are written by internationally renowned researchers in the respective areas. The chapters are co-ordinated and their contents were discussed in joint meetings.

Each chapter has been written using the following procedures:

1. A very detailed table of contents was discussed and co-ordinated at several meetings between authors and editors of related chapters. The discussion was in the form of a series of lectures by the authors to everyone present. Once an agreement was reached on the detailed table of contents the authors wrote a draft and sent it to the editors and to other related authors. For each chapter there is a second reader (the first reader is the author) whose job it has been to scrutinize the

chapter together with the editors. The second reader's role is very important and has required effort and serious involvement with the authors.
Second readers for this volume are:
Chapter 1: Term Rewriting Systems — J.-J. Levy
Chapter 2: Lambda Calculus — R. Hindley
Chapter 3: Algorithmic Proof Systems — R. Milner
Chapter 4: Designing a Theorem Prover — R. Milner
Chapter 5: Modal and Temporal Logics — A. Pneuli and R. Turner.

2. Once this process was completed (i.e. drafts seen and read by a large enough group of authors), there were other meetings on several chapters in which authors lectured on their chapters and faced the criticism of the editors and audience. The final drafts were prepared after these meetings.

3. We attached great importance to group effort and co-ordination in the writing of chapters. The first two parts of each chapter, namely the Introduction–Overview and Main Body, are not completely under the discretion of the author, as he/she had to face the general criticism of all the other authors. Only the third part of the chapter is entirely for the authors' own tastes and preferences.

The Handbook meetings were generously financed by OUP, by SERC contract SO/809/86, by the Department of Computing at Imperial College, and by several anonymous private donations.

We would like to thank our colleagues, authors, second readers, and students for their effort and professionalism in producing the manuscripts for the Handbook. We would particularly like to thank the staff of OUP for their continued and enthusiastic support, and Mrs Jane Spurr, our OUP Administrator for her dedication and efficiency.

London The Editors
May 1992

Contents

Term rewriting systems

Lambda calculi with types

Elements of algorithmic proof

Designing a theorem prover

Modal and temporal logics

Term Rewriting Systems

J. W. Klop[1]

Contents

Abstract

Term rewriting systems (TRSs) play an important role in various areas, such as abstract data type specifications, implementations of functional programming languages and automated deduction. In this chapter we introduce several of the basic concepts and facts for TRSs. Specifically, we discuss abstract reduction systems; general TRSs including an account of Knuth–Bendix completion and (E-)unification; orthogonal TRSs and reduction strategies; strongly sequential orthogonal TRSs. The paper concludes with a discussion of conditional term rewriting systems. The em-

[1]Research partially supported by ESPRIT project 432: Meteor (until Sept. 1989) and ESPRIT BRA projects 3020: Integration and 3074: Semagraph (since July 1989).

phasis throughout the chapter is on providing information of a syntactic nature.

1 Introduction

The concept of a term rewriting system (TRS) is paradigmatic for the study of computational procedures. Already half a century ago, the λ-calculus, probably the most well-known TRS, played a crucial role in mathematical logic with respect to formalizing the notion of computability; much later the same TRS figured in the fundamental work of Scott, Plotkin and others, leading to a break-through in the denotational semantics of programming languages. More recently, the related system of combinatory logic was shown to be a very fruitful tool for the implementation of functional languages. Even more recently another related family of TRSs, that of categorical combinatory logic, has emerged, yielding a remarkable connection between concepts from category theory and elementary steps in machine computations.

Term rewriting systems are attractive because of their simple syntax and semantics—at least those TRSs that do not involve bound variables such as λ-calculus, but involve the rewriting of terms from a first-order language. This simplicity facilitates a satisfactory mathematical analysis. On the other hand they provide a natural medium for implementing computations, and in principle even for parallel computations. This feature makes TRSs interesting for the design of parallel reduction machines.

Another field where TRSs play a fundamental role concerns the analysis and implementation of abstract data type specifications (consistency properties, computability theory, decidability of word problems, theorem proving).

The aim of the present paper is to give an introduction to several key concepts in the theory of term rewriting, providing where possible some of the details. At various places some 'exercises' are included. These contain additional information for which proofs are relatively easy; they are not primarily meant to have an educational purpose, if only because the distribution of the exercises is not very uniform.

The present introduction starts at a level of 'rewriting' which is as abstract as possible and proceeds by considering term rewriting systems which have ever more 'structure'. Thus we start with abstract reduction systems, which are no more than sets equipped with some binary ('rewrite') relations. A number of basic properties and facts can already be stated on this level.

Subsequently, the abstract reductions are specialized to reductions (rewritings) of terms. For such general TRSs a key issue is to prove the termination property; we present one of the major and most powerful termination proof methods, recursive path orderings, in a new formulation designed to facilitate human understanding (rather than practical implementation). Proving termination is of great importance in the area of Knuth–Bendix completions. Here one is concerned, given an equational specification, to construct a TRS which is both confluent and terminating and which proves the same equations as the original specification. If the construction is successful, it yields a positive solution to the validity problem of the original equational specification. (Nowadays there are also several other applications of Knuth–Bendix-like completion methods, such as 'inductionless induction' and 'computing with equations'. For a survey of such applications we refer to [Dershowitz and Jouannaud, 1990].)

Also in Section 2, we explain the basic ideas of Knuth–Bendix completion together with an interesting recent 'abstract' approach of [Bachmair *et al.*, 1986] to prove the correctness of Knuth–Bendix completion algorithms. We also present an elegant unification algorithm, and likewise for 'E-unification'.

In Section 3 we impose more 'structure' on TRSs, in the form of an 'orthogonality' requirement (non-ambiguity and left-linearity). For such orthogonal TRSs a sizeable amount of theory has been developed, both syntactically and semantically. Here we will almost exclusively be concerned with the syntactical aspects; for semantical aspects we refer to [Boudol, 1985], [Berry and Lévy, 1979] , [Guessarian, 1981]. Basic theorems (confluence, the parallel moves lemma, Church's theorem, O'Donnell's theorem) are presented, where possible with some proof sketch. Also in this section we survey the most important facts concerning reduction strategies for orthogonal TRSs, strategies aiming at finding normal forms whenever possible. Section 3 concludes with an explanation of the beautiful theory of [Huet and Lévy, 1979] of (strongly) sequential TRSs. Such TRSs possess a 'good' reduction strategy.

In the final section (4) we consider TRSs with conditional rewrite rules.

Some important topics have not found their way into this introduction. Most notable are: rewriting modulo a set of equations, proof-by-consistency procedures, and graph rewriting. For information about the first two we refer to [Bachmair, 1988] and [Dershowitz and Jouannaud, 1990] (1990), for graph rewriting one may consult [Barendregt *et al.*, 1987].

This chapter is an extension of the short survey/tutorial [Klop, 1987]; also most of the material in [Klop, 1985] is included here.

2 Abstract reduction systems

Many of the basic definitions for and properties of term rewriting systems (TRSs) can be stated more abstractly, viz. for sets equipped with one or more binary relations. As it is instructive to see which definitions and properties depend on the term structure and which are more basic, we start with a section about abstract reduction systems. Moreover, the concepts and properties of abstract reduction systems also apply to other rewrite systems than TRSs, such as string rewrite systems (Thue systems), tree rewrite systems, graph grammars. First we present a sequence of simple definitions.

Definition 2.0.1.

1. An *abstract reduction system* (ARS) is a structure $\mathcal{A} = \langle A, (\rightarrow_\alpha)_{\alpha \in I}\rangle$ consisting of a set A and a sequence of binary relations $\rightarrow_\alpha$ on A, also called reduction or rewrite relations. Sometimes we will refer to $\rightarrow_\alpha$ as α. In the case of just one reduction relation, we also use $\rightarrow$ without more. (An ARS with just one reduction relation is called a 'replacement system' in [Staples, 1975], and a 'transformation system' in [Jantzen, 1988].) If for $a, b \in A$ we have $(a, b) \in \rightarrow_\alpha$, we write $a \rightarrow_\alpha b$ and call b a one-step (α-)*reduct* of a.
2. The transitive reflexive closure of $\rightarrow_\alpha$ is written as $\twoheadrightarrow_\alpha$. (More customary is the notation $\rightarrow^*_\alpha$, but we prefer the double arrow notation as we find it more convenient in diagrams.) So $a \twoheadrightarrow_\alpha b$ if there is a possibly empty, finite sequence of 'reduction steps' $a \equiv a_0 \rightarrow_\alpha a_1 \rightarrow_\alpha \cdots \rightarrow_\alpha a_n \equiv b$. Here $\equiv$ denotes identity of elements of A. The element b is called an (α-)reduct of a. The equivalence relation generated by $\rightarrow_\alpha$ is $=_\alpha$, also called the *convertibility* relation generated by $\rightarrow_\alpha$. The reflexive closure of $\rightarrow_\alpha$ is $\rightarrow^{\equiv}_\alpha$. The transitive closure of $\rightarrow_\alpha$ is $\rightarrow^+_\alpha$. The converse relation of $\rightarrow_\alpha$ is $\leftarrow_\alpha$ or $\rightarrow^{-1}_\alpha$. The union $\rightarrow_\alpha \cup \rightarrow_\beta$ is denoted by $\rightarrow_{\alpha\beta}$. The composition $\rightarrow_\alpha \circ \rightarrow_\beta$ is defined by: $a \rightarrow_\alpha \circ \rightarrow_\beta b$ if $a \rightarrow_\alpha c \rightarrow_\beta b$ for some $c \in A$.
3. If α, β are reduction relations on A, we say that α *commutes weakly* with β if the diagram of Figure 2.1a holds, i.e. if $\forall a, b, c \in A\, \exists d \in A\, (c \leftarrow_\beta a \rightarrow_\alpha b \Rightarrow c \twoheadrightarrow_\alpha d \twoheadleftarrow_\beta b)$, or in a shorter notation: $\leftarrow_\beta \circ \rightarrow_\alpha \subseteq \twoheadrightarrow_\alpha \circ \twoheadleftarrow_\beta$. Further, α *commutes* with β if $\twoheadrightarrow_\alpha$ and $\twoheadrightarrow_\beta$ commute weakly. (This terminology differs from that of [Bachmair and Dershowitz, 1986], where α commutes with β if $\alpha^{-1} \circ \beta \subseteq \beta^{-1} \circ \alpha$.)
4. The reduction relation $\rightarrow$ is called *weakly confluent* or *weakly Church–Rosser* (WCR) if it is weakly self-commuting (see Figure 2.1b), i.e. if $\forall a, b, c \in A\, \exists d \in A\, (c \leftarrow a \rightarrow b \Rightarrow c \twoheadrightarrow d \twoheadleftarrow b)$. (The property WCR is also often called 'local confluence', e.g. in [Jantzen, 1988].)

5. $\to$ is *subcommutative* (notation $\mathrm{WCR}^{\leq 1}$) if the diagram in Figure 2.1c holds, i.e. if $\forall a, b, c \in A\, \exists d \in A\, (c \leftarrow a \to b \Rightarrow c \to^{\equiv} d \leftarrow^{\equiv} b)$.

6. $\to$ is *confluent* or is *Church–Rosser*, has the Church-Rosser property (CR) if it is self-commuting (see Figure 2.1d), i.e. $\forall a, b, c \in A\, \exists d \in A\, (c \twoheadleftarrow a \twoheadrightarrow b \Rightarrow c \twoheadrightarrow d \twoheadleftarrow b)$. Sometimes (6) is called 'confluent' and the situation as in Proposition 2.0.2(6) 'Church–Rosser'.

Proposition 2.0.2. *The following are equivalent:*

1. $\to$ *is confluent*
2. $\twoheadrightarrow$ *is weakly confluent*
3. $\twoheadrightarrow$ *is self-commuting*
4. $\twoheadrightarrow$ *is subcommutative*
5. *the diagram in Figure 2.1e holds, i.e.*

$$\forall a, b, c \in A\, \exists d \in A\, (c \leftarrow a \twoheadrightarrow b \Rightarrow c \twoheadrightarrow d \twoheadleftarrow b)$$

6. $\forall a, b \in A\, \exists c \in A\, (a = b \Rightarrow a \twoheadrightarrow c \twoheadleftarrow b)$ *(Here '=' is the convertibility relation generated by $\to$. See diagram in Figure 2.1f.)*

Definition 2.0.3. Let $\mathcal{A} = \langle A, \to \rangle$ be an ARS.

1. We say that $a \in A$ is a *normal form* if there is no $b \in A$ such that $a \to b$. Further, $b \in A$ *has a normal form* if $b \twoheadrightarrow a$ for some normal form $a \in A$.
2. The reduction relation $\to$ is *weakly normalizing* (WN) if every $a \in A$ has a normal form. In this case we also say that $\mathcal{A}$ is WN.
3. $\mathcal{A}$ (or $\to$) is *strongly normalizing* (SN) if every reduction sequence $a_0 \to a_1 \to \cdots$ eventually must terminate. (Other terminology: $\to$ is *terminating*, or *noetherian*.) If the converse reduction relation $\leftarrow$ is SN, we say that $\mathcal{A}$ (or $\to$) is SN^{-1}.
4. $\mathcal{A}$ (or $\to$) has the *unique normal form property* (UN) if $\forall a, b \in A(a = b$ & a, b are normal forms $\Rightarrow a \equiv b)$.
5. $\mathcal{A}$ (or $\to$) has the *normal form property* (NF) if $\forall a, b \in A(a$ is normal form & $a = b \Rightarrow b \twoheadrightarrow a)$.
6. $\mathcal{A}$ (or $\to$) is *inductive* (Ind) if for every reduction sequence (possibly infinite) $a_0 \to a_1 \to \cdots$ there is an $a \in A$ such that $a_n \twoheadrightarrow a$ for all n.
7. $\mathcal{A}$ (or $\to$) is *increasing* (Inc) if there is a map $|\ |: A \to \mathbb{N}$ such that $\forall a, b \in A\, (a \to b \Rightarrow |\, a\, | < |\, b\, |)$. Here $\mathbb{N}$ is the set of natural numbers with the usual ordering $<$.
8. $\mathcal{A}$ (or $\to$) is *finitely branching* (FB) if for all $a \in A$ the set of one-step reducts of a, $\{b \in A \mid a \to b\}$, is finite. If the converse reduction

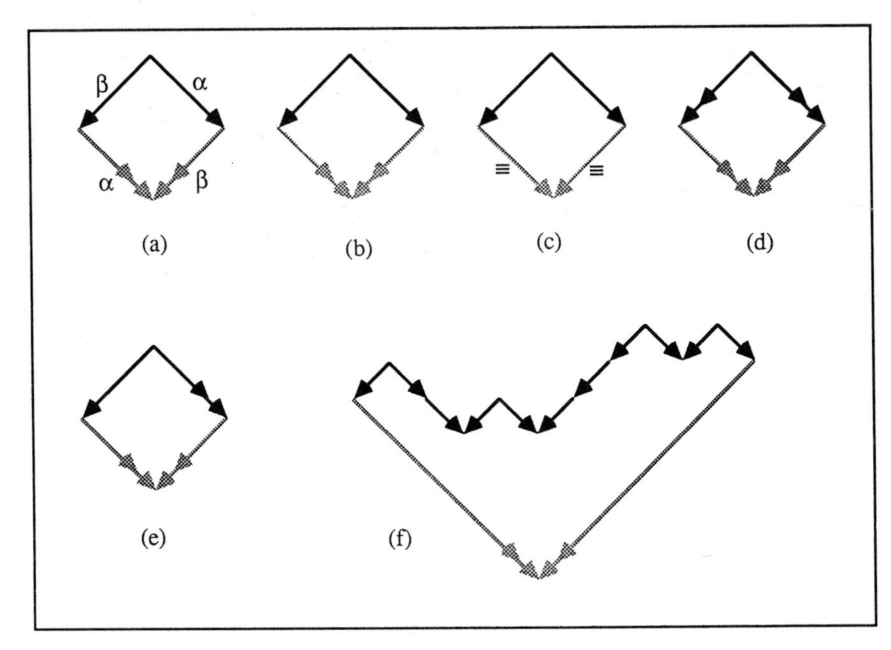

Figure 2.1

relation $\leftarrow$ is FB, we say that $\mathcal{A}$ (or $\rightarrow$) is FB^{-1}. (In [Huet, 1980], FB is called 'locally finite'.)

Exercise 2.0.4. Define: $\mathcal{A}$ (or $\rightarrow$) has the *unique normal form property with respect to reduction* ($\mathrm{UN}^{\rightarrow}$) if $\forall a, b, c \in A\,(a \twoheadrightarrow b \;\&\; a \twoheadrightarrow c \;\&\; b, c$ are normal forms $\Rightarrow b \equiv c)$. Show that $\mathrm{UN} \Rightarrow \mathrm{UN}^{\rightarrow}$, but not conversely.

An ARS which is confluent and terminating (CR & SN) is also called *complete* (other terminology: 'canonical' or 'uniquely terminating').

Before exhibiting several facts about all these notions, let us first introduce some more concepts.

Definition 2.0.5. Let $\mathcal{A} = \langle A, \rightarrow_\alpha \rangle$ and $\mathcal{B} = \langle B, \rightarrow_\beta \rangle$ be two ARSs. Then A is a *sub-ARS* of B, notation $\mathcal{A} \subseteq \mathcal{B}$, if:

1. $A \subseteq B$
2. α is the restriction of β to A, i.e. $\forall a, a' \in A\,(a \rightarrow_\beta a' \Leftrightarrow a \rightarrow_\alpha a')$
3. A is closed under β, i.e. $\forall a \in A\,(a \rightarrow_\beta b \Rightarrow b \in A)$.

The ARS $\mathcal{B}$ is also called an *extension* of $\mathcal{A}$.

Note that all properties introduced so far (CR, WCR, $\mathrm{WCR}^{\leq 1}$, WN, SN, UN, NF, Ind, Inc, FB) are preserved downwards: e.g. if $\mathcal{A} \subseteq \mathcal{B}$ and $\mathcal{B}$

is CR, then also $\mathcal{A}$ is so.

Of particular interest is the sub-ARS determined by an element a in an ARS.

Definition 2.0.6. Let $\mathcal{A} = \langle A, \rightarrow \rangle$ be an ARS, and $a \in A$. Then $\mathcal{G}(a)$, the *reduction graph* of a, is the smallest sub-ARS of $\mathcal{A}$ containing a. So $\mathcal{G}(a)$ has as elements all reducts of a (including a itself) and is structured by the relation $\rightarrow$ restricted to this set of reducts.

We will now collect in one theorem several implications between the various properties of ARSs. The first part (1) is actually the main motivation for the concept of confluence: it guarantees unique normal forms, which is of course a desirable state of affairs in (implementations of) algebraic data type specifications. Apart from the fundamental implication CR $\Rightarrow$ UN, the most important fact is (2), also known as Newman's lemma. The property CP ('cofinality property') is defined in Exercise 2.0.8(13) below.

Theorem 2.0.7.

1. *CR $\Rightarrow$ NF $\Rightarrow$ UN*
2. *SN & WCR $\Rightarrow$ CR (Newman's lemma)*
3. *UN & WN $\Rightarrow$ CR*
4. *UN & WN $\Rightarrow$ Ind*
5. *Ind & Inc $\Rightarrow$ SN*
6. *WCR & WN & Inc $\Rightarrow$ SN*
7. *CR $\Leftrightarrow$ CP for countable ARSs.*

Most of the proofs of (1)–(7) are easy. For Newman's lemma a short proof is given in [Huet, 1980]; an alternative proof, illustrating the notion of 'proof ordering', is given in Section 2.5 (Exercise 2.5.4). Proposition (5) is from [Nederpelt, 1973]; (6) is proved in [Klop, 1980a]; for (7) see Exercise 2.0.8(13) below. The propositions in the statement of the theorem (and some more—for these see Exercises 2.0.8) are displayed also in Figure 2.2; here it is important whether an implication arrow points to the conjunction sign &, or to one of the conjuncts. Likewise for the tail of an implication arrow. (E.g. UN & WN $\Rightarrow$ Ind, SN & WCR $\Rightarrow$ UN & WN, Inc $\Rightarrow$ SN^{-1}, FB^{-1}& SN^{-1} $\Rightarrow$ Inc, CR $\Rightarrow$ UN but not CR $\Rightarrow$ UN & WN.)

It does not seem possible to reverse any of the arrows in this diagram of implications. An instructive counterexample to WCR $\Rightarrow$ CR is the TRS in Figure 2.3 (given by R. Hindley, see also [Huet, 1980]).

There are several other facts about ARSs which often are very helpful e.g. in proving properties of algebraic data type specifications. We present them in the form of the following series of Exercises 2.0.8. For an understanding of the sequel these additional facts are not necessary. Some proofs

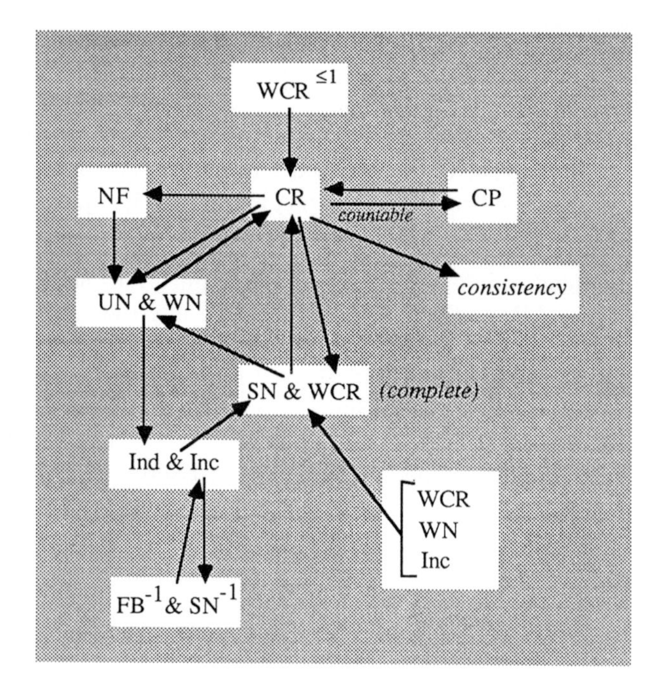

relations between properties of Abstract Reduction Systems

Figure 2.2

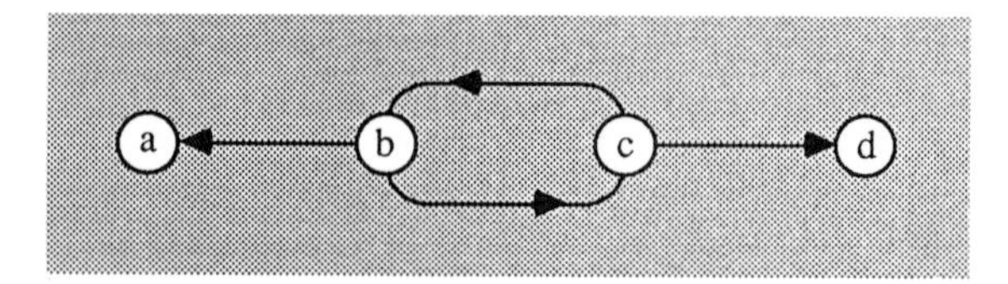

Figure 2.3

require the notion of 'multiset ordering', explained in Exercise 2.3.15.

Exercises 2.0.8.

1. [Rosen, 1973], If $\langle A, \to_1, \to_2 \rangle$ is an ARS such that $\twoheadrightarrow_1 = \twoheadrightarrow_2$ and $\to_1$ is subcommutative, then $\to_2$ is confluent.

2. [Hindley, 1964] Let $\langle A, (\to_\alpha)_{\alpha \in I} \rangle$ be an ARS such that for all $\alpha, \beta \in I, \to_\alpha$ commutes with $\to_\beta$. (In particular, $\to_\alpha$ commutes with itself.) Then the union $\to = \bigcup_{\alpha \in I} \to_\alpha$ is confluent. (This proposition is sometimes referred to as the Lemma of Hindley–Rosen; see e.g. [Barendregt, 1981], Proposition 4.3.5.)

3. [Hindley, 1964] Let $\langle A, \to_1, \to_2 \rangle$ be an ARS. Suppose: $\forall a, b, c \in A\, \exists d \in A\, (a \to_1 b \;\&\; a \to_2 c \Rightarrow b \twoheadrightarrow_2 d \;\&\; c \to_1^{\equiv} d)$. (See Figure 2.4a.) Then $\to_1, \to_2$ commute.

4. [Staples, 1975] Let $\langle A, \to_1, \to_2 \rangle$ be an ARS. Suppose: $\forall a, b, c \in A\, \exists d \in A\, (a \to_1 b \;\&\; a \twoheadrightarrow_2 c \Rightarrow b \twoheadrightarrow_2 d \;\&\; c \twoheadrightarrow_1 d)$. (See Figure 2.4b.) Then $\to_1, \to_2$ commute.

5. [Rosen, 1973] Let $\langle A, \to_1, \to_2 \rangle$ be an ARS. Define: $\to_1$ *requests* $\to_2$ if $\forall a, b, c \in A\, \exists d, e \in A\, (a \twoheadrightarrow_1 b \;\&\; a \twoheadrightarrow_2 c \Rightarrow b \twoheadrightarrow_2 d \;\&\; c \twoheadrightarrow_1 e \twoheadrightarrow_2 d)$. (See Figure 2.4c.) To prove: if $\to_1, \to_2$ are confluent and if $\to_1$ requests $\to_2$, then $\to_{12}$ is confluent.

6. [Rosen, 1973] Let $\langle A, \to_1, \to_2 \rangle$ be an ARS such that $\to_2$ is confluent and $\forall a, b, c \in A\, \exists d, e \in A\, (a \twoheadrightarrow_1 b \;\&\; a \to_2 c \Rightarrow b \twoheadrightarrow_2 d \;\&\; c \twoheadrightarrow_1 e \twoheadrightarrow_2 d)$. (See Figure 2.4d.) Then $\to_1$ requests $\to_2$.

7. [Staples, 1975] Let $\langle A, \to_1, \to_2 \rangle$ be an ARS such that $\to_1$ requests $\to_2$ and $\to_2$ is confluent. Let $\to_3$ be the composition of $\twoheadrightarrow_1$ and $\twoheadrightarrow_2$, i.e. $a \to_3 b$ iff $\exists c\; a \twoheadrightarrow_1 c \twoheadrightarrow_2 b$. Suppose moreover that $\forall a, b, c \in A\, \exists d \in A\, (a \twoheadrightarrow_1 b \;\&\; a \twoheadrightarrow_1 c \Rightarrow b \to_3 d \;\&\; c \to_3 d)$. Then $\to_{12}$ is confluent.

8. (Staples [75]) Define: In the ARS $\langle A, \to_1, \to_2 \rangle$ the reduction relation $\to_2$ is called a *refinement* of $\to_1$ if $\to_1 \subseteq \twoheadrightarrow_2$. If moreover $\forall a, b \in A\, \exists c \in A\, (a \twoheadrightarrow_2 b \Rightarrow a \twoheadrightarrow_1 c \;\&\; b \twoheadrightarrow_1 c)$, then $\to_2$ is a *compatible* refinement of $\to_1$. Let in the ARS $\langle A, \to_1, \to_2 \rangle$ the reduction relation $\to_2$be a refinement of $\to_1$. Prove that $\to_2$ is a compatible refinement of $\to_1$ iff $\forall a, b, c \in A\, \exists d \in A\, (a \to_2 b \;\&\; b \twoheadrightarrow_1 c \Rightarrow c \twoheadrightarrow_1 d \;\&\; a \twoheadrightarrow_1 d)$.

9. [Staples, 1975] Let $\langle A, \to_1, \to_2 \rangle$ be an ARS where $\to_2$ is a compatible refinement of $\to_1$. Then: $\to_1$ is confluent iff $\to_2$ is confluent.

10. [Huet, 1980] DEFINITION: Let $\langle A, \to \rangle$ be an ARS. Then $\to$ is called *strongly confluent* (see Figure 2.4e) if $\forall a, b, c \in A\, \exists d \in A\, (a \to b \;\&\; a \to c \Rightarrow b \twoheadrightarrow d \;\&\; c \to^{\equiv} d)$. Prove that strong confluence implies confluence.

11. Let $\langle A, (\to_\alpha)_{\alpha \in I} \rangle$ be an ARS such that for all $\alpha, \beta \in I, \to_\alpha$ commutes weakly with $\to_\beta$. Define: (a) $\to_\alpha$ is *relatively terminating* if no reduction $a_0 \to a_1 \to a_2 \to \ldots$ (where $\to = \bigcup_{\alpha \in I} \to_\alpha$) contains infinitely many $\alpha-$steps. (b) $\to_\alpha$ *has splitting effect* if there are $a, b, c, \in A$ such that for every $d \in A$ and every $\beta \in I$ with $a \to_\alpha b, a \to_\beta c, c \twoheadrightarrow_\alpha d, b \twoheadrightarrow_\beta d$, the reduction $b \twoheadrightarrow_\beta d$ consists of more than one step. To prove: if every $\to_\alpha$ $(\alpha \in I)$ which has splitting effect is relatively terminating, then $\to$ is confluent. (Note that this is equivalent to Newman's lemma.)

12. [Winkler and Buchberger, 1983] Let $\langle A, \to, > \rangle$ be an ARS where the 'reduction' relation $>$ is a partial order and SN. (So $>$ is well-founded.) Suppose $a \to b$ implies $a > b$. Then the following are equivalent: (a) $\to$ is confluent, (b) whenever $a \to b$ and $a \to c$, there is a $\to$-conversion $b \equiv d_1 \leftrightarrow d_2 \leftrightarrow \ldots \leftrightarrow d_n \equiv c$ (for some $n \geq 1$) between b, c such that $a > d_i$ $(i = 1, \ldots, n)$. Here each $\leftrightarrow$ is $\to$ or $\leftarrow$. (See Figure 2.4f.) (Note that this strengthens Newman's lemma.)

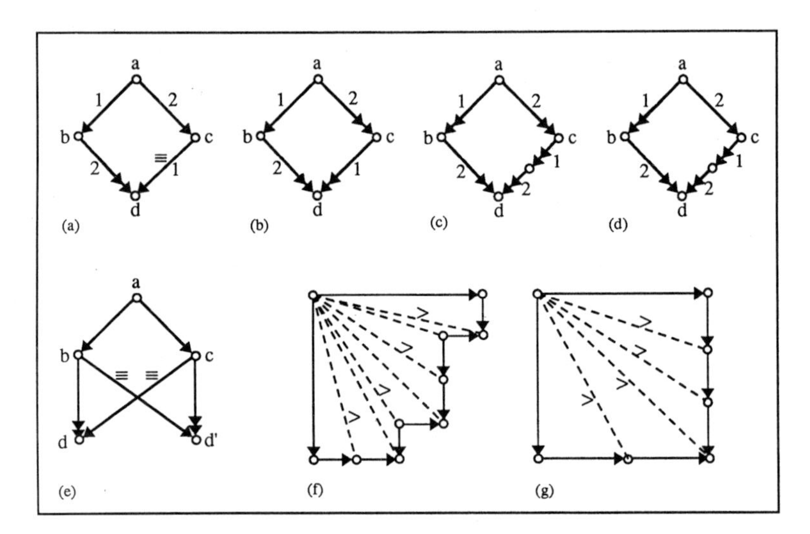

Figure 2.4

13. [Klop, 1980a] Let $\mathcal{A} = \langle A, \rightarrow \rangle$ be an ARS. Let $B \subseteq A$. Then B is *cofinal* in $\mathcal{A}$ if $\forall a \in A\, \exists b \in B\; a \twoheadrightarrow b$. Furthermore, $\mathcal{A}$ is said to have the *cofinality property* (CP) if in every reduction graph $\mathcal{G}(a), a \in A$, there is a (possibly infinite) reduction sequence $a \equiv a_0 \rightarrow a_1 \rightarrow \ldots$ such that $\{a_n \mid n \geq 0\}$ is cofinal in $\mathcal{G}(a)$. Then, for *countable* ARSs: $\mathcal{A}$ is CR $\Leftrightarrow$ $\mathcal{A}$ has CP.

14. Let $\mathcal{A} = \langle A, \rightarrow \rangle$ be an ARS. Define: A is *consistent* if not every pair of elements in A is convertible. Note that if $\mathcal{A}$ is confluent and has two different normal forms, $\mathcal{A}$ is consistent. Further, let $\mathcal{A} = \langle A, \rightarrow_\alpha \rangle, \mathcal{B} = \langle B, \rightarrow_\beta \rangle$ be ARSs such that $A \subseteq B$. Then we define: $\mathcal{B}$ is a *conservative extension* of $\mathcal{A}$ if $\forall a, a' \in A\, (a =_\beta a' \Leftrightarrow a =_\alpha a')$. Note that a conservative extension of a consistent ARS is again consistent. Further, note that a confluent extension $\mathcal{B}$ of $\mathcal{A}$ is conservative.

15. [Newman, 1942] Let WCR^1 be the following property of ARSs $\langle A, \rightarrow \rangle$: $\forall a, b, c \in A\, \exists d \in A\, (c \leftarrow a \rightarrow b \;\&\; b \not\equiv c \Rightarrow c \rightarrow d \leftarrow b)$. (See Figure 2.5a.) Prove that WCR^1 & WN $\Rightarrow$ SN, and give a counterexample to the implication $\mathrm{WCR}^{\leq 1}$ & WN $\Rightarrow$ SN.

16. [Bachmair and Dershowitz, 1986] Let $\langle A, \rightarrow_\alpha, \rightarrow_\beta \rangle$ be an ARS such that $\forall a, b, c \in A \exists d \in A (a \rightarrow_\alpha b \rightarrow_\beta c \Rightarrow a \rightarrow_\beta d \twoheadrightarrow_{\alpha\beta} c)$. (In the terminology of [Bachmair and Dershowitz, 1986] : β *quasi-commutes over* α.) (See Figure 2.5b.) Prove that β/α is SN iff β is SN. (For the definition of β/α, see Exercise 1.0.8(19) below.)

17. [Klop, 1980a] Let $\mathcal{A} = \langle A, \rightarrow_\alpha \rangle$ and $\mathcal{B} = \langle B, \rightarrow_\beta \rangle$ be ARSs. Let $\iota : A \rightarrow B$ and $\kappa : B \rightarrow A$ be maps such that
    (a) $\kappa(\iota(a)) = a$ for all $a \in A$,
    (b) $\forall a, a' \in A \forall b \in B\; \exists b' \in B\; (b \rightarrow_\kappa a \rightarrow_\alpha a' \Rightarrow b \rightarrow_\beta b' \rightarrow_\kappa a')$ (Reductions in $\mathcal{A}$ can be 'lifted' to $\mathcal{B}$.) See Figure 2.5c.

Prove that $\mathcal{B}$ is SN implies that $\mathcal{A}$ is SN.

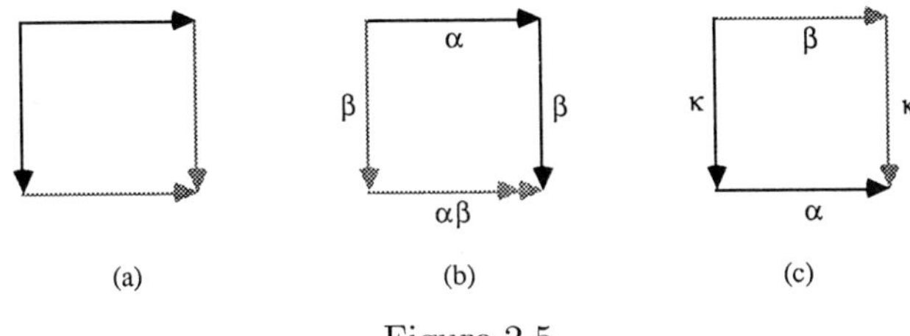

Figure 2.5

18. [Geser, 1990] Let $\langle A, \rightarrow_\alpha, \rightarrow_\beta \rangle$ be an ARS with two reduction relations α, β such that $\alpha \cup \beta$ is transitive. Then: $\alpha \cup \beta$ is SN $\Leftrightarrow$ α is SN and β is SN. (Hint: Use the following infinite version of Ramsey's theorem, in which for a set S the notation $[S]^2$ is used to denote the set $\{\{a, b\} \mid a, b \in S \;\&\; a \neq b\}$ of two-element subsets of S. Furthermore, $\mathbb{N}$ is the set of natural numbers. Theorem: *Let* $[\mathbb{N}]^2$ *be partitioned into subsets* X *and* Y. *Then there is an infinite* $A \subseteq \mathbb{N}$ *such that either* $[A]^2 \subseteq X$ *or* $[A]^2 \subseteq Y$.)

19. [Geser, 1990] This exercise reformulates and slightly generalizes Exercise 2.0.8(11). Let $\langle A, \rightarrow_\alpha, \rightarrow_\beta \rangle$ be an ARS. Define: α/β ('α modulo β') is the reduction relation $\beta^*\alpha\beta^*$. So $a \rightarrow_{\alpha/\beta} b$ iff there are c, d such that $a \twoheadrightarrow_\beta c \rightarrow_\alpha d \twoheadrightarrow_\beta b$. Note that α is relatively terminating (in the sense of Exercise 2.0.8(11)) iff α/β is SN. Define: β is called *non-splitting* (with respect to $\alpha \cup \beta$) if $\forall a, b, c \in A\, \exists d \in A\, (a \rightarrow_\beta b \;\&\; a \rightarrow_{\alpha\cup\beta} c \Rightarrow c \twoheadrightarrow_{\alpha\cup\beta} d \;\&\; b\, (\rightarrow_{\alpha\cup\beta})^{\equiv}\, d)$. Prove: If α/β is SN, α is WCR, and β is non-splitting, then $\alpha \cup \beta$ is confluent.

2.1 Basic notions

Syntax of term rewriting systems

A term rewriting system (TRS) is a pair (Σ, R) of an *alphabet* or *signature* Σ and a set of reduction rules (rewrite rules) R. The alphabet Σ consists of:

1. a countably infinite set of *variables* $x_1, x_2, x_3, \ldots$ also denoted as $x, y, z, x', y', \ldots$
2. a non-empty set of *function symbols* or *operator symbols* $F, G, \ldots,$ each equipped with an 'arity' (a natural number), i.e. the number of 'arguments' it is supposed to have. We not only (may) have unary, binary, ternary, etc., function symbols, but also 0-ary: these are also called *constant symbols*.

The set of terms (or expressions) 'over' Σ is $\mathrm{Ter}(\Sigma)$ and is defined inductively:

1. $x, y, z, \ldots \in \mathrm{Ter}(\Sigma)$,

2. if F is an n-ary function symbol and $t_1, \ldots, t_n \in \text{Ter}(\Sigma)$ $(n \geq 0)$, then $F(t_1, \ldots, t_n) \in \text{Ter}(\Sigma)$. The t_i $(i = 1, \ldots, n)$ are the arguments of the last term.

Terms not containing a variable are called *ground* terms (also: *closed* terms), and $\text{Ter}_0(\Sigma)$ is the set of ground terms. Terms in which no variable occurs twice or more are called *linear.*

Contexts are 'terms' containing one occurrence of a special symbol $\Box$, denoting an empty place. A context is generally denoted by C[ ]. If $t \in \text{Ter}(\Sigma)$ and t is substituted in $\Box$, the result is $C[t] \in \text{Ter}(\Sigma); t$ is said to be a subterm of $C[t]$, notation $t \subseteq C[t]$. Since $\Box$ is itself a context, the trivial context, we also have $t \subseteq t$. Often this notion of subterm is not precise enough, and we have to distinguish *occurrences* of subterms (or symbols) in a term; it is easy to define the notion of occurrence formally, using sequence numbers denoting a 'position' in the term, but here we will be satisfied with a more informal treatment.

Example 2.1.1. Let $\Sigma = \{A, M, S, 0\}$ where the arities are 2,2,1,0 respectively. Then $A(M(x,y),y)$ is a (non-linear) term, $A(M(x,y),z)$ is a linear term, $A(M(S(0),0),S(0))$ is a ground term, $A(M(\Box,0),S(0))$ is a context, $S(0)$ is a subterm of $A(M(S(0),0),S(0))$ having two occurrences: $A(M(\mathbf{S(0)},0),\mathbf{S(0)})$.

A *substitution* σ is a map from $\text{Ter}(\Sigma)$ to $\text{Ter}(\Sigma)$ which satisfies $\sigma(F(t_1, \ldots, t_n)) = F(\sigma(t_1), \ldots, \sigma(t_n))$ for every n-ary function symbol F (here $n \geq 0$). So, σ is determined by its restriction to the set of variables. We also write t^σ instead of $\sigma(t)$.

A *reduction rule* (or rewrite rule) is a pair (t, s) of terms $\in \text{Ter}(\Sigma)$. It will be written as $t \to s$. Often a reduction rule will get a name, e.g. r, and we write $r : t \to s$. Two conditions will be imposed:

1. the LHS (left-hand side) t is not a variable,
2. the variables in the right-hand side s are already contained in t.

A reduction rule $r : t \to s$ determines a set of *rewrites* $t^\sigma \to_r s^\sigma$ for all substitutions σ. The LHS t^σ is called a *redex* (from 'reducible expression'), more precisely an r-redex. A redex t^σ may be replaced by its '*contractum*' s^σ inside a context C[ ]; this gives rise to *reduction steps* (or one-step rewritings)

$$C[t^\sigma] \to_r C[s^\sigma].$$

We call $\to_r$ the *one-step reduction relation* generated by r. Concatenating reduction steps we have (possibly infinite) *reduction sequences* $t_0 \to t_1 \to t_2 \to \cdots$ or *reductions* for short. If $t_0 \to \cdots \to t_n$ we also write $t_0 \twoheadrightarrow t_n$, and t_n is a *reduct* of t_0, in accordance with the notations and concepts introduced in Section 2.0.

Example 2.1.2. Consider Σ as in Example 2.1.1. Let (Σ, R) be the TRS (specifying the natural numbers with addition, multiplication, successor and zero) with reduction rules R given in Table 2.1.

r_1	$A(x, 0)$	$\to$	x
r_2	$A(x, S(y))$	$\to$	$S(A(x, y))$
r_3	$M(x, 0)$	$\to$	0
r_4	$M(x, S(y))$	$\to$	$A(M(x, y), x)$

Table 2.1

Now $M(S(S(0)), S(S(0))) \twoheadrightarrow S(S(S(S(0))))$, since we have the following reduction:

$$\begin{array}{rcl} \mathbf{M(S(S(0)), S(S(0)))} & \to & \mathbf{A(M(S(S(0)), S(0)), S(S(0)))} \\ & \to & S(\mathbf{A(M(S(S(0)), S(0)), S(0))}) \\ & \to & S(S(\mathbf{A(M(S(S(0)), S(0)), 0)})) \\ & \to & S(S(\mathbf{M(S(S(0)), S(0))})) \\ & \to & S(S(A(\mathbf{M(S(S(0)), 0)}, S(S(0))))) \\ & \to & S(S(\mathbf{A(0, S(S(0)))})) \\ & \to & S(S(S(\mathbf{A(0, S(0))}))) \\ & \to & S(S(S(S(\mathbf{A(0, 0)})))) \\ & \to & S(S(S(S(0)))). \end{array}$$

Here in each step the bold-face redex is rewritten. Note that this is not the only reduction from $M(S(S(0)), S(S(0)))$ to $S(S(S(S(0))))$.

Obviously, for each TRS (Σ, R) there is a corresponding ARS, namely $(\mathrm{Ter}(\Sigma), (\rightarrow_r)_{r\in R})$. Here we have to be careful: it may make a big difference whether one discusses the TRS (Σ, R) consisting of all terms, or the TRS restricted to the ground terms (see the next example). We will adopt the convention that (Σ, R) has as corresponding ARS the one mentioned already, and we write $(\Sigma, R)_0$ if the ARS $(\mathrm{Ter}_0(\Sigma), (\rightarrow_r)_{r\in R})$ is meant. Via the associated ARS, all notions considered in Section 1.0 (CR, UN, SN, ...) carry over to TRSs.

Example 2.1.3. Let (Σ, R) be the TRS of Example 2.1.2 and consider (Σ, R') where $R' = R \cup \{A(x,y) \rightarrow A(y,x)\}$; so the extra rule expresses commutativity of addition. Now (Σ, R') is not WN: the term $A(x,y)$ has no normal form. However, $(\Sigma, R')_0$ (the restriction to ground terms) is WN. Whereas $(\Sigma, R)_0$ is SN, $(\Sigma, R')_0$ is no longer so, as witnessed by the infinite reductions possible in the reduction graph in Figure 2.6. The 'bottom' term in that reduction graph is a normal form.

Many-sorted term rewriting systems

TRSs (Σ, R) as we just have defined are sometimes called *homogeneous* [Ganzinger and Giegerich, 1987], as they correspond to algebraic data type specifications (by replacing '$\rightarrow$' by '$=$' in R) where the signature Σ has just one sort (which therefore was not mentioned).

It is straightforward to extend our previous definitions to the *heterogeneous* or *many-sorted* case. The definition of term formation is as usual in many-sorted abstract data type specifications, and is left to the reader. We will stick to the homogeneous case, but note that 'everything' extends at once to the heterogeneous case, at least with respect to the theory in this chapter; of course, the extension to the heterogeneous case presents a whole area of new features and problems (see e.g. [Ehrig and Mahr, 1985], [Drosten, 1989] for a treatment of many-sorted specifications and rewriting).

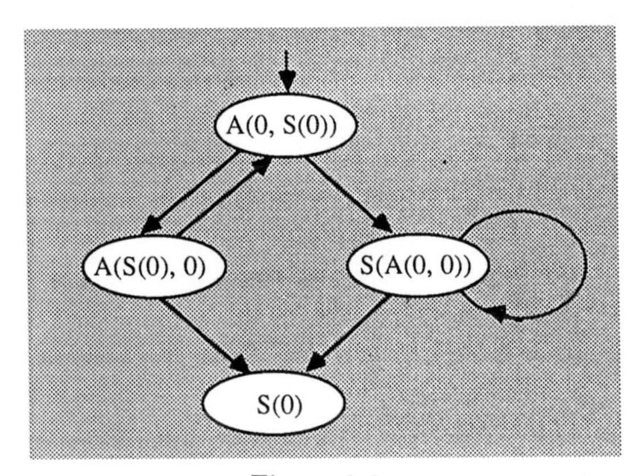

Figure 2.6

Semi-Thue systems

Semi-Thue Systems (STSs), as defined in [Jantzen, 1988], can be 'viewed' in two ways as TRS's. We demonstrate this by the following:

1. Let $T = \{(aba, bab)\}$ be a one-rule STS. Then T corresponds to the TRS R with unary function symbols a, b and a constant o, and the reduction rule $a(b(a(x))) \to b(a(b(x)))$. Now a reduction step in T, e.g.: $bbabaaa \to bbbabaa$, translates in R to the reduction step $b(b(a(b(a(a(a(o))))))) \to b(b(b(a(b(a(a(o)))))))$. It is easy to see that this translation gives an 'isomorphism' between T and R (or more precisely $(R)_0$, the restriction to ground terms).

2. The second way to let an STS correspond to a TRS is by introducing an associative concatenation operator, and letting the symbols of the STS correspond to constant symbols in the TRS. In fact, a 'natural' correspondence in this way requires that we introduce *equational* TRSs, which we will not do here. (See e.g. [Bachmair and Plaisted, 1985] or [Plaisted, 1985].)

Applicative term rewriting systems

In some important TRSs there is a very special binary operator, called *application* (Ap). For example, combinatory logic (CL), based on S, K, I, has the rewrite rules as in Table 2.2. Here S, K, I are constants. Often one uses the infix notation $(t \cdot s)$ instead of $Ap(t, s)$, in which case the rewrite rules of CL read as follows:

As in ordinary algebra, the dot is mostly suppressed; and a further no-

$Ap(Ap(Ap(S,x),y),z)$	$\to$	$Ap(Ap(x,z),Ap(y,z))$
$Ap(Ap(K,x),y)$	$\to$	x
$Ap(I,x)$	$\to$	x

Table 2.2

$((S \cdot x) \cdot y) \cdot z$	$\to$	$(x \cdot z) \cdot (y \cdot z)$
$(K \cdot x) \cdot y$	$\to$	x
$I \cdot x$	$\to$	x

Table 2.3

tational simplification is that many pairs of brackets are dropped in the convention of association to the left. That is, one restores the missing brackets choosing in each step of the restoration the leftmost possibility. Thus the three rules become:

$Sxyz$	$\to$	$xz(yz)$
Kxy	$\to$	x
Ix	$\to$	x

Table 2.4

Note that $xz(yz)$ restores to $(xz)(yz)$, not to $x(z(yz))$. Likewise Kxy restores to $(Kx)y$, not $K(xy)$. Of course not all bracket pairs can be dropped: $xzyz$ is when restored $((xz)y)z$, which is quite different from $xz(yz)$. Note that e.g. SIx does not contain a redex Ix.

It is a convenient fiction to view the S, K, I in the last three equations as 'operators with variable arity' or *varyadic* operators, since they may be followed by an arbitrary number of arguments $t_1, \ldots, t_n (n \geq 0)$. But it needs, in the case of S, at least three arguments to use the rewrite rule for S; e.g.: $St_1t_2t_3t_4t_5t_6 \to t_1t_3(t_2t_3)t_4t_5t_6$.

Example 2.1.4. We have $SII(SII) \to I(SII)(I(SII)) \to SII(I(SII)) \to SII(SII)$. The term $SII(SII)$ has many more reductions, which constitute an interesting reduction graph (see Figure 2.7).

The TRS CL has 'universal computational power': every (partial) recursive function on the natural numbers can be expressed in CL. This feature is used in [Turner, 1979], where CL is used to implement functional

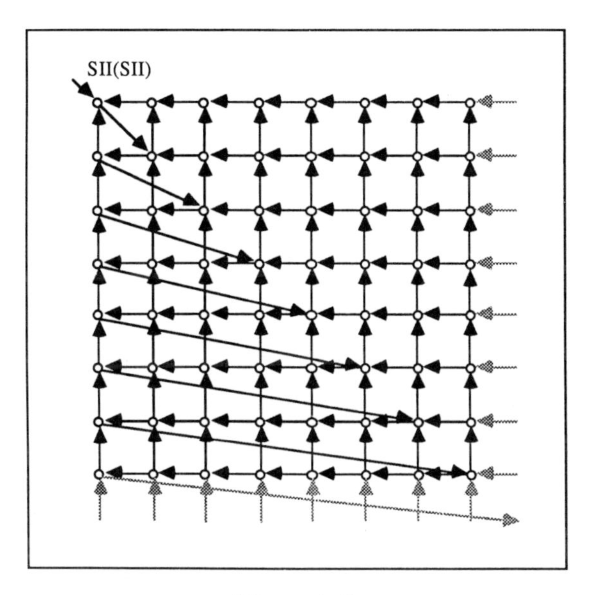

Figure 2.7

programming languages. Actually, an extension of CL is used there, called SKIM (for S,K,I-Machine); it is also an applicative TRS (see Table 2.5). Note that this TRS has infinitely many constants: apart from the constants $S, K, \ldots, \underline{eq}$ there is a constant $\underline{n}$ for each $n \in \mathbb{N}$. There are also infinitely many reduction rules, because the last four rules are actually *rule schemes*; e.g. $\underline{plus}\ \underline{n}\ \underline{m} \rightarrow \underline{n+m}$ stands for all reduction rules like $\underline{plus}\ \underline{0}\ \underline{0} \rightarrow \underline{0}$, $\underline{plus}\ \underline{0}\ \underline{1} \rightarrow \underline{1}, \ldots, \underline{plus}\ \underline{37}\ \underline{63} \rightarrow \underline{100}, \ldots$. In fact, the extra constants in SKIM are there for reasons of efficient implementation; they can all be defined using only S and K. For example, defining B as $S(KS)K$ we have:

$$\begin{aligned} Bxyz \equiv S(KS)Kxyz &\rightarrow KSx(Kx)yz \\ &\rightarrow S(Kx)yz \\ &\rightarrow Kxz(yz) \\ &\rightarrow x(yz) \end{aligned}$$

as we should have. Likewise, defining C as $S(BBS)(KK)$, we have $Cxyz \twoheadrightarrow xzy$ as the reader may check. For the other definitions one may consult [Barendregt, 1981] or [Hindley and Seldin, 1986].

It is harmless to mix the applicative notation with the usual one, as in CL with test for syntactical equality in Table 2.6.
However, some care should be taken: consider the TRS in Table 2.7. where D is now a *constant* (instead of a binary operator) subject to the rewrite rule, in full notation, $Ap(Ap(D, x), x) \rightarrow E$. These two TRSs have

$Sxyz$	$\to$	$xz(yz)$	
Kxy	$\to$	x	
Ix	$\to$	x	
$Cxyz$	$\to$	xzy	
$Bxyz$	$\to$	$x(yz)$	
Yx	$\to$	$x(Yx)$	
$Uz(Pxy)$	$\to$	zxy	
$\underline{cond}\,\underline{true}\,xy$	$\to$	x	
$\underline{cond}\,\underline{false}\,xy$	$\to$	y	
$\underline{plus}\,\underline{n}\,\underline{m}$	$\to$	$\underline{n+m}$	
$\underline{times}\,\underline{n}\,\underline{m}$	$\to$	$\underline{n \cdot m}$	
$\underline{eq}\,\underline{n}\,\underline{n}$	$\to$	$\underline{true}$	
$\underline{eq}\,\underline{n}\,\underline{m}$	$\to$	$\underline{false}$	if $n \neq m$

Table 2.5

$Sxyz$	$\to$	$xz(yz)$
Kxy	$\to$	x
Ix	$\to$	x
$D(x,x)$	$\to$	E

Table 2.6

$Sxyz$	$\to$	$xz(yz)$
Kxy	$\to$	x
Ix	$\to$	x
Dxx	$\to$	E

Table 2.7

very different properties, as we shall see later (the first TRS is confluent, the second is not).

Another interesting example of a TRS in such a mixed notation is Weak Categorical Combinatory Logic, which plays an important role in implementations of functional languages (see [Curien, 1986] and [Hardin, 1989]): Here Id, Fst, Snd, App are constants, $\circ, \langle , \rangle$ and $(\ , \ )$ are binary function symbols and Λ is a unary function symbol. Note that Fst, Snd are not binary symbols and that App is not the 'underlying' application operator

$Id\, x$	$\to$	x
$(x \circ y)z$	$\to$	$x(yz)$
$Fst\,(x, y)$	$\to$	x
$Snd\,(x, y)$	$\to$	y
$\langle x, y\rangle z$	$\to$	(xz, yz)
$App\,(x, y)$	$\to$	xy
$\Lambda(x)yz$	$\to$	$x(y, z)$

Table 2.8

which was called in CL above *Ap*.

2.2 Disjoint sums of term rewriting systems

In view of the need for modularisation of abstract data type specifications, it would be very helpful if some properties of a TRS could be inferred from their validity for 'parts' of that TRS. The simplest possible definition of 'parts' is that obtained by the concept of 'disjoint sum' of TRSs:

Definition 2.2.1. Let R_1, R_2 be TRSs. Then the *disjoint sum* $R_1 \oplus R_2$ of R_1, R_2 is the TRS obtained by taking the disjoint union of R_1 and R_2. That is, if the alphabets of R_1, R_2 are disjoint (R_1, R_2 have no function or constant symbols in common), then the disjoint sum is the ordinary union; otherwise we take renamed copies R_1', R_2' of R_1, R_2 such that these copies have disjoint alphabets and define $R_1 \oplus R_2$ to be the union of these copies.

We have the following useful fact from [Toyama, 1987b]:

Theorem 2.2.2. *$R_1 \oplus R_2$ is confluent iff R_1 and R_2 are confluent.*

So, confluence is a 'modular' property. One might think that the same is true for termination (SN), but [Toyama, 1987a] gives a simple counterexample: take

$$R_1 = \{f(0, 1, x) \to f(x, x, x)\}$$
$$R_2 = \{\underline{or}(x, y) \to x,\ \underline{or}(x, y) \to y\}$$

then R_1, R_2 are both SN, but $R_1 \oplus R_2$ is not, since there is the infinite reduction:

$$\begin{aligned} f(\underline{or}(0,1), \underline{or}(0,1), \underline{or}(0,1)) &\to f(0, \underline{or}(0,1), \underline{or}(0,1)) \\ &\to f(0, 1, \underline{or}(0,1)) \\ &\to f(\underline{or}(0,1), \underline{or}(0,1), \underline{or}(0,1)) \end{aligned}$$

$$\rightarrow \quad \cdots$$

In this counterexample R_2 is not confluent and thus one may conjecture that 'confluent and terminating' (or CR & SN, or complete) is a *modular property* (i.e. $R_1 \oplus R_2$ is complete iff R_1, R_2 are so). Again this is not the case, as a counterexample given by Barendregt and Klop (adapted by Toyama, see [Toyama, 1987a]) shows: R_1 has the eleven rules

$$\begin{array}{lcl} F(4,5,6,x) & \rightarrow & F(x,x,x,x) \\ F(x,y,z,w) & \rightarrow & 7 \end{array}$$

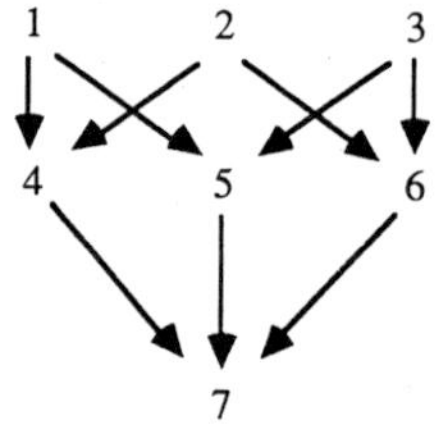

and R_2 has the three rules

$$\begin{array}{lcl} G(x,x,y) & \rightarrow & x \\ G(x,y,x) & \rightarrow & x \\ G(y,x,x) & \rightarrow & x. \end{array}$$

(Similar counterexamples with the additional property of being 'reduced' or 'irreducible'—meaning that both sides of every rule are normal forms with respect to the other rules (see Definition 2.4.18 below for a more accurate definition)—are given in [Toyama, 1987a] and [Ganzinger and Giegerich, 1987].) Now R_1 and R_2 are both complete, but $R_1 \oplus R_2$ is not:

$$\begin{array}{lllll} F(G(1,2,3), & G(1,2,3), & G(1,2,3), & G(1,2,3)) & \twoheadrightarrow \\ F(G(4,4,3), & G(5,2,5), & G(1,6,6), & G(1,2,3)) & \twoheadrightarrow \\ F(\quad 4, & \quad 5, & \quad 6, & G(1,2,3)) & \rightarrow \\ F(G(1,2,3), & G(1,2,3), & G(1,2,3), & G(1,2,3)). & \end{array}$$

Exercise 2.2.3. A simpler counterexample is given in [Drosten, 1989]. Slightly adapted it reads:

$$\begin{array}{llcl} R_1 & F(0,1,x) & \rightarrow & F(x,x,x) \\ & F(x,y,z) & \rightarrow & 2 \\ & 0 & \rightarrow & 2 \\ & 1 & \rightarrow & 2 \end{array}$$

and

$$\begin{array}{llcl} R_2 & D(x,y,y) & \rightarrow & x \\ & D(x,x,y) & \rightarrow & y. \end{array}$$

Now R_1, R_2 are complete; however, their disjoint sum is not. To see this, consider the term $F(M,M,M)$ where $M \equiv D(0,1,1)$ and show that $F(M,M,M)$ has a cyclic reduction.

The last counterexamples involve a non-left-linear TRS. This is essential, as the following theorem indicates. First we define this concept:

Definition 2.2.4.

1. A reduction rule $t \to s$ is *left-linear* if t is a linear term.
2. A TRS is *left-linear* if all its reduction rules are left-linear.

Theorem 2.2.5. [Toyama *et al.*, 1989]). *Let R_1, R_2 be left-linear TRSs. Then: $R_1 \oplus R_2$ is complete iff R_1 and R_2 are complete.*

Some useful information concerning the inference of SN for $R_1 \oplus R_2$ from the SN property for R_1 and R_2 separately is given in [Rusinowitch, 1987a] and [Middeldorp, 1989b], in terms of 'collapsing' and 'duplicating' rewrite rules.

Definition 2.2.6.

1. A rewrite rule $t \to s$ is a *collapsing* rule (c-rule) if s is a variable.
2. A rewrite rule $t \to s$ is a *duplicating* rule (d-rule) if some variable has more occurrences in s than it has in t.

Example 2.2.7. $F(x, x) \to G(x, x)$ is not a d-rule, but $F(x, x) \to H(x, x, x)$ is. Also $P(x) \to G(x, x)$ is a d-rule.

Theorem 2.2.8. *Let R_1 and R_2 be TRSs both with the property SN.*

1. *If neither R_1 nor R_2 contain c-rules, $R_1 \oplus R_2$ is SN.*
2. *If neither R_1 nor R_2 contain d-rules, $R_1 \oplus R_2$ is SN.*
3. *If one of the TRSs R_1, R_2 contains neither c- nor d-rules, $R_1 \oplus R_2$ is SN.*

Statements (1) and (2) are proved in [Rusinowitch, 1987a]; statement (3) is proved in [Middeldorp, 1989b].

Exercise 2.2.9. Prove that WN is a modular property.

Another useful fact, proved in [Middeldorp, 1989a], is that UN is a modular property.

Theorem 2.2.10. *$R_1 \oplus R_2$ is UN iff R_1 and R_2 are so.*

The proof of this theorem employs a lemma of independent interest; see the proof sketch in the following exercises.

Exercises 2.2.11. [Middeldorp, 1990]

1. Let R be a TRS. For $t \in \text{Ter}(R)$, $[t]$ denotes the equivalence class of t with respect to convertibility in R: $[t] = \{t' \mid t =_R t'\}$. Further, $V(t)$ is the

set of variables occurring in t. $EV(t)$ is the set of *essential* variables of t, defined as: $\cap_{t' \in [t]} V(t')$.

2. Now let $t(\vec{x}, \vec{y})$ be a term with essential variables $\vec{x} = x_1, \ldots, x_n$ and non-essential variables $\vec{y} = y_1, \ldots, y_m$. Prove that for arbitrary terms $\vec{s} = s_1, \ldots, s_m$ we have $t(\vec{x}, \vec{s}) =_R t(\vec{x}, \vec{y})$.

3. Let R have the property UN (unique normal forms). Show that a normal form has only essential variables.

4. Let R contain a ground term (i.e., R contains a constant symbol). Show that every convertibility class $[t]$ contains a term s having only essential variables.

5. Let R have the property UN and contain a ground term. Show that there is a choice function φ from $\{[t] \mid t \in \text{Ter}(R)\}$ to $\text{Ter}(R)$, selecting from each equivalence class $[t]$ a term such that

   (a) $\varphi([t]) \in [t]$;
   (b) if $[t]$ contains a normal form t', then $\phi([t]) \equiv t'$;
   (c) $\varphi([t])$ contains only essential variables.

6. Lemma. *Let R be a TRS with property UN and containing a ground term. Then R can be extended to a confluent TRS R' with the same alphabet, the same convertibility and the same normal forms.*
   Prove the lemma by considering R', originating from R by adding the set of reduction rules $\{t \to \varphi([t]) \mid t \in \text{Ter}(R)\ \&\ t \not\equiv \varphi([t])\}$. (Note that the $t \to \varphi([t])$ are added as reduction rules, not merely as reduction steps.)

7. Lemma. *Let R be a TRS with property UN. Then R can be extended to a confluent TRS R' with the same convertibility and the same normal forms.*
   Prove the lemma as follows: in case R contains a constant, (6) applies; if not, we add a constant C and a rule $C \to C$ to yield R''. Now apply (6) on R''.

Exercise 2.2.12. [Middeldorp, 1990] Let R_1, R_2 be disjoint TRSs, both having the property UN. Show that $R_1 \oplus R_2$ has property UN. (Proof sketch: Use the previous exercise to extend R_i to R'_i such that R'_i is confluent and has the same convertibility and the same normal forms as R_i ($i = 1, 2$). Moreover, R'_1 and R'_2 can be taken disjoint from each other. By Toyama's theorem (1.2.2) $R'_1 \oplus R'_2$ is confluent, and hence also UN. Now consider $t, t' \in \text{Ter}(R_1 \oplus R_2)$ such that t, t' are normal forms and convertible in $R_1 \oplus R_2$. Obviously t, t' are also convertible in $R'_1 \oplus R'_2$. The proof is concluded by showing that t, t' are also normal forms in $R'_1 \oplus R'_2$. Hence $t \equiv t'$, and $R_1 \oplus R_2$ is UN.)

Examples 2.2.13.

1. Consider CL $\oplus \{D(x, x) \to E\}$, combinatory logic with binary test for syntactic equality as in Table 2.6. Note that this is indeed a disjoint sum. As we shall see in Section 3.1, CL is confluent. Trivially, the one rule TRS $\{D(x, x) \to E\}$ is confluent. Hence, by Toyama's theorem (2.2.2) the disjoint sum is confluent.

2. By contrast, the union CL $\cup$ $\{Dxx \to E\}$, Combinatory Logic with 'varyadic' test for syntactic equality as in Table 2.7, is *not* confluent. (See [Klop, 1980a].) Note that this combined TRS is merely a union and not a disjoint sum, since CL and $\{Dxx \to E\}$ have the function symbol Ap in common, even though hidden by the applicative notation.

3. Another application of Toyama's theorem (1.2.2): let R consist of the rules

$$\begin{array}{lcl} \underline{if}\ \underline{true}\ \underline{then}\ x\ \underline{else}\ y & \to & x \\ \underline{if}\ \underline{false}\ \underline{then}\ x\ \underline{else}\ y & \to & y \\ \underline{if}\ z\ \underline{then}\ x\ \underline{else}\ x & \to & x \end{array}$$

(Here $\underline{true}, \underline{false}$ are constants and $\underline{if} - \underline{then} - \underline{else}$ is a ternary function symbol.) Then CL $\oplus$ R is confluent. Analogous to the situation in (2), it is essential here that the $\underline{if} - \underline{then} - \underline{else}$ construct is a ternary operator. For the corresponding varyadic operator, the resulting TRS would not be confluent.

Remark 2.2.14. A different approach to modularity is taken by [Kurihara and Kaji, 1988]. Kaji If R_1 and R_2 are disjoint TRSs, it is not allowed in that approach to perform arbitrary interleaving of R_1-steps and R_2-steps; there is the obligation to use as long as possible the rules of the same TRS. Thus, if a rule of say R_1 is applied to term t, we must first normalize t with respect to R_1, before applying rules of R_2, and vice versa. Formally: define relations $\blacktriangleright_i$ $(i = 1, 2)$ for terms $s, t \in \mathrm{Ter}(R_1 \oplus R_2)$ by $s \blacktriangleright_i t$ if $s \to_i^+ t$ and t is a normal form of R_i. Furthermore, $\blacktriangleright$ is the union of $\blacktriangleright_1$ and $\blacktriangleright_2$. Now [Kurihara and Kaji, 1988] prove the following theorem:

1. *Let R_1, R_2 be disjoint TRSs. Then the relation $\blacktriangleright$ is terminating (SN).*

2. *Let R_1, R_2 be disjoint complete TRSs. Then the relation $\blacktriangleright$ is complete.*

Note that in (1) R_1, R_2 need not be SN. We will sketch a proof of (2). Assuming (1), part (2) of the theorem follows in some easy steps: First observe that for $\blacktriangleright$ we have UN $\Leftrightarrow$ CR, using UN & SN $\Rightarrow$ CR, a general fact for ARSs. So to prove UN for $\blacktriangleright$, consider reductions $s \blacktriangleright \cdots \blacktriangleright t_1$ and $s \blacktriangleright \cdots \blacktriangleright t_2$, where t_1, t_2 are $\blacktriangleright$-normal forms. Because the original reductions $\to_i$ $(i = 1, 2)$ in R_i are SN, the terms t_1, t_2 are normal forms with respect to $\to$, the union of $\to_i$ $(i = 1, 2)$. Hence by Toyama's theorem 2.2.2: $t_1 \equiv t_2$.

Exercises 2.2.15. (Middeldorp)

1. Show that the modularity of WN (Exercise 2.2.9) is a corollary of the theorem in Remark 2.2.14.

2. Give an example of disjoint confluent TRSs such that ▶ is not confluent. (Solution by A. Middeldorp of this question in [Kurihara and Kaji, 1988]" Kaji $R_1 = \{F(x,x) \to F(x,x), A \to B\}$; $R_2 = \{e(x) \to x\}$. Now $F(e(A),A) \blacktriangleright_1 F(e(B),B) \blacktriangleright_2 F(B,B)$ and $F(e(A),A) \blacktriangleright_2 F(A,A)$. The terms $F(A,A)$ and $F(B,B)$ are different ▶-normal forms.)

In this introduction to TRSs we will not consider termination properties of combined TRSs $R_1 \cup R_2$ which are not disjoint sums. For results in that area see [Dershowitz, 1981; Dershowitz, 1987], [Bachmair and Dershowitz, 1986], [Toyama, 1988] and, for heterogeneous TRSs, [Ganzinger and Giegerich, 1987]. As to confluence properties of combined TRSs $R_1 \cup R_2$ which are not disjoint sums, we include two facts in the following exercises, which require some concepts from the sequel (namely, the notion of overlapping reduction rules, critical pairs, and λ-calculus).

Exercise 2.2.16. [Raoult and Vuillemin, 1980; Toyama, 1988] Let R_1, R_2 be TRSs. Define: $R_1 \perp R_2$ (R_1 and R_2 are orthogonal to each other) if there is no overlap between a rule of R_1 and one of R_2. (There may be critical pairs due to overlap between R_1-rules, or between R_2-rules.) Prove:

Theorem. *Let R_1, R_2 be left-linear and confluent TRSs such that $R_1 \perp R_2$. Then $R_1 \cup R_2$ is confluent.*

(Proof sketch. Prove that in $R_1 \cup R_2$ we have: (1) R_1-reductions commute; (2) R_2-reductions commute; (3) R_1-reductions commute with R_2-reductions. In order to prove (3), it is sufficient to prove (4) as in Figure 2.8. To prove (4), we need the left-linearity and the orthogonality requirements. The result now follows by an application of the Hindley–Rosen lemma in Exercise 2.0.17(3). The orthogonality is obviously necessary. Note that also the left-linearity cannot be dropped—see Example 2.2.13(2).)

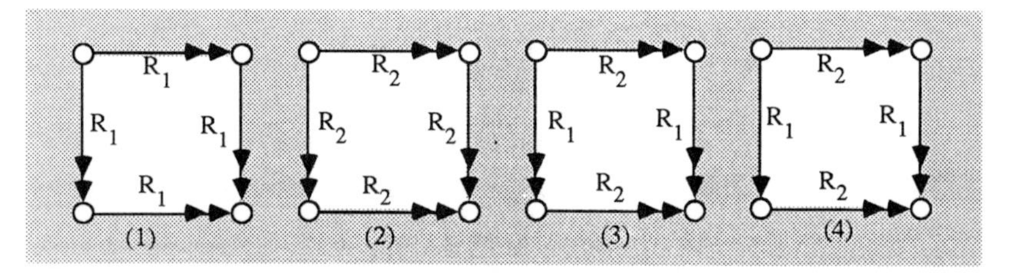

Figure 2.8

Exercises 2.2.17. Prove:

Theorem. *Let R be a left-linear, confluent TRS. Let the signature of R be disjoint from that of λ-calculus, i.e. R does not contain the application operator. Then $\lambda \oplus R$, the disjoint sum of λ-calculus and R, is confluent.*

Proof sketch: by the same strategy as used for Exercise 2.2.16.

Semantics of term rewriting systems

Although we do not enter the subject of *semantics* of TRSs (see e.g. [Boudol, 1985; Guessarian, 1981], , 1985, there is one simple remark that should be made. It concerns a semantical consideration that can be of great help in a proof of UN or CR:

Theorem 2.2.18. *Let $\mathcal{A}$ be an algebra 'for' the TRS R such that for all normal forms t, t' of R:*

$$\mathcal{A} \models t = t' \Rightarrow t \equiv t'.$$

Then R has the property UN (uniqueness of normal forms).

Here the phrase '$\mathcal{A}$ is an algebra for the TRS R' means that $\mathcal{A}$ has the same signature as R, and that reduction in R is sound with respect to $\mathcal{A}$, i.e. $t \twoheadrightarrow_R s$ implies $\mathcal{A} \models t = s$. The terms t, s need not be ground terms.

More 'semantic confluence tests' can be found in [Plaisted, 1985], in the setting of equational TRSs (not treated here).

Decidability of properties in Term Rewriting Systems

We adopt the restriction in this subsection to TRSs R with finite alphabet and finitely many reduction rules. It is undecidable whether for such TRSs the property confluence (CR) holds. (This is so both for R, the TRS of all terms, and $(R)_0$, the TRS restricted to ground terms.)

For *ground TRSs*, i.e. TRSs where in every rule $t \to s$ the terms t, s are ground terms (not to be confused with $(R)_0$ above), confluence is decidable [Dauchet and Tison, 1984; Dauchet *et al.*, 1987; Oyamaguchi, 1987].

For the termination property (SN) the situation is the same. It is undecidable for general TRSs, even for TRSs with only one rule (see for a proof [Dauchet, 1989]). For ground TRSs termination is decidable [Huet and Lankford, 1978].

For particular TRSs it may also be undecidable whether two terms are convertible, whether a term has a normal form, whether a term has an infinite reduction. A TRS where all these properties are undecidable is combinatory logic (CL), in Table 2.4.

Exercise 2.2.19. If $t \in \mathrm{Ter(R)}$, we say 't is SN' if t admits no infinite reduction $t \to t' \to t'' \to \cdots$. Prove: If R is not SN, then there is a redex of R which is not SN. In fact, then there is a redex whose contractum is not SN.

Exercises 2.2.20. (Huet and Lankford [78])

1. Let R be a ground TRS with finitely many rules, $R = \{t_i \to s_i \mid i = 1, \ldots, n\}$. Prove: If R is not SN, then for some $i \in \{1, \ldots, n\}$ and some context $C[\,]$ we have $t_i \to^+ C[t_i]$. (Hint: Use the previous exercise and use induction on n.)

2. Conclude: *SN is decidable for finite ground TRSs.*

Exercise 2.2.21. (Undecidability of SN) In this exercise we will outline a proof that SN is an undecidable property for (finite) TRSs, via a translation of the problem to the (uniform) halting problem for Turing machines. The proof is a slight simplification of the one in [Huet and Lankford, 1978]. (However, that proof employs only constants and unary function symbols; below we use also binary function symbols.) We will not be concerned with the number of reduction rules employed in the translation of a Turing machine to a TRS; for an undecidability proof using a TRS of only two reduction rules, thus establishing that SN is undecidable even for TRSs with only two rules, see [Dershowitz, 1987]. For a (complicated) proof that even for one rule TRSs the property SN is undecidable, see [Dauchet, 1989]. (Even more, for orthogonal one rule TRSs SN is undecidable, as shown in [Dauchet, 1989]. The property 'orthogonal' is defined in Section 3.)

A (deterministic) Turing machine M consists of a triple $\langle Q, S, \delta\rangle$ where Q is a set $\{q_0, \ldots, q_n\}$ of *states*, $S = \{\square, s_1, \ldots, s_m\}$ is the set of *tape symbols* ($\square$ being the empty symbol or 'blank'), and δ is a partial function (the *transition function*) from $Q \times S$ to $Q \times S \times \{L, R\}$. Here L represents a move to the left, R to the right.

An *instantaneous description* or *configuration* is an element of S^*QS^* (in the well-known notation of regular expressions). For example, in Figure 2.9(a) the configuration $\square aqba\square a$ is pictured; the understanding is that in the configuration w_1qw_2 the head is in state q and scans the first symbol to the right of it, i.e. of w_2. Furthermore, the infinite portions of tape which are to the left of w_1 and to the right of w_2, are supposed to be blank. *Equivalent* configurations arise by appending to the left or to the right of the configuration finite portions of empty tape, i.e. elements of $\{\square\}^*$.

The transition function δ determines *transition rules*, of the form

$$qst \rightarrowtail s'q't \quad (\text{for all } t \in S) \text{ whenever } \delta(q,s) = (q', s', R)$$

and

$$tqs \rightarrowtail q'ts' \quad (\text{for all } t \in S) \text{ whenever } \delta(q,s) = (q', s', L).$$

A transition rule of the first type ('R-type') is a move to the right (see Figure 2.9(b)), and of the second type ('L-type') a move to the left. A rule of the first type can also be rendered as

$$qs \rightarrowtail s'q' \text{ whenever } \delta(q,s) = (q', s', R).$$

Transition rules may be applied in a 'context', giving rise to *transitions* between configurations, by appending words $w_1, w_2 \in S^*$ to the left and the right. Thus the transition rule $qst \rightarrowtail s'q'tR$ generates transitions $w_1qstw_2 \rightarrowtail w_1s'q'tw_2$ for all $w_1, w_2 \in S^*$. Note that transitions operate in fact on equivalence classes of configurations.

We will now translate all this in the terminology of TRSs. That is, we associate with the Turing machine $M = \langle Q, S, \delta\rangle$ a TRS R_M as follows. For each $q \in Q$ there is a binary function symbol which we will denote with the same letter. Each $s \in S$ corresponds to a unary function symbol, also denoted with

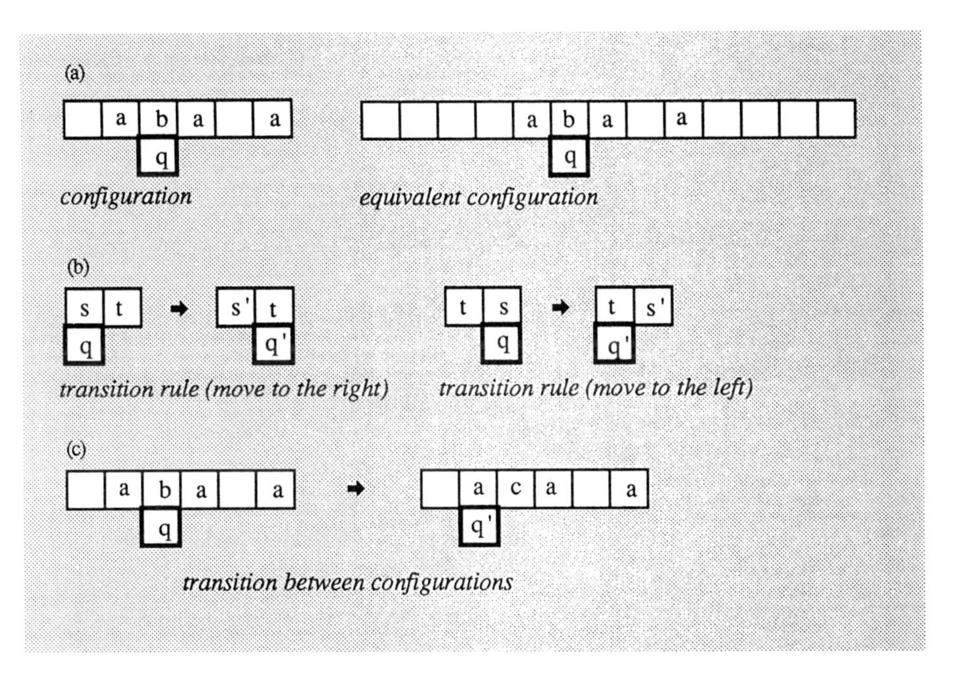

Figure 2.9

the same letter. Furthermore, the alphabet of R_m contains a constant symbol $\blacksquare$. A word $w \in S^*$ is translated into the term $\phi(w)$ as follows:

$$\begin{array}{ll} \phi(\varepsilon) = \blacksquare & (\varepsilon \text{ is the empty word}) \\ \phi(sw) = s(\phi(w)) & \text{for } s \in S, w \in S^*. \end{array}$$

E.g. the translation of $ba\Box a$ is $b(a(\Box(a(\blacksquare))))$. In the sequel of this exercise we will suppress parentheses by association to the right, thus rendering $b(a(\Box(a(\blacksquare))))$ as $ba\Box a\blacksquare$.

A configuration w_1qw_2 will be translated to $q(\phi(w_1^{-1}), \phi(w_2))$. Here w_1^{-1} is w_1 reversed. The reason for this reversal will be clear later. E.g. the configuration $\Box aqba\Box a$ is translated to $q(a\Box\blacksquare, ba\Box a\blacksquare)$.

We will now define the translation of the transition rules of M into reduction rules of R_M. To transition rules of R-type, $qs \rightarrowtail s'q'$, we let correspond the reduction rule

$$q(x, sy) \to q'(s'x, y).$$

In the case that s is $\Box$, so that the rule reads $q\Box \rightarrowtail s'q'$, we add moreover the reduction rule

$$q(x, \blacksquare) \to q'(s'x, \blacksquare).$$

In some sense, the second rule is a degenerate case of the first one; conceiving $\blacksquare$ as a potentially infinite portion of tape, satisfying the equation $\blacksquare = \Box\blacksquare$, it is clear how this rule arises from the first one.

To a rule of L-type, $tqs \rightarrowtail q'ts'$, we let correspond the reduction rule

$$q(tx, sy) \to q'(x, ts'y).$$

Again we have some extra rules for the 'degenerate' cases. If $tqs \rightarrowtail q'ts'$ is in fact $\Box qs \rightarrowtail q'ts'$ we add moreover

$$q(\blacksquare, sy) \to q'(\blacksquare, \Box s'y).$$

If $tqs \rightarrowtail q'ts'$ is in fact $tq\Box \rightarrowtail q'ts'$ we add moreover

$$q(tx, \blacksquare) \to q'(x, ts'\blacksquare).$$

If $tqs \rightarrowtail q'ts'$ is $\Box q\Box \rightarrowtail q'\Box s'$ we add moreover

$$q(\blacksquare, \blacksquare) \to q'(\blacksquare, \Box s'\blacksquare).$$

(So the transition rule $\Box q\Box \rightarrowtail q'\Box s'$ corresponds to four reduction rules.)

1. Now it is not hard to prove that for configurations α, β we have:

$$\alpha \rightarrowtail \beta \Leftrightarrow \phi(\alpha) \to \phi(\beta).$$

2. Prove that, given a TRS R and a term t in R, the problem to determine whether t has an infinite reduction in R, is undecidable. This means: there is no algorithm that accepts as inputs pairs (R, t) of a TRS R (given by a finite set of rewrite rules) and a term $t \in \mathrm{Ter}(R)$, and that yields as output the answer 'yes' if t has an infinite reduction in R, and 'no' otherwise. (Using (1), reduce this problem to the well-known undecidable halting problem for Turing machines with empty tape as initial configuration.)
3. To each ground term in R_M of the form $q(t_1, t_2)$ where t_1, t_2 are terms in which no $q' \in Q$ occurs (call such a term 'restricted'), there corresponds a configuration of M; but this is not so without that restriction. Prove that if some term t in R_M has an infinite reduction in R_M, then there is also a restricted ground term t' in R_M having an infinite reduction, and thus yielding a corresponding infinite run of the Turing machine M.
4. Prove, using (3) and referring to the well-known undecidable *uniform* halting problem for Turing machines, that the problem to determine whether a given TRS is SN (strongly normalizing) is undecidable. The uniform halting problem for Turing machines is the problem to decide whether a given Turing machine halts on every input as initial configuration.

2.3 A termination proof technique

As Newman's lemma (WCR & SN $\Rightarrow$ CR) shows, termination (SN) is a useful property. In general, as noted in Exercise 2.2.21, it is undecidable whether a TRS is SN; but in many instances SN can be proved and various techniques have been developed to do so. (See [Huet and Oppen, 1980; Dershowitz, 1987].) We will present in this section one of the most powerful of such termination proof techniques: the method of *recursive path orderings*, as developed by Dershowitz on the basis of a beautiful theorem of Kruskal. (See also the similar concept of 'path of subterm ordering' in [Plaisted, 1978], discussed in [Rusinowitch, 1987b].) In fact we will use the presentation of [Bergstra and Klop, 1985], where the rather complicated inductive definitions of the usual presentation are replaced by a reduction procedure which is to our taste easier to grasp.

Definition 2.3.1.

1. Let $\mathbb{T}$ be the set of commutative finite trees with nodes labelled by natural numbers. Example: see Figure 2.10(a). This tree will also be denoted by: $3(5, 7(9), 8(0(1, 5)))$. Commutativity means that the 'arguments' may be permuted; thus $3(8(0(5, 1)), 5, 7(9))$ denotes the same commutative tree.
2. Let $\mathbb{T}^*$ be the set of such trees where some of the nodes may be marked with (a single) *. So $\mathbb{T} \subseteq \mathbb{T}^*$. Example: see Figure 2.10(b); this tree will be denoted by $3^*(5, 7(9^*), 8^*(0(1, 5)))$.

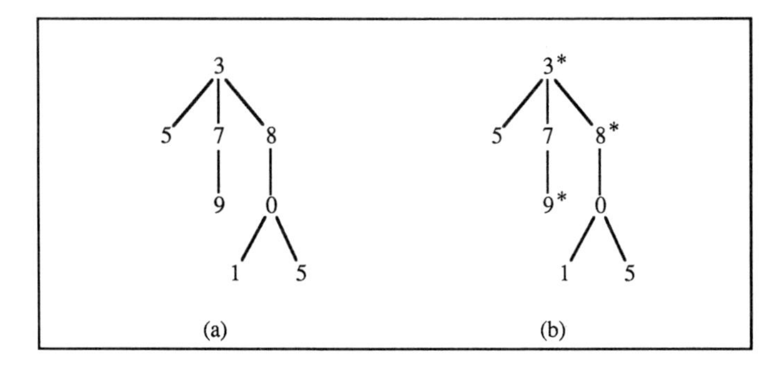

Figure 2.10

Notation 2.3.2. $n(t_1, \ldots, t_k)$ will be written as $n(\vec{t})$. The t_i $(i = 1, \ldots, k)$ are elements of $\mathbb{T}^*$. Further, if $t \equiv n(t_1, \ldots, t_k)$ then t^* stands for $n^*(t_1, \ldots, t_k)$.

Definition 2.3.3. On $\mathbb{T}^*$ we define a reduction relation $\Rightarrow$ as follows.

1. *place marker at the top:*
   $n(\vec{t}) \Rightarrow n^*(\vec{t}) \qquad (\vec{t} = t_1, \ldots, t_k; k \geq 0)$
2. *make copies below lesser top:*
   if $n > m$, then $n^*(\vec{t}) \Rightarrow m(n^*(\vec{t}), \ldots, n^*(\vec{t}))$ ($j \geq 0$ copies of $n^*(\vec{t})$)
3. *push marker down:*
   $n^*(s, \vec{t}) \Rightarrow n(s^*, \ldots, s^*, \vec{t}) \qquad (j \geq 0$ copies of $s^*)$
4. *select argument:*
   $n^*(t_1, \ldots, t_k) \Rightarrow t_i \qquad (i \in \{1, \ldots, k\}, k \geq 1)$

It is understood that these reductions may take place in a context, i.e. if $t \Rightarrow s$, then $n(—, t, —) \Rightarrow n(—, s, —)$

We write $\Rightarrow^+$ for the transitive (but not reflexive) closure of $\Rightarrow$.

Example 2.3.4. Figure 2.11 displays a reduction in $\mathbb{T}^*$.

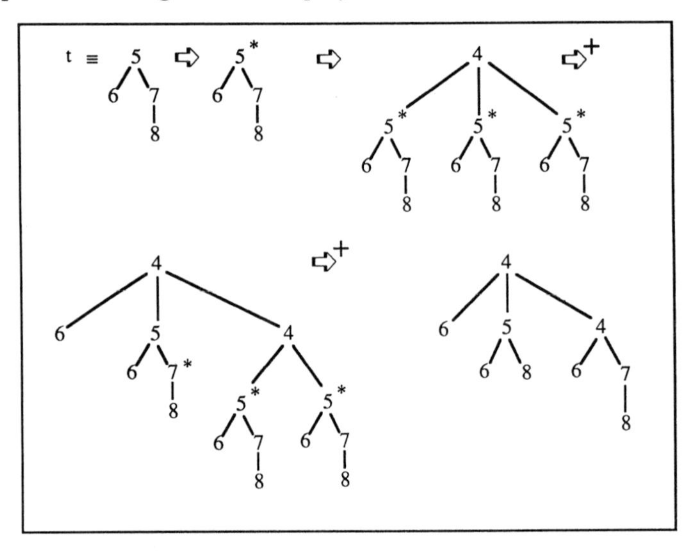

Figure 2.11

Clearly, the reduction $\Rightarrow$ is not SN in $\mathbb{T}^*$; for, consider the second step in Figure 2.11: there the right-hand side contains a copy of the left-hand side. However:

Theorem 2.3.5. *The relation $\Rightarrow^+$, restricted to $\mathbb{T}$, is a well-founded partial ordering. Or, rephrased, the relation $\Rightarrow^+$, restricted to $\mathbb{T}$, is SN.*

So there is no infinite sequence $t_0 \Rightarrow^+ t_1 \Rightarrow^+ t_2 \Rightarrow^+ \cdots$ of terms t_i $(i \geq 0)$ without markers. The proof of Theorem 2.3.5 is based on Kruskal's tree theorem; we will give the main argument.

In order to introduce the next notion of 'embedding', we must make the definition of trees $t \in \mathbb{T}$ somewhat more precise. An element $t \in \mathbb{T}$ is a pair $(\langle D, \leq, \alpha_0 \rangle, \mathcal{L})$ where D is a finite set $\{\alpha_0, \beta, \gamma, \ldots\}$ with distinguished element α_0, called the root or the top of t, and partially ordered by $\leq$. We require that:

1. $\alpha_0 \geq \beta$ for all $\beta \in D$,
2. $\beta \leq \gamma$ and $\beta \leq \delta \Rightarrow \gamma \leq \delta$ or $\delta \leq \gamma$, for all $\beta, \gamma, \delta \in D$.

The set D is also called NODES(t). Furthermore, $\mathcal{L}$: $D \to \mathbb{N}$ is a map assigning labels (natural numbers) to the nodes of t. Finally, we use the notation $\alpha \wedge \beta$ for the supremum (least upper bound) of $\alpha, \beta \in D$. (The actual names $\alpha, \beta, \ldots$ of the nodes are not important, which is why they were suppressed in the pictorial representation of $t \in \mathbb{T}$ above.)

Definition 2.3.6. Let $t, t' \in \mathbb{T}$. We say that t is *(homeomorphically) embedded in* t', notation $t \preceq t'$, if there is a map φ: NODES(t) $\to$ NODES(t') such that:

1. φ is *injective*,
2. φ is *monotonic* $(\alpha \leq \beta \Rightarrow \varphi(\alpha) \leq \varphi(\beta))$,
3. φ is *sup preserving* $(\varphi(\alpha \wedge \beta) = \varphi(\alpha) \wedge \varphi(\beta))$,
4. φ is *label increasing* $(\mathcal{L}(\alpha) \leq \mathcal{L}'(\varphi(\alpha))$, where $\mathcal{L}, \mathcal{L}'$ are the labelling maps of t, t' respectively; $\leq$ is the ordering on natural numbers).

Actually, (2) is superfluous as it follows from (3).

Example 2.3.7.

1. $2(9, 7(0, 4)) \preceq 1(3(8(0(5, 1)), 9, 5(9)), 2)$ as the embedding in Figure 2.12 shows.
2. Note that we do *not* have $1(0, 0) \preceq 1(0(0, 0))$.

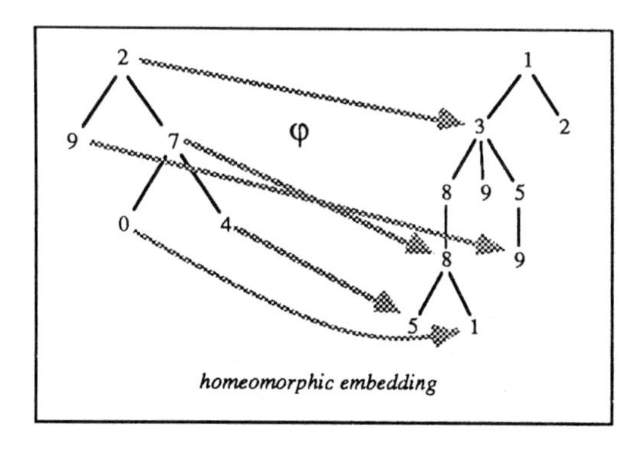

Figure 2.12

Clearly, $\preceq$ is a partial order on $\mathbb{T}$. Moreover it satisfies the following remarkable property:

Theorem 2.3.8. (Kruskal's tree theorem) *Let $t_0, t_1, t_2, \ldots$ be a sequence of trees in $\mathbb{T}$. Then for some $i < j$: $t_i \preceq t_j$.*

The proof of this theorem, as given in [Kruskal, 1960], is extremely complicated. Proofs are given in [Dershowitz, 1979] and [Dershowitz and Jouannaud, 1990]. See also Exercise 2.3.12 for a detailed proof sketch of a restricted case which is sufficient for the present purpose.

Now we have the following proposition (of which (1) is non-trivial to prove):

Proposition 2.3.9.

1. *$\Rightarrow^+$ is a strict partial order on $\mathbb{T}$,*
2. *if $s \preceq t$, then $t \Rightarrow^* s$.*

(Here $\Rightarrow^*$ is the transitive-reflexive closure of $\Rightarrow$.) Combining 2.3.8 and 2.3.9, we have Theorem 2.3.5. For, suppose there is an infinite sequence

$$t_0 \Rightarrow^+ t_1 \Rightarrow^+ t_2 \Rightarrow^+ \cdots \Rightarrow^+ t_i \Rightarrow^+ \cdots \Rightarrow^+ t_j \Rightarrow^+ \cdots$$

then for some $i < j$ we have $t_i \preceq t_j$, hence $t_j \Rightarrow^* t_i$, so $t_i \Rightarrow^+ t_i$, which is impossible as $\Rightarrow^+$ is a strict partial order.

Application 2.3.10 ([Dershowitz, 1987]). Let a TRS R as in Table 2.9 be given. To prove that R is SN, choose a 'weight' assignment $\vee \mapsto 1$, $\wedge \mapsto 2$,

$\neg\neg x$	$\to$	x
$\neg(x \vee y)$	$\to$	$(\neg x \wedge \neg y)$
$\neg(x \wedge y)$	$\to$	$(\neg x \vee \neg y)$
$x \wedge (y \vee z)$	$\to$	$(x \wedge y) \vee (x \wedge z)$
$(y \vee z) \wedge x$	$\to$	$(y \wedge x) \vee (z \wedge x)$

Table 2.9

$\neg \mapsto 3$. Now a reduction in R corresponds to a $\Rightarrow^+$ reduction in $\mathbb{T}$ (and hence it is also SN) as follows:

$$\begin{array}{lll}
3(3(t)) & \Rightarrow^+ & t \\
3(1(t,s)) & \Rightarrow^+ & 2(3(t),3(s)) \\
3(2(t,s)) & \Rightarrow^+ & 1(3(t),3(s)) \\
2(t,1(s,r)) & \Rightarrow^+ & 1(2(t,s),2(t,r)) \\
2(1(s,r),t) & \Rightarrow^+ & 1(2(s,t),2(r,t))
\end{array}$$

E.g. the second rule:

$$\begin{array}{rcl} 3(1(t,s)) & \Rightarrow & 3^*(1(t,s)) \\ & \Rightarrow & 2(3^*(1(t,s)), 3^*(1(t,s))) \\ & \Rightarrow^+ & 2(3(1^*(t,s)), 3(1^*(t,s))) \\ & \Rightarrow^+ & 2(3(t), 3(s)). \end{array}$$

Remark 2.3.11.

1. The termination proof method above does not work when a rule is present of which the left-hand side is embedded (in the sense of Definition 2.3.6) in the right-hand side, as in $f(s(x)) \to g(s(x), f(p(s(x))))$. For an extension of Kruskal's theorem, leading to a method which also can deal with this case, see [Kamin and Lévy, 1980] and [Puel, 1986].
2. Another example where the method above does not work directly, is found in the TRSs corresponding to process algebra axiomatizations as in [Bergstra and Klop, 1984; Bergstra and Klop, 1985]. For instance in the axiom system PA there are the rewrite rules

$$\begin{array}{lcl} x \| y & \to & (x \mathbin{⌊\!⌊} y) + (y \mathbin{⌊\!⌊} x) \\ (x+y) \mathbin{⌊\!⌊} z & \to & (x \mathbin{⌊\!⌊} z) + (y \mathbin{⌊\!⌊} z) \\ (a \cdot x) \mathbin{⌊\!⌊} y & \to & a \cdot (x \| y). \end{array}$$

Here we want to order the operators as follows: $\| > ⌊\!⌊ > \cdot, +$, but then we get stuck at the third rule with the re-emergence of the 'heavy' operator $\|$. In [Bergstra and Klop, 1985] the solution was adopted to introduce infinitely many operators $\|_n$ and $⌊\!⌊_n$, where n refers to some complexity measure of the actual arguments of the operators in a reduction. In fact, the operator + does not contribute to the problem, and forgetting about it and writing $x \| y$ as $g(x,y)$, $x \mathbin{⌊\!⌊} y$ as $h(x,y)$, $a \cdot x$ as $f(x)$, we have Example 16 in [Dershowitz, 1987] where this problem takes the following form and is solved by a lexicographical combination of recursive path orderings:

$$\begin{array}{lcl} g(x,y) & \to & h(x,y) \\ h(f(x),y) & \to & f(g(x,y)). \end{array}$$

The termination proof as in [Bergstra and Klop, 1985] amounts to the following for the present example. Define a norm $|\ |$ on terms by: $|\,t\,|$ is the length of t in symbols; then introduce normed operators g_n and $h_n (n \geq 2)$; order the operators thus: $g_n > h_n > f, h_{n+1} > g_n$. Then replace in a term t every subterm $h(s,r)$ by $h_{|s|+|r|}(s,r)$ and likewise for $g(s,r)$. Now the recursive path ordering as before is applicable. Caution is required here: the norm must be chosen such that the norm of a term t is not increased by reduction of a subterm of t. (For this reason, taking $| t |$ as the length of t in symbols would not work for the process algebra example above.)

3. A third example where the proof method above does not work, is when an associativity rule

$$(x \cdot y) \cdot z \quad \rightarrow \quad x \cdot (y \cdot z)$$

is present. The same problem occurs in the TRS for Ackermann's function:

$$\begin{array}{lcl} A(0,x) & \rightarrow & S(x) \\ A(S(x),0) & \rightarrow & A(x,S(0)) \\ A(S(x),S(y)) & \rightarrow & A(x,A(S(x),y)) \end{array}$$

What we need here is the *lexicographic path ordering* of [Kamin and Lévy, 1980], see [Dershowitz, 1987]. Essentially this says that a reduction in complexity in the first argument of A outweighs an increase (strictly bounded by the complexity of the original term) in the second argument. In fact, an ordering with the same effect can easily be described in the framework of reduction with markers * as explained above: all one has to do is give up the commutativity of the trees in $\mathbb{T}$ and $\mathbb{T}^*$ and require that an embedding (Definition 2.3.6) respects also the left–right ordering; Kruskal's tree theorem works also for this case of non-commutative trees.

Next, the rules in Definition 2.3.3 are restricted such that the arities of the operators are respected; in Definition 2.3.3 the operators were treated 'varyadic'. So rule (3) becomes: $n^*(t_1,\ldots,t_i,\ldots,t_k) \Rightarrow n(t_1,\ldots,t_i^*,\ldots,t_k)$ $(1 \leq i \leq k)$. Further, we add to the rules in Definition 2.3.3 (with (3) amended) the rule

5. *simplify left argument:*
   $n^*(\vec{t}) \Rightarrow n(t_1^*, n^*(\vec{t}),\ldots,n^*(\vec{t}))$
   $(\vec{t} = t_1,\ldots,t_k$ $(k \geq 1)$; $k-1$ copies of $n^*(\vec{t}))$

Example:

$$\begin{array}{rcl} A(S(x),S(y)) & \Rightarrow & A^*(S(x),S(y)) \\ & \Rightarrow & A(S^*(x),A^*(S(x),S(y))) \\ & \Rightarrow & A(x,A^*(S(x),S(y))) \\ & \Rightarrow & A(x,A(S(x),S^*(y))) \\ & \Rightarrow & A(x,A(S(x),y)). \end{array}$$

Exercise 2.3.12. In this exercise we outline a short proof of a restricted version of Kruskal's tree theorem 2.3.8, which is sufficient for termination proofs of TRSs where the function symbols have arities uniformly bounded by some natural number N. (There may be infinitely many function symbols, as e.g. the g_n, h_n in the preceding Remark 2.3.11.) *A fortiori* this is the case for TRSs with finite alphabet.

The proof below is similar to that in [Dershowitz, 1979]; the proof in [Dershowitz and Jouannaud, 1990] is similar but for a short-cut there appealing to a special case of the tree theorem known as Higman's lemma. These proofs are originally due to [Nash-Williams, 1963]. First we define:

1. The *branching degree* of a node s in $t \in \mathbb{T}$ is the number of immediate successor nodes of s.
2. $\mathbb{T}_N$ is the subset of $\mathbb{T}$ consisting of trees where all nodes have branching degree $\leq N$. Likewise we define $\mathbb{T}^*_N$.

We will now outline a proof of Kruskal's tree theorem 2.3.8 where $\mathbb{T}$ is restricted to $\mathbb{T}_N$.

1. Claim. *Each infinite sequence of natural numbers* $n_0, n_1, n_2, \ldots$ *has a weakly ascending infinite subsequence.*
   This means that there is a subsequence $n_{f(0)}, n_{f(1)}, n_{f(2)}, \ldots$ with $f(0) < f(1) < f(2) < \ldots$ such that $n_{f(0)} \leq n_{f(1)} \leq n_{f(2)} \leq \ldots$. The proof is simple.
2. Definition.
   (a) Let $t \in \mathbb{T}_N$. Then $|\, t \,|$ is the number of nodes of t.
   (b) Notation: an infinite sequence of trees $t_0, t_1, \ldots$ will be written as $\mathbf{t}$. The initial segment $t_0, \ldots, t_{n-1}$ is $(\mathbf{t})_n$. The set of infinite sequences of trees from $\mathbb{T}_N$ is $\mathbb{T}^\omega_N$.
   (c) Let $D \subseteq \mathbb{T}^\omega_N$. Then the sequence $\mathbf{t} \in D$ is *minimal in* D if $\forall \mathbf{s} \in D\ (\mathbf{s})_n = (\mathbf{t})_n \Rightarrow |\, s_n \,| \geq |\, t_n \,|$.
   (d) Furthermore, we say that $\mathbf{s}, \mathbf{t} \in \mathbb{T}^\omega_N$ have distance 2^{-n} if $(\mathbf{s})_n = (\mathbf{t})_n$ but $(\mathbf{s})_{n+1} \neq (\mathbf{t})_{n+1}$. This induces a metric on $\mathbb{T}^\omega_N$.
3. Claim. *Let* $D \subseteq \mathbb{T}^\omega_N$ *be non-empty and closed w.r.t. the metric just defined. Then* D *contains a minimal element (with respect to* D*).*
   The proof of Claim 3 is easy.
4. Notation.
   (a) Let $\mathbf{s}, \mathbf{t} \in \mathbb{T}^\omega_N$. Then $\mathbf{s} \subseteq \mathbf{t}$ means that $\mathbf{s}$ is a subsequence of $\mathbf{t}$.
   (b) Let $\mathbf{t} = t_0, t_1, \ldots$ and let $\mathbf{s} = s_{f(0)}, s_{f(1)}, \ldots$ be a subsequence of $\mathbf{t}$, such that for all i, $s_{f(i)}$ is a *proper* subtree of $t_{f(i)}$. Then we write $\mathbf{s} \subseteq\subseteq \mathbf{t}$ and call $\mathbf{s}$ a subsubsequence of $\mathbf{t}$. (See Figure 2.13.)
5. Definition. $\mathbf{s} = s_0, s_1, s_2, \ldots$ is a *chain* if $s_0 \preceq s_1 \preceq s_2 \preceq \ldots$, where $\preceq$ is the embedding relation as in Kruskal's tree theorem.

We will now suppose, for a proof by contradiction, that there is a counterexample sequence to the restricted version of Kruskal's Tree Theorem that we want to prove. That is, the set $C \subseteq \mathbb{T}^\omega_N$ of sequences $\mathbf{s}$ such that for no $i < j$ we have $s_i \preceq s_j$, is supposed to be non-empty. Note that C is closed in the sense of Definition 2(d).

6. CLAIM. *Let* $\mathbf{t}$ *be a minimal element from* C. *Suppose* $\mathbf{s} \subseteq\subseteq \mathbf{t}$.
   (a) *Then for some* $i < j$: $s_i \preceq s_j$.

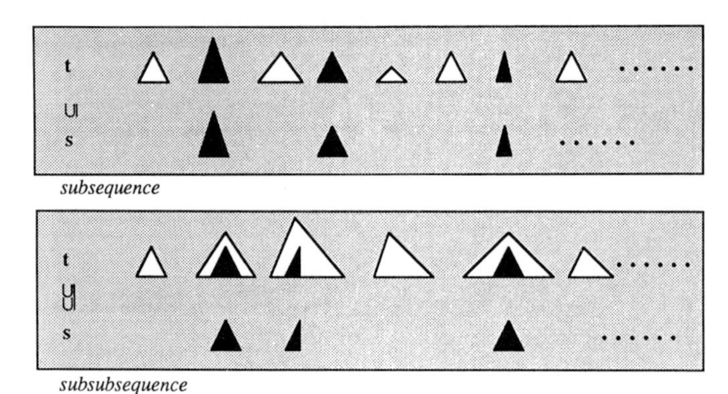

Figure 2.13

(b) *Even stronger,* $\mathbf{s}$ *contains a subsequence which is a chain.*

Proof of Claim 6(a). (Note that a minimal element $\mathbf{t}$ exists by the assumption $C \neq \varnothing$ and by Claim 3.) Let $\mathbf{s}$, $\mathbf{t}$ be as in Claim 6. Let s_0 be a proper subtree of $t_{f(0)} = t_k$. Consider the sequence $t_0, \ldots, t_{k-1}, s_0, s_1, s_2, \ldots$, that is, $(\mathbf{t})_k$ followed by $\mathbf{s}$. By minimality of $\mathbf{t}$, this sequence is not in C. Hence it contains an embedded pair of elements (the earlier one embedded in the later one). The embedded pair cannot occur in the prefix $(\mathbf{t})_k$ because $\mathbf{t} \in C$. It can also not be of the form $t_i \preceq s_j$, since then $\mathbf{t}$ would contain the embedded pair $t_i \preceq t_{f(j)}$. So, the embedded pair must occur in the postfix $\mathbf{s}$.

As to part (b) of the claim, suppose $\mathbf{s}$ does not contain an infinite chain as subsequence. Then $\mathbf{s}$ contains an infinite number of finite chains, each starting to the right of the end of the previous finite chain and each maximal in the sense that it cannot be prolonged by an element occurring to the right of it in $\mathbf{s}$. Now consider the last elements of these finite chains. These last elements constitute an infinite subsubsequence of $\mathbf{t}$, containing by (a) of the claim an embedded pair. But that means that one of the maximal finite chains can be prolonged, a contradiction.

7. Claim. *Let* $\mathbf{t}$ *be minimal in* C *and suppose* $\mathbf{s} \subseteq\subseteq \mathbf{r} \subseteq \mathbf{t}$. *Then* $\mathbf{s}$ *contains an infinite chain as subsequence.*

The proof of Claim 7 is trivial. We will now apply a sieve procedure to the minimal counterexample sequence $\mathbf{t} \in C$. By Claim 1 we can take a subsequence $\mathbf{t}'$ of $\mathbf{t}$ such that the root labels are weakly ascending. Of $\mathbf{t}'$ we take a subsequence $\mathbf{t}^*$ with the property that the branching degrees of the roots are a weakly ascending sequence. By Claim 6 every subsubsequence of $\mathbf{t}^*$ still contains an infinite embedding chain.

Let us 'freeze' the elements in $\mathbf{t}'$, that is, we impose an ordering of the successors of each node in some arbitrary way. So the frozen trees in $\mathbf{t}'$ are no longer commutative trees, and we can speak of the first, second etc. 'arguments' of a node. (An argument of a node α is the subtree with as root a successor node β of α.)

The next step in the sieve procedure is done by considering the sequence of first arguments of (the roots of) the elements in t^*. As this is a subsubsequence, it contains an infinite chain. Accordingly, we thin t^* out, to the subsequence t^{**}. This sequence has the property that its first arguments form a chain. Next, t^{**} is thinned out by considering the sequence of the second arguments of t^{**}. Again, this sequence contains a chain, and thinning t^{**} accordingly yields the subsequence t^{***}.

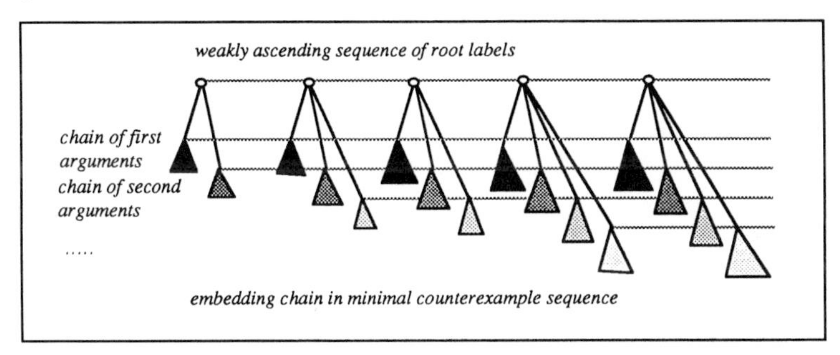

Figure 2.14

After at most N steps of the last kind, we are through. The result is then a chain, since the roots already satisfied the embedding condition (they form a weakly ascending chain), and the arguments are also related as chains. (See Figure 2.14.) However, this contradicts the assumption that **t** contains no embedded pair. Hence C is empty, and the restricted version of Kruskal's tree theorem is proved.

Exercise 2.3.13. [Kruskal, 1960] In this exercise we introduce the terminology of *well-quasi-orders* which is often used to formulate Kruskal's tree theorem.

1. Definition. The binary relation $\leq$ is a *quasi-order* (q.o.) if it is reflexive and transitive. (So the relation $\twoheadrightarrow$ in a TRS is a q.o.) If in addition $\leq$ is anti-symmetric (i.e. $x \leq y$ & $y \leq x \Rightarrow x = y$ for all x, y) then $\leq$ is a partial order (p.o.).
2. Definition. Let $\langle X, \leq \rangle$ be a q.o. A subset $Y \subseteq X$ is called a *cone* if $x \in Y$ & $x \leq y \Rightarrow y \in Y$ for all $x, y \in X$. The cone *generated by* $Y \subseteq X$, notation $Y\uparrow$, is the set $\{x \in X \mid \exists y \in Y\ y \leq x\}$. (It is the intersection of all cones containing Y.) A cone Z is *finitely generated* if $Z = Y\uparrow$ for some finite Y.
3. Definition. Let $\langle X, \leq \rangle$ be a q.o. (p.o., respectively). Then $\langle X, \leq \rangle$ is a *well-quasi-order* (w.q.o.) or *well-partial-order* (w.p.o.) respectively, if every cone of X is finitely generated.
4. Definition. Let $\langle X, \leq \rangle$ be a qo. A subset $Y \subseteq X$ is an *anti-chain* if the elements of Y are pairwise incomparable, i.e. for all $x, y \in Y$ such that $x \neq y$ we have neither $x \leq y$ nor $y \leq x$.

Prove the following lemma:

5. Lemma. *Let $\langle X, \leq \rangle$ be a q.o. Then the following conditions are equivalent:*

(a) *$\langle X, \leq \rangle$ is a w.q.o.;*

(b) *X contains no infinite descending chains $x_0 > x_1 > x_2 > \cdots$ and all anti-chains of X are finite;*

(c) *for every infinite sequence of elements $x_0, x_1, x_2, \ldots$ in X there are i, j such that $i < j$ and $x_i \leq x_j$.*

So, Kruskal's tree theorem as stated in Theorem 2.3.8 can be reformulated as follows: $\langle \mathbb{T}, \preceq \rangle$ *is a well-quasi-order.* Prove that $\langle \mathbb{T}, \preceq \rangle$ is in fact a partial order; so Kruskal's theorem states that $\langle \mathbb{T}, \preceq \rangle$ is even a well-partial-order.

Exercise 2.3.14.

1. Show that the well-partial-order $\langle \mathbb{T}, \preceq \rangle$ is not a linear order.

2. Show that $\Rightarrow^+$ is a linear order. As it is well founded (Theorem 2.3.5), it corresponds to an ordinal. For connections with the ordinal Γ_0, the first impredicative ordinal, see [Dershowitz, 1987]. For more about Kruskal's tree theorem and the connection with large ordinals, as well as a version of the tree theorem which is independent from Peano's Arithmetic, see [Smoryn̂ski, 1982] and [Gallier, 1987].

Exercise 2.3.15. (Multiset orderings) Very useful for termination proofs (used in some of the Exercises 2.0.8) are the *multiset orderings*; these are particular cases of the well-founded ordering $\langle \mathbb{T}, \Rightarrow^+ \rangle$ discussed above, namely by restricting the domain $\mathbb{T}$.

1. *Multisets.* Let $\langle X, < \rangle$ be a strict partial order. Then the p.o. of *multisets over* X, or the *multiset extension of* X, notation $\langle X^\mu, <^\mu \rangle$, is obtained as follows. The elements of X^μ are finite 'sets' of elements from X with the understanding that multiplicity of occurrences is taken into account, other than in ordinary sets. A multiset will be denoted by square brackets [ ]. For example, if $a, b \in X$ then $[a, a, b]$ and $[a, b]$ are different multisets; but $[a, a, b]$ and $[a, b, a]$ denote the same multiset. Stated differently, a multiset is a finite sequence of elements where the order of occurrences in the sequence is disregarded. Giving a more formal definition is left to the reader. A multiset is also known as a *bag*. We use in this exercise $\alpha, \beta, \ldots$ as variables for multisets.

   Now we define the following relation $>_1$ between elements of X^μ by the two clauses:

   (a) $[a] >_1 [b_1, \ldots, b_n]$ for all $a, b_1, \ldots, b_n \in X$ $(n \geq 0)$ such that $a > b_i$ $(i = 1, \ldots, n)$;

   (b) $\alpha >_1 \beta \Rightarrow \alpha \cup \gamma >_1 \beta \cup \gamma$. Here $\cup$ denotes multiset union, defined in the obvious way as a union where the multiplicities of the elements are respected. For example, $[a, a, b] \cup [a, b, c] = [a, a, a, b, b, c]$. Thus, a multiset gets smaller by replacing an element in it by arbitrarily many (possibly 0) elements which are less in the original ordering. The converse of $>_1$ is $<_1$.

   Furthermore, we define:

   (c) $<^\mu$ is the transitive closure of $<_1$.

Now prove the following statements:

(a) If $\langle X, < \rangle$ is a strict partial order, then so is its multiset extension $\langle X^\mu, <^\mu \rangle$. If $\langle X, < \rangle$ is moreover a linear order, then so is $\langle X^\mu, <^\mu \rangle$.

(b) [Dershowitz and Manna, 1979] $\langle X, < \rangle$ is a well-founded p.o. $\Leftrightarrow \langle X^\mu, <^\mu \rangle$ is a well-founded p.o. (The p.o. $\langle X, < \rangle$ is well-founded if there are no infinite descending chains $x_0 > x_1 > \ldots$.)

(c) Let $\langle X, < \rangle$ be a well-founded linear order with order type α. Then $\langle X^\mu, <^\mu \rangle$ has order type ω^α.

2. *Nested multisets.* Let $\langle X, < \rangle$ be a p.o. Then the p.o. of *nested multisets over* X, notation: $\langle X^{\mu^*}, <^{\mu^*} \rangle$, is defined as follows. The domain X^{μ^*} is the least set Y such that $X \subseteq Y$ and $Y^\mu = Y$. Or, inductively:

(a) $X_0 = X$;

(b) $X_{n+1} = (X_0 \cup \cdots \cup X_n)^\mu$;

(c) $X^{\mu^*} = \cup_{n \geq 0} X_n$.

Note that the elements of X^{μ^*} can be represented as finite commutative trees, with terminal nodes labelled by elements from X, and non-terminal nodes with a label representing the multiset operator. The *depth* of $\alpha \in X^{\mu^*}$ is the stage of the inductive definition in which it is generated, or in the tree representation, the maximum of the lengths of the branches of the tree corresponding to α.

Furthermore, the ordering $<^{\mu^*}$ is the least relation R extending $<$ and satisfying:

(a) $x \, R \, \alpha$ for all $x \in X$ and multisets $\alpha \in X^{\mu^*} - X$;

(b) $[\alpha] \, R \, [\beta_1, \ldots, \beta_n]$ for all $\alpha, \beta_1, \ldots, \beta_n \in X^{\mu^*}$ $(n \geq 0)$ such that $\alpha_i \, R \, \beta_i$ $(i = 1, \ldots, n)$;

(c) $\alpha \, R \, \beta \Rightarrow \alpha \cup \gamma \, R \, \beta \cup \gamma$ for all multisets $\alpha, \beta, \gamma \in X^{\mu^*} - X$.

Now:

(a) Let $\langle X, < \rangle$ be a p.o. Prove that $\langle X^{\mu^*}, <^{\mu^*} \rangle$ is a p.o. If moreover $\langle X, < \rangle$ is a linear order, then so is $\langle X^{\mu^*}, <^{\mu^*} \rangle$.

(b) Let $\alpha, \beta \in \langle X^{\mu^*}, <^{\mu^*} \rangle$. Prove that if the depth of α is greater than the depth of β, we have $\alpha <^{\mu^*} \beta$.

(c) [Dershowitz and Manna, 1979]
$\langle X, < \rangle$ is well-founded $\Leftrightarrow \langle X^{\mu^*}, <^{\mu^*} \rangle$ is well-founded.

(d) Let $\langle \mathbb{N}, < \rangle$ be the natural numbers with the usual ordering. Prove that $\langle \mathbb{N}^{\mu^*}, >^{\mu^*} \rangle$, the nested multisets over the natural numbers, is in fact a restriction of the recursive path ordering $\langle \mathbb{T}, \Rightarrow^+ \rangle$ if the non-terminal nodes of the tree representation of $\alpha \in \mathbb{N}^{\mu^*}$ are taken to be 0. That is, for $\alpha, \beta \in \mathbb{N}^{\mu^*} \subseteq \mathbb{T}$ we then have: $\alpha >^{\mu^*} \beta \Leftrightarrow \alpha \Rightarrow^+ \beta$.

(e) Show that the order type of the well-founded linear ordering $\langle \mathbb{N}^{\mu^*}, <^{\mu^*} \rangle$ is ϵ_0. Note that $\langle \mathbb{N}^{\mu^*}, <^{\mu^*} \rangle$ is isomorphic to $\langle \{0\}^{\mu^*}, <^{\mu^*} \rangle$. Here '$<$' in the last occurrence of $<^{\mu^*}$ is the restriction of $<$ to $\{0\}$ (which in fact is the empty relation). Figure 2.15 gives an example of two multisets α, β over $\{0\}$, such that $\alpha >^{\mu^*} \beta$, or equivalently, $\alpha \Rightarrow^+ \beta$. All labels at the nodes can be taken 0, and are omitted in the figure. Note that the procedure using the markers may employ all clauses in Definition 2.3.3 except clause (2).

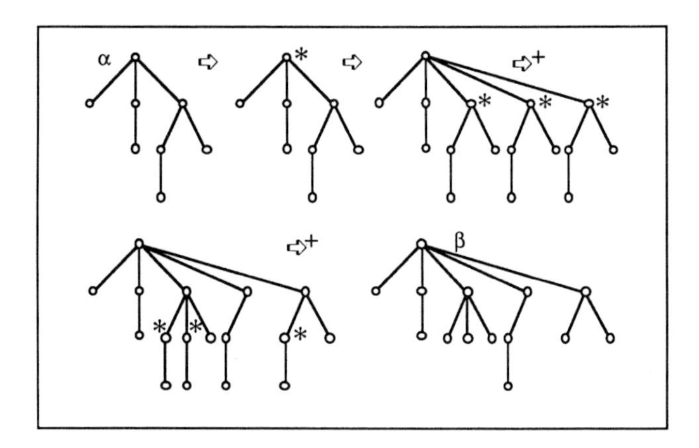

Figure 2.15

2.4 Completion of equational specifications

In this section we will give an introduction to Knuth–Bendix completion of equational specifications. First we will introduce the latter concept.

Equational specifications: syntax and semantics

We can be short about introducing the syntax of equational specifications: an equational specification is just a TRS 'without orientation'. More precisely, an equational specification is a pair (Σ, E) where the signature (or alphabet) Σ is as in Section 2.1 for TRSs (Σ, R), and where E is a set of equations $s = t$ between terms $s, t \in \mathrm{Ter}(\Sigma)$.

If an equation $s = t$ is *derivable* from the equations in E, we write $(\Sigma, E) \vdash s = t$ or $s =_E t$. Formally, derivability is defined by means of the inference system of Table 2.10.

Exercise 2.4.1. (Equational deduction systems) Often the inference system in Table 2.10 is presented slightly differently, as follows. Prove the equivalence of the two versions below with the system above. Axioms (in addition to the equations in E):

$$t = t \quad \textit{reflexivity}$$

Rules:

$$(\Sigma, E) \vdash s = t \qquad \text{if } s = t \in E$$

$$\frac{(\Sigma, E) \vdash s = t}{(\Sigma, E) \vdash s^{\sigma} = t^{\sigma}} \qquad \text{for every substitution } \sigma$$

$$\frac{(\Sigma, E) \vdash s_1 = t_1, \ldots, (\Sigma, E) \vdash s_n = t_n}{(\Sigma, E) \vdash F(s_1, \ldots, s_n) = F(t_1, \ldots, t_n)} \qquad \text{for every } n\text{-ary } F \in \Sigma$$

$$(\Sigma, E) \vdash t = t$$

$$\frac{(\Sigma, E) \vdash t_1 = t_2, (\Sigma, E) \vdash t_2 = t_3}{(\Sigma, E) \vdash t_1 = t_3}$$

$$\frac{(\Sigma, E) \vdash s = t}{(\Sigma, E) \vdash t = s}$$

Table 2.10

$$\frac{t_1 = t_2}{t_2 = t_2} \qquad \textit{symmetry}$$

$$\frac{t_1 = t_2,\ t_2 = t_3}{t_1 = t_3} \qquad \textit{transitivity}$$

$$\frac{t_1 = t_2}{t_1[x := t] = t_2[x := t]} \qquad \textit{substitution}(1)$$

$$\frac{t_1 = t_2}{t[x := t_1] = t[x := t_2]} \qquad \textit{substitution}(2)$$

Here $[x := t]$ denotes substitution of t for all occurrences of x. (The assignment notation is chosen to avoid the usual confusion between $[x/t], [t/x], [x\backslash t], [t\backslash x]$.) An equivalent formulation is to combine the two substitution rules in one:

$$\frac{t_1 = t_2,\ t = t'}{t_1[x := t] = t_2[x := t']} \qquad \textit{substitution}$$

If Σ is a signature, a Σ-*algebra* $\mathcal{A}$ is a set A together with functions $F^{\mathcal{A}} : A^n \to A$ for every n-ary function symbol $F \in \Sigma$. (If F is 0-ary, i.e. F is a constant, then $F^{\mathcal{A}} \in A$.) An equation $s = t$ $(s, t \in \mathrm{Ter}(\Sigma))$ is assigned a meaning in $\mathcal{A}$ by interpreting the function symbols in s, t via the corresponding functions in $\mathcal{A}$. Variables in $s = t$ are (implicitly) universally quantified. If the universally quantified statement corresponding to $s = t$ ($s, t \in \mathrm{Ter}(\Sigma)$) is true in $\mathcal{A}$, we write $\mathcal{A} \models s = t$ and say that $s = t$ is *valid* in $\mathcal{A}$. $\mathcal{A}$ is called a *model* of a set of equations E if every equation in E is valid in $\mathcal{A}$. Abbreviation: $\mathcal{A} \models E$. The *variety* of Σ-algebras defined by an equational specification (Σ, E), notation $\mathrm{Alg}(\Sigma, E)$, is the class of all Σ-algebras $\mathcal{A}$ such that $\mathcal{A} \models E$. Instead of $\forall \mathcal{A} \in \mathrm{Alg}(\Sigma, E)\ \mathcal{A} \models F$, where F is a set of equations between Σ-terms, we will write $(\Sigma, E) \models F$. There is the well-known completeness theorem for equational logic of [Birkhoff, 1935]:

Theorem 2.4.2. *Let (Σ, E) be an equational specification. Then for all $s, t \in \mathrm{Ter}(\Sigma)$:*

$$(\Sigma, E) \vdash s = t \ \Leftrightarrow\ (\Sigma, E) \models s = t.$$

Now the *validity problem* or *uniform word problem* for (Σ, E) is:

> *Given an equation $s = t$ between Σ-terms, decide whether or not $(\Sigma, E) \models s = t$.*

According to Birkhoff's completeness theorem for equational logic this amounts to deciding $(\Sigma, E) \vdash s = t$. Now we can state why *complete* TRSs (i.e. TRSs which are SN and CR) are important. Suppose for the equational specification (Σ, E) we can find a complete TRS (Σ, R) such that for all terms $s, t \in \mathrm{Ter}(\Sigma)$:

$$t =_R s \ \Leftrightarrow\ E \vdash t = s \qquad (*)$$

Then (if R has finitely many rewrite rules only) we have a positive solution of the validity problem. The decision algorithm is simple:

1. *Reduce s and t to their respective normal forms s', t'*
2. *Compare s' and t': $s =_R t$ iff $s' \equiv t'$.*

We are now faced with the question how to find a complete TRS R for a given set of equations E such that $(*)$ holds. In general this is not possible, since not every E (even if finite) has a solvable validity problem. The most famous example of such an E with unsolvable validity problem is the set of equations obtained from CL, combinatory logic, in Tables 2.3, 2.4 above after replacing '$\rightarrow$' by '$=$': see Table 2.11.

$Sxyz$	$=$	$xz(yz)$
Kxy	$=$	x
Ix	$=$	x

Table 2.11

(For a proof of the unsolvability see [Barendregt, 1981].) So the validity problem of (Σ, E) can be solved by providing a complete TRS (Σ, R) for

(Σ, E). Note however, that there are equational specifications (Σ, E) with decidable validity problem but without a complete TRS (Σ, R) satisfying $(*)$: see the following Exercise.

Exercise 2.4.3. Let (Σ, E) be the specification given by the equations

$$\begin{array}{lcl} x + 0 & = & x \\ x + S(y) & = & S(x + y) \\ x + y & = & y + x \end{array}$$

Prove that there is no complete TRS R 'for' E, i.e. such that for all terms $s, t \in \text{Ter}(\Sigma) : s =_R t \Leftrightarrow s =_E t$. (Consider in a supposed complete TRS R, the normal forms of the open terms $x + y$ and $y + x$.)

It is important to realize that we have considered up to now equations $s = t$ between possibly *open* Σ-terms (i.e. possibly containing variables). If we restrict attention to equations $s = t$ between *ground* terms s, t, we are considering the *word problem* for (Σ, E), which is the following decidability problem:

> *Given an equation $s = t$ between ground terms $s, t \in \text{Ter}(\Sigma)$, decide whether or not $(\Sigma, E) \models s = t$ (or equivalently, $(\Sigma, E) \vdash s = t$).*

Also for the word problem, complete TRSs provide a positive solution. In fact, we require less than completeness (SN and CR) for all terms, but only for ground terms. (See Example 2.1.3 for an example where this makes a difference.) It may be (as in Exercise 2.4.3) that a complete TRS for E cannot be found with respect to all terms, while there does exist a TRS which is complete for the restriction to ground terms.

Exercise 2.4.4. Consider the specification as in the previous exercise and find a TRS (Σ, R) such that $(\Sigma, R)_0$ (i.e. the restriction of (Σ, R) to ground terms) is complete.

Remark 2.4.5. Note that there are finite equational specifications (Σ, E) which have a decidable word problem (so for ground terms) for which no complete TRS R (complete with respect to ground terms) exists. This strengthens the observation in Exercise 2.4.3. The simplest such (Σ, E) is the specification consisting of a single binary commutative operator $+$ and a constant 0, and equations $E = \{x + y = y + x\}$. According to Exercise 2.4.3 (which also works for the present simpler specification) no complete TRS R can be found such that for all (open) s, t we have $s =_R t \Leftrightarrow s =_E t$. According to the next exercise, we also have the stronger result that no TRS R exists which is complete for ground terms and such that for ground terms s, t we have $s =_R t \Leftrightarrow s =_E t$.

Exercise 2.4.6. (Bergstra and Klop) Prove the following fact:

Theorem. *Let* (Σ, E) *be the specification with* $\Sigma = \{0, +\}$ *and* $E = \{x+y = y+x\}$. *Then there is no finite TRS R such that the restriction to ground terms,* $(R)_0$, *is complete and such that* $=_R$ *and* $=_E$ *coincide on ground terms.*

Proof Sketch. Define terms $t_0 \equiv 0$, $t_{n+1} \equiv t_n + t_n$ $(n \geq 0)$. Suppose R is a TRS with finitely many rewrite rules such that $=_R$ and $=_E$ coincide on ground terms. Let N be the maximum of the depths of the left-hand sides of the rewrite rules in R. (Here 'depth' refers to the height of the corresponding term formation tree.)

Consider the terms $t^* \equiv t_N + t_{2N}$ and $t^{**} \equiv t_{2N} + t_N$. Clearly, $t^* =_E t^{**}$. In fact, $\{t^*, t^{**}\}$ is an E-equivalence class, hence also an R-convertibility class. Therefore there must be a rewrite rule r such that t^* is an r-redex or t^{**} is an r-redex (since there are only two elements in the convertibility class) and such that $t^* \rightarrow_r t^{**}$. Say t^* is an r-redex. Now one can easily show that $t^* \rightarrow_r t^{**} \rightarrow_r t^*$. Hence R is not even SN on ground terms.

Term rewriting and initial algebra semantics

We will now make more explicit the connection between term rewriting and initial algebra semantics. We suppose familiarity with the concept of an initial algebra in the class of models of an equational specification (Σ, E), i.e. the variety $\mathrm{Alg}(\Sigma, E)$, as defined by universal properties in terms of homomorphisms. (See e.g. [Meinke and Tucker, 1992], [Goguen and Meseguer, 1985].) Although the initial algebra is only determined up to isomorphism, we will speak of 'the' initial algebra and use the notation $I(\Sigma, E)$ for it. It is well known that $I(\Sigma, E)$ can be obtained from the set of ground terms $\mathrm{Ter}_0(\Sigma)$ by dividing out the congruence relation $=_E$. Thus we can equate the initial algebra $I(\Sigma, E)$ with the quotient algebra $\mathrm{Ter}_0(\Sigma)/{=_E}$.

Now suppose that (Σ, R) is a TRS 'for' (Σ, E), that is, $=_R$ coincides with $=_E$. (So the initial algebra of (Σ, E) can also be written as $\mathrm{Ter}_0(\Sigma)/{=_R}$.) If R is a *complete* TRS, then $I(\Sigma, E)$ is in fact a *computable* algebra. This is merely a rephrasing of: the word problem (for ground terms) for (Σ, E) is solvable. As noted in Exercise 2.4.6, the reverse is not necessarily the case; for some (Σ, E) with computable initial algebra there does not exist a complete TRS—at least not *in the same signature*. However, a remarkable theorem of Bergstra and Tucker states that if we allow an extension of the signature with some functions and constants (no new sorts), then a complete TRS can always be found. (This result also follows from the simulation of Turing Machines by a TRS—consisting of two rules—as in [Dershowitz, 1987].) More precisely:

Definition 2.4.7.

1. The algebra $\mathcal{A} \in \mathrm{Alg}(\Sigma, E)$ is *minimal*, if it is (isomorphic to) a quotient algebra $\mathrm{Ter}(\Sigma)/\equiv$ for some congruence $\equiv$. In particular, $I(\Sigma, E)$ is a minimal algebra. In other words, an algebra is minimal if

its elements are generated by functions and constants in the signature.

2. A minimal algebra $\mathcal{A}$ is *computable*, if its equality is decidable, i.e. if the relation $\mathcal{A} \models t = s$ for ground terms $t, s \in \mathrm{Ter}(\Sigma)$ is decidable.

Theorem 2.4.8. [Bergstra and Tucker, 1980] *Let $\mathcal{A}$ be a minimal Σ-algebra, Σ a finite signature. Then the following are equivalent:*

1. *$\mathcal{A}$ is a computable algebra;*
2. *there is an extension of Σ to a finite Σ', obtained by adding some function and constant symbols, and there is a complete TRS (Σ', R) such that*

$$\mathcal{A} \equiv I(\Sigma', R^{=}) \mid_{\Sigma} .$$

Here $R^{=}$ is the equational specification obtained by viewing the reduction rules in R as equations, and $|_{\Sigma}$ is the restriction to the signature Σ. So $\mathcal{A}$ is a '*reduct*' (see [Meinke and Tucker, 1992]) of an initial algebra given by a complete TRS. (The TRS R as in the theorem is not only ground complete, but complete with respect to all terms. Actually, it is an orthogonal TRS as defined in the next chapter; and for orthogonal TRSs possessing at least one ground term, ground completeness implies completeness.) The functions (including the constants as 0-ary functions) to be added to Σ are sometimes referred to as '*hidden functions*'. Note that according to the statement in the theorem no new sorts are needed, thus the present theorem has also a bearing on the homogeneous (i.e. one-sorted) case that we are considering in this chapter.

For more information concerning the connection between term rewriting and computability aspects of initial algebra semantics (and 'final' algebra semantics), also for the heterogeneous (many-sorted) case, we refer to the very complete survey by [Goguen and Meseguer, 1985].

Critical pair completion

We resume the question how to find a complete TRS (for the case of open terms, henceforth) for an equational specification (Σ, E). This is in fact what the Knuth–Bendix completion algorithm is trying to do. We will now explain the essential features of the completion algorithm first by an informal, 'intuition-guided' completion of the equational specification E of groups:

First we give these equations a 'sensible' orientation:

1. $e \cdot x \to x$
2. $I(x) \cdot x \to e$
3. $(x \cdot y) \cdot z \to x \cdot (y \cdot z)$

(Note that the orientation in rules 1, 2 is forced, by the restrictions on rewrite rules in Section 2.1. As to the orientation of rule 3, the other

$e \cdot x$	$=$	x
$I(x) \cdot x$	$=$	e
$(x \cdot y) \cdot z$	$=$	$x \cdot (y \cdot z)$

Table 2.12

direction is just as 'sensible'.) These rules are not confluent, as can be seen by superposition of e.g. 2 and 3. Redex $I(x) \cdot x$ can be unified with a *non-variable* subterm of redex $\underline{(x \cdot y)} \cdot z$ (the underlined subterm), with result $(I(x) \cdot x) \cdot z$. This term is subject to two possible reductions: $(I(x) \cdot x) \cdot z \to_2 e \cdot z$ and $(I(x) \cdot x) \cdot z \to_3 I(x) \cdot (x \cdot z)$. The pair of reducts $\langle e \cdot z, I(x) \cdot (x \cdot z) \rangle$ is called a *critical pair*, since the confluence property depends on the reduction possibilities of the terms in this pair. Formally, we have the following definition which at a first reading is not easily digested. For the concept of a 'most general unifier' we refer to Section 2.6 below.

Definition 2.4.9. Let $\alpha \to \beta$ and $\gamma \to \delta$ be two rewrite rules such that α is *unifiable* (after renaming of variables) with a subterm of γ which is not a variable (a non-variable subterm). This means that there is a context $C[\,]$, a non-variable term t and a 'most general unifier' σ such that $\gamma \equiv C[t]$ and $t^\sigma \equiv \alpha^\sigma$. The term $\gamma^\sigma \equiv C[t]^\sigma$ can be reduced in two possible ways: $C[t]^\sigma \to C[\beta]^\sigma$ and $\gamma^\sigma \to \delta^\sigma$. Now the pair of reducts $\langle C[\beta]^\sigma, \delta^\sigma \rangle$ is called a *critical pair* obtained by the superposition of $\alpha \to \beta$ on $\gamma \to \delta$. If $\alpha \to \beta$ and $\gamma \to \delta$ are the same rewrite rule, we furthermore require that α is unifiable with a proper (i.e. $\not\equiv \alpha$) non-variable subterm of $\gamma \equiv \alpha$.

Definition 2.4.10. A critical pair $\langle s, t \rangle$ is called *convergent* if s and t have a common reduct.

Our last critical pair $\langle e \cdot z, I(x) \cdot (x \cdot z) \rangle$ is not convergent: $I(x) \cdot (x \cdot z)$ is a normal form and $e \cdot z$ only reduces to the normal form z. So we have the problematic pair of terms $z, I(x) \cdot (x \cdot z)$; problematic because their equality is derivable from E, but they have no common reduct with respect to the reduction available so far. Therefore we adopt a new rule

4. $\quad I(x) \cdot (x \cdot z) \to z$

Now we have a superposition of rules 2 and 4: $I(I(y)) \cdot (I(y) \cdot y) \to_4 y$ and $I(I(y)) \cdot (I(y) \cdot y) \to_2 I(I(y)) \cdot e$. This yields the critical pair $\langle y, I(I(y)) \cdot e \rangle$ which cannot further be reduced. Adopt new rule:

5. $\quad I(I(y)) \cdot e \to y$ *cancelled later*

As it will turn out, in a later stage this last rule will become superfluous. We go on searching for critical pairs. Superposition of 4,1: $I(e) \cdot (e \cdot z) \to_4 z$

and $I(e) \cdot (e \cdot z) \to_1 I(e) \cdot z$. Adopt new rule:

6. $I(e) \cdot z \to z$ *cancelled later*

Superposition of 3, 5: $(I(Iy)) \cdot e) \cdot x \to_3 I(I(y)) \cdot (e \cdot x)$ and $(I(Iy)) \cdot e) \cdot x \to_5 y \cdot x$. Adopt new rule:

7. $(I(Iy)) \cdot x \to y \cdot x$ *cancelled later*

Superposition of 5, 7: $I(I(y)) \cdot e \to_7 y.e$ and $I(I(y)) \cdot e \to_5 y$. Adopt new rule:

8. $y \cdot e \to y$

Superposition of 5, 8: $I(I(y)) \cdot e \to_5 y$ and $I(I(y)) \cdot e \to_8 I(I(y))$. Adopt new rule

9. $I(I(y)) \to y$ *cancel 5 and 7*

(Rule 5 is now no longer necessary to ensure that the critical pair $\langle y, I(I(y)) \cdot e\rangle$ has a common reduct, because: $I(I(y)) \cdot e \to_9 y \cdot e \to_8 y$. Likewise for rule 7.) Superposition of 6, 8: $I(e) \cdot e \to_6 e$ and $I(e) \cdot e \to_8 I(e)$. Adopt new rule

10. $I(e) \to e$ *cancel 6*

Superposition of 2, 9: $I(I(y)) \cdot I(y) \to_2$ eand $I(I(y)) \cdot I(y) \to_9 y \cdot I(y)$. Adopt new rule

11. $y \cdot I(y) \to e$

Superposition of 3, 11: $(y \cdot I(y)) \cdot x \to_3 y \cdot (I(y) \cdot x)$ and $(y \cdot I(y)) \cdot x \to_{11} e \cdot x$. Adopt new rule

12. $y \cdot (I(y) \cdot x) \to x$

Superposition (again) of 3, 11: $(x \cdot y) \cdot I(x \cdot y) \to_{11} e$ and $(x \cdot y) \cdot I(x \cdot y) \to_3 x \cdot (y \cdot I(x \cdot y))$. Adopt new rule

13. $x \cdot (y \cdot (y \cdot I(x \cdot y)) \to e)$ *cancelled later*

Superposition of 13, 4: $I(x) \cdot (x \cdot (y \cdot I(x \cdot y))) \to_4 y \cdot I(x \cdot y)$ and $I(x) \cdot (x \cdot (y \cdot I(x \cdot y))) \to_{13} I(x) \cdot e$. Adopt new rule

14. $y \cdot I(x \cdot y) \to I(x)$ *cancelled later* *cancel 13*

Superposition of 4, 14: $I(y) \cdot (y \cdot I(x \cdot y)) \to_4 I(x \cdot y)$ and $I(y) \cdot (y \cdot I(x \cdot y)) \to_{14} I(y) \cdot I(x)$. Adopt new rule

15. $I(x \cdot y) \to I(y) \cdot I(x)$ *cancel 14*

At this moment the TRS has only convergent critical pairs. The significance of this fact is stated in the following lemma.

Lemma 2.4.11. (critical pair lemma; [Knuth and Bendix, 1970; Huet, 1980] and *A TRS R is WCR iff all critical pairs are convergent.*

Exercise 2.4.12. Prove the critical pair lemma. (The proof is not hard, after distinguishing cases as in Figure 2.16, after [Le Chénadec, 1986] where the proof also can be found. Some care has to be taken to deal with repeated variables in left-hand sides of reduction rules.)

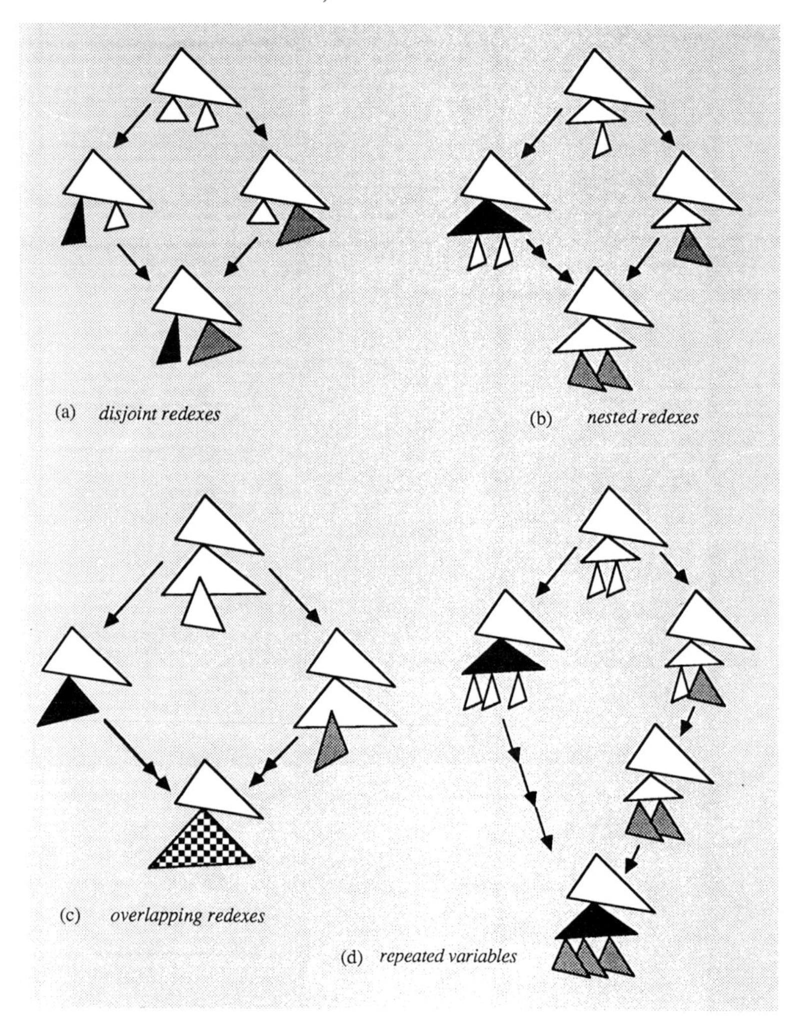

Figure 2.16

Exercise 2.4.13. Prove, using the critical pair lemma: if the TRS R has finitely many rules and is SN, then WCR and CR are decidable.

So the TRS R_c with rewrite rules as in Table 2.13 is WCR.

1.	$e \cdot x$	$\to$	x
2.	$I(x) \cdot x$	$\to$	e
3.	$(x \cdot y) \cdot z$	$\to$	$x \cdot (y \cdot z)$
4.	$I(x) \cdot (x \cdot z)$	$\to$	z
8.	$y \cdot e$	$\to$	y
9.	$I(I(y))$	$\to$	y
10.	$I(e)$	$\to$	e
11.	$y \cdot I(y)$	$\to$	e
12.	$y \cdot (I(y) \cdot x)$	$\to$	x
15.	$I(x \cdot y)$	$\to$	$I(y) \cdot I(x)$

Table 2.13

Furthermore, one can prove SN for R_c by a 'Knuth–Bendix ordering' (not treated here) or by the recursive path ordering explained in Section 2.3. (In fact we need the extended lexicographic version of Remark 2.3.11(3), due to the presence of the associativity rule.) According to Newman's lemma (2.0.7(2)) R_c is therefore CR and hence complete. We conclude that the validity problem for the equational specification of groups is solvable.

The following theorem of Knuth and Bendix is an immediate corollary of the critical pair lemma 2.4.11 and Newman's lemma:

Corollary 2.4.14. [Knuth and Bendix, 1970] *Let R be a TRS which is SN. Then R is CR iff all critical pairs of R are convergent.*

The completion procedure above by hand was naive, since we were not very systematic in searching for critical pairs, and especially since we were guided by an intuitive sense only of what direction to adopt when generating a new rule. In most cases there was no other possibility (e.g. at 4: $z \to I(x) \cdot (x \cdot z)$ is not a reduction rule due to the restriction that the left-hand side is not a single variable), but in case 15 the other direction was at least as plausible, as it is even length-decreasing. However, the other direction $I(y) \cdot I(x) \to I(x \cdot y)$ would have led to disastrous complications (described in [Knuth and Bendix, 1970]). Bendix

The problem of what direction to choose is solved in the actual Knuth–Bendix algorithm and its variants by preordaining a 'reduction ordering' on the terms.

Definition 2.4.15. A *reduction ordering* $>$ is a well-founded partial ordering on terms, which is closed under substitutions and contexts, i.e. if $s > t$ then $s^\sigma > t^\sigma$ for all substitutions σ, and if $s > t$ then $C[s] > C[t]$ for all contexts C[ ].

We now have immediately the following fact (noting that if R is SN, then $\to_R^+$ satisfies the requirements of Definition 2.4.15):

Proposition 2.4.16. *A TRS R is SN iff there is a reduction ordering $>$ such that $\alpha > \beta$ for every rewrite rule $\alpha \to \beta$ of R.*

Simple version of the Knuth–Bendix completion algorithm

Input: – an equational specification (Σ, E)
– a reduction ordering $>$ on $\mathrm{Ter}(\Sigma)$
(i.e. a program which computes $>$)

Output: - a complete TRS R such that for all
$s, t \in \mathrm{Ter}(\Sigma) : s =_R t \Leftrightarrow (\Sigma, E) \vdash s = t$

```
R := ∅;
while E ≠ ∅ do
    choose an equation s = t ∈ E;
    reduce s and t to respective normal forms s' and t'
    with respect to R;
    if s' ≡ t' then
        E := E − {s = t}
    else
        if s' > t' then
            α := s'; β := t'
        else if t' > s' then
            α := t'; β := s'
        else
            failure
        fi;
        CP := {P = Q | ⟨P, Q⟩ is a critical pair between
                    the rules in R and α → β};
        R := R ∪ {α → β};
        E := E ∪ CP − {s = t}
    fi
od;
success
```

Figure 2.17

In Figure 2.17 a simple version of the Knuth–Bendix completion algorithm is presented. As to the reduction ordering $>$ on $\mathrm{Ter}(\Sigma)$ which is an input to the algorithm: finding this is a matter of ingenuity, or experimentation. (Also without reduction ordering, computer systems for Knuth–Bendix completion equipped with an interactive question for orientation of equations into rewrite rules are of great help.)

The program of Figure 2.17 has three possibilities: it may (1) terminate successfully, (2) loop infinitely, or (3) fail because a pair of terms s, t cannot be oriented (i.e. neither $s > t$ nor $t > s$). The third case gives the most important restriction of the Knuth–Bendix algorithm: equational specifications with commutative operators cannot be completed.

Exercise 2.4.17. Show that there exists no complete TRS for the specification of abelian groups as in Table 2.14. (Consider in a supposed complete TRS the normal forms of the open terms $x + y$ and $y + x$.)

$0 + x$	$=$	x
$(-x) + x$	$=$	0
$(x + y) + z$	$=$	$x + (y + z)$
$x + y$	$=$	$y + x$

Table 2.14

If one still wants to deal with equational specifications having commutative/associative operators as in Exercise 2.4.17, one has to work modulo the equations of associativity and commutativity. For completion modulo such equations we refer to [Peterson and Stickel, 1981] and [Jouannaud and Kirchner, 1986].

In case (1) the resulting TRS is complete. To show this requires a nontrivial proof, see e.g. [Huet, 1981]. In the next section we will give an abstract formulation of Knuth–Bendix completion, following [Bachmair *et al.*, 1986], which streamlines considerably this kind of correctness proofs.

The completion program of Figure 2.17 does not 'simplify' the rewrite rules themselves. Such an optimization can be performed after termination of the program, as follows.

Definition 2.4.18. A TRS R is called *irreducible* if for every rewrite rule $\alpha \to \beta$ of R the following holds:

1. β is a normal form with respect to R,
2. α is a normal form with respect to $R - \{\alpha \to \beta\}$.

Exercise 2.4.19. Prove that every irreducible ground TRS is complete. (Hint: Use Exercise 2.2.19 and Corollary 2.4.14.)

Theorem 2.4.20. [Métivier, 1983] *Let R be a complete TRS. Then we can find an irreducible complete TRS R' such that the convertibilities $=_R$ and $=_{R'}$ coincide.*

Exercise 2.4.21. A proof of Theorem 2.4.20 can be given along the following lines. Let R_1 be the TRS $\{\alpha \to \beta' \mid \alpha \to \beta \in R$ and β' is the normal form of β with respect to $R\}$. We may assume that R_1 does not contain rewrite rules that are a renaming of another rewrite rule. Further, define $R' = \{\alpha \to \beta \in R_1 \mid \alpha$ is a normal form with respect to $R_1 - \{\alpha \to \beta\}\}$. Now the proof that $s =_R t \Leftrightarrow s =_{R'} t$ follows from the (easy) proofs of the sequence of statements:

1. if $s \to_{R_1} t$ then $s \to_R^+ t$;
2. R and R_1 define the same set of normal forms;
3. R_1 is SN;
4. if $s \twoheadrightarrow_R t$ and t is a normal form then $s \twoheadrightarrow_{R_1} t$;
5. $s =_R t \Leftrightarrow s =_{R_1} t$;
6. R_1 is CR;
7. if $s \to_{R'} t$ then $s \to_{R_1} t$;
8. R_1 and R' define the same set of normal forms;
9. R' is SN;
10. if $s \twoheadrightarrow_{R_1} t$ and t is a normal form then $s \twoheadrightarrow_{R'} t$;
11. $s =_{R_1} t \Leftrightarrow s =_{R'} t$;
12. R' is CR;
13. R' is irreducible.

Instead of optimizing the TRS which is the output of the above simple completion algorithm *after* the completion, it is more efficient to do this *during* the completion. Figure 2.18 contains a more efficient Knuth–Bendix completion algorithm, which upon successful termination yields irreducible TRSs as output.

We conclude this section with a theorem stating that the Knuth–Bendix completion algorithm, given an equational specification and a reduction ordering, cannot generate two different complete irreducible TRSs. According to [Dershowitz *et al.*, 1988b] the theorem is originally due to M. Ballantyne, but first proved in [Métivier, 1983].

Definition 2.4.22. Let $>$ be a reduction ordering. We call a TRS R *compatible* with $>$ if for every rewrite rule $\alpha \to \beta$ of R we have $\alpha > \beta$.

Theorem 2.4.23. [Métivier, 1983] *Let R_1 and R_2 be two complete irreducible TRSs compatible with a given reduction ordering $>$. Suppose R_1 and R_2 define the same convertibility. Then R_1 and R_2 are equal (modulo a renaming of variables).*

Exercise 2.4.24. [Huet, 1980] In this exercise we collect some criteria for confluence in terms of properties of critical pairs, as well as some counterexamples, from [Huet, 1980]. Also some questions are listed which are, as far as we know, open. See Table 2.15.

1. In row 1 of the table the critical pair lemma 2.4.11 is stated: if every critical pair $\langle t, s\rangle$ is convergent (notation: $t \downarrow s$), then WCR holds. However, CR

More efficient version of the Knuth–Bendix completion algorithm

---

Input: – an equational specification (Σ, E)
– a reduction ordering $>$ on $\mathrm{Ter}(\Sigma)$

Output: - a complete irreducible TRS R such that for all
$s, t \in \mathrm{Ter}(\Sigma) : s =_R t \Leftrightarrow (\Sigma, E) \vdash s = t$

```
R := ∅;
while E ≠ ∅ do
    choose an equation s = t ∈ E;
    reduce s and t to respective normal forms s' and t'
    with respect to R;
    if s' ≡ t' then
        E := E − {s = t}
    else
        if s' > t' then
            α := s'; β := t'
        else if t' > s' then
            α := t'; β := s'
        else
            failure
        fi;
        R := {γ → δ' | γ → δ ∈ R and δ' is a normal form of δ
                with respect to R ∪ {α → β}};
        CP := {P = Q | ⟨P, Q⟩ is a critical pair between
                the rules in R and α → β};
        E := E ∪ CP ∪ {γ = δ | γ → δ ∈ R and γ is reducible by
                α → β} − {s = t};
        R := R ∪ {α → β} − {γ → δ | γ is reducible by α → β}
    fi
od;
success
```

Figure 2.18

1	$\langle t, s \rangle$	$t \downarrow s$	WCR	¬CR
2	$\langle t, s \rangle$	$t \downarrow s$ & SN	WCR	CR
3	$\langle t, s \rangle$	LL & RL & strongly closed	strongly confluent	CR
4	$\langle t, s \rangle$	LL & strongly closed	WCR	¬CR
5	$\langle t, s \rangle$	LL & $t \to_{\|} s$	$\to_{\|}$ is WCR$^{\leq 1}$	CR
6	$\langle t, s \rangle$	LL & $s \to_{\|} t$	WCR	**CR?**
7	$\langle t, s \rangle$	LL & $s \to^{\equiv} t$	WCR	**CR?**
8	$\langle t, s \rangle$	LL & $t \to^{\equiv} s$ or $s \to^{\equiv} t$	WCR	**CR?**

Table 2.15

need not hold; a counterexample is given by the TRS with four constants a, b, c, d and rules as in Figure 2.3.

2. Row 2 of the table is Theorem 2.4.14 of Knuth and Bendix.

3. In row 3, LL means that the TRS is left-linear, RL right-linear (i.e. no right-hand side of a reduction rule contains repetitions of a variable). Strongly confluent is defined in Exercise 2.0.8(10).

We furthermore define:
Definition. A TRS is *strongly closed* if for every every critical pair $\langle t, s \rangle$ there are t', t' such that $t \twoheadrightarrow t' \leftarrow^{\equiv} s$ and $s \twoheadrightarrow t' \leftarrow^{\equiv} t$. Prove that 'strongly closed' is not

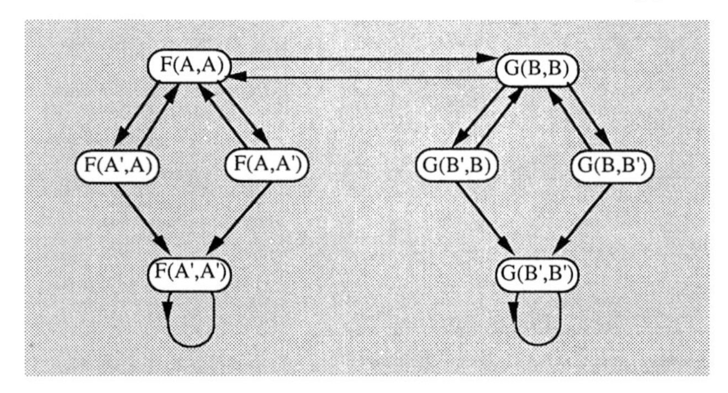

Figure 2.19

sufficient to guarantee CR, by considering the non-left-linear TRS $\{F(x,x) \to A,\ F(x, G(x)) \to B,\ C \to G(C)\}$. However, if the TRS is left-linear, right-linear and strongly closed, then CR holds (for a proof see Huet [80]); in fact, we then have strong confluence.

4. In (3), RL cannot be dropped. A nice counterexample is in [Huet, 1980], given by J.-J. Lévy: it contains the following eight left-linear rules. See also Figure 2.19.

$$\begin{array}{lcllcl} F(A,A) & \to & G(B,B) & G(B,B) & \to & F(A,A) \\ A & \to & A' & B & \to & B' \\ F(A',x) & \to & F(x,x) & G(B',x) & \to & G(x,x) \\ F(x,A') & \to & F(x,x) & G(x,B') & \to & G(x,x) \end{array}$$

Check that CR does not hold, and that the TRS is strongly closed.

5. This is a remarkable fact: if the TRS is left-linear, and for every critical pair $\langle t, s\rangle$ we have $t \to_{||} s$, then $\mathrm{WCR}^{\leq 1}$ holds, and hence CR. Here $\to_{||}$ (parallel reduction) denotes a sequence of redex contractions at disjoint occurrences.

6,7,8. If in (5) we replace $t \to_{||} s$ by $s \to_{||} t$, then the CR question is open. Likewise (7) if $t \to_{||} s$ is replaced by $s \to^{\equiv} t$, or (8) replaced by $t \to^{\equiv} s$ or $s \to^{\equiv} t$.

Exercise 2.4.25. [Knuth and Bendix, 1970] contains completions of two specifications which closely resemble the specification of groups (see Table 2.16), called 'L-R theory' and 'R-L theory'. Prove, using the completions, that $x \cdot e = x$ is not derivable in L-R theory and that in R-L theory the equations $e \cdot x = x$ and $x \cdot I(x) = e$ are not derivable. Furthermore, in L-R theory the equation $x \cdot e = x$ is not derivable. Hence the three theories are different, i.e. determine different varieties of algebras. In fact, note that the variety of groups is a proper subset of both the variety of L-R algebras and that of R-L algebras, and that the latter two varieties are incomparable with respect to set inclusion.

2.5 An abstract formulation of completion

(This section is taken from [Klop and Middeldorp, 1988].)

There are many completion algorithms such as the two above (in Figures 2.17 and 2.18), differing in order of execution or ways of optimization. The question is, how to prove that these algorithms are correct, i.e. deliver upon successful termination indeed a TRS R with the same equality as the one generated by the original set of equations E. As there is a whole family of completion algorithms, one needs to extract the 'abstract principles' of such algorithms; and this is done indeed by [Bachmair *et al.*, 1986]. Their method for proving correctness of completion algorithms starts with the introduction of a derivation system where the objects are pairs (E, R); each derivation step from (E, R) to (E', R') preserves equality: $=_{E\cup R}$ coincides with $=_{E'\cup R'}$, and moreover, along a sequence of derivations the actual proofs of equations $s = t$ will be getting 'better and better', with as optimal proof format that of a 'rewrite proof'. See Figure 2.20, where it is shown how E (that is the pair $(E, \varnothing)$) is gradually transformed via pairs (E', R')

group theory	*L-R theory:*	*R-L theory:*
$e \cdot x = x$	$e \cdot x = x$	$x \cdot e = x$
$I(x) \cdot x = e$	$x \cdot I(x) = e$	$I(x) \cdot x = e$
$(x \cdot y) \cdot z = x \cdot (y \cdot z)$	$(x \cdot y) \cdot z = x \cdot (y \cdot z)$	$(x \cdot y) \cdot z = x \cdot (y \cdot z)$
completion:	*completion:*	*completion:*
$e \cdot x \to x$	$e \cdot x \to x$	
$x \cdot e \to x$		$x \cdot e \to x$
$I(x) \cdot x \to e$		$I(x) \cdot x \to e$
$x \cdot I(x) \to e$	$x \cdot I(x) \to e$	
$(x \cdot y) \cdot z \to x \cdot (y \cdot z)$	$(x \cdot y) \cdot z \to x \cdot (y \cdot z)$	$(x \cdot y) \cdot z \to x \cdot (y \cdot z)$
$I(e) \to e$	$I(e) \to e$	$I(e) \to e$
$I(x \cdot y) \to I(y) \cdot I(x)$	$I(x \cdot y) \to I(y) \cdot I(x)$	$I(x \cdot y) \to I(y) \cdot I(x)$
$x \cdot (I(x) \cdot y) \to y$	$x \cdot (I(x) \cdot y) \to y$	
		$e \cdot x \to I(I(x))$
$I(x) \cdot (x \cdot y) \to y$	$I(x) \cdot (x \cdot y) \to y$	
		$x \cdot I(I(y)) \to x \cdot y$
$I(I(x)) \to x$		
	$x \cdot e \to I(I(x))$	
	$I(I(I(x))) \to I(x)$	$I(I(I(x))) \to I(x)$
		$x \cdot (y \cdot I(y)) \to x$
	$I(I(x)) \cdot y \to x \cdot y$	
		$x \cdot (I(I(y)) \cdot z) \to x \cdot (y \cdot z)$
		$x \cdot (y \cdot (I(y) \cdot z)) \to x \cdot z$
		$I(x) \cdot (x \cdot y) \to I(I(y))$

Table 2.16

to a TRS R (that is the pair $(\varnothing, R)$); along the way the two example proofs in Figure 2.20 get more and more oriented until they are in rewrite form. (Here direction is downward; horizontal steps are without direction.)

There are two crucial ideas in this recent approach. One is the concept of a derivation system on pairs (E, R) as discussed above. The other is the concept of ordering the proofs of equations $s = t$ according to their degree of orientation. We will now proceed to a more formal explanation.

Definition 2.5.1. Let (Σ, E) be an equational specification. If $s =_E t$ by application of exactly one equation in E we write $s \leftrightarrow_E t$. So $s \leftrightarrow_E t$ iff there exists a context $C[\ ]$, a substitution σ and an equation $u = v$ (or $v = u$) in E such that $s \equiv C[u^\sigma]$ and $t \equiv C[v^\sigma]$.

Definition 2.5.2. Let (Σ, E) be an equational specification and R a TRS

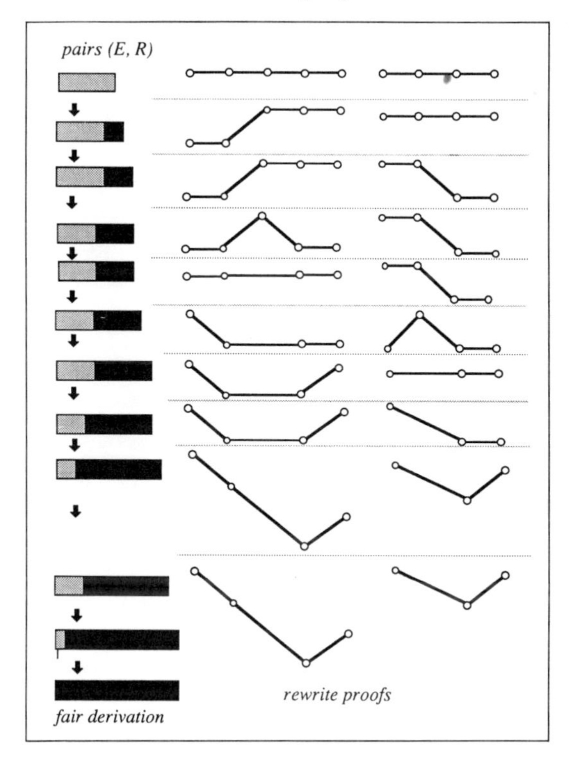

Figure 2.20

with signature Σ.

1. A *proof* in $E \cup R$ of an equation $s = t$ between terms $s, t \in \mathrm{Ter}(\Sigma)$ is a sequence of terms $(s_0, \ldots, s_n)$ such that $s_0 \equiv s$, $s_n \equiv t$, and for all $0 < i \leq n$ we have $s_{i-1} \leftrightarrow_E s_i$, $s_{i-1} \rightarrow_R s_i$ or $s_{i-1} \leftarrow_R s_i$.
2. A *subproof* of $P \equiv (s_0, \ldots, s_n)$ is a proof $P' \equiv (s_i, \ldots, s_j)$ with $0 \leq i \leq j \leq n$. The notation $P[P']$ means that P' is a subproof of P. (Actually, an occurrence of a subproof of P.)
3. A proof of the form $s_0 \twoheadrightarrow_R s_k \twoheadleftarrow_R s_n$ is called a *rewrite proof*.

By definition, $P \equiv (s)$ is a proof of $s = s$. Figure 2.21 contains an example of a proof.

Knuth–Bendix completion aims at transforming every proof $(s_0, \ldots, s_n)$ into a rewrite proof $s_0 \twoheadrightarrow t \twoheadleftarrow s_n$. We now present an inference system for Knuth–Bendix completion. The objects of this system are pairs (E, R). The inference system $\mathcal{BC}$ (*basic completion*) has the following rules (see Table 2.17); $>$ is a reduction ordering.

The notation $s =' t$ means $s = t$ or $t = s$; the symbol $\cup'$ denotes disjoint union. A $\mathcal{BC}$-derivation is a finite or infinite sequence $(E_0, R_0) \Rightarrow$

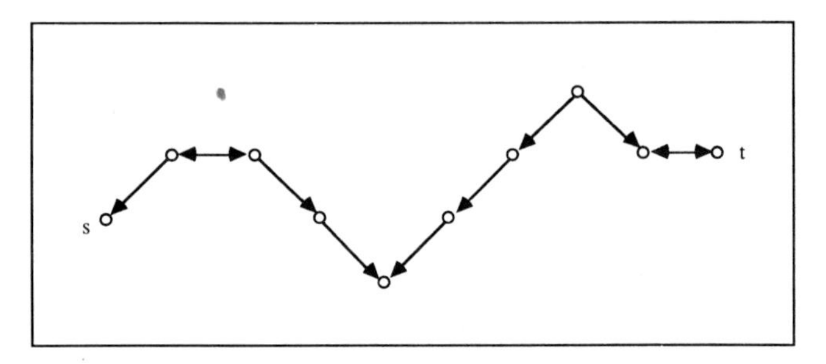

Figure 2.21

(C_1)	*orienting an equation*			
	$(E \cup' \{s =' t\}, R)$	$\Rightarrow$	$(E, R \cup \{s \to t\})$	if $s > t$
(C_2)	*adding an equation*			
	(E, R)	$\Rightarrow$	$(E \cup \{s = t\}, R)$	if $s \leftarrow_R u \to_R t$
(C_3)	*simplifying an equation*			
	$(E \cup' \{s =' t\}, R)$	$\Rightarrow$	$(E \cup \{u = t\}, R)$	if $s \to_R u$
(C_4)	*deleting a trivial equation*			
	$(E \cup' \{s = s\}, R)$	$\Rightarrow$	(E, R)	

Table 2.17

$(E_1, R_1) \Rightarrow (E_2, R_2) \Rightarrow \cdots$. We write $\Rightarrow^+$ for the transitive closure of $\Rightarrow$.

It is easily seen that, given a derivation step $(E, R) \Rightarrow (E', R')$, if R is SN then so is R', and furthermore $=_{E \cup R}$ coincides with $=_{E' \cup R'}$. However, proofs in $E' \cup R'$ are in general 'simpler' than in $E \cup R$. For example, by adding equations to E by inference rule C_2 some subproofs $s \leftarrow_R u \to_R t$ can be replaced by $s \leftrightarrow_{E'} t$. To formalize this reduction in complexity we introduce orderings on proofs.

Definition 2.5.3. A binary relation $\rightarrowtail$ on proofs is *monotonic* if $Q \rightarrowtail Q'$ implies $P[Q] \rightarrowtail P[Q']$ for all proofs P, Q and Q'. The relation $\rightarrowtail$ is *stable* if

$$P \equiv (s, \ldots, u_i, \ldots, t) \rightarrowtail (s, \ldots, v_j, \ldots, t) \equiv Q$$

implies that

$$(C[s^\sigma], \ldots, C[u_i^\sigma], \ldots, C[t^\sigma]) \rightarrowtail (C[s^\sigma], \ldots, C[v_j^\sigma], \ldots, C[t^\sigma])$$

for all proofs P and Q, contexts $C[\,]$ and substitutions σ. A *proof ordering* is a stable, monotonic, well-founded partial ordering on proofs.

Exercise 2.5.4. To illustrate the concept of proof ordering we will give an alternative proof of Newman's lemma 2.0.7(2) using this notion. ('alternative' with respect to the proofs that we have seen in the literature. The present proof is nevertheless well known.) See also Exercise 2.3.15 for our multiset notations.

Let R be a TRS which is SN and WCR. Let $P \equiv (s_0, \ldots, s_n)$ be a proof of the conversion $s_0 = s_n$. We define the *complexity* $\mid P \mid$ of the proof P as the multiset $[s_0, \ldots, s_n]$. The ordering $\rightarrowtail$ which we will use is induced by the multiset extension of $\rightarrow_R^+$, notation: $(\rightarrow_R^+)^\mu$. So

$$P \rightarrowtail P' \text{ iff } \mid P \mid (\rightarrow_R^+)^\mu \mid P' \mid .$$

(This means that $P \rightarrowtail P'$ if the multiset $\mid P' \mid$ arises from the multiset $\mid P \mid$ by repeatedly replacing an element of the multiset by arbitrarily many elements which are less in the sense of the well-founded ordering $\rightarrow_R^+$, i.e. by repeatedly replacing a term t in the multiset of terms by a number (≥ 0) of proper reducts of t.)

1. Prove that $\rightarrowtail$ is a proof ordering.
2. If $P \equiv (s_0, \ldots, s_n)$ is not a rewrite proof, then there is a proof P' of the equation $s_0 = s_n$ such that $P \rightarrowtail P'$. (Hint: Consider a 'peak' in the conversion P, and replace it by a 'valley', using WCR. See Figure 2.22.)
3. Conclude that R is CR.

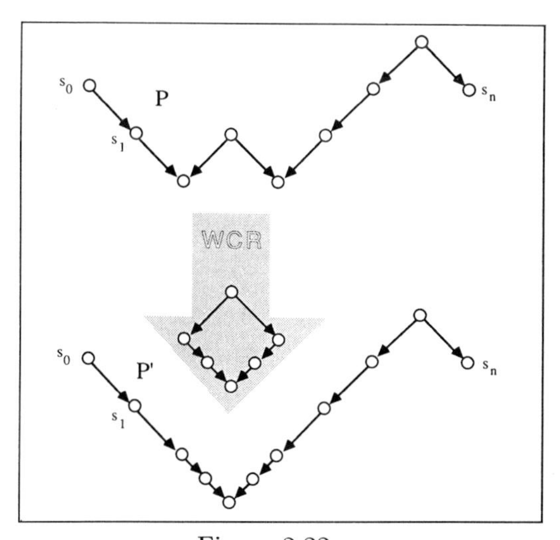

Figure 2.22

The proof ordering which we use for completion is based on the given reduction ordering and on the elementary steps ($\rightarrow_R, \leftarrow_R$ or $\leftrightarrow_E$) in a proof.

Definition 2.5.5.

1. The *complexity* $\mid P \mid$ of a proof $P \equiv (s_0, \ldots, s_n)$ is the multiset $[c(s_0, s_1), \ldots, c(s_{n-1}, s_n)]$ where $c(s_{i-1}, s_i)$, the complexity of an elementary proof step, is defined by

$$c(s_{i-1}, s_i) = \begin{cases} [s_{i-1}] & \text{if } s_{i-1} \to_R s_i \\ [s_i] & \text{if } s_{i-1} \leftarrow_R s_i \\ [s_{i-1}, s_i] & \text{if } s_{i-1} \leftrightarrow_E s_i \end{cases}$$

2. To compare the complexities of the elementary proof steps we use the multiset extension $>^\mu$ of the reduction ordering $>$. (See Exercise 2.3.15.) To compare proof complexities we use the multiset extension of $>^\mu$, notation: $>^{\mu\mu}$. Now we define:

$$P \rightarrowtail_{\mathcal{BC}} P' \Leftrightarrow |P| >^{\mu\mu} |P'|\,.$$

Definition 2.5.6. A proof ordering $\rightarrowtail$ is *compatible with* $\mathcal{BC}$ if $(E, R) \Rightarrow^+ (E', R')$ implies that for every proof P in $E \cup R$ of an equation $s = t$ there exists a proof P' of $s = t$ in $E' \cup R'$ such that $P \rightarrowtail P'$ or $P \equiv P'$.

The following proposition has a straightforward proof, which follows from considering Figure 2.23 and applying stability and monotonicity of $\rightarrowtail_{\mathcal{BC}}$. Figure 2.23 suggests how proofs are reduced in complexity by application of a transformation step according to $C_1, \ldots, C_4$. For instance, in the case of C_2 (see Figure 2.23) the complexity of the subproof $t \leftarrow_R s \to_R u$ is $[[s], [s]]$ which decreases to the complexity of the subproof $t \leftrightarrow_R u$, namely $[[t, u]]$. This is indeed a decrease since $[s] >^\mu [t, u]$.

Proposition 2.5.7. *The ordering $\rightarrowtail_{\mathcal{BC}}$ is a proof ordering, which moreover is compatible with $\mathcal{BC}$.*

So in a $\mathcal{BC}$-derivation $(E_0, R_0) \Rightarrow (E_1, R_1) \Rightarrow (E_2, R_2) \Rightarrow \cdots$ the proofs in $E_j \cup R_j$ are no more difficult than corresponding proofs in $E_i \cup R_i$, for all $j > i$. The following fairness property of $\mathcal{BC}$-derivations implies that moreover every proof in $E_i \cup R_i$ of an equation $s = t$ which is not yet a rewrite proof, can be simplified to a rewrite proof of $s = t$ in $E_j \cup R_j$ for some $j > i$.

Definition 2.5.8. A $\mathcal{BC}$-derivation $(E_0, R_0) \Rightarrow (E_1, R_1) \Rightarrow (E_2, R_2) \Rightarrow \cdots$ is called *fair* if

1. $\bigcap_{j>i} E_j = \varnothing$ for all $i \geq 0$, and
2. if $\langle c, d\rangle \in \bigcap_{j \geq i} CP_j$ for some $i \geq 0$ then $c = d \in E_k$ for some $k \geq 0$. (CP_j is the set of all critical pairs between the rewrite rules of R_j.)

So, according to (2) every critical pair which arises will be (or was) an equation at some time, and by (1) every equation will be 'considered' eventually, that is, oriented in a rewrite rule, simplified, or deleted. The following fact can now be proved routinely.

Proposition 2.5.9. *Let $(E_0, R_0) \Rightarrow (E_1, R_1) \Rightarrow (E_2, R_2) \Rightarrow \cdots$ be a fair $\mathcal{BC}$-derivation and let P be a proof of $s = t$ in $E_i \cup R_i$. If P is not yet a*

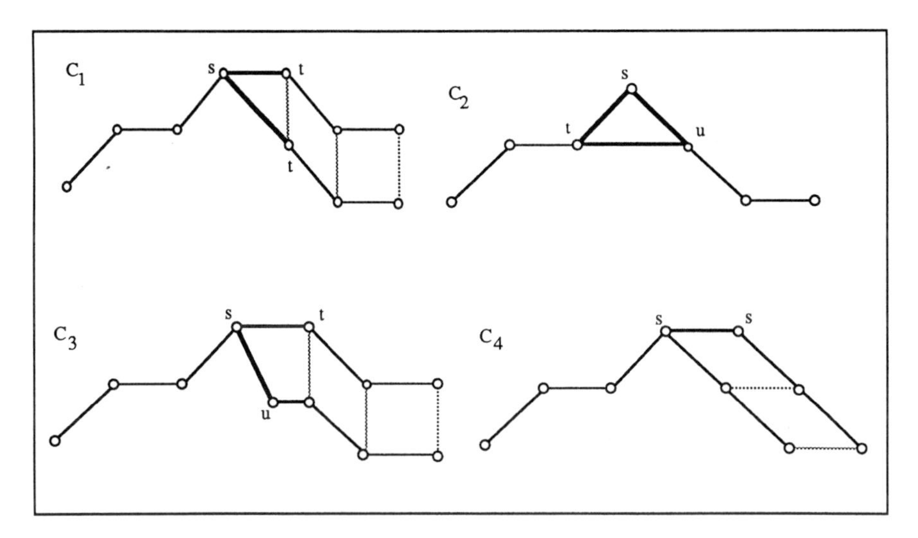

Figure 2.23

rewrite proof then for some $j \geq i$ there exists a proof P' in $E_j \cup R_j$ of $s = t$ such that $P \rightarrowtail_{\mathcal{BC}} P'$.

By a *completion procedure* we mean a strategy for applying the inference rules of $\mathcal{BC}$ to inputs (Σ, E) and reduction ordering $>$, in order to generate a $\mathcal{BC}$-derivation $(E_0, R_0) \Rightarrow (E_1, R_1) \Rightarrow \cdots$ with $(E_0, R_0) = (E, \varnothing)$. Because for some inputs a fair derivation may not be possible, we allow for a completion procedure to fail. We say that a completion procedure is *fair* if it generates only fair derivations unless it fails. We now have:

Theorem 2.5.10. [Bachmair *et al.*, 1986] *Let* **C** *be a fair completion procedure that does not fail on input (Σ, E) and $>$.*

1. *If $s =_E t$ then* **C** *will generate a pair (E_i, R_i) such that s and t have a common reduct in R_i.*
2. *R^∞ $(= \bigcup_n R_n)$ is a complete TRS.*

2.6 Unification

In the preceding sections about completion algorithms, we have used as a 'subroutine' the determination of a *most general unifier* of two terms. In the present section we will describe a version of a unification algorithm, due to [Martelli and Montanari, 1982]; this nondeterministic algorithm to compute mgu's is itself phrased in the terminology of rewriting. We start with presenting the rewrite rules for 'syntactic unification', and afterwards extend these rules to include 'semantic unification' or 'E-unification'.

Syntactic unification

Before presenting the syntactic unification algorithm, we introduce some more concepts about substitutions, which were defined in Section 2.1 as homomorphisms (with respect to term formation) from the set of terms Ter(R) of the TRS R to Ter(R). The composition of substitutions σ, τ is the usual one for functions: $(\tau \circ \sigma)(t) = \tau(\sigma(t))$ for $t \in$ Ter(R); however, $\tau \circ \sigma$ will be written as $\sigma\tau$, and in accordance with our earlier notation convention, $\sigma(t)$ as t^σ. Note that this notation is unambiguous: $(t^\sigma)^\tau = t^{(\sigma\tau)}$.

The *support* of substitution σ is the restriction of σ to the set of those variables x_i for which $x_i \not\equiv x_i^\sigma$. Usually, the support will be finite, and in this case we write σ (by some 'abus de langage') as its support, which is a finite list of 'bindings' of terms to variables:

$$\{x_{i_1} := t_i, \ldots, x_{i_n} := t_n\}.$$

A *renaming substitution* is a bijective substitution. This implies that a renaming, restricted to the set of variables $Var = \{x_i \mid i \geq 0\}$, is a permutation of Var. Note that the composition $\sigma\tau$ of renamings σ, τ is again a renaming, and that the inverse σ^{-1} of a renaming σ exists and is again a renaming. Terms s, t differing by a renaming, i.e. $t^\sigma \equiv s$ for some renaming σ, are called *variants* (of each other).

If t, s are terms such that $t^\sigma \equiv s$ for some substitution σ, we write $t \leq s$. The relation $\leq$ is not yet a partial ordering; it is a quasi-ordering, also called the *subsumption* relation. One easily proves for all $s, t \in$ Ter(R): $s \leq t$ & $t \leq s \Leftrightarrow s, t$ are variants. For substitutions σ, τ we write $\sigma \leq \tau$ if $\tau = \sigma\rho$ for some substitution ρ. In this case σ is called *more general than* τ. (The 'overloading' of the symbol $\leq$ will cause no confusion.) Analogous to the case of terms, one easily proves: $\sigma \leq \tau$ and $\tau \leq \sigma \Leftrightarrow \sigma, \tau$ differ by a renaming ($\sigma\rho = \tau$ for some renaming ρ).

We call σ a *unifier* of a set of terms $\mathcal{T} = \{t_1, \ldots, t_n\}$ if $t_1^\sigma \equiv t_n^\sigma$. It is a *most general unifier* (mgu) of $\mathcal{T}$ if for every unifier τ of $\mathcal{T}$ we have $\sigma \leq \tau$. Each finite set of terms which can be unified (has a unifier) has a mgu; it is unique *modulo renamings*.

The task of finding a most general unifier of two terms $F(t_1, \ldots, t_n)$ and $F(s_1, \ldots, s_n)$ can be viewed as the task of solving the set of equations $\{t_1 = s_1, \ldots, t_n = s_n\}$. A very elegant algorithm exploiting this representation was given by [Martelli and Montanari, 1982]. It consists of rules which transform one set of equations into another one. To conform with the notation in 'equational logic programming' as in [Hölldobler, 1989], we write instead of $\{t_1 = s_1, \ldots, t_n = s_n\}$:

$$\Leftarrow t_1 = s_1, \ldots, t_n = s_n,$$

called also an *equational goal.* The empty goal (empty set of equations) will be denoted as $\Box$. The algorithm to be presented transforms, non-deterministically, goals into goals; just as in logic programming we intend to end a sequence of transformations in the empty goal:

$$G_0 \rightarrowtail G_1 \rightarrowtail \cdots \rightarrowtail \Box.$$

Here $\rightarrowtail$ denotes an elementary 'derivation' step; $G_0, G_1, \ldots$ are equational goals. Actually, at some of the $\rightarrowtail$-steps we may obtain as a 'side-effect' a substitution σ; it will be denoted as a subscript, so that such a step has the form $G \rightarrowtail_\sigma G'$. So a derivation may have the form, e.g.:

$$G_0 \rightarrowtail G_1 \rightarrowtail_{\sigma_1} G_2 \rightarrowtail_{\sigma_2} G_3 \rightarrowtail G_4 \rightarrowtail G_5 \rightarrowtail_{\sigma_5} G_6 \rightarrowtail \cdots \rightarrowtail \Box.$$

Derivation sequences ending in $\Box$ are *successful*; it will also be possible that a derivation is stuck and cannot be prolonged to reach $\Box$, because no transformation rule applies. In that case we conclude the sequence after the goal where the sequence got stuck, with the symbol $\blacksquare$ (for 'failure'):

$$G_0 \rightarrowtail G_1 \rightarrowtail \cdots \rightarrowtail \quad \blacksquare.$$

In the case of a successful derivation, we can obtain the 'harvest' by composing all the substitutions that are found, in their order of appearance; in the example above: $\sigma_1\sigma_2\sigma_5 \cdots$. This substitution is the *computed answer substitution* of the successful derivation that we are considering.

We will now present the four derivation rules for equational goals that together constitute a unification algorithm. With some adaptations, these 'Martelli–Montanari rules' (MM rules) are as follows. Here $\Leftarrow t = s,\ E$ stands for an equational goal containing the equation $t = s$; with E we denote the remaining equations in the goal.

1. **Term decomposition**

$$\Leftarrow F(t_1,\ldots,t_n) = F(s_1,\ldots,s_n),\ E$$
$$\rightarrowtail$$
$$\Leftarrow t_1 = s_1,\ldots,t_n = s_n,\ E$$

2. **Removal of trivial equations**

$$\Leftarrow x = x,\ E \quad \rightarrowtail \quad \Leftarrow E$$

3. **Swap**

$$\Leftarrow t = x,\ E \quad \rightarrowtail \quad \Leftarrow x = t,\ E$$
if t is not a variable

4. **Variable elimination**

$$\Leftarrow x = t,\ E \quad \rightarrowtail_{\{x:=t\}} \quad \Leftarrow E^{\{x:=t\}}$$
if $x \notin t$

(If E is $t_1 = s_1,\ldots,t_n = s_n$, then E^σ is $t_1^\sigma = s_1^\sigma,\ldots,t_n^\sigma = s_n^\sigma$. With '$\in$' we abbreviate 'occurs in'. Note that only in transformation rule (4) a substitution is delivered.)

We have the following well-known 'completeness' theorem:

Theorem 2.6.1. (Unification theorem) *Let G be an equational goal $\Leftarrow t_1 = s_1,\ldots,t_n = s_n$. Then the following are equivalent:*

1. *the equations in G can be unified;*
2. *there is an mgu σ such that $t_1^\sigma \equiv s_1^\sigma,\ldots,t_n^\sigma \equiv s_n^\sigma$;*
3. *the derivation tree with root G and constructed with the MM rules is finite and has only success branches, all yielding an mgu of the equations in G as computed answer substitution.*

Furthermore, if the equations in G cannot be unified, the MM-derivation tree with root G is also finite, but now with all branches ending unsuccessfully.

(It will be clear what is meant in the statement of the theorem above with derivation *tree*; it arises because the rules can be applied nondeterministically.) In the original presentation of Martelli and Montanari, the following two rules are also included; they enhance efficiency, by pruning the MM-derivation tree of some unsuccessful subtrees. But we don't need them for the completeness of this (nondeterministic) unification algorithm. (Also, when extending the set of rules to deal with E-unification, as we will do below, (5) and (6) must be omitted.)

5. **Failure rule**

$$\Leftarrow F(t_1, \ldots, t_n) = G(s_1, \ldots, s_m),\ E \ \rightarrowtail \ \blacksquare$$

6. **Occur check**

$$\begin{array}{l} \Leftarrow x = t,\ E \ \rightarrowtail \ \blacksquare \\ \textit{if } x \not\equiv t \textit{ and } x \in t \end{array}$$

It is not hard to prove that the MM rules are indeed terminating, as stated by the unification theorem. (See [Martelli and Montanari, 1982], [Apt, 1990], or [Dershowitz and Jouannaud, 1990].)

If t, s are unifiable terms we will denote with $mgu(s,t)$ a particular mgu of $\{s,t\}$, obtained by performing the MM transformations according to some fixed strategy.

Example 2.6.2.

1. We want to determine 'the' mgu of the terms $F(G(x), H(x,u))$ and $F(z, H(F(y,y),z))$. The MM rules yield the following successful derivation:

$$\begin{array}{lll} \Leftarrow & F(G(x), H(x,u)) = F(z, H(F(y,y),z)) & \rightarrowtail_{(1)} \\ \Leftarrow & G(x) = z,\ H(x,u) = H(F(y,y),z) & \rightarrowtail_{(3)} \\ \Leftarrow & z = G(x),\ H(x,u) = H(F(y,y),z) & \rightarrowtail_{(4),\{z:=G(x)\}} \\ \Leftarrow & H(x,u) = H(F(y,y),G(x)) & \rightarrowtail_{(1)} \\ \Leftarrow & x = F(y,y),\ u = G(x) & \rightarrowtail_{(4),\{x:=F(y,y)\}} \\ \Leftarrow & u = G(F(y,y)) & \rightarrowtail_{(4),\{u:=G(F(y,y))\}} \\ \square & & \end{array}$$

with computed answer substitution $\{z := G(x)\}\{x := F(y,y)\}\{u := G(F(y,y))\} = \{z := G(F(y,y)), x := F(y,y), u := G(F(y,y))\}$. Indeed this is an mgu of the original pair of terms.

2. A failing unification attempt:

$$\begin{array}{lll} \Leftarrow & F(x,y) = F(y, G(x)) & \rightarrowtail_{(1)} \\ \Leftarrow & x = y,\ y = G(x) & \rightarrowtail_{(2),\{x:=y\}} \\ \Leftarrow & y = G(y) & \rightarrowtail_{(6)} \\ \blacksquare & & \end{array}$$

Semantic unification

In the previous section we have presented an algorithm to solve equations $t_1 = t_2$ 'syntactically'; this is a particular case of the important problem to solve equations 'semantically', i.e. modulo some equational theory E (for this reason semantic unification is also called E-unification). More precisely, in the presence of an equational theory E, and given an equation $t_1 = t_2$, we want to find substitutions σ such that $E \models t_1^\sigma = t_2^\sigma$ or equivalently (see Theorem 2.4.2) $E \vdash t_1^\sigma = t_2^\sigma$. So syntactic unification is E-unification with empty E.

The situation is now much more complicated than for the case of syntactic unification, since in general there will not be a most general unifier σ for t_1, t_2. We will not really enter the vast area of unification theory (see [Siekmann, 1984], but will mention two algorithms for E-unification which are pertinent to term rewriting. Both algorithms operate under the assumption that E, the underlying equational theory, is a *complete* TRS (or rather corresponds to one after orienting the equality axioms of E into rewrite rules). So here we have another important application of Knuth–Bendix completion: it prepares the way for equation solving over E, by delivering a complete TRS for E (if possible).

Narrowing

A well-known technique to solve equations $t_1 = t_2$ in the presence of an equational theory E uses the 'narrowing' transformation on terms. We will give an 'intuitive' explanation first, which also explains why narrowing is called 'narrowing'.

If (Σ, E) is an equational theory, we write $[t = s]_E$ for the set of solutions of the equation $t = s$ in E, i.e. $\{\sigma \mid E \vdash t^\sigma = s^\sigma\}$. A solution σ is a substitution as defined earlier, i.e. a map from Var, the set of variables, to $\mathrm{Ter}(\Sigma)$. Let SUB be the set of all substitutions, and if $X \subseteq$ SUB, let σX denote $\{\sigma\tau \mid \tau \in X\}$. Now noting that for every σ we have $[t = s]_E \supseteq \sigma[t^\sigma = s^\sigma]_E$, there is in principle the possibility of a stepwise determination of $[t = s]_E$. This stepwise determination consists of two kinds of steps. The first is as just described: guess a component σ of a solution and narrow $[t = s]_E$ to $\sigma[t^\sigma = s^\sigma]_E$. The second is: apply an equation of E in one of the sides of the equation $t = s$ under consideration. Clearly, a step of the second kind preserves equality of the solution set. By an iteration of such steps, alternating between steps of the first kind and steps of the second kind, we may reach the solution set of a trivial equation $r = r$ (which is SUB):

$$\begin{aligned} [t = s]_E &\supseteq \sigma[t^\sigma = s^\sigma]_E = \sigma[r = s^\sigma]_E \\ &\supseteq \sigma\sigma^1[r^{\sigma^1} = s^{\sigma\sigma^1}]_E = \cdots \\ &\supseteq \cdots \\ &\supseteq \sigma\sigma^1 \cdots \sigma^n[r = r]_E. \end{aligned}$$

The last solution set $\sigma\sigma^1 \cdots \sigma^n[r = r]_E$ of this 'narrowing' chain has as a most general element the substitution $\sigma\sigma^1 \cdots \sigma^n$. The word 'narrowing' has been given a formal content: it denotes a certain method, based on term rewriting, to perform a stepwise determination of $[t = s]_E$ as described. A narrowing step combines a step of the first kind and one of the second. Actually, the narrowing relation is first defined on terms rather than equations, as in the following definition, where we suppose that R is a TRS equivalent to E (i.e. $=_R$ coincides with $=_E$). Note that narrowing is a generalization of reduction: any reductions step in a TRS is also a narrowing step. Formally:

Definition 2.6.3. Let term t contain the subterm u, so $t \equiv C[u]$ for some context $C[\,]$. In the presence of a TRS R we say that t is *narrowable* to t' at the (nonvariable) subterm $u \subseteq t$ using rewrite rule $r : t_1 \to t_2 \in R$, via $\sigma = mgu(u, t_1)$, if $t' \equiv C[t_2]^\sigma$. Notation: $t \leadsto_{u,r,\sigma} t'$. (Sometimes we will drop mention of u, r; but not of σ.)

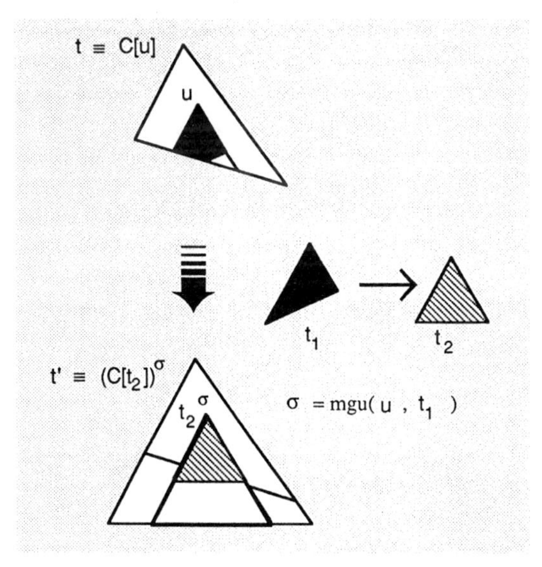

narrowing step on terms

Figure 2.24

We now extend the narrowing transformation, which was defined on terms, to equations: if $t \leadsto_\sigma t'$, then $t = s \leadsto_\sigma t' = s$ and likewise $s = t \leadsto_\sigma s = t'$ are said to be narrowing steps (on equations). As we have seen, the word narrowing actually refers to the solution sets: if $t = s \leadsto_\sigma t' = s^\sigma$ then $[t = s]_R \supseteq \sigma[t^\sigma = s^\sigma]_R$. Note how narrowing cuts down the search space for determining the solution set, first by using the directional aspect of a TRS, and second by performing substitutions which are as 'small' (as general) as possible. However, there is a price to be paid: to ensure completeness of the narrowing method for solving equations, we must require that the underlying TRS is ... complete. More precisely (as stated in Hullot [80]): in order to solve an equation $t_1 = t_1'$ in an equational theory E, corresponding to a complete TRS R, we can construct all possible narrowing derivations starting from the given equation until an equation $t_n = t_n'$ is obtained such that t_n and t_n' are syntactically unifiable. In fact, we are sure to find all possible solutions of the equation. We will make this more precise, via the following definition.

Definition 2.6.4. Let τ, σ be substitutions and E an equational theory. Then $\tau \leq_E \sigma$ if for some ρ we have $\tau\rho =_E \sigma$. (Here $\tau\rho =_E \sigma$ means: $E \vdash x^{\tau\rho} = x^\sigma$ for all x.)

Now we have the following completeness theorem for narrowing plus syntactic unification. (See [Martelli *et al.*, 1986], Theorem 2. See also [Hölldobler, 1989] for a proof of this theorem and many related facts.) The formulation of the theorem refers to a slightly more general setting than in our discussion of narrowing above: the narrowing procedure may be applied not only to single equations, but to equational goals $\Leftarrow t_1 = s_1, \ldots, t_n = s_n$.

Theorem 2.6.5. *Let R be a complete TRS. Suppose $t_1^\sigma =_R t_2^\sigma$ (i.e. σ is a solution of the equation $t_1 = t_2$). Then there is a successful derivation sequence starting with $\Leftarrow t_1 = t_2$ and using narrowing steps and MM steps (1–4), such that the computed answer substitution τ of this sequence 'improves' σ, i.e. $\tau \leq_R \sigma$.*

Remark 2.6.6.

1. Note that the subscript R in $\tau \leq_R \sigma$ is necessary. (Example: $R = \{f(b) \to g(b),\ a \to b\}$. Now $\sigma = \{x/a\}$ is a solution for $\Leftarrow f(x) = g(x)$, but as computed answer substitution we only find $\tau = \{x/b\}$.)
2. Also completeness of R is necessary.
   (a) To see that *confluence* of R is necessary, consider the TRS $R = \{a \to b,\ a \to c\}$ (so R is not confluent). Now the equation $\Leftarrow b = c$ cannot be solved, i.e. we do not find the expected computed answer substitution ϵ (the identity substitution). However, if we turn R into a confluent system, e.g. by adding the rewrite rules $b \to d$ and $c \to d$, then narrowing (together with syntactic unification) gives a refutation of $\Leftarrow b = c$:

   $$\Leftarrow \mathbf{b} = c \leadsto_\epsilon \Leftarrow d = \mathbf{c} \leadsto_\epsilon \Leftarrow \mathbf{d} = \mathbf{d} \rightarrowtail_1 \square.$$

   (b) To see that *termination* of R is necessary, consider the confluent but nonterminating TRS with one rule: $c \to f(c)$. Now narrowing plus syntactic unification is not complete: the equation $x = f(x)$ has a solution, $\{x := c\}$, but cannot be resolved, because the only subterm where narrowing may be applied is $f(x)$ (narrowing may not be performed on a variable) and this does not unify with c. (Also syntactic unification does not help, since x occurs in $f(x)$.) So we do not find a computed answer substitution.

3. Theorem 2.6.5 can be improved in the following sense: we can drop the termination requirement on R, thus only requiring R to be confluent, if we consider only *normalizable* solutions σ (as in the statement of the theorem above). Here σ is called normalizable if all terms x^σ (x a variable) have a normal form. (Note that the solution $\{x := c\}$ in 2(b) was not normalizable.) If moreover we consider not only normalizable solutions σ, but *normal* σ (meaning that every x^σ is in normal form), then we can even drop the subscript R in $\tau \leq_R \sigma$, in the statement of the theorem above.

Lazy term rewriting as a complete E-unification algorithm

An interesting complete E-unification algorithm is given by [Martelli *et al.*, 1986], also for the case where E corresponds after orienting the equations to a *complete* TRS R. The nondeterministic algorithm consists of the four derivation rules (1)–(4) for syntactic unification as given above together with a single rule called 'term rewriting' in [Martelli *et al.*, 1986]. Of course derivation rules 5 (failure rule) and 6 (occur check) are not included now. Actually, this rule does not resemble what is usually called term rewriting. Here we will call the present rule 'lazy term rewriting'.

7. **Lazy term rewriting**

$$\begin{array}{c} \Leftarrow C[F(t_1, \ldots, t_n)] = s,\ E \\ \rightarrowtail \\ \Leftarrow C[t] = s,\ t_1 = s_1, \ldots, t_n = s_n,\ E \\ \textit{if } F(s_1, \ldots, s_n) \to t \end{array}$$

and likewise with the reverse of the equations $C[F(t_1, \ldots, t_n)] = s$ and $C[t] = s$. Here $C[\;]$ is some context, and $F(s_1, \ldots, s_n) \to t$ is a rewrite rule from the complete TRS R.

Note how amazingly little is 'done' in a lazy term rewriting step, as compared to the rather complicated narrowing procedure.

3 Orthogonal Term Rewriting Systems

In the preceding sections we have considered general properties of TRSs and how these properties are related; among them the most important property, confluence, with its consequence of uniqueness of normal forms.

We will now consider a special class of TRSs, the orthogonal ones (in the literature mostly known as non-ambiguous and left-linear TRSs), which all have the confluence property as well as various other desirable properties concerned with reduction strategies.

A remark concerning the choice of the word 'orthogonal': to avoid the cumbersome phrase 'non-ambiguous and left-linear', [Klop, 1980a] introduced the abbreviation 'regular'. This terminology is also used in e.g. [O'Donnell, 1985], [Kennaway, 1989] [Klop, 1987], and in early versions of [Dershowitz and Jouannaud, 1990]. On a proposal of Dershowitz and Jouannaud the word 'regular' has been replaced in the present chapter by 'orthogonal'; this in view of the fact that many authors found the terminology 'regular' objectionable. Indeed, the word 'orthogonal' has the right intuitive connotations.

3.1 Basic theory of orthogonal Term Rewriting Systems

Definition 3.1.1.

1. A TRS R is *orthogonal* if the reduction rules of R are *left-linear* (R is left-linear) and there are *no critical pairs.*
2. R is *weakly orthogonal* if R is left-linear and R contains only trivial critical pairs, i.e. if $\langle t, s\rangle$ is a critical pair then $t \equiv s$.

We recall that a reduction rule $t \to s$ is left-linear if t is linear, i.e. no variable occurs twice or more in t. E.g. the rule $D(x, x) \to E$ is not left-linear; nor is the rule $\underline{\text{if}}\ x\ \underline{\text{then}}\ y\ \underline{\text{else}}\ y \to y$. A TRS R without critical pairs is also called *non-ambiguous* or *non-overlapping.* One problem with non-left-linear rules is that their application requires a test for syntactic equality of the arguments substituted for the variables occurring more than once. As terms may be very large, this may be very laborious. Another problem is that the presence of non-left-linear rules may destroy the CR property.

Exercise 3.1.2. Let R consist of the rules $D(x, x) \to E$, $C(x) \to D(x, C(x))$, $A \to C(A)$. To show: R is WCR, but not CR; for, we have reductions $C(A) \twoheadrightarrow E$ and $C(A) \twoheadrightarrow C(E)$ but $C(E)$, E have no common reduct. There are no critical pairs in R. Hence, in view of our later theorem stating that orthogonal TRSs are confluent, the non-confluence of R is caused by the non-left-linear rule $D(x, x) \to E$.

In the preceding section (Definition 2.4.9) we have already defined the notion of 'critical pair'. Since that definition is often found difficult, we will now explain the *absence* of critical pairs in a more 'intuitive' way. Let R be the TRS as in Table 3.1:

r_1	$F(G(x, S(0)), y, H(z))$	$\to$	x
r_2	$G(x, S(S(0)))$	$\to$	0
r_3	$P(G(x, S(0)))$	$\to$	$S(0)$

Table 3.1

Call the context $F(G(\square, S(0)), \square, H(\square))$ the *pattern* of rule r_1. (Earlier, we defined a context as a term with exactly one hole $\square$, but it is clear what a context with more holes is.) In tree form the pattern is the shaded area as in Figure 3.1. For a left-linear rule it is only its pattern that 'counts'.

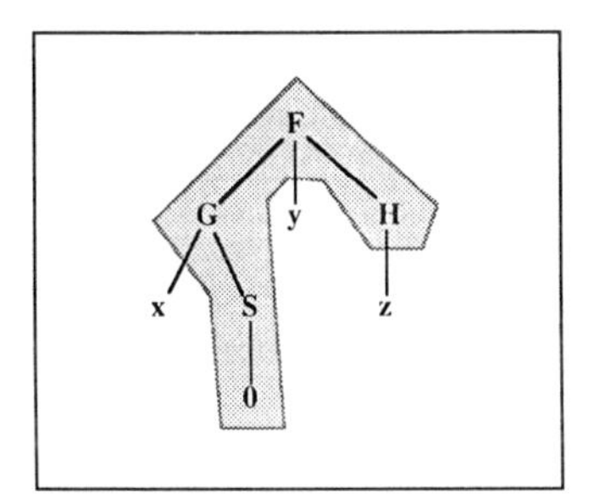

Figure 3.1

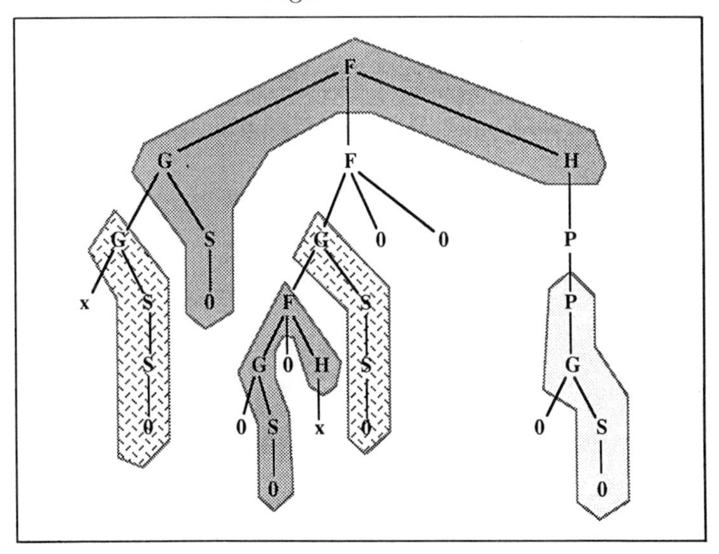

Figure 3.2

The TRS R in Table 3.1 has the property that *in no term patterns can overlap*, i.e. R has the non-overlapping or non-ambiguity property. Figure 3.2 shows a term in R with all patterns indicated, and indeed they do not overlap.

Overlap can already occur in one rule, e.g. in the rule $L(L(x)) \to 0$; see Figure 3.3(a). An overlap at the root (of the tree corresponding to a term), arising from the rules $F(0, x, y) \to 0$, $F(x, 1, y) \to 1$, is shown in Figure 3.3(b). Another overlap at the root, arising from the rules for the non-deterministic $\underline{or}$: $\underline{or}(x, y) \to x$, $\underline{or}(x, y) \to y$, is shown in Figure 3.3(c).

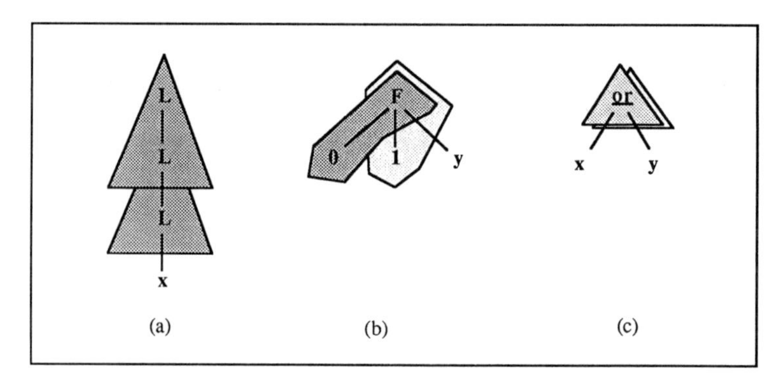

Figure 3.3

We will now formulate and sketch the proofs of the basic theorems for orthogonal TRSs. To that end, we need the notion of '*descendant*' in a reduction. Somewhat informally, this notion can be introduced as follows: Let t be a term in a orthogonal TRS R, and let $s \subseteq t$ be a redex whose head symbol we will give a marking, say by underlining it, to be able to 'trace' it during a sequence of reduction (rewrite) steps. Thus if $s \equiv F(t_1, \ldots, t_n)$, it is marked as $\underline{F}(t_1, \ldots, t_n)$. First consider the rewrite step $t \to_{s'} t'$, obtained by contraction of redex s' in t. We wish to know what has happened in this step to the marked redex s. The following cases can be distinguished, depending on the relative positions of s and s' in t:

Case 1. The occurrences of s' and s in t are disjoint. Then we find back the marked redex s, unaltered, in t'.

Case 2. The occurrences of s and s' coincide. Then the marked redex has disappeared in t'; t' does not contain an underlined symbol.

Case 3. s' is a proper subterm of the marked redex s (so s' is a subterm of one of the arguments of s). Then we find back the marked redex, with some possible change in one of the arguments. (Here we need the orthogonality of R; otherwise the marked redex could have stopped being a redex in t' after the 'internal' contraction of s'.)

Case 4. s is a proper subterm of s'. Then the marked redex s is n times multiplied for some $n \geq 0$; if $n = 0$, s is erased in t'. The reduct t' now contains n copies of the marked redex, all of them still marked.

Now the marked redexes in t' are called the *descendants* of $s \subseteq t$ in the reduction step $t \to_{s'} t'$. It is obvious how to extend this definition by transitivity to sequences of rewrite steps $t \rightarrow_{s'} t' \rightarrow_{s''} t'' \rightarrow \cdots \rightarrow t^{(n-1)} \rightarrow_{s^{(n)}} t^{(n)}$.

Proposition 3.1.3. *Let R be a orthogonal TRS, $t \in Ter(R)$. Let t contain, possibly among others, the mutually disjoint redexes $s_1, \ldots, s_n$. Let these redexes be marked by underlining their head symbol. Furthermore, suppose that $t \twoheadrightarrow t'$ is the sequence of n rewrite steps obtained by contraction of all redexes s_i (in some order), and let $t \rightarrow_s t''$ be a rewrite step obtained from contracting redex s. (See Figure 3.4(a).) Then a common reduct t''' of t', t'' can be found by contracting in t'' all marked redexes (which still are mutually disjoint). The reduction $t' \twoheadrightarrow t'''$ consists of the contraction of all descendants of s in t' after the reduction $t \twoheadrightarrow t'$.*

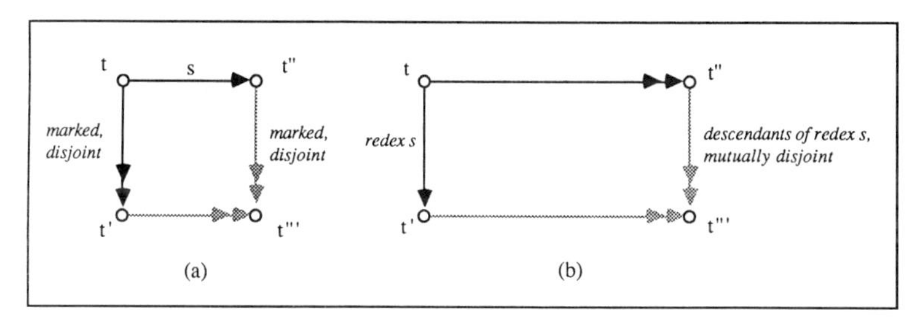

Figure 3.4

The proof is a matter of easy casuistics, left to the reader. An immediate corollary is the 'parallel moves lemma':

Lemma 3.1.4. (parallel moves lemma) *We consider reductions in an orthogonal TRS. Let $t \twoheadrightarrow t''$, and let $t \rightarrow_s t'$ be a one step reduction by contraction of redex s. Then a common reduct t''' of t', t'' can be found by contraction in t'' of all descendants of redex s, which are mutually disjoint. (See Figure 3.4(b).)*

By repeated application of the parallel moves lemma we now have:

Theorem 3.1.5. *Every orthogonal TRS is confluent.*

Theorem 3.1.5 also holds for weakly orthogonal TRSs. The earliest proof of Theorem 3.1.5 is probably that of [Rosen, 1973]; but earlier proofs of the confluence of CL (combinatory logic), work just as well for orthogonal TRSs in general. The confluence theorem for (weakly) orthogonal TRSs is also a special case of a theorem of Huet (mentioned already in Exercise 2.4.24), stated here without proof. We need a definition first:

Definition 3.1.6. (parallel reduction) $t \rightarrow_{\parallel} s$ if $t \twoheadrightarrow s$ via a reduction of disjoint redexes.

Theorem 3.1.7. [Huet, 1980] *Let R be a left-linear TRS. Suppose for every critical pair $\langle t, s\rangle$ we have $t \to_{||} s$. Then $\to_{||}$ is strongly confluent, hence R is confluent.*

(For the definition of 'strongly confluent' see Exercise 2.0.8(10). In fact, the proof in [Huet, 1980] yields more: $\to_{||}$ is even *subcommutative*—see Definition 2.0.1(5).)

Exercises 3.1.8.

1. Combinatory logic (Table 2.4) has rule patterns as in Figure 3.5; they cannot overlap. As CL is left-linear, it is therefore orthogonal and hence confluent.

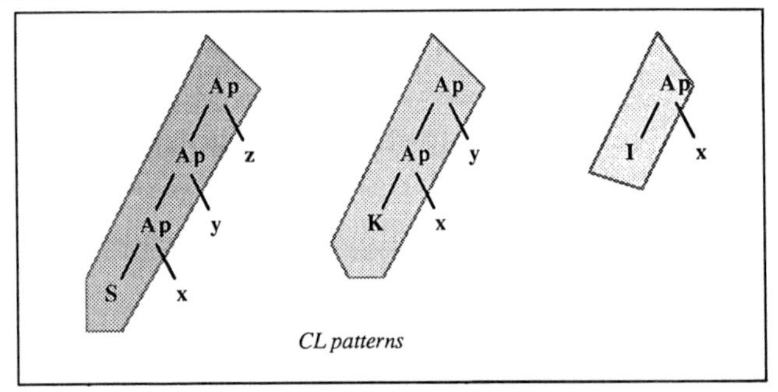

Figure 3.5

2. SKIM, in Table 2.5, is orthogonal. Likewise for the TRSs CL with test for equality, binary or applicative, in Tables 2.6, 2.7 respectively. Also Weak categorical combinatory logic in Table 2.8 is orthogonal.
3. A recursive program scheme (RPS) is a TRS with
   (a) a finite set of function symbols $\mathcal{F} = \{F_1, \dots, F_n\}$ (the 'unknown' functions), where F_i has arity $m_i \geq 0$ $(i = 1, \dots, n)$, and
   (b) a finite set $\mathcal{G} = \{G_1, \dots, G_k\}$ (the 'known' or 'basic' functions), disjoint from $\mathcal{F}$, where G_j has arity $p_j \geq 0$ $(j = 1, \dots, k)$,
   (c) reduction rules of the form

$$F_i(x_1 \dots, x_{m_i}) \to t_i \qquad (i = 1, \dots, n)$$

   where all the displayed variables are pairwise different and where t_i is an arbitrary term built from operators in $\mathcal{F}, \mathcal{G}$ and the displayed variables. For each F_i $(i = 1, \dots, n)$ there is exactly one rule.

Every RPS is orthogonal, hence confluent. For an extensive treatise on semantical aspects of recursive program schemes, see [Courcelle, 1990].

Exercise 3.1.9. For a deterministic Turing machine M, the TRS R_M as defined in Exercise 2.2.21 is orthogonal.

Apart from confluence, many interesting facts can be proved for orthogonal TRSs.

Definition 3.1.10.

1. A TRS is *non-erasing* if in every rule $t \to s$ the same variables occur in t and in s. (E.g. CL is not non-erasing, due to the rule $Kxy \to x$.)
2. A TRS is *weakly innermost normalizing* (WIN) if every term has a normal form which can be reached by an *innermost* reduction. (In an innermost reduction a redex may only be 'contracted' if it contains no proper subredexes.)

The next theorem was proved in [Church, 1941] for the case of the non-erasing version of λ-calculus, the λI-calculus, where the restriction on term formation is adopted saying that in every abstraction term $\lambda x.M$ the variable x must have a free occurrence in M.

Theorem 3.1.11. *Let R be orthogonal and non-erasing. Then: R is WN iff R is SN.*

Another useful theorem, which also reduces the burden of a termination (SN) proof for orthogonal TRSs, is:

Theorem 3.1.12. [O'Donnell, 1977] *Let R be an orthogonal TRS. Then: R is WIN iff R is SN.*

The last two theorems can be refined to terms: call a term WN if it has a normal form, SN if it has no infinite reductions, WIN if it has a normal form reachable by an innermost reduction. The 'local' version of Theorem 3.1.11 then says that for a term in an orthogonal, non-erasing TRS the properties WN and SN coincide. Likewise there is a local version of Theorem 3.1.12. Thus, if in CL a term can be normalized via an innermost reduction, all its reductions are finite.

Exercise 3.1.13. In this exercise we sketch a proof of Theorem 3.1.11 and O'Donnell's Theorem 3.1.12.

1. The following proposition has an easy proof:

   Proposition. *Let t be a term in an orthogonal TRS, containing mutually disjoint redexes $s_1, \ldots, s_n$, and a redex s. Let $t \twoheadrightarrow t'$ be the n-step reduction obtained by contraction, in some order, of the redexes $s_1, \ldots, s_n$. Suppose s has after the reduction $t \twoheadrightarrow t'$ no descendants in t'. Then for some $i \in \{1, \ldots, n\}$, $s \subseteq s_i$. This means that either s coincides with some s_i, or is contained in an argument of some s_i.*

2. We write '$\infty(t)$' if the term t has an infinite reduction $t \to \to \cdots$. So $\infty(t)$ iff t is not SN. Using the proposition in (1) one can now prove (the proof is non-trivial):

   Lemma. *Let t be a term in an orthogonal TRS such that $\infty(t)$. Let $t \to_s t'$ be a reduction step such that $\neg\infty(t')$. Then the redex s must contain a proper subterm p with $\infty(p)$ that is erased in the step $t \to_s t'$ (i.e. has no* *descendants in t').*

3. Using the lemma it is now easy to prove Theorem 3.1.11: 'critical' steps $t \to t'$ in which $\infty(t)$ but $\neg\infty(t')$, cannot occur in a non-erasing TRS.
4. Theorem 3.1.12 follows from the lemma in (2) by observing that an innermost contraction cannot erase a proper subterm which admits an infinite reduction, since otherwise the contracted redex would not have been innermost.

Exercise 3.1.14. STS's (Semi-Thue systems), viewed as TRSs as explained in Section 2.1, are always non-erasing (since the left-hand side and right-hand side of every rule end in x, in their TRS version). Also, if there are no critical pairs in the STS, it is orthogonal. So if a STS has no critical pairs, the properties SN and WN coincide.

This rather trivial observation could have been more easily made by noting that for a STS without critical pairs the property WCR^1 holds, as defined in Exercise 2.0.8(15), whence WN $\Leftrightarrow$ SN.

Exercise 3.1.15. (Klop [80a]) Let t_0 be a term in an orthogonal TRS. Suppose t_0 has a normal form, but has also an infinite reduction $t_0 \to t_1 \to t_2 \to \cdots$. Show that t_0 has also an infinite 'expansion' (the reverse of a reduction) $\cdots \to t_{-2} \to t_{-1} \to t_0$. (Hint: Use the lemma in Exercise 3.1.13, and note that an 'erasing redex' can be used to 'pump' an infinite expansion.)

Exercise 3.1.16. [Klop, 1985]

1. Let R be orthogonal, and suppose R is WN (i.e. every term has a normal form), but not SN. Let $t \in \mathrm{Ter}(R)$ be a term with an infinite reduction. Then $\mathcal{G}(t)$, the reduction graph of t, contains an infinite expansion (by confluence, there must then also be an infinite expansion of the normal form t_0 of t inside $\mathcal{G}(t)$). In fact, $\mathcal{G}(t)$ contains reductions as follows:

$$t \twoheadrightarrow t_1 \twoheadrightarrow t_2 \twoheadrightarrow \cdots \qquad \text{and} \qquad t_0 \twoheadleftarrow t'_1 \twoheadleftarrow t'_2 \twoheadleftarrow \cdots$$

   such that $t_n \to t'_n$ for all $n \geq 1$ and such that the t_i $(n \geq 1)$ are pairwise distinct, and likewise the t'_j $(n \geq 1)$ are pairwise distinct.
2. Let t be a term in an orthogonal TRS. Prove: if $\mathcal{G}(t)$ contains an infinite reduction but contains no infinite acyclic expansion, then t reduces to a context $C[\;]$ of a term s without normal form. (The set of s such that $t \twoheadrightarrow C[s]$ for some $C[\,]$, is called in [Barendregt, 1981] the *family* of t.) (In particular the conclusion holds if $\mathcal{G}(t)$ is finite but contains a reduction cycle. Curiously, in CL as in Table 2.4 this is impossible, i.e. finite reduction graphs in CL based on S, K, I are acyclic; see [Klop, 1980b].)
3. The following figure displays the reduction graph of a term t in an orthogonal TRS R. Give an example of such t, R. Conclude, using (2), that t must have a term without normal form in its family. A fortiori, such a reduction graph cannot occur in an orthogonal TRS which is WN.

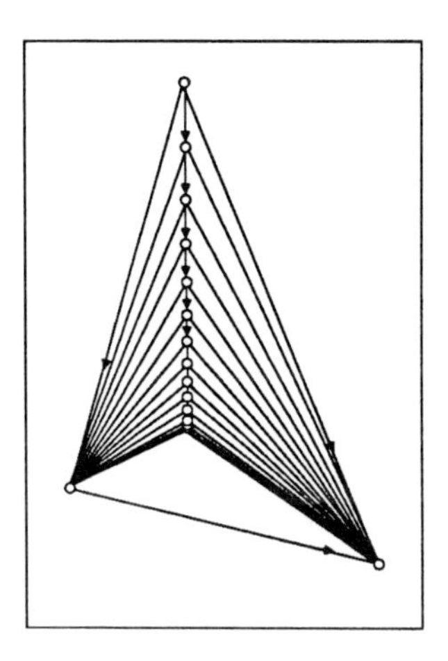

Figure 3.6

Exercise 3.1.17. (Klop [80a]) Prove for all orthogonal TRSs R with finite alphabet and finitely many rules:

1. R is non-erasing $\Leftrightarrow$ R has the property FB^{-1}. (See Definition 2.0.3(8) for FB^{-1}.)
2. R has the property SN^{-1} $\Leftrightarrow$ R has the property Inc. (See Definition 2.0.3.) (Hint: Prove SN^{-1} $\Rightarrow$ non-erasing, use (1) and use the implication FB^{-1} & SN^{-1} $\Rightarrow$ Inc; see Figure 2.2.)

3.2 Reduction strategies for orthogonal Term Rewriting Systems

Terms in a TRS may have a normal form as well as admitting infinite reductions. So, if we are interested in finding normal forms, we should have some strategy at our disposal telling us what redex to contract in order to achieve that desired result. We will in this section present some strategies which are guaranteed to find the normal form of a term whenever such a normal form exists. We will adopt the restriction to orthogonal TRSs; for general TRSs there does not seem to be any result about the existence of 'good' reduction strategies.

The strategies below will be of two kinds: one step or sequential strategies (which point in each reduction step to just one redex as the one to contract) and many step strategies (in which a set of redexes is contracted simultaneously). Of course all strategies must be computable.

Apart from the objective of finding a normal form, we will consider the objective of finding a 'best possible' reduction even if the term at hand does not have a normal form.

Definition 3.2.1. Let R be a TRS.

1. A *one step reduction strategy* $\mathbb{F}$ *for* R is a map $\mathbb{F}$: Ter(R) $\to$ Ter(R) such that
   (a) $t \equiv \mathbb{F}(t)$ if t is a normal form,
   (b) $t \to \mathbb{F}(t)$ otherwise.
2. A *many step reduction strategy* $\mathbb{F}$ *for* R is a map $\mathbb{F}$: Ter(R) $\to$ Ter(R) such that
   (a) $t \equiv \mathbb{F}(t)$ if t is a normal form,
   (b) $t \to^+ \mathbb{F}(t)$ otherwise.

Here $\to^+$ is the transitive (but not reflexive) closure of $\to$. Instead of 'one step strategy' we will also say 'sequential strategy'.

Definition 3.2.2.

1. A reduction strategy (one step or many step) $\mathbb{F}$ for R is *normalizing* if for each term t in R having a normal form, the sequence $\{\mathbb{F}^n(t) \mid n \geq 0\}$ contains a normal form.
2. $\mathbb{F}$ is *cofinal* if for each t the sequence $\{\mathbb{F}^n(t) \mid n \geq 0\}$ is cofinal in $\mathcal{G}(t)$, the reduction graph of t. (See Exercise 2.0.8(13) for 'cofinal' and see Figure 3.7.)

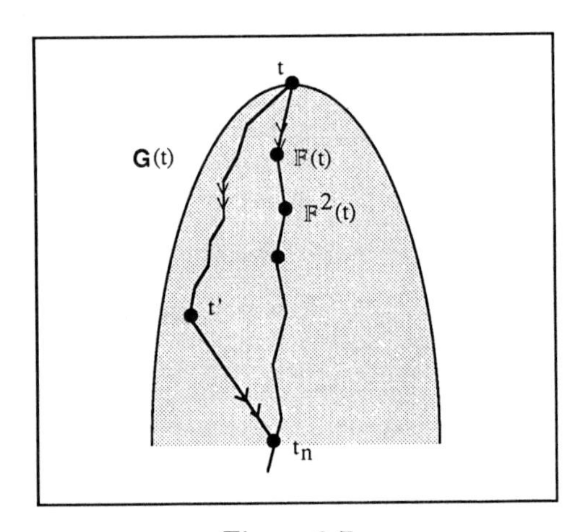

Figure 3.7

A normalizing reduction strategy is good, but a cofinal one is even better: it finds, when applied on term t, the best possible reduction sequence starting from t (or rather, a best possible) in the following sense. Consider a reduction $t \to s$ as a gain in information; thus normal forms have maximum information. In case there is no normal form in $\mathcal{G}(t)$, one can still consider infinite reductions as developing more and more information. Now the cofinal reductions $t \equiv t_0 \to t_1 \to t_2 \to \cdots$ are optimal since for every t' in $\mathcal{G}(t)$ they contain a t_n with information content no less than that of t' (since $t' \twoheadrightarrow t_n$ for some t_n, by definition of 'cofinal'). In a sense, a cofinal reduction plays the role of a kind of 'infinite normal form'. See e.g. [Berry and Lévy, 1979] and [Boudol, 1985], where spaces of finite and infinite reductions modulo the so-called permutation equivalence are studied; this gives rise to cpo's or even complete lattices where the bottom point corresponds to the empty reduction of t, i.e. to t itself, and the top point corresponds to the normal form (or rather the equivalence class of reductions to the normal form), if it exists, and otherwise to the equivalence class of cofinal reductions.

We now present some well-known reduction strategies.

Definition 3.2.3.

1. The *leftmost-innermost* (one step) strategy is the strategy in which in each step the leftmost of the minimal or innermost redexes is contracted (reduced).
2. The *parallel-innermost* (many step) strategy reduces simultaneously all innermost redexes. Since these are pairwise disjoint, this is no problem.
3. The *leftmost-outermost* (one step) strategy: in each step the leftmost redex of the maximal (or outermost) redexes is reduced. Notation: $\mathbb{F}_{\mathrm{lm}}$.
4. The *parallel-outermost* (many step) strategy reduces simultaneously all maximal redexes; since these are pairwise disjoint, this is no problem. Notation: $\mathbb{F}_{\mathrm{po}}$.
5. The *full substitution rule* (or *Kleene reduction*, or *Gross–Knuth reduction*): this is a many step strategy in which all redexes are simultaneously reduced. Notation: $\mathbb{F}_{\mathrm{GK}}$.

Strategies (1)–(4) are well-defined for general TRSs. Strategy (5) is only defined for orthogonal TRSs, since for a general TRS it is not possible to define an unequivocal result of simultaneous reduction of a set of possibly nested redexes. The five strategies are illustrated in Figure 3.8 (taken from [Bergstra *et al.*, 1989]), for the following TRS:

$$\begin{array}{lcl} and(true, x) & \to & x \\ and(false, x) & \to & false \\ or(true, x) & \to & true \\ or(false, x) & \to & true \end{array}$$

We will be mainly interested here in the strategies (3)–(5), for a reason that will be clear by inspection of Table 3.2 below. We have the following facts (for proofs see [O'Donnell, 1977] or [Klop, 1980a]):

leftmost-innermost

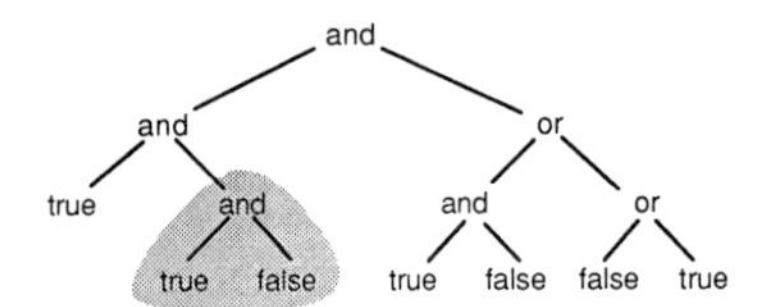

leftmost-outermost

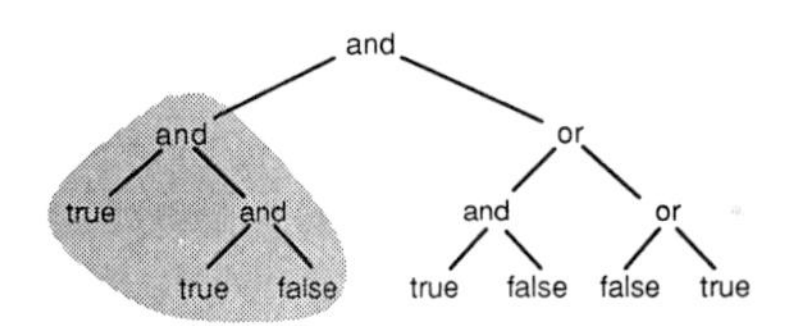

parallel-innermost

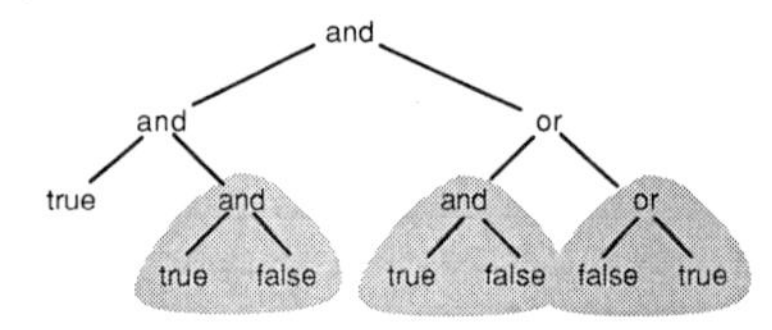

parallel-outermost

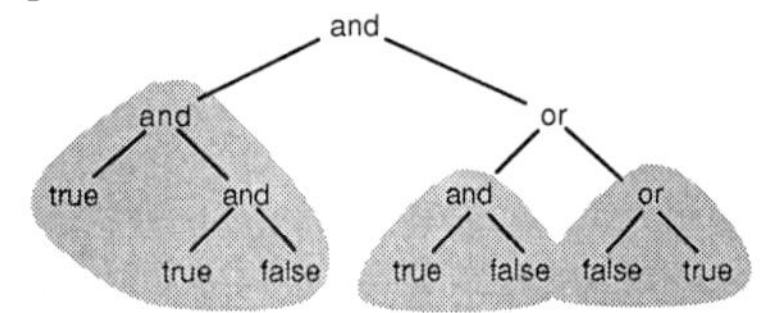

full substitution rule

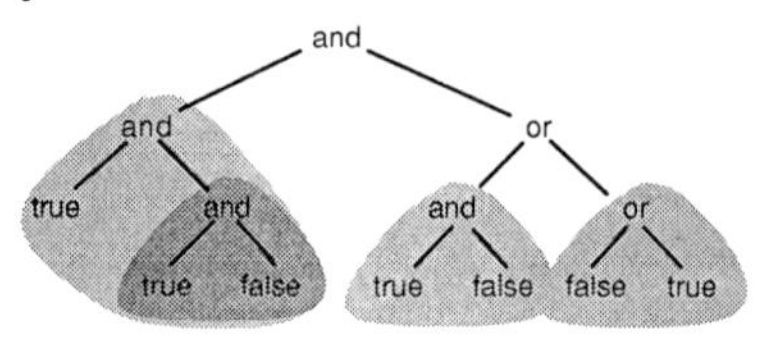

Figure 3.8 (after [Bergstra *et al.*, 1989])

Theorem 3.2.4. *For orthogonal TRSs:*

1. $\mathbb{F}_{GK}$ *is a cofinal reduction strategy.*
2. $\mathbb{F}_{po}$ *is a normalizing reduction strategy.*

Remark 3.2.5. For λ-calculus this theorem also holds. Moreover, $\mathbb{F}_{lm}$ is there also a normalizing strategy, just as it is for the orthogonal TRS CL (combinatory logic). However, in general $\mathbb{F}_{lm}$ is not a normalizing strategy for orthogonal TRSs (see Exercise 3.2.6).

Exercise 3.2.6.

1. An example showing that the leftmost-outermost strategy is not normalizing in general is given in [Huet and Lévy, 1979]: take the orthogonal TRS $\{F(x, B) \to D,\ A \to B,\ C \to C\}$ and consider the term $F(C, A)$. Check that this term has a normal form which is not found by the leftmost-outermost strategy.

2. An example (by N. Dershowitz) showing that parallel-outermost reduction need not be cofinal can be found in the TRS $\{A \to F(A),\ G(x) \to G(x)\}$.

Even though $\mathbb{F}_{\mathrm{lm}}$ is in general for orthogonal TRSs not normalizing, there is a large class of orthogonal TRSs for which it is:

Definition 3.2.7. [O'Donnell, 1977] An orthogonal TRS is *left-normal* if in every reduction rule $t \to s$ the constant and function symbols in the left-hand side t precede (in the linear term notation) the variables.

Example 3.2.8.

1. CL (combinatory logic) is left-normal.
2. RPSs (recursive program schemes) as defined in Exercise 3.1.8(3) are all left-normal.
3. $F(x, B) \to D$ is not left-normal; $F(B, x) \to D$ is left-normal.

Exercise 3.2.9. (Primitive recursive functions) The primitive recursive functions from $\mathbb{N}$ to $\mathbb{N}$ are defined by the following inductive definition [Shoenfield, 1967]:

1. The *constant* functions $C_{n,k}$, the *projection* functions $P_{n,i}$ and the *successor* function S are primitive recursive. (Here $C_{n,k}(x_1, \ldots, x_n) = k$, $P_{n,i}(x_1, \ldots, x_n) = x_i$, $S(x) = x + 1$.)
2. If $G, H_1, \ldots, H_k$ are primitive recursive, then F defined by

$$F(\vec{x}\,) = G(H_1(\vec{x}\,), \ldots, H_k(\vec{x}\,))$$

(where $\vec{x} = x_1, \ldots, x_n$) is primitive recursive.

3. If G and H are primitive recursive, then F defined by

$$\begin{array}{lcl} F(0, \vec{x}\,) & = & G(\vec{x}\,) \\ F(S(y), \vec{x}\,) & = & H(F(y, \vec{x}\,), y, \vec{x}\,) \end{array}$$

is primitive recursive.

Show that, by replacing every '=' by '→' in the defining equations, every primitive recursive function is defined by a terminating, left-normal, orthogonal constructor TRS. (For the definition of 'constructor TRS', see the end of Section 3.3.)

Theorem 3.2.10. [O'Donnell, 1977; Klop, 1980a] *Let R be a left-normal orthogonal TRS. Then $\mathbb{F}_{\mathrm{lm}}$ is a normalizing reduction strategy for R.*

Exercise 3.2.11. (Hindley)

1. Consider CL extended with Recursor, where Recursor $= \{Rxy0 \to x,$ $Rxy(Sz) \to yz(Rxyz)\}$. Note that this applicative TRS is not left-normal, and show that $\mathbb{F}_{\mathrm{lm}}$ is not normalizing.
2. However, for the TRS CL ∪ Recursor* where Recursor* $= \{R^*0xy \to x,\ R^*(Sz)xy \to yz(Rzxy)\}$ the strategy $\mathbb{F}_{\mathrm{lm}}$ is normalizing.

In the reduction strategy $\mathbb{F}_{GK}$ (full substitution) every redex is 'killed' *as soon as it arises*, and this repeatedly. Suppose we relax this requirement, and allow ourselves some time (i.e. some number of reduction steps) before getting rid of a particular redex—but with the obligation to deal with it *eventually.* The reductions arising in this way are all cofinal.

Definition 3.2.12.

1. Let $\mathcal{R} = t_0 \to t_1 \to \cdots$ be a finite or infinite reduction sequence. Consider some redex s in some term t_n of $\mathcal{R}$. We say that s is *secured in* $\mathcal{R}$ if eventually there are no descendants of s left, i.e.

$$\exists m > n \; (t_m \text{ contains no descendants } s', s'', \ldots \text{ of } s \subseteq t_n).$$

2. $\mathcal{R}$ is *fair* if every redex in $\mathcal{R}$ is secured.

Theorem 3.2.13. *For reductions $\mathcal{R}$ in orthogonal TRSs: $\mathcal{R}$ is fair $\Rightarrow$ $\mathcal{R}$ is cofinal.*

Note that Theorem 3.2.4(1) is a corollary of the present theorem, since evidently reductions obtained by applying $\mathbb{F}_{GK}$ are fair. A similar relaxation of constraints applies to the other two strategies $\mathbb{F}_{po}$ and $\mathbb{F}_{lm}$:

Definition 3.2.14.

1. A reduction $\mathcal{R}$ is *leftmost-fair* if $\mathcal{R}$ ends in a normal form or infinitely many times the leftmost outermost redex is contracted in $\mathcal{R}$.
2. $\mathcal{R} = t_0 \to t_1 \to \cdots$ is *outermost-fair* if $\mathcal{R}$ does not contain a term t_n with an outermost redex which stays an outermost redex for an infinite time but which is never contracted.

Theorem 3.2.15. *Let R be an orthogonal TRS. Then:*

1. *Outermost-fair reductions are normalizing.*
2. *If R is moreover left-normal, then leftmost-fair reductions are normalizing.*

We will now summarize some of the main properties of the various reduction strategies (and their 'relaxed' versions) in Table 3.2. Before doing so, we introduce one more property of strategies:

Definition 3.2.16. A reduction strategy $\mathbb{F}$ for R is *perpetual* if for all t: $\infty(t) \Rightarrow \infty(\mathbb{F}(t))$.

Here $\infty(t)$ means that t has an infinite reduction, i.e. not $\mathrm{SN}(t)$. So a perpetual strategy is the opposite of a normalizing one; it tries to avoid normal forms whenever possible, and could therefore also be called 'anti-normalizing'.

In Table 3.2 p, n, c stand for perpetual, normalizing, cofinal respectively. In case a property is not mentioned, it does not hold generally. Note that for the leftmost-outermost strategy, when applied to orthogonal TRSs in general, none of the three properties holds generally. Proofs that leftmost-outermost reduction is normalizing for left-normal orthogonal TRSs and that parallel-outermost reduction is normalizing for all orthogonal TRSs can be found in [O'Donnell, 1977]. The latter fact is also proved in [Bergstra and Klop, 1986] (Appendix).

	orthogonal TRSs	*orthogonal left-normal TRSs*	*orthogonal non-erasing TRSs*
leftmost-innermost	p	p	p n
parallel-innermost	p	p	p n
leftmost-outermost (leftmost-fair)		n	p n
parallel-outermost (outermost-fair)	n	n	p n
full substitution (fair)	n c	n c	p n c

Table 3.2

Computable reduction strategies

A strategy is *recursive* or *computable* if it is, after a coding of the terms into natural numbers, a recursive function. Obviously we are primarily interested in computable strategies; and indeed all five strategies in Definition 3.2.3 are computable. We may now ask whether there is always for an orthogonal TRS a *computable one-step normalizing* reduction strategy. A priori this is not at all clear, in view of TRSs such as the one given by G. Berry: CL extended with rules

$$\begin{array}{lcl} FABx & \to & C \\ FBxA & \to & C \\ FxAB & \to & C \end{array}$$

which is an orthogonal TRS. This TRS seems to require a parallel reduction strategy (so, not a one-step or sequential strategy), because in a term of the form $FMNL$ we have no way to see the 'right' argument for computation: a step in the third argument may be unnecessary, namely if the first and second argument evaluate to A and B respectively (which is undecidable due to the presence of CL); likewise a step in the other arguments may be unnecessary. In the next section about sequential TRSs this problem will be analysed extensively.

When we want to be more liberal, we can consider the same problem for the weakly orthogonal TRS obtained by extending CL with parallel-or:

$$\begin{array}{lcl} or(true, x) & \to & true \\ or(x, true) & \to & true \end{array}$$

It has been claimed by some authors that such TRSs require a parallel evaluation. However, there is the following surprising fact.

Theorem 3.2.17. [Kennaway, 1989] *For every weakly orthogonal TRS there exists a computable sequential normalizing reduction strategy.*

The algorithm involved is however too complicated to be of more than theoretical interest.

Standard reductions in orthogonal TRSs

For λ-calculus and CL there is a very convenient tool: the Standardization Theorem (see [Barendregt, 1981; Klop, 1980a]). For orthogonal TRSs there is unfortunately not a straightforward generalization of this theorem (however, see [Huet and Lévy, 1979] for a generalization). The obstacle is the same as for the normalizing property of the leftmost reduction strategy, discussed in the previous section. When we restrict ourselves again to left-normal orthogonal TRSs, there is a straightforward generalization.

Definition 3.2.18. (Standard reductions) Let R be a TRS and $\mathcal{R} = t_0 \to t_1 \to \cdots$ be a reduction in R. Mark in every step of $\mathcal{R}$ all redex head symbols to the left of the head symbol of the contracted redex, with '$*$'. Furthermore, markers are persistent in subsequent steps.

Then $\mathcal{R}$ is a *standard reduction* if in no step a redex is contracted with a marked head operator.

Exercise 3.2.19. Consider CL $\cup$ Pairing, where Pairing $= \{D_0(Dxy) \to x,\ D_1(Dxy) \to y\}$.

1. Show that the reduction $D_0(D(KII)I) \to D_0(DII) \to I$ is not standard.
2. Show that $D_0(D(KII)I) \to KII \to I$ is standard.

Exercise 3.2.20. (Hindley) Consider in the applicative TRS $R = \{PxQ \to xx,\ R \to S,\ Ix \to x\}$ the reduction

$$\mathcal{R} = PR(IQ) \to PRQ \to RR \to SR$$

and show that there is no standard reduction for $\mathcal{R}$ (i.e. a reduction $PR(IQ) \twoheadrightarrow SR$ which is standard).

Theorem 3.2.21. (Standardization theorem for left-normal orthogonal TRSs) *Let R be a left-normal orthogonal TRS. Then: if $t \twoheadrightarrow s$ there is a standard reduction in R from t to s.*

For a proof see [Klop, 1980a]. A corollary is our earlier theorem stating that $\mathbb{F}_{lm}$ is a normalizing strategy for left-normal orthogonal TRSs; this fact is also known as the *normalization theorem* in λ-calculus and CL literature.

Exercise 3.2.22. Prove the normalization theorem for left-normal orthogonal TRSs from the standardization theorem. (Hint: Suppose t has a normal form t_0. By the standardization theorem, there is a standard reduction from t to t_0. This is in fact the reduction as given by $\mathbb{F}_{lm}$.)

3.3 Sequential orthogonal Term Rewriting Systems

An important feature of orthogonal TRSs is whether they are 'sequential'. The property of sequentiality is relevant both for the existence of normalizing reduction strategies and for the definability (implementability) in λ-calculus or CL.

That a TRS is sequential does of course not mean that it is impossible to rewrite redexes in a parallel way. It means that there are also adequate sequential reduction strategies, i.e. it is not *necessary* to rewrite in a parallel way in order to find normal forms. Sequentiality is a desirable property, but unfortunately it is an undecidable property. However, there is a stronger version, 'strong sequentiality', which is decidable and which guarantees the existence of a recursive one-step normalizing reduction strategy. This was shown in [Huet and Lévy, 1979]. In this section we follow this paper, as well as [Klop and Middeldorp, 1989]. We note that here we are primarily interested in 'mathematical' properties of strong sequentiality, and are not concerned with *efficiency* of decision algorithms; for the latter see [Huet and Lévy, 1979].

As remarked in [Kennaway, 1989], one can ask whether 'sequential' is the right terminology, in view of his theorem (3.2.17) stating that every orthogonal TRS has a computable, sequential, normalizing strategy. Yet we feel that the terminology is right, if we are interested in 'feasibly sequential' (admitting a sequential normalizing strategy that is computable in a 'feasible' way).

Definition 3.3.1. Let ($t \in \text{Ter}R$), R orthogonal. Let $s \subseteq t$ be a redex. Then s is a *needed* redex (needed for the computation of the normal form, if it exists) iff in all reductions $t \to \cdots \to t'$ such that t' is a normal form, some descendant of s is contracted. (So, trivially, any redex in a term without normal form is needed.)

Exercise 3.3.2. Show that the leftmost outermost redex in ($t \in \text{Ter}R$) where R is a left-normal orthogonal TRS, is a needed redex.

Theorem 3.3.3. [Huet and Lévy, 1979] *Let t be a term in an orthogonal TRS R.*

1. *If t is not in normal form, t contains a needed redex.*
2. *Repeated contraction of a needed redex leads to the normal form, if it exists. (So, needed reduction is normalizing.)*

The proof involves quite some effort and is not included here. (For a proof different from the one of Huet and Lévy, see [Kennaway and Sleep, 1989].)

Exercise 3.3.4.

1. The present theory about needed reductions in orthogonal TRSs trivializes for non-erasing TRSs: Show that in a non-erasing orthogonal TRS *every* redex in a term is needed.
2. [Kennaway, 1989] Furthermore the present theory does not have a straightforward generalization to *weakly* orthogonal TRSs: Show that Theorem 3.3.3 does not hold for weakly orthogonal TRSs, by considering $\{or(true, x) \to true, or(x, true) \to true\}$. (However, see [O'Donnell, 1985].)

Thus, Theorem 3.3.3 gives us a normalizing reduction strategy: just contract some needed redex. However, the definition of 'needed' refers to all reductions to normal form, so in order to determine what the needed redexes are, we have to inspect the normalizing reductions first, which is not a very good recipe for a normalizing reduction strategy. In other words, the determination of needed redexes involves *look-ahead*, and it is this necessity for look-ahead that we wish to eliminate. Before we do so, first the following observation, which is easy to prove:

Proposition 3.3.5. *Let ($t \in$ Ter$R$), R orthogonal. Let s and s' be redexes in t such that $s \subseteq s'$. Then: s is needed $\Rightarrow$ s' is needed.*

Corollary 3.3.6. *Let t be a term not in normal form. Then some outermost redex of t is needed.*

Now let $C[\ ,\dots,\ ]$ denote a context with n holes. Denote by σ a substitution of redexes $s_1, \dots, s_n$ in the holes $1, \dots, n$. Then the last corollary states:

$$\forall C[\ ,\dots,\ ] \text{ in normal form } \forall \sigma\ \exists i\ s_i \text{ is needed in } C[s_1, \dots, s_n].$$

So which s_i is needed may depend on σ, i.e. from the other s_j. A more pleasant state of affairs would be when the TRS R would satisfy the following property:

Definition 3.3.7. Let R be an orthogonal TRS. Then R is *sequential** if

$$\forall C[\ ,\dots,\ ] \text{ in normal form } \exists i\ \forall \sigma;\ s_i \text{ is needed in } C[s_1, \dots, s_n].$$

Exercise 3.3.8. (Middeldorp)

1. Show that the orthogonal TRS (where CL is combinatory logic)

$$\mathrm{CL} \oplus \{F(A,B,x) \to C,\ F(B,x,A) \to C,\ F(x,A,B) \to C\}$$

(due to G. Berry) is not sequential*.

2. Show that the TRS $\{F(A,B,x) \to C,\ F(B,x,A) \to C,\ F(x,A,B) \to C\}$ is sequential*.
3. Conclude that 'sequential*' is not a modular property.

The concept 'sequential*' is only introduced for expository purposes. It is not a satisfactory property as it is undecidable. As it will turn out, a more satisfactory property is 'strongly sequential*', defined as follows.

Definition 3.3.9.

1. Let R be an orthogonal TRS and $C[\,]$ a context. Then a reduction relation $\to_?$ (*possible reduction*) is defined as follows. For every redex s and every term t:

$$C[s] \to_? C[t]$$

As usual, $\twoheadrightarrow_?$ is the transitive reflexive closure. The concept of 'descendant' is defined for $\to_?$ in the obvious way.

2. Let s be a redex in t. Then s is *strongly needed* if in every reduction $t \to_? \ldots \to_? t'$ where t' is a normal form, a descendant of s is contracted. Clearly: s is strongly needed $\Rightarrow$ s is needed.
3. R is *strongly sequential** if $\forall C[\ ,\ldots,\ ]$ in normal form $\exists i\ \forall \sigma\ s_i$ is strongly needed in $C[s_1,\ldots,s_n]$.

This property of 'strong sequentiality*' may be rather subtle, as the following example of [Huet and Lévy, 1979] in Exercise 3.3.10 shows.

Exercise 3.3.10. Let R have rewrite rules, written in tree notation, as in Figure 3.9(a) (the RHSs are irrelevant). Show that R is not strongly sequential*, by considering the context as in Figure 3.9(b).

Now the situation takes a pleasant turn since, as we will prove, it is decidable whether a orthogonal TRS is strongly sequential*, and moreover, there is a simple algorithm to compute an i as in the definition. Actually, Huet and Lévy define concepts 'sequential' and 'strongly sequential' in a different way; our 'sequential*' does not exactly coincide with 'sequential' but 'strongly sequential*' is equivalent to 'strongly sequential'. We will define these concepts now. We need some preliminary definitions:

Definition 3.3.11.

1. Let R be a orthogonal TRS. Then the set $\mathrm{Ter}_\Omega(R)$ of *Ω-terms* of R consists of those terms that can be built from function and constant

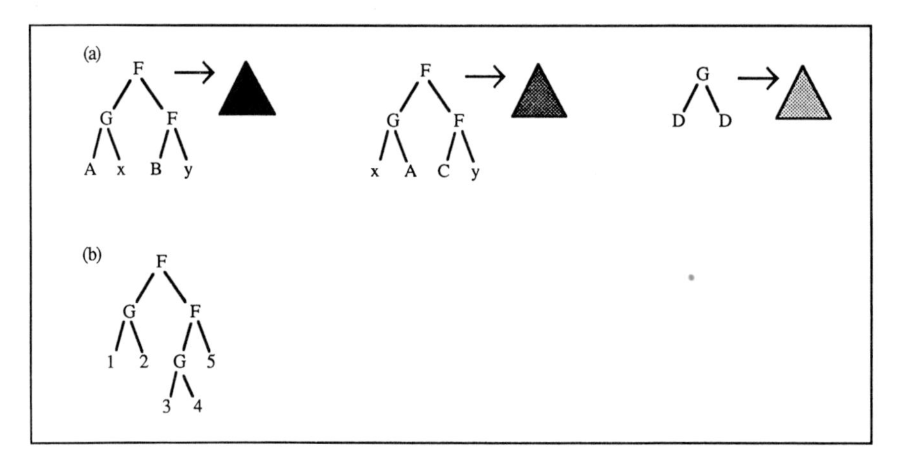

Figure 3.9

symbols from R together with a new constant Ω. Reduction relations $\to$ and $\to_?$ are extended to $\mathrm{Ter}_\Omega(R)$ in the obvious way. As before, we say that t is a normal form if $t \in \mathrm{Ter}_\Omega(R)$, t contains no Ω and t contains no redexes. Further, t is an Ω-normal form if t contains no redexes (but t may contain occurrences of Ω).

2. On $\mathrm{Ter}_\Omega(R)$ we define a partial order $\preceq$ by:
   (a) $\Omega \preceq t$ for all $t \in \mathrm{Ter}_\Omega(R)$,
   (b) $t_i \preceq t'_i$ $(i = 1, \ldots, n) \Rightarrow F(t_1, \ldots, t_n) \preceq F(t'_1, \ldots, t'_n)$.
   Clearly, $t \preceq s$ iff $t \equiv C[\Omega, \ldots, \Omega]$ and $s \equiv C[t_1, \ldots, t_n]$ for some context $C[\ ,\ldots,\ ]$ not containing Ω, and some $t_i \in \mathrm{Ter}_\Omega(R)$ $(i = 1, \ldots, n;\ n \geq 0)$.
3. A predicate P on $\mathrm{Ter}_\Omega(R)$ is *monotone* if $t \preceq t'$ implies $P(t) \Rightarrow P(t')$.
4. The predicate nf is defined on $\mathrm{Ter}_\Omega(R)$ as follows:

   $nf(t)$ holds if $t \twoheadrightarrow n$ where n is a normal form (so without Ω).

5. The predicate $nf_?$ is defined on $\mathrm{Ter}_\Omega(R)$ as follows:

   $nf_?(t)$ holds if $t \twoheadrightarrow_? n$ where n is a normal form.

6. Let P be a monotone predicate on $\mathrm{Ter}_\Omega(R)$. Let $t \equiv C[\Omega, \ldots, \underline{\Omega}, \ldots, \Omega]$ where all Ωs in t are displayed. Then the underlined occurrence of Ω is an *index with respect to* P (or P-index) if for all s such that $t \preceq s$, where $s \equiv C[t_1, \ldots, t_i, \ldots, t_n]$, we have: $P(s) \Rightarrow t_i \not\equiv \Omega$. (Note that in particular, if t has a P-index, then $P(t)$ does not hold.)

It is easily proved that the predicates nf and $nf_?$ are monotone. Now we define (after [Huet and Lévy, 1979]):

Definition 3.3.12.

1. The orthogonal TRS R is *sequential* if every $t \in \mathrm{Ter}_\Omega(R)$ in Ω-normal form, but not in normal form, has an nf-index.
2. The orthogonal TRS R is *strongly sequential* if every $t \in \mathrm{Ter}_\Omega(R)$ in Ω-normal form, but not in normal form, has an $nf_?$-index.

Exercise 3.3.13. (Middeldorp)

1. Show that: R is sequential $\Rightarrow$ R is sequential*, but not vice versa. Hint: Consider the TRS as in Exercise 3.3.8(2), with the term $F(\Omega, \Omega, \Omega)$.
2. Show that: R is strongly sequential $\Leftrightarrow$ R is strongly sequential*.

Exercise 3.3.14. Let $t \equiv C[\Omega, \ldots, \underline{\Omega}, \ldots, \Omega] \in \mathrm{Ter}_\Omega(R)$, R not necessarily strongly sequential. The i-th occurrence of Ω in t is underlined. Suppose that this underlined occurrence is an $nf_?$-index of t. Show then that in $C[s_1, \ldots, s_i, \ldots, s_n]$, where s_i is a redex and the other s_j are arbitrary terms, the redex s_i is strongly needed.

To link the beginning of this section, which used the terminology of contexts, with the present set-up via Ω-terms, we note that a context in normal form, containing at least one hole, corresponds with an Ω-term in Ω-normal form, but not in normal form. Before devoting the rest of this section to an exposition of the long proof that strong sequentiality is a decidable property, we will first show how to find an$nf_?$-index. First, we need some definitions.

Definition 3.3.15. Let $t \in \mathrm{Ter}_\Omega(R)$.

1. t is a *redex compatible* Ω-term if t can be refined to a redex (i.e. $t \preceq t'$ for some redex t').
2. *Ω-reduction* replaces a redex compatible subterm $\not\equiv \Omega$ by Ω, notation: $\rightarrow_\Omega$. So, $C[t] \rightarrow_\Omega C[\Omega]$ if t is redex compatible and $t \not\equiv \Omega$.
3. The *fixed part* $\omega(t)$ of an Ω-term t is the result of maximal application of Ω-reductions. (In other words, the normal form with respect to Ω-reduction.)

Exercise 3.3.16. Show that $\omega(t)$ is well-defined, by proving that Ω-reduction is confluent and terminating.

Now let $t \equiv C[\Omega, \ldots, \underline{\Omega}, \ldots, \Omega]$ be an Ω-normal form containing at least one Ω. We wish to test whether the i-th occurrence of Ω, the underlined one, is an $nf_?$-index of t. To this end we replace it by a fresh constant symbol, p. Result: $t' \equiv C[\Omega, \ldots, p, \ldots, \Omega]$.

Claim 3.3.17. $\underline{\Omega}$ is an $nf_?$-index in t $\Leftrightarrow$ p occurs in $\omega(t')$. (See Figure 3.10.)

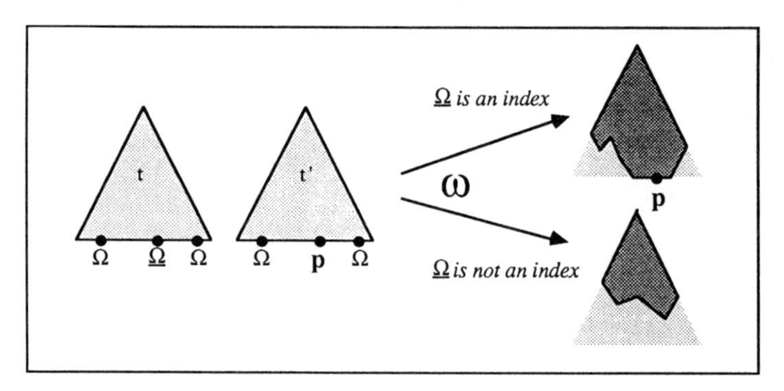

Figure 3.10

The proof of the claim is routine and we omit it. Intuitively, the persistence of the test symbol p in $\omega(t')$ means that whatever the redexes (or even general terms, cf. Exercise 3.3.14) in the other places are, and whatever their reducts might be, the p does not vanish, is not erasable by the action of the other redexes (or general terms). So if instead of p an actual redex s_i was present, the only way to normalize the term at hand is to reduce s_i itself, eventually. [Huet and Lévy, 1979] gives an efficient algorithm for executing the 'p-test', i.e. for finding $nf_?$-indexes (and hence, strongly needed redexes, cf. Exercise 3.3.14).

The decision procedure for the strong sequentiality property itself is much more difficult. We will now present a proof (in a slightly informal way) which is a simplification of the one in [Huet and Lévy, 1979], but where we do not pay any attention to the efficiency of the decision procedure.

In the following we will refer to a $nf_?$-index as an 'index' for short. An Ω-occurrence which is not an index will be called 'free'. A term in which all Ωs are free is called free.

The main 'problem' is that we do *not* have the following transitivity property for indexes, which on first sight one might expect to hold: if in the Ω-terms $C_1[\Omega], C_2[\Omega]$, where in both terms the displayed occurrence of Ω is an index (there may be other Ω's occurring), then the displayed Ω in $C_1[C_2[\Omega]]$ is again an index.

Example 3.3.18. Counterexample to transitivity for indexes. Consider the TRS as in Exercise 3.3.10, and the term $F(G(\Omega,\Omega),\underline{\Omega})$. The underlined occurrence is an index, as is easily seen by applying the 'p-test': $\omega(F(G(\Omega,\Omega),p)) = F(\Omega,p)$. However, substituting the same term in the index position, with result $F(G(\Omega,\Omega),F(G(\Omega,\Omega),\Omega))$, we have the 'context' in Figure 3.9(b), which is as shown, essentially, in Exercise 3.3.10, a free term.

However, some 'partial' transitivity properties for the propagation of indexes do hold, notably the one in Proposition 3.3.21 below. We will now make explicit some properties of index propagation. To this end we employ the following notational convention: instead of '*the displayed occurrence of* Ω *in* $C[\Omega]$ *is an index*' (here the Ω-term $C[\Omega]$ may contain other Ω's) we will just write '$C[\Omega\!\downarrow]$'. However, the absence of an arrow as e.g. in $C[\Omega, \Omega\!\downarrow]$ does not mean that (in this case) the first Ω is not an index. Furthermore we stipulate that in $C[\Omega, \ldots, \Omega]$ (or a version with arrow annotations) more occurrences of Ω may occur than the ones displayed, unless specified explicitly otherwise. Finally, the notations $s, t, C[\Omega, \ldots, \Omega]$ (possibly with arrow annotations) will refer to Ω-terms, which we sometimes call just 'terms'.

Proposition 3.3.19.

1. $C_1[C_2[\Omega\!\downarrow]] \Rightarrow C_1[\Omega\!\downarrow]$ *and* $C_2[\Omega\!\downarrow]$.
2. *The reverse implication does not hold generally.*

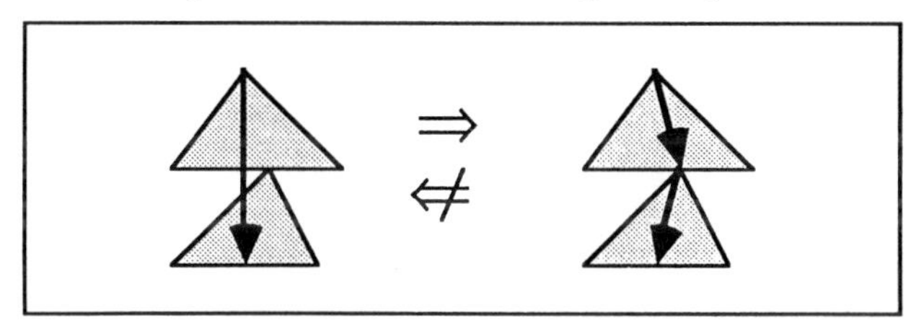

Figure 3.11

Proof. See Figure 3.11, where an arrow points to an index Ω. Part (2) is the counterexample in 3.3.18. Part (1) follows by an easy argument using the p-test criterion for indexes.

Proposition 3.3.20.

1. *Let* $\omega(t) = \Omega$. *Then* $C[t, \Omega\!\downarrow] \Rightarrow [\Omega, \Omega\!\downarrow]$.
2. *The reverse implication holds for all* t: $C[t, \Omega\!\downarrow] \Leftarrow C[\Omega, \Omega\!\downarrow]$.

Proof. (See Figure 3.12.) Simple applications of the p-test.

The following proposition (from [Klop and Middeldorp, 1989]) states the 'partial transitivity' for index propagation mentioned before. Here ρ refers to the *maximal height* of the trees corresponding to the redex schemes (i.e., the left-hand-sides of reduction rules) of R. Furthermore, the *depth* of an occurrence in a term is the length of the branch leading from the root symbol to that occurrence.

Proposition 3.3.21. *Let the depth of* Ω *in* $C_2[\Omega]$ *be at least* ρ. *Then:*

$$C_1[C_2[\Omega\!\downarrow]] \text{ and } C_2[C_3[\Omega\!\downarrow]] \;\Rightarrow\; C_1[C_2[C_3[\Omega\!\downarrow]]].$$

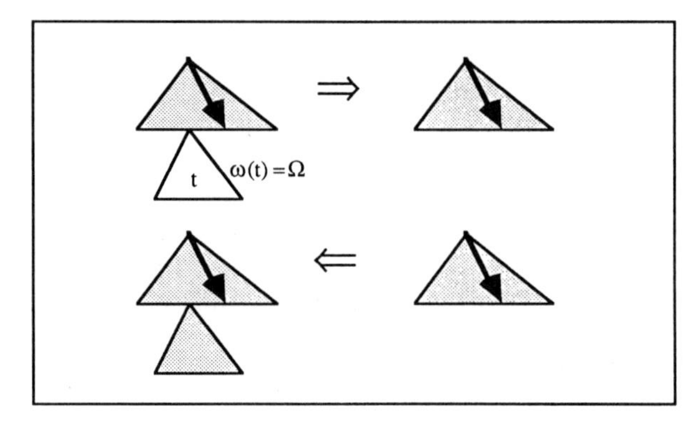

Figure 3.12

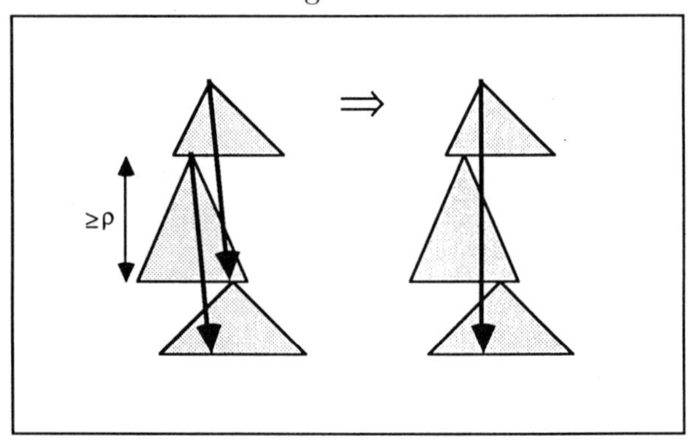

Figure 3.13

Proof sketch. Suppose contexts $C_i[\Omega]$ $(i = 1, 2, 3)$ as in the proposition are given. Consider $\omega(C_1[C_2[C_3[p]]])$. We claim that p is still present in this term. For if not, consider an Ω-reduction leading to $\omega(C_1[C_2[C_3[p]]])$ and especially the Ω-reduction step in which the symbol p is lost. The redex compatible subterm which is removed in this step has a root symbol s. Now s cannot occur in the subterm $C_2[C_3[p]]$ of $C_1[C_2[C_3[p]]]$, for otherwise p would not occur in $\omega(C_2[C_3[p]])$. But s can also not occur in the C_1-part of $C_1[C_2[C_3[p]]]$, for then p would not occur in $\omega(C_1[C_2[p]])$ due to the assumption referring to ρ.

In the following propositions, a *rigid* term t is a term t such that $\omega(t) = t$. Terms t such that $\omega(t) = \Omega$ will be called *soft*; they 'melt away' completely by Ω-reduction. It is not hard to prove that every term has a unique decomposition into a top part which is rigid and some subterms which are soft. (The top context may be trivial, i.e. equal to Ω.)

Proposition 3.3.22. *Every term $t \in \mathrm{Ter}_\Omega(R)$ can be written, uniquely, as $C[t_1, \ldots, t_n]$ such that $C[\Omega, \ldots, \Omega]$ is rigid and the t_i $(i = 1, \ldots, n)$ are soft.*

Proposition 3.3.23. *Suppose $C[t_1, \ldots, t_n]$ is a term such that $C[\Omega, \ldots, \Omega]$ is rigid and t_k is soft for $k = 1, \ldots, n$. Let $t_i \equiv C'[\Omega]$. Then:*

$$C'[\Omega\!\downarrow] \Rightarrow C[t_1, \ldots, t_{i-1}, C'[\Omega\!\downarrow], t_{i+1}, \ldots, t_n].$$

Proof. (See Figure 3.14.) By routine arguments involving the p-test.

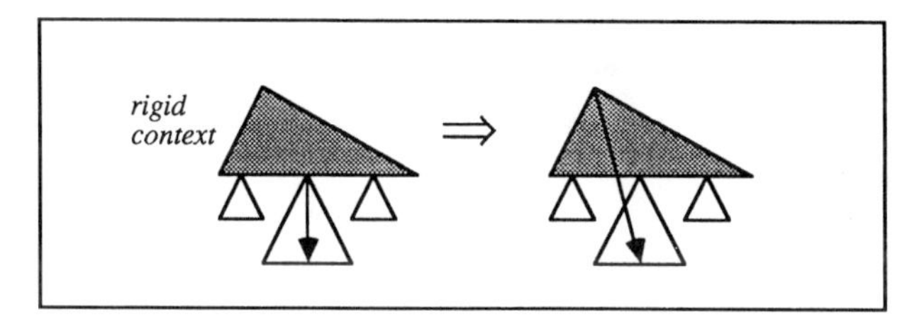

Figure 3.14

In an attempt to decide whether the TRS R is strongly sequential, we will try to construct a term $t \in \mathrm{Ter}_\Omega(R)$ in Ω-normal form but not in normal form, which is free, i.e. has no indexes. If such a free term exists, then and only then R is not strongly sequential. Especially we will look for a *minimal* free term, minimal with respect to the length. According to the last proposition, we may suppose that a minimal free term, if it exists, is soft. So, such a minimal free term is built from redex compatible terms (i.e. originates, starting from a redex compatible term, by repeatedly substituting redex compatible terms for Ωs)—this follows at once from the definition of 'soft' and Ω-reduction. (See Figure 3.15(a).) However, this observation is not yet sufficient for a sensible attempt to construct a minimal free term, for there are in general infinitely many redex compatible terms which may be the building blocks of the minimal free term we are looking for. Fortunately, we may even suppose that a minimal free term is built from a special kind of redex compatible terms, the *preredexes*, of which only finitely many exist if the TRS R has finitely many reduction rules as was our assumption. (See Figure 3.15(b).)

Definition 3.3.24.

1. A *redex scheme* (or *redex pattern*) is a left-hand side of a reduction rule where all variables are replaced by Ω.
2. A *preredex* is a term which can be refined to a redex scheme. (See Figure 3.16.)

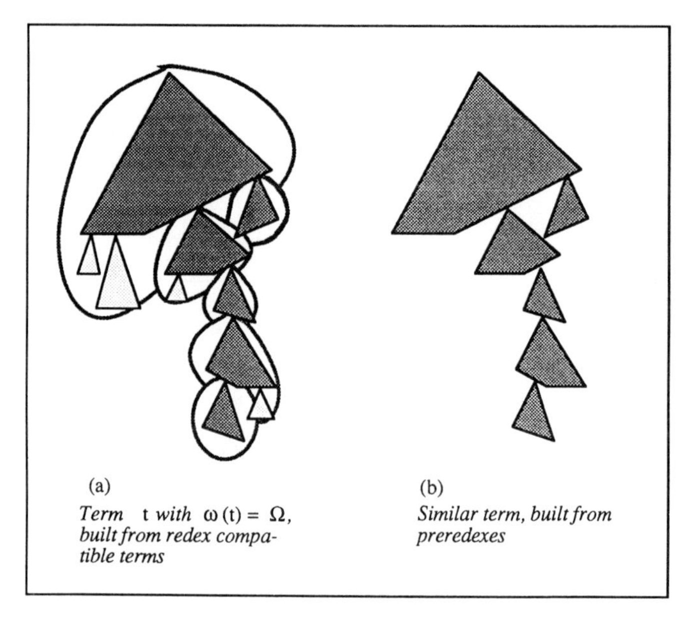

(a)
Term t with ω (t) = Ω, built from redex compatible terms
(b)
Similar term, built from preredexes

Figure 3.15

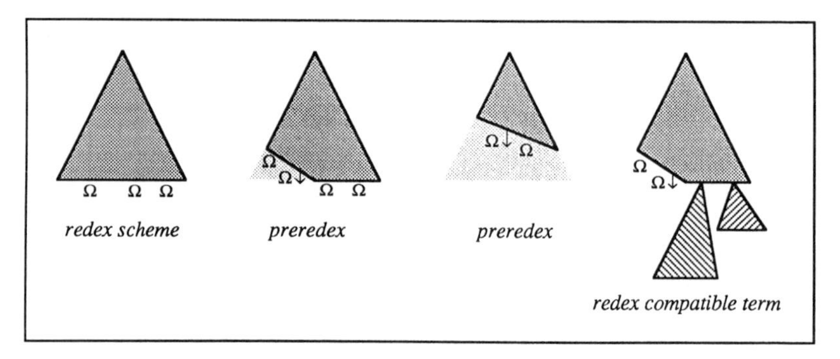

Figure 3.16

So, a redex scheme itself is a preredex; every preredex is also a redex compatible term. If the TRS R has finitely many rules, there are only finitely many preredexes. The Ωs in a redex scheme are all free; the Ωs arising by 'truncating' a redex scheme and thus forming a preredex, may be free or an index depending on other redex schemes. The 'old' Ωs in the truncation, if there are any, remain free. All this follows immediately from the definitions and the p-test.

We have already noted that a minimal free term t may be supposed to be built from redex compatible terms, as in Figure 3.15(a). This 'partition' in redex compatible terms need not be unique, but that does not matter.

Suppose a certain partition of t is given, corresponding to some Ω-reduction from t to Ω. Each redex compatible term from which t is built, and which is removed in this Ω-reduction, consists of a preredex refined with some 'extra' subterms. (the subterms that make the difference between Figure 3.15(a) and (b)). Now we remove from t all these extra subterms. (See Figure 3.17.)

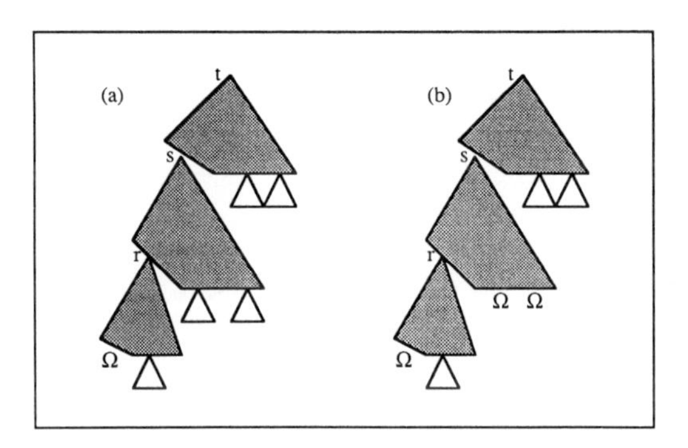

Figure 3.17

We claim that the term t', originating after removing all 'extra' subterms, is again free. To see this, consider the example in Figure 3.16, and remove the two extra subterms of the redex compatible subterm s. The Ωs that arise after this removal are free in s; this follows easily by applying the p-test and noting that subterm r is soft. But then these Ωs are also free in t; this follows from Proposition 3.3.19(1). Furthermore, the present removal of the extra subterms of s also does not turn free Ωs at other places into indexes, by Proposition 3.3.20(2).

We will now try to construct a minimal free term t in a tree-like procedure, as suggested in Figure 3.18.

Of course, we want t to be in Ω-normal form—cf. Definition 3.3.12(2). We start, therefore, with the finitely many proper preredexes, where a preredex is 'proper' if it is not a redex scheme. Now at every index Ω, we again attach in the next construction step a proper preredex. This nondeterministic procedure is repeated. A branch in the thus originating tree of construction terminates 'successfully' if a free term is reached. In that case the TRS R is not strongly sequential. However, there may arise infinite branches in the construction tree. But these we may 'close', eventually, by some form of 'loop checking' in the following way. First a definition.

Definition 3.3.25.

1. Let $C_i[\Omega]$ be preredexes ($i = 1, \ldots, n$). Then the term

$$\tau \equiv C_1[C_2[\ldots[C_n[\Omega]]\ldots]]$$

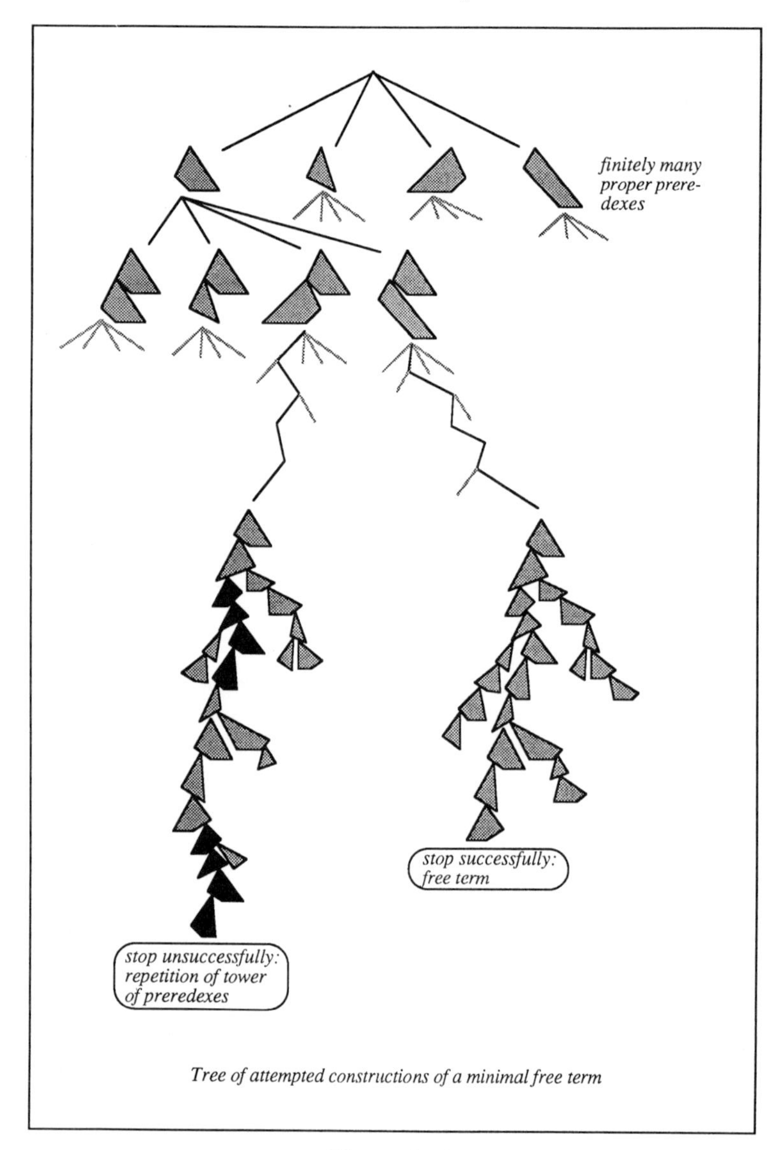

Figure 3.18

is called a *tower of preredexes.* If $1 \leq i < j \leq n$, we say that tower τ contains the subtower $\tau' \equiv C_i[C_{i+1}[\ldots[C_j[\Omega]]\ldots]]$.

2. Let ρ be the maximal height of redex schemes of R. A tower $\tau \equiv C_1[\ldots[C_n[\Omega]]\ldots]$ of preredexes is *sufficiently high* if the depth of the displayed Ω in τ is at least ρ.

3. Let t be a term built from preredexes. A *main tower* in τ is a tower (arising after removing some subterms of t) containing a complete branch in the tree corresponding to t (i.e. from the root to some 'final' symbol).

Now if in the construction tree we observe at some construction branch the arising of a term which has a main tower containing two disjoint sufficiently high *identical* subtowers, that construction branch is stopped unsuccessfully.

So every branch of the construction tree terminates, either successfully in a free term, or unsuccessfully. Because the construction tree is finitely branching, the result is a finite construction tree. Now if all construction branches terminate unsuccessfully, the TRS R is strongly sequential; otherwise the presence of a free term at the end of a successful branch reveals that TRS R is not strongly sequential. Hence strong sequentiality is decidable.

We still have to prove that our decision procedure is correct, in particular we have to justify the correctness of the 'loop check' for unsuccessfully closing branches at which a repetition of subtowers occurs. To this end, consider the term s at some point (node) in the construction tree, and consider a successor s' obtained by adjoining a proper preredex π at some index position of s. In general, π will contain some free Ωs as well as some index Ωs (with respect to π). The free Ωs remain free with respect to the whole term s' (Proposition 3.3.19(1)). What about the indexes of π? They may become free in s'. Now what happens with them is entirely determined by the main tower of proper preredexes in s' leading to the Ω in s where π will be adjoined. This follows from Proposition 3.3.20 stating that removal of soft terms does not affect the index or non-index status of other Ωs.

In fact, what happens with the indexes of π is already determined by the subtower of height $\geq \rho$ immediately above the adherence point Ω. This follows from Proposition 3.3.21. But then it is easy to see that in a minimal free term there will not be a repetition of two identical sufficiently large disjoint subtowers (see Figure 3.19). For, if such a repetition occurs in a minimal free term, we can construct a smaller one by cutting away part of the term as in Figure 3.19, contradicting the minimality. This ends the proof of decidability of strong sequentiality.

Many TRSs arising in 'practice' are *constructor* TRSs. For such TRSs it is easy to decide strong sequentiality. A constructor TRS is a TRS in which the set of function symbols can be partitioned into a set $\mathcal{D}$ of *defined* function symbols and a set $\mathcal{C}$ of *constructors*, such that for every rewrite rule $t \to s$, the left-hand side t has the form $F(t_1, \ldots, t_n)$ with $F \in \mathcal{D}$ and $t_1, \ldots, t_n \in \mathrm{Ter}(\mathcal{C}, \mathcal{V})$, the set of terms built from variables and constructors.

The reason why it is easy to decide strong sequentiality for constructor

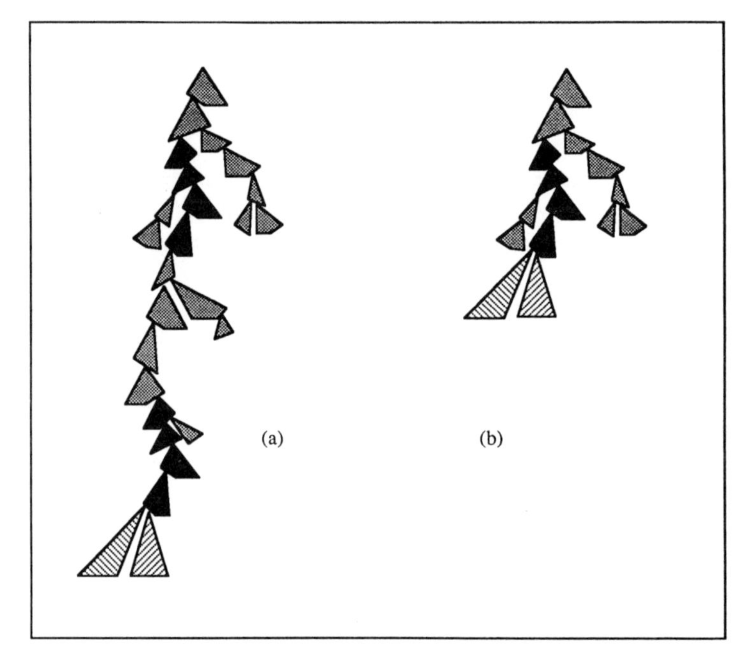

Figure 3.19

TRSs is that we do have transitivity of indexes now, in contrast with the case of general TRSs (cf. Counterexample 3.3.18).

Proposition 3.3.26. *Let R be an orthogonal constructor TRS. Let* $C_2[\Omega]$ *start with a defined function symbol. Then:* $C_1[\Omega\downarrow]$ *and* $C_2[\Omega\downarrow]$ *implies* $C_1[C_2[\Omega\downarrow]]$.

Proof. Straightforward, using the p-test for finding indexes.

Corollary 3.3.27. *A constructor TRS is strongly sequential iff every proper preredex has an index.*

So, in order to decide whether a constructor TRS R is strongly sequential, we only have to compute the indexes of its finitely many proper preredexes. (R is supposed to have only finitely many rewrite rules.) Also, the computation of these indexes is very easy: Let $C[\Omega,\ldots,\Omega,\ldots,\Omega]$ be a preredex of R. Now it is not difficult to see that $C[\Omega,\ldots,\Omega\downarrow,\ldots,\Omega]$ iff $C[\Omega,\ldots,p,\ldots,\Omega]$ is not redex compatible.

Exercise 3.3.28. Let R be an orthogonal constructor TRS. Show that R is strongly sequential if every proper preredex P has an Ω-occurrence which is in *all* redex schemes S such that $P \preceq S$, more defined (i.e. replaced by an Ω-term

$\not\equiv \Omega$).

Exercise 3.3.29. [Huet and Lévy, 1979] Let R be a left-normal orthogonal TRS. Show that R is strongly sequential. Show that, in fact, in $C[\Omega, \ldots, \Omega]$ (where $C[, \ldots,]$ is an Ω-free context in normal form) the leftmost occurrence of Ω is an index.

Exercise 3.3.30. [Klop and Middeldorp, 1989] Show that strong sequentiality is a modular property of orthogonal TRSs, i.e. if R_1, R_2 are orthogonal TRSs with disjoint alphabet, then:

$R_1 \oplus R_2$ is strongly sequential $\Leftrightarrow$ R_1 and R_2 are strongly sequential.

Exercise 3.3.31. [Thatte, 1987] Let R_1, R_2 be orthogonal TRSs. Define R_1, R_2 to be *left-equivalent* if the rewrite rules of R_1, R_2 have identical left-hand sides. An orthogonal TRS R is called *left-sequential* if all TRSs which are left-equivalent with R are sequential (Definition 3.3.12(1)).

Let R be an orthogonal TRS and $C[\Omega, \ldots, \Omega]$ a context in Ω-normal form. The i-th occurrence of Ω is called an *index with respect to left-sequentiality* if this Ω is an index with respect to sequentiality for all TRSs left-equivalent with R.

1. Let R be the TRS with rules $\{F(A,B,x) \to x,\ F(x,A,B) \to x,\ F(B,x,A) \to x,\ G(A) \to A\}$. Show that the third occurrence of Ω in $F(G(\Omega), G(\Omega), \Omega)$ is an index with respect to left-sequentiality, but not with respect to strong sequentiality.
2. Prove that strong sequentiality implies left-sequentiality.

*3. (Open problem.) Does the reverse of (2) also hold, i.e. is every left-sequential TRS strongly sequential?

4 Conditional Term Rewriting Systems

Of growing importance in the field of term rewriting are the *conditional* term rewriting systems (CTRSs). CTRSs have originally arisen from universal algebra (see [Meinke and Tucker, 1992]) and in the theory of abstract data types, as implementations of specifications containing *positive conditional equations*

$$t_1(\vec{x}) = s_1(\vec{x}) \wedge \cdots \wedge t_n(\vec{x}) = s_n(\vec{x}) \Rightarrow t_0(\vec{x}) = s_0(\vec{x}) \qquad (*)$$

(If $n = 0$, the equation is called unconditional.) Here $\vec{x} = x_1, \ldots, x_k$; not every t_i, s_i needs to contain all those variables. In $(*)$ we implicitly use universal quantification over $\vec{x}$, i.e. $(*)$ is meant to be

$$\forall \vec{x} \,(\bigwedge_{i=1,..,n} t_i(\vec{x}) = s_i(\vec{x}) \Rightarrow t_0(\vec{x}) = s_0(\vec{x})).$$

Hence the variables appearing in the conditions $t_i(\vec{x}) = s_i(\vec{x})$, $i = 1, \ldots, n$, but not in the consequent $t_0(\vec{x}) = s_0(\vec{x})$ have an 'existential' meaning; e.g.

$$E(x,y) = true \ \wedge \ E(y,z) = true \ \Rightarrow \ E(x,z) = true$$

is by elementary predicate logic equivalent to

$$\exists y\,(E(x,y) = true \ \wedge \ E(y,z) = true) \ \Rightarrow \ E(x,z) = true.$$

Henceforth we will, to conform with the notation often used in 'equational logic programming', write instead of (*)

$$t_0(\vec{x}) = s_0(\vec{x}) \ \Leftarrow \ t_1(\vec{x}) = s_1(\vec{x}), \ldots, t_n(\vec{x}) = s_n(\vec{x}).$$

Example 4.0.1. A specification of *gcd* on natural numbers with 0 and successor S, using conditional equations:

$$\begin{array}{lcllcl}
0 < 0 & = & 0 & & S(x) - S(y) & = \ x - y \\
0 < S(x) & = & S(0) & & 0 - x & = \ 0 \\
S(x) < 0 & = & 0 & & x - 0 & = \ x \\
S(x) < S(y) & = & x < y & & & \\
gcd(x,y) & = & gcd(x-y,y) & \Leftarrow & y < x = S(0) & \\
gcd(x,y) & = & gcd(x,y-x) & \Leftarrow & x < y = S(0) & \\
gcd(x,x) & = & x & & &
\end{array}$$

(To keep the specification one-sorted, 0 and $S(0)$ are used as booleans *false* and *true* respectively. Furthermore, '$-$' is cut-off subtraction.)

The satisfaction relation $\mathcal{A} \models \varphi$, for an equational implication or as we will call them henceforth, *conditional equation* φ, is clear; see also [Meinke and Tucker, 1992], where it is also shown that analogous to the equational case we can develop initial algebra semantics for conditional equations. Conditional equations not only facilitate some specifications, they also are a strictly stronger specification mechanism. In [Bergstra and Meyer, 1984] a conditional specification is given with an initial algebra that cannot be specified (in the same signature) by means of equations.

Again we can ask whether there exists a deduction system and a corresponding completeness theorem, in analogy with Birkhoffs theorem 2.4.2 for equational logic.

Conditional equational deduction

[Selman, 1972] presents a sound and complete deduction system for, as they are called there, *equation conjunction implication (ECI) languages*, or as we will say, for conditional equational logic. We state this deduction system in a considerably simplified way, by considering in a conditional equation

$t = s \Leftarrow E$ where $E = t_1 = s_1, \ldots, t_n = s_n$ $(n \geq 0)$, the sequence of conditions E as a set rather than an ordered tuple as in Selman [72], and by admitting empty E. (See Table 4.1.) Adapting the inference system to the case where E is a multiset or even an ordered tuple is straightforward.

axioms

$$t = s \Leftarrow t = s,\ t' = s'$$

$$t = t \Leftarrow$$

$$t = s \Leftarrow t = r,\ s = r$$

$$F(t_1, \ldots, t_n) = F(s_1, \ldots, s_n) \Leftarrow t_1 = s_1, \ldots, t_n = s_n$$

for every n-ary F

rules

$$\frac{t = s \Leftarrow t' = s',\ E,\quad t' = s' \Leftarrow F}{t = s \Leftarrow E,\ F}$$

$$\frac{t = s \Leftarrow E}{t^\sigma = s^\sigma \Leftarrow E^\sigma} \quad \text{for every substitution } \sigma$$

Table 4.1

Here $E = \{t_1 = s_1, \ldots, t_n = s_n\}$ $(n \geq 0)$, $F = \{t'_1 = s'_1, \ldots, t'_m = s'_m\}$ $(m \geq 0)$; $E^\sigma = \{t_1^\sigma = s_1^\sigma, \ldots, t_n^\sigma = s_n^\sigma\}$.

Operational semantics of conditional equations

In the unconditional case, there is no problem in the transition from equations to directed equations, i.e. rewrite rules: $t_0(\vec{x}) = s_0(\vec{x})$ is replaced by $t_0(\vec{x}) \to s_0(\vec{x})$, provided the left-hand side is not a single variable and variables occurring in the right-hand side do also occur in the left-hand side. (Of course, choosing the 'right' direction may be a problem—see our discussion of Knuth–Bendix completion.)

In the conditional case the transition from conditional equations to conditional rewrite rules does present a problem, or at least some choices. [Dershowitz *et al.*, 1988b] make the following distinctions, thereby extending a classification introduced in [Bergstra and Klop, 1986]. First we introduce some notation.

Definition 4.0.2. Let $\to$ be a rewrite relation.

1. $t \downarrow s$ (t, s are *joinable*) if $t \twoheadrightarrow u$ and $s \twoheadrightarrow u$ for some term u. (So $\to$ is confluent if $=$ (convertibility) and $\downarrow$ coincide.)
2. $s \twoheadrightarrow_! t$ if $s \twoheadrightarrow t$ and t is a ground normal form.

Now there are several choices for evaluating the conditions of CTRSs. In the terminology of [Dershowitz *et al.*, 1988b] we can distinguish (among others) the following types of CTRSs:

1. *semi-equational* systems

$$t_0 \to s_0 \Leftarrow t_1 = s_1, \ldots, t_n = s_n$$

2. *join* systems

$$t_0 \to s_0 \Leftarrow t_1 \downarrow s_1, \ldots, t_n \downarrow s_n$$

3. *normal* systems

$$t_0 \to s_0 \Leftarrow t_1 \twoheadrightarrow_! s_1, \ldots, t_n \twoheadrightarrow_! s_n$$

4. *generalized* systems

$$t_0 \to s_0 \Leftarrow P_1, \ldots, P_n.$$

In the last type of CTRSs, the P_i ($i = 1, \ldots, n$) are conditions formulated in a general mathematical framework, e.g. in some first-order language, involving the variables occurring in the consequent (and possibly others).

In [Bergstra and Klop, 1986] semi-equational systems were said to be of Type I, join systems of Type II, and normal systems of Type III$_n$. Actually, [Bergstra and Klop, 1986] define: $t \twoheadrightarrow_! s$ if s is a ground normal form even with respect to the *unconditional part* from the CTRS R (obtained by removing all conditions). This is necessary since otherwise the reduction relation may not be well-defined.

Note that in the cases (1)–(3), the definition of $\to$ is circular since it depends on conditions involving in some way or another a reference to $\to$; but it is not hard to see that in fact $\to$ is well defined since all conditions of type (1)–(3) are positive. Hence the rewrite rules constitute a positive induction definition of $\to$. In the case of generalized CTRSs we have to take care in formulating the conditions, in order to ensure that $\to$ is well-defined.

Remark 4.0.3. In a rewrite rule $t \to s$ one requires that in s no new variables appear with respect to t. The same requirement is made for conditional rewrite rules $t \to s \Leftarrow C$. But, as observed in [Dershowitz *et al.*, 1988b], for CTRSs it would make good sense to lift this requirement, as e.g. in the following perfectly natural conditional rewrite specification of the Fibonacci numbers:

$$\begin{array}{lcl} Fib(0) & \to & \langle 0, 1\rangle \\ Fib(x+1) & \to & \langle z, y+z\rangle \quad \Leftarrow \quad Fib(x) \downarrow \langle y, z\rangle. \end{array}$$

We will not study this more liberal format here, since it introduces a considerable complication of the theory.

We will now discuss several confluence criteria for CTRSs. The first one is a generalization due to Middeldorp [91] (also in Middeldorp [90]) of Toyamas theorem 2.2.2, stating that confluence is a modular property of TRSs, to CTRSs:

Theorem 4.0.4. *Let R_1, R_2 be both semi-equational CTRSs or both join CTRSs or both normal CTRSs with disjoint alphabet. Then:*

$$R_1, R_2 \text{ are confluent} \Leftrightarrow R_1 \oplus R_2 \text{ is confluent.}$$

(The disjoint sum $R_1 \oplus R_2$ is defined analogously to the unconditional case: simply join the sets of rewrite rules.) The proof is a nontrivial application of Toyamas theorem 2.2.2.

Orthogonal Conditional Term Rewriting Systems

We will now state some confluence criteria for orthogonal CTRSs.

Definition 4.0.5.

1. Let R be a CTRS (of any type, semi-equational, join, ...). Then R_u, the *unconditional version* of R, is the TRS which arises from R by deleting all conditions.
2. The CTRS R is called *(non-)left-linear* if R_u is so; likewise for *(weakly) orthogonal.* (See Section 2.1 for orthogonal TRSs.)

Definition 4.0.6.

1. Let R be a CTRS with rewrite relation $\to$, and let P be an n-ary predicate on the set of terms of R. Then P is *closed with respect to* $\to$ if for all terms t_i, t_i' such that $t_i \twoheadrightarrow t_i'$ $(i = 1, \ldots, n)$:
$$P(t_1, \ldots, t_n) \Rightarrow P(t_1', \ldots, t_n').$$
2. Let R be a CTRS with rewrite relation $\to$. Then R is *closed* if all conditions (appearing in some conditional rewrite rule of R), viewed as predicates with the variables ranging over R-terms, are closed with respect to $\to$.

Theorem 4.0.7. [O'Donnell, 1977] *Let R be a generalized, weakly orthogonal CTRS which is closed. Then R is confluent.*

The proof is a rather straightforward generalization of the confluence proof for weakly orthogonal TRSs.

Obviously, the convertibility conditions $t_i = s_i$ $(i = 1, \ldots, n)$ in a rewrite rule of a semi-equational CTRS are closed. Hence:

Corollary 4.0.8. *Weakly orthogonal semi-equational CTRSs are confluent.*

Example 4.0.9. Let R be the orthogonal, semi-equational CTRS obtained by extending combinatory logic with a 'test for convertibility':

$$\begin{array}{lcll} Sxyz & \to & xz(yz) & \\ Kxy & \to & x & \\ Ix & \to & x & \\ Dxy & \to & E & \Leftarrow \quad x = y. \end{array}$$

Then R is confluent.

The question now arises whether analogous facts hold for the other types of CTRSs. Indeed, this is the case for normal conditions. The following theorem is a slight generalization of a result in [Bergstra and Klop, 1986]:

Theorem 4.0.10. *Weakly orthogonal normal CTRSs are confluent.*

Remark 4.0.11.

1. Orthogonal join CTRSs are in general not confluent, and even in general not weakly confluent. In [Bergstra and Klop, 1986] the following counterexample is given:

$$\begin{array}{lcll} C(x) & \to & E & \Leftarrow \quad x \downarrow C(x) \\ B & \to & C(B). & \end{array}$$

   See Figure 4.1. $C(E) \downarrow E$ does not hold, since this would require

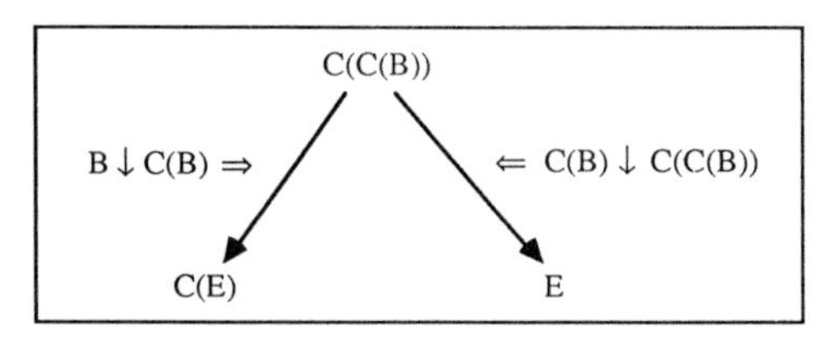

Figure 4.1

   $C(E) \to E$, i.e. $C(E) \downarrow E$.

2. The counterexample in (1) exhibits an interesting phenomenon, or rather, makes a pitfall explicit. According to Corollary 4.0.8 above, the semi-equational CTRS with rules

$$\begin{array}{llll} C(x) & \to & E & \Leftarrow \; x = C(x) \\ B & \to & C(B) & \end{array}$$

is confluent. Hence its convertibility, $=$, coincides with the joinability relation, $\downarrow$. So $x = C(x)$ iff $x \downarrow C(x)$. Yet the join CTRS obtained by replacing the condition $x = C(x)$ by $x \downarrow C(x)$, is according to (1) of this remark *not* confluent.

The complexity of normal forms

Whereas in the unconditional case, being in 'normal form' is an easily decidable property, this needs no longer to be so in the case of CTRSs. In fact, there are semi-equational orthogonal CTRSs for which the set of normal forms is undecidable (and hence not even r.e., since the complement of the set of normal forms is r.e.). The same holds for normal orthogonal CTRSs, and for join CTRSs. The proof is short and instructive enough to be included:

Consider CL (combinatory logic); it is well known (cf. [Barendregt, 1981]) that there is a *representation* $\underline{n}$, a ground CL-term in normal form, of the natural number n for each $n \geq 0$, together with a *computable coding* $\#$ from the set of ground CL-terms into natural numbers, and an '*enumerator*' E (also a ground CL-term in normal form) such that $E\underline{\#(M)} \twoheadrightarrow M$ for every ground CL-term M. Now let R be the normal CTRS obtained by extending CL with a new constant symbol F and the rule

$$Fx \to \underline{1} \;\Leftarrow\; Ex \twoheadrightarrow \underline{0}.$$

(Note that the reduction relation $\to$ of R satisfies $Fx \to \underline{1} \;\Leftrightarrow\; Ex \twoheadrightarrow \underline{0}$.) If R had decidable normal forms, then in particular the set $\{\underline{n} \mid F\underline{n} \twoheadrightarrow \underline{1}\}$ would be decidable, i.e. the set $\{\underline{n} \mid E\underline{n} \twoheadrightarrow \underline{0}\}$ would be so. However, then the set

$$\mathcal{X} = \{M \text{ a ground CL-term} \mid M \twoheadrightarrow \underline{0}\}$$

is decidable; for, given M we compute $\#(M)$ and decide whether $E(\underline{\#(M)}) \twoheadrightarrow \underline{0}$ or not. (By confluence for R it follows from $E(\underline{\#(M)}) \twoheadrightarrow \underline{0}$ and $E\underline{\#(M)} \twoheadrightarrow M$ that $M \twoheadrightarrow \underline{0}$.) But this contradicts the fact that $\mathcal{X}$ is undecidable; this follows from a theorem of Scott stating that *any nonempty proper subset of the set of ground CL-terms which is closed under convertibility in CL must be undecidable.*

For a condition guaranteeing decidability of normal forms, we refer to the notion 'decreasing' below.

Exercise 4.0.12. Adapt the proof above such that it holds for normal CTRSs, and for join CTRSs.

Exercise 4.0.13. [Bergstra and Klop, 1986] In this exercise we give a criterion for decidability of normal forms which does not imply termination (as the criterion 'decreasing' does).

Let R be a normal CTRS. If r: $t \to s \Leftarrow t_1 \twoheadrightarrow n_1, \ldots, t_k \twoheadrightarrow n_k$ is a rule of R, then an instance t^σ (σ some substitution) is called a *candidate r-redex* of R. (Of course it depends on the validity of the instantiated conditions $t_i^\sigma \twoheadrightarrow n_i$ of r whether t^σ is an actual r-redex or not.)

We define inductively the set NF_n of normal forms of order n for all $n \geq 0$ as follows: NF_0 is the set of normal forms of R_u, the unconditional part of R. Suppose NF_i $(i \leq n)$ have been defined. Then $M \in \mathrm{NF}_{n+1}$ if for every candidate r-redex $t^\sigma \subseteq M$, r as above, the left-hand side of one of the conditions, t_i^σ, evaluates to a 'wrong' normal form m_i, i.e. $m_i \not\equiv n_i$, such that m_i is of order $\leq n$. Furthermore, NF is the set of all normal forms of R. We say that $\mathrm{NF} - \bigcup_{n \geq 0} \mathrm{NF}_n$ contains the normal forms of *infinite order.*

1. Show that if NF is undecidable, then there must be some normal form of infinite order.
2. Suppose for every rule r (as above) of R we have $t_i \subset t$ (t_i is a proper subterm of t), $i = 1, \ldots, k$. Then we say that R *has subterm conditions.* Show that if R has subterm conditions, there are no normal forms of infinite order. Hence NF is decidable.

Non-orthogonal conditional rewriting

Following [Dershowitz *et al.*, 1988b] (see also [Dershowitz and Okada, 1990]), we will now consider CTRSs which are not orthogonal (i.e. may have 'critical pairs') and formulate some conditions ensuring confluence.

Definition 4.0.14. (Critical pairs)

1. Let R be a CTRS containing the two conditional rewrite rules

$$t_i \to s_i \Leftarrow E_i \quad (i = 1, 2).$$

   (Suppose these are 'standardized apart', i.e. have no variables in common.) Suppose t_2 can be unified with the nonvariable subterm u in $t_1 \equiv C[u]$, via $\sigma = mgu(t_2, u)$. Then the conditional *equation*(!)

$$s_1^\sigma = C[t_2]^\sigma \Leftarrow (E_1, E_2)^\sigma$$

   is a *critical pair* of the two rules.
2. A critical pair is an *overlay* if in (1), t_1 and t_2 unify at the root, i.e. $t_1 \equiv u$.
3. A CTRS is *non-overlapping* (or non-ambiguous) if it has no critical pairs.
4. A critical pair $s = t \Leftarrow E$ is *joinable* if for all substitutions σ such that E^σ is true, we have $s^\sigma \downarrow t^\sigma$.

Theorem 4.0.15. [Dershowitz *et al.*, 1988b]

1. *Let R be a semi-equational CTRS. Then: If R is terminating and all critical pairs are joinable, R is confluent.*
2. *Let R be a join system. Then: If R is decreasing and all critical pairs are joinable, R is confluent.*
3. *Let R be a join system. Then: If R is terminating and all critical pairs are overlays and joinable, R is confluent.*

This theorem contains the unexplained notion of a 'decreasing' CTRS:

Definition 4.0.16. [Dershowitz *et al.*, 1988b] Let R be a CTRS.

1. $>$ is a *decreasing* ordering for R if
   (a) $>$ is a well-founded ordering on the set of terms of R (i.e. there are no descending chains $t_0 > t_1 > t_2 > \cdots$);
   (b) $t \subset s \Rightarrow t < s$ (here $\subset$ is the proper subterm ordering);
   (c) $t \to s \Rightarrow t > s$;
   (d) for each rewrite rule $t \to s \Leftarrow t_1 \downarrow s_1, \ldots, t_n \downarrow s_n$ $(n \geq 0)$ and each substitution σ we have: $t^\sigma > t_i^\sigma, s_i^\sigma$ $(i = 1, \ldots, n)$. (Likewise for other CTRSs than join CTRSs.)
2. A CTRS is decreasing if it has a decreasing ordering.

A consequence of 'decreasing' is termination. Moreover, the notions $\to, \twoheadrightarrow, \downarrow$, and normal form are decidable.

Remark 4.0.17. Related notions are *fair* or *simplifying* CTRSs [Kaplan, 1984; Kaplan, 1987] and *reductive* CTRSs [Jouannaud and Waldmann, 1986]. In fact: reductive $\Rightarrow$ simplifying $\Rightarrow$ decreasing; see also [Dershowitz and Okada, 1990].

We conclude this section by mentioning a useful fact:

Theorem 4.0.18. [Dershowitz *et al.*, 1988b] *Let $R^=$ be a decreasing semi-equational CTRS. Let $R^\downarrow$ be the corresponding join CTRS (where conditions $t_i = s_i$ are changed into $t_i \downarrow s_i$). Then:*

$$R^= \textit{ is confluent } \Rightarrow R^\downarrow \textit{ is confluent.}$$

Acknowledgements

I am grateful to several persons for their support in writing this chapter. In particular I would like to thank Henk Barendregt, Nachum Dershowitz,

Ronan Sleep, Roel de Vrijer, as well as editors and co-authors of this Handbook. Special thanks to Aart Middeldorp for several contributions, and to Jean-Jacques Lévy for his close scrutiny of a previous version including many helpful comments. Finally, many thanks to Aart Middeldorp, Vincent van Oostrom, Jane Spurr and Fer-Jan de Vries for the heroic struggle to transform an early Macintosh version into LaTeX.

References

[Apt, 1990] K. R. Apt. Logic programming. In J. van Leeuwen, editor, *Formal Models and Semantics. Handbook of Theoretical Computer Science. Vol. B*, pages 495–574. Elsevier – MIT Press, 1990.

[Bachmair and Dershowitz, 1986] L. Bachmair and N. Dershowitz. Commutation, transformation, and termination. In J. H. Siekmann, editor, *Proc. 8th Conference on Automated Deduction*, volume 230 of *Lecture Notes in Computer Science*, pages 5–20, Oxford, 1986. Springer.

[Bachmair and Plaisted, 1985] L. Bachmair and D. A. Plaisted. Associative path orderings. In J.-P. Jouannaud, editor, *Proc. 1st International Conference on Rewriting Techniques and Applications*, volume 202 of *Lecture Notes in Computer Science*, pages 241–254, Dijon, 1985. Springer.

[Bachmair *et al.*, 1986] L. Bachmair, N. Dershowitz, and J. Hsiang. Orderings for equational proofs. In *Proc. 1st IEEE Symposium on Logic in Computer Science*, pages 346–357, Cambridge, Massachusetts, 1986.

[Bachmair, 1988] L Bachmair. Proof by consistency in equational theories. In *Proc. 3rd IEEE Symposium on Logic in Computer Science*, pages 228–233, Edinburgh, 1988. IEEE.

[Bachmair, 1989] L. Bachmair. *Canonical Equational Proofs*. Birkhäuser, Boston, 1989.

[Barendregt *et al.*, 1987] H. P. Barendregt, M. C. J. D. van Eekelen, J. R. W. Glauert, J. R. Kennaway, M. J. Plasmeijer, and M. R. Sleep. Term graph rewriting. In *Proc. 1st Conference on Parallel Architectures and Languages Europe (PARLE). Vol. II*, volume 259 of *Lecture Notes in Computer Science*, pages 141–158, Eindhoven, 1987. Springer.

[Barendregt, 1981] H. P. Barendregt. *The Lambda Calculus. Its Syntax and Semantics*. North-Holland, Amsterdam, 2nd (1984) edition, 1981.

[Barendregt, 1989] H. P. Barendregt. Functional programming and lambda calculus. In J. van Leeuwen, editor, *Handbook of Theoretical Computer Science*. North-Holland, Amsterdam, 1989.

[Bergstra and Klop, 1984] J. A. Bergstra and J. W. Klop. Process algebra for synchronous communication. *Information and Control*, 60(1/3):109–137, 1984.

[Bergstra and Klop, 1985] J. A. Bergstra and J. W. Klop. Algebra of communicating processes with abstraction. *Theor. Comput. Sci.*, 37(1):171–199, 1985.

[Bergstra and Klop, 1986] J. A. Bergstra and J. W. Klop. Conditional rewrite rules: confluence and termination. *J. Comput. System Sci.*, 32(3):323–362, 1986.

[Bergstra and Meyer, 1984] J. A. Bergstra and J.-J.Ch. Meyer. On specifying sets of integers. *Elektronische Informationsverarbeitung und Kybernetik*, 20(10/11):531–541, 1984.

[Bergstra and Tucker, 1980] J. A. Bergstra and J. V. Tucker. A characterisation of computable data types by means of a finite equational specification method. In J. W. de Bakker and J. van Leeuwen, editors, *Proc. 7th International Colloquium on Automata, Languages and Programming*, volume 85 of *Lecture Notes in Computer Science*, pages 76–90, Amsterdam, 1980. Springer.

[Bergstra *et al.*, 1989] J. A. Bergstra, J. Heering, and P. Klint, editors. *Algebraic specification*. Addison-Wesley, Reading, Massachusetts, 1989.

[Berry and Lévy, 1979] G. Berry and J.-J. Lévy. Minimal and optimal computations of recursive programs. *J. Assoc. Comput. Mach.*, 26:148–175, 1979.

[Birkhoff, 1935] G. Birkhoff. On the structure of abstract algebras. *Proc. Cambridge Philos. Soc.*, 31:433–454, 1935.

[Boudol, 1985] G. Boudol. Computational semantics of term rewriting systems. In M. Nivat and J. C. Reynolds, editors, *Algebraic methods in semantics*, pages 169–236. Cambridge University Press, 1985.

[Church, 1941] A. Church. *The calculi of lambda conversion*, volume 6 of *Annals of Mathematics Studies*. Princeton University Press, 1941.

[Courcelle, 1990] B. Courcelle. Recursive application schemes. In J. van Leeuwen, editor, *Formal Models and Semantics. Handbook of Theoretical*

Computer Science. Vol. B, pages 459–492. Elsevier – The MIT Press, Amsterdam, 1990.

[Curien, 1986] P.-L. Curien. *Categorical Combinators, Sequential Algorithms and Functional Programming.* Research Notes in Theoretical Computer Science. Pitman, London, 1986.

[Dauchet and Tison, 1984] M. Dauchet and S. Tison. Decidability of Confluence for Ground Term Rewriting Systems. Report, Université de Lille I, 1984.

[Dauchet *et al.*, 1987] M. Dauchet, S. Tison, T. Heuillard, and P. Lescanne. Decidability of the confluence of ground term rewriting systems. In *Proc. 2nd Symposium on Logic in Computer Science*, pages 353–359, Ithaca, NY, 1987.

[Dauchet, 1989] M. Dauchet. Simulation of Turing machines by a left-linear rewrite rule. In *Proc. 3rd International Conference on Rewriting Techniques and Applications*, volume 355 of *Lecture Notes in Computer Science*, pages 109–120, Chapel Hill, 1989. Springer.

[Dershowitz and Jouannaud, 1990] N. Dershowitz and J.-P. Jouannaud. Rewrite systems. In J. van Leeuwen, editor, *Formal Models and Semantics. Handbook of Theoretical Computer Science. Vol. B*, pages 243–320. Elsevier – The MIT Press, Amsterdam, 1990.

[Dershowitz and Manna, 1979] N. Dershowitz and Z. Manna. Proving termination with multiset orderings. *Comm. ACM*, 22(8):465–476, 1979.

[Dershowitz and Okada, 1990] N. Dershowitz and M. Okada. A rationale for conditional equational programming. *Theor. Comput. Sci.*, 75:111–138, 1990.

[Dershowitz *et al.*, 1988a] N. Dershowitz, L. Marcus, and A. Tarlecki. Existence, uniqueness, and construction of rewrite systems. *SIAM J. Comput.*, 17(4):629–639, 1988.

[Dershowitz *et al.*, 1988b] N. Dershowitz, M. Okada, and G. Sivakumar. Canonical Conditional Rewrite Systems. In *Proc. 9th Conference on Automated Deduction*, volume 310 of *Lecture Notes in Computer Science*, pages 538–549, Argonne, 1988. Springer.

[Dershowitz, 1979] N. Dershowitz. A note on simplification orderings. *Information Processing Letters*, 9(5):212–215, 1979.

[Dershowitz, 1981] N. Dershowitz. Termination of linear rewriting systems. In S. Even and O. Kariv, editors, *Proc. 8th International Colloquium on*

Automata, Languages and Programming, volume 115 of *Lecture Notes in Computer Science*, pages 448–458. Springer, 1981.

[Dershowitz, 1985] N. Dershowitz. Computing with rewrite systems. *Information and Control*, 65:122–157, 1985.

[Dershowitz, 1987] N. Dershowitz. Termination of rewriting. *J. Symbolic Computation*, 3(1):69–116, 1987. Corrigendum: 4(3):409–410.

[Drosten, 1989] K. Drosten. *Termersetzungssysteme*, volume 210 of *Informatik-Fachberichte*. Springer, 1989. In German.

[Ehrig and Mahr, 1985] H. Ehrig and B. Mahr. *Fundamentals of Algebraic Specification 1. Equations and Initial Semantics.* Springer-Verlag, Berlin, 1985.

[Gallier, 1987] J. H. Gallier. What's so special about Kruskal's Theorem and the ordinal γ_0. Technical report MS-CIS-87-27, University of Pennsylvania, Philadelphia, 1987.

[Ganzinger and Giegerich, 1987] H. Ganzinger and R. Giegerich. A note on termination in combinations of heterogeneous term rewriting systems. *Bull. European Association for Theoretical Computer Science*, 31:22–28, 1987.

[Geser, 1990] A. Geser. *Relative Termination.* PhD thesis, University of Passau, 1990.

[Goguen and Meseguer, 1985] J. A. Goguen and J. Meseguer. Initiality, induction, and computability. In M. Nivat and J. C. Reynolds, editors, *Algebraic Methods in Semantics*, pages 459–542. Cambridge University Press, 1985.

[Guessarian, 1981] I. Guessarian. *Algebraic Semantics*, volume 99 of *Lecture Notes in Computer Science.* Springer, 1981.

[Hardin, 1989] T. Hardin. Confluence results for the pure Strong Categorical Logic CCL; λ-calculi as subsystems of CCL. *Theor. Comput. Sci., Fundamental Studies*, 65(3):291–342, 1989.

[Hindley and Seldin, 1986] J. R. Hindley and J. P. Seldin. *Introduction to Combinators and λ-Calculus*, volume 1 of *London Mathematical Society Student Texts.* Cambridge University Press, 1986.

[Hindley, 1964] J. R. Hindley. *The Church-Rosser property and a result in combinatory logic.* PhD thesis, University of Newcastle-upon-Tyne, 1964.

[Hölldobler, 1989] S. Hölldobler. *Foundations of Equational Logic Programming*, volume 353 of *Lecture Notes in Computer Science*. Springer, 1989.

[Huet and Lankford, 1978] G. Huet and D. S. Lankford. On the Uniform Halting Problem for Term Rewriting Systems. Rapport Laboria 283, IRIA, 1978.

[Huet and Lévy, 1979] G. Huet and J.-J. Lévy. Call-by-need Computations in Non-ambiguous Linear Term Rewriting Systems. Rapport 359, INRIA, 1979. To appear as: 'Computations in orthogonal term rewriting systems' in J.-L. Lassez and G. Plotkin, editors, *Computational Logic, Essays in Honour of Alan Robinson*, MIT Press, Cambridge, Massachusetts.

[Huet and Oppen, 1980] G. Huet and D. C. Oppen. Equations and rewrite rules: A survey. In R. V. Book, editor, *Formal Language Theory: Perspectives and Open Problems*, pages 349–405. Academic Press, London, 1980.

[Huet, 1980] G. Huet. Confluent reductions: Abstract properties and applications to term rewriting systems. *J. Assoc. Comput. Mach.*, 27(4):797–821, 1980.

[Huet, 1981] G. Huet. A complete proof of correctness of the Knuth-Bendix completion algorithm. *J. Comput. System Sci*, 23:11–21, 1981.

[Hullot, 1980] J. M. Hullot. Canonical forms and unification. In *Proc. 5th Conference on Automated Deduction*, pages 318–334, Les Arcs, France, 1980.

[Jantzen, 1988] M. Jantzen. *Confluent String Rewriting and Congruences*, volume 14 of *European Association for Theoretical Computer Science. Monographs on Theoretical Computer Science.* Springer-Verlag, Berlin, 1988.

[Jouannaud and Kirchner, 1986] J.-P. Jouannaud and H. Kirchner. Completion of a set of rules modulo a set of equations. *SIAM J. Comp*, 15(4):1155–1194, 1986.

[Jouannaud and Waldmann, 1986] J.-P. Jouannaud and B. Waldmann. Reductive conditional Term Rewriting Systems. In *Proc. 3rd IFIP Working Conference on Formal Description of Programming Concepts*, pages 223–244, Ebberup, 1986.

[Kamin and Lévy, 1980] S. Kamin and J.-J. Lévy. Two Generalizations of the Recursive Path Ordering. Unpublished manuscript, University of Illinois, 1980.

[Kaplan, 1984] S. Kaplan. Conditional rewrite rules. *Theor. Comput. Sci.*, 33(2/3), 1984.

[Kaplan, 1987] S. Kaplan. Simplifying conditional term rewriting systems: unification, termination and confluence. *J. of Symbolic Computation*, 4(3):295–334, 1987.

[Kennaway and Sleep, 1989] J. R. Kennaway and M. R. Sleep. Neededness is Hypernormalizing in Regular Combinatory Reduction Systems. Preprint, School of Information Systems, University of East Anglia, Norwich, 1989.

[Kennaway, 1989] J. R. Kennaway. Sequential evaluation strategies for parallel-or and related reduction systems. *Annals of Pure and Applied Logic*, 43:31–56, 1989.

[Klop and Middeldorp, 1988] J. W. Klop and A. Middeldorp. An introduction to Knuth-Bendix completion. *CWI Quarterly*, 1(3):31–52, 1988.

[Klop and Middeldorp, 1989] J. W. Klop and A. Middeldorp. Sequentiality in Orthogonal Term Rewriting Systems. Report CS-R8932, CWI – Centre for Mathematics and Computer Science, Amsterdam, 1989. To appear in *J. Symbolic Computation*.

[Klop, 1980a] J. W. Klop. *Combinatory Reduction Systems*, volume 127 of *Mathematical Centre Tracts*. CWI, Amsterdam, 1980.

[Klop, 1980b] J. W. Klop. Reduction cycles in Combinatory Logic. In J. P. Seldin and J. R. Hindley, editors, *To H. B. Curry: Essays on Combinatory Logic, Lambda Calculus and Formalism*, pages 193–214. Academic Press, London, 1980.

[Klop, 1985] J. W. Klop. Term rewriting systems. Unpublished, 1985. Notes for the Seminar on Reduction Machines, Ustica.

[Klop, 1987] J. W. Klop. Term rewriting systems: a tutorial. *Bulletin of the EATheor. Comput. Sci.*, 32:143–182, 1987.

[Knuth and Bendix, 1970] D. E. Knuth and P. B. Bendix. Simple word problems in universal algebras. In J. Leech, editor, *Computational Problems in Abstract Algebra*, pages 263–297. Pergamon Press, 1970.

[Kruskal, 1960] J. B. Kruskal. Well-quasi-ordering, the tree theorem, and Vazsonyi's conjecture. *Trans. AMS*, 95:210–225, 1960.

[Kurihara and Kaji, 1988] M. Kurihara and I. Kaji. Modular term rewriting systems: Termination, confluence and strategies. Report, Hokkaido

University, 1988. Abridged version: 'Modular term rewriting systems and the termination' in *Information Processing Letters* 34:1–4.

[Lankford, 1979] D. S. Lankford. On proving term rewriting systems are noetherian. Memo MTP-3, Mathematical Department, Louisiana Technical University, Ruston, Louisiana, 1979.

[Le Chénadec, 1986] P. Le Chénadec. *Canonical Forms in Finitely Presented Algebras.* Research Notes in Theoretical Computer Science. Pitman, London, 1986.

[Martelli and Montanari, 1982] A. Martelli and U. Montanari. An efficient unification algorithm. *Trans. on Programming Languages and Systems*, 4(2):258–282, 1982.

[Martelli *et al.*, 1986] A. Martelli, C. Moiso, and C. F. Rossi. An algorithm for unification in equational theories. In *Proc. Symposium on Logic Programming*, pages 180–186, 1986.

[Meinke and Tucker, 1992] K. Meinke and J. V. Tucker. Universal algebra. In S. Abramsky, D. Gabbay, and T. Maibaum, editors, *Handbook of Logic in Computer Science. Vol. 1.* Oxford University Press, 1992.

[Métivier, 1983] Y. Métivier. About the rewriting systems produced by the Knuth-Bendix completion algorithm. *Information Processing Letters*, 16:31–34, 1983.

[Middeldorp, 1989a] A. Middeldorp. Modular aspects of properties of term rewriting systems related to normal forms. In *Proc. 3rd International Conference on Rewriting Techniques and Applications*, volume 355 of *Lecture Notes in Computer Science*, pages 263–277, Chapel Hill, 1989. Springer.

[Middeldorp, 1989b] A. Middeldorp. A sufficient condition for the termination of the direct sum of term rewriting systems. In *Proc. 4th IEEE Symposium on Logic in Computer Science*, pages 396–401, Pacific Grove, 1989. IEEE Press.

[Middeldorp, 1990] A. Middeldorp. *Modular properties of term rewriting systems.* PhD thesis, Vrije Universiteit, Amsterdam, 1990.

[Nash-Williams, 1963] C. St. J. A. Nash-Williams. On well-quasi-ordering finite trees. *Proc. Cambridge Philosophical Society*, 59(4):833–835, 1963.

[Nederpelt, 1973] R. P. Nederpelt. *Strong normalization for a typed lambda calculus with lambda structured types.* PhD thesis, Technische Hogeschool, Eindhoven, The Netherlands, 1973.

[Newman, 1942] M. H. A. Newman. On theories with a combinatorial definition of "equivalence". *Annals of Math.*, 43(2):223–243, 1942.

[O'Donnell, 1977] M. J. O'Donnell. *Computing in Systems Described by Equations*, volume 58 of *Lecture Notes in Computer Science.* Springer, 1977.

[O'Donnell, 1985] M. J. O'Donnell. *Equational Logic as a Programming Language.* The MIT Press, Cambridge, Massachusetts, 1985.

[Oyamaguchi, 1987] M. Oyamaguchi. The Church-Rosser property for ground term rewriting systems is decidable. *Theor. Comput. Sci.*, 49(1):43–79, 1987.

[Peterson and Stickel, 1981] G. E. Peterson and M. E. Stickel. Complete sets of reductions for some equational theories. *J. ACM*, 28(2):233–264, 1981.

[Plaisted, 1978] D. A. Plaisted. A recursively defined ordering for proving termination of term rewriting systems. Report R-78-943, University of Illinois, Urbana, Illinois, 1978.

[Plaisted, 1985] D. A. Plaisted. Semantic confluence tests and completion methods. *Information and Control*, 65:182–215, 1985.

[Puel, 1986] L. Puel. Using unavoidable sets of trees to generalize Kruskal's theorem. *J. of Symbolic Computation*, 8(4):335–382, 1986.

[Raoult and Vuillemin, 1980] J.-C. Raoult and J. Vuillemin. Operational and semantic equivalence between recursive programs. *Journal of the ACM*, 27(4):772–796, 1980.

[Rosen, 1973] B. K. Rosen. Tree-manipulating systems and Church-Rosser theorems. *Journal of the ACM*, 20(1):160–187, 1973.

[Rusinowitch, 1987a] M. Rusinowitch. On termination of the direct sum of term rewriting systems. *Information Processing Letters*, 26:65–70, 1987.

[Rusinowitch, 1987b] M. Rusinowitch. Path of subterms ordering and recursive decomposition ordering revisited. *J. of Symbolic Computation*, 3:117–131, 1987.

[Selman, 1972] A. Selman. Completeness of calculii for axiomatically defined classes of algebras. *Algebra Universalis*, 2:20–32, 1972.

[Shoenfield, 1967] J. R. Shoenfield. *Mathematical Logic.* Addison-Wesley, Reading, Massachusetts, 1967.

[Siekmann, 1984] J. Siekmann. Universal unification. In R. E. Shostak, editor, *Proc. 7th International Conference on Automated Deduction*, volume

170 of *Lecture Notes in Computer Science*, pages 1–42, Napa, California, 1984. Springer.

[Smoryǹski, 1982] C. Smoryǹski. The variety of arboreal experience. *The Mathematical Intelligencer*, 4(4):182–189, 1982.

[Staples, 1975] J. Staples. Church-Rosser theorems for replacement systems. In J. Crosley, editor, *Algebra and Logic*, volume 450 of *Lecture Notes in Mathematics*, pages 291–307. Springer, 1975.

[Thatte, 1987] S. Thatte. A refinement of strong sequentiality for term rewriting with constructors. *Information and Computation*, 72:46–65, 1987.

[Toyama *et al.*, 1989] Y. Toyama, J. W. Klop, and H. P. Barendregt. Termination for the direct sum of left-linear term rewriting systems. In *Proc. 3rd International Conference on Rewriting Techniques and Applications*, volume 355 of *Lecture Notes in Computer Science*, pages 477–491. Springer, Chapel Hill, 1989. Extended version: Report CS-R8923, CWI, Amsterdam.

[Toyama, 1987a] Y. Toyama. Counterexamples to termination for the direct sum of Term Rewriting Systems. *Information Processing Letters*, 25:141–143, 1987.

[Toyama, 1987b] Y. Toyama. On the Church-Rosser property for the direct sum of term rewriting systems. *Journal of the ACM*, 34(1):128–143, 1987.

[Toyama, 1988] Y. Toyama. Commutativity of Term Rewriting Systems. In K. Fuchi and L. Kott, editors, *Programming of Future Generation Computer II*, pages 393–407. North-Holland, Amsterdam, 1988.

[Turner, 1979] D. A. Turner. A new implementation technique for applicative languages. *Software Practice and Experience*, 9:31–49, 1979.

[Winkler and Buchberger, 1983] F. Winkler and B. Buchberger. A criterion for eliminating unnecessary reductions in the Knuth-Bendix algorithm. In *Proc. of the Colloquium on Algebra, Combinatorics and Logic in Computer Science*, Györ, Hungary, 1983.

Lambda Calculi with Types

H.P. Barendregt

Contents

This work is dedicated to

Nol and Riet Prager

the musician/philosopher and the poet.

1 Introduction

The lambda calculus was originally conceived by Church [Church, 193233] as part of a general theory of functions and logic, intended as a foundation for mathematics. Although the full system turned out to be inconsistent, as shown in [Kleene and Rosser, 1935], the subsystem dealing with functions only became a successful model for the computable functions. This system is called now the *lambda calculus.* Books on this subject e.g. are [Church, 1941], [Curry and Feys, 1958], [Curry *et al.*, 1972], [Barendregt, 1984], [Hindley and Seldin, 1986] and [Krivine, 1990].

In [Kleene and Rosser, 1935] it is proved that all recursive functions can be represented in the lambda calculus. On the other hand, in [Turing, 1937] it is shown that exactly the functions computable by a Turing machine can be represented in the lambda calculus. Representing computable functions as λ-terms, i.e. as expressions in the lambda calculus, gives rise to so-called *functional programming.* See [Barendregt, 1990] for an introduction and references.

The lambda calculus, as treated in the references cited above, is usually refered to as a *type-free* theory. This is so, because every expression (considered as a function) may be applied to every other expression (considered as an argument). For example, the identity function $\mathsf{I} = \lambda x.x$ may be applied to any argument x to give as result that same x. In particular I may be applied to itself.

There are also typed versions of the lambda calculus. These are introduced essentially in [Curry, 1934] (for the so-called combinatory logic, a variant of the lambda calculus) and in [Church, 1940]. Types are usually objects of a syntactic nature and may be assigned to lambda terms. If M is such a term and, a type A is assigned to M, then we say '*M has type A*' or '*M in A*'; the notation used for this is $M : A$. For example in most systems with types one has $\mathsf{I} : (A{\rightarrow}A)$, that is, the identity I may get as type $A{\rightarrow}A$. This means that if x being an argument of I is of type A, then also the value $\mathsf{I}x$ is of type A. In general $A{\rightarrow}B$ is the type of functions from A to B.

Although the analogy is not perfect, the type assigned to a term may be compared to the dimension of a physical entity. These dimensions prevent us from wrong operations like adding 3 volts to 2 ampères. In a similar way types assigned to lambda terms provide a partial specification of the algorithms that are represented and are useful for showing partial correctness.

Types may also be used to improve the efficiency of compilation of terms representing functional algorithms. If for example it is known (by looking at types) that a subexpression of a term (representing a funtional program) is purely arithmetical, then fast evaluation is possible. This is because the expression then can be executed by the ALU of the machine and not in the slower way in which symbolic expressions are evaluated in general.

The two original papers of Curry and Church introducing typed versions of the lambda calculus give rise to two different families of systems. In the typed lambda calculi *à la* Curry terms are those of the type-free theory. Each term has a set of possible types. This set may be empty, be a singleton or consist of several (possibly infinitely many) elements. In the systems *à la* Church the terms are annotated versions of the type-free terms. Each term has a type that is usually unique (up to an equivalence relation) and that is derivable from the way the term is annotated.

The Curry and Church approaches to typed lambda calculus correspond to two paradigms in programming. In the first of these a program may be written without typing at all. Then a compiler should check whether a type can be assigned to the program. This will be the case if the program is correct. A well-known example of such a language is ML, see [Milner, 1984]. The style of typing is called 'implicit typing'. The other paradigm in programming is called 'explicit typing' and corresponds to the Church version of typed lambda calculi. Here a program should be written together with its type. For these languages type-checking is usually easier, since no types have to be constructed. Examples of such languages are ALGOL 68 and PASCAL. Some authors designate the Curry systems as 'lambda calculi *with type assignment*' and the Church systems as 'systems of *typed* lambda calculus'.

Within each of the two paradigms there are several versions of typed lambda calculus. In many important systems, especially those *à la* Church, it is the case that terms that do have a type always possess a normal form. By the unsolvability of the halting problem this implies that not all computable functions can be represented by a typed term, see [Barendregt, 1990], theorem 4.2.15. This is not so bad as it sounds, because in order to find such computable functions that cannot be represented, one has to stand on one's head. For example in $\lambda 2$, the second-order typed lambda calculus, only those partial recursive functions cannot be represented that happen to be total, but not provably so in mathematical analysis (second-order arithmetic).

Considering terms and types as programs and their specifications is not the only possibility. A type A can also be viewed as a proposition and a term M in A as a proof of this proposition. This so-called propositions-as-types interpretation is independently due to [de Bruijn, 1970] and [Howard, 1980] (both papers were conceived in 1968). Hints in this direction were given in Curry and Feys [Curry and Feys, 1958] and in [Läuchli, 1970]. Several systems of proof checking are based on this interpretation of propositions-as-types and of proofs-as-terms. See e.g. [de Bruijn, 1980] for a survey of the so-called AUTOMATH proof checking system. Normalization of terms corresponds in the formulas-as-types interpretation to normalisation of proofs in the sense of [Prawitz, 1965]. Normal proofs often give useful proof theoretic information, see e.g. [Schwichtenberg, 1977]. In this chapter several typed lambda calculi will be introduced, both *à la* Curry and *à la* Church. Since in the last two decades several dozens of systems have appeared, we will make a selection guided by the following methodology.

> *Only the simplest versions of a system will be considered. That is, only with β-reduction, but not with e.g. η-reduction. The Church systems will have types built up using only $\rightarrow$ and Π, not using e.g. $\times$ or Σ. The Curry systems will have types built up using only $\rightarrow$, $\cap$ and μ.*

(For this reason we will not consider systems of constructive type theory as developed e.g. in [Martin-Löf, 1984], since in these theories Σ plays an essential role.) It will be seen that there are already many interesting systems in this simple form. Understanding these will be helpful for the understanding of more complicated systems. No semantics of the typed lambda calculi will be given in this chapter. The reason is that, especially for the Church systems, the notion of model is still subject to intensive investigation. [Lambek and Scott, 1986] and [Mitchell, 1990], a chapter on typed lambda calculus in another handbook, do treat semantics but only for one of the systems given in the present chapter. For the Church systems several proposals for notions of semantics have been proposed. These have been neatly unified using fibred categories in [Jacobs, 1991]. See also [Pavlović, 1990]. For the semantics of the Curry systems see [Hindley, 1983] and [Coppo, 1985]. A later volume of this handbook will contain a chapter on the semantics of typed lambda calculi.

[Barendregt and Hemerik, 1990] and [Barendregt, 1991] are introductory versions of this chapter. Books including material on typed lambda calculus are [Girard *et al.*, 1989] (treats among other things semantics of the Church version of $\lambda 2$), [Hindley and Seldin, 1986] (Curry and Church versions of $\lambda\!\rightarrow$), [Krivine, 1990] (Curry versions of $\lambda 2$ and $\lambda\cap$), [Lambek and Scott, 1986] (categorical semantics of $\lambda\!\rightarrow$) and the forthcoming [Barendregt and Dekkers, to appear] and [Nerode and Odifreddi, to appear].

Section 2 of this chapter is an introduction to type-free lambda-calculus and may be skipped if the reader is familiar with this subject. Section 3 explains in more detail the Curry and Church approach to lambda calculi with types. Section 4 is about the Curry systems and Section 5 is about the Church systems. These two sections can be read independently of each other.

2 Type-free lambda calculus

The introduction of the type-free lambda calculus is necessary in order to define the system of Curry type assignment on top of it. Moreover, although the Church style typed lambda calculi can be introduced directly, it is nevertheless useful to have some knowledge of the type-free lambda calculus. Therefore this section is devoted to this theory. For more information see [Hindley and Seldin, 1986] or [Barendregt, 1984].

2.1 The system

In this chapter the type-free lambda calculus will be called 'λ-calculus' or simply λ. We start with an informal description.

Application and abstraction

The λ-calculus has two basic operations. The first one is application. The expression

$$F.A$$

(usually written as FA) denotes the data F considered as algorithm applied to A considered as input. The theory λ is *type-free*: it is allowed to consider expressions like FF, that is, F applied to itself. This will be useful to simulate recursion.

The other basic operation is *abstraction*. If $M \equiv M[x]$ is an expression containing ('depending on') x, then $\lambda x.M[x]$ denotes the intuitive map

$$x \mapsto M[x],$$

i.e. to x one assigns $M[x]$. The variable x does not need to occur actually in M. In that case $\lambda x.M[x]$ is a constant function with value M.

Application and abstraction work together in the following intuitive formula:

$$(\lambda x.x^2 + 1)3 = 3^2 + 1 \ \ (= 10).$$

That is, $(\lambda x.x^2 + 1)3$ denotes the function $x \mapsto x^2 + 1$ applied to the argument 3 giving $3^2 + 1$ (which is 10). In general we have

$$(\lambda x.M[x])N = M[N].$$

This last equation is preferably written as

$$(\lambda x.M)N = M[x := N], \qquad (\beta)$$

where $[x := N]$ denotes substitution of N for x. This equation is called β-conversion. It is remarkable that although it is the only essential axiom of the λ-calculus, the resulting theory is rather involved.

Free and bound variables

Abstraction is said to *bind* the *free* variable x in M. For example, we say that $\lambda x.yx$ has x as bound and y as free variable. Substitution $[x := N]$ is only performed in the free occurrences of x:

$$yx(\lambda x.x)[x := N] = yN(\lambda x.x).$$

In integral calculus there is a similar variable binding. In $\int_a^b f(x,y)dx$ the variable x is bound and y is free. It does not make sense to substitute 7 for x, obtaining $\int_b^a f(7,y)d7$; but substitution for y does make sense, obtaining $\int_b^a f(x,7)dx$.

For reasons of hygiene it will always be assumed that the bound variables that occur in a certain expression are different from the free ones. This can be fulfilled by renaming bound variables. For example, $\lambda x.x$ becomes $\lambda y.y$. Indeed, these expressions act the same way:

$$(\lambda x.x)a = a = (\lambda y.y)a$$

and in fact they denote the same intended algorithm. Therefore expressions that differ only in the names of bound variables are identified. Equations like $\lambda x.x \equiv \lambda y.y$ are usually called α-conversion.

Functions of several arguments

Functions of several arguments can be obtained by iteration of application. The idea is due to Schönfinkel [Schönfinkel, 1924] but is often called 'currying', after H.B. Curry who introduced it independently. Intuitively, if $f(x,y)$ depends on two arguments, one can define

$$\begin{array}{rcl} F_x & = & \lambda y.f(x,y) \\ F & = & \lambda x.F_x. \end{array}$$

Then

$$(Fx)y = F_x y = f(x,y). \tag{1}$$

This last equation shows that it is convenient to use *association to the left* for iterated application:

$$FM_1 \ldots M_n \text{ denotes } (..((FM_1)M_2)\ldots M_n).$$

The equation (1) then becomes

$$Fxy = f(x,y).$$

Dually, iterated abstraction uses *association to the right:*

$$\lambda x_1 \cdots x_n.f(x_1,\ldots,x_n) \text{ denotes } \lambda x_1.(\lambda x_2.(\ldots(\lambda x_n.f(x_1,\ldots,x_n))..)).$$

Then we have for F defined above

$$F = \lambda xy.f(x,y)$$

and (1) becomes

$$(\lambda xy.f(x,y))xy = f(x,y).$$

For n arguments we have

$$(\lambda x_1 \ldots x_n.f(x_1,\ldots,x_n))x_1 \ldots x_n = f(x_1,\ldots,x_n),$$

by using (β) n times. This last equation becomes in convenient vector notation

$$(\lambda \vec{x}.f(\vec{x}))\vec{x} = f(\vec{x});$$

more generally one has

$$(\lambda \vec{x}.f(\vec{x}))\vec{N} = f(\vec{N}).$$

Now we give the formal description of the λ-calculus.

Definition 2.1.1. The set of λ-*terms*, notation Λ, is built up from an infinite set of variables $V = \{v, v', v'', \ldots\}$ using application and (function) abstraction:

$$\begin{array}{lcl} x \in V & \Rightarrow & x \in \Lambda, \\ M, N \in \Lambda & \Rightarrow & (MN) \in \Lambda, \\ M \in \Lambda, x \in V & \Rightarrow & (\lambda x M) \in \Lambda. \end{array}$$

Using abstract syntax one may write the following.

$$\begin{array}{l} V ::= v \mid V' \\ \Lambda ::= V \mid (\Lambda\Lambda) \mid (\lambda V \Lambda) \end{array}$$

Example 2.1.2. The following are λ-terms:

$$\begin{array}{l} v; \\ (vv''); \\ (\lambda v(vv'')); \\ ((\lambda v(vv''))v'); \\ ((\lambda v'((\lambda v(vv''))v'))v'''). \end{array}$$

Convention 2.1.3.

1. $x, y, z, \ldots$ denote arbitrary variables;
   $M, N, L, \ldots$ denote arbitrary λ-terms.

2. As already mentioned informally, the following abbreviations are used:

$$FM_1 \ldots M_n \text{ stands for } (..((FM_1)M_2) \ldots M_n)$$

   and

$$\lambda x_1 \cdots x_n.M \text{ stands for } (\lambda x_1(\lambda x_2(\ldots(\lambda x_n(M))..))).$$

3. Outermost parentheses are not written.

Using this convention, the examples in 2.1.2 now may be written as follows:

$$\begin{array}{l} x;\, xz;\, \lambda x.xz; \\ (\lambda x.xz)y; \\ (\lambda y.(\lambda x.xz)y)w. \end{array}$$

Note that $\lambda x.yx$ is $(\lambda x(yx))$ and not $((\lambda xy)x)$.

Notation 2.1.4. $M \equiv N$ denotes that M and N are the same term or can be obtained from each other by renaming bound variables. For example,

$$\begin{array}{rcl} (\lambda x.x)z & \equiv & (\lambda x.x)z; \\ (\lambda x.x)z & \equiv & (\lambda y.y)z; \\ (\lambda x.x)z & \not\equiv & (\lambda x.y)z. \end{array}$$

Definition 2.1.5.

1. The set of *free variables* of M, (notation $FV(M)$), is defined inductively as follows:

$$\begin{array}{rcl} FV(x) & = & \{x\}; \\ FV(MN) & = & FV(M) \cup FV(N); \\ FV(\lambda x.M) & = & FV(M) - \{x\}. \end{array}$$

2. M is a *closed* λ*-term* (or *combinator*) if $FV(M) = \emptyset$. The set of closed λ-terms is denoted by Λ^0.

3. The result of *substitution* of N for (the free occurrences of) x in M, notation $M[x := N]$, is defined as follows: Below $x \not\equiv y$.

$$\begin{aligned}
x[x := N] &\equiv N;\\
y[x := N] &\equiv y;\\
(PQ)[x := N] &\equiv (P[x := N])(Q[x := N]);\\
(\lambda y.P)[x := N] &\equiv \lambda y.(P[x := N]), \text{ provided } y \not\equiv x;\\
(\lambda x.P)[x := N] &\equiv (\lambda x.P).
\end{aligned}$$

In the λ-term

$$y(\lambda xy.xyz)$$

y and z occur as free variables; x and y occur as bound variables. The term $\lambda xy.xxy$ is closed.

Names of bound variables will be always chosen such that they differ from the free ones in a term. So one writes $y(\lambda xy'.xy'z)$ for $y(\lambda xy.xyz)$. This so-called 'variable convention' makes it possible to use substitution for the λ-calculus without a proviso on free and bound variables.

Proposition 2.1.6 (Substitution lemma). *Let $M, N, L \in \Lambda$. Suppose $x \not\equiv y$ and $x \notin FV(L)$. Then*

$$M[x := N][y := L] \equiv M[y := L][x := N[y := L]].$$

Proof. By induction on the structure of M. ∎

Now we introduce the λ-calculus as a formal theory of equations between λ-terms.

Definition 2.1.7.

1. The principal axiom scheme of the λ-calculus is

$$(\lambda x.M)N = M[x := N] \qquad (\beta)$$

   for all $M, N \in \Lambda$. This is called *β-conversion.*

2. There are also the 'logical' axioms and rules:

$$\begin{aligned}
& M = M;\\
M = N &\Rightarrow N = M;\\
M = N, N = L &\Rightarrow M = L;\\
M = M' &\Rightarrow MZ = M'Z;
\end{aligned}$$

$$\begin{aligned} M = M' &\Rightarrow ZM = ZM'; \\ M = M' &\Rightarrow \lambda x.M = \lambda x.M'. \end{aligned} \qquad (\xi)$$

3. If $M = N$ is provable in the λ-calculus, then we write $\lambda \vdash M = N$ or sometimes just $M = N$.

Remarks 2.1.8.

1. We have identified terms that differ only in the names of bound variables. An alternative is to add to the λ-calculus the following axiom scheme of *α-conversion*.

   $$\lambda x.M = \lambda y.M[x := y], \qquad (\alpha)$$

   provided that y does not occur in M. The axiom (β) above was originally the second axiom; hence its name. We prefer our version of the theory in which the identifications are made on a syntactic level. These identifications are done in our mind and not on paper.

2. Even if initially terms are written according to the variable convention, α-conversion (or its alternative) is necessary when rewriting terms. Consider e.g. $\omega \equiv \lambda x.xx$ and $1 \equiv \lambda yz.yz$. Then

   $$\begin{aligned} \omega 1 &\equiv (\lambda x.xx)(\lambda yz.yz) \\ &= (\lambda yz.yz)(\lambda yz.yz) \\ &= \lambda z.(\lambda yz.yz)z \\ &\equiv \lambda z.(\lambda yz'.yz')z \\ &= \lambda zz'.zz' \\ &\equiv \lambda yz.yz \\ &\equiv 1. \end{aligned}$$

3. For implementations of the λ-calculus the machine has to deal with this so called α-conversion. A good way of doing this is provided by the 'name-free notation' of N.G. de Bruijn, see [Barendregt, 1984], Appendix C. In this notation $\lambda x(\lambda y.xy)$ is denoted by $\lambda(\lambda 21)$, the 2 denoting a variable bound 'two lambdas above'.

The following result provides one way to represent recursion in the λ-calculus.

Theorem 2.1.9 (Fixed point theorem).

1. $\forall F \exists X FX = X$.
   (This means that for all $F \in \Lambda$ there is an $X \in \Lambda$ such that $\lambda \vdash FX = X$.)

2. *There is a fixed point combinator*

$$\mathsf{Y} \equiv \lambda f.(\lambda x.f(xx))(\lambda x.f(xx))$$

such that

$$\forall F\ F(\mathsf{Y}F) = \mathsf{Y}F.$$

Proof. 1. Define $W \equiv \lambda x.F(xx)$ and $X \equiv WW$. Then
$X \equiv WW \equiv (\lambda x.F(xx))W = F(WW) \equiv FX$.

2. By the proof of (1). Note that
$\mathsf{Y}F = (\lambda x.F(xx))(\lambda x.F(xx)) \equiv X$. ∎

Corollary 2.1.10. *Given a term $C \equiv C[f,x]$ possibly containing the displayed free variables, then*

$$\exists F \forall X\ FX = C[F,X].$$

Here $C[F,X]$ is of course the substitution result $C[f := F][x := X]$.

Proof. Indeed, we can construct F by supposing it has the required property and calculating back:

$$\begin{array}{rrcl} & \forall X\ FX & = & C[F,X] \\ \Leftarrow & Fx & = & C[F,x] \\ \Leftarrow & F & = & \lambda x.C[F,x] \\ \Leftarrow & F & = & (\lambda fx.C[f,x])F \\ \Leftarrow & F & \equiv & \mathsf{Y}(\lambda fx.C[f,x]). \end{array}$$

∎

This also holds for more arguments: $\exists F \forall \vec{x}\ F\vec{x} = C[F,\vec{x}]$.

As an application, terms F and G can be constructed such that for all terms X and Y

$$\begin{array}{rcl} FX & = & XF, \\ GXY & = & YG(YXG). \end{array}$$

2.2 Lambda definability

In the lambda calculus one can define numerals and represent numeric functions on them.

Definition 2.2.1.

1. $F^n(M)$ with $n \in \mathbb{N}$ (the set of natural numbers) and $F, M \in \Lambda$, is defined inductively as follows:

$$\begin{aligned} F^0(M) &\equiv M; \\ F^{n+1}(M) &\equiv F(F^n(M)). \end{aligned}$$

2. The *Church numerals* $\mathbf{c}_0, \mathbf{c}_1, \mathbf{c}_2, \ldots$ are defined by

$$\mathbf{c}_n \equiv \lambda fx.f^n(x).$$

Proposition 2.2.2 (J. B. Rosser). *Define*

$$\begin{aligned} \mathsf{A}_+ &\equiv \lambda xypq.xp(ypq); \\ \mathsf{A}_* &\equiv \lambda xyz.x(yz); \\ \mathsf{A}_{exp} &\equiv \lambda xy.yx. \end{aligned}$$

Then one has for all $n, m \in \mathbb{N}$

1. $\mathsf{A}_+\mathbf{c}_n\mathbf{c}_m = \mathbf{c}_{n+m}$.

2. $\mathsf{A}_*\mathbf{c}_n\mathbf{c}_m = \mathbf{c}_{n.m}$.

3. $\mathsf{A}_{exp}\mathbf{c}_n\mathbf{c}_m = \mathbf{c}_{(n^m)}$, *except for $m = 0$ (Rosser starts at 1).*

Proof. We need the following lemma.

Lemma 2.2.3.

1. $(\mathbf{c}_n x)^m(y) = x^{n*m}(y)$;

2. $(\mathbf{c}_n)^m(x) = \mathbf{c}_{(n^m)}(x)$, *for $m > 0$.*

Proof. 1. By induction on m. If $m = 0$, then LHS $= y =$ RHS. Assume (1) is correct for m (Induction Hypothesis: IH). Then

$$\begin{array}{rcl}(\mathbf{c}_n x)^{m+1}(y) & = & \mathbf{c}_n x((\mathbf{c}_n x)^m(y)) \\ & =_{IH} & \mathbf{c}_n x(x^{n*m}(y)) \\ & = & x^n(x^{n*m}(y)) \\ & \equiv & x^{n+n*m}(y) \\ & \equiv & x^{n*(m+1)}(y).\end{array}$$

2. By induction on $m > 0$. If $m = 1$, then LHS $\equiv \mathbf{c}_n x \equiv$ RHS. If (2) is correct for m, then

$$\begin{array}{rcl}\mathbf{c}_n^{m+1}(x) & = & \mathbf{c}_n(\mathbf{c}_n^m(x)) \\ & =_{IH} & \mathbf{c}_n(\mathbf{c}_{(n^m)}(x)) \\ & = & \lambda y.(\mathbf{c}_{(n^m)}(x))^n(y) \\ & =_{(1)} & \lambda y.x^{n^m * n}(y) \\ & = & \mathbf{c}_{(n^{m+1})}x.\end{array}$$

■

Now the proof of the proposition.

1. By induction on m.
2. Use the lemma (1).
3. By the lemma (2) we have for $m > 0$

$$\mathbf{A}_{exp}\mathbf{c}_n\mathbf{c}_m = \mathbf{c}_m\mathbf{c}_n = \lambda x.\mathbf{c}_n{}^m(x) = \lambda x.\mathbf{c}_{(n^m)}x = \mathbf{c}_{(n^m)},$$

since $\lambda x.Mx = M$ if $M = \lambda y.M'[y]$ and $x \notin FV(M)$. Indeed,

$$\begin{array}{rcl}\lambda x.Mx & = & \lambda x.(\lambda y.M'[y])x \\ & = & \lambda x.M'[x] \\ & \equiv & \lambda y.M'[y] \\ & = & M.\end{array}$$

■

We have seen that the functions plus, times and exponentiation on $\mathbb{N}$ can be represented in the λ-calculus using Church's numerals. We will show that all computable (recursive) functions can be represented.

Boolean truth values and a conditional can be represented in the λ-calculus.

Definition 2.2.4 (Booleans, conditional).

1. **true** $\equiv \lambda xy.x$, **false** $\equiv \lambda xy.y$.
2. If B is a Boolean, i.e. a term that is either **true**, or **false**, then

$$\textbf{if } B \textbf{ then } P \textbf{ else } Q$$

can be represented by BPQ. Indeed, $\textbf{true}PQ = P$ and $\textbf{false}PQ = Q$.

Definition 2.2.5 (Pairing). For $M, N \in \Lambda$ write

$$[M, N] \equiv \lambda z.zMN.$$

Then

$$[M, N]\,\textbf{true} = M$$
$$[M, N]\,\textbf{false} = N$$

and hence $[M, N]$ can serve as an ordered pair.

Definition 2.2.6.

1. A *numeric function* is a map $f : \mathbb{N}^p \to \mathbb{N}$ for some p.
2. A numeric function f with p arguments is called λ-*definable* if one has for some combinator F

$$F\mathbf{c}_{n_1} \ldots \mathbf{c}_{n_p} = \mathbf{c}_{f(n_1,\ldots,n_p)} \tag{1}$$

for all $n_1, \ldots, n_p \in \mathbb{N}$. If (1) holds, then f is said to be λ-*defined* by F.

Definition 2.2.7.

1. The *initial functions* are the numeric functions U^i_r, S^+, Z defined by:

$$\begin{aligned} U^i_r(x_1, \ldots, x_r) &= x_i, \quad 1 \leq i \leq r; \\ S^+(n) &= n + 1; \\ Z(n) &= 0. \end{aligned}$$

2. Let $P(n)$ be a numeric relation. As usual

$$\mu m.P(m)$$

denotes the least number m such that $P(m)$ holds if there is such a number; otherwise it is undefined.

As we know from Chapter 2 in this handbook, the class $\mathcal{R}$ of recursive functions is the smallest class of numeric functions that contains all initial functions and is closed under composition, primitive recursion and minimalization. So $\mathcal{R}$ is an inductively defined class. The proof that all recursive functions are λ-definable is by a corresponding induction argument. The result is originally due to Kleene [Kleene, 1936].

Lemma 2.2.8. *The initial functions are λ-definable.*

Proof. Take as defining terms

$$\begin{array}{lcl} \mathsf{U}_p^i & \equiv & \lambda x_1 \cdots x_p.x_i; \\ \mathsf{S}^+ & \equiv & \lambda xyz.y(xyz) \quad (= \mathsf{A}_+\mathbf{c}_1); \\ \mathsf{Z} & \equiv & \lambda x.\mathbf{c}_0. \end{array}$$

∎

Lemma 2.2.9. *The λ-definable functions are closed under composition.*

Proof. Let $g, h_1, \ldots, h_m$ be λ-defined by $G, H_1, \ldots, H_m$ respectively. Then

$$f(\vec{n}) = g(h_1(\vec{n}), \ldots, h_m(\vec{n}))$$

is λ-defined by

$$F \equiv \lambda\vec{x}.G(H_1\vec{x})\ldots(H_m\vec{x}).$$

∎

Lemma 2.2.10. *The λ-definable functions are closed under primitive recursion.*

Proof. Let f be defined by

$$\begin{array}{l} f(0, \vec{n}) = g(\vec{n}) \\ f(k+1, \vec{n}) = h(f(k, \vec{n}), k, \vec{n}) \end{array}$$

where g, h are λ-defined by G, H respectively. We have to show that f is λ-definable. For notational simplicity we assume that there are no parameters $\vec{n}$ (hence $G = \mathbf{c}_{f(0)}$.) The proof for general $\vec{n}$ is similar.

If k is not an argument of h, then we have the scheme of iteration. Iteration can be represented easily in the λ-calculus, because the Church numerals are iterators. The construction of the representation of f is done in two steps. First primitive recursion is reduced to iteration using ordered pairs; then iteration is represented. Here are the details. Consider

$$T \equiv \lambda p.[\mathsf{S}^+(p\mathbf{true}), H(p\mathbf{false})(p\mathbf{true})].$$

Then for all k one has

$$\begin{array}{rcl} T([\mathbf{c}_k, \mathbf{c}_{f(k)}]) & = & [\mathbf{f}\mathsf{S}^+\mathbf{c}_k, H\mathbf{c}_{f(k)}\mathbf{c}_k] \\ & = & [\mathbf{c}_{k+1}, \mathbf{c}_{f(k+1)}]. \end{array}$$

By induction on k it follows that

$$[\mathbf{c}_k, \mathbf{c}_{f(k)}] = T^k[\mathbf{c}_0, \mathbf{c}_{f(0)}].$$

Therefore

$$\mathbf{c}_{f(k)} = \mathbf{c}_k T[\mathbf{c}_0, \mathbf{c}_{f(0)}]\ \mathbf{false},$$

and f can be λ-defined by

$$F \equiv \lambda k.kT[\mathbf{c}_0, G]\ \mathbf{false}.$$

∎

Lemma 2.2.11. *The λ-definable functions are closed under minimalization.*

Proof. Let f be defined by $f(\vec{n}) = \mu m[g(\vec{n}, m) = 0]$, where $\vec{n} = n_1, \ldots, n_k$ and g is λ-defined by G. We have to show that f is λ-definable. Define

$$\mathbf{zero} \equiv \lambda n.n(\mathbf{true\ false})\mathbf{true}.$$

Then

$$\begin{array}{rcl} \mathbf{zero}\ \mathbf{c}_0 & = & \mathbf{true}, \\ \mathbf{zero}\ \mathbf{c}_{n+1} & = & \mathbf{false}. \end{array}$$

By Corollary 2.1.10 there is a term H such that

$$H\vec{n}y = \ \mathbf{if}\ (\mathbf{zero}(G\vec{n}y))\ \mathbf{then}\ y\ \mathbf{else}\ H\vec{n}(\mathsf{S}^+y).$$

Set $F = \lambda\vec{n}.H\vec{x}\mathbf{c}0$. Then F λ-defines f:

$$\begin{array}{rcll} F\mathbf{c}_{\vec{x}} & = & H\mathbf{c}_{\vec{n}}\mathbf{c}_0 & \\ & = & \mathbf{c}_0, & \text{if } G\mathbf{c}_{\vec{n}}\mathbf{c}_0 = \mathbf{c}_0, \\ & = & H\mathbf{c}_{\vec{n}}\mathbf{c}_1 & \text{else;} \\ & = & \mathbf{c}_1, & \text{if } G\mathbf{c}_{\vec{n}}\mathbf{c}_1 = \mathbf{c}_0, \\ & = & H\mathbf{c}_{\vec{n}}\mathbf{c}_2 & \text{else;} \\ & = & \mathbf{c}_2, & \text{if } \ldots \\ & = & \ldots & \end{array}$$

Here $\mathbf{c}_{\vec{n}}$ stands for $\mathbf{c}_{n_1} \ldots \mathbf{c}_{n_k}$. ∎

Theorem 2.2.12. *All recursive functions are λ-definable.*

Proof. By 2.2.8-2.2.11. ∎

The converse also holds. The idea is that if a function is λ-definable, then its graph is recursively enumerable because equations derivable in the λ-calculus can be enumerated. It then follows that the function is recursive. So for numeric functions we have f is recursive iff f is λ-definable. Moreover also for partial functions a notion of λ-definability exists and one has ψ is partial recursive iff ψ is λ-definable. The notions λ-definable and recursive both are intended to be formalizations of the intuitive concept of computability. Another formalization was proposed by Turing in the form of Turing computable. The equivalence of the notions recursive, λ-definable and Turing computable (for the latter see besides the original [Turing, 1937], e.g., [Davis, 1958]) Davis provides some evidence for the Church–Turing thesis that states that 'recursive' is the proper formalization of the intuitive notion 'computable'.

We end this subsection with some undecidability results. First we need the coding of λ-terms. Remember that the collection of variables is $\{v, v', v'', \ldots\}$.

Definition 2.2.13.

1. Notation. $v^{(0)} = v$; $v^{(n+1)} = v^{(n)\prime}$.

2. Let $\langle\ ,\ \rangle$ be a recursive coding of pairs of natural numbers as a natural number. Define

$$\begin{aligned} \sharp(v^{(n)}) &= \langle 0, n\rangle; \\ \sharp(MN) &= \langle 2, \langle \sharp(M), \sharp(N)\rangle\rangle; \\ \sharp(\lambda x.M) &= \langle 3, \langle \sharp(x), \sharp(M)\rangle\rangle. \end{aligned}$$

3. Notation

$$\ulcorner M \urcorner = \mathbf{c}_{\sharp M}.$$

Definition 2.2.14. Let $\mathcal{A} \subseteq \Lambda$.

1. $\mathcal{A}$ *is closed under* $=$ if

$$M \in \mathcal{A},\ \lambda \vdash M = N \ \Rightarrow\ N \in \mathcal{A}.$$

2. $\mathcal{A}$ *is non-trivial* if $\mathcal{A} \neq \emptyset$ and $\mathcal{A} \neq \Lambda$.

3. $\mathcal{A}$ *is recursive* if $\sharp\mathcal{A} = \{\sharp M \mid M \in \mathcal{A}\}$ is recursive.

The following result due to Scott is quite useful for proving undecidability results.

Theorem 2.2.15. *Let $\mathcal{A} \subseteq \Lambda$ be non-trivial and closed under $=$. Then $\mathcal{A}$ is not recursive.*

Proof. (J. Terlouw) Define

$$\mathcal{B} = \{M \mid M\ulcorner M\urcorner \in \mathcal{A}\}.$$

Suppose $\mathcal{A}$ is recursive; then by the effectiveness of the coding also $\mathcal{B}$ is recursive (indeed, $n \in \sharp\mathcal{B} \Leftrightarrow \langle 2, \langle n, \sharp\mathbf{c}_n\rangle\rangle \in \sharp\mathcal{A}$). It follows that there is an $F \in \Lambda^0$ with

$$\begin{array}{lcl} M \in \mathcal{B} & \Leftrightarrow & F\ulcorner M\urcorner = \mathbf{c}_0; \\ M \notin \mathcal{B} & \Leftrightarrow & F\ulcorner M\urcorner = \mathbf{c}_1. \end{array}$$

Let $M_0 \in \mathcal{A}, M_1 \notin \mathcal{A}$. We can find a $G \in \Lambda$ such that

$$\begin{array}{lcl} M \in \mathcal{B} & \Leftrightarrow & G\ulcorner M\urcorner = M_1 \notin \mathcal{A}, \\ M \notin \mathcal{B} & \Leftrightarrow & G\ulcorner M\urcorner = M_0 \in \mathcal{A}. \end{array}$$

[Take $Gx =$ **if zero**(Fx) **then** M_1 **else** M_0, with **zero** defined in the proof of 2.2.11.] In particular

$$\begin{array}{lclcl} G \in \mathcal{B} & \Leftrightarrow & G\ulcorner G\urcorner \notin \mathcal{A} & \Leftrightarrow_{\text{Def}} & G \notin \mathcal{B}, \\ G \notin \mathcal{B} & \Leftrightarrow & G\ulcorner G\urcorner \in \mathcal{A} & \Leftrightarrow_{\text{Def}} & G \in \mathcal{B}, \end{array}$$

a contradiction. ∎

The following application shows that the lambda calculus is not a decidable theory.

Corollary 2.2.16 (Church). *The set*

$$\{M \mid M = \mathbf{true}\}$$

is not recursive.

Proof. Note that the set is closed under $=$ and is nontrivial. ∎

2.3 Reduction

There is a certain asymmetry in the basic scheme (β). The statement

$$(\lambda x.x^2 + 1)3 = 10$$

can be interpreted as '10 is the result of computing $(\lambda x.x^2 + 1)3$', but not vice versa. This computational aspect will be expressed by writing

$$(\lambda x.x^2 + 1)3 \twoheadrightarrow 10$$

which reads '$(\lambda x.x^2 + 1)3$ *reduces to* 10'.

Apart from this conceptual aspect, reduction is also useful for an analysis of convertibility. The Church–Rosser theorem says that if two terms are convertible, then there is a term to which they both reduce. In many cases the inconvertibility of two terms can be proved by showing that they do not reduce to a common term.

Definition 2.3.1.

1. A binary relation R on Λ is called *compatible* (w.r.t. operations) if

$$\begin{array}{rcl} M\,R\,N & \Rightarrow & (ZM)\,R\,(ZN), \\ & & (MZ)\,R\,(NZ), \text{ and} \\ & & (\lambda x.M)\,R\,(\lambda x.N). \end{array}$$

2. A *congruence* relation on Λ is a compatible equivalence relation.

3. A *reduction* relation on Λ is a compatible, reflexive and transitive relation.

Definition 2.3.2. The binary relations $\rightarrow_\beta, \twoheadrightarrow_\beta$ and $=_\beta$ on Λ are defined inductively as follows:

1. (a) $(\lambda x.M)N \rightarrow_\beta M[x := N]$;
   (b) $M \rightarrow_\beta N \;\Rightarrow\; ZM \rightarrow_\beta ZN,\; MZ \rightarrow_\beta NZ$ and $\lambda x.M \rightarrow_\beta \lambda x.N$.
2. (a) $M \twoheadrightarrow_\beta M$;
   (b) $M \rightarrow_\beta N \;\Rightarrow\; M \twoheadrightarrow_\beta N$;
   (c) $M \twoheadrightarrow_\beta N, N \twoheadrightarrow_\beta L \;\Rightarrow\; M \twoheadrightarrow_\beta L$.
3. (a) $M \twoheadrightarrow_\beta N \;\Rightarrow\; M =_\beta N$;
   (b) $M =_\beta N \;\Rightarrow\; N =_\beta M$;
   (c) $M =_\beta N, N =_\beta L \;\Rightarrow\; M =_\beta L$.

These relations are pronounced as follows:

$M \twoheadrightarrow_\beta N$: M *β-reduces to* N;
$M \rightarrow_\beta N$: M *β-reduces to* N *in one step*;
$M =_\beta N$: M is *β-convertible to* N.

By definition $\rightarrow_\beta$ is compatible. The relation $\twoheadrightarrow_\beta$ is the reflexive transitive closure of $\rightarrow_\beta$ and therefore a reduction relation. The relation $=_\beta$ is a congruence relation.

Proposition 2.3.3. $M =_\beta N \;\Leftrightarrow\; \lambda \vdash M = N$.

Proof. ($\Leftarrow$) By induction on the generation of $\vdash$. ($\Rightarrow$) By induction one shows

$$\begin{array}{lcl} M \to_\beta N & \Rightarrow & \lambda \vdash M = N; \\ M \twoheadrightarrow_\beta N & \Rightarrow & \lambda \vdash M = N; \\ M =_\beta N & \Rightarrow & \lambda \vdash M = N. \end{array}$$

■

Definition 2.3.4.

1. A *β-redex* is a term of the form $(\lambda x.M)N$. In this case $M[x := N]$ is its *contractum*.
2. A λ-term M *is* a *β-normal form* (β-nf) if it does not have a β-redex as subexpression.
3. A term M *has* a β-normal form if $M =_\beta N$ and N is a β-nf, for some N.

Example 2.3.5. $(\lambda x.xx)y$ is not a β-nf, but has as β-nf the term yy.

An immediate property of nf's is the following.

Lemma 2.3.6. *Let* $M, M', N, L \in \Lambda$.

1. *Suppose* M *is a β-nf. Then*

$$M \twoheadrightarrow_\beta N \;\Rightarrow\; N \equiv M.$$

2. *If* $M \to_\beta M'$, *then* $M[x := N] \to_\beta M'[x := N]$.

Proof. 1. If M is a β-nf, then M does not contain a redex. Hence never $M \to_\beta N$. Therefore if $M \twoheadrightarrow_\beta N$, then this must be because $M \equiv N$.

2. By induction on the generation of $\to_\beta$. ■

Theorem 2.3.7 (Church–Rosser theorem). *If* $M \twoheadrightarrow_\beta N_1, M \twoheadrightarrow_\beta N_2$, *then for some* N_3 *one has* $N_1 \twoheadrightarrow_\beta N_3$ *and* $N_2 \twoheadrightarrow_\beta N_3$; *in diagram*

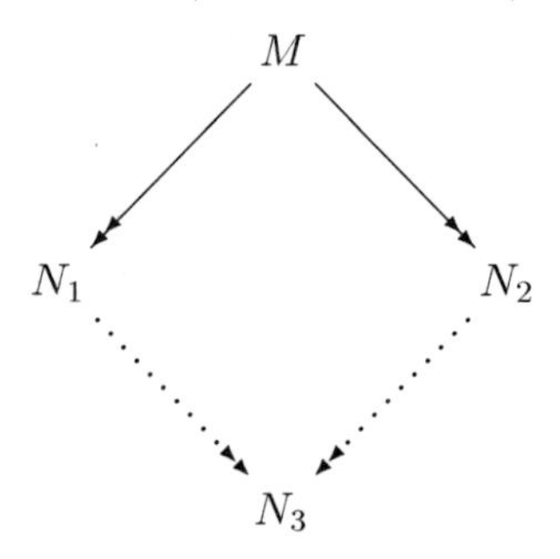

The proof is postponed until 2.3.17.

Corollary 2.3.8. *If $M =_\beta N$, then there is an L such that $M \twoheadrightarrow_\beta L$ and $N \twoheadrightarrow_\beta L$.*

Proof. Induction on the generation of $=_\beta$.

Case 1. $M =_\beta N$ because $M \twoheadrightarrow_\beta N$. Take $L \equiv N$.

Case 2. $M =_\beta N$ because $N =_\beta M$. By the IH there is a common β-reduct L_1 of N, M. Take $L \equiv L_1$.

Case 3. $M =_\beta N$ because $M =_\beta N', N' =_\beta N$. Then

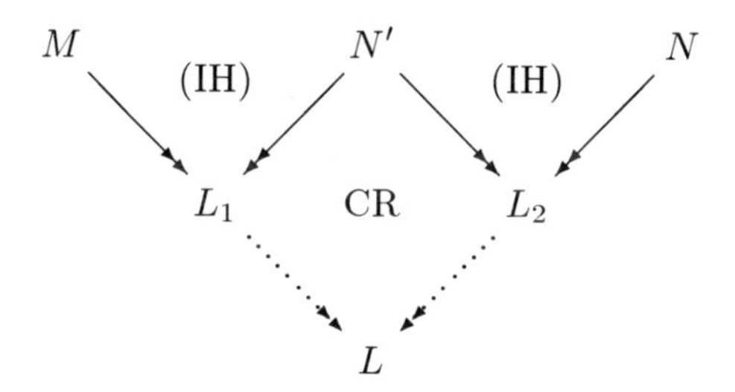

■

Corollary 2.3.9.

1. *If M has N as β-nf, then $M \twoheadrightarrow_\beta N$.*
2. *A λ-term has at most one β-nf.*

Proof.
1. Suppose $M =_\beta N$ with N in β-nf. By corollary 2.3.8 one has $M \twoheadrightarrow_\beta L$ and $N \twoheadrightarrow_\beta L$ for some L. But then $N \equiv L$, by Lemma 2.3.6, so $M \twoheadrightarrow_\beta N$.
2. Suppose M has β-nf's N_1, N_2. Then $N_1 =_\beta N_2$ ($=_\beta M$). By Corollary 2.3.8 one has $N_1 \twoheadrightarrow_\beta L, N_2 \twoheadrightarrow_\beta L$ for some L. But then $N_1 \equiv L \equiv N_2$ by Lemma 2.3.6(1). ■

Some consequences.

1. The λ-calculus is consistent, i.e. $\lambda \nvdash$ **true** = **false**. Otherwise **true** $=_\beta$ **false** by Proposition 2.3.3, which is impossible by Corollary 2.3.8

since **true** and **false** are distinct β-nf's. This is a syntactical consistency proof.

2. $\Omega \equiv (\lambda x.xx)(\lambda x.xx)$ has no β-nf. Otherwise $\Omega \twoheadrightarrow_\beta N$ with N in β-nf. But Ω only reduces to itself and is not in β-nf.

3. In order to find the β-nf of a term, the various subexpressions of it may be reduced in different orders. If a β-nf is found, then by Corollary 2.3.9 (2) it is unique. Moreover, one cannot go wrong: every reduction of a term can be continued to the β-nf of that term (if it exists). See also Theorem 2.3.20.

Proof of the Church–Rosser theorem
This occupies 2.3.10 - 2.3.17. The idea of the proof is as follows. In order to prove the theorem, it is sufficient to show the following strip lemma:

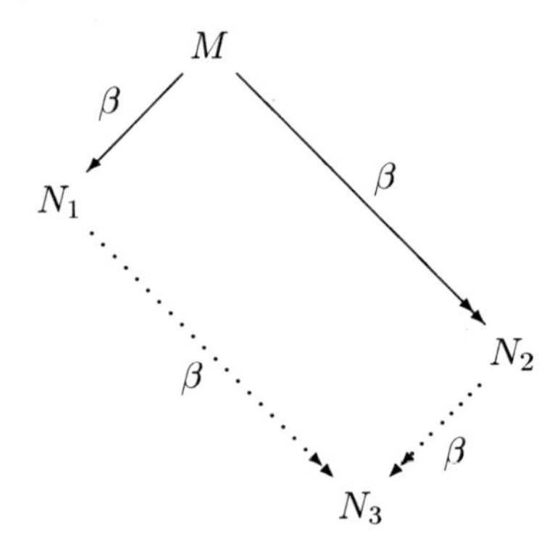

In order to prove this lemma, let $M \to_\beta N_1$ be a one step reduction resulting from changing a redex R in M in its contractum R' in N_1. If one makes a bookkeeping of what happens with R during the reduction $M \twoheadrightarrow N_2$, then by reducing all 'residuals' of R in N_2 the term N_3 can be found. In order to do the necessary bookkeeping an extended set $\underline{\Lambda} \supseteq \Lambda$ and reduction $\underline{\beta}$ is introduced. The underlining is used in a way similar to 'radioactive tracing isotopes' in experimental biology.

Definition 2.3.10 (Underlining).

1. $\underline{\Lambda}$ is the set of terms defined inductively as follows:

$$\begin{array}{rcl} x \in V & \Rightarrow & x \in \underline{\Lambda}; \\ M, N \in \underline{\Lambda} & \Rightarrow & (MN) \in \underline{\Lambda}; \\ M \in \underline{\Lambda}, x \in V & \Rightarrow & (\lambda x.M) \in \underline{\Lambda}; \\ M, N \in \underline{\Lambda}, x \in V & \Rightarrow & ((\underline{\lambda} x.M)N) \in \underline{\Lambda}. \end{array}$$

2. Underlined (one step) reduction ($\to_{\underline{\beta}}$ and) $\twoheadrightarrow_{\underline{\beta}}$ are defined starting with the contraction rules

$$(\lambda x.M)N \rightarrow M[x := N],$$

$$(\underline{\lambda} x.M)N \rightarrow M[x := N].$$

Then $\rightarrow$ is extended to the compatible relation $\rightarrow_{\underline{\beta}}$ (also w.r.t. $\underline{\lambda}$-abstraction) and $\twoheadrightarrow_{\underline{\beta}}$ is the transitive reflexive closure of $\rightarrow_{\underline{\beta}}$.

3. If $M \in \underline{\Lambda}$, then $|M| \in \Lambda$ is obtained from M by leaving out all underlinings. For example, $|(\lambda x.x)((\underline{\lambda} x.x)(\lambda x.x))| \equiv \mathsf{I}(\mathsf{II})$.

4. Substitution for $\underline{\Lambda}$ is defined by adding to the schemes in definition 2.1.5(3) the following:

$$((\underline{\lambda} x.M)N)[y := L] \equiv (\underline{\lambda} x.M[y := L])(N[y := L]).$$

Definition 2.3.11. A map $\varphi{:}\underline{\Lambda} \rightarrow \Lambda$ is defined inductively as follows:

$$\begin{array}{rcl} \varphi(x) & \equiv & x; \\ \varphi(MN) & \equiv & \varphi(M)\varphi(N), \text{ if } M, N \in \underline{\Lambda}; \\ \varphi(\lambda x.M) & \equiv & \lambda x.\varphi(M); \\ \varphi((\underline{\lambda} x.M)N) & \equiv & \varphi(M)[x := \varphi(N)]. \end{array}$$

In other words, the map φ contracts all redexes that are underlined, from the inside to the outside.

Notation 2.3.12. If $|M| \equiv N$ or $\varphi(M) \equiv N$, then this will be denoted by respectively

$$M \xrightarrow[\;|\;|\;]{} N \text{ or } M \xrightarrow[\varphi]{} N.$$

Lemma 2.3.13.

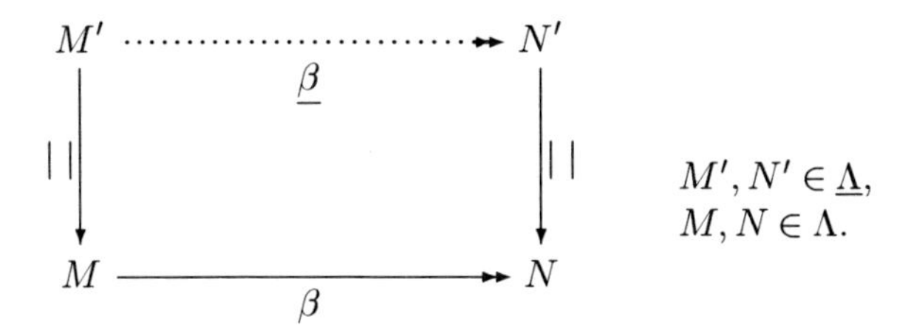

$M', N' \in \underline{\Lambda}$,
$M, N \in \Lambda$.

Proof. First suppose $M \rightarrow_{\beta} N$. Then N is obtained by contracting a redex in M and N' can be obtained by contracting the corresponding redex in M'. The general statement follows by transitivity. ∎

Lemma 2.3.14. *Let* $M, M', N, L \in \underline{\Lambda}$. *Then*

1. *Suppose* $x \not\equiv y$ *and* $x \notin FV(L)$. *Then*

$$M[x := N][y := L] \equiv M[y := L][x := N[y := L]].$$

2.

$$\varphi(M[x := N]) \equiv \varphi(M)[x := \varphi(N)].$$

3.

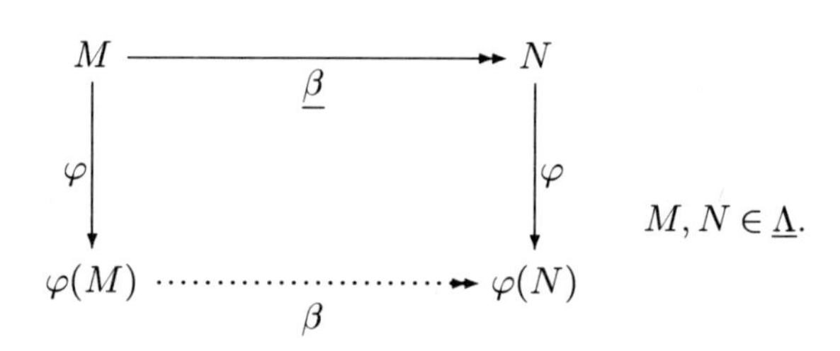

Proof. 1. By induction on the structure of M.

2. By induction on the structure of M, using (1) in case $M \equiv (\underline{\lambda} y.P)Q$. The condition of (1) may be assumed to hold by our convention about free variables.

3. By induction on the generation of $\twoheadrightarrow_{\underline{\beta}}$, using (2). ∎

Lemma 2.3.15.

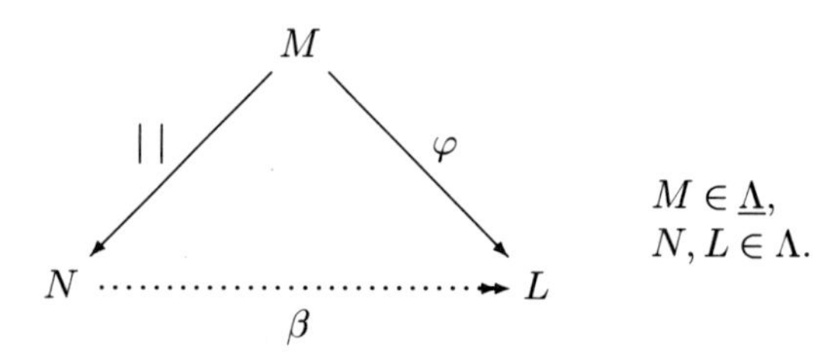

Proof. By induction on the structure of M. ∎

Lemma 2.3.16 (Strip lemma).

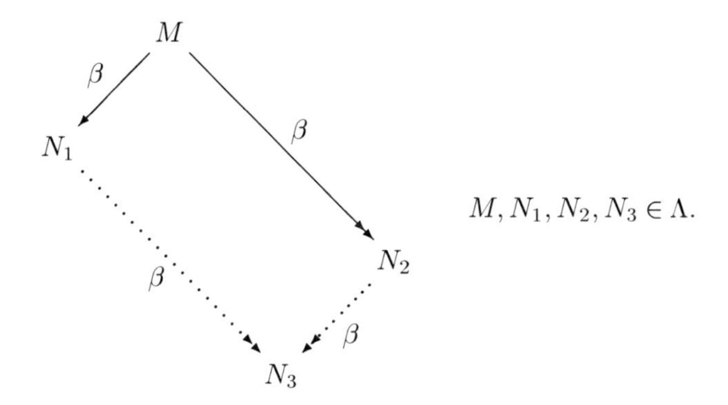

Proof. Let N_1 be the result of contracting the redex occurrence $R \equiv (\lambda x.P)Q$ in M. Let $M' \in \underline{\Lambda}$ be obtained from M by replacing R by $R' \equiv (\underline{\lambda} x.P)Q$. Then $|M'| \equiv M$ and $\varphi(M') \equiv N_1$. By Lemmas 2.3.12, 2.3.13 and 2.3.14 we can construct the following diagram which proves the strip lemma.

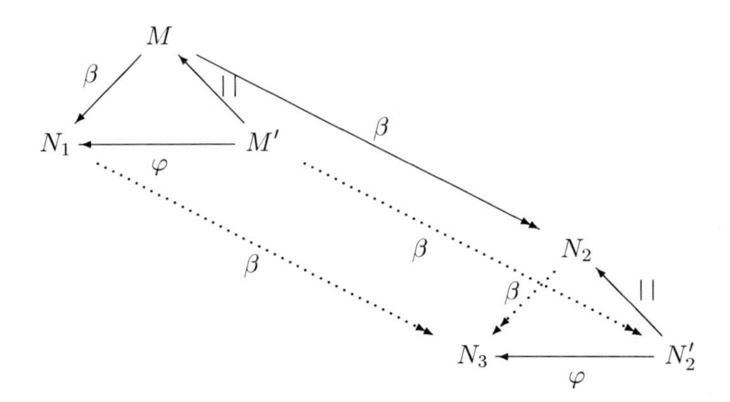

∎

Theorem 2.3.17 (Church-Rosser theorem). *If* $M \twoheadrightarrow_\beta N_1, M \twoheadrightarrow_\beta N_2$, *then for some* N_3 *one has* $N_1 \twoheadrightarrow_\beta N_3$ *and* $N_2 \twoheadrightarrow_\beta N_3$.

Proof. If $M \twoheadrightarrow_\beta N_1$, then $M \equiv M_0 \rightarrow_\beta M_1 \rightarrow_\beta \ldots M_n \equiv N_1$. Hence the CR property follows from the strip lemma and a simple diagram chase:

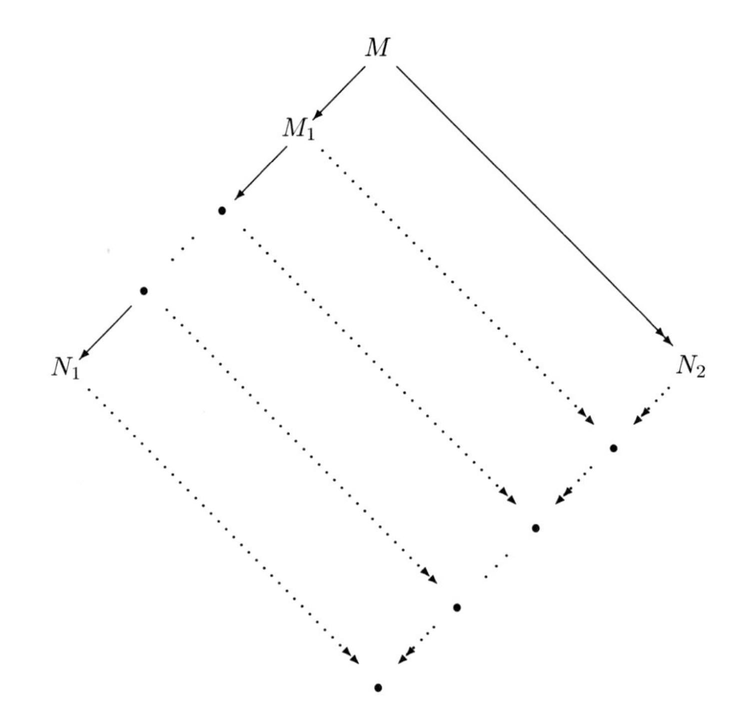

■

Normalization

Definition 2.3.18. For $M \in \Lambda$ the *reduction graph* of M, notation $G_\beta(M)$, is the directed multigraph with vertices $\{N \mid M \twoheadrightarrow_\beta N\}$ and directed by $\to_\beta$. We have a multigraph because contractions of different redexes are considered as different edges.

Example 2.3.19. $G_\beta(\mathsf{I}(\mathsf{I}a))$ is

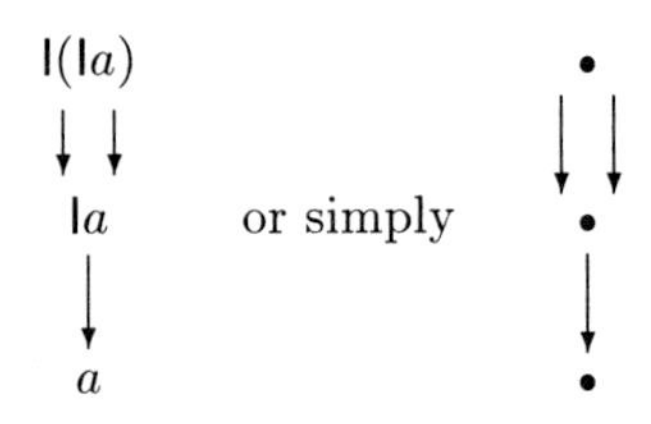

A lambda term M is called *strongly normalizing* iff all reduction sequences starting with M terminate (or equivalently iff $G_\beta(M)$ is finite). There are terms that do have an nf, but are not strongly normalizing because they have an infinite reduction graph. Indeed, let $\Omega \equiv (\lambda x.xx)(\lambda x.xx)$.

Then

$$\Omega \to_\beta \Omega \to_\beta \Omega \to_\beta \Omega \to_\beta \ldots.$$

Now $\mathsf{K}\mathsf{I}\Omega =_\beta \mathsf{I}$, but the left hand side also has an infinite reduction graph. Therefore a so-called *strategy* is necessary in order to find normal forms.

We state the following theorem due to Curry; for a proof see [Barendregt, 1984], theorem 13.2.2.

Theorem 2.3.20 (Normalization theorem). *If M has a normal form, then iterated contraction of the leftmost redex (i.e. with its main lambda leftmost) leads to that normal form.*

In other words: the leftmost reduction strategy is *normalizing*.

The functional language (pure) LISP uses an *eager* or *applicative* evaluation strategy, i.e. whenever an expression of the form FA has to be evaluated, A is reduced to normal form first, before 'calling' F. In the λ-calculus this strategy is not normalizing as is shown by the two reduction paths for $\mathsf{K}\mathsf{I}\Omega$ above. There is, however, a variant of the lambda calculus, called the $\lambda\mathsf{I}$-calculus, in which the eager evaluation strategy is normalizing. See [Barendregt, 1984], Ch 9, and §11.3. In this $\lambda\mathsf{I}$-calculus terms like K, 'throwing away' Ω in the reduction $\mathsf{K}\mathsf{I}\Omega \twoheadrightarrow \mathsf{I}$, do not exist. The 'ordinary' λ-calculus is sometimes referred to as $\lambda\mathsf{K}$-calculus.

In several lambda calculi with types one has that typable terms are strongly normalizing, see subsections 4.3 and 5.3.

Böhm trees and approximation

We end this subsection on reduction by introducing Böhm trees, a kind of 'infinite normal form'.

Lemma 2.3.21. *Each $M \in \Lambda$ is either of the following two forms.*

1. $M \equiv \lambda x_1 \ldots x_n.yN_1 \ldots N_m$, *with $n, m \geq 0$, and y a variable.*
2. $M \equiv \lambda x_1 \ldots x_n.(\lambda y.N_0)N_1 \ldots N_m$, *with $n \geq 0, m \geq 1$.*

Proof. By definition a λ-term is either a variable, or of the form PQ (an application) or $\lambda x.P$ (an abstraction).

If M is a variable, then M is of the form (1) with $n = m = 0$.

If M is an application, then $M \equiv P_0P_1 \ldots P_m$ with P_0 not an application. Then M is of the form (1) or (2) with $n = 0$, depending on whether P_0 is a variable (giving (1)) or an abstraction (giving (2)).

If M is an abstraction, then a similar argument shows that M is of the right form. ∎

Definition 2.3.22.

1. A λ-term M is a *head normal form* (hnf) if M is of the form (1) in Lemma 2.3.21. In that case y is called the *head variable* of M.

2. M has an hnf if $M =_\beta N$ for some N that is an hnf.

3. If M is of the form (2) in 2.3.21, then $(\lambda y.N_0)N_1$ is called the *head redex* of M.

Lemma 2.3.23. *If $M =_\beta M'$ and*

$$M \text{ has hnf } M_1 \equiv \lambda x_1 \cdots x_n.yN_1 \ldots N_m,$$

$$M' \text{ has hnf } M_1' \equiv \lambda x_1 \cdots x_{n'}.y'N_1' \ldots N_{m'}',$$

then $n = n', y \equiv y', m = m'$ and $N_1 =_\beta N_1', \ldots, N_m =_\beta N_{m'}'$.

Proof. By the corollary to the Church–Rosser theorem 2.3.8 M_1 and M_1' have a common reduct L. But then the only possibility is that

$$L \equiv \lambda x_1 \cdots x_{n''}.y''N_1'' \ldots N_{m''}''$$

with

$$n = n' = n', \; y = y'' = y', \; m = m'' = m' \text{ and } N_1 =_\beta N_1'' =_\beta N_1', \ldots .$$

∎

The following definitions give the flavour of the notion of Böhm tree. The definitions are not completely correct, because there should be an ordering in the direct successors of a node. However, this ordering is displayed in the drawings of the trees. For a precise definition, covering this order, see [Barendregt, 1984], Ch.10.

Definition 2.3.24.

1. A *tree* has the form depectied in the following figure

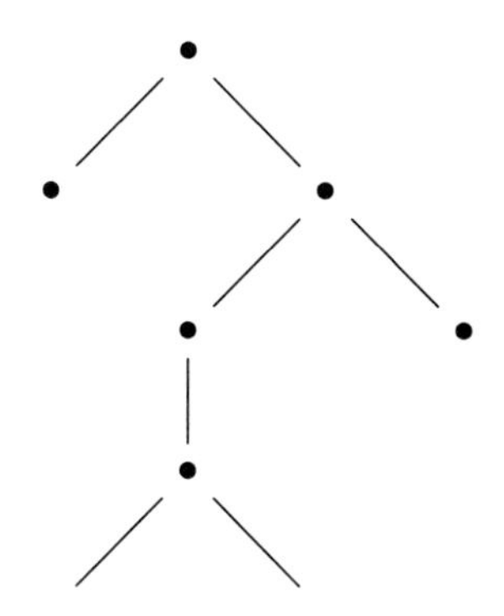

That is, a tree is a partially ordered set such that

(a) there is a root;

(b) each node (point) has finitely many direct successors;

(c) the set of predecessors of a node is finite and is linearly ordered.

2. A *labelled* tree is a tree with symbols at some of its nodes.

Definition 2.3.25. Let $M \in \Lambda$. The *Böhm tree* of M, notation $BT(M)$, is the labelled tree defined as follows:

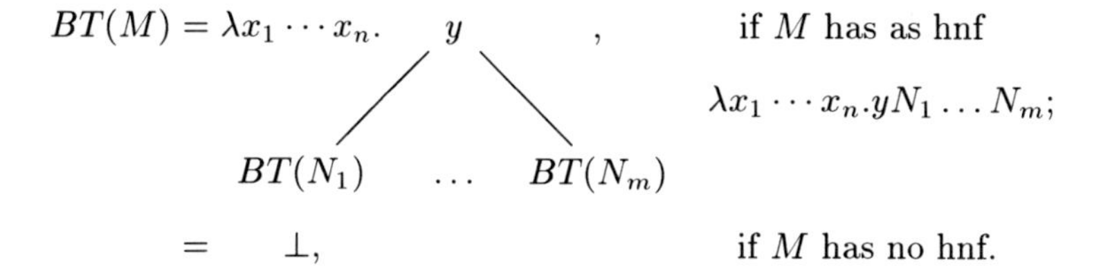

$BT(M) = \lambda x_1 \cdots x_n.\ y$,
$BT(N_1)$ ... $BT(N_m)$
if M has as hnf
$\lambda x_1 \cdots x_n . y N_1 \ldots N_m$;
$= \quad \perp,$
if M has no hnf.

Example 2.3.26.

1.

$BT(\lambda abc.ac(bc)) = \lambda abc.\ a$

$c \qquad b$

c

2.

$$BT((\lambda x.xx)(\lambda x.xx)) = \perp .$$

3.

$$BT(\mathsf{Y}) = \lambda f.\ \begin{array}{c} f \\ | \\ f \\ | \\ \vdots \end{array}\ .$$

This is because $\mathsf{Y} = \lambda f.\omega_f \omega_f$ with $\omega_f \equiv \lambda x.f(xx)$.
Therefore $\mathsf{Y} = \lambda f.f(\omega_f \omega_f)$ and

$$BT(\mathsf{Y}) = \lambda f.\ \begin{array}{c} f \\ | \\ BT(\omega_f \omega_f) \end{array}\ ;$$

now $\omega_f \omega_f = f(\omega_f \omega_f)$ so

$$BT(\omega_f \omega_f) = \begin{array}{c} f \\ | \\ BT(\omega_f \omega_f) \end{array} = \begin{array}{c} f \\ | \\ f \\ | \\ \vdots \end{array}\ .$$

Remark 2.3.27. Note that Definition 2.3.25 is not an inductive definition of $BT(M)$. The $N_1, \ldots, N_m$ in the tail of an hnf of a term may be more complicated than the term itself. See again [Barendregt, 1984], Ch.10.

Proposition 2.3.28. *$BT(M)$ is well defined and*

$$M =_\beta N \ \Rightarrow \ BT(M) = BT(N).$$

Proof. What is meant is that $BT(M)$ is independent of the choice of the hnf's. This and the second property follow from Lemma 2.3.23. ∎

Definition 2.3.29.

1. $\lambda\bot$ is the extension of the lambda calculus defined as follows. One of the variables is selected for use as a constant and is given the name $\bot$. Two contraction rules are added:

$$\lambda x.\bot \rightarrow \bot;$$

$$\bot M \rightarrow \bot.$$

The resulting reduction relation is called $\beta\bot$- reduction and is denoted by $\twoheadrightarrow_{\beta\bot}$.

2. A $\beta\bot$- *normal form* is such that it cannot be $\beta\bot$-reduced

3. Böhm trees for $\lambda\bot$ are defined by requiring that a $\lambda\bot$-term

$$\lambda x_1 \cdots x_n.yN_1 \ldots N_m$$

is only in $\beta\bot$-hnf if $y \not\equiv \bot$ or if $n = m = 0$.

Note that if M has a β-nf or β-hnf, then M also has a $\beta\bot$-hnf. This is because an hnf $\lambda x_1 \ldots x_n.yN_1 \ldots N_m$ is also a $\beta\bot$-hnf unless $y = \bot$. But in that case $\lambda x_1 \ldots x_n.yN_1 \ldots N_m \twoheadrightarrow_{\beta\bot} \bot$ and hence M has a β-hnf.

Definition 2.3.30.

1. Let A and B be Böhm trees of some $\lambda\bot$-terms. Then A is *included* in B, notation $A \subseteq B$, if A results from B by cutting off some subtrees, leaving an empty node. For example,

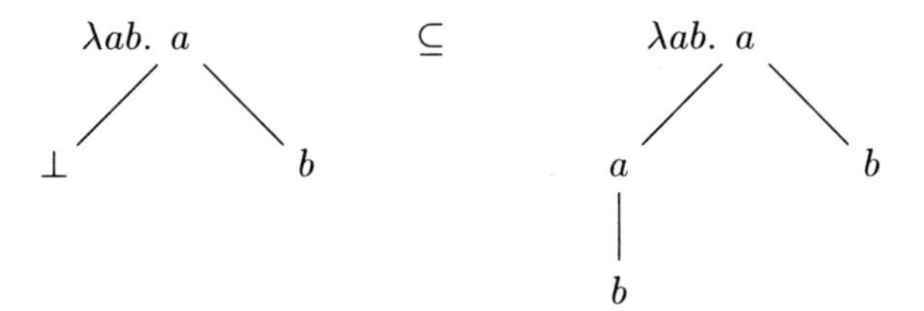

2. Let P, Q be $\lambda\bot$- terms. Then P *approximates* Q, notation $P \subseteq Q$, if $BT(P) \subseteq BT(Q)$.

3. Let P be a $\lambda\bot$-term. The set of *approximate normal forms* (anf's) of P, is defined as

$$\mathcal{A}(P) \quad = \quad \{Q \subseteq P \mid Q \text{ is a } \beta\bot\text{-nf}\}.$$

Example 2.3.31. The set of anf's of the fixedpoint operator Y is

$$\mathcal{A}(\mathsf{Y}) = \{\bot, \lambda f.f\bot, \lambda f.f^2\bot, \ldots\}.$$

Without a proof we mention the following 'continuity theorem', due to Wadsworth [Wadsworth, 1971].

Proposition 2.3.32. *Let $F, M \in \Lambda$ be given. Then*

$$\forall P \in \mathcal{A}(FM)\, \exists Q \in \mathcal{A}(M) \quad P \in \mathcal{A}(FQ).$$

See [Barendregt, 1984], proposition 14.3.19, for the proof and a topological explanation of the result.

3 Curry versus Church typing

In this section the system $\lambda\!\rightarrow$ of simply typed lambda calculus will be introduced. Attention is focused on the difference between typing *à la* Curry and *à la* Church by introducing $\lambda\!\rightarrow$ in both ways. Several other systems of typed lambda calculus exist both in a Curry and a Church version. However, this is not so for all systems. For example, for the Curry system $\lambda\cap$ (the system of intersection types, introduced in 4.1) it is not clear how to define a Church version. And for the Church system λC (calculus of constructions) it is not clear how to define a Curry version. For the systems that exist in both styles there is a clear relation between the two versions, as will be explained for $\lambda\!\rightarrow$.

3.1 The system $\lambda\!\rightarrow$-Curry

Originally the implicit typing paradigm was introduced in [Curry, 1934] for the theory of combinators. In [Curry and Feys, 1958], Curry *et al.* [Curry *et al.*, 1972] the theory was modified in a natural way to the lambda calculus assigning elements of a given set $\mathbb{T}$ of types to type free lambda terms. For this reason these calculi *à la* Curry are sometimes called *systems of type assignment.* If the type $\sigma \in \mathbb{T}$ is assigned to the term $M \in \Lambda$ one writes $\vdash M : \sigma$, often with a subscript under $\vdash$ to denote the particular system. Usually a set of assumptions Γ is needed to derive a type assignment and one writes $\Gamma \vdash M : \sigma$ (pronounce this as 'Γ yields M in σ'). A particular Curry type assignment system depends on two parameters, the set $\mathbb{T}$ and the rules of type assignment. As an example we now introduce the system $\lambda\!\rightarrow$-Curry.

Definition 3.1.1. The set of *types* of $\lambda\!\rightarrow$, notation Type($\lambda\!\rightarrow$), is inductively defined as follows. We write $\mathbb{T}=$ Type($\lambda\!\rightarrow$).

$$\begin{array}{ll} \alpha, \alpha', \ldots \in \mathbb{T} & \text{(type variables);} \\ \sigma, \tau \in \mathbb{T} \Rightarrow (\sigma\!\rightarrow\!\tau) \in \mathbb{T} & \text{(function space types).} \end{array}$$

Such definitions will occur more often and it is convenient to use the following abstract syntax to form $\mathbb{T}$:

$$\mathbb{T} = \mathbb{V} \mid \mathbb{T} {\rightarrow} \mathbb{T}$$

with $\mathbb{V}$ defined by

$$\mathbb{V} = \alpha \mid \mathbb{V}' \quad \text{(type variables).}$$

Notation 3.1.2.

1. If $\sigma_1, \ldots, \sigma_n \in \mathbb{T}$ then

$$\sigma_1 {\rightarrow} \sigma_2 {\rightarrow} \cdots {\rightarrow} \sigma_n$$

   stands for

$$(\sigma_1 {\rightarrow} (\sigma_2 {\rightarrow} \cdots {\rightarrow} (\sigma_{n-1} {\rightarrow} \sigma_n)..));$$

   that is, we use association to the right.

2. $\alpha, \beta, \gamma, \ldots$ denote arbitrary type variables.

Definition 3.1.3 ($\lambda{\rightarrow}$-Curry).

1. A *statement* is of the form $M : \sigma$ with $M \in \Lambda$ and $\sigma \in \mathbb{T}$. This statement is pronounced as '$M \in \sigma$'. The type σ is the *predicate* and the term M is the *subject* of the statement.

2. A *declaration* is a statement with as subject a (term) variable.

3. A *basis* is a set of declarations with distinct variables as subjects.

Definition 3.1.4. A statement $M : \sigma$ is *derivable from* a basis Γ , notation

$$\Gamma \vdash_{\lambda\rightarrow\text{-Curry}} M : \sigma$$

(or

$$\Gamma \vdash_{\lambda\rightarrow} M : \sigma$$

or

$$\Gamma {\vdash} M : \sigma$$

if there is no danger for confusion) if $\Gamma \vdash M : \sigma$ can be produced by the following rules.

λ→-Curry (version 0)

$$
\begin{array}{rcl}
(x{:}\sigma) \in \Gamma & \Rightarrow & \Gamma \vdash x : \sigma; \\
\Gamma \vdash M : (\sigma \to \tau),\ \ \Gamma \vdash N : \sigma & \Rightarrow & \Gamma \vdash (MN) : \tau; \\
\Gamma,\ x{:}\sigma \vdash M : \tau & \Rightarrow & \Gamma \vdash (\lambda x.M) : (\sigma \to \tau).
\end{array}
$$

Here $\Gamma, x{:}\sigma$ stands for $\Gamma \cup \{x{:}\sigma\}$. If $\Gamma = \{x_1{:}\sigma_1, \ldots, x_n{:}\sigma_n\}$ (or $\Gamma = \varnothing$) then instead of $\Gamma \vdash M : \sigma$ one writes $x_1{:}\sigma_1, \ldots, x_n{:}\sigma_n \vdash M : \sigma$ (or $\vdash M : \sigma$). Pronounce $\vdash$ as 'yields'.

The rules given in Definition 3.1.3 are usually notated as follows:

λ→-Curry (version 1)

(axiom)	$\Gamma \vdash x : \sigma,$	if $(x{:}\sigma) \in \Gamma$;
(→-elimination)	$\dfrac{\Gamma \vdash M : (\sigma \to \tau) \quad \Gamma \vdash N : \sigma}{\Gamma \vdash (MN) : \tau}\,;$	
(→-introduction)	$\dfrac{\Gamma, x{:}\sigma \vdash M : \tau}{\Gamma \vdash (\lambda x.M) : (\sigma \to \tau)}\,.$	

Another notation for these rules is the natural deduction formulation.

λ→-Curry (version 2)

Elimination rule	Introduction rule
$\dfrac{M : (\sigma \to \tau) \quad N : \sigma}{MN : \tau}$	$\begin{array}{c}\not{x : \sigma}\\ \vdots \\ \dfrac{M : \tau}{(\lambda x.M) : (\sigma \to \tau)}\end{array}$

In this version the axiom of version 0 or 1 is considered as implicit and is not notated. The notation

$$
\begin{array}{c} x : \sigma \\ \vdots \\ M : \tau \end{array}
$$

means that from the assumption $x{:}\sigma$ (together with a set Γ of other statements) one can derive $M : \tau$. The introduction rule in the table states that from this one may infer that $(\lambda x.M) : (\sigma{\rightarrow}\tau)$ is derivable even without the assumption $x{:}\sigma$ (but still using Γ). This process is called *cancellation* of an assumption and is indicated by striking through the statement $\cancel{(x{:}\sigma)}$.

Examples 3.1.5.

1. Using version 1 of the system, the *derivation*

$$\dfrac{\dfrac{x{:}\sigma, y{:}\tau \vdash x : \sigma}{x{:}\sigma \vdash (\lambda y.x) : (\tau{\rightarrow}\sigma)}}{\vdash (\lambda xy.x) : (\sigma{\rightarrow}\tau{\rightarrow}\sigma)}$$

shows that $\vdash (\lambda xy.x) : (\sigma{\rightarrow}\tau{\rightarrow}\sigma)$ for all $\sigma, \tau \in \mathbb{T}$.

A *natural deduction* derivation (for version 2 of the system) of the same type assignment is

$$\dfrac{\dfrac{\dfrac{\cancel{x{:}\sigma}\ 2 \qquad \cancel{y{:}\tau}\ 1}{x{:}\sigma}}{(\lambda y.x)\ :\ (\tau{\rightarrow}\sigma)}\,1}{(\lambda xy.x)\ :\ (\sigma{\rightarrow}\tau{\rightarrow}\sigma)}\,2$$

The indices 1 and 2 are bookkeeping devices that indicate at which application of a rule a particular assumption is being cancelled.

A more explicit way of dealing with cancellations of statements is the 'flag-notation' used by Fitch [Fitch, 1952] and in the languages AUTOMATH of de Bruijn [de Bruijn, 1980]. In this notation the above derivation becomes as follows.

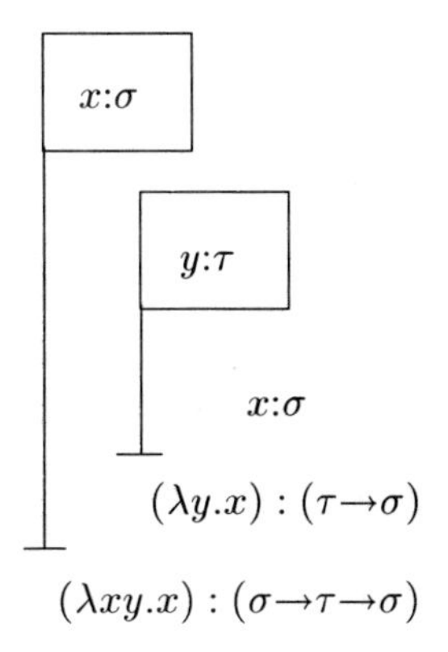

As one sees, the bookkeeping of cancellations is very explicit; on the other hand it is less obvious how a statement is derived from previous statements.

2. Similarly one can show for all $\sigma \in \mathbb{T}$

$$\vdash (\lambda x.x) : (\sigma \to \sigma).$$

3. An example with a non-empty basis is the following

$$y{:}\sigma \vdash (\lambda x.x)y : \sigma.$$

In the rest of this chapter we usually will introduce systems of typed lambda calculi in the style of version 1 of $\lambda{\to}$-Curry.

Pragmatics of constants

In applications of typed lambda calculi often one needs constants. For example in programming one may want a type constant **nat** and term constants **0** and **suc** representing the set of natural numbers, zero and the successor function. The way to do this is to take a type variable and two term variables and give these the names **nat**, **0** and **suc**. Then one forms as basis

$$\Gamma_0 = \{\mathbf{0}{:}\mathbf{nat}, \mathbf{suc}{:}(\mathbf{nat} \to \mathbf{nat})\}.$$

This Γ_0 will be treated as a so called 'initial basis'. That is, only bases Γ will be considered that are extensions of Γ_0. Moreover one promises not to bind the variables in Γ_0 by changing e.g.

$$\mathbf{0}{:}\mathbf{nat},\ \mathbf{suc}{:}(\mathbf{nat} \to \mathbf{nat}) \vdash M : \sigma$$

into

$$\vdash (\lambda \mathbf{0} \lambda \mathbf{suc}.M) : (\mathbf{nat} \to (\mathbf{nat} \to \mathbf{nat}) \to \sigma).$$

(If one does not keep the promise no harm is done, since then **0** and **suc** become ordinary bound variables.)

The programming language ML, see [Milner, 1984], is essentially $\lambda{\to}$-Curry extended with a constant Y and type assignment $\mathsf{Y} : ((\sigma \to \sigma) \to \sigma)$ for all σ.

Properties of $\lambda{\to}$-Curry

Several properties of type assignment in $\lambda{\to}$ are valid. The first one analyses how much of a basis is necessary in order to derive a type assignment.

Properties of $\lambda{\to}$*-Curry*

Several properties of type assignment in $\lambda{\to}$ are valid. The first one analyses how much of a basis is necessary in order to derive a type assignment.

Definition 3.1.6. Let $\Gamma = \{x_1{:}\sigma_1, \ldots, x_n{:}\sigma_n\}$ be a basis.

1. Write $\text{dom}(\Gamma) = \{x_1, \ldots, x_n\}$; $\sigma_i = \Gamma(x_i)$. That is, Γ is considered as a partial function.
2. Let V_0 be a set of variables. Then $\Gamma \restriction V_0 = \{x{:}\sigma \mid x \in V_0 \;\&\; \sigma = \Gamma(x)\}$.
3. For $\sigma, \tau \in \mathbb{T}$ substitution of τ for α in σ is denoted by $\sigma[\alpha := \tau]$.

Proposition 3.1.7 (Basis lemma for $\lambda{\to}$-Curry).
Let Γ be a basis.

1. *If $\Gamma' \supseteq \Gamma$ is another basis, then* $\Gamma \vdash M : \sigma \Rightarrow \Gamma' \vdash M : \sigma$.
2. $\Gamma \vdash M : \sigma \Rightarrow FV(M) \subseteq \text{dom}\,\Gamma$.
3. $\Gamma \vdash M : \sigma \Rightarrow \Gamma \restriction FV(M) \vdash M : \sigma$.

Proof. 1. By induction on the derivation of $M : \sigma$. Since such proofs will occur frequently we will spell it out in this simple situation in order to be briefer later on.

Case 1. $M : \sigma$ is $x{:}\sigma$ and is element of Γ. Then also $x{:}\sigma \in \Gamma'$ and hence $\Gamma' \vdash M : \sigma$.

Case 2. $M : \sigma$ is $(M_1 M_2) : \sigma$ and follows directly from $M_1 : (\tau{\to}\sigma)$ and $M_2 : \tau$ for some τ. By the IH one has $\Gamma' \vdash M_1 : (\tau{\to}\sigma)$ and $\Gamma' \vdash M_2 : \tau$. Hence $\Gamma' \vdash (M_1 M_2) : \sigma$.

Case 3. $M : \sigma$ is $(\lambda x.M_1) : (\sigma_1{\to}\sigma_2)$ and follows directly from $\Gamma, x{:}\sigma_1 \vdash M_1 : \sigma_2$. By the variable convention it may be assumed that the bound variable x does not occur in dom Γ'. Then $\Gamma', x{:}\sigma_1$ is also a basis which extends $\Gamma, x{:}\sigma_1$. Therefore by the IH one has $\Gamma', x{:}\sigma_1 \vdash M_1 : \sigma_2$ and so $\Gamma' \vdash (\lambda x.M_1) : (\sigma_1{\to}\sigma_2)$.

2. By induction on the derivation of $M : \sigma$. We only treat the case that $M : \sigma$ is $(\lambda x.M_1) : (\sigma_1{\to}\sigma_2)$ and follows directly from $\Gamma, x{:}\sigma_1 \vdash M_1 : \sigma_2$. Let $y \in FV(\lambda x.M_1)$, then $y \in FV(M_1)$ and $y \not\equiv x$. By the IH one has $y \in \text{dom}(\Gamma, x{:}\sigma_1)$ and therefore $y \in$ dom Γ.

3. By induction on the derivation of $M : \sigma$. We only treat the case that $M : \sigma$ is $(M_1 M_2) : \sigma$ and follows directly from $M_1 : (\tau{\to}\sigma)$ and

$M_2 : \tau$ for some τ. By the IH one has $\Gamma \restriction FV(M_1) \vdash M_1 : (\tau{\rightarrow}\sigma)$ and $\Gamma \restriction FV(M_2) \vdash M_2 : \tau$. By (1) it follows that $\Gamma \restriction FV(M_1 M_2) \vdash M_1 : (\tau{\rightarrow}\sigma)$and $\Gamma \restriction FV(M_1 M_2) \vdash M_2 : \tau$ and hence $\Gamma \restriction FV(M_1 M_2) \vdash (M_1 M_2) : \sigma$.

■

The second property analyses how terms of a certain form get typed. It is useful among other things to show that certain terms have no types.

Proposition 3.1.8 (Generation lemma for $\lambda{\rightarrow}$-Curry).

1. $\Gamma \vdash x : \sigma \Rightarrow (x{:}\sigma) \in \Gamma$.
2. $\Gamma \vdash MN : \tau \Rightarrow \exists \sigma\ [\Gamma \vdash M : (\sigma{\rightarrow}\tau)\ \&\ \Gamma \vdash N : \sigma]$.
3. $\Gamma \vdash \lambda x.M : \rho \Rightarrow \exists \sigma, \tau\ [\Gamma, x{:}\sigma \vdash M : \tau\ \&\ \rho \equiv (\sigma{\rightarrow}\tau)]$.

Proof. By induction on the length of derivation. ■

Proposition 3.1.9 (Typability of subterms in $\lambda{\rightarrow}$-Curry). *Let M' be a subterm of M. Then $\Gamma \vdash M : \sigma \Rightarrow \Gamma' \vdash M' : \sigma'$ for some Γ' and σ'. The moral is: if M has a type, i.e. $\Gamma \vdash M : \sigma$ for some Γ and σ, then every subterm has a type as well.*

Proof. By induction on the generation of M. ■

Proposition 3.1.10 (Substitution lemma for $\lambda{\rightarrow}$-Curry).

1. $\Gamma \vdash M : \sigma \Rightarrow \Gamma[\alpha := \tau] \vdash M : \sigma[\alpha := \tau]$.
2. *Suppose* $\Gamma, x{:}\sigma \vdash M : \tau$ *and* $\Gamma \vdash N : \sigma$. *Then* $\Gamma \vdash M[x := N] : \tau$.

Proof. 1. By induction on the derivation of $M : \sigma$.

2. By induction on the generation of $\Gamma, x{:}\sigma \vdash M : \tau$.

■

The following result states that the set of $M \in \Lambda$ having a certain type in $\lambda{\rightarrow}$ is closed under reduction.

Proposition 3.1.11 (Subject reduction theorem for $\lambda\!\rightarrow$-Curry). *Suppose $M \twoheadrightarrow_\beta M'$. Then*

$$\Gamma \vdash M : \sigma \;\Rightarrow\; \Gamma \vdash M' : \sigma.$$

Proof. Induction on the generation of $\twoheadrightarrow_\beta$ using Propositions 3.1.8 and 3.1.10. We treat the prime case, namely that $M \equiv (\lambda x.P)Q$ and $M' \equiv P[x := Q]$. Well, if

$$\Gamma \vdash (\lambda x.P)Q : \sigma,$$

then it follows by the generation lemma 3.1.8 that for some τ one has

$$\Gamma \vdash (\lambda x.P) : (\tau\!\rightarrow\!\sigma) \text{ and } \Gamma \vdash Q : \tau.$$

Hence once more by Proposition 3.1.8 that

$$\Gamma, x{:}\tau \vdash P : \sigma \text{ and } \Gamma \vdash Q : \tau$$

and therefore by the substitution lemma 3.1.10

$$\Gamma \vdash P[x := Q] : \sigma.$$

■

Terms having a type are not closed under expansion. For example

$$\vdash \mathsf{I} : (\sigma\!\rightarrow\!\sigma), \text{ but } \nvdash \mathsf{KI}(\lambda x.xx) : (\sigma\!\rightarrow\!\sigma).$$

See Exercise 3.1.13. One even has the following stronger failure of subject expansion, as is observed in [van Bakel, 1991].

Observation 3.1.12. There are $M, M' \in \Lambda$ and $\sigma, \sigma' \in \mathbb{T}$ such that $M' \twoheadrightarrow_\beta M$ and

$$\vdash M : \sigma,$$
$$\vdash M' : \sigma',$$

but

$$\nvdash M' : \sigma.$$

Proof. Take $M \equiv \lambda xy.y$, $M' \equiv \mathsf{SK}$, $\sigma \equiv \alpha\!\rightarrow\!(\beta\!\rightarrow\!\beta)$ and $\sigma' \equiv (\beta\!\rightarrow\!\alpha)\!\rightarrow\!(\beta\!\rightarrow\!\beta)$; do Exercise 3.1.13. ■

Exercises 3.1.13.

- Let $\mathsf{I} = \lambda x.x, \mathsf{K} = \lambda xy.x$ and $\mathsf{S} = \lambda xyz.xz(yx)$.
  - ∗ Show that for all $\sigma, \tau, \rho \in \mathbb{T}$ one has
    $\vdash \mathsf{S} : (\sigma\!\rightarrow\!\tau\!\rightarrow\!\rho)\!\rightarrow\!(\sigma\!\rightarrow\!\tau)\!\rightarrow\!(\sigma\!\rightarrow\!\rho)$
    $\vdash \mathsf{SK} : (\sigma\!\rightarrow\!\tau)\!\rightarrow\!\sigma\!\rightarrow\!\sigma;$
    $\vdash \mathsf{KI} : (\tau\!\rightarrow\!\sigma\!\rightarrow\!\sigma)$
  - ∗ Show that $\nvdash \mathsf{SK} : (\tau\!\rightarrow\!\sigma\!\rightarrow\!\sigma)$.
  - ∗ Show that $\lambda x.xx$ and $\mathsf{KI}(\lambda x.xx)$ have no type in $\lambda\!\rightarrow$.

3.2 The system $\lambda\!\to$-Church

Before we give the formal definition, let us explain right away what is the difference between the Church and Curry versions of the system $\lambda\!\to$. One has

$$\vdash_{\text{Curry}} (\lambda x.x) : (\sigma\!\to\!\sigma),$$

but on the other hand

$$\vdash_{\text{Church}} (\lambda x{:}\sigma.x) : (\sigma\!\to\!\sigma).$$

That is, the term $\lambda x.x$ is annotated in the Church system by '$:\sigma$'. The intuitive meaning is that $\lambda x{:}\sigma.x$ takes the argument x from the type (set) σ. This explicit mention of types in a term makes it possible to decide whether a term has a certain type. For some Curry systems this question is undecidable.

Definition 3.2.1. Let $\mathbb{T}$ be some set of types. The set of $\mathbb{T}$-*annotated* λ-*terms* (also called *pseudoterms*), notation $\Lambda_{\mathbb{T}}$, is defined as follows:

$$\Lambda_{\mathbb{T}} = V \mid \Lambda_{\mathbb{T}}\Lambda_{\mathbb{T}} \mid \lambda x{:}\mathbb{T}\Lambda_{\mathbb{T}}$$

Here V denotes the set of term variables.

The same syntactic conventions for $\Lambda_{\mathbb{T}}$ are used as for Λ. For example

$$\lambda x_1{:}\sigma_1 \cdots x_n{:}\sigma_n.M \equiv (\lambda x_1{:}\sigma_1(\lambda x_2{:}\sigma_2 \ldots (\lambda x_n{:}\sigma_n(M)))).$$

This term may also be abbreviated as

$$\lambda\vec{x}{:}\vec{\sigma}.M.$$

Several systems of typed lambda calculi *à la* Church consist of a choice of the set of types $\mathbb{T}$ and of an assignment of types $\sigma \in \mathbb{T}$ to terms $M \in \Lambda_{\mathbb{T}}$. However, as will be seen in Section 5, this is not the case in all systems *à la* Church. In systems with so-called (term) dependent types the sets of terms and types are defined simultaneously. Anyway, for $\lambda\!\to$-Church the separate definition of the types and terms is possible and one has as choice of types the same set $\mathbb{T} = \text{Type}\,(\lambda\!\to)$ as for $\lambda\!\to$-Curry.

Definition 3.2.2. The typed lambda calculus $\lambda\!\to$-Church is defined as follows:

1. The set of types $\mathbb{T} = \text{Type}\,(\lambda\!\to)$ is defined by

$$\mathbb{T} = \mathbb{V} \mid \mathbb{T}\!\to\!\mathbb{T}.$$

2. A *statement* is of the form $M : \sigma$ with $M \in \Lambda_{\mathbb{T}}$ and $\sigma \in \mathbb{T}$.

3. A *basis* is again a set of statements with only dinstinct variables as subjects.

Definition 3.2.3. A statement $M : \sigma$ is *derivable* from the basis Γ, notation $\Gamma \vdash M : \sigma$, if $M : \sigma$ can be produced using the following rules.

$\lambda{\rightarrow}$-Church

(axiom)	$\Gamma \vdash x : \sigma,$	if $(x{:}\sigma) \in \Gamma$;
($\rightarrow$-elimination)	$\dfrac{\Gamma \vdash M : (\sigma{\rightarrow}\tau) \quad \Gamma \vdash N : \sigma}{\Gamma \vdash (MN) : \tau}\,;$	
($\rightarrow$-introduction)	$\dfrac{\Gamma, x{:}\sigma \vdash M : \tau}{\Gamma \vdash (\lambda x{:}\sigma.M) : (\sigma{\rightarrow}\tau)}\,.$	

As before, derivations can be given in several styles. We will not need to be explicit about this.

Definition 3.2.4. The set of *(legal) $\lambda{\rightarrow}$-terms*, notation $\Lambda(\lambda{\rightarrow})$, is defined by

$$\Lambda(\lambda{\rightarrow}) = \{M \in \Lambda_{\mathbb{T}} \mid \exists \Gamma, \sigma \;\; \Gamma \vdash M : \sigma\}.$$

In order to refer specifically to $\lambda{\rightarrow}$-Church, one uses the notation

$$\Gamma \vdash_{\lambda\rightarrow\text{Church}} M : \sigma.$$

If there is little danger of ambiguity one uses also $\vdash_{\lambda\rightarrow}, \vdash_{\text{Church}}$ or just $\vdash$.

Examples 3.2.5. In $\lambda{\rightarrow}$-Church one has

1. $\vdash (\lambda x{:}\sigma.x) : (\sigma{\rightarrow}\sigma)$;

2. $\vdash (\lambda x{:}\sigma \lambda y{:}\tau.x) : (\sigma{\rightarrow}\tau{\rightarrow}\sigma)$;

3. $x{:}\sigma \vdash (\lambda y{:}\tau.x) : (\tau{\rightarrow}\sigma)$.

As for the type-free theory one can define reduction and conversion on the set of pseudoterms $\Lambda_{\mathbb{T}}$.

Definition 3.2.6. On $\Lambda_{\mathbb{T}}$ the binary relations *one-step β-reduction*, *many-step β-reduction* and *β-convertibility*, notations $\rightarrow_\beta$, $\twoheadrightarrow_\beta$ and $=_\beta$ respectively, are generated by the contraction rule

$$(\lambda x{:}\sigma.M)N \;\rightarrow\; M[x := N] \qquad (\beta)$$

For example one has

$$(\lambda x{:}\sigma.x)(\lambda y{:}\tau.yy) \rightarrow_\beta \lambda y{:}\tau.yy.$$

Without a proof we mention that the Church–Rosser theorem 2.3.7 for $\twoheadrightarrow_\beta$ also holds on $\Lambda_{\mathbb{T}}$. The proof is similar to that for Λ; see Barendregt and Dekkers (to appear) for the details. The following results for $\lambda\!\rightarrow$-Church are essentially the same as Propositions 3.1.7 - 3.1.11 for $\lambda\!\rightarrow$-Curry. Therefore proofs are omitted.

Proposition 3.2.7 (Basis lemma for $\lambda\!\rightarrow$-Church). *Let Γ be a basis.*

1. *If $\Gamma' \supseteq \Gamma$ is another basis, then $\Gamma \vdash M : \sigma \Rightarrow \Gamma' \vdash M : \sigma$.*
2. *$\Gamma \vdash M : \sigma \Rightarrow FV(M) \subseteq$ dom (Γ).*
3. *$\Gamma \vdash M : \sigma \Rightarrow \Gamma \restriction FV(M) \vdash M : \sigma$.*

Proposition 3.2.8 (Generation lemma for $\lambda\!\rightarrow$-Church).

1. *$\Gamma \vdash x : \sigma \;\Rightarrow\; (x{:}\sigma) \in \Gamma$.*
2. *$\Gamma \vdash MN : \tau \;\Rightarrow\; \exists\sigma\, [\Gamma \vdash M : (\sigma\rightarrow\tau)$ and $\Gamma \vdash N : \sigma]$*
3. *$\Gamma \vdash (\lambda x{:}\sigma.M) : \rho \Rightarrow \exists\tau\, [\rho = (\sigma\rightarrow\tau)$ and $\Gamma, x{:}\sigma \vdash M : \tau]$.*

Proposition 3.2.9 (Typability of subterms in $\lambda\!\rightarrow$-Church). *If M has a type, then every subterm of M has a type as well.*

Proposition 3.2.10 (Substitution lemma for $\lambda\!\rightarrow$-Church).

1. *$\Gamma \vdash M : \sigma \Rightarrow \Gamma[\alpha := \tau] \vdash M[\alpha := \tau] : \sigma[\alpha := \tau]$.*
2. *Suppose $\Gamma, x{:}\sigma \vdash M : \tau$ and $\Gamma \vdash N : \sigma$. Then $\Gamma \vdash M[x := N] : \tau$.*

Proposition 3.2.11 (Subject reduction theorem for $\lambda\!\rightarrow$-Church). *Let $M \twoheadrightarrow_\beta M'$. Then*

$$\Gamma \vdash M : \sigma \Rightarrow \Gamma \vdash M' : \sigma.$$

This proposition implies that the set of legal expressions is closed under reduction. It is not closed under expansion or conversion. Take for example

$\mathsf{I} =_\beta \mathsf{K}\mathsf{I}\Omega$ annotated with the appropriate types; it follows from proposition 3.2.9 that $\mathsf{K}\mathsf{I}\Omega$ has no type. On the other hand convertible *legal* terms have the same type with respect to a given basis.

Proposition 3.2.12 (Uniqueness of types lemma for $\lambda\rightarrow$-Church).

1. *Suppose* $\Gamma \vdash M : \sigma$ *and* $\Gamma \vdash M : \sigma'$. *Then* $\sigma \equiv \sigma'$.
2. *Suppose* $\Gamma \vdash M : \sigma$, $\Gamma \vdash M' : \sigma'$ *and* $M =_\beta M'$. *Then* $\sigma \equiv \sigma'$.

Proof. 1. Induction on the structure of M.

2. By the Church–Rosser theorem for $\Lambda_{\mathbb{T}}$, the subject reduction theorem 3.2.11 and (1).

■

As observed in 3.1.12 this proposition does not hold for $\lambda\rightarrow$-Curry.

Original version of $\lambda\rightarrow$

Church defined his $\lambda\rightarrow$ in a slightly different, but essentially equivalent, way. He defined the set of (legal) terms directly and not as a subset of the pseudoterms $\Lambda_{\mathbb{T}}$. Each variable carries its own type. The set of terms of type σ, notation $\Lambda_\sigma(\lambda\rightarrow)$ or simply Λ_σ, is defined inductively as follows. Let V be the set of variables.

$$\begin{array}{lcl} \sigma \in \mathbb{T},\ x \in V & \Rightarrow & x^\sigma \in \Lambda_\sigma; \\ M \in \Lambda_{\sigma\rightarrow\tau}, N \in \Lambda_\sigma & \Rightarrow & (MN) \in \Lambda_\tau; \\ M \in \Lambda_\tau & \Rightarrow & (\lambda x^\sigma.M) \in \Lambda_{\sigma\rightarrow\tau}. \end{array}$$

Then Church's definition of legal terms was

$$\Lambda(\lambda\rightarrow) = \cup_{\sigma\in\mathbb{T}}\Lambda_\sigma(\lambda\rightarrow).$$

The following example shows that our version is equivalent to the original one.

Example 3.2.13. The statement in $\lambda\rightarrow$-Church

$$x{:}\sigma \vdash (\lambda y{:}\tau.x) : (\tau\rightarrow\sigma)$$

becomes in the original system of Church

$$(\lambda y^\tau.x^\sigma) \in \Lambda_{\tau\rightarrow\sigma}.$$

It turns out that this original notation is not convenient for more complicated typed lambda calculi. The problem arises if types themselves become subject to reduction. Then one would expect that

$$\begin{aligned}\sigma \twoheadrightarrow_\beta \tau \quad &\Rightarrow \quad x^\sigma \twoheadrightarrow_\beta x^\tau \\ &\Rightarrow \quad \lambda x^\sigma.x^\sigma \twoheadrightarrow_\beta \lambda x^\sigma.x^\tau.\end{aligned}$$

However, in the last term it is not clear how to interpret the binding effect of λx^σ (is x^τ bound by it?). Therefore we will use the notation of definition 3.2.1.

Relating the Curry and Church systems

For typed lambda calculi that can be described both *à la* Curry and *à la* Church, there is often a simple relation between the two versions. This will be explained for $\lambda\!\rightarrow$.

Definition 3.2.14. There is a 'forgetful' map $|\cdot| : \Lambda_{\mathbb{T}} \rightarrow \Lambda$ defined as follows:

$$\begin{aligned}|x| &\equiv x;\\ |MN| &\equiv |M||N|;\\ |\lambda x{:}\sigma.M| &\equiv \lambda x.|M|.\end{aligned}$$

The map $|\cdot|$ just erases all type ornamentations of a term in $\Lambda_{\mathbb{T}}$. The following result states that ornamented legal terms in the Church version 'project' to legal terms in the Curry version of $\lambda\!\rightarrow$; conversely, legal terms in $\lambda\!\rightarrow$-Curry can be 'lifted' to legal terms in $\lambda\!\rightarrow$-Church.

Proposition 3.2.15.

1. *Let $M \in \Lambda_{\mathbb{T}}$. Then*

$$\Gamma \vdash_{\text{Church}} M : \sigma \quad \Rightarrow \quad \Gamma \vdash_{\text{Curry}} |M| : \sigma.$$

2. *Let $M \in \Lambda$. Then*

$$\Gamma \vdash_{\text{Curry}} M : \sigma \quad \Rightarrow \quad \exists M' \in \Lambda_{\mathbb{T}}\, [\Gamma \vdash_{\text{Church}} M' : \sigma \;\&\; |M'| \equiv M].$$

Proof. (1), (2). By induction on the given derivation. ∎

Corollary 3.2.16. *In particular, for a type $\sigma \in \mathbb{T}$ one has*

$$\sigma \text{ is inhabited in } \lambda\!\rightarrow\text{-Curry} \quad \Leftrightarrow \quad \sigma \text{ inhabited in } \lambda\!\rightarrow\text{-Church}.$$

Proof. Immediate. ∎

4 Typing *à la* Curry

4.1 The systems

In this subsection the main systems for assigning types to type-free lambda terms will be introduced. The systems to be discussed are $\lambda{\to}$, $\lambda 2$, $\lambda\mu$ and $\lambda\cap$. Moreover, there are also two extra derivation rules EQ and $\mathcal{A}$ that can be added to each of these systems. In Figure 1 the systems are represented in a diagram.

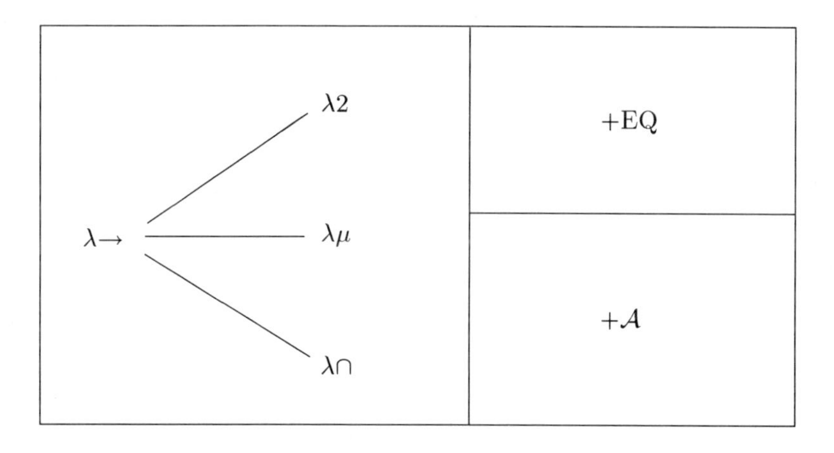

Fig. 1. The sytems *à la* Curry

The systems $\lambda 2$, $\lambda\mu$ and $\lambda\cap$ are all extensions of $\lambda{\to}$-Curry. Several stronger systems can be defined by forming combinations like $\lambda 2\mu$ or $\lambda\mu\cap$. However, such systems will not be studied in this chapter.

Now we will first describe the rules EQ and $\mathcal{A}$ and then the systems $\lambda 2$, $\lambda\mu$ and $\lambda\cap$.

Definition 4.1.1.

1. The *equality rule*, notation EQ is the rule

$$\frac{M : \sigma \qquad M =_\beta N}{N : \sigma}$$

2. The *approximation rule*, notation $\mathcal{A}$, consists of the following two rules. These rules are defined for $\lambda\bot$ introduced in Definition 2.3.29. The constant $\bot$ plays a special role in the rule $\mathcal{A}$.

Rule $\mathcal{A}$

$$\frac{\Gamma \vdash P : \sigma \text{ for all } P \in \mathcal{A}(M)}{\Gamma \vdash M : \sigma};$$

$$\frac{}{\Gamma \vdash \bot : \sigma}.$$

See 2.3.30 for the definition of $\mathcal{A}(M)$. Note that in these rules the requirements $M =_\beta N$ and $P \in \mathcal{A}(M)$ are not statements, but are, so to speak, side conditions. The last rule states that $\bot$ has any type.

Notation 4.1.2.

1. $\lambda -^+$ is $\lambda -$ extended by rule EQ.
2. $\lambda - \mathcal{A}$ is $\lambda -$ extended by rule $\mathcal{A}$.

So for example $\lambda 2^+ = \lambda 2 + \text{EQ}$ and $\lambda\mu\mathcal{A} = \lambda\mu + \mathcal{A}$.

Examples 4.1.3.

1. One has
$$\vdash_{\lambda\to^+} (\lambda pq.(\lambda r.p)(qp)) : (\sigma\to\tau\to\sigma)$$
since $\lambda pq.(\lambda r.p)(qp) = \lambda pq.p$. Note, however, that this statement is in general not provable in $\lambda\to$ itself. The term has in $\lambda\to$ only types of the form $\sigma\to(\sigma\to\tau)\to\sigma$, as follows form the generation lemma.

2. Let Y be the fixed point operator $\lambda f.(\lambda x.f(xx))(\lambda x.f(xx))$. Then
$$\vdash_{\lambda\to\mathcal{A}} \mathsf{Y} : ((\sigma\to\sigma)\to\sigma),$$
Indeed, the approximants of Y are
$$\{\bot, \lambda f.f\bot, \ldots, \lambda f.f^n\bot, \ldots\}$$
and these all have type $((\sigma\to\sigma)\to\sigma)$. Again, this statement is not derivable in $\lambda\to$ itself. (In $\lambda\to$ all typable terms have a normal form as will be proved in Section 4.2)

Now it will be shown that the rule EQ follows from the rule $\mathcal{A}$. So in general one has $\lambda-\mathcal{A}^+ = \lambda-\mathcal{A}$.

Proposition 4.1.4. *In all systems of type assignment λ–$\mathcal{A}$ one has the following.*

1. $\Gamma \vdash M : \sigma$ *and* $P \in \mathcal{A}(M) \Rightarrow \Gamma \vdash P : \sigma$.

2. *Let* $BT(M) = BT(M')$. *Then*

$$\Gamma \vdash M : \sigma \;\Rightarrow\; \Gamma \vdash M' : \sigma$$

3. *Let* $M =_\beta M'$. *Then*

$$\Gamma \vdash M : \sigma \;\Rightarrow\; \Gamma \vdash M' : \sigma.$$

Proof. 1. If P is an approximation of M, then P results from $BT(M)$ by replacing some subtrees by $\bot$ and writing the result as a λ-term. Now $\bot$ may assume arbitrary types, by one of the rules $\mathcal{A}$. Therefore P has the same type as M. [Example. Let $M \equiv \mathsf{Y}$, the fixedpoint combinator and let $P \equiv \lambda f.f(f\bot)$ be an approximant. We have $\vdash \mathsf{Y} : (\sigma{\rightarrow}\sigma){\rightarrow}\sigma$. By choosing σ as type for $\bot$, one obtains $\vdash P : (\sigma{\rightarrow}\sigma){\rightarrow}\sigma$.]

2. Suppose $BT(M) = BT(M')$; then $\mathcal{A}(M) = \mathcal{A}(M')$. Hence

$$\begin{aligned}\Gamma \vdash M : \sigma &\Rightarrow \forall P \in \mathcal{A}(M) = \mathcal{A}(M')\ \Gamma \vdash P : \sigma, \text{ by } (1),\\ &\Rightarrow \Gamma \vdash M' : \sigma, \text{ by rule } \mathcal{A}\end{aligned}$$

3. If $M =_\beta M'$, then $BT(M) = BT(M')$, by proposition 2.3.28. Hence the result follows from (2).

∎

The system $\lambda 2$

The system $\lambda 2$ was introduced independently in [Girard, 1972] and [Reynolds, 1974]. In these papers the system was introduced in the Church paradigm. Girard's motivation to introduce $\lambda 2$ was based on proof theory. He extended the dialectica translation of Gödel, see [Troelstra, 1973], to analysis, thereby relating provability in second-order arithmetic to expressibility in $\lambda 2$. Reynolds' motivation to introduce $\lambda 2$ came from programming. He wanted to capture the notion of explicit polymophism.

Other names for $\lambda 2$ are

- polymorphic typed lambda calculus
- second-order typed lambda calculus
- second-order polymorphic typed lambda calculus
- system F.

Usually these names refer to $\lambda 2$-Church. In this section we will introduce the Curry version of $\lambda 2$, leaving the Church version to Section 5.1.

The idea of polymorphism is that in $\lambda\!\rightarrow$

$$(\lambda x.x) : (\alpha\!\rightarrow\!\alpha)$$

for arbitrary α. So one stipulates in $\lambda 2$

$$(\lambda x.x) : (\forall\alpha.(\alpha\!\rightarrow\!\alpha))$$

to indicate that $\lambda x.x$ has all types $\sigma\!\rightarrow\!\sigma$.

As will be seen later, the mechanism is rather powerful.

Definition 4.1.5. The set of types of $\lambda 2$, notation $\mathbb{T} = \text{Type}(\lambda 2)$, is defined by the following abstract grammar:

$$\mathbb{T} = \mathbb{V} \mid \mathbb{T}\!\rightarrow\!\mathbb{T} \mid \forall\mathbb{V}\mathbb{T}$$

Notation 4.1.6.

1. $\forall\alpha_1 \cdots \alpha_n.\sigma$ stands for $(\forall\alpha_1(\forall\alpha_2 \ldots (\forall\alpha_n(\sigma))\ldots))$.
2. $\forall$ binds more strongly than $\rightarrow$.

So $\forall\alpha\sigma\!\rightarrow\!\tau \equiv (\forall\alpha\sigma)\!\rightarrow\!\tau$; but $\forall\alpha.\sigma\!\rightarrow\!\tau \equiv \forall\alpha(\sigma\!\rightarrow\!\tau)$.

Definition 4.1.7. Type assignment in $\lambda 2$-Curry is defined by the following natural deduction system:

$\lambda 2$

(start rule)	$\dfrac{(x{:}\sigma) \in \Gamma}{\Gamma \vdash x : \sigma}$;
($\to$-elimination)	$\dfrac{\Gamma \vdash M : (\sigma{\to}\tau) \qquad \Gamma \vdash N : \sigma}{\Gamma \vdash (MN) : \tau}$;
($\to$-introduction)	$\dfrac{\Gamma, x : \sigma \vdash M : \tau}{\Gamma \vdash (\lambda x.M) : (\sigma{\to}\tau)}$;
($\forall$-elimination)	$\dfrac{\Gamma \vdash M : (\forall\alpha.\sigma)}{\Gamma \vdash M : (\sigma[\alpha := \tau])}$;
($\forall$-introduction)	$\dfrac{\Gamma \vdash M : \sigma}{\Gamma \vdash M : (\forall\alpha.\sigma)}, \ \alpha \notin FV(\Gamma)$.

Examples 4.1.8. In $\lambda 2$-Curry one has the following.

$$\begin{array}{lll}
1. & \vdash (\lambda x.x) & : & (\forall\alpha.\alpha{\to}\alpha); \\
2. & \vdash (\lambda xy.y) & : & (\forall\alpha\beta.\alpha{\to}\beta{\to}\beta); \\
3. & \vdash (\lambda fx.f^n x) & : & (\forall\alpha.(\alpha{\to}\alpha){\to}\alpha{\to}\alpha); \\
4. & \vdash (\lambda x.xx) & : & (\forall\beta.\forall\alpha\alpha{\to}\beta); \\
5. & \vdash (\lambda x.xx) & : & (\forall\beta.\forall\alpha\alpha{\to}(\beta{\to}\beta)); \\
6. & \vdash (\lambda x.xx) & : & (\forall\alpha\alpha){\to}(\forall\alpha\alpha).
\end{array}$$

Example (3) shows that the Church numerals $\mathbf{c}_n \equiv \lambda fx.f^n x$ have type $\forall\alpha.(\alpha{\to}\alpha){\to}\alpha{\to}\alpha$. This type is sometimes called 'polynat'. One reason for the strength of $\lambda 2$ is that the Church numerals may not only be used as iterators for functions of a fixed type $\alpha{\to}\alpha$, but also for iteration on $\sigma{\to}\sigma$ for arbitrary σ. This makes it possible to represent in $\lambda 2$ the term R for primitive recursion of Gödel's T and many other computable functions, see subsection 5.4.

In subsection 4.3 it will be shown that only strongly normalizing terms have a type in $\lambda 2$.

The system $\lambda\mu$

The system $\lambda\mu$ is that of *recursive types.* These come together with an equivalence relation $\approx$ on them. The type assignment rules are such that if $M : \sigma$ and $\sigma \approx \sigma'$, then $M : \sigma'$. A typical example of a recursive type is a σ_0 such that

$$\sigma_0 \approx \sigma_0 \to \sigma_0. \tag{1}$$

This σ_0 can be used to type arbitrary elements $M \in \Lambda$. For example

$$\begin{array}{l} x{:}\sigma_0 \vdash x : \sigma_0 \to \sigma_0 \\ x{:}\sigma_0 \vdash xx : \sigma_0 \\ \vdash \lambda x.xx : \sigma_0 \to \sigma_0 \\ \vdash \lambda x.xx : \sigma_0 \\ \vdash (\lambda x.xx)(\lambda x.xx) : \sigma_0 \end{array}$$

A proof in natural deduction notation of the last statement is the following:

$$\dfrac{\dfrac{\dfrac{\dfrac{[x : \sigma_0]^1}{x : \sigma_0 \to \sigma_0} \qquad x : \sigma_0}{(xx) : \sigma_0}}{(\lambda x.xx) : \sigma_0 \to \sigma_0}\,1}{(\lambda x.xx) : \sigma_0 \to \sigma_0 \qquad (\lambda x.xx) : \sigma_0}$$

$$(\lambda x.xx)(\lambda x.xx) : \sigma_0$$

In fact, equation (1) is like a recursive domain equation $D \cong [D \to D]$ that enables us to interpret elements of Λ. In order to construct a type σ_0 satisfying (1), there is an operator μ such that putting $\sigma_0 \equiv \mu\alpha.\alpha \to \alpha$ implies (1).

Definition 4.1.9.

1. The set of types of $\lambda\mu$, notation $\mathbb{T} = \text{Type}(\lambda\mu)$, is defined by the following abstract grammar.

$$\mathbb{T} = \mathbb{V} \mid \mathbb{T} \to \mathbb{T} \mid \mu\mathbb{V}.\mathbb{T}$$

2. Let $\sigma \in T$. The *tree of* σ, notation $T(\sigma)$, is defined as follows:

$$\begin{array}{llll} T(\alpha) & = & \alpha, & \text{if } \alpha \text{ a is type variable;} \\ T(\sigma \to \tau) & = & \begin{array}{c} \to \\ \swarrow \quad \searrow \\ T(\sigma) \qquad T(\tau) \end{array} & ; \\ T(\mu\alpha.\sigma) & = & \bot, & \text{if } \sigma \equiv \mu\beta_1 \ldots \mu\beta_n.\alpha \\ & & & \text{for some } n \geq 0; \\ & = & T(\sigma[\alpha := \mu\alpha.\sigma]), & \text{else.} \end{array}$$

3. For $\sigma, \tau \in \mathbb{T}$ one defines

$$\sigma \approx \tau \quad \Leftrightarrow \quad T(\sigma) = T(\tau).$$

Examples 4.1.10.

1. If $\tau \equiv \mu\alpha.\alpha \rightarrow \gamma$, then

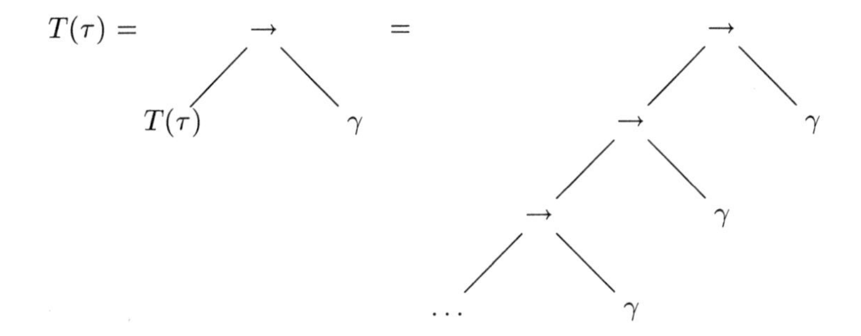

2. If $\sigma \equiv (\mu\alpha.\alpha \rightarrow \gamma) \rightarrow \mu\delta\mu\beta.\beta$, then

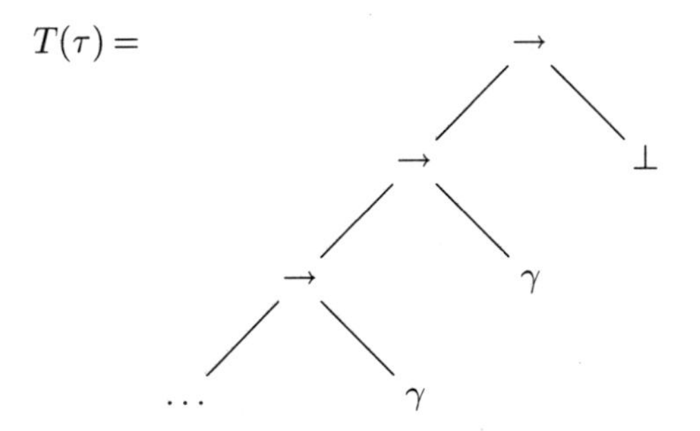

3. $(\mu\alpha.\alpha \rightarrow \gamma) \approx (\mu\alpha(\alpha \rightarrow \gamma) \rightarrow \gamma)$.

4. $\mu\alpha.\sigma \approx \sigma[\alpha := \mu\alpha.\sigma]$ for all σ, even if $\sigma \equiv \mu\vec{\beta}.\alpha$.

Definition 4.1.11. The type assignment system $\lambda\mu$ is defined by the natural deduction system shown in the following figure.

$\lambda\mu$

(start rule)	$\dfrac{(x{:}\sigma) \in \Gamma}{\Gamma \vdash x : \sigma}\,;$
($\to$-elimination)	$\dfrac{\Gamma \vdash M : (\sigma{\to}\tau) \quad \Gamma \vdash N : \sigma}{\Gamma \vdash (MN) : \tau}\,;$
($\to$-introduction)	$\dfrac{\Gamma, x{:}\sigma \vdash M : \tau}{\Gamma \vdash (\lambda x.M) : (\sigma{\to}\tau)}\,;$
($\approx$-rule)	$\dfrac{\Gamma \vdash M : \sigma \quad \sigma \approx \tau}{\Gamma \vdash M : \tau}\,.$

The following result is taken from [Coppo, 1985].

Proposition 4.1.12.
Let σ be an arbitrary type of $\lambda\mu$. Then one can derive in $\lambda\mu$

1. $\vdash \mathsf{Y} : (\sigma{\to}\sigma){\to}\sigma$;
2. $\vdash \Omega : \sigma$.

Proof. 1. Let $\tau \equiv \mu\alpha.\alpha{\to}\sigma$. Then $\tau \approx \tau{\to}\sigma$.
Then the following is a derivation for

$$\mathsf{Y} \equiv \lambda f.(\lambda x.f(xx))(\lambda x.f(xx)) : (\sigma{\to}\sigma){\to}\sigma.$$

$$\dfrac{\dfrac{\dfrac{\dfrac{\cancel{f : \sigma{\to}\sigma}^{\,2} \qquad \dfrac{\dfrac{\cancel{x : \tau}^{\,1}}{x : \tau{\to}\sigma \qquad x : \tau}}{xx : \sigma}}{f(xx) : \sigma}\,1}{\dfrac{\lambda x.f(xx) : \tau{\to}\sigma}{\lambda x.f(xx) : \tau{\to}\sigma \quad \lambda x.f(xx) : \tau}}}{(\lambda x.f(xx))(\lambda x.f(xx)) : \sigma}}{\mathsf{Y} \equiv \lambda f.(\lambda x.f(xx))(\lambda x.f(xx)) : (\sigma{\to}\sigma){\to}\sigma}\,2$$

2. Note that $\mathsf{YI} \twoheadrightarrow_\beta \Omega$ and prove and use the subject reduction theorem for $\lambda\mu$; or show $\vdash \Omega : \sigma$ directly.

■

The System $\lambda\cap$

The system $\lambda\cap$ of *intersection types* is sometimes called the *Torino system*, since the initial work on this system was done in that city, for example by Coppo, Dezani and Venneri [Coppo *et al.*, 1981], Barendregt, Coppo and Dezani [Barendregt *et al.*, 1983], Coppo, Dezani, Honsell and Longo [Coppo *et al.*, 1984], Dezani and Margaria [Dezani-Ciancaglini and Margaria, 1987] and Coppo, Dezani and Zacchi [Coppo *et al.*, 1987]. See also [Hindley, 1983].

The system makes it possible to state that a variable x has two types σ and τ at the same time. This kind of polymorphism is to be contrasted to that which is present in $\lambda 2$. In that system the polymorphism is parametrized. For example the type assignment

$$(\lambda x.x) : (\forall\alpha.\alpha{\rightarrow}\alpha)$$

states that $\lambda x.x$ has type $\alpha{\rightarrow}\alpha$ *uniformly* in α. The assignment $x : \sigma\cap\tau$ states only that x has both type σ and type τ.

Definition 4.1.13.

1. The set of types of $\lambda\cap$, notation $\mathbb{T} = \text{Type}(\lambda\cap)$, is defined as follows:

$$\mathbb{T} = \mathbb{V} \mid \mathbb{T}{\rightarrow}\mathbb{T} \mid \mathbb{T}\cap\mathbb{T}$$

2. One of the type variables will be selected as a constant and is notated as ω.

In order to define the rules of type assignment, it is necessary to introduce a preorder on $\mathbb{T}$.

Definition 4.1.14.

1. The relation $\leq$ is defined on $\mathbb{T}$ by the following axioms and rules:
   $\sigma \leq \sigma$;
   $\sigma \leq \tau, \tau \leq \rho \;\Rightarrow\; \sigma \leq \rho$
   $\sigma \leq \omega$;
   $\omega \leq \omega{\rightarrow}\omega$;
   $(\sigma{\rightarrow}\rho)\cap(\sigma{\rightarrow}\tau) \leq (\sigma{\rightarrow}(\rho\cap\tau))$;
   $\sigma\cap\tau \leq \sigma, \sigma\cap\tau \leq \tau$;
   $\sigma \leq \tau, \sigma \leq \rho \;\Rightarrow\; \sigma \leq \tau\cap\rho$;
   $\sigma \leq \sigma', \tau \leq \tau' \;\Rightarrow\; \sigma'{\rightarrow}\tau \leq \sigma{\rightarrow}\tau'$.

2. $\sigma \sim \tau \;\Leftrightarrow\; \sigma \leq \tau \;\&\; \tau \leq \sigma$.

For example one has

$$\omega \sim (\omega {\to} \omega);$$

$$((\sigma{\to}\tau) \cap (\sigma'{\to}\tau)) \leq ((\sigma \cap \sigma'){\to}\tau).$$

Definition 4.1.15. The system of type assignment $\lambda\cap$ is defined by the following axioms and rules:

$\lambda\cap$

(start rule)	$\dfrac{(x{:}\sigma) \in \Gamma}{\Gamma \vdash x : \sigma};$
($\to$-elimination)	$\dfrac{\Gamma \vdash M : (\sigma{\to}\tau) \quad \Gamma \vdash N : \sigma}{\Gamma \vdash (MN) : \tau};$
($\to$-introduction)	$\dfrac{\Gamma, x{:}\sigma \vdash M : \tau}{\Gamma \vdash (\lambda x.M) : (\sigma{\to}\tau)};$
($\cap$-elimination)	$\dfrac{\Gamma \vdash M : (\sigma \cap \tau)}{\Gamma \vdash M : \sigma \quad \Gamma \vdash M : \tau};$
($\cap$-introduction)	$\dfrac{\Gamma \vdash M : \sigma \quad \Gamma \vdash M : \tau}{\Gamma \vdash M : (\sigma \cap \tau)};$
(ω-introduction)	$\dfrac{}{\Gamma \vdash M : \omega};$
($\leq$-rule)	$\dfrac{\Gamma \vdash M : \sigma \quad \sigma \leq \tau}{\Gamma \vdash M : \tau}.$

Examples 4.1.16. In $\lambda\cap$ one has

1. $\vdash \lambda x.xx : ((\sigma{\to}\tau) \cap \sigma){\to}\tau$
2. $\vdash \Omega : \omega$
3. $\vdash (\lambda pq.(\lambda r.p)(qp)) : (\sigma{\to}(\tau{\to}\sigma))$.

Proof. 1. The following derivation proves the statement:

$$\dfrac{\dfrac{\dfrac{\cancel{x:(\sigma{\to}\tau)\cap\sigma}^{1}}{x:\sigma{\to}\tau \quad x:\sigma}}{(xx):\tau}}{(\lambda x.xx):((\sigma{\to}\tau)\cap\sigma){\to}\tau}\,1$$

2. Obvious. In fact it can be shown that M has no head normal form iff only ω is a type for M, see [Barendregt *et al.*, 1983].

3.

$$\dfrac{\dfrac{\dfrac{\dfrac{\cancel{q{:}\tau}^{2} \quad \cancel{p{:}\sigma}^{3} \quad \cancel{r{:}\omega}^{1}}{(\lambda r.p):(\omega{\to}\sigma)}\,1 \qquad \dfrac{}{(qp):\omega}}{(\lambda r.p)(qp):\sigma}}{(\lambda q.(\lambda r.p)(qp)):(\tau{\to}\sigma)}\,2}{(\lambda pq.(\lambda r.p)(qp)):(\sigma{\to}(\tau{\to}\sigma))}\,3$$

∎

In [van Bakel, 1991] it is observed that assignment (3) in Example 4.1.16 is not possible in $\lambda{\to}$.

Also for $\lambda\cap$ there are some variants for the system. For example one can delete the rule (axiom) that assigns ω to any term. In [van Bakel, 1991] several of these variants are studied; see theorem 4.3.12.

Combining the systems à la Curry

The system $\lambda 2, \lambda\mu$ and $\lambda\cap$ are all extensions of $\lambda{\to}$. An extension $\lambda 2\mu\cap$ including all these systems and moreover cartesian products and direct sums is studied in [MacQueen *et al.*, 1984].

Basic Properties

The Curry systems $\lambda{\to}$, $\lambda 2$, $\lambda\mu$ and $\lambda\cap$ enjoy several properties. The most immediate ones, valid for all four systems, will be presented now. In subsection 4.2 it will be shown that subject reduction holds for all systems. Some other properties like strong normalization are valid for only some of these systems and will be presented in subsections 4.2, 4.3 and 4.4.

In the following $\vdash$ refers to one of the Curry systems $\lambda{\to}$, $\lambda 2$, $\lambda\mu$ and $\lambda\cap$. The following three properties are proved in the same way as is done in section 3.1 for $\lambda{\to}$.

Proposition 4.1.17 (Basis lemma for the Curry systems). *Let* Γ *be a basis.*

1. *If* $\Gamma' \supseteq \Gamma$ *is another basis, then* $\Gamma \vdash M : \sigma \;\Rightarrow\; \Gamma' \vdash M : \sigma$.
2. $\Gamma \vdash M : \sigma \;\Rightarrow\; FV(M) \subseteq \text{dom}(\Gamma)$.
3. $\Gamma \vdash M : \sigma \;\Rightarrow\; \Gamma \upharpoonright FV(M) \vdash M : \sigma$.

Proposition 4.1.18 (Subterm lemma for the Curry systems). *Let* M' *be a subterm of* M. *Then*

$$\Gamma \vdash M : \sigma \;\Rightarrow\; \Gamma' \vdash M' : \sigma' \text{ for some } \Gamma' \text{ and } \sigma'.$$

The moral is: If M *has a type, then every subterm has a type as well.*

Proposition 4.1.19 (Substitution lemma for the Curry systems).

1. $\Gamma \vdash M : \sigma \Rightarrow \Gamma[\alpha := \tau] \vdash M : \sigma[\alpha := \tau]$.
2. *Suppose* $\Gamma, x{:}\sigma \vdash M : \tau$ and $\Gamma \vdash N : \sigma$. *Then*

$$\Gamma \vdash M[x := N] : \tau.$$

Exercise 4.1.20. Show that for each of the systems $\lambda{\rightarrow}$, $\lambda 2$, $\lambda\mu$ and $\lambda\cap$ one has $\nvdash \mathsf{K} : (\alpha{\rightarrow}\alpha)$ in that system.

4.2 Subject reduction and conversion

In this subsection it will be shown that for the main systems of type assignment *à la* Curry, viz. $\lambda{\rightarrow}$, $\lambda 2$, $\lambda\mu$ and $\lambda\cap$ with or without the extra rules $\mathcal{A}$ and EQ, the subject reduction theorem holds. That is,

$$\Gamma \vdash M : \sigma \text{ and } M \twoheadrightarrow_\beta M' \quad\Rightarrow\quad \Gamma \vdash M' : \sigma.$$

Subject conversion or closure under the rule EQ is stronger and states that

$$\Gamma \vdash M : \sigma \text{ and } M =_\beta M' \quad\Rightarrow\quad \Gamma \vdash M' : \sigma.$$

This property holds only for the systems including $\lambda\cap$ or rule $\mathcal{A}$ (or trivially if rule EQ is included).

Subject reduction

We start with proving the subject reduction theorem for all the systems. For $\lambda\!\rightarrow$ this was already done in 3.1.11. In order to prove the result for $\lambda 2$ some definitions and lemmas are needed. This is because for example Proposition 3.1.8 is not valid for $\lambda 2$. So for the time being we focus on $\lambda 2$ and $\mathbb{T} = \text{Type}(\lambda 2)$.

Definition 4.2.1.

1. Write $\sigma > \tau$ if either

$$\tau \equiv \forall\alpha.\sigma, \text{ for some } \alpha,$$

   or

$$\sigma \equiv \forall\alpha.\sigma_1 \text{ and } \tau \equiv \sigma_1[\alpha := \pi] \text{ for some } \pi \in \mathbb{T}.$$

2. $\geq$ is the reflexive and transitive closure of $>$.

3. A map $o : \mathbb{T}\rightarrow\mathbb{T}$ is defined by

$$\begin{array}{lcll} \alpha^o & = & \alpha, & \text{if } \alpha \text{ is a type variable;} \\ (\sigma\rightarrow\tau)^o & = & \sigma\rightarrow\tau; & \\ (\forall\alpha.\sigma)^o & = & \sigma^o. & \end{array}$$

Note that there are exactly two deduction rules for $\lambda 2$ in which the subject does not change: the $\forall$ introduction and elimination rules. Several of these rules may be applied consecutively, obtaining

$$\frac{M : \sigma}{\begin{array}{c}\vdots\\ \vdots\end{array}}\qquad \frac{}{M : \tau}$$

The definition of $\geq$ is such that in this case $\sigma \geq \tau$. Also one has the following.

Lemma 4.2.2. *Let $\sigma \geq \tau$ and suppose no free type variable in σ occurs in Γ. Then*

$$\Gamma \vdash M : \sigma \;\Rightarrow\; \Gamma \vdash M : \tau$$

Proof. Suppose $\Gamma \vdash M : \sigma$ and $\sigma \geq \tau$. Then $\sigma \equiv \sigma_1 > \cdots > \sigma_n \equiv \tau$ for some $\sigma_1, \ldots, \sigma_n$. By possibly renaming some variables it may be assumed that for $1 \leq i < n$ one has

$$\sigma_{i+1} \equiv \forall\alpha.\sigma_i \;\;\Rightarrow\;\; \alpha \notin FV(\Gamma)$$

By definition of the relation $>$ and the rules of $\lambda 2$ it follows that for all $i < n$ one has $\Gamma \vdash M : \sigma_i \;\Rightarrow\; \Gamma \vdash M : \sigma_{i+1}$. Therefore $\Gamma \vdash M : \sigma_n \equiv \tau$. ■

Lemma 4.2.3 (Generation lemma for $\lambda 2$-Curry).

1. *$\Gamma \vdash x : \sigma \;\Rightarrow\; \exists \sigma' \geq \sigma\ (x{:}\sigma') \in \Gamma$.*
2. *$\Gamma \vdash (MN) : \tau \;\Rightarrow\; \exists\sigma\exists\tau' \geq \tau\ [\Gamma \vdash M : \sigma{\to}\tau'$ and $\Gamma \vdash N : \sigma]$.*
3. *$\Gamma \vdash (\lambda x.M) : \rho \;\Rightarrow\; \exists\sigma,\tau\ [\Gamma, x{:}\sigma \vdash M : \tau$ and $\sigma{\to}\tau \geq \rho]$.*

Proof. By induction on derivations. ■

Lemma 4.2.4.

1. *Given σ, τ there exists a τ' such that $(\sigma[\alpha := \tau])^o \equiv \sigma^o[\alpha := \tau']$.*
2. *$\sigma_1 \geq \sigma_2 \;\;\Rightarrow\;\; \exists\vec{\alpha}\,\exists\vec{\tau}\ \ \sigma_2^o \equiv \sigma_1^o[\vec{\alpha} := \vec{\tau}]$.*
3. *$(\sigma{\to}\rho) \geq (\sigma'{\to}\rho') \;\;\Rightarrow\;\; \exists\vec{\alpha}\,\exists\vec{\tau}\ \ \sigma'{\to}\rho' \equiv (\sigma{\to}\rho)[\vec{\alpha} := \vec{\tau}]$.*

Proof. 1. Induction on the structure of σ.

2. It suffices to show this for $\sigma_1 > \sigma_2$.
   Case 1. $\sigma_2 \equiv \forall\alpha.\sigma_1$. Then $\sigma_2^o \equiv \sigma_1^o$.
   Case 2. $\sigma_1 \equiv \forall\alpha.\rho$ and $\sigma_2 \equiv \rho[\alpha := \tau]$.
   Then by (1) one has $\sigma_2^o \equiv \rho^o[\alpha := \tau'] \equiv \sigma_1^o[\alpha := \tau']$.

3. By (2) we have

$$(\sigma'{\to}\rho') \equiv (\sigma'{\to}\rho')^o \equiv (\sigma{\to}\rho)^o[\vec{\alpha} := \vec{\tau}] \equiv (\sigma{\to}\rho)[\vec{\alpha} := \vec{\tau}].$$

■

Theorem 4.2.5 (Subject reduction theorem for $\lambda 2$-Curry). *Let $M \twoheadrightarrow_\beta M'$. Then for $\lambda 2$-Curry one has $\Gamma \vdash M : \sigma \;\Rightarrow\; \Gamma \vdash M' : \sigma$.*

Proof. Induction on the derivation of $M \twoheadrightarrow_\beta M'$. We will treat only the case that $M \equiv (\lambda x.P)Q$ and $M' \equiv P[x := Q]$. Now

$$\begin{array}{ll} & \Gamma \vdash ((\lambda x.P)Q) : \sigma \\ \Rightarrow & \exists\rho\exists\sigma' \geq \sigma\, [\Gamma \vdash (\lambda x.P) : (\rho{\to}\sigma') \& \ \Gamma \vdash Q : \rho] \\ \Rightarrow & \exists\rho'\exists\sigma'' \geq \sigma\, [\Gamma, x{:}\rho' \vdash P : \sigma'' \& \ \rho'{\to}\sigma'' \geq \rho{\to}\sigma' \& \ \Gamma \vdash Q : \rho] \end{array}$$

by Lemma 4.2.4 (3) it follows that

$$(\rho{\to}\sigma') \equiv (\rho'{\to}\sigma'')[\vec{\alpha} := \vec{\tau}]$$

and hence by Lemma 4.1.19 (1)

$$\begin{array}{ll} \Rightarrow & \Gamma, x{:}\rho \vdash P : \sigma',\ \Gamma \vdash Q : \rho \text{ and } \sigma' \geq \sigma, \\ \Rightarrow & \Gamma \vdash P[x := Q] : \sigma' \text{ and } \sigma' \geq \sigma, \text{ by Lemma 4.1.19 (2)} \\ \Rightarrow & \Gamma \vdash P[x := Q] : \sigma, \text{ by Lemma 4.2.2.} \end{array}$$

■

In [Mitchell, 1988] a semantic proof of the subject reduction theorem for $\lambda 2$ is given.

The proof of the subject reduction theorem for $\lambda\mu$ is somewhat easier than for $\lambda 2$.

Theorem 4.2.6 (Subject reduction theorem for $\lambda\mu$).
Let $M \twoheadrightarrow_\beta M'$. Then for $\lambda\mu$ one has

$$\Gamma \vdash M : \sigma \ \Rightarrow\ \Gamma \vdash M' : \sigma.$$

Proof. As for $\lambda 2$, but using the relation $\approx$ instead of $\geq$. ■

The subject reduction theorem holds also for $\lambda\cap$. This system is even closed under the rule EQ as we will see soon.

Subject conversion

For the systems $\lambda\cap$ and λ–$\mathcal{A}$ we will see that the subject conversion theorem holds. It is interesting to understand the reason why $\lambda\cap$ is closed under β-expansion. This is not so for $\lambda{\to}$, $\lambda 2$ and $\lambda\mu$. Let $M \equiv (\lambda x.P)Q$ and $M' \equiv P[x := Q]$. Suppose $\Gamma \vdash_{\lambda\cap} M' : \sigma$ in order to show that $\Gamma \vdash_{\lambda\cap} M : \sigma$. Now Q occurs $n \geq 0$ times in M' , each occurrence having type τ_i, say, for $1 \leq i \leq n$. Define $\tau \equiv \tau_1 \cap \cdots \cap \tau_n$ if $n > 0$ and $\tau \equiv \omega$ if $n = 0$. Then $\Gamma \vdash Q : \tau$ and $\Gamma, x : \tau \vdash P : \sigma$. Hence $\Gamma \vdash (\lambda x.P) : (\tau{\to}\sigma)$ and $\Gamma \vdash (\lambda x.P)Q : \sigma$.

In $\lambda\rightarrow$, $\lambda 2$ and $\lambda\mu$ it may not be possible to find a common type for the different occurrences of Q. Note also that the type ω is essential in case $x \notin FV(P)$.

Theorem 4.2.7 (Subject conversion theorem for $\lambda\cap$). *Let $M =_\beta M'$. Then for $\lambda\cap$ one has*

$$\Gamma \vdash M : \sigma \quad \Rightarrow \quad \Gamma \vdash M' : \sigma.$$

Proof. See [Barendregt *et al.*, 1983], corollary 3.8. ∎

Exercise 4.2.8. Let $M \equiv \lambda pq.(\lambda r.p)(qp)$.

- Show that although $M =_\beta \lambda pq.p : (\alpha\rightarrow\beta\rightarrow\alpha)$ in $\lambda\rightarrow$, the term M does not have $\alpha\rightarrow\beta\rightarrow\alpha$ as type in $\lambda\rightarrow$, $\lambda 2$ or $\lambda\mu$.
- Give a derivation in $\lambda\cap$ of $\vdash M : (\alpha\rightarrow\beta\rightarrow\alpha)$.

4.3 Strong normalization

Remember that a lambda term M is called *strongly normalizing* iff all reduction sequences starting with M terminate. For example KIK is strongly normalizing, while $\mathsf{KI}\Omega$ not. In this subsection it will be examined in which systems of type assignment *à la* Curry one has that the terms that do have a type are strongly normalizing. This will be the case for $\lambda\rightarrow$ and $\lambda 2$ but of course not for $\lambda\mu$ and $\lambda\cap$ (since in the latter systems all terms are typable). However, there is a variant $\lambda\cap^-$ of $\lambda\cap$ such that one even has

$$M \text{ is strongly normalizing} \quad \Leftrightarrow \quad M \text{ is typable in } \lambda\cap^-.$$

Turing proved that all terms typable in $\lambda\rightarrow$ are normalizing; this proof was only first published in [Gandy, 1980]. As was discussed in Section 2, normalization of terms does not imply in general strong normalization. However, for $\lambda\rightarrow$ and several other systems one does have strong normalization of typable terms. Methods of proving strong normalization from (weak) normalization due to Nederpelt [Nederpelt, 1973] and Gandy [Gandy, 1980] are described in [Klop, 1980].

Also in [Tait, 1967] it is proved that all terms typable in $\lambda\rightarrow$ are normalizing. This proof uses the so called method of 'computable terms' and was already presented in the unpublished [Stanford Report, 1963]. In fact, using Tait's method one can also prove strong normalization and applies to other systems as well, in particular to Gödel's T; see [Troelstra, 1973].

Girard [Girard, 1972] gave an 'impredicative twist' to Tait's method in order to show normalization for terms typable in (the Church version of)

$\lambda 2$ and in the system $\lambda\omega$ to be discussed in Section 5. Girard's proof was reformulated in [Tait, 1975] and we follow the general flavour of that paper.

We start with the proof of SN for $\lambda\!\rightarrow$.

Definition 4.3.1.

1. $\mathrm{SN} = \{M \in \Lambda \mid M \text{ is strongly normalizing}\}$.
2. Let $A, B \subseteq \Lambda$. Define $A \rightarrow B$ a subset of Λ by
$$A \rightarrow B = \{F \in \Lambda \mid \forall a \in A\ Fa \in B\}.$$
3. For every $\sigma \in \mathrm{Type}(\lambda\!\rightarrow)$ a set $[\![\sigma]\!] \subseteq \Lambda$ is defined as follows:
$$\begin{array}{rcl} [\![\alpha]\!] & = & \mathrm{SN}, \text{ where } \alpha \text{ is a type variable;} \\ [\![\sigma \rightarrow \tau]\!] & = & [\![\sigma]\!] \rightarrow [\![\tau]\!]. \end{array}$$

Definition 4.3.2.

1. A subset $X \subseteq \mathrm{SN}$ is called *saturated* if
   (a) $\forall n \geq 0\, \forall R_1, \ldots, R_n \in \mathrm{SN}\ \ x\vec{R} \in X$,
   where x is any term variable;
   (b) $\forall n \geq 0\, \forall R_1, \ldots, R_n \in \mathrm{SN} \forall Q \in \mathrm{SN}$
$$P[x := Q]\vec{R} \in X \quad \Rightarrow \quad (\lambda x.P)Q\vec{R} \in X.$$
2. $\mathrm{SAT} = \{X \subseteq \Lambda \mid X \text{ is saturated}\}$.

Lemma 4.3.3.

1. $\mathrm{SN} \in \mathrm{SAT}$.

2. $A, B \in \mathrm{SAT} \;\Rightarrow\; A \rightarrow B \in \mathrm{SAT}$.

3. Let $\{A_i\}_{i \in I}$ *be a collection of members of* SAT, *then* $\bigcap_{i \in I} A_i \in \mathrm{SAT}$.

4. For all $\sigma \in$ *Type*$(\lambda\!\rightarrow)$ *one has* $[\![\sigma]\!] \in \mathrm{SAT}$.

Proof. 1. One has $\mathrm{SN} \subseteq \mathrm{SN}$ and satisfies condition (a) in the definition of saturation. As to condition (b), suppose
$$P[x := Q]\vec{R} \in \mathrm{SN} \text{ and } Q, \vec{R} \in \mathrm{SN} \tag{1}$$
We claim that also
$$(\lambda x.P)Q\vec{R} \in \mathrm{SN} \tag{2}$$
Indeed, reductions inside P, Q or the $\vec{R}$ must terminate since these terms are SN by assumption ($P[x := Q]$ is a subterm of a term in

SN, by (1), hence itself SN; but then P is SN); so after finitely many steps reducing the term in (2) we obtain $(\lambda x.P')Q'\vec{R}'$ with $P \twoheadrightarrow_\beta P'$ etcetera. Then the contraction of $(\lambda x.P')Q'\vec{R}'$ gives

$$P'[x := Q']\vec{R}'. \tag{3}$$

This is a reduct of $P[x := Q]\vec{R}$ and since this term is SN also (3) and the term $(\lambda x.P)Q$ are SN.

2. Suppose $A, B \in \text{SAT}$. Then by definition $x \in A$ for all variables x. Therefore

$$\begin{array}{rcl} F \in A \to B & \Rightarrow & Fx \in B \\ & \Rightarrow & Fx \in \text{SN} \\ & \Rightarrow & F \in \text{SN}. \end{array}$$

So indeed $A \to B \subseteq \text{SN}$. As to condition 1 of saturation, let $\vec{R} \in \text{SN}$. We must show for a variable x that $x\vec{R} \in A \to B$. This means

$$\forall Q \in A \;\; x\vec{R}Q \in B,$$

which is true since $A \subseteq \text{SN}$ and B is saturated.

3. Similarly.

4. By induction on the generation of σ, using (1) and (2).

■

Definition 4.3.4.

1. A *valuation* in Λ is a map $\rho: V \to \Lambda$, where V is the set of term variables.

2. Let ρ be a valuation in Λ. Then

$$[\![M]\!]_\rho = M[x_1 := \rho(x_1), \ldots, x_n := \rho(x_n)],$$

where $\vec{x} = x_1, \ldots, x_n$ is the set of free variables in M.

3. Let ρ be a valuation in Λ. Then ρ *satisfies* $M : \sigma$, notation $\rho \models M : \sigma$, if $[\![M]\!]_\rho \in [\![\sigma]\!]$.

If Γ is a basis, then ρ *satisfies* Γ, notation $\rho \models \Gamma$, if $\rho \models x : \sigma$ for all $(x{:}\sigma) \in \Gamma$.

4. A basis Γ *satisfies* $M : \sigma$, notation $\Gamma \models M : \sigma$, if

$$\forall \rho\, [\rho \models \Gamma \Rightarrow \rho \models M : \sigma].$$

Proposition 4.3.5 (Soundness).

$$\Gamma \vdash_{\lambda\to} M : \sigma \;\Rightarrow\; \Gamma \models M : \sigma.$$

Proof. By induction on the derivation of $M : \sigma$.

Case 1. $\Gamma \vdash M : \sigma$ with $M \equiv x$ follows from $(x{:}\sigma) \in \Gamma$.
Then trivially $\Gamma \models x : \sigma$.

Case 2. $\Gamma \vdash M : \sigma$ with $M \equiv M_1 M_2$ is a direct consequence of $\Gamma \vdash M_1 : \tau\to\sigma$ and $\Gamma \vdash M_2 : \tau$.
Suppose $\rho \models \Gamma$ in order to show $\rho \models M_1 M_2 : \sigma$. Then $\rho \models M_1 : \tau\to\sigma$ and $\rho \models M_2 : \tau$, i.e. $[\![M_1]\!]_\rho \in [\![\tau\to\sigma]\!] = [\![\tau]\!]\to[\![\sigma]\!]$ and $[\![M_2]\!]_\rho \in [\![\tau]\!]$. But then $[\![M_1 M_2]\!]_\rho = [\![M_1]\!]_\rho [\![M_2]\!]_\rho \in [\![\sigma]\!]$, i.e. $\rho \models M_1 M_2 : \sigma$.

Case 3. $\Gamma \vdash M : \sigma$ with $M \equiv \lambda x.M'$ and $\sigma \equiv \sigma_1\to\sigma_2$ is a direct consequence of $\Gamma, x{:}\sigma_1 \vdash M' : \sigma_2$.
By the IH one has

$$\Gamma, x : \sigma_1 \models M' : \sigma_2 \tag{1}$$

Suppose $\rho \models \Gamma$ in order to show $\rho \models \lambda x.M' : \sigma_1\to\sigma_2$. That is, we must show

$$[\![\lambda x.M']\!]_\rho N \in [\![\sigma_2]\!] \text{ for all } N \in [\![\sigma_1]\!].$$

So suppose that $N \in [\![\sigma_1]\!]$. Then $\rho(x := N) \models \Gamma, x : \sigma_1$, and hence

$$[\![M']\!]_{\rho(x:=N)} \in [\![\sigma_2]\!],$$

by (1). Since

$$\begin{array}{rcl} [\![\lambda x.M']\!]_\rho N & \equiv & (\lambda x.M')[\vec{y} := \rho(\vec{y})]N \\ & \to_\beta & M'[\vec{y} := \rho(\vec{y}), x := N] \\ & \equiv & [\![M']\!]_{\rho(x:=N)}, \end{array}$$

it follows from the saturation of $[\![\sigma_2]\!]$ that $[\![\lambda x.M']\!]_\rho N \in [\![\sigma_2]\!]$.

∎

Theorem 4.3.6 (Strong normalization for $\lambda\to$-Curry). *Suppose $\Gamma \vdash_{\lambda\to} M : \sigma$. Then M is strongly normalizing.*

Proof. Suppose $\Gamma \vdash M : \sigma$. Then $\Gamma \models M : \sigma$. Define $\rho_o(x) = x$ for all x. Then $\rho_o \models \Gamma$ (since $x \in [\![\tau]\!]$ holds because $[\![\tau]\!]$ is saturated). Therefore $\rho_o \models M : \sigma$, hence $M \equiv [\![M]\!]_{\rho_o} \in [\![\sigma]\!] \subseteq \text{SN}$. ∎

The proof of SN for $\lambda\!\rightarrow$ has been given in such a way that a simple generalization of the method proves the result for $\lambda 2$. This generalization will be given now.

Definition 4.3.7.

1. A *valuation* in SAT is a map

   $\xi : \mathbb{V} \rightarrow \text{SAT}$

   where $\mathbb{V}$ is the set of type variables.

2. Given a valuation ξ in SAT one defines for every $\sigma \in \text{Type}(\lambda 2)$ a set $[\![\sigma]\!]_\xi \subseteq \Lambda$ as follows:

$$\begin{aligned} [\![\alpha]\!]_\xi &= \xi(\alpha), \text{ where } \alpha \in \mathbb{V}; \\ [\![\sigma \rightarrow \tau]\!]_\xi &= [\![\sigma]\!]_\xi \rightarrow [\![\tau]\!]_\xi; \\ [\![\forall \alpha.\sigma]\!]_\xi &= \bigcap_{X \in \text{SAT}} [\![\sigma]\!]_{\xi(\alpha:=X)} \end{aligned}$$

Lemma 4.3.8. *Given a valuation ξ in* SAT *and a σ in Type($\lambda 2$), then* $[\![\sigma]\!]_\xi \in \text{SAT}$.

Proof. As for Lemma 4.3.3(4) using also that SAT is closed under arbitrary intersections. ∎

Definition 4.3.9.

1. Let ρ be a valuation in Λ and ξ be a valuation in SAT. Then

$$\rho, \xi \models M : \sigma \quad \Leftrightarrow \quad [\![M]\!]_\rho \in [\![\sigma]\!]_\xi .$$

2. For such ρ, ξ one writes

$$\rho, \xi \models \Gamma \quad \Leftrightarrow \quad \rho, \xi \models x : \sigma \text{ for all } x{:}\sigma \text{ in } \Gamma.$$

3. $\Gamma \models M : \sigma \;\Leftrightarrow\; \forall \rho, \xi \;[\rho, \xi \models \Gamma \;\Rightarrow\; \rho, \xi \models M : \sigma]$.

Proposition 4.3.10.

$$\Gamma \vdash_{\lambda 2} M : \sigma \Rightarrow \Gamma \models M : \sigma.$$

Proof. As for Proposition 4.3.5 by induction on the derivation of $\Gamma \vdash M : \sigma$. There are two new cases corresponding to the $\forall$-rules.

Case 4. $\Gamma \vdash M : \sigma$ with $\sigma \equiv \sigma_0[\alpha := \tau]$ is a direct consequence of $\Gamma \vdash M : \forall\alpha.\sigma_0$. By the IH one has

$$\Gamma \models M : \forall\alpha.\sigma_0. \tag{1}$$

Now suppose $\rho, \xi \models \Gamma$ in order to show that $\rho, \xi \models M : \sigma_0[\alpha := \tau]$. By (1) one has

$$[\![M]\!]_\rho \in [\![\forall\alpha.\sigma_0]\!]_\xi = \bigcap_{X \in \mathrm{SAT}} [\![\sigma_0]\!]_{(\alpha:=X)}.$$

Hence

$$[\![M]\!]_\rho \in [\![\sigma_0]\!]_{\xi(\alpha:=[\![\tau]\!]_\xi)}.$$

We are done since

$$[\![\sigma_0]\!]_{\xi(\alpha:=[\![\tau]\!]_\xi)} = [\![\sigma_0[\alpha := \tau]]\!]_\rho$$

as can be proved by induction on $\sigma_0 \in$ Type($\lambda 2$) (some care is needed in case $\sigma_0 \equiv \forall\beta.\tau_0$).

Case 5. $\Gamma \vdash M : \sigma$ with $\sigma \equiv \forall\alpha.\sigma_0$ and $\alpha \notin FV(\Gamma)$ is a direct consequence of $\Gamma \vdash M : \sigma_0$. By the IH one has

$$\Gamma \models M : \sigma_0. \tag{2}$$

Suppose $\rho, \xi \models \Gamma$ in order to show $\rho, \xi \models \forall\alpha.\sigma_0$. Since $\alpha \notin FV(\Gamma)$ one has for all $X \in$ SAT that also $\rho, \xi(\alpha := X) \models \Gamma$. Therefore

$$[\![M]\!]_\rho \in [\![\sigma_0]\!]_{\xi(\alpha:=X)} \text{ for all } X \in \mathrm{SAT},$$

by (2), hence

$$[\![M]\!]_\rho \in [\![\forall\alpha.\sigma_0]\!]_\xi,$$

i.e. $\rho, \xi \models M : \forall\alpha.\sigma_0$.

■

Theorem 4.3.11 (Strong normalization for $\lambda 2$-Curry).

$$\Gamma \vdash_{\lambda 2} M : \sigma \Rightarrow M \textit{ is strongly normalizing.}$$

Proof. Similar to the proof of Theorem 4.3.6 ■

Although the proof of SN for $\lambda 2$ follows the same pattern as for $\lambda\!\to$, there is an essential difference. The proof of SN($\lambda\!\to$) can be formalized in Peano arithmetic. However, as was shown in [Girard, 1972], the proof of SN($\lambda 2$) cannot even be formalized in the rather strong system A_2 of 'mathematical analysis' (second order arithmetic); see also [Girard *et al.*, 1989]. The reason is that SN($\lambda 2$) implies (within Peano arithmetic) the consistency of A_2 and hence Gödel's second incompleteness theorem applies. An attempt to formalize the given proof of SN($\lambda 2$) breaks down at the point trying to formalize the predicate '$M \in [\![\sigma]\!]_\xi$'. The problem is that SAT is a third-order predicate.

The property SN does not hold for the systems $\lambda\mu$ and $\lambda\cap$. This is obvious, since all lambda terms can be typed in these two systems. However, there is a restriction of $\lambda\cap$ that does satisfy SN.

Let $\lambda\cap^-$ be the system $\lambda\cap$ without the type constant ω. The following result is an interesting characterization of strongly normalizing terms.

Theorem 4.3.12 (van Bakel; Krivine).

$$M \textit{ can be typed in } \lambda\cap^- \quad \Leftrightarrow \quad M \textit{ is strongly normalizing.}$$

Proof. See [van Bakel, 1991], theorem 3.4.11 or [Krivine, 1990], p. 65. ∎

4.4 Decidability of type assignment

For the various systems of type assignment several questions may be asked. Note that for $\Gamma = \{x_1{:}\sigma_1, \ldots, x_n{:}\sigma_n\}$ one has

$$\Gamma \vdash M : \sigma \quad \Leftrightarrow \vdash (\lambda x_1{:}\sigma_1 \ldots \lambda x_n{:}\sigma_n.M) : (\sigma_1 \rightarrow \ldots \rightarrow \sigma_n \rightarrow \sigma),$$

therefore in the following one has taken $\Gamma = \varnothing$. Typical questions are

1. Given M and σ, does one have $\vdash M : \sigma$?

2. Given M, does there exists a σ such that $\vdash M : \sigma$?

3. Given σ, does there exists an M such that $\vdash M : \sigma$?

These three problems are called *type checking*, *typability* and *inhabitation* respectively and are denoted by $M : \sigma?$, $M : ?$ and $? : \sigma$.

In this subsection the decidabiltiy of these three problems will be examined for the various systems. The results can be summarized as follows:

Decidability of type checking, typability and inhabitation

	$M : \sigma?$	$M : ?$	$? : \sigma$
$\lambda\rightarrow$	yes	yes	yes
$\lambda 2$	??	??	no
$\lambda\mu$	yes	yes, always	yes, always
$\lambda\cap$	no	yes, always	??
$\lambda\rightarrow^{+}$	no	no	yes
$\lambda 2^{+}$	no	no	no
$\lambda\mu^{+}$	no	yes, always	yes, always
$\lambda\rightarrow\mathcal{A}$	no	no	yes, always
$\lambda 2\mathcal{A}$	no	no	yes, always
$\lambda\mu\mathcal{A}$	no	yes, always	yes, always
$\lambda\cap\mathcal{A}$	no	yes, always	yes, always

Remarks 4.4.1. The system $\lambda\cap^{+}$ is the same as $\lambda\cap$ and therefore it is not mentioned. The two question marks for $\lambda 2$ indicate—to quote Robin Milner—'embarrassing open problems'. For partial results concerning $\lambda 2$ and related systems see [Pfenning, 1988], [Giannini and Ronchi della Roca, 1988], [Henglein, 1990], and [Kfoury *et al.*, 1990]. In 4.4.10 it will be shown that for $\lambda 2$ the decidability of type checking implies that of typability. It is generally believed that both problems are undecidable for $\lambda 2$.

Sometimes a question is trivially decidable, simply because the property always holds. Then we write 'yes, always'. For example in $\lambda\cap$ every term M has ω as type. For this reason it is more interesting to ask whether terms M are typable in a weaker system $\lambda\cap^{-}$. However, by theorem 4.3.12 this question is equivalent to the strong normalization of M and hence undecidable.

We first will show the decidabiltity of the three questions for $\lambda\rightarrow$. This occupies 4.4.2 - 4.4.13 and in these items $\mathbb{T}$ stands for Type($\lambda\rightarrow$) and $\vdash$ for $\vdash_{\lambda\rightarrow\text{-Curry}}$.

Definition 4.4.2.

1. A substitutor is an operation
$$*:\mathbb{T}\rightarrow\mathbb{T}$$
such that
$$*(\sigma\rightarrow\tau) \equiv *(\sigma)\rightarrow *(\tau).$$
2. We write σ^* for $*(\sigma)$.
3. Usually a substitution $*$ has a finite support, that is, for all but finitely many type variables α one has $\alpha^* \equiv \alpha$ (the support of $*$ being $\sup(*) = \{\alpha \mid \alpha^* \not\equiv \alpha\}$).

In that case we write

$$*(\sigma) = \sigma[\alpha_1 := \alpha_1^*, \ldots, \alpha_n := \alpha_n^*],$$

where $\{\alpha_1, \ldots, \alpha_n\}$ is the support of $*$. We also write

$$* = [\alpha_1 := \alpha_1^*, \ldots, \alpha_n := \alpha_n^*].$$

Definition 4.4.3.

1. Let $\sigma, \tau \in T$. A *unifier* for σ and τ is a substitutor $*$ such that $\sigma^* \equiv \tau^*$.
2. The substitutor $*$ is a most general unifier for σ and τ if
   (a) $\sigma^* \equiv \tau^*$
   (b) $\sigma^{*_1} \equiv \tau^{*_1} \;\Rightarrow\; \exists *_2 \;\; *_1 \equiv *_2 \circ *.$
3. Let $E = \{\sigma_1 = \tau_1, \ldots, \sigma_n = \tau_n\}$ be a finite set of equations between types. The equations do not need to be valid. A *unifier* for E is a substitutor $*$ such that $\sigma_1^* \equiv \tau_1^* \;\&\; \cdots \;\&\; \sigma_n^* \equiv \tau_n^*$. In that case one writes $* \models E$. Similarly one defines the notion of a most general unifier for E.

Examples 4.4.4. The types $\beta{\rightarrow}(\alpha{\rightarrow}\beta)$ and $(\gamma{\rightarrow}\gamma){\rightarrow}\delta$ have a unifier. For example $* = [\beta := \gamma{\rightarrow}\gamma,\ \delta := \alpha{\rightarrow}(\gamma{\rightarrow}\gamma)]$ or $*_1 = [\beta := \gamma{\rightarrow}\gamma,\ \alpha := \varepsilon{\rightarrow}\varepsilon,\ \delta := \varepsilon{\rightarrow}\varepsilon{\rightarrow}(\gamma{\rightarrow}\gamma)]$. The unifier $*$ is most general, $*_1$ is not.

Definition 4.4.5. σ is a *variant* of τ if for some $*_1$ and $*_2$ one has

$$\sigma = \tau^{*_1} \text{ and } \tau = \sigma^{*_2}.$$

Example 4.4.6. $\alpha{\rightarrow}\beta{\rightarrow}\beta$ is a variant of $\gamma{\rightarrow}\delta{\rightarrow}\delta$ but not of $\alpha{\rightarrow}\beta{\rightarrow}\alpha$.

Note that if $*_1$ and $*_2$ are both most general unifiers of say σ and τ, then σ^{*_1} and σ^{*_2} are variants of each other and similarly for τ.

The following result due to Robinson [Robinson, 1965] states that unifiers can be constructed effectively.

Theorem 4.4.7 (Unification theorem).

1. *There is a recursive function U having (after coding) as input a pair of types and as output either a substitutor or* fail *such that*

$$\sigma \text{ and } \tau \text{ have a unifier} \quad\Rightarrow\quad U(\sigma,\tau) \text{ is a most general unifier}$$

$$\begin{array}{rcl} & & \text{for } \sigma \text{ and } \tau; \\ \sigma \text{ and } \tau \text{ have no unifier} & \Rightarrow & U(\sigma,\tau) = \mathsf{fail}. \end{array}$$

2. *There is (after coding) a recursive function U having as input finite sets of equations between types and as output either a substitutor or* fail *such that*

$$\begin{array}{rcl} E \text{ has a unifier} & \Rightarrow & U(E) \text{ is a most general unifier for } E; \\ E \text{ has no unifier} & \Rightarrow & U(E) = \mathsf{fail}. \end{array}$$

Proof. Note that $\sigma_1 \to \sigma_2 \equiv \tau_1 \to \tau_2$ holds iff $\sigma_1 \equiv \tau_1$ and $\sigma_2 \equiv \tau_2$ hold.

1. Define $U(\sigma, \tau)$ by the following recursive loop, using case distinction.

$$\begin{array}{rcll} U(\alpha,\tau) & = & [\alpha := \tau], & \text{if } \alpha \notin \mathrm{FV}(\tau), \\ & = & Id, \text{ the identity}, & \text{if } \tau = \alpha, \\ & = & \mathsf{fail}, & \text{else}; \\ U(\sigma_1 \to \sigma_2, \alpha) & = & U(\alpha, \sigma_1 \to \sigma_2); & \\ U(\sigma_1 \to \sigma_2, \tau_1 \to \tau_2) & = & U(\sigma_1^{U(\sigma_2,\tau_2)}, \tau_1^{U(\sigma_2,\tau_2)}) \circ U(\sigma_2, \tau_2). & \end{array}$$

where this last expression is considered to be fail if one of its parts is. Let $\#_{var}(\sigma, \tau)$ ='the number of variables in $\sigma \to \tau$' and $\#_{\to}(\sigma, \tau)$='the number of arrows in $\sigma \to \tau$'. By induction on $(\#_{var}(\sigma, \tau), \#_{\to}(\sigma, \tau))$ ordered lexicographically one can show that $U(\sigma, \tau)$ is always defined. Moreover U satisfies the specification.

2. If $E = \{\sigma_1 = \tau_1, \ldots, \sigma_n = \tau_n\}$, then define $U(E) = U(\sigma, \tau)$, where $\sigma = \sigma_1 \to \cdots \to \sigma_n$ and $\tau = \tau_1 \to \cdots \to \tau_n$.

∎

See Section 7 in Klop's chapter in this handbook for more on unification. The following theorem is essentially due to Wand [Wand, 1987] and simplifies the proof of the decidability of type checking and typability for $\lambda\to$.

Proposition 4.4.8. *For every basis Γ, term $M \in \Lambda$ and $\sigma \in \mathbb{T}$ such that $\mathrm{FV}(M) \subseteq \mathrm{dom}(\Gamma)$ there is a finite set of equations $E = E(\Gamma, M, \sigma)$ such that for all substitutors $*$ one has*

$$* \models E(\Gamma, M, \sigma) \quad \Rightarrow \quad \Gamma^* \vdash M : \sigma^*, \tag{1}$$

$$\Gamma^* \vdash M : \sigma^* \quad \Rightarrow \quad *_1 \models E(\Gamma, M, \sigma), \tag{2}$$

for some $*_1$ such that $*$ and $*_1$ have the same effect on the type variables in Γ and σ.

Proof. Define $E(\Gamma, M, \sigma)$ by induction on the structure of M:

$$\begin{array}{rcl} E(\Gamma, x, \sigma) & = & \{\sigma = \Gamma(x)\}; \\ E(\Gamma, MN, \sigma) & = & E(\Gamma, M, \alpha{\rightarrow}\sigma) \cup E(\Gamma, N, \alpha), \\ & & \quad \text{where } \alpha \text{ is a fresh variable;} \\ E(\Gamma, \lambda x.M, \sigma) & = & E(\Gamma \cup \{x{:}\alpha\}, M, \beta) \cup \{\alpha{\rightarrow}\beta = \sigma\}, \\ & & \quad \text{where } \alpha, \beta \text{ are fresh.} \end{array}$$

By induction on M one can show (using the generation lemma (3.1.8)) that (1) and (2) hold. ∎

Definition 4.4.9.

1. Let $M \in \Lambda$. Then (Γ, σ) is a *principal pair* (pp) for M if

   (1) $\Gamma \vdash M : \sigma$.

   (2) $\Gamma' \vdash M : \sigma' \Rightarrow \exists * \, [\Gamma^* \subseteq \Gamma' \;\&\; \sigma^* \equiv \sigma']$.

   Here $\{x_1{:}\sigma_1, \ldots\}^* = \{x_1{:}\sigma_1^*, \ldots\}$.

2. Let $M \in \Lambda$ be closed. Then σ is a *principal type* (pt) for M if

   (1) $\vdash M : \sigma$

   (2) $\vdash M : \sigma' \Rightarrow \exists * \; [\sigma^* \equiv \sigma']$.

Note that if (Γ, σ) is a *pp* for M, then every variant (Γ', σ') of (Γ, σ), in the obvious sense, is also a *pp* for M. Conversely if (Γ, σ) and (Γ', σ') are *pp*'s for M, then (Γ', σ') is a variant of (Γ, σ). Similarly for closed terms and *pt*'s. Moreover, if (Γ, σ) is a *pp* for M, then $\mathrm{FV}(M) = \mathrm{dom}(\Gamma)$.

The following result is independently due to Curry [Curry, 1969], Hindley [Hindley, 1969] and Milner [Milner, 1978]. It shows that for $\lambda\!\rightarrow$ the problems of type checking and typability are decidable.

Theorem 4.4.10 (Principal type theorem for $\lambda\!\rightarrow$-Curry).

1. *There exists (after coding) a recursive function pp such that one has*

$$M \text{ has a type} \quad \Rightarrow \quad pp(M) = (\Gamma, \sigma), \text{ where } (\Gamma, \sigma) \text{ is a } pp \text{ for } M;$$

$$M \text{ has no type} \quad \Rightarrow \quad pp(M) = \mathsf{fail}.$$

2. *There exists (after coding) a recursive function pt such that for closed terms M one has*

$$\begin{aligned} M \text{ has a type} &\Rightarrow pt(M) = \sigma, \text{ where } \sigma \text{ is a } pt \text{ for } M; \\ M \text{ has no type} &\Rightarrow pt(M) = \mathsf{fail}. \end{aligned}$$

Proof. 1. Let $\mathrm{FV}(M) = \{x_1, \ldots, x_n\}$ and set $\Gamma_0 = \{x_1{:}\alpha_1, \ldots, x_n{:}\alpha_n\}$ and $\sigma_0 = \beta$. Note that

$$\begin{aligned} M \text{ has a type} &\Leftrightarrow \exists \Gamma\, \exists \sigma \;\; \Gamma \vdash M : \sigma \\ &\Leftrightarrow \exists * \;\; \Gamma_0^* \vdash M : \sigma_0^* \\ &\Leftrightarrow \exists * \;\; * \models E(\Gamma_0, M, \sigma_0). \end{aligned}$$

Define

$$\begin{aligned} pp(M) &= (\Gamma_0^*, \sigma_0^*), && \text{if } U(E(\Gamma_0, M, \sigma_0)) = *; \\ &= \mathsf{fail}, && \text{if } U(E(\Gamma_0, M, \sigma_0)) = \mathsf{fail}. \end{aligned}$$

Then $pp(M)$ satisfies the requirements. Indeed, if M has a type, then $U(E(\Gamma_0, M, \sigma_0)) = *$ is defined and $\Gamma_0^* \vdash M : \sigma_0^*$ by (1) in proposition 4.4.8. To show that (Γ_0^*, σ_0^*) is a pp, suppose that also $\Gamma' \vdash M : \sigma'$. Let $\widetilde{\Gamma} = \Gamma' \upharpoonright \mathrm{FV}(M)$; write $\widetilde{\Gamma} = \Gamma_0^{*_0}$ and $\sigma' = \sigma_0^{*_0}$. Then also $\Gamma_0^{*_0} \vdash M : \sigma_0^{*_0}$. Hence by (2) in proposition 4.4.8 for some $*_1$ (acting the same as $*_0$ on Γ_0, σ_0) one has $*_1 \models E(\Gamma_0, M, \sigma_0)$. Since $*$ is a most general unifier (proposition 4.4.7) one has $*_1 = *_2 \circ *$ for some $*_2$. Now indeed

$$(\Gamma_0^*)^{*_2} = \Gamma_0^{*_1} = \Gamma_0^{*_0} = \widetilde{\Gamma} \subseteq \Gamma'$$

and

$$(\sigma_0^*)^{*_2} = \sigma_0^{*_1} = \sigma_0^{*_0} = \sigma'.$$

If M has no type, then $\neg\exists * \;\; * \models E(\Gamma_0, M, \sigma_0)$ hence

$$U(\Gamma_0, M, \sigma_0) = \mathsf{fail} = pp(M).$$

2. Let M be closed and $pp(M) = (\Gamma, \sigma)$. Then $\Gamma = \emptyset$ and we can put $pt(M) = \sigma$. ∎

Corollary 4.4.11. *Type checking and typability for $\lambda\!\rightarrow$ are decidable.*

Proof. As to type checking, let M and σ be given. Then

$$\vdash M : \sigma \iff \exists * \, [\sigma = pt(M)^*].$$

This is decidable (as can be seen using an algorithm—*pattern matching*—similar to the one in Theorem 4.4.7).

As to the question of typability, let M be given. Then M has a type iff $pt(M) \neq \mathsf{fail}$. ∎

Theorem 4.4.12. *The inhabitation problem for $\lambda{\rightarrow}$, i.e.*

$$\exists M \in \Lambda \ \vdash_{\lambda\rightarrow} M : \sigma$$

is a decidable property of σ.

Proof. One has by Corollary 3.2.16 that

$$\begin{aligned} \sigma \text{ inhabited in } \lambda{\rightarrow}\text{-Curry} &\iff \sigma \text{ inhabited in } \lambda{\rightarrow}\text{-Church} \\ &\iff \sigma \text{ provable in PROP}, \end{aligned}$$

where PROP is the minimal intuitionistic proposition calculus with only $\rightarrow$ as connective and σ is considered as an element of PROP, see Section 5.4. Using finite Kripke models it can be shown that the last statement is decidable. Therefore the first statement is decidable too. ∎

Without a proof we mention the following result of [Hindley, 1969].

Theorem 4.4.13 (Second principal type theorem for $\lambda{\rightarrow}$-Curry). *Every type $\sigma \in \mathbb{T}$ there exists a basis Γ and term $M \in \Lambda$ such that (Γ, σ) is a pp for M.*

Now we consider $\lambda 2$. The situation is as follows. The question whether type checking and typability are decidable is open. However, one has the following result by Malecki [Malecki, 1989].

Proposition 4.4.14. *In $\lambda 2$ the problem of typability can be reduced to that of type checking. In particular*

$$\{(M : \sigma) \mid \vdash_{\lambda 2} M : \sigma\} \text{ is decidable} \Rightarrow \{M \mid \exists \sigma \vdash_{\lambda 2} M : \sigma\} \text{ is decidable.}$$

Proof. One has

$$\exists \sigma \vdash M : \sigma \ \Leftrightarrow \ \vdash (\lambda xy.y)M : (\alpha{\rightarrow}\alpha).$$

The implication $\Rightarrow$ is obvious, since $\vdash (\lambda xy.y) : (\sigma{\rightarrow}\alpha{\rightarrow}\alpha)$ for all σ. The implication $\Leftarrow$ follows from Proposition 4.1.18. ∎

Theorem 4.4.15. *The inhabitation problem for $\lambda 2$ is undecidable.*

Proof. As for $\lambda\!\!\rightarrow$ one can show that

$$\begin{aligned}\sigma \text{ inhabited in } \lambda 2\text{-Curry} &\iff \sigma \text{ inhabited in } \lambda 2\text{-Church}\\ &\iff \sigma \text{ provable in PROP2,}\end{aligned}$$

where PROP2 is the constructive second-order proposition calculus. In [Löb, 1976] it is proved that this last property is undecidable. ∎

Proposition 4.4.16. *For $\lambda\mu$ one has the following:*

1. *Type checking is decidable.*
2. *Typability is trivially decidable: every λ-term has a type.*
3. *The inhabitation problem for $\lambda\mu$ is trivially decidable: all types are inhabited.*

Proof.
1. See [Coppo and Cardone, 1991] who use the same method as for $\lambda\!\!\rightarrow$ and the fact that $T(\sigma) = T(\tau)$ is decidable.
2. Let $\sigma_0 = \mu\alpha.\alpha\!\rightarrow\!\alpha$. Then every $M \in \Lambda$ has type σ_0, see the example before 4.1.
3. All types are inhabited by Ω, see 4.1.12 (2).

∎

Lemma 4.4.17. *Let $\lambda-$ be a system of type assignment that satisfies subject conversion, i.e.*

$$\Gamma \vdash_{\lambda-} M : \sigma \;\&\; M =_\beta N \;\Rightarrow\; \Gamma \vdash_{\lambda-} N : \sigma.$$

1. *Suppose some closed terms have type $\alpha\!\rightarrow\!\alpha$, others not. Then the problem of type checking is undecidable.*
2. *Suppose some terms have a type, other terms not. Then the problem of typability is undecidable.*

Proof.
1. If the set $\{(M, \sigma) \mid \vdash M : \sigma\}$ is decidable, then so is $\{M \mid \vdash M : \alpha\!\rightarrow\!\alpha\}$. But this set is by assumption closed under $=$ and non-trivial, contradicting Scott's theorem 2.2.15.
2. Similarly. ∎

Proposition 4.4.18. *For $\lambda\cap$ one has the following:*

1. *Type checking problem is undecidable.*
2. *Typability is trivially decidable: all terms have a type.*

Proof. 1. Lemma 4.4.17(1) applies by 4.2.7, the fact that $\vdash \mathsf{I} : \alpha \to \alpha$ and Exercise 4.1.20.

2. For all M one has $M : \omega$. ∎

It is not known whether inhabitation in $\lambda\cap$ is decidable.

Lemma 4.4.19. *Let $\lambda-$ be one of the systems à la Curry. Then*

1. $\Gamma \vdash_{\lambda-^{+}} M : \sigma \;\Leftrightarrow\; \exists M' \, [M \twoheadrightarrow_\beta M' \;\&\; \Gamma \vdash_{\lambda-} M' : \sigma]$.
2. σ *is inhabited in* $\lambda-^{+}$ $\Leftrightarrow$ σ *is inhabited in* $\lambda-$.

Proof. 1. ($\Leftarrow$) Trivial, since $M \twoheadrightarrow_\beta M'$ implies $M =_\beta M'$. ($\Rightarrow$) By induction on the derivation of $M : \sigma$. The only interesting case is when the last applied rule is an application of rule EQ. So let it be

$$\frac{M_1 : \sigma \quad M_1 = M}{M : \sigma}.$$

The induction hypothesis says that for some M_1' with $M_1 \twoheadrightarrow_\beta M_1'$ one has $\Gamma \vdash_{\lambda-} M_1' : \sigma$. By the Church–Rosser theorem 2.3.7 M_1' and M have a common reduct, say M'. But then by the subject reduction theorem one has $\Gamma \vdash_{\lambda-} M' : \sigma$ and we are done.

2. By (1). ∎

Proposition 4.4.20. *For the systems $\lambda-^{+}$ one has the following:*

1. *Type checking is undecidable.*
2. *Typability is undecidable for $\lambda\!\to^{+}$ and $\lambda 2^{+}$, but trivially decidable for $\lambda\mu^{+}$ and $\lambda\cap^{+}$.*
3. *The status of the inhabitation problem for $\lambda-^{+}$ is the same as for $\lambda-$.*

Proof. 1. By definition subject conversion holds for the systems $\lambda-^{+}$. In all systems $\mathsf{I} : \alpha \to \alpha$. From Lemma 4.4.19(1) and Exercise 4.1.20 it follows that Lemma 4.4.17(1) applies.

2. By Theorems 4.3.6 and 4.3.11 terms without an nf have no type in $\lambda\!\to$ or $\lambda 2$. Hence by Lemma 4.4.19(1) these terms have no type in

$\lambda{\rightarrow}^+$ or $\lambda 2^+$. Since for these systems there are terms having a type lemma 4.4.17(2) applies.

In $\lambda\mu^+$ and $\lambda\cap^+$ all terms have a type.

3. By Lemma 4.4.19(2). ∎

Lemma 4.4.21. *Let M be a term in nf. Then*

$$\vdash_{\lambda-\mathcal{A}} M : \sigma \ \Rightarrow \vdash_{\lambda-} M : \sigma.$$

Proof. By induction on the given derivation, using that $M \in \mathcal{A}(M)$. ∎

Proposition 4.4.22. *For the systems $\lambda - \mathcal{A}$ the situation is as follows:*

1. *The problem of type checking is undecidable for the systems $\lambda{\rightarrow}\mathcal{A}$, $\lambda 2\mathcal{A}$, $\lambda\mu\mathcal{A}$ and $\lambda\cap\mathcal{A}$.*
2. *The problem of typability is undecidable for the system $\lambda{\rightarrow}\mathcal{A}$ and $\lambda 2\mathcal{A}$ but trivially decidable for the systems $\lambda\mu\mathcal{A}$ and $\lambda\cap\mathcal{A}$ (all terms are typable).*
3. *The problem of inhabitation is trivially decidable for all four systems including rule $\mathcal{A}$ (all types are inhabited).*

Proof. 1. By Lemma 4.4.21 and Exercise 4.1.20 one has $\nvdash \mathsf{K} : \alpha{\rightarrow}\alpha$. Hence 4.4.17(1) applies.

2. Similarly.

3. The inhabitation problem becomes trivial: in all four systems one has

$$\vdash \Omega : \sigma$$

for all types σ. This follows from Example 4.1.3(2) and the facts that $\mathsf{YI} =_\beta \Omega$ and $\lambda - \mathcal{A}$ is closed under the rule EQ. ∎

The results concerning decidability of type checking, typability and inhabitation are summarised in the table at the beginning of this subsection.

5 Typing *à la* Church

In this section several systems of typed lambda calculus will be described in a uniform way. Church versions will be given for the systems $\lambda\!\rightarrow$ and $\lambda 2$, already encountered in the Curry style. Then a collection of eight lambda-calculi *à la* Church is given, the so called λ-*cube*. Two of the cornerstones of this cube are essentially $\lambda\!\rightarrow$ and $\lambda 2$ and another system is among the family of AUTOMATH languages of [de Bruijn, 1980]. The λ-cube forms a natural fine structure of the *calculus of constructions* of [Coquand and Huet, 1988] and is organized according to the possible 'dependencies' between terms and types. This will be done in 5.1.

The description method of the systems in the λ-cube is generalized in subsection 5.2, obtaining the so called 'pure type systems' (PTSs). In preliminary versions of this chapter PTSs were called 'generalized type systems' (GTSs). Several elementary properties of PTS's are derived.

In subsection 5.3 it is shown that all terms in the systems of the λ-cube are strongly normalizing. However in 5.5 it turns out that this is not generally true in PTS's.

In subsection 5.4 a cube of eight logical systems will be described. Each logical system L_i corresponds to one of the systems λ_i on the λ-cube. One has for sentences A

$$\vdash_{L_i} A \;\Rightarrow\; \exists M\, \Gamma \vdash_{\lambda_i} M : [\![A]\!]$$

where Γ depends on the similarity type of the language of L_i and $[\![A]\!]$ is a canonical interpretation of A in λ_i. Moreover, the term M can be found uniformly from the proof of A in L_i. The map $[\![-]\!]$ is called the *propositions-as-types* interpretation. It turns out also that the logical systems can be described as PTSs and that in this way the propositions-as-type interpretation becomes a very simple forgetful map from the logical cube into the λ-cube.

As an application of the propositions-as-types interpretation one can represent in a natural way data types in $\lambda 2$. Data types correspond to inductively defined sets and these can be naturally represented in second-order predicate logic, one of the systems on the logical cube. Then, by means of a map from predicate to proposition logic and by the propositions-as-types interpretation one obtains an interpretation of data types in $\lambda 2$.

5.1 The cube of typed lambda calculi

In this subsection we introduce in a uniform way the eight typed lambda calculi $\lambda\!\rightarrow$, $\lambda 2$, $\lambda\underline{\omega}$, $\lambda\omega$, λP, λP2, λP$\underline{\omega}$, and λPω. (The system λPω is often called λC.) The eight systems form a cube as follows:

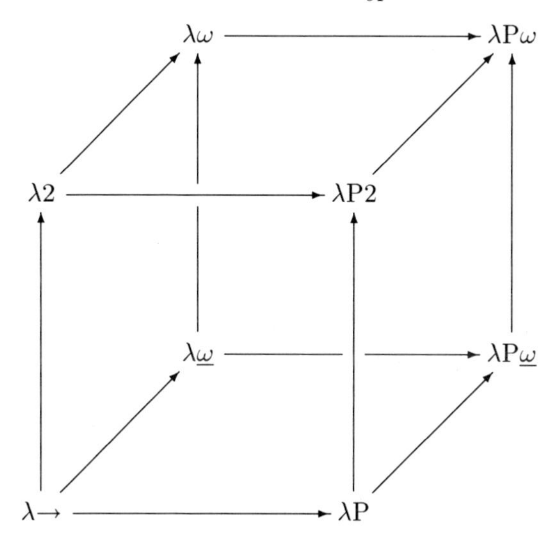

Fig. 2. The λ-cube.

where each edge → respresents the inclusion relation ⊆. This cube will be referred to as the λ-*cube*.

The system λ→ is the simply typed lambda calculus, already encountered in section 3.2. The system λ2 is the *polymorphic* or *second order* typed lambda calculus and is essentially the system F of [Girard, 1972]; the system has been introduced independently in [Reynolds, 1974]. The Curry version of λ2 was already introduced in Section 4.1. The system λω is essentially the system $F\omega$ of [Girard, 1972]. The system λP reasonably corresponds to one of the systems in the family of AUTOMATH languages, see [de Bruijn, 1980]. (A more precise formulation of several AUTOMATH systems can be given as PTSs, see subsection 5.2.) This system λP appears also under the name *LF* in Harper *et al.* [Harper *et al.*, 1987]. The system λP2 is studied in [Longo and Moggi, 1988] under the same name. The system λC = λPω is one of the versions of the calculus of constructions introduced by [Coquand and Huet, 1988]. The system $\lambda\underline{\omega}$ is related to a system studied by [Renardel de Lavalette, 1991]. The system $\lambda P\underline{\omega}$ seems not to have been studied before. (For $\lambda\underline{\omega}$ and $\lambda P\underline{\omega}$ read: 'weak λω' and 'weak λPω' respectively.)

As we have seen in Section 4, the system λ→ and λ2 can be given also *à la* Curry. A Curry version of λω appears in [Giannini and Ronchi della Roca, 1988] and something similar can probably be done for $\lambda\underline{\omega}$. On the other hand, no natural Curry versions of the systems λP, λP2, $\lambda P\underline{\omega}$ and λC seem possible.

Now first the systems λ→ and λ2 *à la* Church will be introduced in the usual way. Also $\lambda\underline{\omega}$ and λP will be defined. Then the λ-cube will be defined in a uniform way and two of the systems on it turn out to be equivalent to $\lambda\!\rightarrow$ and $\lambda 2$.

$\lambda\!\rightarrow$-Church

Although this system has been introduced already in subsection 3.2, we will repeat its definition in a stylistic way, setting the example for the definition of the other systems.

Definition 5.1.1. The system $\lambda\!\rightarrow$-Church consists of a set of types $\mathbb{T} = \text{type}(\lambda\!\rightarrow)$, a set of pseudoterms $\Lambda_{\mathbb{T}}$, a set of bases, a conversion (and reduction) relation on $\Lambda_{\mathbb{T}}$ and a type assignment relation $\vdash$.

The sets $\mathbb{T}$ and $\Lambda_{\mathbb{T}}$ are defined by an abstract syntax, bases are defined explicitly, the conversion relation is defined by a contraction rule and $\vdash$ is defined by a deduction system as follows:

1. Types	$\mathbb{T} = \mathbb{V} \mid \mathbb{T}\rightarrow\mathbb{T}$;
2. Pseudoterms	$\Lambda_{\mathbb{T}} = V \mid \Lambda_{\mathbb{T}}\Lambda_{\mathbb{T}} \mid \lambda V{:}\mathbb{T}.\Lambda$;
3. Bases	$\Gamma = \{x_1{:}A_1, \ldots, x_n{:}A_n\}$,
	with all x_i distinct and all $A_i \in \mathbb{T}$;
4. Contraction rule	$(\lambda x{:}A.M)N \rightarrow_\beta M[x := N]$;
5. Type assignment	$\Gamma \vdash M : A$ is defined as follows.

$\lambda\!\rightarrow$

(start-rule)	$\dfrac{(x{:}A) \in \Gamma}{\Gamma \vdash x{:}A}$;
($\rightarrow$-elimination)	$\dfrac{\Gamma \vdash M : (A\rightarrow B) \quad \Gamma \vdash N : A}{\Gamma \vdash (MN) : B}$;
($\rightarrow$-introduction)	$\dfrac{\Gamma,\ x{:}A \vdash M{:}B}{\Gamma \vdash (\lambda x{:}A.M) : (A\rightarrow B)}$.

Remarks 5.1.2.

1. In 1 the character $\mathbb{V}$ denotes the syntactic category of type variables. Similarly in 2 the character V denotes the category of term variables. In 4 the letter x denotes an arbitrary term variable. In 3 the $x_1, \ldots, x_n$ are distinct term variables. In 4 and 5 the letters A, B denote arbitrary types and M, N arbitrary pseudoterms. The basis $\Gamma, x{:}A$ stands for $\Gamma \cup \{x{:}A\}$, where it is necessary that x is a variable that does not occur in Γ.

2. A pseudoterm M is called *legal* if for some Γ and A one has $\Gamma \vdash M{:}A$.

Typical examples of type assignments in $\lambda{\rightarrow}$ are the following. Let $A, B \in \mathbb{T}$.

$$\begin{array}{rcl} & \vdash & (\lambda a{:}A.a) : (A{\rightarrow}A); \\ b{:}B & \vdash & (\lambda a{:}A.b) : (A{\rightarrow}B); \\ b{:}A & \vdash & ((\lambda a{:}A.a)b) : A; \\ c{:}A, b{:}B & \vdash & (\lambda a{:}A.b)c : B; \\ & \vdash & (\lambda a{:}A.\lambda b{:}B.a) : (A{\rightarrow}B{\rightarrow}A). \end{array}$$

The system λT

Type and term constants are not officially introduced in this chapter. However, these are useful to make axiomatic extensions of $\lambda{\rightarrow}$ in which certain terms and types play a special role. We will simulate constants via variables. For example one may select a type variable $\mathbf{0}$ and term variables $0, S$ and R_σ for each σ in $\mathbb{T}$ as constants: one postulates in an initial context the following.

$$\begin{array}{rcl} 0 & : & \mathbf{0}; \\ S & : & \mathbf{0}{\rightarrow}\mathbf{0}; \\ R_\sigma & : & (\sigma{\rightarrow}(\sigma{\rightarrow}\mathbf{0}{\rightarrow}\sigma){\rightarrow}\mathbf{0}{\rightarrow}\sigma). \end{array}$$

Further one extends the definitional equality by adding to the β-contraction rule the following contraction rule for R_σ.

$$\begin{array}{rcl} R_\sigma MN0 & \rightarrow & M; \\ R_\sigma MN(Sx) & \rightarrow & N(R_\sigma MNx)x. \end{array}$$

This extension of $\lambda{\rightarrow}$ is called λT or *Gödel's theory T of primitive recursive functionals* ('Gödel's T'). The type $\mathbf{0}$ stands for the natural numbers with element 0 and successor function S; the R_σ stand for the recursion operator creating recursive functionals of type $\mathbf{0}{\rightarrow}\sigma$. In spite of the name, more than just the primitive recursive functions are representable. This is because recursion is allowed on higher functionals; see e.g. [Barendregt, 1984], appendix A.2.1. and [Terlouw, 1982] for an analysis.

λ2-*Church*

Definition 5.1.3. The system λ2-Church is defined as follows:

$\lambda 2$

(start-rule)	$\dfrac{(x{:}A) \in \Gamma}{\Gamma \vdash x : A}$,
(→-elimination)	$\dfrac{\Gamma \vdash M : (A{\to}B) \quad \Gamma \vdash N : A}{\Gamma \vdash (MN) : B}$;
(→-introduction)	$\dfrac{\Gamma, a{:}A \vdash M : B}{\Gamma \vdash (\lambda a{:}A.M) : (A{\to}B)}$;
(∀-elimination)	$\dfrac{\Gamma \vdash M : (\forall\alpha.A)}{\Gamma \vdash MB : A[\alpha := B]}$, $B \in \mathbb{T}$;
(∀-introduction)	$\dfrac{\Gamma \vdash M : A}{\Gamma \vdash (\Lambda\alpha.M) : (\forall\alpha.A)}$, $\alpha \notin \mathrm{FV}(\Gamma)$.

1. Types $\mathbb{T} = \mathbb{V} \mid \mathbb{T}{\to}\mathbb{T} \mid \forall\mathbb{V}\mathbb{T}$;
2. Pseudoterms $\Lambda_{\mathbb{T}} = V \mid \Lambda_{\mathbb{T}}\Lambda_{\mathbb{T}} \mid \Lambda_{\mathbb{T}}\mathbb{T} \mid \lambda V{:}\mathbb{T}\Lambda_{\mathbb{T}} \mid \Lambda\mathbb{V}\Lambda_{\mathbb{T}}$;
3. Bases $\Gamma = \{x_1{:}A_1, \ldots, x_n{:}A_n\}$, with $\vec{x}$ distinct and $\vec{A} \in \mathbb{T}$;
4. Contraction rules $(\lambda a{:}A.M)N \to_\beta M[a := N]$ $(\Lambda\alpha.M)A \to_\beta M[\alpha := A]$
5. Type assignment $\Gamma \vdash M : A$ is defined as follows.

Typical assignments in $\lambda 2$ are the following:

$$\begin{aligned} &\vdash (\lambda a{:}\alpha.a) : (\alpha{\to}\alpha);\\ &\vdash (\Lambda\alpha\lambda a{:}\alpha.a) : (\forall\alpha.\alpha{\to}\alpha);\\ &\vdash (\Lambda\alpha\lambda a{:}\alpha.a)A : (A{\to}A);\\ b{:}A\ &\vdash (\Lambda\alpha\lambda a{:}\alpha.a)Ab : A; \end{aligned}$$

{of course the following reduction holds:

$$(\Lambda\alpha\lambda a{:}\alpha.a)Ab \to (\lambda a{:}A.a)b \to b;\ \}$$
$$\vdash (\Lambda\beta\lambda a{:}(\forall\alpha.\alpha).a((\forall\alpha.\alpha){\to}\beta)a) : (\forall\beta.(\forall\alpha.\alpha){\to}\beta);$$

{for this last example one has to think twice to see that it is correct; a simpler term of the same type is the following}

$$\vdash (\Lambda\beta\lambda a{:}(\forall\alpha{:}\alpha).a\beta) : (\forall\beta.(\forall\alpha.\alpha)\rightarrow\beta).$$

Without a proof we mention that the Church–Rosser property holds for reduction on pseudoterms in $\lambda 2$.

Dependency

Types and terms are mutually dependent; there are

terms depending on terms;
terms depending on types;
types depending on terms;
types depending on types.

The first two sorts of dependency we have seen already. Indeed, in $\lambda\rightarrow$ we have

$$F : A\rightarrow B \quad M : A \quad \Rightarrow \quad FM : B.$$

Here FM is a term depending on a term (e.g. on M). For $\lambda 2$ we saw

$$G : \forall\alpha.\alpha\rightarrow\alpha \quad A \text{ a type} \quad \Rightarrow \quad GA : A\rightarrow A.$$

Hence for $G = \Lambda\alpha\lambda a{:}\alpha.a$ one has that GA is a term depending on the type A.

In $\lambda\rightarrow$ and $\lambda 2$ one has also function abstraction for the two dependencies. For the two examples above

$$\lambda m{:}A.Fm : A\rightarrow B,$$

$$\Lambda\alpha.G\alpha : \forall\alpha.\alpha\rightarrow\alpha.$$

Now we shall define two other systems $\lambda\underline{\omega}$ and λP with *types* FA (FM resp) depending on types (respectively terms). We will also have function abstraction for these dependencies in $\lambda\underline{\omega}$ and λP.

Types depending on types; the system $\lambda\underline{\omega}$

A natural example of a type depending on another type is $\alpha\rightarrow\alpha$ that depends on α. In fact it is natural to define $f = \lambda\alpha \in \mathbb{T}.\alpha\rightarrow\alpha$ such that $f(\alpha) = \alpha\rightarrow\alpha$. This will be possible in the system $\lambda\underline{\omega}$. Another feature of $\lambda\underline{\omega}$ is that types are generated by the system itself and not in the informal metalanguage. There is a constant $*$ such that $\sigma : *$ corresponds to $\sigma \in \mathbb{T}$. The informal statement

$$\alpha, \beta \in \mathbb{T} \Rightarrow (\alpha\rightarrow\beta) \in \mathbb{T}$$

now becomes the formal

$$\alpha{:}*, \beta{:}* \vdash (\alpha{\to}\beta) : *.$$

For the f above we then write $f \equiv \lambda\alpha{:}*.\alpha{\to}\alpha$. The question arises where this f lives. Neither on the level of the terms, nor among the types. Therefore a new category $\mathbb{K}$ (of kinds) is introduced

$$\mathbb{K} = * \mid \mathbb{K}{\to}\mathbb{K}.$$

That is $\mathbb{K} = \{*, *{\to}*, *{\to}*{\to}*, \ldots\}$. A constant $\Box$ will be introduced such that $k : \Box$ corresponds to $k \in \mathbb{K}$. If $\vdash k : \Box$ and $\vdash F : k$, then F is called a *constructor* of kind k. We will see that $\vdash (\lambda\alpha{:}*.\alpha{\to}\alpha) : (*{\to}*)$, i.e. our f is a constructor of kind $*{\to}*$. Each element of $\mathbb{T}$ will be a constructor of kind $*$.

Although types and terms of $\lambda\underline{\omega}$ can be kept separate, we will consider them as subsets of one general set $\mathcal{T}$ of pseudo expressions. This is a preparation to 5.1.8, 5.1.9 and 5.1.10 in which it is essential that types and terms are being mixed.

Definition 5.1.4 (Types and terms of $\lambda\underline{\omega}$).

1. A set of pseudo-expressions $\mathcal{T}$ is defined as follows

$$\mathcal{T} = V \mid C \mid \mathcal{T}\mathcal{T} \mid \lambda V{:}\mathcal{T}.\mathcal{T} \mid \mathcal{T}{\to}\mathcal{T}$$

   where V is an infinite collection of variables and C of constants.

2. Among the constants C two elements are selected and given the names $*$ and $\Box$. These so called *sorts* $*$ and $\Box$ are the main reason to introduce constants.

Because types and terms come from the same set $\mathcal{T}$, the definition of a statement is modified accordingly. Bases have to become linearly ordered. The reason is that in $\lambda\underline{\omega}$ one wants to derive

$$\begin{array}{rcl} \alpha{:}*, x{:}\alpha & \vdash & x : \alpha; \\ \alpha{:}* & \vdash & (\lambda x{:}\alpha.x) : (\alpha{\to}\alpha) \end{array}$$

but not

$$\begin{array}{rcl} x{:}\alpha, \alpha{:}* & \vdash & x : \alpha; \\ x{:}\alpha & \vdash & (\lambda\alpha{:}*.x) : (*{\to}\alpha) \end{array}$$

in which α occurs both free and bound.

Definition 5.1.5 (Contexts for $\lambda\underline{\omega}$).

1. A *statement* of $\lambda\underline{\omega}$ is of the form $M : A$ with $M, A \in \mathcal{T}$.
2. A *context* is a finite linearly ordered set of statements with distinct variables as subjects. $\Gamma, \Delta, \ldots$ range over contexts.
3. $<>$ denotes the empty context. If $\Gamma = <x_1{:}A_1, \ldots, x_n{:}A_n>$ then $\Gamma, y{:}B = <x_1{:}A_1, \ldots, x_n{:}A_n, y{:}B>$.

Definition 5.1.6 (Typing rules for $\lambda\underline{\omega}$). The notion $\Gamma \vdash_{\lambda\underline{\omega}} M : A$ is defined by the following axiom and rules. The letter s ranges over $\{*, \Box\}$.

$\lambda\underline{\omega}$

(axiom)	$<> \vdash * : \Box;$
(start-rule)	$\dfrac{\Gamma \vdash A : s}{\Gamma, x{:}A \vdash x : A},\ x \notin \Gamma;$
(weakening rule)	$\dfrac{\Gamma \vdash A : B \quad \Gamma \vdash C : s}{\Gamma, x{:}C \vdash A : B},\ x \notin \Gamma;$
(type/kind formation)	$\dfrac{\Gamma \vdash A : s \quad \Gamma \vdash B : s}{\Gamma \vdash (A \to B) : s}.$
(application rule)	$\dfrac{\Gamma \vdash F : (A \to B) \quad \Gamma \vdash a : A}{\Gamma \vdash Fa : B};$
(abstraction rule)	$\dfrac{\Gamma, x{:}A \vdash b : B \quad \Gamma \vdash (A \to B) : s}{\Gamma \vdash (\lambda x{:}A.b) : (A \to B)};$
(conversion rule)	$\dfrac{\Gamma \vdash A : B \quad \Gamma \vdash B' : s \quad B =_\beta B'}{\Gamma \vdash A : B'}.$

Example 5.1.7.

$$
\begin{array}{rll}
\alpha{:}*, \beta{:}* & \vdash_{\lambda\underline{\omega}} & (\alpha \to \beta) : *; \\
\alpha{:}*, \beta{:}*, x{:}(\alpha \to \beta) & \vdash_{\lambda\underline{\omega}} & x : (\alpha \to \beta); \\
\alpha{:}*, \beta{:}* & \vdash_{\lambda\underline{\omega}} & (\lambda x{:}(\alpha \to \beta).x) : ((\alpha \to \beta) \to (\alpha \to \beta)).
\end{array}
$$

Write $D \equiv \lambda\beta{:}*.\beta \to \beta$. Then the following hold.

$$
\begin{array}{rll}
 & \vdash_{\lambda\underline{\omega}} & D : (* \to *). \\
\alpha{:}* & \vdash_{\lambda\underline{\omega}} & (\lambda x{:}D\alpha.x) : D(D\alpha).
\end{array}
$$

Types depending on terms; the system λP

An intuitive example of a type depending on a term is $A^n \rightarrow B$ with n a natural number. In order to formalize the possibility of such 'dependent types' in the system λP, the notion of kind is extended such that if A is a type and k is a kind, then $A \rightarrow k$ is a kind. In particular $A \rightarrow *$ is a kind. Then if $f : A \rightarrow *$ and $a : A$, one has $fa : *$. This fa is a term dependent type. Moreover one has function abstraction for this dependency.

Another idea important for a system with dependent types is the formation of *cartesian products*. Suppose that for each $a : A$ a type B_a is given and that there is an element $b_a : B_a$. Then we may want to form the function

$$\lambda a{:}A.b_a$$

that should have as type the cartesian product

$$\Pi a{:}A.B_a$$

of the B_a's. Once these product types are allowed, the function space type of A and B can be written as

$$(A \rightarrow B) \equiv \Pi a{:}A.B (\equiv B^A, \text{ informally}),$$

where a is a variable not occurring in B. This is analogous to the fact that a product of equal numbers is a power:

$$\prod_{i=1}^{n} b_i = b^n$$

provided that $b_i = b$ for $1 \leq i \leq n$. So by using products, the type constructor $\rightarrow$ can be eliminated.

Definition 5.1.8 (Types and terms of λP).

1. The set of pseudo-expressions of λP, notation, $\mathcal{T}$ is defined as follows

   $$\mathcal{T} = V \mid C \mid \mathcal{T}\mathcal{T} \mid \lambda V{:}\mathcal{T}.\mathcal{T} \mid \Pi V{:}\mathcal{T}.\mathcal{T}$$

   where V is the collection of variables and C that of constants. No distinction between type- and term-variables is made.

2. Among the constants C two elements are called $*$ and $\square$.

Definition 5.1.9 (Assignment rules for λP). Statements and contexts are defined as for $\lambda\underline{\omega}$ (statements are of the form $M{:}A$ with $M, A \in \mathcal{T}$;

contexts are finite linearly ordered statements).
The notion $\vdash$ is defined by the following axiom and rules. Again the letter s ranges over $\{*, \square\}$.

λP

(axiom)	$<> \vdash * : \square;$
(start-rule)	$\dfrac{\Gamma \vdash A : s}{\Gamma, x{:}A \vdash x : A}, \ x \notin \Gamma;$
(weakening rule)	$\dfrac{\Gamma \vdash A : B \quad \Gamma \vdash C : s}{\Gamma, x{:}C \vdash A : B}, \ x \notin \Gamma;$
(type/kind formation)	$\dfrac{\Gamma \vdash A : * \quad \Gamma, x{:}A \vdash B : s}{\Gamma \vdash (\Pi x{:}A.B) : s}.$
(application rule)	$\dfrac{\Gamma \vdash F : (\Pi x{:}A.B) \quad \Gamma \vdash a : A}{\Gamma \vdash Fa : B[x := a]};$
(abstraction rule)	$\dfrac{\Gamma, x{:}A \vdash b : B \quad \Gamma \vdash (\Pi x{:}A.B) : s}{\Gamma \vdash (\lambda x{:}A.b) : (\Pi x{:}A.B)};$
(conversion rule)	$\dfrac{\Gamma \vdash A : B \quad \Gamma \vdash B' : s \quad B =_\beta B'}{\Gamma \vdash A : B'}.$

Typical assignments in λP are the following:

$$\begin{array}{rcl}
A{:}* & \vdash & (A \to *) : \square; \\
A{:}*, P{:}A \to *, a{:}A & \vdash & Pa : *; \\
A{:}*, P{:}A \to *, a{:}A & \vdash & Pa \to * : \square; \\
A{:}*, P{:}A \to * & \vdash & (\Pi a{:}A.Pa \to *) : \square; \\
A{:}*, P{:}A \to * & \vdash & (\lambda a{:}A \lambda x{:}Pa.x) : (\Pi a{:}A.(Pa \to Pa))
\end{array}$$

Pragmatics of λP

Systems like λP have been introduced by N.G. de Bruijn [de Bruijn, 1970; de Bruijn, 1980] in order to represent mathematical theorems and their proofs. The method is as follows. One assumes there is a set prop of propositions that is closed under implication. This is done by taking as context Γ_0 defined as

$$\text{prop}{:}*, \text{Imp}{:}\text{prop} \to \text{prop} \to \text{prop}.$$

Write $\varphi \supset \psi$ for Imp$\,\varphi\psi$. In order to express that a proposition is valid a variable T : prop$\rightarrow *$ is declared and φ : prop is defined to be valid if $\mathrm{T}\varphi$ is inhabited, i.e. $M : \mathrm{T}\varphi$ for some M. Now in order to express that implication has the right properties, one assumes $\supset_e$ and $\supset_i$ such that

$$\supset_e\varphi\psi : \mathrm{T}(\varphi \supset \psi)\rightarrow\mathrm{T}\varphi\rightarrow\mathrm{T}\psi.$$

$$\supset_i\varphi\psi : (\mathrm{T}\varphi\rightarrow\mathrm{T}\psi)\rightarrow\mathrm{T}(\varphi \supset \psi).$$

So for the representation of implicational proposition logic one wants to work in context Γ_{prop} consisting of Γ_0 followed by

$$\begin{array}{lcl} \mathrm{T} & : & \mathrm{prop}\rightarrow * \\ \supset_e & : & \Pi\varphi{:}\mathrm{prop}\Pi\psi{:}\mathrm{prop}.\mathrm{T}(\varphi \supset \psi)\rightarrow\mathrm{T}\varphi\rightarrow\mathrm{T}\psi \\ \supset_i & : & \Pi\varphi{:}\mathrm{prop}\Pi\psi{:}\mathrm{prop}.(\mathrm{T}\varphi\rightarrow\mathrm{T}\psi)\rightarrow\mathrm{T}(\varphi \supset \psi). \end{array}$$

As an example we want to formulate that $\varphi \supset \varphi$ is valid for all propositions. The translation as type is $\mathrm{T}(\varphi \supset \varphi)$ which indeed is inhabited

$$\Gamma_{\mathrm{prop}} \vdash_{\lambda\mathrm{P}} (\supset_i\varphi\varphi(\lambda x{:}\mathrm{T}\varphi.x)) : \mathrm{T}(\varphi \supset \varphi).$$

(Note that since $\vdash \mathrm{T}\varphi : *$ one has $\vdash (\lambda x{:}\mathrm{T}\varphi.x) : (\mathrm{T}\varphi\rightarrow\mathrm{T}\varphi)$.)

Having formalized many valid statements de Bruijn realized that it was rather tiresome to carry around the T. He therefore proposed to use $*$ itself for prop, the constructor $\rightarrow$ for $\supset$ and the identity for T. Then for $\supset_e\varphi\psi$ one can use

$$\lambda x{:}(\varphi\rightarrow\psi)\lambda y{:}\varphi.xy$$

and for $\supset_i\varphi\psi$

$$\lambda x{:}(\varphi\rightarrow\psi).x.$$

In this way the $\{\rightarrow, \forall\}$ fragment of (manysorted constructive) predicate logic can be interpreted too. A predicate P on a set (type) A can be represented as a $P{:}(A\rightarrow *)$ and for $a{:}A$ one defines Pa to be valid if it is inhabited. Quantification $\forall x \in A.Px$ is translated as $\Pi x{:}A.Px$. Now a formula like

$$[\forall x \in A\forall y \in A.Pxy]\rightarrow[\forall x \in A.Pxx]$$

can be seen to be valid because its translation is inhabited

$$\begin{array}{rcl} A{:}*, P{:}A\rightarrow A\rightarrow * & \vdash & (\lambda z{:}(\Pi x{:}A\Pi y{:}A.Pxy)\lambda x{:}A.zxx) : \\ & & ([\Pi x{:}A\Pi y{:}A.Pxy]\rightarrow[\Pi x{:}A.Pxx]). \end{array}$$

The system $\lambda\mathrm{P}$ is given that name because predicate logic can be interpreted in it. The method interprets propositions (or formulas) as types and proofs as inhabiting terms and is the basis of several languages in the family AUTOMATH designed and implemented by de Bruijn and coworkers for the automatic verification of proofs. Similar projects inspired by AUTOMATH are described in [Constable *et al.*, 1986] (NUPRL), [Harper *et al.*, 1987] (LF) and [Coquand and Huet, 1988] (calculus of constructions). The project LF uses the interpretation of formulas using T:(prop→∗) like the original use in AUTOMATH. In [Martin-Löf, 1984] the proposition-as-types paradigm is used for formulating results in the foundation of mathematics.

The λ-cube

We will now introduce a cube of eight systems of typed lambda calculi. This so called 'λ-cube' forms a natural framework in which several known systems *à la* Church, including λ→, λ2, $\lambda\underline{\omega}$ and λP are given in a uniform way. It provides a finestructure of the calculus of constructions, which is the strongest system in the cube. The differentiation between the systems is obtained by controlling the way in which abstractions are allowed.

The systems λ→ and λ2 in the λ-cube are not given in their original version, but in a equivalent variant. Also for some of the other known systems the versions on the cube are only in essence equivalent to the original ones. The point is that there are some choices for the precise formulation of the systems and in the cube these choices are made uniformly.

Definition 5.1.10 (Systems of the λ-cube).

1. The systems of the λ-cube are based on a set of pseudo-expressions $\mathcal{T}$ defined by the following abstract syntax.

$$\mathcal{T} = V \mid C \mid \mathcal{T}\mathcal{T} \mid \lambda V{:}\mathcal{T}.\mathcal{T} \mid \Pi V{:}\mathcal{T}.\mathcal{T}$$

   where V and C are infinite collections of variables and constants respectively. No distinction between type- and term-variables is made.

2. On $\mathcal{T}$ the notions of β-conversion and β-reduction are defined by the following contraction rule:

$$(\lambda x{:}A.B)C \to B[x := C].$$

3. A *statement* is of the form $A : B$ with $A, B \in \mathcal{T}$. A is the *subject* and B is the *predicate* of $A : B$. A *declaration* is of the form $x{:}A$ with $A \in \mathcal{T}$ and x a variable. A *pseudo-context* is a finite ordered sequence of declarations, all with distinct subjects. The empty context is denoted by $<>$. If $\Gamma = < x_1{:}A_1, \ldots, x_n{:}A_n >$, then

$$\Gamma, x{:}B = < x_1{:}A_1, \ldots, x_n{:}A_n, x{:}B > .$$

Usually we do not write the <> .

4. The rules of type assignment will axiomatize the notion

$$\Gamma \vdash A : B$$

stating that $A : B$ can be derived from the pseudo-context Γ; in that case A and B are called (legal) expressions and Γ is a (legal) context.

The rules are given in two groups:

(a) the general axiom and rules, valid for all systems of the λ-cube;

(b) the specific rules, differentiating between the eight systems; these are parametrized Π-introduction rules.

Two constants are selected and are given the names $*$ and $\Box$. These two constants are called *sorts*. Let $\mathcal{S} = \{*, \Box\}$ and s, s_1, s_2 range over $\mathcal{S}$.

We use $A, B, C, a, b, \ldots$ for abitrary pseudo-terms and $x, y, z, \ldots$ for arbitrary variables.

Systems in the λ-cube

1. General axiom and rules.

(axiom) $<> \vdash * : \Box$;

(start rule) $$\frac{\Gamma \vdash A : s}{\Gamma, x{:}A \vdash x : A}, \; x \notin \Gamma;$$

(weakening rule) $$\frac{\Gamma \vdash A : B \quad \Gamma \vdash C : s}{\Gamma, x{:}C \vdash A : B}, \; x \notin \Gamma;$$

(application rule) $$\frac{\Gamma \vdash F : (\Pi x{:}A.B) \quad \Gamma \vdash a : A}{\Gamma \vdash Fa : B[x := a]};$$

(abstraction rule) $$\frac{\Gamma, x{:}A \vdash b : B \quad \Gamma \vdash (\Pi x{:}A.B) : s}{\Gamma \vdash (\lambda x{:}A.b) : (\Pi x{:}A.B)};$$

(conversion rule) $$\frac{\Gamma \vdash A : B \quad \Gamma \vdash B' : s \quad B =_\beta B'}{\Gamma \vdash A : B'}.$$

2. The specific rules

(s_1, s_2) rule $$\frac{\Gamma \vdash A : s_1, \quad \Gamma, x{:}A \vdash B : s_2}{\Gamma \vdash (\Pi x{:}A.B) : s_2}.$$

5. *The eight systems of the* λ-cube are defined by taking the general rules plus a specific subset of the set of rules $\{(*,*), (*,\Box), (\Box,*), (\Box,\Box)\}$.

System	Set of specific rules			
λ→	$(*,*)$			
λ2	$(*,*)$	$(\Box,*)$		
λP	$(*,*)$		$(*,\Box)$	
λP2	$(*,*)$	$(\Box,*)$	$(*,\Box)$	
$\lambda\underline{\omega}$	$(*,*)$			$(\Box,\Box)$
λω	$(*,*)$	$(\Box,*)$		$(\Box,\Box)$
$\lambda P\underline{\omega}$	$(*,*)$		$(*,\Box)$	$(\Box,\Box)$
λPω=λC	$(*,*)$	$(\Box,*)$	$(*,\Box)$	$(\Box,\Box)$

The λ-cube will usually be drawn in the *standard orientation* displayed as follows; the inclusion relations are often left implicit.

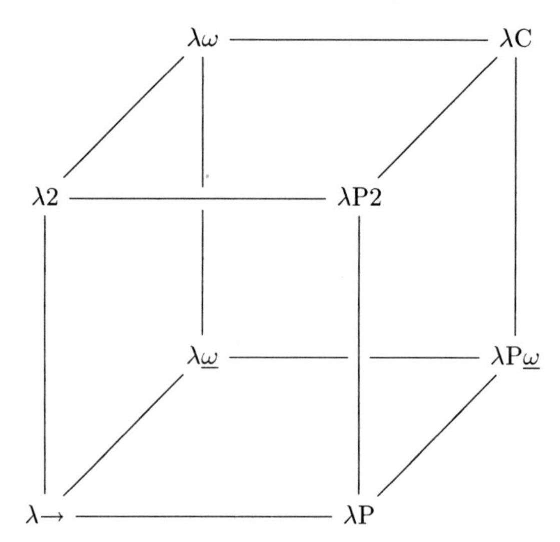

Remark 5.1.11. Most of the systems in the λ-cube appear elsewhere in the literature, often in some variant form.

System	*related system(s)*	*names and references*
$\lambda\!\to$	λ^{τ}	simply typed lambda calculus; [Church, 1940], [Barendregt, 1984], Appendix A, [Hindley and Seldin, 1986], Ch 14.
$\lambda 2$	F	scond order (typed) lambda calculus; [Girard, 1972], [Reynolds, 1974].
λP	AUT-QE; LF	[de Bruijn, 1970]; [Harper *et al.*, 1987].
$\lambda P2$		[Longo and Moggi, 1988].
$\lambda\underline{\omega}$	POLYREC	[Renardel de Lavalette, 1991].
$\lambda\omega$	$F\omega$	[Girard, 1972].
$\lambda P\omega = \lambda C$	CC	calculus of constructions; [Coquand and Huet, 1988].

Remarks 5.1.12.

1. The expression $(\Pi\alpha{:}*.(\alpha\to\alpha))$ in $\lambda 2$ being a cartesian product of types will also be a type, so $(\Pi\alpha{:}*.(\alpha\to\alpha)) : *$. But since it is a

product over all possible types α, including the one *in statu nascendi* (i.e. $(\Pi\alpha{:}*.(\alpha\to\alpha))$ itself is among the types in $*$), there is an essential impredicativity here.

2. Note that in $\lambda\!\to$ one has also in some sense terms depending on types and types depending on types:

$$\lambda x{:}A.x \text{ is a term depending on the type } A,$$
$$A\to A \text{ is a type depending on the type } A.$$

But in $\lambda\!\to$ one has no function abstraction for these dependencies. Note also that in $\lambda\!\to$ (and even in $\lambda 2$ and $\lambda\underline{\omega}$) one has no types depending on terms. The types are given beforehand. The right-hand side of the cube is essentially more difficult then the left-hand side because of the mixture of types and terms.

The two versions of $\lambda\!\to$ *and* $\lambda 2$

Now we have given the definition of the λ-cube, we want to explain why $\lambda\!\to$ and $\lambda 2$ in the cube are essentially the same as the systems with the same name defined in 5.1.1 and 5.1.3 respectively.

Definition 5.1.13. In the systems of the λ-cube we use the following notation:

$$A\to B \equiv \Pi x{:}A.B, \text{ where } x \text{ is fresh (not in } A, B).$$

Lemma 5.1.14. *Consider* $\lambda\!\to$ *in the* λ*-cube. If* $\Gamma \vdash A : *$ *in this system, then* A *is built up from the set* $\{B \mid (B : *) \in \Gamma\}$ *using only* $\to$ *(as defined in 5.1.13).*

Proof. By induction on the generation of $\vdash$. ∎

Notice that the application rule implies the $\to$-elimination rule:

$$\frac{\Gamma \vdash F : (A\to B)(\equiv \Pi x{:}A.B) \quad \Gamma \vdash a : A}{\Gamma \vdash (Fa) : B[x := a] \equiv B},$$

since x does not occur in B. It follows that if e.g. in $\lambda\!\to$ in the λ-cube one derives

$$A{:}*, B{:}*, a{:}A, b{:}B \vdash M : C : *$$

then

$$a{:}A, b{:}B \vdash M : C$$

is derivable in the system $\lambda\!\to$ as defined in 5.1.1.

Similarly one shows that both variants of $\lambda 2$ are the same by first defining in the λ-cube

$$\forall\alpha.A \equiv \Pi\alpha{:}{*}.A,$$

$$\Lambda\alpha.M \equiv \lambda\alpha{:}{*}.M.$$

Of course the use of the greek letter α is only suggestive; after all, it is a bound variable and its name is irrelevant.

Some derivable type assignments in the λ-cube

We end this subsection by giving some examples of type assignment for the systems in the λ-cube. The examples for $\lambda\!\rightarrow$ and $\lambda 2$ given before are essentially repeated in the new style of the systems.

The reader is invited to carefully study these examples in order to gain some intuition in the systems of the λ-cube. Some of the examples are followed by a comment {in curly brackets}. In order to understand the intended meaning for the systems on the right plane in the λ-cube (i.e. the rule pair $(*, \Box)$ is present), some of the elements of $*$ have to be considered as sets and some as propositions. The examples show that the systems in the λ-cube are related to logical systems and form a preview of the propositions-as-type interpretation described in subsection 5.4. Names of variables are chosen freely as either Roman or Greek letters, in order to follow the intended interpretation. The notation $\Gamma \vdash A : B : C$ stands for the conjunction of $\Gamma \vdash A : B$ and $\Gamma \vdash B : C$.

Examples 5.1.15.

1. In $\lambda\!\rightarrow$ the following can be derived:

$$\begin{array}{rcl} A{:}* & \vdash & (\Pi x{:}A.A) : *; \\ A{:}* & \vdash & (\lambda a{:}A.a) : (\Pi x{:}A.A); \\ A{:}*, B{:}*, b{:}B & \vdash & (\lambda a{:}A.b) : (A{\rightarrow}B), \\ & & \text{where } (A{\rightarrow}B) \equiv (\Pi x{:}A.B); \\ A{:}*, b{:}A & \vdash & ((\lambda a{:}A.a)b) : A; \\ A{:}*, B{:}*, c{:}A, b{:}B & \vdash & ((\lambda a{:}A.b)c) : B; \\ A{:}*, B{:}* & \vdash & (\lambda a{:}A\lambda b{:}B.a) : (A{\rightarrow}(B{\rightarrow}A)) : *. \end{array}$$

2. In $\lambda 2$ the following can be derived:

$$\begin{array}{rcl} \alpha{:}* & \vdash & (\lambda a{:}\alpha.a) : (\alpha{\rightarrow}\alpha); \\ & \vdash & (\lambda\alpha{:}*\lambda a{:}\alpha.a) : (\Pi\alpha{:}*.(\alpha{\rightarrow}\alpha)) : *; \\ A{:}* & \vdash & (\lambda\alpha{:}*\lambda a{:}\alpha.a)A : (A{\rightarrow}A); \\ A{:}*, b{:}A & \vdash & (\lambda\alpha{:}*\lambda a{:}\alpha.a)Ab : A; \end{array}$$

of course the following reduction holds:

$$\begin{array}{rcl}(\lambda\alpha{:}*\lambda a{:}\alpha.a)Ab & \to & (\lambda a{:}A.a)b \\ & \to & b.\end{array}$$

The following two examples show a connection with second-order proposition logic.

$$\vdash (\lambda\beta{:}*\lambda a{:}(\Pi\alpha{:}*.\alpha).a((\Pi\alpha{:}*.\alpha)\to\beta)a) : (\Pi\beta{:}*.(\Pi\alpha{:}*.\alpha)\to\beta).$$

{For this last example one has to think twice to see that it is correct; a simpler term of the same type is the following; write $\bot \equiv (\Pi\alpha{:}*.\alpha)$, which is the second-order definition of falsum.}

$$\vdash (\lambda\beta{:}*\lambda a{:}\bot.a\beta) : (\Pi\beta{:}*.\bot\to\beta).$$

{The type considered as proposition says: *ex falso sequitur quodlibet*, i.e. anyting follows from a false statement; the term in this type is its proof.}

3. In $\lambda\underline{\omega}$ the following can be derived

$$\vdash (\lambda\alpha{:}*.\alpha\to\alpha) : (*\to*) : \Box$$

{$(\lambda\alpha{:}*.\alpha\to\alpha)$ is a constructor mapping types into types};

$$\begin{array}{l}\beta{:}* \vdash (\lambda\alpha{:}*.\alpha\to\alpha)\beta : *; \\ \beta{:}*, x{:}\beta \vdash (\lambda y{:}\beta.x) : (\lambda\alpha{:}*.\alpha\to\alpha)\beta\end{array}$$

{note that $(\lambda y{:}\beta.x)$ has type $\beta\to\beta$ in the given context};

$$\begin{array}{l}\alpha{:}*, f{:}*\to* \vdash f(f\alpha) : *; \\ \alpha{:}* \vdash (\lambda f{:}*\to*.f(f\alpha)) : (*\to*)\to*\end{array}$$

{in this way higher-order constructors are formed}.

4. In λP the following can be derived:

$$A{:}* \vdash (A\to*) : \Box$$

{if A is a type considered as set, then $A\to*$ is the kind of predicates on A};

$$A{:}*, P{:}(A\to*), a{:}A \vdash Pa : *$$

{if A is a set, $a \in A$ and P is a predicate on A, then Pa is a type considered as proposition (true if inhabited; false otherwise)};

$$A{:}*, P{:}(A\to A\to*) \vdash (\Pi a{:}A.Paa) : *$$

{if P is a binary predicate on the set A, then $\forall a \in A\ Paa$ is a proposition};

$$A{:}*, P{:}A{\to}*, Q{:}A{\to}* \vdash (\Pi a{:}A.(Pa{\to}Qa)) : *$$

{this proposition states that the predicate P considered as a set is included in the predicate Q};

$$A{:}*, P{:}A{\to}* \vdash (\Pi a{:}A.(Pa{\to}Pa)) : *$$

{this proposition states the reflexivity of inclusion};

$$A{:}*, P{:}A{\to}* \vdash (\lambda a{:}A\lambda x{:}Pa.x) : (\Pi a{:}A.(Pa{\to}Pa)) : *$$

{the subject in this assignment provides the 'proof' of reflexivity of inclusion};

$$A{:}*, P{:}A{\to}*, Q{:}* \vdash ((\Pi a{:}A.Pa{\to}Q){\to}(\Pi a{:}A.Pa){\to}Q) : *$$

$$\begin{aligned} A{:}*, P{:}A{\to}*, Q{:}*, a_0{:}A \vdash\ & (\lambda x{:}(\Pi a{:}A.Pa{\to}Q)\lambda y{:}(\Pi a{:}A.Pa).xa_o(ya_o)) : \\ & (\Pi x{:}(\Pi a{:}A.Pa{\to}Q)\Pi y{:}(\Pi a{:}A.Pa).Q) \equiv \\ & \quad (\Pi a{:}A.Pa{\to}Q){\to}(\Pi a{:}A.Pa){\to}Q \end{aligned}$$

{this proposition states that the proposition

$$(\forall a \in A.Pa{\to}Q){\to}(\forall a \in A.Pa){\to}Q$$

is true in non-empty structures A; notice that the lay out explains the functioning of the λ–rule; in this type assignment the subject is the 'proof' of the previous true proposition; note that in the context the assumption $a_0{:}A$ is needed in this proof.}

5. In $\lambda\omega$ the following can be derived.
   Let $\alpha\&\beta \equiv \Pi\gamma{:}*.(\alpha{\to}\beta{\to}\gamma){\to}\gamma$, then

$$\alpha{:}*, \beta{:}* \vdash \alpha\&\beta : *$$

{this is the 'second-order definition of &' and is definable already in $\lambda 2$}.

Let AND $\equiv \lambda\alpha{:}{*}\lambda\beta{:}{*}.\alpha\&\beta$ and $K \equiv \lambda\alpha{:}{*}\lambda\beta{:}{*}\lambda x{:}\alpha\lambda y{:}\beta.x$, then

$$\begin{array}{l} \vdash \ \mathrm{AND} : ({*}\to{*}\to{*}), \\ \vdash K : (\Pi\alpha{:}{*}\Pi\beta{:}{*}.\alpha\to\beta\to\alpha). \end{array}$$

{Note that $\alpha\&\beta$ and K can be derived already in $\lambda 2$, but the term AND cannot}.

$$\alpha{:}{*}, \beta{:}{*} \vdash (\lambda x{:}\mathrm{AND}\alpha\beta.x\alpha(K\alpha\beta)) : (\ \mathrm{AND}\alpha\beta\to\alpha) : {*}$$

{the subject is a proof that $\mathrm{AND}\alpha\beta\to\alpha$ is a tautology}.

6. In λP2 {corresponding to second-order predicate logic} the following can be derived.

$$\begin{array}{rcl} A{:}{*}, P{:}A\to{*} & \vdash & (\lambda a{:}A.Pa\to\bot) : (A\to{*}) \\ A{:}{*}, P{:}A\to A\to{*} & \vdash & [(\Pi a{:}A\Pi b{:}A.Pab\to Pba\to\bot) \\ & & \to(\Pi a{:}A.Paa\to\bot)] : {*} \end{array}$$

{the proposition states that a binary relation that is asymmetric is irreflexive}

7. In λP$\underline{\omega}$ the following can be derived.

$$A{:}{*} \vdash (\lambda P{:}A\to A\to{*}\lambda a{:}A.Paa) : ((A\to A\to{*})\to(A\to{*})) : \Box$$

{this constructor assigns to a binary predicate P on A its 'diagonalization'};

$$\vdash (\lambda A{:}{*}\lambda P{:}A\to A\to{*}\lambda a{:}A.Paa) : (\Pi A{:}{*}\Pi P{:}A\to A\to{*}\Pi a{:}A.{*}) : \Box$$

{the same is done uniformly in A}.

8. In λPω = λC the following can be derived.

$$\vdash (\lambda A{:}{*}\lambda P{:}A\to{*}\lambda a{:}A.Pa\to\bot) : (\Pi A{:}{*}.(A\to{*})\to(A\to{*})) : \Box$$

{this constructor assigns to a type A and to a predicate P on A the negation of P}.

Let ALL $\equiv (\lambda A{:}{*}\lambda P{:}A{\to}{*}.\Pi a{:}A.Pa)$; then

$$A{:}{*}, P{:}A{\to}{*} \vdash \ \text{ALL}\, AP : * \text{ and } (\text{ALL}\, AP) =_\beta (\Pi a{:}A.Pa)$$

{universal quantification done uniformly}.

Exercise 5.1.16.

1. Define $\neg \equiv \lambda\alpha{:}{*}.\alpha{\to}\bot$. Construct a term M such that in $\lambda\omega$

$$\alpha : *, \beta : * \vdash M : ((\alpha{\to}\beta){\to}(\neg\beta{\to}\neg\alpha)).$$

2. Find an expression M such that in λP2

$$A{:}{*}, P{:}(A{\to}A{\to}{*}) \vdash$$

$$M : [(\Pi a{:}A\Pi b{:}A.Pab{\to}Pba{\to}\bot){\to}(\Pi a{:}A.Paa{\to}\bot)] : *.$$

3. Find a term M such that in λC

$$A{:}{*}, P{:}A{\to}{*}, a{:}A \vdash M : (\text{ALL}\, AP{\to}Pa).$$

5.2 Pure type systems

The method of generating the systems in the λ-cube has been generalized independently by [Berardi, 1989] and [Terlouw, 1989]. This resulted in the notion of *pure type system* (PTS). Many systems of typed lambda calculus *à la* Church can be seen as PTSs. Subtle differences between systems can be described neatly using the notation for PTSs.

One of the successes of the notion of PTS's is concerned with logic. In subsection 5.4 a cube of eight logical systems will be introduced that is in a close correspondence with the systems on the λ-cube. This result is the so called 'propositions-as-types' interpretation. It was observed by [Berardi, 1989] that the eight logical systems can each be described as a PTS in such a way that the propositions-as-types interpretation obtains a canonical simple form.

Another reason for introducing PTSs is that several propositions about the systems in the λ-cube are needed. The general setting of the PTSs makes it nicer to give the required proofs. Most results in this subsection are taken from [Geuvers and Nederhof, 1991] and also serve as a preparation for the strong normalization proof in Section 5.3.

The pure type systems are based on the set of pseudo-terms $\mathcal{T}$ for the λ-cube. We repeat the abstract syntax for $\mathcal{T}$.

$$\mathcal{T} = V \mid C \mid \mathcal{T}\mathcal{T} | \lambda V{:}\mathcal{T}\mathcal{T} \mid \Pi V{:}\mathcal{T}\mathcal{T}$$

Definition 5.2.1. The *specification of a* PTS consists of a triple S = (S, A, R) where

1. S is a subset of C, called the *sorts*;

2. A is a set of *axioms* of the form

$$c : s$$

   with $c \in \mathcal{C}$ and $s \in \mathcal{S}$;

3. $\mathcal{R}$ is a set of rules of the form

$$(s_1, s_2, s_3)$$

   with $s_1, s_2, s_3 \in \mathcal{S}$.

It is useful to divide the set V of variables into disjoint infinite subsets V_s for each sort $s \in \mathcal{S}$. So $V = \cup\{V_s \mid s \in \mathcal{S}\}$. The members of V_s are denoted by ${}^s x, {}^s y, {}^s z, \ldots$. Arbitrary variables are often still denoted by $x, y, z, \ldots$; however if necessary one writes $x \equiv {}^s x$ to indicate that $x \in V_s$. The first version of $\lambda 2$ introduced in 5.1.3 can be understood as $x, y, z, \ldots$ ranging over V_* and $\alpha, \beta, \gamma, \ldots$ over $V_\Box$.

Definition 5.2.2. The PTS determined by the specification S = $(\mathcal{S}, \mathcal{A}, \mathcal{R})$, notation λS=$\lambda(\mathcal{S}, \mathcal{A}, \mathcal{R})$, is defined as follows. Statements and contexts are defined as for the λ-cube. The notion of type derivation $\Gamma \vdash_{\lambda \mathrm{S}} A : B$ (we just write $\Gamma \vdash A : B$) is defined by the following axioms and rules:

$\lambda(\mathcal{S}, \mathcal{A}, \mathcal{R})$

(axioms)	$<>\vdash c : s,$	if $(c : s) \in \mathcal{A}$;
(start)	$\dfrac{\Gamma \vdash A : s}{\Gamma, x : A \vdash x : A},$	if $x \equiv {}^s x \notin \Gamma$;
(weakening)	$\dfrac{\Gamma \vdash A : B \quad \Gamma \vdash C : s}{\Gamma, x : C \vdash A : B},$	if $x \equiv {}^s x \notin \Gamma$;
(product)	$\dfrac{\Gamma \vdash A : s_1 \quad \Gamma, x{:}A \vdash B : s_2}{\Gamma \vdash (\Pi x{:}A.B) : s_3},$	if $(s_1, s_2, s_3) \in \mathcal{R}$;
(application)	$\dfrac{\Gamma \vdash F : (\Pi x{:}A.B) \quad \Gamma \vdash a : A}{\Gamma \vdash Fa : B[x := a]};$	
(abstraction)	$\dfrac{\Gamma, x{:}A \vdash b : B \quad \Gamma \vdash (\Pi x{:}A.B) : s}{\Gamma \vdash (\lambda x{:}A.b) : (\Pi x{:}A.B)};$	
(conversion)	$\dfrac{\Gamma \vdash A : B \quad \Gamma \vdash B' : s \quad B =_\beta B'}{\Gamma \vdash A : B'}.$	

In the above we use the following conventions.

s ranges over $\mathcal{S}$, the set of sorts;

x ranges over variables.

The proviso in the conversion rule ($B =_\beta B'$) is a priori not decidable. However it can be replaced by the decidable condition

$$B' \twoheadrightarrow_\beta B \text{ or } B \twoheadrightarrow_\beta B'$$

without changing the set of derivable statements.

Definition 5.2.3.

1. The rule (s_1, s_2) is an abbreviation for (s_1, s_2, s_2). In the λ-cube only systems with rules of this simpler form are used.

2. The PTS $\lambda(\mathcal{S}, \mathcal{A}, \mathcal{R})$ is called *full* if

$$\mathcal{R} = \{(s_1, s_2) \mid s_1, s_2 \in \mathcal{S}\}.$$

Examples 5.2.4.

1. $\lambda 2$ is the PTS determined by:

$$\begin{array}{rcl} \mathcal{S} & = & \{*, \Box\} \\ \mathcal{A} & = & \{* : \Box\} \\ \mathcal{R} & = & \{(*, *), (\Box, *)\}. \end{array}$$

Specifications like this will be given more stylistically as follows.

$$\lambda 2 \begin{array}{|ll|} \hline \mathcal{S} & *, \Box \\ \mathcal{A} & * : \Box \\ \mathcal{R} & (*, *), (\Box, *) \\ \hline \end{array}$$

2. λC is the full PTS with

$$\lambda C \begin{array}{|ll|} \hline \mathcal{S} & *, \Box \\ \mathcal{A} & * : \Box \\ \mathcal{R} & (*, *), (\Box, *), (*, \Box), (\Box, \Box) \\ \hline \end{array}$$

3. A variant $\lambda C'$ of λC is the full PTS with

$$\lambda C' \begin{array}{|ll|} \hline \mathcal{S} & *^t, *^p, \Box \\ \mathcal{A} & *^t : \Box, *^p : \Box \\ \mathcal{R} & \mathcal{S}^2, \text{ i.e. all pairs} \\ \hline \end{array}$$

4. $\lambda\!\rightarrow$ is the PTS determined by

$$\lambda\!\rightarrow \begin{array}{|ll|} \hline \mathcal{S} & *, \Box \\ \mathcal{A} & * : \Box \\ \mathcal{R} & (*, *) \\ \hline \end{array}$$

5. A variant of $\lambda\!\rightarrow$, called λ^τ in [Barendregt, 1984] Appendix A, is the PTS determined by

$$\lambda^\tau \begin{array}{|ll|} \hline \mathcal{S} & * \\ \mathcal{A} & 0 : * \\ \mathcal{R} & (*, *) \\ \hline \end{array}$$

The difference with $\lambda\!\rightarrow$ is that in λ^τ no type variables are possible but only has constant types like $0, 0\!\rightarrow\!0, 0\!\rightarrow\!0\!\rightarrow\!0, \ldots$.

6. The system $\lambda *$ in which $*$ is the sort of all types, including itself, is specified by

$\lambda *$		
	$\mathcal{S}$	$*$
	$\mathcal{A}$	$* : *$
	$\mathcal{R}$	$(*, *)$

In subsection 5.5 it will be shown that the system $\lambda *$ is 'inconsistent', in the sense that all types are inhabited. This result is known as Girard's paradox. One may think that the result is caused by the circularity in $* : *$, however [Girard, 1972] showed that also the following system is inconsistent in the same sense, see Section 5.5.

λU		
	$\mathcal{S}$	$*, \Box, \Delta$
	$\mathcal{A}$	$* : \Box, \Box : \Delta$
	$\mathcal{R}$	$(*, *), (\Box, *), (\Box, \Box), (\Delta, \Box), (\Delta, *)$

7. [Geuvers, 1990] The system of higher-order logic in [Church, 1940] can be described by the following PTS; see Ssection 5.4 for its use.

λHOL		
	$\mathcal{S}$	$*, \Box, \Delta$
	$\mathcal{A}$	$* : \Box, \Box : \Delta$
	$\mathcal{R}$	$(*, *), (\Box, *), (\Box, \Box)$

8. [van Benthem Jutting, 1990] So far none of the rules has been of the form (s_1, s_2, s_3). Several members of the AUTOMATH family, see [van Daalen, 1980; de Bruijn, 1980], can be described as PTSs with such rules. The sort Δ serves as a 'parking place' for certain terms.

λAUT-68		
	$\mathcal{S}$	$*, \Box, \Delta$
	$\mathcal{A}$	$* : \Box$
	$\mathcal{R}$	$(*, *), (*, \Box, \Delta), (\Box, *, \Delta)$
		$(\Box, \Box, \Delta), (*, \Delta, \Delta), (\Box, \Delta, \Delta)$

This system is a strengthening of $\lambda\!\rightarrow$ in which there are more powerful contexts.

λAUT-QE		
	$\mathcal{S}$	$*, \Box, \Delta$
	$\mathcal{A}$	$* : \Box$
	$\mathcal{R}$	$(*, *), (*, \Box), (\Box, *, \Delta)$
		$(\Box, \Box, \Delta), (*, \Delta, \Delta), (\Box, \Delta, \Delta)$

This system corresponds to λP.

λPAL		
	$\mathcal{S}$	$*, \square, \Delta$
	$\mathcal{A}$	$* : \square$
	$\mathcal{R}$	$(*, *, \Delta), (*, \square, \Delta), (\square, *, \Delta)$ $(\square, \square, \Delta), (*, \Delta, \Delta), (\square, \Delta, \Delta)$

This system is a subsystem of $\lambda{\to}$. An interesting conjecture of de Bruijn states that mathematics from before the year 1800 can all be formalized in λPAL.

In subsection 5.4 we will encounter rules of the form (s_1, s_2, s_3) in order to represent first-order but not higher-order functions.

Properties of arbitrary PTS*s*

Now we will state and prove some elementary properties of PTSs. In 5.2.5 - 5.2.17 the notions of context, derivability etc. refer to $\lambda\mathrm{S} = \lambda(\mathcal{S}, \mathcal{A}, \mathcal{R})$, an arbitrary PTS. The results are taken from [Geuvers and Nederhof, 1991].

Notation 5.2.5.

1. $\Gamma \vdash A : B : C$ means $\Gamma \vdash A : B \& \Gamma \vdash B : C$.
2. Let $\Delta \equiv u_1{:}B_1, \ldots, u_n{:}B_n$ with $n \geq 0$ be a pseudocontext. Then $\Gamma \vdash \Delta$ means $\Gamma \vdash u_1{:}B_1$ & ... & $\Gamma \vdash u_n{:}B_n$.

Definition 5.2.6. Let Γ be a pseudocontext and A be a pseudoterm.

1. Γ is called *legal* if $\exists P, Q \in \mathcal{T}\, \Gamma \vdash P : Q$.
2. A is called a Γ-*term* if $\exists B \in \mathcal{T}[\Gamma \vdash A : B$ or $\Gamma \vdash B : A]$.
3. A is called a Γ-*type* if $\exists s \in \mathcal{S}[\Gamma \vdash A : s]$.
4. If $\Gamma \vdash A : s$, then A is called a Γ-*type of sort* s.
5. A is called a Γ-*element* if $\exists B \in \mathcal{T} \exists s \in \mathcal{S}[\Gamma \vdash A : B : s]$.
6. If $\Gamma \vdash A : B : s$ then A is called a Γ-*element of type* B *and of sort* s.
7. $A \in \mathcal{T}$ is called *legal* if $\exists \Gamma, B\ [\Gamma \vdash A : B$ or $\Gamma \vdash B : A]$.

Definition 5.2.7. Let $\Gamma \equiv x_1{:}A_1, \ldots, x_n{:}A_n$ and $\Delta \equiv y_1{:}B_1, \ldots, y_m{:}B_m$ be pseudo-contexts.

1. A statement $x{:}A$ *is in* Γ, notation $(x{:}A) \in \Gamma$, if $x \equiv x_i$ and $A \equiv A_i$ for some i.

2. Γ is *part* of Δ, notation $\Gamma \subseteq \Delta$, if every $x{:}A$ in Γ is also in Δ.

3. Let $1 \le i \le n+1$. Then the *restriction* of Γ to i, notation $\Gamma \upharpoonright i$, is $x_1{:}A_1, \ldots, x_{i-1}{:}A_{i-1}$.

4. Γ is an *initial segment* of Δ, notation $\Gamma \le \Delta$, if for some $j \le m+1$ one has $\Gamma \equiv \Delta \upharpoonright j$.

Lemma 5.2.8 (Free variable lemma for PTS's).
Let $\Gamma \equiv x_1{:}A_1, \ldots, x_n{:}A_n$ be a legal context, say $\Gamma \vdash B : C$. Then the following hold.

1. *The $x_1, \ldots, x_n$ are all distinct.*

2. *$FV(B), FV(C) \subseteq \{x_1, \ldots, x_n\}$.*

3. *$FV(A_i) \subseteq \{x_1, \ldots, x_{i-1}\}$ for $1 \le i \le n$.*

Proof. (1), (2), (3). By induction on the derivation of $\Gamma \vdash B : C$. ∎

The following lemmas show that legal contexts behave as expected.

Lemma 5.2.9 (Start lemma for PTS's). *Let Γ be a legal context. Then*

1. *$(c : s)$ is an axiom $\Rightarrow$ $\Gamma \vdash c : s$;*

2. *$(x{:}A) \in \Gamma$ $\Rightarrow$ $\Gamma \vdash x : A$.*

Proof. (1), (2). By assumption $\Gamma \vdash B : C$ for some B and C. The result follows by induction on the derivation of $\Gamma \vdash B : C$. ∎

Lemma 5.2.10 (Transitivity lemma for PTS's). *Let Γ and Δ be contexts of which Γ is legal. Then*

$$[\Gamma \vdash \Delta \ \&\ \Delta \vdash A : B] \Rightarrow \Gamma \vdash A : B.$$

Proof. By induction on the derivation of $\Delta \vdash A : B$.
We treat two cases:

Case 1. $\Delta \vdash A : B$ is $<> \vdash c : s$ with $c : s$ an axiom. Then by the start lemma 5.2.9 (1) we have $\Gamma \vdash c : s$, since Γ is legal. (Note that trivially $\Gamma \vdash <>$, so one needs to postulate that Γ is legal.)

Case 2. $\Delta \vdash A : B$ is $\Delta \vdash (\Pi x{:}A_1.A_2) : s_3$ and is a direct consequence of $\Delta \vdash A_1 : s_1$ and $\Delta, x{:}A_1 \vdash A_2 : s_2$ for some $(s_1, s_2, s_3) \in \mathcal{R}$. It may be assumed that x does not occur in Γ. Write $\Gamma^+ \equiv \Gamma, x{:}A_1$. Then by the induction hypothesis $\Gamma \vdash A_1 : s_1$, so $\Gamma^+ \vdash \Delta, x{:}A_1$. Hence

$$\Gamma, x{:}A_1 \vdash A_2 : s_2$$

and hence by the product rule

$$\Gamma \vdash (\Pi x_1{:}A_1.A_2){:}s_3$$

i.e. $\Gamma \vdash A : B$.

∎

Lemma 5.2.11 (Substitution lemma for PTS's). *Assume*

$$\Gamma, x{:}A, \Delta \vdash B : C \tag{1}$$

and

$$\Gamma \vdash D : A. \tag{2}$$

Then

$$\Gamma, \Delta[x := D] \vdash B[x := D] : C[x := D].$$

Proof. By induction on the derivation of (1). We treat two cases. Write M^* for $M[x := D]$.

Case 1. The last rule used to obtain (1) is the start rule.

Subcase 1.1. $\Delta = <>$. Then the last step in the derivation of (1) is

$$\frac{\Gamma \vdash A : s}{\Gamma, x{:}A \vdash x : A},$$

so in this subcase $(B : C) \equiv (x : A)$. We have to show

$$\Gamma \vdash (x : A)^* \equiv (D : A)$$

which holds by assumption (2).

Subcase 1.2. $\Delta = \Delta_1, y{:}E$ and the last step in the derivation of (1) is

$$\frac{\Gamma, x{:}A, \Delta_1 \vdash E : s}{\Gamma, x{:}A, \Delta_1, y{:}E \vdash y : E}.$$

We have to show

$$\Gamma, \Delta_1^*, y{:}E^* \vdash y : E^*,$$

but this follows directly from the induction hypothesis $\Gamma, \Delta_1^* \vdash E^* : s$.

Case 2. The last applied rule to obtain (1) is the application rule, i.e.

$$\frac{\Gamma, x{:}A, \Delta, \vdash B_1 : (\Pi y{:}C_1.C_2) \quad \Gamma, x{:}A, \Delta \vdash B_2 : C_1}{\Gamma, x{:}A, \Delta \vdash (B_1 B_2) : C_2[y := B_2]}.$$

By the induction hypothesis one has

$$\Gamma, \Delta^* \vdash B_1^* : (\Pi y{:}C_1^*.C_2^*) \text{ and } \Gamma, \Delta^* \vdash B_2^* : C_1^*$$

and hence

$$\Gamma, \Delta^* \vdash (B_1^* B_2^*) : (C_2^*[y := B_2^*])$$

so by the substitution lemma for terms, 2.1.6, one has

$$\Gamma, \Delta^* \vdash (B_1 B_2)^* : (C_2[y := B_2])^*.$$

∎

Lemma 5.2.12 (Thinning lemma for PTS's). *Let Γ and Δ be legal contexts such that $\Gamma \subseteq \Delta$. Then*

$$\Gamma \vdash A : B \Rightarrow \Delta \vdash A : B.$$

Proof. By induction on the length of derivation of $\Gamma \vdash A : B$. We treat two cases.
Case 1. $\Gamma \vdash A : B$ is the axiom $<> \vdash c : s$. Then by the start lemma 5.2.9 one has $\Delta \vdash c : s$.
Case 2. $\Gamma \vdash A : B$ is an $\Gamma \vdash (\Pi x{:}A_1.A_2) : s_3$ and follows from $\Gamma \vdash A_1 : s_1$ and $\Gamma, x{:}A_1 \vdash A_2 : s_2$. By the IH one has $\Delta \vdash A_1 : s_1$ and since it may be assumed that x does not occur in Δ it follows that $\Delta, x{:}A_1 \vdash x : A_1$,i.e. $\Delta, x{:}A_1$ is legal. But then again by the IH $\Delta, x{:}A_1 \vdash A_2 : s_2$ and hence $\Delta \vdash (\Pi x{:}A_1.A_2) : s_3$.

∎

The following result analyses how a type assignment $\Gamma \vdash A : B$ can be obtained, according to whether A is a variable, a constant, an application, a λ-abstraction or a Π-abstraction.

Lemma 5.2.13 (Generation lemma for PTS's).

1. $\Gamma \vdash c : C \quad \Rightarrow \quad \exists s \in \mathcal{S}\ [C =_\beta s\ \&\ (c : s)$ *is an axiom*$]$.
2. $\Gamma \vdash x : C \quad \Rightarrow \quad \exists s \in \mathcal{S} \exists B =_\beta C\ [\Gamma \vdash B : s\ \&\ (x{:}B) \in \Gamma\ \&\ x \equiv {}^s x]$.
3. $\Gamma \vdash (\Pi x{:}A.B) : C \quad \Rightarrow \quad \exists (s_1, s_2, s_3) \in \mathcal{R}\ [\Gamma \vdash A : s_1\ \&\ \Gamma, x{:}A \vdash B : s_2\ \&\ C =_\beta s_3]$.
4. $\Gamma \vdash (\lambda x{:}A.b) : C \quad \Rightarrow \quad \exists s \in \mathcal{S} \exists B\ [\Gamma \vdash (\Pi x{:}A.B){:}s\ \&\ \Gamma, x{:}A \vdash b : B\ \&\ C =_\beta (\Pi x{:}A.B)]$.
5. $\Gamma \vdash (Fa) : C \quad \Rightarrow \quad \exists A, B\ [\Gamma \vdash F : (\Pi x{:}A.B)\ \&\ \Gamma \vdash a : A\ \&\ C =_\beta B[x := a]]$.

Proof. Consider a derivation of $\Gamma \vdash A : C$ in one of the cases. The rules weakening and conversion do not change the term A. We can follow the branch of the derivation until the term A is introduced the first time. This can be done by

- an axiom for 1;
- the start rule for 2
- the product-rule for 3;
- the application rule for 4;
- the abstraction-rule for 5.

In each case the conclusion of the axiom or rule is $\Gamma' \vdash A : B'$ with $\Gamma' \subseteq \Gamma$ and $B' =_\beta B$. The statement of the lemma follows by inspection of the used axiom or rule and the thinning lemma 5.2.12.

∎

The following corollary states that every Γ-term is a sort, a Γ-type or a Γ-element. Note however that the classes of sorts, Γ-types and Γ-elements overlap. For example, in $\lambda\!\to$ with context $\Gamma \equiv \alpha : *$ one has that $\alpha\to\alpha$ is both a Γ-type and a Γ-element; indeed,

$$\Gamma \vdash (\lambda x{:}\alpha.x) : (\alpha\to\alpha) : * \text{ and } \Gamma \vdash (\alpha\to\alpha) : * : \Box.$$

Also it follows that subexpressions of legal terms are again legal. Subexpressions are defined as usual. (M sub A iff $M \in \mathrm{Sub}(A)$, where $\mathrm{Sub}(A)$, the set of subexpressions of A, is defined as follows.

$\mathrm{Sub}(A) = \{A\}$, if A is one of the constants (including the sorts) or variables;
$= \{A\} \cup \mathrm{Sub}(P) \cup \mathrm{Sub}(Q)$, if A is of the form $\Pi x{:}P.Q$, $\lambda x{:}P.Q$ or PQ.)

Corollary 5.2.14. *In every* PTS*one has the following.*

1. $\Gamma \vdash A : B \Rightarrow \exists s[B \equiv s \text{ or } \Gamma \vdash B : s]$
2. $\Gamma \vdash A : (\Pi x{:}B_1.B_2) \Rightarrow \exists s_1, s_2[\Gamma \vdash B_1 : s_1 \ \& \ \Gamma_1, x : B_1 \vdash B_2 : s_2]$.
3. *If A is a Γ-term, then A is a sort, a Γ-type or a Γ-element.*
4. *If A is legal and B sub A, then B is legal.*

Proof. 1. By induction on the derivation of $\Gamma \vdash A : B$.

2. By (1) and (4) of the generation lemma (notice that $(\Pi x{:}B_1.B_2) \not\equiv s$).
3. By (1), distinguishing the cases $\Gamma \vdash A : C$ and $\Gamma \vdash C : A$.
4. Let A be legal. By definition either $\Gamma \vdash A : C$ or $\Gamma \vdash C : A$, for some Γ and C. If the first case does not hold, then by (1) it follows that $A \equiv s$, hence $B \equiv A$ is legal. So suppose $\Gamma \vdash A : B$. It follows by induction on the structure of A, using the generation lemma, that any subterm of A is also legal.

∎

Theorem 5.2.15 (Subject reduction theorem for PTS's).

$$\Gamma \vdash A : B \ \& \ A \twoheadrightarrow_\beta A' \quad \Rightarrow \quad \Gamma \vdash A' : B.$$

Proof. Write $\Gamma \rightarrow_\beta \Gamma'$ iff $\Gamma = x_1{:}A_1, \ldots, x_n{:}A_n, \Gamma' = x_1{:}A'_1, \ldots, x_n{:}A'_n$ and for some i one has $A_i \rightarrow A'_i$ and $A_j \equiv A'_j$ for $j \neq i$. Consider the statements

$$\Gamma \vdash A : B \ \& \ A \rightarrow_\beta A' \quad \Rightarrow \quad \Gamma \vdash A' : B; \qquad (i)$$

$$\Gamma \vdash A : B \ \& \ \Gamma \rightarrow_\beta \Gamma' \quad \Rightarrow \quad \Gamma' \vdash A : B. \qquad (ii)$$

These will be proved simultaneously by induction on the generation of $\Gamma \vdash A : B$. We treat two cases.

Case 1. The last applied rule is the product rule. Then $\Gamma \vdash A : B$ is $\Gamma \vdash (\Pi x{:}A_1.A_2) : s_3$ and is a direct consequence of $\Gamma \vdash A_1 : s_1$ and $\Gamma, x{:}A_1 \vdash A_2 : s_2$ for some rule (s_1, s_2, s_3). Then (i) and (ii) follow from the IH (for (i) and (ii), and (ii), respectively).

Case 2. The last applied rule is the application rule. Then $\Gamma \vdash A : B$ is $\Gamma \vdash A_1 A_2 : B_2[x := A_2]$ and is a direct consequence of $\Gamma \vdash A_1 : (\Pi x{:}B_1.B_2)$ and $\Gamma \vdash A_2 : B_1$. The correctness of (ii) follows directly from the IH. As to (i), by Corollary 5.2.14 (1) it follows that for some sort s

$$\Gamma \vdash (\Pi x{:}B_1.B_2) : s,$$

hence by the generation lemma

$$\Gamma \vdash B_1 : s_1,$$

$$\Gamma, x{:}B_1 \vdash B_2 : s_2.$$

¿From this it follows with the substitution lemma that

$$\Gamma \vdash B_2[x := A_2] : s_2 \tag{1}$$

Subcase 2.1. $A' \equiv A_1' A_2'$ and $A_1 {\to} A_1'$ or $A_2 {\to} A_2'$. The IH and the application rule give

$$\Gamma \vdash A_1' A_2' : B_2[x := A_2']$$

Therefore by (1) and the conversion rule

$$\Gamma \vdash A_1' A_2' : B_2[x := A_2]$$

which is $\Gamma \vdash A' : B$.

Subcase 2.2. $A_1 \equiv \lambda x{:}A_{11}.A_{12}$ and $A' \equiv A_{12}[x := A_2]$. Then we have

$$\Gamma \vdash (\lambda x{:}A_{11}.A_{12}) : (\Pi x{:}B_1.B_2) \tag{2}$$

$$\Gamma \vdash A_2 : B_1. \tag{3}$$

By the generation lemma applied to (2) we get

$$\Gamma \vdash A_{11} : s_2 \tag{4}$$

$$\Gamma, x{:}A_{11} \vdash A_{12} : B_2' \tag{5}$$

$$\Gamma, x{:}A_{11} \vdash B_2' : s_2$$

$$\Pi x{:}B_1.B_2 = \Pi x{:}A_{11}.B_2' \tag{6}$$

for some B_2' and rule (s_1, s_2, s_3). From (6) and the Church–Rosser property, we obtain

$$B_1 = A_{11} \text{ and } B_2 = B_2' \tag{7}$$

By (3), (4) and (7) it follows from the conversion rule

$$\Gamma \vdash A_2 : A_{11},$$

hence by (5) and the substitution lemma

$$\Gamma \vdash (A_{12}[x := A_2]) : (B_2'[x := A_2]).$$

From this (1) and the conversion rule we finally obtain

$$\Gamma \vdash (A_{12}[x := A_2]) : (B_2[x := A_2])$$

which is $\Gamma \vdash A' : B$

∎

Corollary 5.2.16. *In every* PTS*one has the following.*

1. $[\Gamma \vdash A : B \ \& \ B \twoheadrightarrow_\beta B'] \ \Rightarrow \ \Gamma \vdash A : B'$.
2. *If A is a Γ-term and $A \twoheadrightarrow_\beta A'$, then A' is a Γ-term.*

Proof. 1. If $\Gamma \vdash A : B$, then by Corollary 5.2.14 (1) $B \equiv s$ or $\Gamma \vdash B : s$, for some sort s. In the first case also $B' \equiv s$ and we are done. In the second case one has, by the subject reduction theorem, 5.2.15, $\Gamma \vdash B' : s$ and hence by the conversion rule $\Gamma \vdash A : B'$.

2. By 5.2.15 and (1).

∎

The following result is proved in [van Benthem Jutting, 1990] extending in a nontrivial way a result of [Luo, 1990] for a particular type system. The proof for arbitrary PTSs is somewhat involved and will not be given here.

Lemma 5.2.17 (Condensing lemma for PTS's). *In every* PTS *one has the following:*

$$\Gamma, x{:}A, \Delta \vdash B : C \ \& \ x \notin \Delta, B, C \ \Rightarrow \ \Gamma, \Delta \vdash B : C.$$

Here $x \notin \Delta, \ldots$ means that x is not free in Δ etc.

Corollary 5.2.18 (Decidability of type checking and typability for normalizing PTS's). *Let* $\lambda\mathrm{S} = \lambda(\mathcal{S}, \mathcal{A}, \mathcal{R})$, *with $\mathcal{S}$ finite, be a* PTS *that* *is (weakly or stongly) normalizing. Then the questions of type checking and typability (in the sense of subsection 4.4) are decidable.*

Proof. This is proved in [van Benthem Jutting, 1990] as a corollary to the *method* of lemma 5.2.17, not to the result itself. ∎

On the other hand [Meyer, 1988] shows that for $\lambda *$ these questions are not decidable.

In 5.2.19 - 5.2.22 we will consider results that hold only in special PTS's.

Definition 5.2.19. Let $\lambda S = \lambda(\mathcal{S}, \mathcal{A}, \mathcal{R})$ be a given PTS.
λS is called *singly sorted* if

1. $(c : s_1), (c : s_2) \in \mathcal{A} \;\Rightarrow\; s_1 \equiv s_2$;
2. $(s_1, s_2, s_3), (s_1, s_2, s_3') \in \mathcal{R} \;\Rightarrow\; s_3 \equiv s_3'$.

Examples 5.2.20.

1. All systems in the λ-cube and $\lambda *$ and λU as well are singly sorted.
2. The PTS specified by

$\mathcal{S}$	$*, \Box, \Delta$
$\mathcal{A}$	$* : \Box, * : \Delta$
$\mathcal{R}$	$(*, *), (*, \Box)$

is not singly sorted.

Lemma 5.2.21 (Uniqueness of types lemma for singly sorted PTS's). *Let* λS *be a* PTS*that is singly sorted. Then*

$$\Gamma \vdash A : B_1 \;\&\; \Gamma \vdash A : B_2 \;\Rightarrow\; B_1 =_\beta B_2.$$

Proof. By induction on the structure of A. We treat two cases. Assume $\Gamma \vdash A : B_i$ for $i = 1, 2$.
Case 1. $A \equiv c$, a constant. By the generation lemma it follows that

$$\exists s_i = B_i \; (c : s_i) \text{ is an axiom}$$

for $i = 1, 2$. By the assumption that λS is singly sorted we can conclude that $s_1 \equiv s_2$, hence $B_1 = B_2$.

Case 2. $A \equiv \Pi x{:}A_1.A_2$. By the generation lemma it follows that

$$\Gamma \vdash A_1 : s_1 \;\&\; \Gamma, x : A_1 \vdash A_2 : s_2 \;\&\; B_1 = s_3$$

$$\Gamma \vdash A_1 : s_1' \;\&\; \Gamma, x{:}A_1 \vdash A_2 : s_2' \;\&\; B_2 = s_3'$$

for some rules (s_1, s_2, s_3) and (s_1', s_2', s_2'). By the induction hypothesis it follows that $s_1' = s_1$ and $s_2' = s_2$ hence $s_1' \equiv s_1$ and $s_2' \equiv s_2$. Hence by the fact that λS is singly sorted we can conclude that $s_3' \equiv s_3$. Therefore $B' = B$. ∎

Corollary 5.2.22. *Let* λS *be a singly sorted* PTS.

1. *Suppose* $\Gamma \vdash A : B$ *and* $\Gamma \vdash A' : B'$. *Then*

$$A =_\beta A' \;\;\Rightarrow\;\; B =_\beta B'.$$

2. *Suppose* $\Gamma \vdash B : s, B =_\beta B'$ *and* $\Gamma \vdash A' : B'$. *Then* $\Gamma \vdash B' : s$.

Proof. 1. If $A =_\beta A'$, then by the Church–Rosser theorem $A \twoheadrightarrow_\beta A''$ and $A' \twoheadrightarrow_\beta A''$ for some A''. Hence by the subject reduction theorem 5.2.15

$$\Gamma \vdash A'' : B \text{ and } \Gamma \vdash A'' : B'.$$

But then by uniqueness of types $B =_\beta B'$.

2. By the assumption and Corollary 5.2.14 it follows that $\Gamma \vdash B' : s'$ or $B' \equiv s'$ for some sort s'.

Case 1. $\Gamma \vdash B' : s'$. Since B and B' have a common reduct B'', it follows by the subject reduction theorem that $\Gamma \vdash B'' : s$ and $\Gamma \vdash B'' : s'$. By uniqueness of types one has $s \equiv s'$ and hence $\Gamma \vdash B' : s$.
Case 2. $B' \equiv s'$. Then $B \twoheadrightarrow_\beta s'$, hence by subject reduction $\Gamma \vdash s' : s$, i.e. $\Gamma \vdash B' : s$. ∎

Now we introduce a classification of pseudoterms that is useful for the analysis of legal terms in systems of the λ-cube.

Definition 5.2.23. A map $\sharp : \mathcal{T} \to \{0, 1, 2, 3\}$ is defined as follows:

$$\sharp(\Box) = 3; \sharp(*) = 2; \sharp({}^{\Box}x) = 1; \sharp({}^{*}x) = 0;$$

$$\sharp(s) = \sharp({}^{s}x) = \text{ arbitary, say 0, if } s \not\equiv \Box, *;$$

$$\sharp(\lambda x{:}A.B) = \sharp(\Pi x{:}A.B) = \sharp(BA) = \sharp(B).$$

For $A \in \mathcal{T}$ the value $\sharp(A)$ is called the *degree* of A.

It will be shown for all systems in the λ-cube that if $\Gamma \vdash A : B$, then $\sharp(A) + 1 = \sharp(B)$. This is a folklore result for AUTOMATH-like systems and the proof below is due to van Benthem Jutting. First some lemmas.

Lemma 5.2.24. *In* λC *and hence in all systems of the* λ*-cube one has the following:*

1. $\Gamma \not\vdash \Box : A$.
2. $\Gamma \not\vdash (AB) : \Box$.
3. $\Gamma \not\vdash (\lambda x{:}A.b) : \Box$.

Proof. 1. By induction on derivations one shows

$$\Gamma \vdash B : A \Rightarrow B \not\equiv \Box$$

2. Similarly one shows $\Gamma \vdash (AB) : C \Rightarrow C \not\equiv \Box$.
   We treat the case that the application rule is used last.

$$\frac{\Gamma \vdash A : (\Pi x{:}P.Q) \quad \Gamma \vdash B : P}{\Gamma \vdash (AB) : Q[x := B](\equiv C)}$$

   By 5.2.14 (1) one has $\Gamma \vdash (\Pi x{:}P.Q) : s$. hence by the generation lemma $\Gamma, x{:}P \vdash Q : s$. Therefore by $\Gamma \vdash B : P$ and the substitution lemma

$$\Gamma \vdash C \equiv Q[x := B] : s$$

   By (1) it follows that $C \not\equiv \Box$.

3. If $\Gamma \vdash (\lambda x{:}A.b) : \Box$, then by the generation lemma for some B one has $(\Pi x{:}A.B) =_\beta \Box$, contradicting the Church–Rosser theorem.

∎

Lemma 5.2.25.

1. $\Gamma \vdash_{\lambda C} A : \Box \Rightarrow \sharp(A) = 2$.
2. $\Gamma \vdash_{\lambda C} A : B \ \&\ \sharp(A) \in \{2, 3\} \quad \Rightarrow \quad B \equiv \Box$.

Proof. 1. By induction on derivations.

2. Similarly. We treat two cases (that turn out to be impossible).

Case 1. The abstraction rule is used last:

$$\frac{\Gamma, x{:}A_1 \vdash b : B_1 \quad \Gamma \vdash (\Pi x{:}A_1.B_1) : s}{\Gamma \vdash (\lambda x{:}A_1.b) : (\Pi x{:}A_1.B_1)}.$$

Since $\sharp(b) = \sharp(\lambda x{:}A_1.b) \in \{2,3\}$ one has by the IH that $B_1 \equiv \square$. By the generation lemma it follows that $\Gamma, x{:}A_1 \vdash B_1 : s'$, which is impossible by 5.2.24 (1).

Case 2. The conversion rule is used last:

$$\frac{\Gamma \vdash A : b' \quad \Gamma \vdash B' : s \quad B' =_\beta B}{\Gamma \vdash A : B}.$$

By the IH one has $B' \equiv \square$. But then $B \twoheadrightarrow_\beta \square$ so by subject reduction $\Gamma \vdash \square : s$. Again this contradicts 5.2.24 (i).

■

Lemma 5.2.26. *If* $\sharp(x) = \sharp(Q)$. *Then* $\sharp(P[x := Q]) = \sharp(P)$.

Proof. Induction in the structure of P. ■

Definition 5.2.27.

1. A statement $A : B$ is *ok* if $\sharp(A) + 1 = \sharp(B)$.
2. A statement $A : B$ is *hereditarily ok*, notation hok, if it is ok and moreover all substatements $y : P$ (occurring just after a symbol 'λ' or 'Π') in A and B are ok.

Proposition 5.2.28. *Let* $\Gamma \vdash_{\lambda C} A : B$. *Then* $A : B$ *and all statements in* Γ *are hok.*

Proof. By induction on the derivation of $\Gamma \vdash A : B$. We treat four cases.

Case 1. (axiom). The statement in $<> \vdash * : \square$ is hok.

Case 2. (start rule). Suppose all statements in $\Gamma \vdash A : s$ are *hok*. Then also in $\Gamma, {}^s x{:}A \vdash {}^s x{:}A$, since $\sharp({}^s x) = \sharp(s) - 2$ and $\sharp(A) = \sharp(s) - 1$.

Case 3. (application rule). Suppose that the statements in $\Gamma \vdash F : (\Pi x{:}A.B)$ and $\Gamma \vdash a : A$ are *hok*. We have to show that $(Fa) : (B[x := a])$ is *hok*. This statement is ok since

$$\sharp(Fa) + 1 = \sharp(F) + 1 = \sharp(\Pi x{:}A.B) = \sharp(B) = \sharp(B[x := a])$$

by Lemma 5.2.26 and the fact that $x : A$ and $a : A$ are ok (so that $\sharp(x) = \sharp(a)$). The statement is also *hok* since all parts $y : P$ occur already in $\Gamma, F, (\Pi x{:}A.B)$ or a.

Case 4. (conversion rule). Suppose that all statements in $\Gamma \vdash A : B, \Gamma \vdash B' : s$ are *hok* and that $B =_\beta B'$. If we can show that

$\sharp(B) = \sharp(B')$ it follows that also $A : B'$ is *hok* and we are done. By Lemma 5.2.22 (2) one has $\Gamma \vdash B : s$.

Subcase 4.1. $s \equiv \Box$. Then $\sharp(B) = 2 = \sharp(B')$ by Lemma 5.2.25(1)

Subcase 4.2. $s \equiv *$. Then $\Gamma \vdash B : *$ and hence by Lemma 5.2.25(2) one has $\sharp(B) \notin \{2, 3\}$. Since $A : B$ is ok, we must have $\sharp(B) = 1$. Moreover $B' : s \equiv *$ is ok, hence also $\sharp(B') = 1$.

∎

Corollary 5.2.29. $\Gamma \vdash_{\lambda C} A : B \Rightarrow \sharp(A) + 1 = \sharp(B)$.

Proposition 5.2.30.

1. *Let* $(\lambda x{:}A.b)a$ *be legal in* λC. *Then* $\sharp(x) = \sharp(a)$.
2. *Let* A *be legal in* λC. *Then*

$$A \twoheadrightarrow_\beta B \quad \Rightarrow \quad \sharp(A) = \sharp(B).$$

Proof. 1. By Corollary 5.2.14(1) one has $\Gamma \vdash (\lambda x{:}A.b)a : B$ for some Γ and B. Using the generation lemma once it follows that

$$\Gamma \vdash (\lambda x{:}A.b) : (\Pi x{:}A'.B') \text{ and } \Gamma \vdash a : A',$$

and using it once more that $\Gamma \vdash A : s$ and $(\Pi x{:}A.B'') =_\beta (\Pi x{:}A'.B')$, for some s and B''. Then $A =_\beta A'$, by the Church-Rosser theorem. Hence by the conversion rule $\Gamma \vdash a : A$. Therefore $a : A$ is ok. But also $x : A$ is ok. Thus it follows that $\sharp(x) = \sharp(a)$.

2. By induction on the generation of $A \twoheadrightarrow_\beta B$, using (1) and lemma 5.2.26.

∎

Finally we show that PTS's extending $\lambda 2$ the type $\bot \equiv (\Pi\alpha{:}*.\alpha)$ can be inhabited only by non normalizing terms. Hence, if one knows that the system is normalizing—as is the case for e.g. $\lambda 2$ and λC—then this implies that $\bot$ is not inhabited. On the other hand if in a PTS the type $\bot$ is inhabited—as is the case for e.g. $\lambda *$—then not all typable terms are normalizing.

Proposition 5.2.31. *Let* λS *be a PTS extending* $\lambda 2$. *Suppose* $\vdash_{\lambda S} M : \bot$. *Then* M *has no normal form.*

Proof. Suppose towards a contradiction that M has a nf N. Then by the subject reduction theorem 5.2.15 one has $\vdash_{\lambda S} N : \bot$. By the generation lemma N cannot be constant or a term starting with Π, since both kinds of terms should belong to a sort, but $\bot$ is not a sort. Moreover N is not a variable since the context is empty. Suppose N is an application; write $N \equiv N_1 N_2 \ldots N_k$, where N_1 is not an application anymore. By a reasoning as before N_1 cannot be a variable or a term starting with Π. But then $N_1 \equiv (\lambda x{:}A.P)$; hence N contains the redex $(\lambda x{:}A.P)N_2$, contradicting the fact that N is a nf. Therefore N neither can be an application. The only remaining possibility is that N starts with a λ. Then $N \equiv \lambda a{:} * .B$ and since $\vdash N : \bot$ one has $a{:}* \vdash B : a$. Again by the generation lemma B cannot be a constant nor a term starting with Π or λ. The only remaining possibility is that $B \equiv xC_1 \ldots C_k$. But then $x \equiv a$ and $k = 0$. Hence $a{:}* \vdash a : a$ which implies $a = *$, a contradiction. (The sets V and C are disjoint.) ∎

5.3 Strong normalization for the λ-cube

Recall that a pseudo-term M is called strongly normalizing, notation SN(M), if there is no infinite reduction starting from M.

Definition 5.3.1. Let λS be a PTS. Then λS is *strongly normalizing*, notation
λS ⊨ SN, if all legal terms of λS are SN, i.e.

$$\Gamma \vdash A : B \Rightarrow \mathrm{SN}(A)\ \&\ \mathrm{SN}(B).$$

In this subsection it will be proved that all systems in the λ-cube satisfy SN. For this it is sufficient to show λC ⊨ SN. This was first proved by [Coquand, 1985]. We follow a proof due to [Geuvers and Nederhof, 1991] which is modular: first it is proved that

$$\lambda\omega \models \mathrm{SN} \quad \Rightarrow \quad \lambda\mathrm{C} \models \mathrm{SN} \tag{1}$$

and then

$$\lambda\omega \models \mathrm{SN} \tag{2}$$

The proof of (2) is due to [Girard, 1972] and is a direct generalization of his proof of λ2 ⊨ SN as presented in subsection 4.3. Although the proof is relatively simple, it is ingenious and cannot be carried out in higher-order arithmetic. On the other hand the proof of (1) can be carried out in Peano arithmetic. This has as consequence that λω ⊨ SN and λC ⊨ SN are provably equivalent in Peano arithmetic, a fact that was first shown by [Berardi, 1989] using proof theoretic methods. The proof of Geuvers and

Nederhof uses a translation between λC and $\lambda\omega$ preserving reduction. This translation is inspired by the proof of [Harper *et al.*, 1987] showing that

$$\lambda\!\rightarrow\ \models \text{SN} \quad \Rightarrow \quad \lambda\text{P} \models \text{SN}$$

using a similar translation. Now (1) and (2) will be proved. The proof is rather technical and the readers may skip it when first reading this chapter.

Proof of $\lambda\omega \models SN \;\Rightarrow\; \lambda\text{C} \models SN$

This proof occupies 5.3.2 – 5.3.14. Two partial maps $\tau{:}\mathcal{T}\rightarrow\mathcal{T}$ and $[\![\ ]\!]{:}\mathcal{T}\rightarrow\mathcal{T}$ will be defined. Then τ will be extended to contexts and it will be proved that

$$\Gamma \vdash_{\lambda C} A : B \quad \Rightarrow \quad \tau(\Gamma) \vdash_{\lambda\omega} [\![A]\!] : \tau(B)$$

and

$$A \rightarrow_\beta A' \quad \Rightarrow \quad [\![A]\!] \twoheadrightarrow_{\neq 0} [\![A']\!].$$

($M \twoheadrightarrow_{\neq 0} N$ means that $M \twoheadrightarrow_\beta N$ in at least one reduction step. Then assuming that $\lambda\omega \models \text{SN}$ one has

$$\begin{array}{rcl} \Gamma \vdash_{\lambda C} A : B & \Rightarrow & \text{SN}([\![A]\!]) \\ & \Rightarrow & \text{SN}(A). \end{array}$$

as is not difficult to show. This implies that we are done since by Corollary 5.2.14 it follows that also

$$\Gamma \vdash_{\lambda C} A : B \quad \Rightarrow \quad \text{SN}(B).$$

In order to fulfill this program, next to τ and $[\![\ ]\!]$ another partial map ρ is needed.

Definition 5.3.2.

1. Write $\mathcal{T}_i = \{M \in \mathcal{T} \mid \sharp(M) = i\}$ and $\mathcal{T}_{i,j} = \mathcal{T}_i \cup \mathcal{T}_j$; similarly $\mathcal{T}_{i,j,k}$ is defined.

2. Let $A \in \mathcal{T}$. In λC one uses the following terminology.

$$\begin{array}{lcl} A \text{ is a } \textit{kind} & \Leftrightarrow & \exists\Gamma[\Gamma \vdash A : \Box]; \\ A \text{ is a } \textit{constructor} & \Leftrightarrow & \exists\Gamma, B[\Gamma \vdash A : B : \Box]; \\ A \text{ is a } \textit{type} & \Leftrightarrow & \exists\Gamma[\Gamma \vdash A : *]; \\ A \text{ is an } \textit{object} & \Leftrightarrow & \exists\Gamma, B[\Gamma \vdash A : B : *]. \end{array}$$

Note that types are constructors and that for A legal in λC one has

$$\begin{array}{lcl} A \text{ is kind} & \Leftrightarrow & \sharp(A) = 2; \\ A \text{ is constructor or type} & \Leftrightarrow & \sharp(A) = 1; \\ A \text{ is object} & \Leftrightarrow & \sharp(A) = 0. \end{array}$$

Moreover for legal A one has $\sharp(A) = 3$ iff $A \equiv \Box$.

Definition 5.3.3. A map $\rho:\mathcal{T}_{2,3}\to\mathcal{T}$ is defined as follows:

$$\begin{array}{rcll}
\rho(\square) & = & *; & \\
\rho(*) & = & *; & \\
\rho(\Pi x{:}A.B) & = & \rho(A)\to\rho(B), & \text{if } \sharp(A)=2; \\
 & = & \rho(B), & \text{if } \sharp(A)\neq 2; \\
\rho(\lambda x{:}A.B) & = & \rho(B); & \\
\rho(BA) & = & \rho(B). &
\end{array}$$

It is clear that if $\sharp(A)\in\{2,3\}$, then $\rho(A)$ is defined and moreover $FV(\rho(A)) = \varnothing$.

Lemma 5.3.4.

1. $\Gamma\vdash_{\lambda C} A:\square \quad\Rightarrow\quad \vdash_{\lambda\omega}\rho(A):\square$.
2. *Let* $A\in\mathcal{T}_{2,3}$ *and* $\sharp(a)=\sharp(x)$. *Then* $\rho(A[x:=a])\equiv\rho(A)$.
3. *Let* $A\in\mathcal{T}_{2,3}$ *be legal and* $A\twoheadrightarrow_\beta B$. *Then* $\rho(A)\equiv\rho(B)$.
4. *Let* $\Gamma\vdash_{\lambda C} A_i:\square, i=1,2$. *Then*

$$A_1 =_\beta A_2 \quad\Rightarrow\quad \rho(A_1)\equiv\rho(A_2).$$

Proof. 1. By induction on the generation of $A:\square$. We treat two cases.
Case 1. $\Gamma\vdash_{\lambda C} A:\square$ is $\Gamma', x{:}C\vdash_{\lambda C} A:\square$ and follows directly from $\Gamma'\vdash_{\lambda C} A:\square$ and $\Gamma'\vdash_{\lambda C} C:s$. By the induction hypothesis one has $\vdash_{\lambda\omega}\rho(A):\square$.
Case 2. $\Gamma\vdash_{\lambda C} A:\square$ is $\Gamma\vdash_{\lambda C}(A_1A_2):B[x:=A_2]$ and follows directly from $\Gamma\vdash_{\lambda C} A_1:(\Pi x{:}C.B)$ and $\Gamma\vdash_{\lambda C} A_2:C$. Then either $B\equiv\square$, which is impossible by Lemma 5.2.24(2), or $B\equiv x$ and $A_2\equiv\square$. But also $\Gamma\vdash_{\lambda C}\square:C$ is impossible.

2. By induction on the structure of A.
3. By induction on the relation $\twoheadrightarrow$, using (2) and Proposition 5.2.30 for the case $A\equiv(\lambda x{:}D.P)Q$ and $B\equiv P[x:=Q]$.
4. By (3).

∎

A special variable 0 with $0:*$ will be used in the definition of τ. Moreover, in order to define the required map from λC to $\lambda\omega$ 'canonical' constants in types are needed. For this reason a fixed context Γ_0 will be introduced from which it follows that every type has an inhabitant.

Definition 5.3.5.

1. Γ_0 is the $\lambda\omega$ context

$$0{:}*, c{:}\bot,$$

where $\bot \equiv \Pi x{:}*.x$.

2. If $\Gamma \vdash_{\lambda\omega} B : *$, then c^B is defined as cB.

3. If $\Gamma \vdash_{\lambda\omega} B : \Box$, then c^B is defined inductively as follows; note that if $B \not\equiv *$, then it follows from the generation Lemma 5.2.13 that $B \equiv B_1 \rightarrow B_2$. Therefore we can define

$$\begin{array}{rcl} c^* & \equiv & 0; \\ c^{B_1 \rightarrow B_2} & \equiv & \lambda x{:}B_1.c^{B_2}. \end{array}$$

Lemma 5.3.6. *If* $\Gamma \vdash_{\lambda\omega} B : s$, *then* $\Gamma_0, \Gamma \vdash_{\lambda\omega} c^B : B$.

Proof. If $s \equiv *$, then $c^B \equiv cB$ and the conclusion clearly holds. If $s \equiv \Box$, then the result follows by induction on B. ∎

Definition 5.3.7.

1. A map $\tau{:}\mathcal{T}_{1,2,3} \rightarrow \mathcal{T}$ is defined as follows.

$$\begin{array}{lcll} \tau(\Box) & = & 0; & \\ \tau(*) & = & 0; & \\ \tau({}^\Box x) & = & {}^\Box x; & \\ \tau(\Pi x{:}A.B) & = & \Pi x{:}\rho(A).\tau(A) \rightarrow \tau(B), & \text{if } \sharp(A) = 2; \\ & = & \Pi x{:}\tau(A).\tau(B), & \text{if } \sharp(A) = 1; \\ & = & \tau(B), & \text{else;} \\ \tau(\lambda x{:}A.B) & = & \lambda x{:}\rho(A).\tau(B), & \text{if } \sharp(A) = 2; \\ & = & \tau(B), & \text{else;} \\ \tau(BA) & = & \tau(B), & \text{if } \sharp(A) = 0; \\ & = & \tau(B)\tau(A), & \text{else.} \end{array}$$

2. The map τ is extended to pseudo-contexts as follows.

$$\tau({}^*x{:}A) = {}^*x{:}\tau(A); \tau({}^\Box x{:}A) = {}^\Box x{:}\rho(A), {}^*x{:}\tau(A).$$

Let $\Gamma \equiv x_1{:}A_1, \ldots, x_n{:}A_n$ be a pseudo-context. Then

$$\tau(\Gamma) = \Gamma_0, \tau(x_1{:}A_1), \ldots, \tau(x_n{:}A_n).$$

By induction on the structure of A it follows that if $A \in \mathcal{T}_{1,2,3}$, then $\tau(A)$ is defined and moreover ${}^*x \notin FV(\tau(A))$.

Lemma 5.3.8.

1. *Let* $B \in \mathcal{T}_{1,2,3}$ *and* $\sharp(a) = \sharp(x)$. *Then*

$$\begin{array}{rcll} \tau(B[x := a]) & = & \tau(B)[x := \tau(a)], & \textit{if } x \equiv {}^{\Box}x; \\ & = & \tau(B), & \textit{if } x \equiv {}^{*}x. \end{array}$$

2. *If* $A \in \mathcal{T}_{1,2,3}$ *is legal and* $A \twoheadrightarrow B$, *then* $\tau(A) \twoheadrightarrow \tau(B)$.

Proof. 1. By induction on the structure of B, using Lemma 5.3.4(3).

2. By induction on the generation of $A \twoheadrightarrow B$. We only treat the case $A \equiv (\lambda x{:}D.b)a$ and $B \equiv b[x := a]$. By the generation lemma it follows that $\Gamma \vdash D : s$ with $s \equiv *$ or $s \equiv \Box$. In the first case one has $x \equiv {}^{*}x$ and by (1)

$$\tau((\lambda x{:}D.b)a) \equiv \tau(b) \equiv \tau(b[x := a]) \equiv \tau(B).$$

In the second case one has $x \equiv {}^{\Box}x$ and by (1)

$$\begin{array}{rcl} \tau(A) & \equiv & (\lambda x{:}\rho(D).\tau(b))\tau(a) \\ & \to & \tau(b)[x := \tau(a)] \\ & \equiv & \tau(B). \end{array}$$

■

Lemma 5.3.9. *Let* $\Gamma \vdash_{\lambda C} B : \Box$ *or* $B \equiv \Box$. *Then*

$$\Gamma \vdash_{\lambda C} A : B \Rightarrow \tau(\Gamma) \vdash_{\lambda\omega} \tau(A) : \rho(B).$$

Proof. By induction on the proof of $\Gamma \vdash_{\lambda C} A : B$. We treat three cases.

Case 1. $\Gamma \vdash_{\lambda C} A : B$ is $\Gamma', x{:}C \vdash_{\lambda C} A : B$ and follows from $\Gamma' \vdash_{\lambda C} A : B$ and $\Gamma' \vdash_{\lambda C} C : s$ by the weakening rule. By the IH one has

$$\tau(\Gamma') \vdash_{\lambda\omega} \tau(A) : \rho(B) \;\&\; \tau(\Gamma') \vdash_{\lambda\omega} \tau(C) : *.$$

We must show

$$\tau(\Gamma'), \tau(x{:}C) \vdash_{\lambda\omega} \tau(A) : \rho(B). \tag{1}$$

If $x \equiv {}^{*}x$, then $\tau(x{:}C) \equiv x{:}\tau(C)$ and (1) follows from the IH by weakening. If $x \equiv {}^{\Box}x$, then $\tau(x{:}C) \equiv {}^{\Box}x{:}\rho(C), {}^{*}x{:}\tau(C)$ and (1) follows from the IH by weakening twice. (Note that in this case $\Gamma' \vdash_{\lambda C} C : \square$, so by Lemma 5.3.4 (1) one has $\vdash_{\lambda\omega} \rho(C) : \square$.)

Case 2. $\Gamma \vdash_{\lambda C} A : B$ is $\Gamma \vdash_{\lambda C} (\lambda x{:}D.b) : (\Pi x{:}D.B)$ and follows from $\Gamma \vdash_{\lambda C} (\Pi x{:}D.B) : s$ and $\Gamma, x{:}D \vdash_{\lambda C} b : B$. By the assumption of the theorem one has $s \equiv \square$.

Subcase 2.1. $\sharp(D) = 2$. By the IH it follows among other things that

$$\tau(\Gamma) \vdash_{\lambda\omega} [\Pi x{:}\rho(D).\tau(D) {\rightarrow} \tau(B)] : *$$

$$\tau(\Gamma), {}^{\square}x{:}\rho(D), {}^{*}x{:}\tau(D) \vdash_{\lambda\omega} \tau(b) : \rho(B). \tag{2}$$

We must show

$$\tau(\Gamma) \vdash_{\lambda\omega} (\lambda x{:}\rho(D).\tau(D)) : (\rho(D) {\rightarrow} \rho(B)).$$

Now ${}^{*}x$ does not occur in $\rho(B)$ since it is closed, nor in $\tau(b)$. Therefore, by (2) and the substitution lemma, using $c^{\tau(D)}$ in context $\Gamma_0 \subseteq \tau(\Gamma)$, one has

$$\tau(\Gamma), {}^{\square}x{:}\rho(D) \vdash_{\lambda\omega} \tau(b) : \rho(B)$$

and hence

$$\begin{aligned} \tau(\Gamma) \vdash_{\lambda\omega} (\lambda x{:}\rho(D).\tau(b)) : (\Pi x{:}\rho(D).\rho(B)) &\equiv \rho(D) {\rightarrow} \rho(B) \\ &\equiv \rho(\Pi x{:}D.B), \end{aligned}$$

since $\rho(B)$ is closed.

Subcase 2.2. $\sharp(D) = 1$. Similarly.

Case 3. $\Gamma \vdash_{\lambda C} A : B$ is $\Gamma \vdash_{\lambda C} (\Pi x{:}D.E) : s_2$ and follows directly from $\Gamma \vdash_{\lambda C} D : s_1$ and $\Gamma, x{:}D \vdash_{\lambda C} E : s_2$.

Subcase 3.1. $s_1 \equiv *$. The IH states

$$\begin{aligned} &\tau(\Gamma) \vdash_{\lambda\omega} \tau(D) : *; \\ &\tau(\Gamma), x{:}\tau(D) \vdash_{\lambda\omega} \tau(E) : *. \end{aligned}$$

We have to show

$$\tau(\Gamma) \vdash_{\lambda\omega} (\Pi x{:}\tau(D).\tau(E)) : *;$$

but this follows immediately from the IH.

Subcase 3.2. $s_1 \equiv \Box$. The IH states now

$$\tau(\Gamma) \vdash_{\lambda\omega} \tau(D) : *,$$
$$\tau(\Gamma), {}^{\Box}x{:}\rho(D), {}^{*}x{:}\tau(D) \vdash_{\lambda\omega} \tau(E) : *.$$

We have to show

$$\tau(\Gamma) \vdash_{\lambda\omega} (\Pi x{:}\rho(D).\tau(D){\rightarrow}\tau(E)) : *;$$

this follows from the IH and the fact that the fresh variable ${}^{*}x$ does not occur in $\tau(E)$.

∎

Now the third partial map on pseudo-terms will be defined.

Definition 5.3.10. The map $[\![-]\!]{:}\mathcal{T}_{0,1,2}{\rightarrow}\mathcal{T}$ is defined as follows. Remember that in the context $\Gamma_0 \equiv 0{:}*, c{:}\bot$ we defined expressions c^A such that $\Gamma \vdash A : s \Rightarrow \Gamma_0, \Gamma \vdash c^A : A$.

$$\begin{array}{rcll}
[\![*]\!] & = & c^0 & \\
[\![{}^{*}x]\!] & = & {}^{*}x & \\
[\![{}^{\Box}x]\!] & = & {}^{*}x; & \\
[\![\Pi x{:}A.B]\!] & = & c^{0\rightarrow 0\rightarrow 0}[\![A]\!]([\![B]\!][{}^{\Box}x := c^{\rho(A)}][{}^{*}x := c^{\tau(A)}]), & \text{if } \sharp(A) = 2; \\
 & = & c^{0\rightarrow 0\rightarrow 0}[\![A]\!]([\![B]\!][{}^{*}x := c^{\tau(A)}]), & \text{if } \sharp(A) \neq 2; \\
[\![\lambda x{:}A.B]\!] & = & (\lambda z{:}0\lambda^{\Box}x{:}\rho(A)\lambda^{*}x{:}\tau(A).[\![B]\!])[\![A]\!], & \text{if } \sharp(A) = 2; \\
 & = & (\lambda z{:}0\lambda^{*}x{:}\tau(A).[\![B]\!])[\![A]\!], & \text{if } \sharp(A) \neq 2; \\
[\![BA]\!] & = & [\![B]\!]\tau(A)[\![A]\!], & \text{if } \sharp(A) = 2. \\
 & = & [\![B]\!][\![A]\!], & \text{if } \sharp(A) \neq 2.
\end{array}$$

In the above $z \equiv {}^{*}z$ is fresh.

Proposition 5.3.11.

$$\Gamma \vdash_{\lambda C} A : B \quad \Rightarrow \quad \tau(\Gamma) \vdash_{\lambda\omega} [\![A]\!] : \tau(B).$$

Proof. By induction on the derivation of $A : B$. We treat two cases.

Case 1. $\Gamma \vdash_{\lambda C} A : B$ is $\Gamma \vdash_{\lambda C} (\Pi x{:}D.E) : s_2$ and follows from $\Gamma \vdash_{\lambda C} D : s_1$ and $\Gamma, x{:}D \vdash E : s_2$. By the IH one has $\tau(\Gamma) \vdash_{\lambda\omega} [\![D]\!] : 0$ and $\tau(\Gamma, x{:}D) \vdash_{\lambda\omega} [\![E]\!] : 0$. By Lemma 5.3.9 one has $\tau(\Gamma) \vdash_{\lambda\omega} \tau(D) : *$, hence $\tau(\Gamma) \vdash_{\lambda\omega} c^{\tau(D)} : \tau(D)$.

If $s_1 \equiv *$, then $x \equiv {}^*x$ and $\tau(\Gamma, x{:}D) \equiv \tau(\Gamma), x{:}\tau(D)$. Therefore by the substitution lemma

$$\tau(\Gamma) \vdash_{\lambda\omega} [\![E]\!][x := c^{\tau(D)}] : 0.$$

Hence by the application rule twice

$$\tau(\Gamma) \vdash_{\lambda\omega} c^{0\to0\to0}[\![D]\!]([\![E]\!][x := c^{\tau(D)}]) : 0.$$

If $s_1 \equiv \square$, then $x \equiv {}^{\square}x$ and $\tau(\Gamma, x{:}D) \equiv \tau(\Gamma), {}^{\square}x{:}\rho(D), {}^*x{:}\tau(D)$. Therefore by the substitution lemma

$$\tau(\Gamma) \vdash_{\lambda\omega} [\![E]\!][{}^{\square}x := c^{\rho(D)}][{}^*x := c^{\tau(D)}] : 0.$$

Hence by the application rule twice

$$\tau(\Gamma) \vdash_{\lambda\omega} c^{0\to0\to0}[\![D]\!]([\![E]\!][{}^{\square}x := c^{\rho(D)}][{}^*x := c^{\tau(D)}]) : 0.$$

In both cases one has

$$\tau(\Gamma) \vdash_{\lambda\omega} [\![\Pi x{:}D.E]\!] : 0$$

Case 2. $\Gamma \vdash_{\lambda C} A : B$ is $\Gamma \vdash_{\lambda C} (\lambda x{:}D.b) : (\Pi x{:}D.B)$ and follows from

$$\Gamma, x{:}D \vdash_{\lambda C} b : B$$

and

$$\Gamma \vdash_{\lambda C} (\Pi x{:}D.B) : s.$$

By the generation lemma (and the Church-Rosser theorem) one has for some sort s_1

$$\Gamma \vdash_{\lambda C} D : s_1 \ \&\ \Gamma, x : D \vdash_{\lambda C} B : s.$$

By the IH one has

$$\tau(\Gamma, x{:}D) \vdash_{\lambda\omega} [\![b]\!] : \tau(B)$$

and

$$\tau(\Gamma) \vdash_{\lambda\omega} [\![D]\!] : 0.$$

By Lemma 5.3.9 one has

$$\tau(\Gamma) \vdash_{\lambda\omega} \tau(D) : *$$

and

$$\tau(\Gamma, x{:}D) \vdash_{\lambda\omega} \tau(B) : *.$$

If $s_1 \equiv *$, then $x \equiv {}^*x$ and $\tau(\Gamma, x{:}D) \equiv \tau(\Gamma), x{:}\tau(D)$.

Therefore by two applications of the abstraction rule and one application of the product rule one obtains

$$\tau(\Gamma) \vdash_{\lambda\omega} ((\lambda z{:}0\lambda x{:}\tau(D).[\![b]\!])[\![D]\!]) : (\tau(D) \to \tau(B)).$$

If $s_1 \equiv \Box$, then a similar argument shows

$$\tau(\Gamma) \vdash_{\lambda\omega} (\lambda z{:}0\lambda^{\Box}x{:}\rho(D)\lambda^{*}x{:}\tau(D).[\![b]\!])[\![D]\!] : (\Pi x{:}\rho(D).\tau(D) \to \tau(B)).$$

In both cases one has

$$\tau(\Gamma) \vdash_{\lambda\omega} [\![\lambda x{:}D.b]\!] : \tau(\Pi x{:}D.B).$$

∎

Lemma 5.3.12. *Let $A.B \in T$. Then*

1. $x \equiv {}^{*}x \Rightarrow [\![A[{}^{*}x := B]]\!] \equiv [\![A]\!][{}^{*}x := [\![B]\!]]$
2. $x \equiv {}^{\Box}x \Rightarrow [\![A[{}^{\Box}x := B]]\!] \equiv [\![A]\!][{}^{\Box}x := \tau(B), {}^{*}x := [\![B]\!]]$.

Proof. 1. By induction on the structure of A. We treat one case: $A \equiv \Pi y{:}D.E$. Write $P^{+} \equiv P[x := B]$. Now

$$\begin{aligned} [\![A^{+}]\!] &\equiv [\![\Pi y{:}D^{+}.E^{+}]\!] \\ &\equiv c^{0\to0\to0}[\![D^{+}]\!][\![E^{+}]\!][y := c^{\tau(D^{+})}] \\ &\equiv (c^{0\to0\to0}[\![D]\!][\![E]\!][y := c^{\tau(D)}])[x := [\![B]\!]] \\ &\equiv [\![\Pi y{:}D.E]\!][x := [\![B]\!]], \end{aligned}$$

by the induction hypothesis, the substitution lemma and the fact that $\tau(D[{}^{*}x := B]) \equiv \tau(D)$.

2. Similarly.

∎

Lemma 5.3.13. *Let $A, B \in \mathcal{T}_{0,1,2}$. Then*

$$A \to B \quad \Rightarrow \quad [\![A]\!] \twoheadrightarrow_{\neq 0} [\![B]\!].$$

where $\twoheadrightarrow_{\neq 0}$ denotes that the reduction takes at least one step.

Proof. By induction on the generation of $A \rightarrow B$. We treat only the case that $A \rightarrow B$ is

$$(\lambda x{:}D.P)Q \rightarrow P[x := Q].$$

If $x \equiv {}^*x$, then

$$\begin{array}{rcl} [\![(\lambda x{:}D.P)Q]\!] & \equiv & (\lambda z{:}0\lambda x{:}\tau(D).[\![P]\!])[\![D]\!][\![Q]\!] \\ & \twoheadrightarrow_{\neq 0} & [\![P]\!][x := [\![Q]\!]] \\ & \equiv & [\![P[x := Q]]\!]. \end{array}$$

If $x \equiv {}^{\Box}x$, then

$$\begin{array}{rcl} [\![(\lambda x{:}D.P)Q]\!] & \equiv & (\lambda z{:}0\lambda^{\Box}x{:}\rho(D)\lambda^{*}x{:}\tau(D).[\![P]\!])[\![D]\!]\tau(Q)[\![Q]\!] \\ & \twoheadrightarrow_{\neq 0} & [\![P]\!][{}^{\Box}x := \tau(Q), {}^{*}x := [\![Q]\!]] \\ & \equiv & [\![P[x := Q]]\!]. \end{array}$$

∎

Theorem 5.3.14. $\lambda\omega \models SN \Rightarrow \lambda\mathrm{C} \models SN$.

Proof. Suppose $\lambda\omega \models \mathrm{SN}$. Let M be a legal $\lambda\mathrm{C}$ term. By Corollary 5.2.14 it is sufficient to assume $\Gamma \vdash_{\lambda C} M : A$ in order to show $\mathrm{SN}(M)$. Consider a reduction starting with $M \equiv M_0$

$$M_0 \rightarrow M_1 \rightarrow M_2 \rightarrow \cdots$$

One has $\Gamma \vdash_{\lambda C} M_i : A$, and therefore $\Gamma \vdash_{\lambda\omega} [\![M_i]\!] : \tau(A)$ for all i, by Proposition 5.3.11. By lemma 5.3.13 one has

$$[\![M_0]\!] \twoheadrightarrow_{\neq 0} [\![M_1]\!] \twoheadrightarrow_{\neq 0} \cdots$$

But then $[\![M]\!]$ is a legal $\lambda\omega$ term and hence the sequence is finite. ∎

Corollary 5.3.15 (Berardi). *In HA, the system of intuitionistic arithmetic, one can prove*

$$\lambda\omega \models SN \;\Leftrightarrow\; \lambda\mathrm{C} \models SN.$$

Proof. The implication $\Leftarrow$ is trivial. By inspecting the proof of 5.3.14 it can be verified that everything is formalizable in HA. ∎

This corollary was first proved in [Berardi, 1989] by proof theoretic methods. The present proof of Geuvers and Nederhof gives a more direct argument.

The proof of $\lambda\omega \models SN$
occupies 5.3.16 -5.3.32. The result will be proved using the following steps:

1. A map $|-|:\mathcal{T}_0 \to \Lambda$ will be defined such that
$$\Gamma \vdash_{\lambda\omega} A : B : * \Rightarrow \mathrm{SN}(|A|);$$
2. $\Gamma \vdash_{\lambda\to} A : B : * \Rightarrow \mathrm{SN}(A);$
3. $\Gamma \vdash_{\lambda\omega} A : B : \Box \Rightarrow \mathrm{SN}(A);$
4. $\Gamma \vdash_{\lambda\omega} A : B : * \Rightarrow \mathrm{SN}(A);$
5. $\Gamma \vdash_{\lambda\omega} A : B \Rightarrow \mathrm{SN}(A) \& \mathrm{SN}(B).$

Definition 5.3.16. A map $|-|:\mathcal{T}_0 \to \Lambda$ is defined as follows:

$$\begin{array}{lcll} |{}^*x| & = & x; & \\ |\lambda x{:}A.B| & = & \lambda x.|B|, & \text{if } \sharp(A) = 1; \\ & = & |B|, & \text{else}; \\ |BA| & = & |B||A|, & \text{if } \sharp(A) = 0; \\ & = & |B|, & \text{else}; \\ |\Pi x{:}A.B| & = & |B|. & \end{array}$$

The last clause is not used essentially, since legal terms $\Pi x{:}A.B$ never have degree 0. Typical examples of $|-|$ are the following.

$$\begin{array}{l} |\lambda x{:}\alpha.x| = \lambda x.x; \\ |\lambda \alpha{:}*.\lambda x{:}\alpha.x| = \lambda x.x; \\ |(\lambda x{:}\alpha.x)y| = (\lambda x.x)y; \\ |(\lambda \alpha{:}*.\lambda x{:}\alpha.x)\beta| = \lambda x.x. \end{array}$$

The following lemma shows what kinds exist in $\lambda\omega$ and what kinds and objects in $\lambda\to$.

Lemma 5.3.17. *Let K be the set of pseudo-terms defined by the abstract syntax $K = * \mid K \to K$. So $K = \{*, *\to*, *\to*\to*, \ldots\}$. Then*

1. $\Gamma \vdash_{\lambda\omega} A : \Box \Rightarrow A \in K.$
2. $\Gamma \vdash_{\lambda\omega} B : A : \Box \Rightarrow A, B$ *do not contain any* ${}^*x$.
3. $\Gamma \vdash_{\lambda\to} A : \Box \Rightarrow A \equiv *.$
4. $\Gamma \vdash_{\lambda\to} A : * \Rightarrow A$ *is an nf.*

Proof. By induction on derivations. ∎

Lemma 5.3.18. *Let $A \equiv \Box$ or $\Gamma \vdash_{\lambda\omega} A : \Box$. Then for all terms B legal in $\lambda\omega$ one has*

$$A =_\beta B \Rightarrow A \equiv B.$$

Proof. First let $A \equiv \Box$. Suppose B is legal and $A =_\beta B$. By the Church–Rosser theorem one has $B \twoheadrightarrow_\beta \Box$. Then the last step in this reduction must be

$$(\lambda x{:}A_1.A_2)A_3 \rightarrow_\beta A_2[x := A_3] \equiv \Box.$$

Case 1. $A_2 \equiv x$ and $A_3 \equiv \Box$. Then by 5.2.30 one has $\sharp(\Box) = \sharp(x)$, which is impossible.
Case 2. $A_2 \equiv \Box$. Then $(\lambda x{:}A_1.\Box)$ is legal, hence $\Gamma \vdash (\lambda x{:}A_1.\Box) : C$ for some Γ, C. But then by 5.2.29 one has $\sharp(C) = \sharp(\lambda x{:}A_1.\Box) + 1 = 4$, a contradiction.

If $\Gamma \vdash_{\lambda\omega} A : \Box$, then $A \in K$ as defined in 5.3.17 and similarly a contradiction is obtained. (In case 2 one has $\Gamma \vdash (\lambda x{:}A_1.A) : (\Pi x{:}A_1.\Box)$, but then $\Gamma \vdash (\Pi x{:}A_1.\Box) : s$.) ∎

Now it will be proved in 5.3.19 - 5.3.24 that if $\Gamma \vdash_{\lambda\omega} A : B : *$, then $\mathrm{SN}(|A|)$. The proof is related to the one for $\lambda 2$–Curry in section 4.3. Although the proof is not very complicated, it cannot be carried out in higher-order arithmetic PA^ω (because as [Girard, 1972] shows $\mathrm{SN}(\lambda\omega)$ implies $\mathrm{Con}(PA^\omega)$ and Gödels second incompleteness theorem applies).

We work in ZF-set theory. Let $\mathcal{U}$ be a large enough set. (If syntax is coded via arithmetic in the set of natural numbers ω, hence the set of type-free λ-terms Λ is a subset of ω, then $\mathcal{U} = \mathcal{V}_{\omega 2}$ will do; it is closed under the operations powerset, function spaces and under syntactic operations. Here $\mathcal{V}_\alpha$ is the usual set-theoretic hierarchy defined by $\mathcal{V}_0 = \varnothing, \mathcal{V}_{\alpha+1} = P(\mathcal{V}_\alpha)$ and $\mathcal{V}_\lambda = \cup_{\alpha\in\lambda}\mathcal{V}_\alpha$; moreover $\omega 2$ is the ordinal $\omega + \omega$.)

Definition 5.3.19.

1. A valuation is a map $\rho{:}V \rightarrow \mathcal{U}$.

2. Given a valuation ρ a map $[\![-]\!]_\rho{:}\mathcal{T} \rightarrow \mathcal{U} \cup \{\mathcal{U}\}$ is defined as follows: Remember that $X \rightarrow Y = \{F \in \Lambda \mid \forall M \in X\ FM \in Y\}$and that $\mathrm{SAT} = \{X \subseteq \Lambda \mid X \text{ is saturated}\}$.

$$\begin{aligned}
[\![\Box]\!]_\rho &= \mathcal{U};\\
[\![*]\!]_\rho &= \mathrm{SAT};\\
[\![x]\!]_\rho &= \rho(x);
\end{aligned}$$

$$
\begin{array}{rcll}
[\![\Pi x{:}A.B]\!]_\rho & = & [\![A]\!]_\rho \rightarrow [\![B]\!]_\rho & \text{if } \sharp(A) = \sharp(B) = 1, \\
 & = & [\![B]\!]_\rho^{[\![A]\!]_\rho}, & \text{if } \sharp(A) = \sharp(B) = 2, \\
 & = & \cap\{[\![B]\!]_{\rho[x:=f]} \mid f \in [\![A]\!]_\rho\}, & \text{if } \sharp(A) = 2, \sharp(B) = 1, \\
 & = & \varnothing, & \text{else;} \\
[\![\lambda x{:}A.B]\!]_\rho & = & \lambda x.[\![B]\!]_{\rho[x:=x]}, & \text{if } \sharp(A) = 1, \sharp(B) = 0, \\
 & = & \lambda f \in [\![A]\!]_\rho.[\![B]\!]_{\rho[x:=f]}, & \text{if } \sharp(A) = 2, \sharp(B) = 1, \\
 & = & [\![B]\!]_\rho, & \text{if } \sharp(A) = 2, \sharp(B) = 0, \\
 & = & \varnothing, & \text{else;} \\
[\![BA]\!]_\rho & = & [\![B]\!]_\rho [\![A]\!]_\rho, & \text{if } \sharp(A) = \sharp(B) = 0, \\
 & = & [\![B]\!]_\rho([\![A]\!]_\rho), & \text{if } \sharp(A) = \sharp(B) = 1, \\
 & = & [\![B]\!]_\rho, & \text{if } \sharp(A) = 1, \sharp(B) = 0, \\
 & = & \varnothing, & \text{else.}
\end{array}
$$

Comment 5.3.20. In the first clauses of the definitions of $[\![\Pi x{:}A.B]\!]_\rho$, $[\![\lambda x{:}A.B]\!]_\rho$ and $[\![BA]\!]_\rho$ a syntactic operation (as coded in set theory) is used ($\rightarrow$ as defined in 4.3.1.(2) extended to sets, λ abstraction and application as syntactic operations extended to $\mathcal{U}$). In the second clauses some set theoretic operations are used (function spaces, lambda abstraction, function application). In the third clause in the definition of $[\![\Pi x{:}A.B]\!]_\rho$ an essential impredicativity – the 'Girard trick' – occurs: $[\![\Pi x{:}A.B]\!]_\rho$ for a fixed ρ is defined in terms of $[\![B]\!]_\rho$ for arbitrary ρ. The fourth clauses are not used essentially.

Definition 5.3.21. Let ρ be a valuation.

- $\rho \vDash A : B \;\Leftrightarrow\; [\![A]\!]_\rho \in [\![B]\!]_\rho$.

- $\rho \vDash \Gamma \;\Leftrightarrow\; \rho \vDash x : A$ for each $(x{:}A) \in \Gamma$.

- $\Gamma \vDash A : B \;\Leftrightarrow\; \forall \rho\, [\rho \vDash \Gamma \Rightarrow \rho \vDash A : B]$.

Lemma 5.3.22. *Let ρ be a valuation with $\rho \vDash \Gamma$.*

1. *Assume that A is legal in $\lambda\omega$ and $\sharp(A) = 0$. Then*

$$[\![A]\!]_\rho = |A|[\vec{x} := \rho(\vec{x})] \in \Lambda.$$

2. *Assume $\sharp(x) = \sharp(a)$. Then*

$$[\![B[x := a]]\!]_\rho = [\![B]\!]_{\rho[x:=[\![a]\!]_\rho]}.$$

3. *Let B be legal in $\lambda\omega$. Suppose either $\sharp(B) = 0$ and $\sharp(a) = \sharp(x) = 1$ or $\sharp(B) = 1$ and $\sharp(a) = \sharp(x) = 0$. Then*

$$[\![B[x := a]]\!]_\rho = [\![B]\!]_\rho$$

4. *Let A, A' be legal in $\lambda\omega$ and $\sharp(A) = \sharp(A') \neq 0$. Then for all ρ*

$$A =_\beta A' \;\Rightarrow\; [\![A]\!]_\rho = [\![A']\!]_\rho.$$

Proof. 1. By induction on the structure of A.

2. By induction on the structure of B.
3. By induction on the structure of B.
4. Show that if A legal, $\sharp(A) \neq 0$ and $A \twoheadrightarrow_\beta A'$, then $[\![A]\!]_\rho = [\![A']\!]_\rho$. ∎

Proposition 5.3.23.

$$\Gamma \vdash_{\lambda\omega} A : B \;\Rightarrow\; \Gamma \models A : B.$$

Proof. By induction on the derivation of $A : B$. Since these proofs should be familiar by now, the details are left to the reader. ∎

Corollary 5.3.24.

1. $\Gamma \vdash_{\lambda\omega} A : B : * \;\Rightarrow\; SN(|A|)$.
2. $\Gamma \vdash_{\lambda\rightarrow} A : B : * \;\Rightarrow\; SN(A)\ \&\ SN(B)$.

Proof. For each kind k a canonical element $f^k \in [\![k]\!]_\rho$ will be defined.

$$\begin{aligned} f^* &= \mathrm{SN} \\ f^{k_1\to k_2} &= \lambda f \in [\![k_1]\!].f^{k_2}. \end{aligned}$$

Assume $\Gamma \vdash A : B : *$. Define $\rho(=\rho_\Gamma)$ by

$$\begin{aligned} \rho({}^\square x) &= f^A && \text{if } (x{:}A) \in \Gamma; \\ &= f^*, && \text{if } x \notin Dom(\Gamma); \end{aligned}$$

$$\rho({}^{*}x) \quad = \quad {}^{*}x.$$

Then $\rho \models \Gamma$, because if ${}^{*}x{:}A$ is in Γ, then $\Gamma \vdash A : *$ hence $[\![A]\!]_\rho \in [\![*]\!]_\rho = \text{SAT}$ and therefore $\rho(x) = x \in [\![A]\!]_\rho$ by the definition of saturation; if ${}^{\Box}x{:}A$ is in Γ, then $\rho \models {}^{\Box}x : A$ since $\rho({}^{\Box}x) = f^A \in [\![A]\!]_\rho$.

1. By 5.3.21 one has $[\![A]\!]_\rho \in [\![B]\!]_\rho \in \text{SAT}$ and therefore

$$|A|[\vec{x} := \rho(\vec{x})] \in [\![B]\!]_\rho \subseteq \text{SN}$$

so $|A|[\vec{x} := \rho(\vec{x})] \in \text{SN}$ and hence $|A| \in \text{SN}$.

2. By (1) one has $|A| \in \text{SN}$. From this it follows that $A \in \text{SN}$, since for legal terms of $\lambda\!\to$ one has

$$A \to_\beta A' \quad \Rightarrow \quad |A| \to_\beta |A'|.$$

(This is not true for $\lambda\omega$; for example

$$(\lambda x{:}(\lambda\alpha{:}*.\alpha\to\alpha)\beta.x) \to_\beta (\lambda x{:}\beta\to\beta.x)$$

but the absolute values are both $\lambda x.x$.)

■

¿From the previous result we will derive that constructors in $\lambda\omega$ are strongly normalizing by interpreting kinds and constructors in $\lambda\omega$ as respectively types and elements in $\lambda\!\to$. The kind $*$ will be translated as a fixed $0{:}*$. The following examples give the intuition.

valid in $\lambda\omega$	translation valid in $\lambda\!\to$
$\alpha{:}* \vdash (\lambda\beta{:}*.\alpha) : (*\to*) : \Box$	$0{:}*, a{:}0 \vdash (\lambda b{:}0.a) : (0\to0) : *;$
$\alpha{:}*, f{:}(*\to*) \vdash (f\alpha \to f\alpha) : *$	$0{:}*, a{:}0, f{:}(0\to0) \vdash c^{0\to0\to0}(fa)(fa) : 0;$
$\alpha{:}* \vdash (\Pi\beta{:}*.\beta\to\alpha) : *$	$0{:}*, a{:}0 \vdash c^{0\to0\to0}c^0 a : 0.$

Definition 5.3.25. A map $()^{-}{:}\mathcal{T}_{1,2,3} \to \mathcal{T}_{0,1,2}$ is defined as follows:

$$\begin{array}{rcll} (\Box)^{-} & = & *; & \\ (*)^{-} & = & 0; & \\ ({}^{\Box}x)^{-} & = & {}^{*}x; & \\ (BA)^{-} & = & B^{-}A^{-}, & \text{if } \sharp(A) \neq 0, \\ & = & B^{-}, & \text{else;} \end{array}$$

$$
\begin{array}{rcll}
(\lambda x{:}A.B)^- & = & (\lambda x^-{:}A^-.B^-), & \text{if } \sharp(A) \neq 0, \sharp(x) \neq 0, \\
& = & B^-, & \text{else;} \\
(\Pi x{:}A.B)^- & = & (\Pi x^-{:}A^-.B^-), & \text{if } \sharp(A) = \sharp(B) = 2, \\
& = & c^{0\to 0\to 0} A^- B^-, & \text{if } \sharp(A) = \sharp(B) = 1, \\
& = & B^-[x^- := c^{A^-}], & \text{if } \sharp(A) = 2, \sharp(B) = 1, \\
& = & B^-, & \text{else.}
\end{array}
$$

For pseudo-contexts one defines the following (remember $\Gamma_0 = \{0{:}*, c{:}\bot\}$).

$$
\begin{array}{rcl}
({}^{\Box}x{:}A)^- & = & x{:}A^-; \\
({}^{*}x{:}A)^- & = & <>; \\
(x_1{:}A_1, \ldots, x_n{:}A_n)^- & = & \Gamma_0, (x_1{:}A_1)^-, \ldots, (x_n{:}A_n)^-.
\end{array}
$$

Then one can prove by induction on derivations

$$\Gamma \vdash_{\lambda\omega} A : B \;\&\; \sharp(A) \neq 0 \quad \Rightarrow \quad \Gamma^- \vdash_{\lambda\to} A^- : B^-.$$

Lemma 5.3.26.

1. *For $\sharp(A) \neq 0$ and $\sharp(a) = \sharp(x) \neq 0$ one has*

$$(A[x := a])^- \equiv A^-[x^- := a^-].$$

2. *For A legal in $\lambda\omega$ with $\sharp(A) = 1$ one has*

$$A \to_\beta B \;\Rightarrow\; A^- \to_\beta B^-.$$

Proof. Both by induction on the structure of A. ∎

Proposition 5.3.27.

$$\Gamma \vdash_{\lambda\omega} A : B : \Box \;\Rightarrow\; SN(A).$$

Proof.

$$
\begin{array}{rcl}
\Gamma \vdash_{\lambda\omega} A : B : \Box & \Rightarrow & \Gamma^- \vdash_{\lambda\to} A^- : B^- : * \\
& \Rightarrow & \mathrm{SN}(A^-)
\end{array}
$$

$$\Rightarrow \quad \mathrm{SN}(A).$$

∎

Definition 5.3.28. Let $M \equiv (\lambda x{:}A.B)C$ be a legal $\lambda\omega$-term.

1. M is a *0-redex* if $\sharp(B) = 0$ and $\sharp(A) = 1$;
2. M is a *2-redex* if $\sharp(B) = 0$ and $\sharp(A) = 2$;
3. M is an *ω-redex* if $\sharp(B) = 1$ and $\sharp(A) = 2$;
4. A 2-λ is the first lambda occurrence in a 2-redex.

The three different kinds of redexes give rise to three different notions of contraction and reduction and will be denoted by $\rightarrow_0, \rightarrow_2$ and $\rightarrow_\omega$ respectively. Note that β-reduction is $0, 2, \omega$-reduction, in the obvious sense. We will prove that β-reduction of legal $\lambda\omega$-terms is SN by first proving the same for $2, \omega$-reduction.

Lemma 5.3.29. *Let $A, B \in T_0$ be legal terms in $\lambda\omega$. Then*

1. $(A \rightarrow_2 B) \;\Rightarrow\;$ *(number of 2-λs in A)>(number of 2-λs in B).*

2. $(A \rightarrow_\omega B) \;\Rightarrow\;$ *(number of 2-λs in A) =(number of 2-λs in B).*

3. $A \rightarrow_{2,\omega} B \;\Rightarrow\; |A| \equiv |B|$.

4. $A \rightarrow_0 B \;\Rightarrow\; |A| \rightarrow_\beta |B|$.

Proof. 1. Contracting a 2-redex $(\lambda x{:}A_0.B_0)C_0$ removes one 2-λ in A, removes A_0 and moves around C_0, possibly with duplications. A 2-λ is always part of $(\lambda x{:}A_1.B_1)$ with degree 0. A kind or constructor does not contain objects, in particular no 2-redexes. Therefore removing A_0, or moving around C_0 does not change the number of 2-λ's and we have the result.

2. Similarly.

3. If $M \equiv (\lambda x{:}A_0.B_0)C_0$ in A is a 2-redex, then C_0 is a constructor and $|M| \equiv |B_0|$. Remark that a constructor in an object M can occur only as subterm of A_1 occurring in $\lambda y{:}A_1.B_1$ in M. By the definition of $|-|$ constructors are removed in $|M|$. Therefore also $|B_0[x := C_0]| \equiv |B_0|$. We can conclude $|A| \equiv |B|$.

If $M \equiv (\lambda x{:}A_0.B_0)C_0$ in A is an ω-redex, then M and its contractum M' are both constructors. Therefore $|A| \equiv |B|$, again by the fact that constructors are eliminated by $|-|$.

4. If $M \equiv (\lambda x{:}A_0.B_0)C_0$ is a 0-redex with contractum $M' \equiv B_0[x := C_0]$, then $|M| \equiv (\lambda x.|B_0|)|C_0|$ and $|M'| \equiv |B_0[x := C_0]| \equiv |B_0|[x ::= |C_0|]$ as can be proved by induction on the structure of B_0. Therefore $|M| \rightarrow_\beta |M'|$. More generally $|A| \rightarrow_\beta |B|$ if $A \rightarrow_0 B$.

∎

Lemma 5.3.30. *Suppose M is legal in $\lambda\omega$ and $\sharp(M) = 0$. Then M is strongly normalizing for*

1. *ω-reduction;*
2. *$2, \omega$-reduction.*

Proof. 1. M is not of the form $\Pi x{:}A.B$. Therefore it follows that either

$$M \equiv \lambda x_1{:}A_1 \cdots \lambda x_n{:}A_n.yB_1 \cdots B_m, n, m \geq 0.$$

or

$$M \equiv \lambda x_1{:}A_1 \cdots \lambda x_n{:}A_n.(\lambda y{:}C_0.C_1)B_1 \cdots B_m, n \geq 0, m \geq 1.$$

In the second case $\sharp(M) = \sharp(C_1)$. Therefore $(\lambda y{:}C_o.C_1)B_1$ is not an ω-redex. So in both cases ω-reduction starting with M must take place within the constructors that are subterms of the A_i, B_i or C_i, thus leaving the overall structure of M the same. Since β-reduction on constructors is SN by 5.3.27 it follows that ω-reduction on objects is SN.

2. Suppose

$$M_0 \rightarrow_{2,\omega} M_1 \rightarrow_{2,\omega} \cdots$$

is an infinite $2, \omega-$reduction. By 5.3.29 (1), (2) it follows that after some steps we have

$$M_k \rightarrow_\omega M_{k+1} \rightarrow_\omega \cdots$$

which is impossible by (1).

∎

Corollary 5.3.31. *Suppose $\sharp(A) = 0$ and SN($|A|$). Then SN(A).*

Proof. An infinite reduction starting with A must by 5.3.30 2 be of the form

$$A \twoheadrightarrow_{2,\omega} A_1 \rightarrow_0 A_2 \twoheadrightarrow_{2,\omega} A_3 \rightarrow_0 A_4 \twoheadrightarrow_{2,\omega} \cdots.$$

But then by 5.3.29 3,4 we have

$$|A| \equiv |A_1| \rightarrow_\beta |A_2| \equiv |A_3| \rightarrow_\beta |A_4| \equiv \cdots.$$

contradicting SN($|A|$). ∎

Proposition 5.3.32.

$$\Gamma \vdash_{\lambda\omega} A : B \;\Rightarrow\; SN(A)\;\&\;SN(B).$$

Proof. If $\Gamma \vdash_{\lambda\omega} A : B : *$, then $\sharp(A) = 0$ by 5.2.28 and SN($|A|$) by 5.3.24(1) hence SN(A) by 5.3.31; also $\Gamma \vdash_{\lambda\omega} B : * : \Box$ and therefore by 5.3.27 one has SN(B). If on the other hand $\Gamma \vdash_{\lambda\omega} A : B : \Box$, then SN($A$) by 5.3.27 and SN($B$) since B is in nf by 5.3.17 (1). ∎

Theorem 5.3.33 (Strong normalization for the λ-cube). *For all systems in the λ-cube one has the following:*

1. $\Gamma \vdash A : B \;\Rightarrow\; SN(A)\;\&\;SN(B)$.
2. $x_1{:}A_1, \ldots, x_n{:}A_n \vdash B : C \;\Rightarrow\; A_1, \ldots, A_n, B, C$ *are SN.*

Proof. 1. It is sufficient to prove this for the strongest system λC and hence by 5.3.15 for $\lambda\omega$. This is done in 5.3.32.

2. By induction on derivations, using (1).

∎

5.4 Representing logics and data-types

In this section eight systems of intuitionistic logic will be introduced that correspond in some sense to the systems in the λ-cube. The systems are the following; there are four systems of proposition logic and four systems of many-sorted predicate logic.

PROP	proposition logic;
PROP2	second-order proposition logic;
PROP$\underline{\omega}$	weakly higher-order proposition logic;
PROPω	higher-order proposition logic;
PRED	predicate logic;
PRED2	second-order predicate logic;
PRED$\underline{\omega}$	weakly higher-order predicate logic;
PREDω	higher-order predicate logic.

All these systems are minimal logics in the sense that the only logical operators are → and ∀. However, for the second- and higher-order systems the operators $\neg, \&, \vee$ and $\exists$, as well as Leibniz's equality, are all definable, see 5.4.17. Weakly higher-order logics have variables for higher-order propositions or predicates but no quantification over them; a higher-order proposition has lower order propositions as arguments. Classical versions of the logics in the upper plane are obtained easily (by adding as axiom $\forall\alpha.\neg\neg\alpha\rightarrow\alpha$). The systems form a cube as shown in the fowwowing Figure. 3.

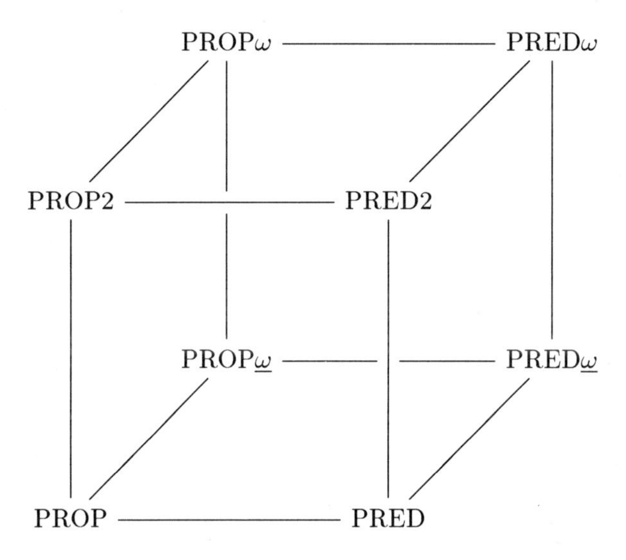

Fig. 3. The logic-cube.

This cube will be referred to as the logic-cube. The orientation of the logic-cube as drawn is called the standard orientation. Each system L_i on the logic-cube corresponds to the system λ_i on the λ-cube on the corresponding vertex (both cubes in standard orientation). The edges of the logic-cube represent inclusions of systems in the same way as on the λ-cube.

A formula A in a logic L_i on the logic-cube can be interpreted as a type $[\![A]\!]$ in the corresponding λ_i on the λ-cube. The transition $A \mapsto [\![A]\!]$ is called the *propositions-as-types* interpretation of [de Bruijn, 1970] and Howard [Howard, 1980], first formulated for extensions of PRED and λP. The method has been extended by [Martin-Löf, 1984] who added to λP types $\Sigma x{:}A.B$ corresponding to (strong) constructive existence and a constructor $=_A : A\rightarrow A\rightarrow *$ corresponding to equality on a type A. Since Martin-Löf's principal objective is to give a constructive foundation of mathematics, he does not consider the impredicative rules $(\Box, *)$.

The propositions-as-types interpretation satisfies the following soundness result: if A is provable in PRED, then $[\![A]\!]$ is inhabited in λP. In fact, an inhabitant of $[\![A]\!]$ in λP can be found canonically from a proof of A in PRED; different proofs of A are interpreted as different terms of type $[\![A]\!]$. The interpretation has been extended to several other systems, see e.g. [Stenlund, 1972], [Martin-Löf, 1984] and [Luo, 1990]. In [Geuvers, 1988] it is verified that for all systems L_i on the logic-cube soundness holds with respect to the corresponding system λ_i on the λ-cube: if A is provable in L_i, then $[\![A]\!]$ is inhabited in λ_i. [Barendsen, 1989] verifies that a proof D of such A can be canonically translated to $[\![D]\!]$ being an inhabitant of $[\![A]\!]$.

After seeing [Geuvers, 1988], it was realized by Berardi [Berardi, 1988a; Berardi, 1990] that the systems in the logic-cube can be considered as PTSs. Doing this, the propositions-as-types interpretation obtains a simple canonical form. We will first give a description of PRED in its usual form and then in its form as a PTS.

The soundness result for the propositions-as-type interpretation raises the question whether one has also completeness in the sense that if a formula A of a logic L_i is such that $[\![A]\!]$ is inhabited in λ_i, then A is provable in L_i. For the proposition logics this is trivially true. For PRED completeness with respect to λP is proved in [Martin-Löf, 1971], [Barendsen and Geuvers, 1989] and [Berardi, 1990] (see also [Swaen, 1989]). For PREDω completeness with respect to λC fails, as is shown in [Geuvers, 1989] and [Berardi, 1989].

This subsection ends with a representation of data types in λ2. The method is due to [Leivant, 1983] and coincides with an algorithm given later by [Böhm and Berarducci, 1985] and by [Fokkinga, 1987]. Some results are stated about the representability of computable functions on data types represented in λ2.

Many sorted predicate logic

Many sorted predicate logic will be introduced in its minimal form: formulas are built up from atomic ones using only → and ∀ as logical operators.

Definition 5.4.1.

1. The notion of a *many sorted structure* will be defined by an example. The following sequence is a typical many sorted structure

$$\mathcal{A} = \langle A, B, f, g, P, Q, c\rangle,$$

where

A, B are non-empty sets, the *sorts* of $\mathcal{A}$
$f : (A{\to}(A{\to}A))$ and $g : A{\to}B$ are functions;
$P \subseteq A$ and $Q \subseteq A \times B$ are relations;
$c \in A$ is a constant.

The name 'sorts' for A and B is standard terminology; in the context of PTSs it is better to call these the 'types' of $\mathcal{A}$.

2. The *signature* of $\mathcal{A}$ is $\langle 2; \langle 1,1,1\rangle, \langle 1,2\rangle; \langle 1\rangle, \langle 1,2\rangle; 1\rangle$ stating that there are two sorts; two functions, the first of which has signature $\langle 1,1,1\rangle$, i.e. having as input two elements of the first sort and as output an element of the first sort, the second of which has signature $\langle 1,2\rangle$, i.e. having an element of the first sort as input and an element of the second sort as output; etc.

Definition 5.4.2. Given the many sorted structure $\mathcal{A}$ of 5.4.1 the *language* $L_{\mathcal{A}}$ *of (minimal) many sorted predicate logic over* $\mathcal{A}$ is defined as follows. In fact this language depends only on the signature of $\mathcal{A}$.

1. $L_{\mathcal{A}}$ has the following special symbols.
   - $\mathbf{A}, \mathbf{B}$ sort symbols;
   - $\mathbf{f}, \mathbf{g}$ function symbols;
   - $\mathbf{P}, \mathbf{Q}$ relation symbols;
   - $\mathbf{c}$ constant symbol.
2. The set of variables of $L_{\mathcal{A}}$ is
$$V = \{x^{\mathbf{A}} \mid x \text{ variable}\} \cup \{x^{\mathbf{B}} \mid x \text{ variable}\}.$$
3. The set of terms of sort A and of sort B, notation $\text{Term}_{\mathbf{A}}$ and $\text{Term}_{\mathbf{B}}$ respectively, are defined inductively as follows:
   - $x^{\mathbf{A}} \in \text{Term}_{\mathbf{A}}, x^{\mathbf{B}} \in \text{Term}_{\mathbf{B}}$;
   - $\mathbf{c} \in \text{Term}_{\mathbf{A}}$;
   - $s \in \text{Term}_{\mathbf{A}}$ and $t \in \text{Term}_{\mathbf{A}} \Rightarrow \mathbf{f}(s,t) \in \text{Term}_{\mathbf{A}}$;
   - $s \in \text{Term}_{\mathbf{A}} \Rightarrow \mathbf{g}(s) \in \text{Term}_{\mathbf{B}}$.
4. The set of formulae of $L_{\mathcal{A}}$, notation Form, is defined inductively as follows:
   - $s \in \text{Term}_{\mathbf{A}} \Rightarrow \mathbf{P}(s) \in \text{Form}$;
   - $s \in \text{Term}_{\mathbf{A}}, t \in \text{Term}_{\mathbf{B}} \Rightarrow \mathbf{Q}(s,t) \in \text{Form}$;
   - $\varphi \in \text{Form}, \psi \in \text{Form} \Rightarrow (\varphi \rightarrow \psi) \in \text{Form}$;
   - $\varphi \in \text{Form} \Rightarrow (\forall x^{\mathbf{A}}.\varphi) \in \text{Form}$ and $(\forall x^{\mathbf{B}}.\varphi) \in \text{Form}$.

Definition 5.4.3. Let $\mathcal{A}$ be a many sorted structure. The *(minimal) many sorted predicate logic over* $\mathcal{A}$, notation $\text{PRED} = \text{PRED}_{\mathcal{A}}$, is defined as follows. If Δ is a set of formulae, then $\Delta \vdash \varphi$ denotes that φ is derivable from the assumptions Δ. This notion is defined inductively as follows (C ranges over A and B, and the corresponding $\mathbf{C}$ over $\mathbf{A}, \mathbf{B}$):

$$\begin{array}{rcl} \varphi \in \Gamma & \Rightarrow & \Gamma \vdash \varphi \\ \Gamma \vdash \varphi \to \psi, \Gamma \vdash \varphi & \Rightarrow & \Gamma \vdash \psi \\ \Gamma, \varphi \vdash \psi & \Rightarrow & \Gamma \vdash \varphi \to \psi \\ \Gamma \vdash \forall x^{\mathbf{C}}.\varphi,\ t \in \mathrm{Term}_{\mathbf{C}} & \Rightarrow & \Gamma \vdash \varphi[x := t] \\ \Gamma \vdash \varphi,\ x^{\mathbf{C}} \notin FV(\Gamma) & \Rightarrow & \Gamma \vdash \forall x^{\mathbf{C}}.\varphi, \end{array}$$

where $[x := t]$ denotes substitution of t for x and FV is the set of free variables in a term, formula or collection of formulae. For $\varnothing \vdash \varphi$ one writes simply $\vdash \varphi$ and one says that φ is a *theorem.*

These rules can be remembered best in the following natural deduction form.

$$\frac{\varphi \to \psi \quad \varphi}{\psi}; \qquad \frac{\begin{array}{c}\not\varphi \\ \vdots \\ \psi\end{array}}{\varphi \to \psi};$$

$$\frac{\forall x^{\mathbf{C}}.\varphi}{\varphi[x := t]},\ t \in \mathrm{term}_{\mathbf{C}}; \qquad \frac{\varphi}{\forall x^{\mathbf{C}}\varphi},\ x \text{ not free in the assumptions.}$$

Some examples of terms, formulae and theorems are the following. The expressions $x^{\mathbf{A}}, \mathbf{c}, \mathbf{f}(x^{\mathbf{A}}, \mathbf{c})$ and $\mathbf{f}(\mathbf{c}, \mathbf{c})$ are all in $\mathrm{Term}_{\mathbf{A}}$; $\mathbf{g}(x^{\mathbf{A}})$ is in $\mathrm{Term}_{\mathbf{B}}$. Moreover

$$\forall x^{\mathbf{A}} \mathbf{P}(\mathbf{f}(x^{\mathbf{A}}, x^{\mathbf{A}})), \tag{1}$$

$$\forall x^{\mathbf{A}} [\mathbf{P}(x^{\mathbf{A}}) \to \mathbf{P}(\mathbf{f}(x^{\mathbf{A}}, \mathbf{c}))], \tag{2}$$

$$\forall x^{\mathbf{A}} [\mathbf{P}(x^{\mathbf{A}}) \to \mathbf{P}(\mathbf{f}(x^{A}, \mathbf{c}))] \to \forall x^{\mathbf{A}} \mathbf{P}(x^{\mathbf{A}}) \to \mathbf{P}(\mathbf{f}(\mathbf{c}, \mathbf{c})) \tag{3}$$

are formulae. The formula (3) is even a theorem. A derivation of (3) is as follows:

$$\dfrac{\dfrac{\dfrac{\dfrac{\cancel{\forall x^{\mathbf{A}}[\mathbf{P}(x^{\mathbf{A}})\to\mathbf{P}(f(x^{\mathbf{A}},\mathbf{c}))]}2}{\mathbf{P}(\mathbf{c})\to\mathbf{P}(\mathbf{f}(\mathbf{c},\mathbf{c}))} \qquad \dfrac{\cancel{\forall x^{\mathbf{A}}\mathbf{P}(x^{\mathbf{A}})}1}{\mathbf{P}(\mathbf{c})}}{\mathbf{P}(\mathbf{f}(\mathbf{c},\mathbf{c}))}}{\forall x^{\mathbf{A}}\mathbf{P}(x^{\mathbf{A}})\to\mathbf{P}(\mathbf{f}(\mathbf{c},\mathbf{c}))}\,1}{\forall x^{\mathbf{A}}[\mathbf{P}(x^{\mathbf{A}})\to\mathbf{P}(\mathbf{f}(x^{\mathbf{A}},\mathbf{c}))]\to\forall x^{\mathbf{A}}\mathbf{P}(x^{\mathbf{A}})\to\mathbf{P}(\mathbf{f}(\mathbf{c},\mathbf{c}))}\,2$$

the numbers 1, 2 indicating when a cancellation of an assumption is being made. A simpler derivation of the same formula is

$$\dfrac{\cancel{\forall x^{\mathbf{A}}[\mathbf{P}(x^{\mathbf{A}})\to\mathbf{P}(\mathbf{f}(x^{\mathbf{A}},\mathbf{c}))]}2 \qquad \dfrac{\dfrac{\cancel{\forall x^{\mathbf{A}}\mathbf{P}(x^{\mathbf{A}})}1}{\mathbf{P}(\mathbf{f}(\mathbf{c},\mathbf{c}))}}{\forall x^{\mathbf{A}}\mathbf{P}(x^{\mathbf{A}})\to\mathbf{P}(\mathbf{f}(\mathbf{c},\mathbf{c}))}\,1}{\forall x^{\mathbf{A}}[\mathbf{P}(x^{\mathbf{A}})\to\mathbf{P}(\mathbf{f}(x^{\mathbf{A}},\mathbf{c}))]\to\forall x^{\mathbf{A}}\mathbf{P}(x^{\mathbf{A}})\to\mathbf{P}(\mathbf{f}(\mathbf{c},\mathbf{c}))}\,2$$

Now we will explain, first somewhat informally, the *propositions-as-types* interpretation from PRED into λP. First one needs a context corresponding to the structure $\mathcal{A}$. This is $\Gamma_{\mathcal{A}}$ defined as follows (later $\Gamma_{\mathcal{A}}$ will be defined a bit differently):

$$\begin{aligned}\Gamma_{\mathcal{A}} \quad = \quad & A{:}*, B{:}*, \\ & P{:}A{\to}*, Q{:}A{\to}B{\to}*, \\ & f{:}A{\to}A{\to}A, g{:}A{\to}B, \\ & c{:}A.\end{aligned}$$

For this context one has

$$\Gamma_{\mathcal{A}} \vdash c : A \tag{0'}$$

$$\Gamma_{\mathcal{A}} \vdash (fcc) : A$$

$$\Gamma_{\mathcal{A}} \vdash \Pi x{:}A.P(fxx) : * \tag{1'}$$

$$\Gamma_{\mathcal{A}} \vdash \Pi x{:}A.(Px{\to}P(fxc)) : * \tag{2'}$$

$$\Gamma_{\mathcal{A}} \vdash (\Pi x{:}A.(Px{\to}P(fxc))){\to}((\Pi x{:}A.Px){\to}P(fcc)) : *. \tag{3'}$$

We see how the formulae (1)–(3) are translated as types. The inhabitants of $*$ have a somewhat 'ambivalent' behaviour: they serve both as sets (e.g. $A{:}*$) and as propositions (e.g. $Px : *$ for $x{:}A$). The fact that formulae are translated as types is called the *propositions-as-types* (or also *formulae-as-types*) interpretation. The provability of the formula (3) corresponds to the fact that the type in (3′) is inhabited. In fact

$$\Gamma_{\mathcal{A}} \vdash \lambda p{:}(\Pi x{:}A.(Px \to P(fxc))).\lambda q{:}(\Pi x{:}A.Px).pc(qc) :$$

$$\Pi p{:}(\Pi x{:}A.(Px \to P(fxc))).\Pi q{:}(\Pi x{:}A.Px).P(fcc).$$

A somewhat simpler inhabitant of the type in (3′), corresponding to the second proof of the formula (3) is

$$\lambda p{:}(\Pi x{:}A.(Px \to P(fxc))).\lambda q{:}(\Pi x{:}A.Px).q(fcc).$$

In fact, one has the following result that we state at this moment informally (and in fact not completely correct).

Theorem 5.4.4 (Soundness of the propositions-as-types interpretation). *Let $\mathcal{A}$ be a many sorted structure and let φ be a formula of $L_{\mathcal{A}}$. Suppose*

$$\vdash_{\text{PRED}} \varphi \textit{ with derivation } D;$$

then

$$\Gamma_{\mathcal{A}} \vdash_{\lambda P} [D] : [\varphi] : *,$$

where $[D]$ and $[\varphi]$ are canonical translations of respectively φ and D.

Now it will be shown that up to 'isomorphism' PRED can be viewed as a PTS. This PTS will be called λPRED. The map $\varphi \mapsto [\varphi]$ can be factorized as the composition of an isomorphism PRED →λPRED and a canonical forgetful homomorphism λPRED →λP.

Definition 5.4.5 ([Berardi, 1988a]). PRED considered as a PTS, notation λPRED, is determined by the following specification:

$\mathcal{S}$	$*^s, *^p, *^f, \square^s, \square^p$
$\mathcal{A}$	$*^s : \square^s, *^p : \square^p$
$\mathcal{R}$	$(*^p, *^p), (*^s, *^p), (*^s, \square^p),$ $(*^s, *^s, *^f), (*^s, *^f, *^f)$

Some explanations are called for. The sort $*^s$ is for sets (the 'sorts' of the many sorted logic). The sort $*^p$ is for propositions (the formulae of the logic will become elements of $*^p$). The sort $*^f$ is for first-order functions between the sets in $*^s$. The sort $\square^s$ contains $*^s$ and the sort $\square^p$ contains $*^p$. (There is no $\square^f$, otherwise it would be allowed to have free variables for function spaces.)

The rule $(*^p, *^p)$ allows the formation of implication of two formulae:

$$\varphi{:}*^p, \psi{:}*^p \vdash (\varphi{\to}\psi) \equiv (\Pi x{:}\varphi.\psi) : *^p.$$

The rule $(*^s, *^p)$ allows quantification over sets:

$$A{:}*^s, \varphi{:}*^p \vdash (\forall x^{\mathbf{A}}.\varphi) \equiv (\Pi x{:}A.\varphi) : *^p.$$

The rule $(*^s, \square^p)$ allows the formation of first-order predicates:

$$A{:}*^s \vdash (A{\to}*^p) \equiv (\Pi x{:}A.*^p) : \square^p;$$

hence

$$A{:}*^s, P{:}A{\to}*^p, x{:}A \vdash Px : *^p,$$

i.e. P is a predicate over the set A.

The rule $(*^s, *^s, *^f)$ allows the formation of a function space between the basic sets in $*^s$:

$$A{:}*^s, B{:}*^s \vdash (A{\to}B) : *^f;$$

the rule $(*^s, *^f, *^f)$ allows the formation of curried functions of several arguments in the basic sets:

$$A{:}*^s \vdash (A{\to}(A{\to}A)) : *^f.$$

This makes it possible to have for example $g{:}A{\to}B$ and $f{:}(A{\to}(A{\to}A))$ in a context.

Now it will be shown formally that λPRED is able to simulate the logic PRED. Terms, formulae and derivations of PRED are translated into terms of λ PRED. Terms become elements, formulae become types and a derivation of a formula φ becomes an element of the type corresponding to φ.

Definition 5.4.6. Let $\mathcal{A}$ be as in 5.4.1. The *canonical context* corresponding to $\mathcal{A}$, notation $\Gamma_{\mathcal{A}}$, is defined by

$$\begin{aligned} \Gamma_{\mathcal{A}} = \quad & A{:}*^s, B{:}*^s, \\ & P{:}(A{\to}*^p), Q{:}(A{\to}B{\to}*^p), \\ & f{:}(A{\to}(A{\to}A)), g{:}(A{\to}B), \\ & c{:}A. \end{aligned}$$

Given a term $t \in L_{\mathcal{A}}$, the canonical translation of t, notation $[\![t]\!]$, and the canonical context for t, notation Γ_t, are inductively defined as follows:

t	$[\![t]\!]$	Γ_t
$x^{\mathbf{C}}$	x	$x : C$
$\mathbf{c}$	c	$\langle\rangle$
$\mathbf{f}(s, s')$	$f[\![s]\!][\![s']\!]$	$\Gamma_s \cup \Gamma_{s'}$
$\mathbf{g}(s)$	$g[\![s]\!]$	Γ_s

Given a a formula φ in $L_{\mathcal{A}}$, the canonical translation of φ, notation $[\![\varphi]\!]$, and the canonical context for φ, notation Γ_φ, are inductively defined as follows:

φ	$[\![\varphi]\!]$	Γ_φ
$\mathbf{P}(t)$	$P[\![t]\!]$	Γ_t
$\mathbf{Q}(s, t)$	$Q[\![s]\!][\![t]\!]$	$\Gamma_s \cup \Gamma_t$
$\varphi_1 \rightarrow \varphi_2$	$[\![\varphi_1]\!] \rightarrow [\![\varphi_2]\!]$	$\Gamma_{\varphi_1} \cup \Gamma_{\varphi_2}$
$\forall x^{\mathbf{C}}.\psi$	$\Pi x{:}C.[\![\psi]\!]$	$\Gamma_\psi - \{x{:}C\}$

Lemma 5.4.7.

1. $t \in Term_{\mathbf{C}} \;\Rightarrow\; \Gamma_{\mathcal{A}}, \Gamma_t \vdash_{\lambda\mathrm{PRED}} [\![t]\!] : C.$
2. $\varphi \in Form \;\Rightarrow\; \Gamma_{\mathcal{A}}, \Gamma_\varphi \vdash_{\lambda\mathrm{PRED}} [\![\varphi]\!] : *^p.$

Proof. By an easy induction. ∎

In order to define the canonical translation of derivations, it is useful to introduce some notation. The following definition is a reformulation of 5.4.3, now giving formal notations for derivations.

Definition 5.4.8. In PRED the notion 'D is a *derivation showing* $\Delta \vdash \varphi$', notation $D : (\Delta \vdash \varphi)$, is defined as follows.

$$\begin{array}{rcl} \varphi \in \Delta & \Rightarrow & P_\varphi : (\Delta \vdash \varphi); \\ D_1 : (\Delta \vdash \varphi{\rightarrow}\psi), D_2 : (\Delta \vdash \varphi) & \Rightarrow & (D_1 D_2) : (\Delta \vdash \psi); \\ D : (\Delta, \varphi \vdash \psi) & \Rightarrow & (I\varphi.D) : (\Delta \vdash \varphi{\rightarrow}\psi); \\ D : (\Delta \vdash \forall x^{\mathbf{C}}.\varphi), t \in \mathrm{Term}_{\mathbf{C}} & \Rightarrow & (Dt) : (\Delta \vdash \varphi[x := t]); \\ D : (\Delta \vdash \varphi), x^{\mathbf{C}} \notin FV(\Delta) & \Rightarrow & (Gx^{\mathbf{C}}.D) : (\Delta \vdash \forall x^{\mathbf{C}}.\varphi). \end{array}$$

Here $\mathbf{C}$ is $\mathbf{A}$ or $\mathbf{B}$, P stands for 'projection', $I\varphi$ stands for introduction and has a binding effect on φ and $Gx^{\mathbf{C}}$ stands for 'generalization' (over C) and has a binding effect on $x^{\mathbf{C}}$.

Definition 5.4.9.

1. Let $\Delta = \{\varphi_1, \ldots, \varphi_n\} \subseteq$ Form. Then the *canonical translation* of Δ, notation Γ_Δ, is the context defined by

$$\Gamma_\Delta = \Gamma_{\varphi_1} \cup \cdots \cup \Gamma_{\varphi_n}, x_{\varphi_1}{:}[\![\varphi_1]\!], \cdots, x_{\varphi_n}{:}[\![\varphi_n]\!].$$

2. For $D : (\Delta \vdash \varphi)$ in PRED the canonical translation of D, notation $[\![D]\!]$, and the canonical context for D, notation Γ_D, are inductively defined as follows:

D	$[\![D]\!]$	Γ_D
P_φ	x_φ	$\langle\rangle$
$D_1 D_2$	$[\![D_1]\!][\![D_2]\!]$	$\Gamma_{D_1} \cup \Gamma_{D_2}$
$I\varphi.D_1$	$\lambda x_\varphi{:}[\![\varphi]\!].[\![D_1]\!]$	$\Gamma_{D_1} - \{x_\varphi{:}[\![\varphi]\!]\}$
Dt	$[\![D]\!][\![t]\!]$	$\Gamma_D \cup \Gamma_t$
$Gx^{\mathbf{C}}.D$	$\lambda x{:}C.[\![D]\!]$	$\Gamma_D - \{x{:}C\}$

The following result is valid for the structure $\mathcal{A}$ as given in 5.4.1.

Lemma 5.4.10.

$$D : (\Delta \vdash_{\mathrm{PRED}} \varphi) \;\Rightarrow\; \Gamma_{\mathcal{A}}, \Gamma_\Delta \cup \Gamma_\varphi \cup \Gamma_D \vdash_{\lambda\mathrm{PRED}} [\![D]\!] : [\![\varphi]\!].$$

Proof. By induction on the derivation in PRED. ∎

Barendsen [Barendsen, 1989] observed that in spite of Lemma 5.4.10 one has in general for e.g. a sentence φ (i.e. $FV(\varphi) = \varnothing$)

$$\vdash_{\text{PRED}} \varphi \quad \not\Rightarrow \quad \exists A \, [\Gamma_{\mathcal{A}} \vdash_{\lambda\text{PRED}} A : [\![\varphi]\!]].$$

The point is that in ordinary (minimal, intuitionistic or classical) logic it is always assumed that the universes (the sorts $A, B, \ldots$) of the structure $\mathcal{A}$ are supposed to be non-empty. For example

$$(\forall x^{\mathbf{A}}.(Px{\to}Q)){\to}(\forall x^{\mathbf{A}}.Px){\to}Q)$$

is provable in PRED, but only valid in structures with $A \neq \varnothing$. In so-called *free logic* one allows also structures with empty domains. This logic has been axiomatized by [Peremans, 1949] and [Mostowski, 1951]. The system λPRED is flexible enough to cover also this free logic. The following extended context $\Gamma^+_{\mathcal{A}}$ explicitly states that the domains in question are not empty.

Definition 5.4.11. Given a many sorted structure $\mathcal{A}$ as in 5.4.1, the *extended context*, notation $\Gamma^+_{\mathcal{A}}$, is defined by $\Gamma^+_{\mathcal{A}} = \Gamma_{\mathcal{A}}, a{:}A, b{:}B$.

Not only there is a sound interpretation of PRED into λPRED, there is also a converse. In order to prove this completeness the following lemma, due to Fujita and Tonino, is needed.

Lemma 5.4.12. *Suppose* $\Gamma \vdash_{\lambda\text{PRED}} A : B : *^p$. *Then there is a many sorted structure* $\mathcal{A}$, *a set of formulae* $\Delta \subseteq L_{\mathcal{A}}$, *a formula* $\varphi \in L_{\mathcal{A}}$ *and a derivation D such that*

$$\begin{aligned} &\Gamma \equiv \Gamma_{\mathcal{A}}, \Gamma_{\Delta} \cup \Gamma_{\varphi} \cup \Gamma_D, \\ &A \equiv [\![D]\!], B \equiv [\![\varphi]\!] \\ &D : \Delta \vdash_{\text{PRED}} \varphi. \end{aligned}$$

Proof. See [Fujita and Tonino, 1991]. ∎

Corollary 5.4.13.

1. *Let* φ *be a formula and* Δ *be a set of formulae of* $L_{\mathcal{A}}$. *Then*

$$D : \Delta \vdash_{\text{PRED}} \varphi \quad \Leftrightarrow \quad \Gamma_{\mathcal{A}}, \Gamma_{\Delta} \cup \Gamma_{\varphi} \cup \Gamma_D \vdash_{\lambda\text{PRED}} [\![D]\!] : [\![\varphi]\!].$$

2. *Let* $\Delta \cup \{\varphi\}$ *be a set of sentences of* $L_{\mathcal{A}}$. *Then*

$$\Delta \vdash_{\text{PRED}} \varphi \quad \Leftrightarrow \quad \exists M[\Gamma^+_{\mathcal{A}}, \Gamma_{\Delta} \vdash_{\lambda\text{PRED}} M : [\![\varphi]\!]].$$

3. *Let* φ *be a sentence of* $L_{\mathcal{A}}$. *Then*

$$\vdash_{\text{PRED}} \varphi \quad \Leftrightarrow \quad \exists M[\Gamma_{\mathcal{A}}^{+} \vdash_{\lambda\text{PRED}} M : [\![\varphi]\!]].$$

Proof. 1. By 5.4.10 and 5.4.12 and the fact that $[\![-]\!]$ is injective on derivations and formulae.

2. If the members of Δ and φ are without free variables, then

$$D : (\Delta \vdash_{\text{PRED}} \varphi) \quad \Leftrightarrow \quad \Gamma_{\mathcal{A}}, \Gamma_{\Delta} \cup \Gamma_{D} \vdash_{\lambda\text{PRED}} [\![D]\!] : [\![\varphi]\!].$$

A statement in Γ_D is of the form $x : C$. Since $\Gamma_{\mathcal{A}}^{+} \vdash a : A, b : B$ one has

$$\begin{aligned} \Delta \vdash_{\text{PRED}} \varphi \quad &\Leftrightarrow \quad \exists D[D : (\Delta \vdash_{\text{PRED}} \varphi)] \\ &\Leftrightarrow \quad \exists D[\Gamma_{\mathcal{A}}, \Gamma_{\Delta} \cup \Gamma_{D} \vdash_{\lambda\text{PRED}} [\![D]\!] : [\![\varphi]\!]] \\ &\Leftrightarrow \quad \exists M[\Gamma_{\mathcal{A}}^{+}, \Gamma_{\Delta} \vdash_{\lambda\text{PRED}} M : [\![\varphi]\!]]. \end{aligned}$$

(For the last ($\Rightarrow$) take $M \equiv [\![D]\!][x, y := a, b]$; for ($\Leftarrow$) use Lemma 5.4.12.)

3. By (2), taking $\Delta = \varnothing$. ∎

Now that it has been established that PRED and λPRED are 'isomorphic', the propositions-as-types interpretation from PRED to λP can be factorized in two simple steps: from PRED to λPRED via the isomorphism and from λPRED to λP via a canonical forgetful map.

Definition 5.4.14 (Propositions-as-types interpretation).

1. Define the forgetful map $|-|$: term(λPRED)$\rightarrow$term(λP) by deleting all superscripts in $*$ and $\square$, so:

$$\begin{aligned} *^{s} &\mapsto * \\ *^{p} &\mapsto * \\ *^{f} &\mapsto * \\ \square^{s} &\mapsto \square \\ \square^{p} &\mapsto \square. \end{aligned}$$

E.g. $|\lambda x{:}*^{p}.x| \equiv \lambda x{:}*.x$. Write $|\Gamma| \equiv \langle x_1{:}|A_1|, \ldots\rangle$ for $\Gamma \equiv \langle x_1{:}A_1, \ldots\rangle$.

2. Let $\mathcal{A}$ be a signature and let t, φ, Δ and D be respectively a term, a formula, a set of formulae and a derivation in PRED formulated in $L_{\mathcal{A}}$. Write

$$\begin{array}{rcl}[t] & = & |[\![t]\!]|;\\ [\varphi] & = & |[\![\varphi]\!]|;\\ [D] & = & |[\![D]\!]|;\\ [\Delta] & = & |\Gamma^+_{\mathcal{A}}|, |\Gamma_\Delta|.\end{array}$$

Corollary 5.4.15 (Soundness for the propositions-as-types interpretation).

1. $\Gamma \vdash_{\lambda\mathrm{PRED}} A : B \;\Rightarrow\; |\Gamma| \vdash_{\lambda\mathbf{P}} |A| : |B|$,
2. *For sentences* Δ *and* φ *in* $L_{\mathbf{A}}$ *one has*

$$D{:}\Delta \vdash_{\mathrm{PRED}} \varphi \;\Rightarrow\; [\Delta] \vdash_{\lambda\mathbf{P}} M : [\varphi],\ \textit{for some } M.$$

Proof. 1. By a trivial induction on derivations in λPRED.

2. By 5.4.13(2) and 1.

■

Now that we have seen the equivalence between PRED and λPRED, the other systems on the logic cube will be described directly as a PTS and not as a more traditional logical system. In this way we obtain the so called L-cube isomorphic to the logic-cube.

Definition 5.4.16.

1. The systems λPROP, λPROP2, $\lambda\mathrm{PROP}\underline{\omega}$ and λPROPω are the PTSs specified as follows:

λPROP		
	$\mathcal{S}$	$*^p, \Box^p$
	$\mathcal{A}$	$*^p : \Box^p$
	$\mathcal{R}$	$(*^p, *^p)$

$\lambda\mathrm{PROP2} = \lambda\mathrm{PROP} + (\Box^p, *^p)$.

λPROP2		
	$\mathcal{S}$	$*^p, \Box^p$
	$\mathcal{A}$	$*^p : \Box^p$
	$\mathcal{R}$	$(*^p, *^p), (\Box^p, *^p)$

$\lambda\mathrm{PROP}\underline{\omega} = \lambda PROP + (\Box^p, \Box^p)$.

λPROP$\underline{\omega}$		
	$\mathcal{S}$	$*^p, \Box^p$
	$\mathcal{A}$	$*^p : \Box^p$
	$\mathcal{R}$	$(*^p, *^p), (\Box^p, \Box^p)$

λPROP$\omega = \lambda$PROP $+ (\Box^p, *^p) + (\Box^p, \Box^p)$.

λPROPω		
	$\mathcal{S}$	$*^p, \Box^p$
	$\mathcal{A}$	$*^p : \Box^p$
	$\mathcal{R}$	$(*^p, *^p), (\Box^p, *^p), (\Box^p, \Box^p)$

2. The systems λPRED, λPRED2, λPRED$\underline{\omega}$ and λPREDω are the PTS's specified as follows.

λPRED		
	$\mathcal{S}$	$*^p, *^s, *^f, \Box^p, \Box^s$
	$\mathcal{A}$	$*^p : \Box^p, *^s : \Box^s$
	$\mathcal{R}$	$(*^p, *^p), (*^s, *^p)$
		$(*^s, *^s, *^f), (*^s, *^f, *^f), (*^s, \Box^p)$

λPRED2 $= \lambda$PRED $+ (\Box^p, *^p)$.

λPRED2		
	$\mathcal{S}$	$*^p, *^s, *^f, \Box^p, \Box^s$
	$\mathcal{A}$	$*^p : \Box^p, *^s : \Box^s$
	$\mathcal{R}$	$(*^p, *^p), (*^s, *^p), (\Box^p, *^p)$
		$(*^s, *^s, *^f), (*^s, *^f, *^f), (*^s, \Box^p)$

λPRED$\underline{\omega} = \lambda$PRED $+ (\Box^p, \Box^p)$.

λPRED$\underline{\omega}$		
	$\mathcal{S}$	$*^p, *^s, *^f, \Box^p, \Box^s$
	$\mathcal{A}$	$*^p : \Box^p, *^s : \Box^s$
	$\mathcal{R}$	$(*^p, *^p), (*^s, *^p)$
		$(*^s, *^s, *^f), (*^s, *^f, *^f), (*^s, \Box^p), (\Box^p, \Box^p)$

λPRED$\omega = \lambda$PRED $+ (\Box^p, *^p) + (\Box^p, \Box^p)$.

λPREDω		
	$\mathcal{S}$	$*^p, *^s, *^f, \Box^p, \Box^s$
	$\mathcal{A}$	$*^p : \Box^p, *^s : \Box^s$
	$\mathcal{R}$	$(*^p, *^p), (*^s, *^p), (\Box^p, *^p)$
		$(*^s, *^s, *^f), (*^s, *^f, *^f), (*^s, \Box^p), (\Box^p, \Box^p)$

The eight systems form a cube as shown in the following figure 4.

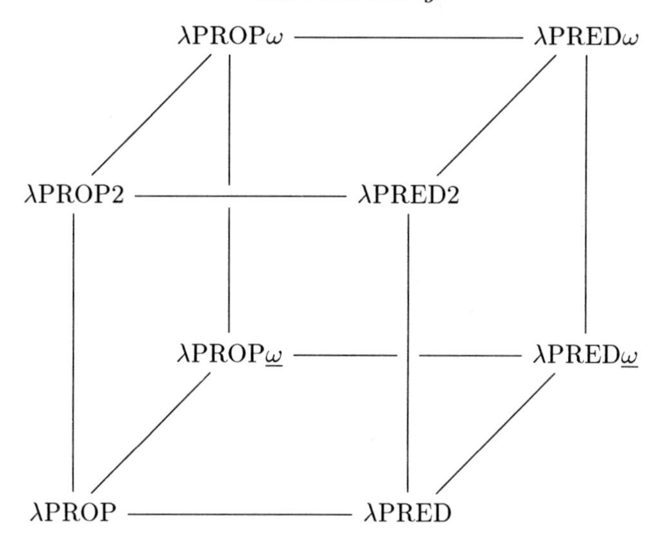

Fig. 4. The L-cube.

Since this description of the logical systems as PTSs is more uniform than the original one, we will considere only this L-cube, rather than the isomorphic one in fig. 3. In particular, fig. 4 displays the standard orientation of the L-cube and each system L_i (ranging over λPROP, λPRED etc.) corresponds to a unique system λ_i on the similar vertex in the λ-cube (in standard orientation).

Now it will be shown how in the upper plane of the L-cube the logical operators $\neg, \&, \vee$ and $\exists$ and also an equality predicate $=_L$ are definable. The relation $=_L$ is called *Leibniz' equality.*

Definition 5.4.17 (Second-order definability of the logical operations).

1. For $A, B{:}*^p$ define

$$\begin{array}{rcl} \bot & \equiv & (\Pi\beta{:}*^p.\beta); \\ \neg A & \equiv & (A{\rightarrow}\bot) \\ A\&B & \equiv & \Pi\gamma{:}*^p.(A{\rightarrow}B{\rightarrow}\gamma){\rightarrow}\gamma; \\ A\vee B & \equiv & \Pi\gamma{:}*^p.(A{\rightarrow}\gamma){\rightarrow}(B{\rightarrow}\gamma){\rightarrow}\gamma. \end{array}$$

2. For $A{:}*^p$ and $S{:}*^s$ define

$$\exists x{:}S.A \equiv \Pi\gamma{:}*^p.(\Pi x{:}S.(A{\rightarrow}\gamma)){\rightarrow}\gamma.$$

3. For $S{:}*^s$ and $x, y{:}S$ define

$$(x =_L y) \equiv \Pi P{:}S{\rightarrow}*^p.Px{\rightarrow}Py.$$

Note that the definition of & and $\vee$ make sense for systems extending λPROP2 and $\exists$ and $=_S$ for systems extending λPRED2. It is a good exercise to verify that the usual logical rules for $\&, \vee, \exists$ and $=_S$ are valid in the appropriate systems.

Example 5.4.18. We show how a part of first order Heyting Arithmetic (HA) can be done in λPRED. That is, we give a context $\Gamma_{\mathcal{A}}, \Gamma_{\Delta}$ such that $\Gamma_{\mathcal{A}}$ fixes the language of HA and Γ_{Δ} fixes a part of the axioms of HA. Take $\Gamma_{\mathcal{A}}$ to be

$$\begin{array}{rcl} N & : & *^s, \\ 0 & : & N, \\ S & : & N{\rightarrow}N, \\ + & : & N{\rightarrow}N{\rightarrow}N, \\ = & : & N{\rightarrow}N{\rightarrow} *^p . \end{array}$$

Take Γ_{Δ} to be

$$\begin{array}{rcl} tr & : & \Pi x, y, z : N.\ x = y \rightarrow y = z \rightarrow x = z, \\ sy & : & \Pi x, y : N.\ x = y \rightarrow y = x, \\ re & : & \Pi x : N.\ x = x, \\ a_1 & : & \Pi x, y : N.\ Sx = Sy \rightarrow x = y, \\ a_2 & : & \Pi x : N.\ x + 0 = x, \\ a_3 & : & \Pi x, y : N.\ x + Sy = S(x + y). \end{array}$$

Note that we do not have $a_4 : [\Pi x{:}N.\ Sx \neq 0]$ and $a_5 : [\Pi x{:}N.\ x \neq 0 \rightarrow \exists y{:}N.x = Sy]$, because the logic is minimal (We can't define $\neg$ and $\exists$ in first order logic.) Also we don't have an induction scheme for the natural numbers, which requires infinitely many axioms or one second order axiom $(a_6 : \Pi P{:}N{\rightarrow} *^p .P0 \rightarrow (\Pi x{:}N.Px \rightarrow P(Sx)) \rightarrow \Pi x{:}N.Px)$. One says that HA is not *finitely first order axiomatizable*. Finally, the atomic equality in λPRED is very weak, e.g. it doesn't satisfy the *substitution property*: if $\varphi(x)$ and $x = y$ hold, then $\varphi(y)$ holds. In second order predicate logic (λPRED2) HA can be axiomatized by adding a_6 and further a_4 and a_5 using the definable $\neg$ and $\exists$. Also the atomic $=$ can be replaced by the (definable) Leibniz equality on N, which does satisfy the substitution property.

Example 5.4.19. The structure of *commutative torsion groups* is not finitely nor infinitely first order axiomatizable. (This example is taken from [Barwise, 1977].) The manysorted structure of a commutative torsion group is $\langle A, =, \star, 0\rangle$ and it has as axioms:

$$\begin{aligned}\forall x, y, z\ \ (x \star y) \star z &= x \star (y \star z),\\ \forall x\ \ x \star 0 &= x,\\ \forall x\ \exists y\ \ x \star y &= 0,\\ \forall x, y\ \ x \star y &= y \star x,\\ \forall x\ \exists n \geq 1\ \ nx &= 0,\end{aligned}$$

where we write

$$nx \text{ for } \underbrace{x \star \cdots \star x}_{n}$$

If one tries to write the last formula in a first order form we get the following.

$$\forall x\ \ (x = 0 \vee 2x = 0 \vee \cdots)$$

So we obtain an 'infinitary' formula, which, can be shown to be not first order, by some use of the compactness theorem. A second order statement (as type) that expresses that the group has torsion is

$$\forall x{:}A\forall P{:}A{\rightarrow}{*}.[Px{\rightarrow}(\forall y{:}A.Py{\rightarrow}P(x \star y)){\rightarrow}P0].$$

Theorem 5.4.20 (Soundness of the propositions-as-types interpretation). *Let L_i be a system on the L-cube and let λ_i be the corresponding system on the λ-cube. The forgetful map $|\ .\ |$ that erases all superscripts in the $*$'s and $\square$'s satisfies the following*

$$\Gamma \vdash_{L_i} A : B : s \ \ \Rightarrow\ \ |\Gamma| \vdash_{\lambda_i} |A| : |B| : |s|.$$

Proof. By a trivial induction on the derivation in L_i. ∎

As was remarked before, completeness for the propositions-as-types interpretation holds for PRED and λP, but not for PREDω and λC.

Theorem 5.4.21 ([Berardi, 1989; Geuvers, 1989]). *Consider the similarity type of the structure $\mathcal{A} = \langle A\rangle$, i.e . there is one set without any relations. Then there is in the signature of $\mathcal{A}$ a sentence φ of* PREDω *such that*

$$\nvdash_{\text{PRED}\omega} \varphi$$

but for some M one has

$$\Gamma_{\mathcal{A}} \vdash_{\lambda\text{C}} M : [\varphi].$$

Proof. (Berardi) Define

$$\text{EXT}\ \equiv \Pi p, p'{:}{*}^p.[(p \leftrightarrow p'){\rightarrow}\Pi Q{:}{*}^p{\rightarrow}{*}^p.(Qp{\rightarrow}Qp')]$$

$$\varphi \equiv\ \text{EXT} \rightarrow \text{`}A \text{ does not have exactly two elements'}$$

Obviously $\nvdash_{\text{PRED}\omega} \varphi$. Claim: interpreted in λC one has

$$\text{EXT} \rightarrow \text{`if } A \text{ is non-empty, then } A \text{ is a type-free } \lambda\text{-model'}.$$

The reason is that if $a{:}A$, then

$$\vdash (\lambda x{:}(A{\rightarrow}A).a) : ((A{\rightarrow}A){\rightarrow}A)$$

and always

$$\vdash (\lambda y{:}A.\lambda z{:}A.z) : (A{\rightarrow}(A{\rightarrow}A)),$$

therefore '$A \leftrightarrow (A{\rightarrow}A)$' and since '$A \cong A$' (i.e. there is a bijection from A to A), it follows by EXT that '$A \cong (A{\rightarrow}A)$', i.e.'$A$ is a type-free λ-model'.

By the claim A cannot have two elements, since only the trivial λ-model is finite. ∎

Proof. (Geuvers) Consider in λPREDω the context Γ and type B defined as follows:

$$\begin{aligned} &\Gamma \equiv A{:}*^s, c{:}A \\ &B \equiv \Pi Q{:}(*^p{\rightarrow}*^p).\Pi q{:}*^p.(Q(\Pi x{:}A.q){\rightarrow}\exists q'{:}*^p.Q(q'{\rightarrow}q)). \end{aligned}$$

Then B considered as formula is not derivable in λPREDω, but its translation $|B|$ in λC is inhabited, i.e.

1. $|\Gamma| \vdash_{\lambda C} C : |B|$, for some C.
2. $\Gamma \not\vdash_{\lambda \mathrm{PRED}\omega} C : B$, for all C.

As to 1, it is sufficient to construct a C_0 such that

$$A{:}*, c{:}A, Q{:}(*{\rightarrow}*), q{:}* \vdash C_0 : (Q(\Pi x{:}A.q){\rightarrow}\exists q'{:}*.Q(q'{\rightarrow}q)).$$

Now note that

$$Q(\Pi x{:}A.q) \equiv Q(A{\rightarrow}q)$$

and the type

$$\begin{aligned} &[Q(\Pi x{:}A.q){\rightarrow}\exists q'{:}*.Q(q'{\rightarrow}q)] \equiv \\ &\equiv Q(A{\rightarrow}q){\rightarrow}[\Pi\alpha{:}*.\Pi q'{:}*.(Q(q'{\rightarrow}q){\rightarrow}\alpha){\rightarrow}\alpha] \end{aligned}$$

is inhabited by

$$\lambda y{:}(Q(A{\rightarrow}q)).\lambda\alpha{:}*.\lambda f{:}(\Pi q'{:}*.(Q(q'{\rightarrow}q){\rightarrow}\alpha)).fAy.$$

As to 2, if $\Gamma \vdash_{\lambda \mathrm{PRED}\omega} C : B$, then also

$$\begin{aligned} &A{:}*^s, c{:}A, Q{:}(*^p{\rightarrow}*^p), q{:}*^p, r{:}(Q(\Pi x{:}A.q)), \alpha{:}*^p, t{:}(\Pi q'{:}*^p.Q(q'{\rightarrow}q){\rightarrow}\alpha) \\ &\vdash CQqr\alpha t : \alpha \end{aligned}$$

By considering the possible forms of the normal form of $CQqr\alpha t$ it can be shown that this is impossible. ∎

The counterexample of Geuvers is shorter (and hence easier to formalize) than that of Berardi, but it is less intuitive.

As is well-known, logical deductions are subject to reduction, see e.g. [Prawitz, 1965] or [Stenlund, 1972]. For example in PRED one has

$$\frac{\dfrac{\begin{array}{c}[\varphi]\\ D_1\\ \psi\end{array}}{\varphi \to \psi} \qquad \begin{array}{c}D_2\\ \varphi\end{array}}{\psi} \equiv (\lambda\varphi.D_1)D_2$$

$$\to_\beta D_1[\varphi:=D_2] \equiv \begin{array}{c}D_2\\ \varphi\\ D_1\\ \psi\end{array}$$

and

Reduction 2

$$\frac{\dfrac{\begin{array}{c}x\\ D\\ \psi\end{array}}{\forall x^C.\psi}}{\psi[x:=t]} \equiv (Gx^C.D)t$$

$$\to_\beta D[x:=t] \equiv \begin{array}{c}t\\ D\\ \psi\end{array}$$

If the deductions are represented in λPRED, then these reductions become ordinary β-reductions:

$$\begin{array}{rl} [\![(I\varphi.D_1)D_2]\!] \equiv & (\lambda x_\varphi{:}[\![\varphi]\!].[\![D_1]\!])[\![D_2]\!] \rightarrow_\beta \\ & [\![D_1]\!][x_\varphi := [\![D_2]\!]] \equiv [\![D_1[P_\varphi := D_2]]\!]; \\ [\![(Gx^{\mathbf{C}}.D)t]\!] \equiv & (\lambda x{:}C.[\![D]\!])[\![t]\!] \rightarrow_\beta \\ & [\![D]\!][x := [\![t]\!]] \equiv [\![D[x := t]]\!]. \end{array}$$

In fact the best way to define the notion of reduction for a logical system on the L-cube is to consider that system as a PTS subject to β-reductions.

Now it follows that reductions in all systems of the L-cube are strongly normalizing.

Corollary 5.4.22. *Deductions in a system on the L-cube are strongly normalizing.*

Proof. The propositions-as-types map

$$|\ \ | : L\text{-cube} \rightarrow \lambda\text{-cube}$$

preserves reduction; moreover the systems on the λ-cube are strongly normalizing. ∎

The following example again shows the flexibility of the notion of PTS.

Example 5.4.23 ([Geuvers, 1990]). The system of higher-order logic in [Church, 1940] can be described by the following PTS:

λHOL		
	$\mathcal{S}$	$*, \Box, \Delta$
	$\mathcal{A}$	$* : \Box, \Box : \Delta$
	$\mathcal{R}$	$(*, *), (\Box, *), (\Box, \Box)$

That is λHOL is $\lambda\omega$ plus $\Box : \Delta$. The sort $\Box$ repesents the universe of domains and the sort $*$ represents the universe of formulae. The sort Δ and the rule $\Box : \Delta$ allow us to make declarations $A : \Box$ in the context. The system λHOL consists of a higher-order term language given by the sorts $* : \Box : \Delta$ and the rule $(\Box, \Box)$ (notice the similarity with $\lambda\rightarrow$) with a higher-order logic on top of it, given by the rules $(*, *)$ and $(\Box, *)$.

A sound interpretation of λPREDω in λHOL is determined by the map given by

$$\begin{array}{lcl} *^p & \mapsto & * \\ *^s & \mapsto & \Box \\ *^f & \mapsto & \Box \\ \Box^p & \mapsto & \Box \\ \Box^s & \mapsto & \Delta. \end{array}$$

[Geuvers, 1990] proves that λHOL is isomorphic with the following extended version of λPREDω,

λPREDω!	$\mathcal{S}$	$*^p, *^s, \square^p, \square^s$
	$\mathcal{A}$	$*^p : \square^p, *^s : \square^s$
	$\mathcal{R}$	$(*^p, *^p), (*^s, *^p), (\square^p, *^p)$
		$(*^s, *^s), (\square^p, *^s), (*^s, \square^p), (\square^p, \square^p)$

where isomorphic means that there are mappings $F : (\lambda\text{PRED}\omega!) \to (\lambda\text{HOL})$ and $G : (\lambda\text{HOL}) \to (\lambda\text{PRED}\omega!)$ such that $G \circ F = \text{Id}$ and $F \circ G = \text{Id}$. (Here the systems (λHOL) and (λPREDω!) are identified with the set of derivable sequents in these systems.) This shows that even completeness holds for the interpretation above.

Representing data types in $\lambda 2$

In this subsection it will be shown that data types can be represented in $\lambda 2$. This result of [Leivant, 1983; Leivant, 1990] will be presented in a modified form due to [Barendsen, 1989].

Definition 5.4.24.

1. A *data structure* is a many sorted structure with no given relations. A sort in a data structure is called a *data set.*
2. A *data system* is the signature of a data structure. A sort in a data system is called a *data type.*

Data systems will often be specified as shown in the following example.

- Sorts

$$\mathbf{A}, \mathbf{B}$$

- Functions

$$\mathbf{f} : \mathbf{A} \to \mathbf{B}$$

$$\mathbf{g} : \mathbf{B} \to \mathbf{A} \to \mathbf{A}$$

- Constants

$$\mathbf{c} \in \mathbf{A}.$$

In a picture:

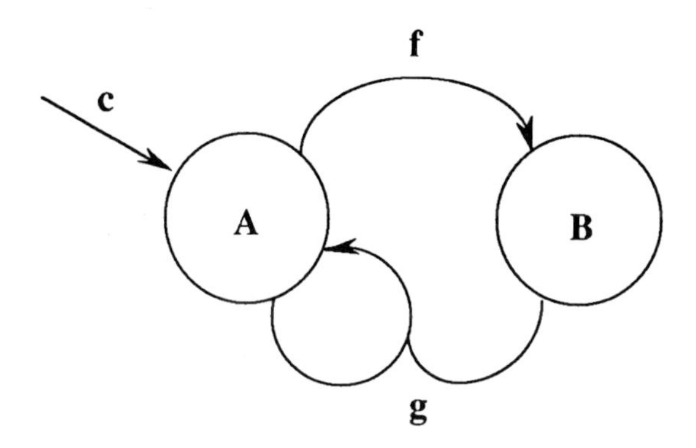

Examples 5.4.25. Two data systems are chosen as typical examples.

1. The data system for the natural numbers **Nat** is specified as follows:

    - Sorts
    $$\mathbf{N};$$
    - Functions
    $$\mathbf{S} : \mathbf{N} \to \mathbf{N};$$
    - Constants
    $$\mathbf{0} \in \mathbf{N}.$$

2. The data system of lists over a sort **A**, notation $\mathbf{List}_{\mathbf{A}}$, is specified as follows:

    - Sorts
    $$\mathbf{A}, \mathbf{L}_{\mathbf{A}};$$
    - Functions
    $$\mathbf{Cons} : \mathbf{A} \to \mathbf{L}_{\mathbf{A}} \to \mathbf{L}_{\mathbf{A}};$$
    - Constants
    $$\mathbf{nil} \in \mathbf{L}_{\mathbf{A}}.$$

Definition 5.4.26.

1. A sort in a data system is called a *parameter sort* if there is no in-going arrow into that sort and also no constant for that sort.

2. A data system is called *parameter-free* if it does not have a parameter sort.

The data system **Nat** is parameter-free. The data system $\mathbf{List_A}$ has the sort $\mathbf{A}$ as a parameter sort.

Definition 5.4.27. Let $\mathcal{D}$ be a data system. The language $L_{\mathcal{D}}$ corresponding to $\mathcal{D}$ is defined in 5.4.2

1. The *(open) termmodel* of $\mathcal{D}$, notation $\mathcal{T}(\mathcal{D})$, consists of the terms (containing free variables) of $L_{\mathcal{D}}$ together with the obvious maps given by the function symbols. That is, for every sort $\mathbf{C}$ of

   $\mathcal{D}$ the corresponding set C consists of the collection of the terms in $L_{\mathcal{D}}$ of sort $\mathbf{C}$; corresponding to a function symbol $\mathbf{f} : \mathbf{C}_1 \to \mathbf{C}_2$ a function $f : C_1 \to C_2$ is defined by

   $$f(t) = \mathbf{f}(t).$$

   A constant $\mathbf{c}$ of sort $\mathbf{C}$ is interpreted as itself; indeed one has also $\mathbf{c} \in C$.

2. Similarly one defines the *closed termmodel* of $\mathcal{D}$, notation $\mathcal{T}^o(\mathcal{D})$, as the substructure of sets of $\mathcal{T}(\mathcal{D})$ given by the closed terms.

For example the closed term model of **Nat** consists of the set

$$\mathbf{0}, \mathbf{S0}, \mathbf{SS0}, \ldots$$

with the successor function and the constant $\mathbf{0}$; this type structure is an isomorphic copy of

$$\langle \{0, 1, 2, \ldots\}, S, 0 \rangle.$$

$\mathcal{T}(\mathbf{List_A})$ consists of the finite lists of variables of type $\mathbf{A}$.

Definition 5.4.28. Given a data system $\mathcal{D}$ with

$$\begin{array}{ll} \mathbf{A}_1, \ldots, \mathbf{A}_n & \text{parameter sorts;} \\ \mathbf{B}_1, \ldots, \mathbf{B}_m & \text{other sorts;} \\ \mathbf{f}_1 : \mathbf{A}_1 \to \mathbf{B}_1 \to \mathbf{B}_2 & \text{(say)} \\ \ldots & \\ \mathbf{c}_1 : \mathbf{B}_1 & \text{(say)} \\ \ldots & \end{array}$$

Write

$$\Gamma_{\mathcal{D}} = A_1{:}*, \ldots, A_n{:}*,$$

$$B_1{:}*, \ldots, B_m{:}*,$$
$$f{:}A_1 \to B_1 \Rightarrow B_2,$$

$$\ldots$$

$$c_1{:}B_1,$$

$$\ldots.$$

For every term $t \in L_{\mathcal{D}}$ define a $\lambda 2$-term $t^{\sim}$ and context Γ_t as follows.

t	$t^{\sim}$	Γ_t
$x^{\mathbf{C}}$	x	$x{:}C$
$\mathbf{f}t_1 \cdots t_n$	$ft_1^{\sim} \cdots t_n^{\sim}$	$\Gamma_{t_1} \cup \cdots \cup \Gamma_{t_n}$
$\mathbf{c}$	c	$\langle\rangle$

Lemma 5.4.29. *For a term $t \in L_{\mathcal{D}}$ of type C one has*

$$\Gamma_{\mathcal{D}}, \Gamma_t \vdash_{\lambda 2} t^{\sim} : C.$$

Proof. By induction on the structure of t. ∎

Given a data system $\mathcal{D}$, then there is a trivial way of representing $\mathcal{T}(\mathcal{D})$ into $\lambda 2$ (or even into $\lambda\to$) by mapping t onto $t^{\sim}$. Take for example the data system **Nat**. Then $\Gamma_{\mathbf{Nat}} = N{:}*, S{:}N \to N, 0{:}N$ and every term $\mathbf{S}^k\mathbf{0}$ can be represented as

$$\Gamma_{\mathbf{Nat}} \vdash (S^k 0) : N.$$

However, for this representation it is not possible to find, for example, a term *Plus* such that, say,

$$Plus(S0)(S0) =_{\beta} SS0.$$

The reason is that S is nothing but a variable and one cannot separate a compound $S0$ or $SS0$ into its parts to see that they represent the numbers one and two. Therefore we want a better form of representation.

Definition 5.4.30. Let $\mathcal{D}$ be a data system as in definition 5.4.28.

1. Write $\Delta_{\mathcal{D}} = \underline{A}_1{:}*, \ldots, \underline{A}_n : *$.
2. A *$\lambda 2$-representation* of $\mathcal{D}$ consists of the following.
   - Types $\underline{B}_1, \ldots, \underline{B}_m$ such that

$$\Delta_{\mathcal{D}} \vdash \underline{B}_1 : *, \ldots, \underline{B}_m : *.$$

- Terms $\underline{f}_1, \ldots, \underline{c}_1, \ldots$ such that

$$\begin{array}{l}\Delta_{\mathcal{D}} \vdash \underline{f}_1 : \underline{A}_1 \to \underline{B}_1 \to \underline{B}_2; \\ \ldots \\ \Delta_{\mathcal{D}} \vdash \underline{c}_1 : \underline{B}_1; \\ \ldots\end{array}$$

- Given a $\lambda 2$-representation of $\mathcal{D}$ there is for each term t of $L_{\mathcal{D}}$ a $\lambda 2$-term $\underline{t}$ and context Δ_t defined as follows.

t	$\underline{t}$	Δ_t
$x^{\mathbf{C}}$	x	$x{:}\underline{C}$
$\mathbf{f}t_1 \cdots t_n$	$\underline{f}\underline{t}_1 \cdots \underline{t}_n$	$\Delta_{t_1} \cup \cdots \cup \Delta_{t_n}$
$\mathbf{c}$	$\underline{c}$	$\langle\rangle$

- The $\lambda 2$-representation of $\mathcal{D}$ is called *free* if moreover for all terms t, s in $L_{\mathcal{D}}$ of the same type one has

$$\underline{t} =_\beta \underline{s} \quad \Leftrightarrow \quad t \equiv s.$$

Notation 5.4.31. Let $\Gamma = x_1{:}A_1, \ldots, x_n{:}A_n$ be a context. Then

$$\begin{array}{rcl}\lambda\Gamma.M & \equiv & \lambda x_1{:}A_1 \cdots \lambda x_n{:}A_n.M; \\ \Pi\Gamma.M & \equiv & \Pi x_1{:}A_1 \cdots \Pi x_n{:}A_n.M; \\ M\Gamma & \equiv & Mx_1 \cdots x_n.\end{array}$$

Theorem 5.4.32 (Representation of data types in $\lambda 2$ [Leivant, 1983; Böhm and Berarducci, 1985; Fokkinga, 1987]). *Let $\mathcal{D}$ be a data system. Then there is a free representation of $\mathcal{D}$ in $\lambda 2$.*

Proof. Let $\mathcal{D}$ be given as in definition 5.4.28. Write

$$\begin{array}{rcl}\Theta_{\mathcal{D}} & = & B_1 : *, \ldots, B_m : *, \\ & & f_1 : A_1 \to B_1 \to B_2, \\ \ldots & & \\ & & c_1 : B_1,\end{array}$$

....

We want a representation such that for terms t in $L_{\mathcal{D}}$ of a non-parameter type

$$\underline{t}\Theta_{\mathcal{D}} =_\beta t^\sim[x_1 := x_1\Theta_{\mathcal{D}}]\cdots[x_n := x_n\Theta_{\mathcal{D}}], \tag{1}$$

where $x_1, \ldots, x_n$ are free variables with non parameter types in t; for terms t of a parameter type one has

$$\underline{t} \equiv t^\sim. \tag{2}$$

Then for terms of the same non-parameter type one has

$$\begin{array}{rcl} \underline{t} =_\beta \underline{s} & \Rightarrow & \underline{t}\Theta_{\mathcal{D}} =_\beta \underline{s}\Theta_{\mathcal{D}} \\ & \Rightarrow & t^{\sim *} =_\beta s^{\sim *} \\ & \Rightarrow & t^\sim =_\beta s^\sim \\ & \Rightarrow & t^\sim \equiv s^\sim \\ & \Rightarrow & t \equiv s, \end{array}$$

where * denotes the substitutor $[x_1 := x_1\Theta_{\mathcal{D}}]\cdots[x_n := x_n\Theta_{\mathcal{D}}]$. For terms of the same parameter type the implication holds also. Now (2) is trivial, since a term t of a parameter type $\mathbf{A}$ is necessarily a variable and hence $t \equiv x^{\mathbf{A}}$, so $t^\sim \equiv x \equiv \underline{t}$. In order to fulfill (1) define

$$\begin{array}{rcl} \underline{B}_i & \equiv & \Pi\Theta_{\mathcal{D}}.B_i \\ \underline{c} & \equiv & \lambda\Theta_{\mathcal{D}}.c \\ \underline{f}_1 & \equiv & \lambda a_1{:}\underline{A}_1\lambda b_1{:}\underline{B}_1\lambda b_2{:}\underline{B}_2\lambda\Theta_{\mathcal{D}}.f a_1(b_1\Theta_{\mathcal{D}})(b_2\Theta_{\mathcal{D}}). \end{array}$$

Then by induction on the structure of t one can derive (1). Induction step:

$$\begin{array}{rcl} \underline{\mathbf{f}_1 t_1 t_2 t_3}\Theta_{\mathcal{D}} & \equiv & \underline{f}_1\underline{t}_1\underline{t}_2\underline{t}_3\Theta_{\mathcal{D}} \\ & =_\beta & f_1\underline{t}_1(\underline{t}_2\Theta_{\mathcal{D}})(\underline{t}_3\Theta_{\mathcal{D}}) \\ & =_\beta & f_1 t_1^\sim t_2^{\sim *} t_3^{\sim *} \\ & \equiv & (\mathbf{f}_1 t_1 t_2 t_3)^{\sim *}. \end{array}$$

∎

Now it will be shown that for a term $t \in L_{\mathcal{D}}$ the representation $\mathbf{t}$ in $\lambda 2$ given by theorem 5.4.32 can be seen as the canonical translation of a proof that t satisfies 'the second order definition of the set of elements of the free structure generated by $\mathcal{D}$'.

Definition 5.4.33.

1. The map $\sharp$: $\mathcal{T}\to\{0,1,2,3\} \times \{s,p\}$ for λC is modified as follows for pseudoterms of λPRED2. Let i range over $\{s,p\}$.

$$\begin{array}{rcll} \sharp(\Box^i) & = & 3^i, & \text{which is a notation for (3,i);} \\ \sharp(*^i) & = & 2^i; & \\ \sharp({}^{\Box^i}x) & = & 1^i; & \\ \sharp({}^{*^i}x) & = & 0^i; & \end{array}$$

$$\sharp(\Pi x{:}A.B) = \sharp(\lambda x{:}A.B) = \sharp(BA) = \sharp(B).$$

2. A map $[\![\ ]\!]$: λPRED2 into λPROP2 is defined as follows.

$$\begin{array}{rcll} [\![\Box^i]\!] & = & \Box; & \\ [\![*^i]\!] & = & *; & \\ [\![{}^{\Box^i}x]\!] & = & {}^{\Box}x; & \\ [\![{}^{*^i}x]\!] & = & {}^{*}x; & \\ [\![\lambda x{:}A.B]\!] & = & [\![B]\!] & \text{if } \sharp A = 1^s, \\ & = & \lambda[\![x]\!]{:}[\![A]\!].[\![B]\!] & \text{else;} \\ [\![\Pi x{:}A.B]\!] & = & [\![B]\!] & \text{if } \sharp A = 1^s, \\ & = & \Pi[\![x]\!]{:}[\![A]\!].[\![B]\!] & \text{else;} \\ [\![BA]\!] & = & [\![B]\!] & \text{if } \sharp A = 1^s, \\ & = & [\![B]\!][\![A]\!] & \text{else.} \\ [\![x{:}A]\!] & = & \langle\rangle & \text{if } \sharp x \in \{0^s, 1^s\}, \\ & = & [\![x]\!]{:}[\![A]\!] & \text{else.} \\ [\![x_1{:}A_1,\ldots,x_n{:}A_n]\!] & = & [\![x_1{:}A_1]\!],\ldots,[\![x_n{:}A_n]\!]. & \end{array}$$

3. A map $|\ |$: λPROP2$\to\lambda$2 is defined as follows.

$$\begin{array}{rcl} |\Box^i| & = & \Box; \\ |*^i| & = & *; \\ |{}^{\Box^i}x| & = & {}^{\Box}x; \\ |{}^{*^i}x| & = & {}^{*}x; \\ |\Pi x{:}A.B| & = & \Pi|x|{:}|A|.|B|; \\ |\lambda x{:}A.B| & = & \lambda|x|{:}|A|.|B|; \end{array}$$

$$|BA| \quad = \quad |B||A|.$$

Finally put

$$\begin{aligned} |x{:}A| &= |x|{:}|A|; \\ |x_1{:}A_1, \ldots, x_n{:}A_n| &= |x_1{:}A_1|, \ldots, |x_n{:}A_n|. \end{aligned}$$

4. A map [ ]: λPRED2$\rightarrow\lambda 2$ is defined by $[A] = |[\![A]\!]|$.

Proposition 5.4.34.

1. $\Gamma \vdash_{\lambda\text{PRED2}} A : B \;\Rightarrow\; [\![\Gamma]\!] \vdash_{\lambda\text{PROP2}} [\![A]\!] : [\![B]\!]$.
2. $\Gamma \vdash_{\lambda\text{PROP2}} A : B \;\Rightarrow\; |\Gamma| \vdash_{\lambda 2} |A| : |B|$.
3. $\Gamma \vdash_{\lambda\text{PRED2}} A : B \;\Rightarrow\; [\Gamma] \vdash_{\lambda 2} [A] : [B]$.

Proof. 1. By induction on derivations using

$$[\![P[x := Q]]\!] = [\![P]\!][[\![x]\!] := [\![Q]\!]].$$

2. Similarly, using $^{*^*}x \notin FV([P])$.

3. By (1) and (2). ∎

Now the alternative construction of $\underline{t}$ for $t \in L_{\mathcal{D}}$ can be given. The method is due to [Leivant, 1983]. Let $\mathcal{D}$ be a datasystem with parameter sorts. To fix the ideas, let $\mathcal{D} = \mathbf{List_A}$. Write $\Gamma_{\mathcal{D}} = A{:}*^s, L_A{:}*^s, nil{:}L_A,\ cons : A{\rightarrow}L_A{\rightarrow}L_A$. For the parameter type $\mathbf{A}$ a predicate $P^A{:}(A{\rightarrow}*^p)$ is declared. For $\mathbf{List_A}$ the predicate

$$\begin{aligned} P^{L_A} \quad = \quad & \lambda z{:}(L_A).\Pi Q{:}(L_A{\rightarrow}*^p). \\ & [Q\,nil{\rightarrow}[\Pi a{:}A\Pi y{:}(L_A).P^A a{\rightarrow}Qy{\rightarrow}Q(cons\,ay)]{\rightarrow}Qz] \end{aligned}$$

says of an element $z{:}L_A$ that z belongs to the set of lists built up from elements of A satisfying the predicate P^A.

Now if $t \in L_{\mathcal{D}}$ is of type $\mathbf{List_A}$, then intuitively $t^{\sim} : L_A$ satisfies P^{L_A}. Indeed, one has for such t

$$\Gamma_{\mathcal{D}}, \Gamma_t \vdash t^{\sim} : L_A \text{ and } \Gamma_{\mathcal{D}}, \Gamma_t \vdash d_t : (P^{L_A} t^{\sim}). \tag{1}$$

for some d_t constructed as follows. Let $\mathbf{C}$ range over $\mathbf{A}$ and $\mathbf{List_A}$ with the corresponding C being A or L_A.

t	$t^\sim$	Γ_t	d_t
$x^{\mathbf{C}}$	x	$x{:}C, a_x{:}(P^C x)$	a_x
nil	*nil*	$\langle\rangle$	$\lambda Q{:}(L_A{\to}*^p)\lambda p{:}(Q\,nil)$ $\lambda q{:}(\Pi a{:}A\Pi y{:}L_A.$ $[P^A a{\to}Qy{\to}Q(cons\,ay)]).p$
$\mathbf{cons}\,t_1t_2$	$cons\,t_1^\sim t_2^\sim$	$\Gamma_{t_1}, \Gamma_{t_2}$	$\lambda Q{:}(L_A{\to}*^p)\lambda p{:}(Q\,nil)$ $\lambda q{:}(\Pi a{:}A\Pi y{:}L_A.$ $[P^A a{\to}Qy{\to}Q(cons\,ay)]).$ $qt_1^\sim t_2^\sim d_{t_1}(d_{t_2}Qpq)$

By induction on the structure of t one verifies (1). By Proposition 5.4.34 it follows that

$$[\Gamma_{\mathcal{D}}, \Gamma_t] \vdash [d_t] : [(P^C t^\sim)]. \tag{2}$$

Write

$$\begin{aligned} \underline{A} &= [P^A], \\ \underline{L}_A &= [P^{L_A}] = \Pi Q{:}*.Q{\to}(\underline{A}{\to}Q{\to}Q){\to}Q, \\ \text{nil} &= [d_{\text{nil}}] = \lambda Q{:}*.\lambda p{:}Q\lambda q{:}(\underline{A}{\to}Q{\to}Q).p, \\ \text{cons} &= \lambda a{:}\underline{A}\lambda x{:}\underline{L}_A\lambda Q{:}*.\lambda p{:}Q\lambda q{:}(\underline{A}{\to}Q{\to}Q).qax. \end{aligned}$$

Notice that this is the same $\lambda 2$-representation of $\mathbf{List}_{\mathbf{A}}$ as given in theorem 5.4.32 and that $\underline{t} =_\beta [d_t]$.

In this way many data types can be represented in $\lambda 2$.

Examples 5.4.35.

1. Lists.

   To be explicit, a *list* $\langle a_1, a_2\rangle \in L_A$ and *cons* are represented as follows.

$$\begin{aligned} \underline{L}_A &= (\Pi L{:}*.L{\to}(A{\to}L{\to}L){\to}L); \\ \langle \underline{a}_1, \underline{a}_2\rangle &= (\lambda L{:}*\lambda nil{:}L\lambda cons{:}A{\to}L{\to}L.cons\,a_1(cons\,a_2 nil))); \\ \text{cons} &= \lambda a{:}A\lambda x{:}(\Pi L{:}*.L{\to}(A{\to}L{\to}L){\to}L) \\ &\quad\ \lambda L{:}*\lambda nil{:}L\lambda cons{:}A{\to}L{\to}L.cons\,(xL\,nil\,cons); \end{aligned}$$

   Moreover

$$A{:}*, a_1{:}A, a_2{:}A \vdash \langle \underline{a}_1, \underline{a}_2\rangle{:}\underline{L}_A.$$

2. Booleans.
   Sorts

Bool
Constants
true, false$\in$Bool

are represented in $\lambda 2$ as follows.

$$\begin{aligned} \underline{Bool} &= \Pi\alpha{:}{*}.\alpha{\rightarrow}\alpha{\rightarrow}\alpha, \\ \underline{true} &= \lambda\alpha{:}{*}\lambda x{:}\alpha\lambda y{:}\alpha.x, \\ \underline{false} &= \lambda\alpha{:}{*}\lambda x{:}\alpha\lambda y{:}\alpha.y. \end{aligned}$$

3. Pairs.
   Sorts

$$\mathbf{A_1}, \mathbf{A_2}, \mathbf{B}$$

   Functions

$$\mathbf{p}{:}\mathbf{A_1}{\rightarrow}\mathbf{A_2}{\rightarrow}\mathbf{B}.$$

   Representation in $\lambda 2$

$$\begin{aligned} \underline{B} &= \Pi\alpha{:}{*}.(A_1{\rightarrow}A_2{\rightarrow}\alpha){\rightarrow}\alpha, \\ \underline{p} &= \lambda x{:}A_1\lambda y{:}A_2\lambda\alpha{:}{*}\lambda z{:}(A_1{\rightarrow}A_2{\rightarrow}\alpha).zxy. \end{aligned}$$

Applying the map $|\ |: terms(\lambda 2){\rightarrow}\Lambda$ defined in 3.2.14 the usual representations of Booleans and pairing in the type-free λ-calculus is obtained. The same applies to the $\lambda 2$ representation of the data type Nat giving the type-free Church numerals.

Now that data types can be represented faithfully in $\lambda 2$, the question arises which functions on these can be represented by λ-terms. Since all terms have an nf, not all recursive functions can be represented in $\lambda 2$, see e.g. [Barendregt, 1990], thm. 4.2.15.

Definition 5.4.36. Let $\mathcal{D}$ be a data structure freely represented in$\lambda 2$ as usual. Consider in the closed term model $\mathcal{T}^o(\mathcal{D})$ a function $f{:}C{\rightarrow}C'$, where C and C' are non-parameter sorts, is called $\lambda 2$-*definable* if there is a term $\underline{f}$ such that

$$\Gamma_D \vdash_{\lambda 2} \underline{f} : (\underline{C}{\rightarrow}\underline{C'})\ \&\ \underline{f}\underline{t} =_\beta \underline{ft} \text{ for all } t \in Term_C.$$

Definition 5.4.37. Let a data system $\mathcal{D}$ be given. A *Herbrand–Gödel system*, formulated in λPRED2, is given by

1. $\Gamma_{\mathcal{D}}$

2. $\Gamma_{f_1,\ldots,f_n}$, a finite set of function declarations of the form $f_1{:}B_1,\ldots,$ $f_n{:}B_n$ with $\Gamma_{\mathcal{D}} \vdash B_i{:}*^f$.

3. $\Gamma_{ax_1,\ldots,ax_m}$, a finite set of axiom declarations of the form $a_1{:}ax_1,\ldots,$ $a_m{:}ax_m$ with each ax_i of the form $f_j(s_1,\ldots,s_p) =_L r$ with the $s_1,\ldots,s_p,r$ terms in $L_{\mathcal{D}}$ of the correct type (see 5.4.17(4) for the definition of $=_L$) .

For such a Herbrand–Gödel system we write

$$HG \equiv \Gamma_{\mathcal{D}}, \Gamma_{\vec{f}}, \Gamma_{\vec{ax}}.$$

In order to emphasize the functions one may write $HG = HG(\vec{f})$. The principal function symbol is the last f_n.

Example 5.4.38. The following is a Herbrand-Gödel system (Note that the principal function symbol f_2 specifies the function $\lambda x \in Nat.x + x$).

$$\begin{aligned} HG_0 \equiv\ & N{:}*^s, 0{:}N, S{:}(N{\rightarrow}N), \\ & f_1{:}N{\rightarrow}N{\rightarrow}N, f_2{:}N{\rightarrow}N_1 \\ & a_1{:}(\Pi x{:}N.f_1 x 0 =_L x), \\ & a_2{:}(f_1 x(Sy) =_L S(f_1 xy)), \\ & a_3{:}(f_2 x =_L f_1 xx). \end{aligned}$$

Definition 5.4.39. Let $\mathcal{A}$ be a data structure having no parameter sorts. Let $f : C{\rightarrow}C'$ be a given external function on $\mathcal{T}(\mathcal{D})$ (similar definitions can be given for functions of more arguments). Let HG be a Herbrand–Gödel system.

1. HG *computes* $f \Leftrightarrow HG = HG(f_1,\ldots,f_n)$ and for all $t{\in}\mathrm{Term}_C$ one has for some p

$$HG \vdash_{\lambda\mathrm{PRED2}} p : (f_n \underline{t} =_L \underline{f(t)}).$$

2. Suppose $HG(f_1,\ldots,f_n)$ computes f. Then f is called *provably type-correct* (in λPRED2) if for some B one has

$$HG \vdash_{\lambda\mathrm{PRED2}} B : [\Pi x{:}\underline{C}.[P^C x{\rightarrow}P^{C'}(f_n x)]].$$

Note that the notion 'provably type correct' is a so-called intensional property: it depends on how the f is given to us as f_n. Now the questions about λ2-definability can be answered in a satisfactory way. This result is due to

[Leivant, 1983]. It generalizes a result due to [Girard, 1972] characterizing the $\lambda 2$-definable functions on Nat as those that are provably total.

Theorem 5.4.40. *Let $\mathcal{D}$ be a parameter-free data structure.*

1. *The basic functions in $\mathcal{D}$ are $\lambda 2$-definable*
2. *A function $f{:}C{\rightarrow}C'$ is recursive iff f is HG computable.*
3. *A function $f{:}C{\rightarrow}C'$ is $\lambda 2$-definable iff f is HG-computable and provably type correct in λPRED2.*

Proof. 1. This was shown in theorem 5.4.32.

2. See [Mendelson, 1987].
3. See [Leivant, 1983; Leivant, 1990].

∎

5.5 Pure type systems not satisfying normalization

In this subsection some pure type systems will be considered in which there are terms of type $\bot \equiv \Pi\alpha{:}{*}.\alpha$. As a consequence there are typable terms without a normal form.

In subsection 5.2 we encountered the system $\lambda *$ which can be seen as a simplification of λC by identifying $*$ and $\square$. It has as peculiarity that $* : *$ and its PTS specification is quite simple.

Definition 5.5.1. The system $\lambda *$ is the PTS determined as follows:

$\lambda *$		
	$\mathcal{S}$	$*$
	$\mathcal{A}$	$* : *$
	$\mathcal{R}$	$(*, *)$

Since all constructions possible in λC can be done also in $\lambda *$ by collapsing $\square$ to $*$, it seems an interesting simplification. However, the system $\lambda *$ turns out to be 'inconsistent' in the sense that every type is inhabited, thus making the propositions-as-types interpretation meaningless. Nevertheless, the system $\lambda *$ is meaningful on the level of conversion of terms. In fact there is a nontrivial model of $\lambda *$, the so-called closure model due to [Scott, 1976], see also e.g. [Barendregt and Rezus, 1983]. For a discussion on the computational relevance of $\lambda *$, see [Coquand, 1986] and [Howe, 1987].

The 'inconsistency' following from $*{:}*$ was first proved by [Girard, 1972]. He also showed that the circularity of $*{:}*$ is not necessary to derive the paradox. For this purpose he introduced the following pure type system λU. Remember its definition.

Definition 5.5.2. The system λU is the PTS defined as follows:

λU		
	$\mathcal{S}$	$*, \Box, \Delta$
	$\mathcal{A}$	$* : \Box, \Box : \Delta$
	$\mathcal{R}$	$(*,*), (\Box,*), (\Box,\Box), (\Delta,\Box), (\Delta,*)$

So λU is an extension of $\lambda\omega$. The next theorem is the main result in this subsection. The proof occupies this whole subsection.

Theorem 5.5.3 (Girard's paradox). *In λU the type $\bot$ is inhabited, i.e. $\vdash M{:}\bot$, for some M.*

Proof. See 5.5.26. ∎

Corollary 5.5.4.

1. *In λU all types are inhabited.*
2. *In λU there are typable terms that have no normal form.*
3. *Results (1) and (2) also hold for $\lambda *$ in place of λU.*

Proof. 1. Let $M{:}\bot$ be provable in λU. Then

$$a{:}* \vdash Ma : a$$

and it follows that every type of sort $*$ in λU is inhabited. Types of sort $\Box$ or Δ are always inhabited; e.g. $\Pi\vec{x}{:}\vec{A}.*$ by $\lambda\vec{x}{:}\vec{A}.\bot$.

2. By proposition 5.2.31

3. By applying the contraction $f(*) = f(\Box) = f(\Delta) = *$ mapping λU onto $\lambda *$.

∎

The proof of Girard's paradox will be given in five steps. Use is made of ideas in [Coquand, 1985], [Howe, 1987] and [Geuvers, 1988].

1. Jumping out of a structure.
2. A paradox in naive set theory.
3. Formalizing.
4. An universal notation system in λU.
5. The paradox in λU.

Step 1. Jumping out of a structure

Usually the method of diagonalization provides a constructive way to 'jump out' of a structure. Hence if we make the (tacit) assumption that everything should be in our structure, then we obtain a contradiction, the paradox. Well known is the Russell paradox obtained by diagonalization. Define the naive set

$$R = \{a \mid a \notin a\}$$

Then

$$\forall a[a \in R \leftrightarrow a \notin a],$$

in particular

$$R \in R \leftrightarrow R \notin R,$$

which is a contradiction. A positive way of rephrasing this result is saying that R does not belong to the universe of sets from which we take the a; thus we are able to jump out of a system. This is the essence of diagonalization first presented in Cantor's theorem. The method of diagonalization yields also undecidable problems and sentences with respect to some given formal system (i.e. neither provable nor unprovable). (If the main thesis in [Hofstadter, 1979] turns out to be correct it may even be the underlying principle of selfconsciousness.)

The following paradox is in its set theoretic form, due to [Mirimanoff, 1917]. We present a game theoretic version by [Zwicker, 1987]. Consider games for two players. Such a game is called *finite* if any run of the game cannot go on forever. For example noughts and crosses is finite. Chess is not finite (a game may go on forever, this in spite of the rule that there is a draw if the same position has appeared on the board three times; that rule is only optional). *Hypergame* is the following game: player I chooses a finite game; player II does the first move in the chosen game; player I does the second move in that game; etc. Claim: hypergame is finite. Indeed, after player I has chosen a finite game, only finitely many moves can be made within that game. Now consider the following run of hypergame.

Player I:	hypergame
Player II:	hypergame
Player I:	hypergame
...	...

Therefore hypergame is not a finite game and we have our paradox. This paradox can be formulated also as a positive result.

Proposition 5.5.5 (Informal). *Let A be a set and let R be a binary relation on A. Define for $a \in A$*

$SN_R a \;\Leftrightarrow\;$ *there is no infinite sequence $a_0, a_1, \ldots \in A$ such that*

$$\ldots\ldots Ra_1 Ra_0 Ra.$$

Then in A we have

$$\neg\exists b \forall a\, [SN_R a \;\leftrightarrow\; aRb].$$

Proof. Suppose towards a contradiction that for some b

$$\forall a\, [SN_R a \leftrightarrow aRb]. \tag{1}$$

Then

$$\forall a\, [aRb \rightarrow SN_R a]. \tag{2}$$

This implies

$$SN_R b,$$

because if there is an infinite sequence under b

$$\ldots Ra_1 Ra_0 Rb$$

then there is also one under $a_0(Rb)$, contadicting (2). But then by (1)

$$bRb$$

Hence $\ldots RbRbRb$ and this means $\neg SN_R b$. Contradiction. ∎

By taking for A the universe of all sets and for R the relation $\in$, one obtains Mirimanoff's paradox. By taking for A the collection of all ordinal numbers and for R again $\in$, one obtains the Burali–Forti paradox.

The construction in 5.5.5 is an alternative way of 'jumping out of a system'. This method and the diagonalization inherent in Cantor's theorem can be seen as limit cases of the following generalized construction. This observation is due to [Quine, 1963], p.36.

Proposition 5.5.6. *Let A be a set and let R be a binary relation on A. For $n = 1, 2, \ldots, \infty$ define*

$$C_n a \;\Leftrightarrow\; \exists a_0, \ldots, a_n \in A[a_0 = a \;\&\; \forall i < n\; a_{i+1} R a_i \;\&\; a_n = a].$$

$$B_n = \{a \in A \mid \neg C_n a\}.$$

{The set B_n consists of those $a \in A$ not on an 'n-cycle'}. Then in A one has

$$\neg\exists b \forall a [B_n a \leftrightarrow aRb].$$

Proof. Exercise. ∎

By taking $n = 1$ one obtains the usual diagonalization method of Cantor. By taking $n = \infty$ one obtains the result 5.5.5. Taking $n = 2$ gives the solution to the puzzle 'the exclusive club' of [Smullyan, 1985], p.21. (A person is a member of this club if and only if he does not shave anyone who shaves him. Show that there is no person that has shaved every member of the exclusive club and no one else.)

Step 2. The paradox in naive set theory

Now we will define a (naive) set T with a binary relation $<$ on it such that

$$\forall a \in T\,[SN_{<}a \quad \leftrightarrow \quad a < b], \tag{!}$$

for some $b \in T$. Together with Proposition 5.5.5 this gives the paradox. The particular choice of T and $<$ is such that the auxiliary lemmas needed can be formalized in λU.

Definition 5.5.7.

1. $T = \{(A, R) \mid A \text{ is a set and } R \text{ is a binary transitive relation on } A\}$
   For $(A, R), (A', R') \in T$ and $f{:}A \rightarrow A'$ write

$$\begin{array}{lcl} (A,R) <_f^- (A',R') & \Leftrightarrow & \forall a,b \in A\,[aRb \rightarrow f(a)R'f(b)]; \\ f \text{ is bounded} & \Leftrightarrow & \exists a' \in A'\forall a \in A. f(a)R'a'; \\ (A,R) <_f (A',R') & \Leftrightarrow & (A,R) <_f^- (A',R')\ \&\ f \text{ is bounded.} \end{array}$$

2. Define the binary relation $<$ on T by

$$(A, R) < (A', R') \;\Leftrightarrow\; \exists f{:}(A \rightarrow A')[(A, R) <_f (A', R')].$$

3. Let $W = \{(A, R) \in T \mid SN_{<}(A, R)\}$.

We will see that $b = (W, <) \in T$ satisfies (!) above. (For notational simplicity we write for the restriction of $<$ to W also $<$.)

Definition 5.5.8. For $(A, R) \in T$ and $a \in A$ write

1. $A_a = \{b \in A \mid bRa\}$;
2. R_a is the restriction of R to A_a.

Lemma 5.5.9. *Let $(A, R) \in T$ and $a, b \in A$. Then*

1. $(A_a, R_a) < (A, R)$;
2. $aRb \rightarrow (A_a, R_a) < (A_b, R_b)$;
3. $aRb \rightarrow SN_R b \rightarrow SN_R a$;
4. $[\forall a \in A SN_R a] \rightarrow SN_{<}(A, R)$.

Proof. 1,2. By using the map $f = \lambda x{:}A_a.x$. For (2) the transitivity of R is needed to ensure that f has codomain A_b. In both cases f is bounded by a.

3. Suppose aRb. If there is an infinite R-chain under a, i.e. $\ldots a_1 R a_o R a$, then there is also one under b; indeed $\ldots a_1 R a_o R a R b$. Therefore $SN_R b$ imlpies $SN_R a$.

4. Suppose there is an infinite $<$-chain under (A, R):

$$\ldots(A_1, R_1) < (A_0, R_0) < (A, R).$$

From the figure 5 it can be seen that using the bounding elements in (A_n, R_n) for the map $f_n{:}A_{n+1}\rightarrow A_n$ (projected via the fs into A) there is an infinite R-chain, below an element of A.

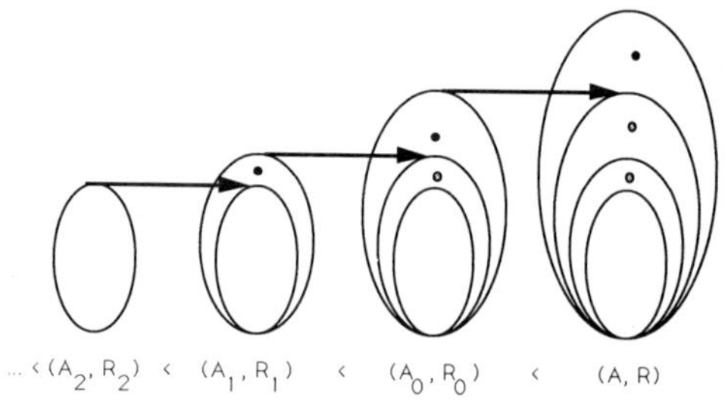

Fig. 5.

This contradicts the assumption $\forall a \in A\ SN_R(a)$.

∎

Proposition 5.5.10.

$$\forall (A, R) \in T[SN_<(A, R) \leftrightarrow (A, R) < (W, <)].$$

Proof. It suffices to show that for $(A, R) \in T$

1. $SN_<(A, R) \ \rightarrow\ (A, R) < (W, <)$;
2. $SN_<(W, <)$.

For then $(A, R) < (W, <) \ \rightarrow\ SN_<(A, R)$ by Lemma 5.5.9 (3).

As to 1, suppose $SN_<(A, R)$. Let $a\in A$ and define $f(a) = (A_a, R_a)$, with R_a defined in 5.5.8. By 5.5.9 (1) one has $f(a) < (A, R)$; by assumption and 5.5.9(3) applied to $(T, <)$ it follows that $SN_<(f(a))$ and hence $f(a) \in W$. Therefore $f{:}A\rightarrow W$. Moreover, $f{:}(A, R) < (W, <)$ by Lemma 5.5.9 (1), (2).

As to 2, note that by definition $\forall (A, R) \in W\ \ SN_<(A, R)$. Hence by Lemma 5.5.9 (4) one has $SN_<(W, <)$. ∎

Step 3. Formalizing

In this step several notions and lemmas from steps 1 and 2 will be formalized. This could be done inside the systems of the cube (in fact inside λP2). However, since we want the eventual contradiction to occur inside λU, a system that is chosen with as few axioms as seems possible, the formalization will be done in λU directly. From now on the notions of context and $\vdash$ refer to λU. Use will be made freely of logical notions (e.g. we write $\forall a{:}A$ instead of $\Pi a{:}A$).

The first task is to define the notion SN_R without referring to the concept of infinity.

Definition 5.5.11.

1. Γ_0 is the context

$$A{:}\Box, R{:}(A \rightarrow A \rightarrow *).$$

2. Write in context Γ_0
   $\text{chain}_{A,R} \equiv \lambda P{:}(A \rightarrow *).\forall a{:}A[Pa \rightarrow \exists b{:}A[Pb \,\&\, bRa]]$
   $SN_{A,R} \equiv \lambda a{:}A.\forall P{:}(A \rightarrow *)[\text{chain}_{A,R}P \rightarrow \neg Pa]$.

Intuitively, $\text{chain}_{A,R}P$ states that $P{:}A \rightarrow *$ is a predicate on (i.e. subset of) A such that for every element a in P there is an element b in P with bRa. Moreover $\text{SN}_{A,R}a$ states that $a{:}A$ is not in a subset $P \subseteq A$ that is a chain.

Lemma 5.5.12. *In λU one can show*

1. $\Gamma_0 \vdash chain_{A,R} : ((A \rightarrow *) \rightarrow *)$.
2. $\Gamma_0 \vdash SN_{A,R} : (A \rightarrow *)$.

Proof. Immediate. ∎

Proposition 5.5.13. *In context Γ_0 the type*

$$\neg \exists b{:}A \forall a{:}A[SN_{A,R}a \leftrightarrow aRb]$$

is in λU inhabited.

Proof. With a little effort the proof of Proposition 5.5.5 can be formalized in λPRED2. Then one can apply the map $f{:}\lambda\text{PRED2} \rightarrow \lambda U$ determined by

$$f(*^p) = *, f(*^s) = f(*^f) = f(\Box^p) = \Box, f(\Box^s) = \Delta.$$

∎

We now need a relativization of Proposition 5.5.13.

Definition 5.5.14.

1. In context Γ_0 write
   $\text{closed}_{A,R} \equiv \lambda Q{:}(A{\rightarrow}*).\forall a,b{:}A\ [Qa{\rightarrow}bRa{\rightarrow}Qb]$.
   {$\text{closed}_{A,R}Q$ says: 'if a is in Q and b is R-below a, then b is in Q'.}

2. In context $\Gamma_0, Q{:}A{\rightarrow}*$, write

$$\forall a{:}A^Q.B \equiv \forall a{:}A[Qa{\rightarrow}B]$$

$$\exists a{:}A^Q.B \equiv \exists a{:}A[Qa\&B].$$

   {This is relativizing to a predicate Q.}

Corollary 5.5.15. *In context $\Gamma_0, Q{:}A{\rightarrow}*$ the type*

$$\mathit{closed}_{A,R}Q{\rightarrow}\exists b{:}A^Q\forall a{:}A^Q\ [SN_{A,R}a \leftrightarrow aRb]$$

is inhabited in λU.

Proof. The proof of Proposition 5.5.5 formalized in PRED2 can be relativized and that proof becomes, after applying the contraction f the required inhabitant. ∎

So far we have formalized the results in Step 1. There are several problems for the formalization of the naive paradox in Step 2 into λU. The main one is that in λU a 'subset' of a type does not form a type again. For example it is not clear how to form $A_a(\subseteq A)$ as a type. This problem is solved by considering instead of a structure (A_a, R_a) the structure (A, R^a) with

$$bR^ac \;\Leftrightarrow\; bRc \;\&\; bRa.$$

In order to formalize Lemma 5.5.9 the definition of $<$ has to be adjusted. Let the *domain* of R be the (naive) subset

$$\text{Dom}_R = \{a{:}A \mid \exists b{:}A\ aRb\}.$$

In the new definition of $<$ it is required that the monotonic map involved is bounded, but only on the domain of R.

A second problem is that T and W are not types and that it is not clear how to realize $(W, <)\in T$. This problem will be solved by constructing in λU a 'universal' kind $\mathbf{U}$ such that all pairs (A, R) can be 'faithfully' embedded into $\mathbf{U}$.

Definition 5.5.16. In λU define two predicates $<^-, <$ of type

$$[\Pi\alpha{:}\Box\Pi r{:}(\alpha\to\alpha\to *)\Pi\alpha'{:}\Box\Pi r'{:}(\alpha'\to\alpha'\to *)\Pi f{:}(\alpha\to\alpha').*]$$

as follows. We write

$$(A, R) <_f^- (A', R') \quad \text{for} \quad <^- ARA'R'f$$

and similarly for $<$.

1. $(A, R) <_f^- (A', R') \ \Leftrightarrow\ \forall a, b{:}A\ [aRb \to (fa)R'(fb)]$.

2.

$$\begin{aligned}(A, R) <_f (A', R') \quad \Leftrightarrow \quad & (A, R) <_f^- (A', R')\ \&\\ & \exists a'{:}A'\ [Dom_{R'}a'\ \&\\ & \forall a{:}A\ [Dom_R a\to(fa)R'a']],\end{aligned}$$

   where $\mathrm{Dom}_R a$ stands for $\exists b{:}A.aRb$.

3. Write for the appropriate A, R and A', R'

$$(A, R) <^- (A', R') \quad \Leftrightarrow \quad \exists f{:}A\to A'\ (A, R) <_f^- (A', R')$$

   and similarly for $<$.

The notion $SN_<$ is not a particular instance of the notion $SN_{A,R}$. This is because the 'set'

$$\{(A, R) \mid A{:}*, R{:}A\to A\to *\}$$

on which $<$ is supposed to act does not form a type. Therefore $SN_<$ has to be defined separately.

Definition 5.5.17.

1. $\text{chain}_< \equiv \lambda P{:}(\Pi\alpha{:}\Box.(\alpha{\to}\alpha{\to}*){\to}*).$

$$[\forall\alpha_1{:}\Box\forall r_1{:}(\alpha_1{\to}\alpha_1{\to}*).$$
$$[P\alpha_1 r_1{\to}\exists\alpha_2{:}\Box\exists r_2{:}(\alpha_2{\to}\alpha_2{\to}*)$$
$$[P\alpha_2 r_2 \& (\alpha_2, r_2) < (\alpha_1, r_1)]$$
$$]$$
$$].$$

2. $SN_< \equiv \lambda\alpha{:}\Box\lambda r{:}(\alpha{\to}\alpha{\to}*).\forall P{:}[\Pi\alpha'{:}\Box.(\alpha'{\to}\alpha'{\to}*){\to}*].$
   $[\text{chain}_< P{\to}\neg(P\alpha r)].$

3. Trans Trans $\equiv \lambda\alpha{:}\Box\lambda r{:}(\alpha{\to}\alpha{\to}*).\forall a, b, c{:}\alpha.[arb{\to}brc{\to}arc].$

4. In context $\Gamma_0, a{:}A$ define

$$R^a \equiv \lambda b, c{:}A.[bRc\&bRa].$$

Proposition 5.5.18. *Let* $A{:}\Box, R{:}(A{\to}A{\to}*), a{:}A, b{:}A$ *and assume*

$$\text{Trans}AR;$$

that is, work in context x :TransAR. *Then the following types are inhabited.*

1. $\text{Dom}_R a \to (A, R^a) < (A, R).$
2. $aRb \to (A, R^a) < (A, R^b).$
3. $aRb \to SN_{A,R}b \to SN_{A,R}a.$
4. $(\forall a{:}A.SN_{A,R}a) \leftrightarrow SN_< AR.$

Proof. 1. Assume $\text{Dom}_R a$. Define $f = \lambda x{:}A.x$. Then $(A, R^a) <_f^- (A, R)$. Moreover a in Dom_R bounds $fx = x$ for x in $\text{Dom}_{(R^a)}$. Indeed, $xR^a y \to xRa$. Therefore $(A, R^a) <_f (A, R)$.

2. Assume Trans AR and aRb. Again define $f = \lambda x{:}A.x$. Then

$$(A, R^a) <_f^- (A, R^b);$$

indeed, $xR^a y \to xRy \;\&\; xRaRb \to xR^b y$ by the transitivity of R. Also a is in $\text{Dom}_{(R^b)}$ and again bounds $fx = x$ for x in $\text{Dom}_{(R^a)}$.

3. Assume aRb and $SN_{A,R}b$. Let $\text{chain}_{A,R}P$ and assume towards a contradiction Pa. Define $P' = \lambda x{:}A.[Px \;\vee\; x =_L b]$. Then also $\text{chain}_{A,R}P'$ and $P'b$, contradicting $SN_{A,R}b$.

4. ($\to$) Assume $(\forall a{:}A.\; SN_{A,R}a)$. Let $\text{chain}_< P$ and assume towards a contradiction PAR. Then for some A' and R' one has $PA'R'$ and $(A', R') < (A, R)$, and therefore for some $a{:}A$ one has

$$\begin{aligned}\mathrm{Dom}_R a \quad \& \quad & \exists f{:}(A'{\to}A)\ [(A',R') <_f^- (A,R) \\ & \& \ \forall y{:}A'[\mathrm{Dom}_{R'} y \to (fy)Ra]]\end{aligned} \tag{1}$$

Define

$$\begin{aligned} P' \quad \equiv \quad & \lambda x{:}A.\mathrm{Dom}_R x \ \& \ [\exists \alpha{:}\Box \exists r{:}(\alpha{\to}\alpha{\to}*). \\ & P\alpha r \ \& \ \exists f{:}(\alpha{\to}A)\ [(\alpha,r) <_f^- (A,R) \\ & \& \ \forall y{:}\alpha\ [\mathrm{Dom}_r y{\to}(fy)Rx]]]. \end{aligned}$$

Then also $\mathrm{chain}_{A,R}P'$. By (1) one has $P'a$, contradicting $SN_{A,R}a$.

($\leftarrow$) Assume $SN_< AR$. Let $a{:}A$ and suppose towards a contradiction that $\mathrm{chain}_{A,R}P$ and Pa. Define

$$P' \equiv \lambda\alpha{:}\Box\lambda r{:}(\alpha{\to}\alpha{\to}*).[\exists b{:}A.Pb \ \& \ (A,R^b) < (\alpha,r)].$$

Then $\mathrm{chain}_< P'$, by (2), and $P'AR$, by (1) and (2), contradicting $SN_< AR$.

∎

Step 4. A universal notation system in λU

In this step the second problem mentioned in Step 3 will be solved. Terms $\mathbf{U}$ and $\mathbf{i}$ will be constructed such that $\mathbf{i}$ faithfully embeds a pair (A,R) with $A{:}n$ and $R{:}(A{\to}A{\to}*)$ into $\mathbf{U}$. Such a pair ($\mathbf{U}$, $\mathbf{i}$) is called a *universal notation system* for orderings and plays the role of the naive set $T = \{(A,R) \mid R{:}A{\to}A{\to}*\}$.

Proposition 5.5.19. *There are terms* $\mathbf{U}$ *and* $\mathbf{i}$ *such that in* λU

1. $\vdash \mathbf{U} : \Box$.
2. $\vdash \mathbf{i} : [\Pi\alpha{:}\Box.(\alpha{\to}\alpha{\to}*){\to}\mathbf{U}]$.
3. *The type {'faithfulness of the map* $\mathbf{i}$*'}*

$$\forall\alpha{:}\Box\forall r{:}(\alpha{\to}\alpha{\to}*)\forall\alpha'{:}\Box\forall r'{:}$$

$$(\alpha'{\to}\alpha'{\to}*)[\mathbf{i}\alpha r =_L \mathbf{i}\alpha' r'{\to}(\alpha',r) <^- (\alpha',r')]$$

is inhabited.

Proof. Define

$$H \quad \equiv \quad \Pi\alpha{:}\Box.[(\alpha{\to}\alpha{\to}*){\to}*];$$

$$\begin{aligned}\mathbf{U} &\equiv H{\rightarrow}*;\\ \mathbf{i} &\equiv \lambda\alpha{:}\Box\lambda r{:}(\alpha{\rightarrow}\alpha{\rightarrow}*)\lambda h{:}H.h\alpha r.\end{aligned}$$

Then clearly one has in λU

$$H:\Box, \mathbf{U}:\Box \text{ and } \mathbf{i}:[\Pi\alpha{:}\Box.(\alpha{\rightarrow}\alpha{\rightarrow}*){\rightarrow}(H{\rightarrow}*)].$$

So we have 1 and 2. As to 3, we must show that in context

$$\alpha{:}\Box, r{:}(\alpha{\rightarrow}\alpha{\rightarrow}*), \alpha'{:}\Box, r'{:}(\alpha'{\rightarrow}\alpha'{\rightarrow}*)$$

the type

$$\mathbf{i}\alpha r =_L \mathbf{i}\alpha' r'{\rightarrow}(\alpha, r) <^- (\alpha', r')$$

is inhabited. Now

$$\begin{aligned} & \mathbf{i}\alpha r =_L \mathbf{i}\alpha' r'\\ \rightarrow\quad & \lambda h{:}H.h\alpha r =_L \lambda h{:}H.h\alpha' r'\\ \rightarrow\quad & h\alpha r =_L h\alpha' r', \text{ for all } h{:}H,\\ \rightarrow\quad & [(\alpha, r) <^- (\alpha', r')] =_L [(\alpha', r') <^- (\alpha', r')],\end{aligned}$$

by taking $h \equiv \lambda\beta{:}\Box\lambda s{:}(\beta{\rightarrow}\beta{\rightarrow}*).(\beta, s) <^- (\alpha', r')$.

Since the right-hand side of the last equation is inhabited it follows that

$$(\alpha, r) <^- (\alpha', r').$$

■

Step 5 The paradox in λU

Using $\mathbf{U}$ in $\mathbf{i}$ of Step 4 we now can formalize the informal paradox derived in step 2.

Definition 5.5.20.

1. On $\mathbf{U}$ define the binary relation $<_\mathbf{i}$ as follows. For $u, u'{:}\mathbf{U}$ let

$$\begin{aligned} u <_\mathbf{i} u' \equiv\ & \exists\alpha{:}\Box\exists r{:}(\alpha{\rightarrow}\alpha{\rightarrow}*)\exists\alpha'{:}\Box\exists r'{:}(\alpha'{\rightarrow}\alpha'{\rightarrow}*).\\ & [u =_L (\mathbf{i}\alpha r)\&u' =_L (\mathbf{i}\alpha' r')\&\\ & \text{Trans } \alpha r\ \&\ \text{Trans } \alpha' r'\ \&\\ & SN_<(\alpha, r)\ \&\\ & SN_<(\alpha', r')\ \&\ (\alpha, r) < (\alpha', r')].\end{aligned}$$

2. On $\mathbf{U}$ define the (unary) predicate $\mathbf{I}$ as follows. For $u{:}\mathbf{U}$ let

$$\begin{aligned}\mathbf{I}u =\ & \exists\alpha{:}\Box\exists r{:}(\alpha{\rightarrow}\alpha{\rightarrow}*).\\ & [u =_L (\mathbf{i}\alpha r)\ \&\ \text{Trans } \alpha r\ \&\ SN_<(\alpha, r)].\end{aligned}$$

Note that $\text{closed}_{\mathbf{U},<_{\mathbf{i}}}\mathbf{I}$.

3. The element $\mathbf{u} : \mathbf{U}$ is defined by $\mathbf{u} \equiv \mathbf{iU} <_{\mathbf{i}}$.

Lemma 5.5.21. *In context* $\alpha{:}\square, r{:}(\alpha{\to}\alpha{\to}*), \alpha'{:}\square, r'{:}(\alpha'{\to}\alpha'{\to}*)$ *the following types are inhabited.*

1. $(\mathbf{i}\alpha r) <_{\mathbf{i}} (\mathbf{i}\alpha' r') \to (\alpha, r) < (\alpha', r')$.
2. $SN_{<}(A, R) \to SN_{\mathbf{U},<_{\mathbf{i}}}(\mathbf{i}AR)$.

Proof. 1. Suppose $(\mathbf{i}\alpha r) <_{\mathbf{i}} (\mathbf{i}\alpha' r')$. Then there are β, s, β', s' of appropriate type such that

$$\mathbf{i}\alpha r =_L \mathbf{i}\beta s \;\&\; \mathbf{i}\alpha' r' =_L \mathbf{i}\beta' s' \;\&\; (\beta, s) < (\beta', s').$$

By the faithfulness of $\mathbf{i}$ and the symmetry of $=_L$ it follows that

$$(\alpha, r) <^{-} (\beta, s) < (\beta', s') <^{-} (\alpha', r')$$

hence

$$(\alpha, r) < (\alpha', r').$$

2. Suppose $SN_{<}(A, R)$. If $\text{chain}_{\mathbf{U},<_{\mathbf{i}}}Q$, then define

$$P\alpha r \;\equiv\; Q(\mathbf{i}\alpha r).$$

Then $\text{chain}_{<}P$. Since $SN_{<}(A, R)$ we have $\neg PAR$. But then $\neg Q(\mathbf{i}AR)$. So we proved

$$\text{chain}_{\mathbf{U},<_{\mathbf{i}}}Q \to \neg Q(\mathbf{i}AR),$$

i.e. $SN_{\mathbf{U},<_{\mathbf{i}}}(\mathbf{i}AR)$.

∎

Corollary 5.5.22. *The type*

$$\forall u{:}\mathbf{U}.SN_{\mathbf{U},<_{\mathbf{i}}}u$$

is inhabited.

Proof. Let u:**U** and suppose towards a contradiction

$$\text{chain}_{\mathbf{U},<_{\mathbf{i}}} P \ \& \ Pu.$$

Then

$$\exists u':\mathbf{U}.(u' <_{\mathbf{i}} u \ \& \ Pu').$$

Now

$$u' <_{\mathbf{i}} u \rightarrow \exists\alpha{:}\Box\exists r{:}(\alpha\rightarrow\alpha\rightarrow *)[u =_L (\mathbf{i}\alpha r) \ \& \ SN_{<}(\alpha, r)].$$

Hence by (2) of the lemma

$$SN_{\mathbf{U},<_{\mathbf{i}}}(\mathbf{i}\alpha r) =_L SN_{\mathbf{U},<_{\mathbf{i}}} u.$$

But then, again using $\text{chain}_{\mathbf{U},<_{\mathbf{i}}} P$, it follows that $\neg(Pu)$. Contradiction. ∎

Lemma 5.5.23. *Let* $A{:}\Box$, $R{:}(A\rightarrow A\rightarrow *)$ *and assume* $\text{Trans}AR$. *Then the following type is inhabited*

$$SN_{<}(A, R)\rightarrow\forall a{:}A.SN_{<}(A, R^a).$$

Proof. Applying 5.5.18(4) one has

$$\begin{array}{rcll} SN_{<}(A,R) & \rightarrow & \forall b{:}A.SN_{A,R}b, & \\ & \rightarrow & \forall b{:}A.\forall a{:}A.SN_{A,(R^a)}b, & \text{see below,} \\ & \rightarrow & \forall a{:}A.SN_{<}(A, R^a). & \end{array}$$

The implication $SN_{A,R}b\rightarrow SN_{A,(R^a)}b$ is proved as follows. Let $SN_{A,R}b$ and assume towards a contradiction that $\text{chain}_{A,(R^a)}P$ and Pb. Then also $\text{chain}_{A,R}P$, contradicting $\text{SN}_{A,R}b$. ∎

Lemma 5.5.24.

1. *Let* $\alpha{:}\Box$ *and* $r{:}\alpha\rightarrow\alpha\rightarrow *$ *and assume* $\text{Trans}\alpha r$ & $SN_{<}(\alpha, r)$. *Then there are* $\alpha^+{:}\Box$ *and* $r^+{:}\alpha^+\rightarrow\alpha^+\rightarrow *$ *such that*

$$\text{Trans}\ \alpha^+ r^+ \ \& \ SN_{<}(\alpha^+, r^+) \ \& \ (\alpha, r) < (\alpha^+, r^+).$$

2. $\forall v{:}\mathbf{U}^{\mathbf{I}}\exists v^+{:}\mathbf{U}^{\mathbf{I}} v <_{\mathbf{i}} v^+.$

Proof. 1. The construction is the one for representing data structures in Section 5.4. Define

$$\alpha^\circ \equiv \Pi\beta{:}\Box.\beta\rightarrow(\alpha\rightarrow\beta)\rightarrow\beta,$$

$$F \equiv \lambda x{:}\alpha\lambda\beta{:}\Box\lambda\infty{:}\beta\lambda f{:}(\alpha\rightarrow\beta).fx,$$

$$\underline{\infty} \equiv \lambda\beta{:}\Box\lambda\infty{:}\beta\lambda f{:}(\alpha\rightarrow\beta).\infty;$$

then $\underline{\infty}{:}\alpha^\circ{:}\Box$ and $F{:}(\alpha\rightarrow\alpha^\circ)$. Intuitively $\alpha^\circ = \alpha\cup\{\underline{\infty}\}$ and F is the canonical imbedding. Indeed, F is injective and $\underline{\infty}$ is not in the range of F. In fact, in the given context one has

$$(\lambda a{:}\alpha\lambda b{:}\alpha\lambda p{:}(Fa =_L Fb)\lambda Q{:}(\alpha{\to}*).p(\lambda x{:}\alpha^\circ.x{*}\bot Q)) \quad : \quad (\forall a, b{:}\alpha.(Fa =_L Fb{\to}a =_L b);$$

$$(\lambda a{:}\alpha\lambda p{:}(Fa =_L \underline{\infty}).p(\lambda x{:}\alpha^\circ.x{*}\bot(\lambda a{:}\alpha.T))(\lambda b{:}\bot.b)) \quad : \quad (\forall a{:}\alpha.Fa \neq_L \underline{\infty});$$

here $T \equiv \bot{\to}\bot$ stands for 'true' and has $(\lambda b{:}\bot.b)$ as inhabiting proof. Define $r^\circ{:}\alpha^\circ{\to}\alpha^\circ{\to}*$ as the canonical extension of r to α^+ making $\underline{\infty}$ larger than the elements of α:

$$r^\circ \equiv \lambda x{:}\alpha^\circ\lambda y{:}\alpha^\circ.[\exists a{:}\alpha\exists b{:}\alpha.rab \;\&\; x =_L Fa \;\&\; y =_L Fb] \vee$$

$$[\exists a{:}\alpha.x =_L Fa \;\&\; y =_L \underline{\infty}].$$

Then Trans $\alpha^\circ r^\circ \& SN_<(\alpha^\circ, r^\circ)$ and $(\alpha, r) <_F^- (\alpha^\circ, r^\circ)$ with bounding element $\underline{\infty}$. This $\underline{\infty}$ is not yet in Dom_{α^+}; but one has $(\alpha, r) <_{F\circ F} (\alpha^{\circ\circ}, r^{\circ\circ})$ with bounding element $F\underline{\infty}$ and therefore one can take $\alpha^+ = \alpha^{\circ\circ}$ and $r^+ = r^{\circ\circ}$.

2. If $v = \mathbf{i}\alpha r$, then take $v^+ = \mathbf{i}\alpha^+ r^+$.

■

Proposition 5.5.25. *The following type is inhabited:*

$$\exists u{:}\mathbf{U}^\mathbf{I}\forall v{:}\mathbf{U}^\mathbf{I}[SN_{\mathbf{U},<_\mathbf{i}}v \quad\leftrightarrow\quad v <_\mathbf{i} u].$$

Proof. For u one can take $\mathbf{u} \equiv (\mathbf{iU} <_\mathbf{i})$. In view of Corollary5.5.22 it is sufficient to show for $v{:}\mathbf{U}$ that {the following types are inhabited}:

1. $\mathbf{Iu}$,
2. $\mathbf{I}v{\to}v <_\mathbf{i} \mathbf{u}$.

As to 1, we know from Corollary 5.5.22

$$\begin{array}{ll} \forall u{:}\mathbf{U} & SN_{\mathbf{U},<_\mathbf{i}}u \\ & {\to}SN_<\mathbf{U} <_\mathbf{i}), \text{ by Proposition 5.5.18(4)}, \\ & {\to}\mathbf{I}(\mathbf{iU} <_\mathbf{i}), \text{ since clearly Trans } \mathbf{U} <_\mathbf{i}, \\ & {\to}\mathbf{Iu}. \end{array}$$

As to 2, assume $\mathbf{I}v$. Then $v =_L (\mathbf{i}\alpha r)$ for some pair α, r with Transαr & $SN_<(\alpha, r)$.

Define

$$f \equiv (\lambda a{:}\alpha.(\mathbf{i}\alpha r^a)) : (\alpha \rightarrow \mathbf{U}).$$

Then for all $a{:}\alpha$ with $\mathrm{Dom}_r a$ one has

$$fa = (\mathbf{i}\alpha r^a) <_{\mathbf{i}} (\mathbf{i}\alpha r) = v,$$

{by 5.5.18(1) one has $(\alpha, r^a) < (\alpha, r)$; use Lemma 5.5.23 and the definition of $<_{\mathbf{i}}$} and similarly for all $a, b{:}\alpha$

$$\begin{array}{lll} arb & \rightarrow (\alpha, r^a) < (\alpha, r^b), & \\ & \rightarrow \mathbf{i}\alpha r^a <_{\mathbf{i}} \mathbf{i}\alpha r^b, & SN_<(\alpha, r^a) \;\&\; SN_<(\alpha, r^b) \text{ since } SN_<(\alpha, r), \\ & \rightarrow fa <_{\mathbf{i}} fb. & \end{array}$$

Therefore $(\alpha, r) <_f^- (\mathbf{U}, <_{\mathbf{i}})$; f on Dom_r is bounded by v. Since $v <_{\mathbf{i}} v^+$ one has $\mathrm{Dom}_{<_{\mathbf{i}}} v$. Therefore $(\alpha, r) <_f (\mathbf{U}, <_{\mathbf{i}})$ and hence $v =_L (\mathbf{i}\alpha r) <_{\mathbf{i}} (\mathbf{i}\mathbf{U} <_{\mathbf{i}}) = \mathbf{u}$. ∎

Theorem 5.5.26 (Girard's paradox). *The type $\perp$ is inhabited in λU and hence in $\lambda *$.*

Proof. Note that Proposition 5.5.25 is in contradiction with Corollary 5.5.15, since $\mathbf{I}$ is closed in $\mathbf{U}, <_{\mathbf{i}}$. This shows that $\perp$ is inhabited in λU, so a fortiori in $\lambda *$. ∎

In [Coquand, 1989b] another term inhabiting $\perp$ is constructed. This proof can be carried out in the system λU^- which is the PTS defined as follows:

λU^-		
	$\mathcal{S}$	$*, \Box, \Delta$
	$\mathcal{A}$	$* : \Box, \Box : \Delta$
	$\mathcal{R}$	$(*, *), (\Box, *), (\Box, \Box), (\Delta, \Box)$

Fully formalized proof of Girard's paradox

As a final souvenir we now show the reader the full term inhabiting $\perp$. The term was presented to us by Leen Helmink who constructed it on an interactive proof development system based on AUTOMATH for arbitrary PTSs. The treatment on his system found an error in an earlier version of this subsection. This kind of use has always been the aim of de Bruijn, who conceived AUTOMATH as a proof checker.

Following the series of intermediate lemmas in this subsection, it became pragmatic to deal with definitions as follows. If we need an expression like

$$C \equiv ---X - X--- \tag{1}$$

where X is defined as M of type A, then we do not fill in the (possibly large) term M for X, but write

$$(\lambda X{:}A.\ ---X - X---)M. \tag{2}$$

This in order to keep expresions manageable. This definition mechanism is also used extensively in functional programming languages like ML. [Helmink, 1991] shows that if all definitions given as β-redexes are contracted, then the length of the term is multiplied by a factor 72 (so that the term will occupy 215 pages, that is more than this chapter).

Due to the presence of depending types, expressions like (2) are not always legal in a PTS, even if (1) is. {For example working in λU we often needed the expression $\alpha \rightarrow *$ for the type of predicates on α. We want to define

$$\text{Pred} \ =_{\text{def}} \lambda\alpha{:}\Box.\alpha \rightarrow *,$$

and use it as follows:

$$[\lambda\text{Pred}{:}(\Box \rightarrow \Box).[\lambda R{:}(\text{Pred}\ \alpha)\ldots](\lambda x{:}\alpha.\bot)---](\lambda\alpha{:}\Box.\alpha \rightarrow *). \tag{3}$$

This is illegal for two reasons. First of all $\Box \rightarrow \Box$ is not allowed in λU. Secondly, the subterm $[\lambda R{:}(\text{Pred}\ \alpha)\ldots](\lambda x{:}\alpha.\bot)$ is ill formed, since $(\lambda x{:}\alpha.\bot)$ is 'not yet' of type $(\text{Pred}\ \alpha)$.} These phenomena were taken into account by de Bruijn and in the AUTOMATH languages expressions like (3) are allowed. The term that follows is for these reasons only legal in a liberal version of λU.

Glancing over the next pages, the attentive reader that has worked through the proofs in this subsection may experience a free association of the whirling details.

(λ(⇒):Πa b:∗ . ∗ . (λ⊥:∗ . (λexfalso:Πa:∗ . ⊥⇒a . (λ⊤:∗ . (λ(¬):Πa:∗ . ∗ . (λ(&):Πa b:∗ . ∗ . (λ&$_{in}$:Πa b:∗ . a⇒b⇒a&b . (λ(⇔):Π
a b:∗ . ∗ . (λ(∨):Πa b:∗ . ∗ . (λ∨$_{inl}$:Πa b:∗ . a⇒a∨b . (λ∨$_{inr}$:Πa b:∗ . a⇒b∨a . (λ∃:Πa:□ . Πp:(a→∗) . ∗ . (λ∃$_{in}$:Πa:□ . Πp:(a→∗) .
Πx:a . (p x)⇒(∃ a p) . (λeq:Πt:□ . (t→t→∗) . (λrefl$_{eq}$:Πt:□ . Πc:t . (eq t c c) . (λsub$_{eq}$:Πt:□ . Πx y:t . Πp:(eq t x y) . Πf:(t→∗) . Π
q:(f x) . (f y) . (λsm$_{eq}$:Πt:□ . Πx y:t . (eq t x y)⇒(eq t y x) . (λtr$_{eq}$:Πt:□ . Πx y z:t . (eq t x y)⇒(eq t y z)⇒(eq t x z) . (λ∀$_{rel}$:Π
A:□ . ΠQ B:(A→∗) . ∗ . (λ∃$_{rel}$:ΠA:□ . ΠQ B:(A→∗) . ∗ . (λch:ΠA:□ . ΠR:(A→A→∗) . ΠP:(A→∗) . ∗ . (λSN:ΠA:□ . ΠR:(A→A
→∗) . Πa:A . ∗ . (λch$_{el}$:ΠA:□ . ΠR:(A→A→∗) . ΠP:(A→∗) . (ch$_{AR}$ P)⇒(Πa:A . (P a)⇒(Πϕ:∗ . (Πb:A . (P b)⇒(R b a)⇒ϕ)⇒ϕ)
) . (λSN$_{el}$:ΠA:□ . ΠR:(A→A→∗) . Πa:A . ΠP:(A→∗) . (SN$_{AR}$ a)⇒(ch$_{AR}$ P)⇒(P a)⇒⊥ . (λL14$_a$:ΠA:□ . ΠR:(A→A→∗) . Π
b:A . ((SN$_{AR}$ b)⇒(R b b))⇒¬(SN$_{AR}$ b) . (λL14$_b$:ΠA:□ . ΠR:(A→A→∗) . Πb:A . (Πa:A . (R a b)⇒(SN$_{AR}$ a))⇒(SN$_{AR}$ b) . (λ
cl:ΠA:□ . ΠR:(A→A→∗) . ΠQ:(A→∗) . ∗ . (λC16:ΠA:□ . ΠR:(A→A→∗) . ΠQ:(A→∗) . (cl$_{AR}$ Q)⇒¬(∃$_{rel}$ A Q (λb:A . (∀$_{rel}$ A
Q (λa:A . (SN$_{AR}$ a)⇔(R a b))))) . (λDom:ΠA:□ . ΠR:(A→A→∗) . Πa:A . ∗ . (λmor$_{<-}$:ΠA:□ . ΠR:(A→A→∗) . ΠA′:□ . Π
R′:(A′→A′→∗) . Πf:A→A′ . ∗ . (λ<⁻:ΠA:□ . ΠR:(A→A→∗) . ΠA′:□ . ΠR′:(A′→A′→∗) . ∗ . (λW$_{<-}$:ΠA:□ . ΠR:(A→A→∗) .
ΠA′:□ . ΠR′:(A′→A′→∗) . Πf:A→A′ . (mor$_{<-}$ A R A′ R′ f)⇒(<⁻ A R A′ R′) . (λdms:ΠA:□ . ΠR:(A→A→∗) . ΠA′:□ . Π
R′:(A′→A′→∗) . Πf:A→A′ . Πa′:A′ . ∗ . (λbd:ΠA:□ . ΠR:(A→A→∗) . ΠA′:□ . ΠR′:(A′→A′→∗) . Πf:A→A′ . ∗ . (λW$_{bd}$:ΠA:□ .
ΠR:(A→A→∗) . ΠA′:□ . ΠR′:(A′→A′→∗) . Πf:A→A′ . Πa′:A′ . (dms A R A′ R′ f a′)⇒(bd A R A′ R′ f) . (λemb$_<$:ΠA:□ . Π
R:(A→A→∗) . ΠA′:□ . ΠR′:(A′→A′→∗) . Πf:A→A′ . ∗ . (λ< :ΠA:□ . ΠR:(A→A→∗) . ΠA′:□ . ΠR′:(A′→A′→∗) . ∗ . (λW$_<$:Π
A:□ . ΠR:(A→A→∗) . ΠA′:□ . ΠR′:(A′→A′→∗) . Πf:A→A′ . (emb$_<$ A R A′ R′ f)⇒(< A R A′ R′) . (λemb:ΠA:□ . ΠR:(A→A
→∗) . ΠA′:□ . ΠR′:(A′→A′→∗) . Πf:A→A′ . Πa′:A′ . ∗ . (λemb_to_< :ΠA:□ . ΠR:(A→A→∗) . ΠA′:□ . ΠR′:(A′→A′→∗) . Π
f:A→A′ . Πa′:A′ . (emb A R A′ R′ f a′)⇒(< A R A′ R′) . (λ< _to_emb:ΠA:□ . ΠR:(A→A→∗) . ΠA′:□ . ΠR′:(A′→A′→∗) . (<
A R A′ R′)⇒(Πϕ:∗ . (Πf:A→A′ . Πa′:A′ . (emb A R A′ R′ f a′)⇒ϕ)⇒ϕ) . (λLDom:ΠA:□ . ΠR:(A→A→∗) . ΠA′:□ . ΠR′:(A′
→A′→∗) . Πf:A→A′ . (mor$_{<-}$ A R A′ R′ f)⇒(Πa:A . (Dom$_{AR}$ a)⇒(Dom$_{A'R'}$ (f a))) . (λrefl$_{<-}$:ΠA:□ . ΠR:(A→A→∗) . (<⁻
A R A R) . (λtr$_{mor}$:ΠA:□ . ΠR:(A→A→∗) . ΠB:□ . ΠS:(B→B→∗) . ΠC:□ . ΠT:(C→C→∗) . Πf:A→B . Πg:B→C . (mor$_{<-}$ A R
B S f)⇒(mor$_{<-}$ B S C T g)⇒(mor$_{<-}$ A R C T (λa:A . (g (f a)))) . (λL1:ΠA:□ . ΠR:(A→A→∗) . ΠB:□ . ΠS:(B→B→∗) . Π
C:□ . ΠT:(C→C→∗) . Πf:A→B . Πg:B→C . Πb:B . (emb A R B S f b)⇒(mor$_{<-}$ B S C T g)⇒(emb A R C T (λa:A . (g (f a)))
(g b)) . (λL2:ΠA:□ . ΠR:(A→A→∗) . ΠB:□ . ΠS:(B→B→∗) . ΠC:□ . ΠT:(C→C→∗) . Πf:A→B . Πg:B→C . Πc:C . (mor$_{<-}$ A R
B S f)⇒(emb B S C T g c)⇒(emb A R C T (λa:A . (g (f a))) c) . (λtr$_{emb}$:ΠA:□ . ΠR:(A→A→∗) . ΠB:□ . ΠS:(B→B→∗) . Π
C:□ . ΠT:(C→C→∗) . Πf:A→B . Πg:B→C . Πb:B . Πc:C . (emb A R B S f b)⇒(emb B S C T g c)⇒(emb A R C T (λa:A . (g (f
a))) (g b)) . (λL3:ΠA:□ . ΠR:(A→A→∗) . ΠB:□ . ΠS:(B→B→∗) . ΠC:□ . ΠT:(C→C→∗) . (<⁻ A R B S)⇒(< B S C T)⇒(< A
R C T) . (λL4:ΠA:□ . ΠR:(A→A→∗) . ΠB:□ . ΠS:(B→B→∗) . ΠC:□ . ΠT:(C→C→∗) . (< A R B S)⇒(< B S C T)⇒(< A R C
T) . (λL5:ΠA:□ . ΠR:(A→A→∗) . ΠB:□ . ΠS:(B→B→∗) . ΠC:□ . ΠT:(C→C→∗) . (< A R B S)⇒(<⁻ B S C T)⇒(< A R C T)
. (λch$_<$:ΠP:Πα:□ . Πr:(α→α→∗) . ∗ . ∗ . (λSN$_<$:Πα:□ . Πr:(α→α→∗) . ∗ . (λTr:Πα:□ . Πr:(α→α→∗) . ∗ . (λrst:ΠA:□ . Πa:A . Π
R:(A→A→∗) . (A→A→∗) . (λLrTr:ΠA:□ . Πa:A . ΠR:(A→A→∗) . (Tr A R)⇒(Tr A (rst A a R)) . (λLch:ΠA:□ . ΠR:(A→A→
∗) . Πa:A . ΠP:(A→∗) . (ch A (rst A a R) P)⇒(ch$_{AR}$ P) . (λL19i:ΠA:□ . ΠR:(A→A→∗) . Πa:A . (Dom$_{AR}$ a)⇒(< A (rst A a R)
A R) . (λL19ii$_a$:ΠA:□ . ΠR:(A→A→∗) . (Tr A R)⇒(Πa b:A . (R a b)⇒(mor$_{<-}$ A (rst A a R) A (rst A b R) (λx:A . x))) . (λ
L19ii$_b$:ΠA:□ . ΠR:(A→A→∗) . (Tr A R)⇒(Πa b:A . (R a b)⇒(bd A (rst A a R) A (rst A b R) (λx:A . x))) . (λL19ii:ΠA:□ . Π
R:(A→A→∗) . (Tr A R)⇒(Πa b:A . (R a b)⇒(< A (rst A a R) A (rst A b R))) . (λQ:ΠA:□ . ΠR:(A→A→∗) . ΠP:Πα:□ . Πr:(α
→α→∗) . ∗ . (A→∗) . (λL19iv$_a$:ΠA:□ . ΠR:(A→A→∗) . ΠP:Πα:□ . Πr:(α→α→∗) . ∗ . (ch_< P)⇒(ch$_{AR}$ (Q A R P)) . (λ
L19iv:ΠA:□ . ΠR:(A→A→∗) . (Πa:A . (SN$_{AR}$ a))⇒(SN$_<$ A R) . (λPP:ΠA:□ . ΠR:(A→A→∗) . ΠP:(A→∗) . Πα:□ . Πr:(α→α
→∗) . ∗ . (λL19iv$_{aux}$:ΠA:□ . ΠR:(A→A→∗) . (Tr A R)⇒(SN$_<$ A R)⇒(Πa:A . (SN$_{AR}$ a)) . (λH:□ . (λ**U**:□ . (λ**i**:Πα:□ . Πr:(α→
α→∗) . **U** . (λ(=):(**U**→**U**→∗) . (λL20:Πα:□ . Πr:(α→α→∗) . Πα′:□ . Πr′:(α′→α′→∗) . (**i** α r)=(**i** α′ r′)⇒(<⁻ α r α′ r′) . (λ
<$_{\mathrm{i}}$:(**U**→**U**→∗) . (λ**I**:(**U**→∗) . (λ**u**:**U** . (λLTr:(Tr **U** <$_{\mathrm{i}}$) . (λL22i:Πα:□ . Πr:(α→α→∗) . Πα′:□ . Πr′:(α′→α′→∗) . (<$_{\mathrm{i}}$ (**i** α r) (**i**
α′ r′))⇒(< α r α′ r′) . (λL22ii:ΠA:□ . ΠR:(A→A→∗) . (SN$_<$ A R)⇒(SN$_{\mathbf{U}<_{\mathrm{i}}}$ (**i** A R)) . (λC23:Πu:**U** . (SN$_{\mathbf{U}<_{\mathrm{i}}}$ u) . (λL24:Π
A:□ . ΠR:(A→A→∗) . (Tr A R)⇒(SN$_<$ A R)⇒(Πb:A . (SN$_<$ A (rst A b R))) . (λα°:Πα:□ . □ . (λF:Πα:□ . α→(α° α) . (λ$\underline{\infty}$:Π
α:□ . (α° α) . (λ$\overline{\underline{\infty}}$:Πα:□ . ((α°α)→(α°α)→∗) . (λmap:Πα:□ . Πr:(α→α→∗) . ((α°α)→(α°α)→∗) . (λr°:Πα:□ . Πr:(α→α→∗)
. ((α°α)→(α°α)→∗) . (λmor$_F$:Πα:□ . Πr:(α→α→∗) . (mor$_{<-}$ α r (α° α) (r° α r) (F α)) . (λinj$_F$:Πα:□ . Πr:(α→α→∗) . Πa
b:α . (eq (α° α) (F α a) (F α b))⇒(eq α a b) . (λL$\underline{\infty}$F:Πα:□ . Πr:(α→α→∗) . Πa:α . ¬(eq (α° α) (F α a) ($\underline{\infty}$ α)) . (λall$\overline{\underline{\infty}}$:Πα:□
. Πr:(α→α→∗) . Πa:α . (r° α r (F α a) ($\underline{\infty}$ α)) . (λMOD:Πα:□ . Πr:(α→α→∗) . ((α°α)→∗)→(α→∗) . (λL6:Πα:□ . Πr:(α→α→
∗) . ΠP:((α°α)→∗) . (ch (α° α) (r° α r) P)⇒(ch$_{\alpha r}$ (MOD α r P)) . (λTrr$^\circ_1$:Πα:□ . Πr:(α→α→∗) . Πtr:(Tr α r) . Πx y z:(α° α) .
(map α r x y)⇒(map α r y z)⇒(map α r x z) . (λTrr$^\circ_2$:Πα:□ . Πr:(α→α→∗) . Πtr:(Tr α r) . Πx y z:(α° α) . (map α r x y)⇒($\overline{\underline{\infty}}$
α y z)⇒($\overline{\underline{\infty}}$ α x z) . (λTrr$^\circ_3$:Πα:□ . Πr:(α→α→∗) . Πtr:(Tr α r) . Πx y z:(α° α) . ($\overline{\underline{\infty}}$ α x y)⇒(map α r y z)⇒⊥ . (λTrr$^\circ_4$:Πα:□ .
Πr:(α→α→∗) . Πtr:(Tr α r) . Πx y z:(α° α) . ($\overline{\underline{\infty}}$ α x y)⇒($\overline{\underline{\infty}}$ α y z)⇒⊥ . (λTrr°:Πα:□ . Πr:(α→α→∗) . Πtr:(Tr α r) . (Tr (α° α
) (r° α r)) . (λSN$_<$_r°:Πα:□ . Πr:(α→α→∗) . Πtr:(Tr α r) . Πsn:(SN$_<$ α r) . (SN$_<$ (α° α) (r° α r)) . (λα⁺:Πα:□ . □ . (λr⁺:Πα
:□ . Πr:(α→α→∗) . ((α⁺ α)→(α⁺ α)→∗) . (λL25:Πα:□ . Πr:(α→α→∗) . (< α r (α⁺ α) (r⁺ α r)) . (λL26i:(**I u**) . (λL26ii$_a$:Πα:□
. Πr:(α→α→∗) . (Tr α r)⇒(SN$_<$ α r)⇒(mor$_{<-}$ α r **U** <$_{\mathrm{i}}$ (λa:α . (**i** α (rst α a r)))) . (λL26ii$_{b.aux}$:Πα:□ . Πr:(α→α→∗) . (Tr α
r)⇒(SN$_<$ α r)⇒(Dom$_{\mathbf{U}<_{\mathrm{i}}}$ (**i** α r)) . (λL26ii$_b$:Πα:□ . Πr:(α→α→∗) . (Tr α r)⇒(SN$_<$ α r)⇒(bd α r **U** <$_{\mathrm{i}}$ (λa:α . (**i** α (rst α a r)
))) . (λL26ii:Πv:**U** . (**I** v)⇒(<$_{\mathrm{i}}$ v **u**) . (λL26:(∃$_{rel}$ **U I** (λu:**U** . (∀$_{rel}$ **U I** (λv:**U** . (SN$_{\mathbf{U}<_{\mathrm{i}}}$ v)⇔(<$_{\mathrm{i}}$ v u))))) . (λL27$_a$:(cl$_{\mathbf{U}<_{\mathrm{i}}}$ I) .
(λTh27:⊥ . Th27) (C16 **U** <$_{\mathrm{i}}$ **I** L27$_a$ L26)) (λa b:**U** . λp:(**I** a) . λp$_1$:(<$_{\mathrm{i}}$ b a) . (p$_1$ (**I** b) (λα:□ . λr:(α→α→∗) . λα′:□ . λr′:(α′→
α′→∗) . λp$_2$:b=(**i** α r) . λp$_3$:(Tr α r) . λp$_4$:(SN$_<$ α r) . λp$_5$:a=(**i** α′ r′) . λp$_6$:(Tr α′ r′) . λp$_7$:(SN$_<$ α′ r′) . λp$_8$:(< α r α′ r′) . λβ:∗
. λp$_9$:Πα$_1$:□ . Πr$_1$:(α$_1$→α$_1$→∗) . b=(**i** α$_1$ r$_1$)⇒(Tr α$_1$ r$_1$)⇒(SN$_<$ α$_1$ r$_1$)⇒β . (p$_9$ α r p$_2$ p$_3$ p$_4$)))))) (∃$_{in}$ **U** (λa:**U** . (**I** a)&((λ
u:**U** . (∀$_{rel}$ **U I** (λv:**U** . (SN$_{\mathbf{U}<_{\mathrm{i}}}$ v)⇔(<$_{\mathrm{i}}$ v u)))) a)) **u** (&$_{in}$ (**I u**) (∀$_{rel}$ **U I** (λv:**U** . (SN$_{\mathbf{U}<_{\mathrm{i}}}$ v)⇔(<$_{\mathrm{i}}$ v **u**))) L26i (λa:**U** . λp:(**I**
a) . (&$_{in}$ ((SN$_{\mathbf{U}<_{\mathrm{i}}}$ a)⇒(<$_{\mathrm{i}}$ a **u**)) ((<$_{\mathrm{i}}$ a **u**)⇒(SN$_{\mathbf{U}<_{\mathrm{i}}}$ a)) (λp$_1$:(SN$_{\mathbf{U}<_{\mathrm{i}}}$ a) . (L26ii a p)) (λp$_1$:(<$_{\mathrm{i}}$ a **u**) . (C23 a))))))) (λv:**U** . λ
p:(**I** v) . (p (<$_{\mathrm{i}}$ v **u**) (λα:□ . λr:(α→α→∗) . λp$_1$:v=(**i** α r) . λp$_2$:(Tr α r) . λp$_3$:(SN$_<$ α r) . λβ:∗ . λp$_4$:Πα$_1$:□ . Πr$_1$:(α$_1$→α$_1$→∗) .
Πα′:□ . Πr′:(α′→α′→∗) . v=(**i** α$_1$ r$_1$)⇒(Tr α$_1$ r$_1$)⇒(SN$_<$ α$_1$ r$_1$)⇒**u**=(**i** α′ r′)⇒(Tr α′ r′)⇒(SN$_<$ α′ r′)⇒(< α$_1$ r$_1$ α′ r′)⇒β
. (p$_4$ α r **U** <$_{\mathrm{i}}$ p$_1$ p$_2$ p$_3$ (refl$_{eq}$ **U u**) LTr (L19iv **U** <$_{\mathrm{i}}$ C23) (W$_<$ α r **U** <$_{\mathrm{i}}$ (λa:α . (**i** α (rst α a r))) (&$_{in}$ (mor$_{<-}$ α r **U** <$_{\mathrm{i}}$ (λ
a:α . (**i** α (rst α a r)))) (bd α r **U** <$_{\mathrm{i}}$ (λa:α . (**i** α (rst α a r)))) (L26ii$_a$ α r p$_2$ p$_3$) (L26ii$_b$ α r p$_2$ p$_3$))))))))) (λα:□ . λr:(α→α→∗)
. λp:(Tr α r) . λp$_1$:(SN$_<$ α r) . (W$_{bd}$ α r **U** <$_{\mathrm{i}}$ (λa:α . (**i** α (rst α a r))) (**i** α r) (&$_{in}$ (Dom$_{\mathbf{U}<_{\mathrm{i}}}$ (**i** α r)) (Πa:α . (Dom$_{\alpha r}$ a)⇒(<$_{\mathrm{i}}$
(**i** α (rst α a r)) (**i** α r))) (L26ii$_{b.aux}$ α r p p$_1$) (λa:α . λp$_2$:(Dom$_{\alpha r}$ a) . λβ:∗ . λp$_3$:Πα$_1$:□ . Πr$_1$:(α$_1$→α$_1$→∗) . Πα′:□ . Πr′:(α′→
α′→∗) . (**i** α (rst α a r))=(**i** α$_1$ r$_1$)⇒(Tr α$_1$ r$_1$)⇒(SN$_<$ α$_1$ r$_1$)⇒(**i** α r)=(**i** α′ r′)⇒(Tr α′ r′)⇒(SN$_<$ α′ r′)⇒(< α$_1$ r$_1$ α′ r′)⇒
β . (p$_3$ α (rst α a r) α r (refl$_{eq}$ **U** (**i** α (rst α a r))) (LrTr α a r p) (L24 α r p p$_1$ a) (refl$_{eq}$ **U** (**i** α r)) p p$_1$ (L19i α r a p$_2$))))))) (λ
α:□ . λr:(α→α→∗) . λp:(Tr α r) . λp$_1$:(SN$_<$ α r) . (∃$_{in}$ **U** (λb:**U** . (<$_{\mathrm{i}}$ (**i** α r) b)) (**i** (α⁺ α) (r⁺ α r)) (λβ:∗ . λp$_2$:Πα$_1$:□ . Π
r$_1$:(α$_1$→α$_1$→∗) . Πα′:□ . Πr′:(α′→α′→∗) . (**i** α r)=(**i** α$_1$ r$_1$)⇒(Tr α$_1$ r$_1$)⇒(SN$_<$ α$_1$ r$_1$)⇒(**i** (α⁺ α) (r⁺ α r))=(**i** α′ r′)⇒(Tr
α′ r′)⇒(SN$_<$ α′ r′)⇒(< α$_1$ r$_1$ α′ r′)⇒β . (p$_2$ α r (α⁺ α) (r⁺ α r) (refl$_{eq}$ **U** (**i** α r)) p p$_1$ (refl$_{eq}$ **U** (**i** (α⁺ α) (r⁺ α r))) (Trr°
(α° α) (r° α r) (Trr° α r p)) (SN$_<$_r° (α° α) (r° α r) (Trr° α r p) (SN$_<$_r° α r p p$_1$)) (L25 α r)))))) (λα:□ . λr:(α→α→∗) . λ
p:(Tr α r) . λp$_1$:(SN$_<$ α r) . λa b:α . λp$_2$:(r a b) . λβ:∗ . λp$_3$:Πα$_1$:□ . Πr$_1$:(α$_1$→α$_1$→∗) . Πα′:□ . Πr′:(α′→α′→∗) . (**i** α (rst α a r)
)=(**i** α$_1$ r$_1$)⇒(Tr α$_1$ r$_1$)⇒(SN$_<$ α$_1$ r$_1$)⇒(**i** α (rst α b r))=(**i** α′ r′)⇒(Tr α′ r′)⇒(SN$_<$ α′ r′)⇒(< α$_1$ r$_1$ α′ r′)⇒β . (p$_3$ α (rst
α a r) α (rst α b r) (refl$_{eq}$ **U** (**i** α (rst α a r))) (LrTr α a r p) (L24 α r p p$_1$ a) (refl$_{eq}$ **U** (**i** α (rst α b r))) (LrTr α b r p) (L24 α r
p p$_1$ b) (L19ii α r p a b p$_2$))))) (λβ:∗ . λp:Πα:□ . Πr:(α→α→∗) . **u**=(**i** α r)⇒(Tr α r)⇒(SN$_<$ α r)⇒β . (p **U** <$_{\mathrm{i}}$ (refl$_{eq}$ **U u**) LTr
(L19iv **U** <$_{\mathrm{i}}$ C23)))) (λα:□ . λr:(α→α→∗) . (W$_<$ α r (α⁺ α) (r⁺ α r) (λx:α . (F (α° α) (F α x))) (&$_{in}$ (mor$_{<-}$ α r (α⁺ α)
(r⁺ α r) (λx:α . (F (α° α) (F α x)))) (bd α r (α⁺ α) (r⁺ α r) (λx:α . (F (α° α) (F α x)))) (tr$_{mor}$ α r (α° α) (r° α r) (α⁺ α)
(r⁺ α r) (F α) (F (α° α)) (mor$_F$ α r) (mor$_F$ (α° α) (r° α r))) (W$_{bd}$ α r (α⁺ α) (r⁺ α r) (λx:α . (F (α° α) (F α x))) (F (α° α)

(∞ α)) (&in (Dom (α+ α) (r+ α r) (F (α° α) (∞ α))) (Πa:α . (Domαr a)⇒(r+ α r (F (α° α) (F α a)) (F (α° α) (∞ α))))
(∃in (α+ α) (λb:(α+ α) . (r+ α r (F (α° α) (∞ α)) b)) (∞̅ (α° α)) (all∞̅ (α° α) (r° α r) (∞ α))) (λa:α . λp:(Domαr a) .
(morF (α° α) (r° α r) (F α a) (∞ α) (all∞̅ α r a)))))))) (λα:□ . λr:(α→α→*) . (r° (α° α) (r° α r)))) (λα:□ . (α° (α° α))))
(λα:□ . λr:(α→α→*) . λtr:(Tr α r) . λsn:(SN< α r) . (L19iv (α° α) (r° α r) (λa:(α° α) . λP:((α°α)→*) . λp:(ch (α° α) (r° α r)
P) . λp1:(P a) . (p a p1 ⊥ (λz:(α° α) . λp2:(P z)&(r° α r z a) . (p2 ⊥ (λp3:(P z) . λp4:(r° α r z a) . (p4 ⊥ (λp5:(map α r z a) . (p5
⊥ (λa1 b:α . λp6:(r a1 b) . λp7:(eq (α° α) z (F α a1)) . λp8:(eq (α° α) a (F α b)) . (SNel α r a1 (MOD α r P) (L19ivaux α r tr sn
a1) (L6 α r P p) (p7 P p3))))) (λp5:(∞̅ α z a) . (p5 ⊥ (λp6:(eq (α° α) a (∞ α)) . λp7:(∃ α (λb:α . (eq (α° α) z (F α b)))) . (p7
⊥ (λz1:α . λp8:(eq (α° α) z (F α z1)) . (SNel α r z1 (MOD α r P) (L19ivaux α r tr sn z1) (L6 α r P p) (p8 P p3))))))))))))))
(λα:□ . λr:(α→α→*) . λtr:(Tr α r) . λa b c:(α° α) . λp:(r° α r a b) . λp1:(r° α r b c) . (p (r° α r a c) (λp2:(map α r a b) . (p1 (r°
α r a c) (λp3:(map α r b c) . (∨inl (map α r a c) (∞̅ α a c) (Trr°1 α r tr a b c p2 p3))) (λp3:(∞̅ α b c) . (∨inr (∞̅ α a c) (map α
r a c) (Trr°2 α r tr a b c p2 p3))))) (λp2:(∞̅ α a b) . (p1 (r° α r a c) (λp3:(map α r b c) . (exfalso (r° α r a c) (Trr°3 α r tr a b c
p2 p3))) (λp3:(∞̅ α b c) . (exfalso (r° α r a c) (Trr°4 α r tr a b c p2 p3)))))))) (λα:□ . λr:(α→α→*) . λtr:(Tr α r) . λx y z:(α° α)
. λp:(∞̅ α x y) . λp1:(∞̅ α y z) . (p ⊥ (λp2:(eq (α° α) y (∞ α)) . λp3:(∃ α (λb:α . (eq (α° α) x (F α b)))) . (p1 ⊥ (λp4:(eq (α° α
) z (∞ α)) . λp5:(∃ α (λb:α . (eq (α° α) y (F α b)))) . (p5 ⊥ (λz1:α . λp6:(eq (α° α) y (F α z1)) . (L∞F α r z1 (treq (α° α) (F α
z1) y (∞ α) (smeq (α° α) y (F α z1) p6) p2)))))))))) (λα:□ . λr:(α→α→*) . λtr:(Tr α r) . λx y z:(α° α) . λp:(∞̅ α x y) . λp1
:(map α r y z) . (p ⊥ (λp2:(eq (α° α) y (∞ α)) . λp3:(∃ α (λb:α . (eq (α° α) x (F α b)))) . (p1 ⊥ (λa b:α . λp4:(r a b) . λp5:(eq
(α° α) y (F α a)) . λp6:(eq (α° α) z (F α b)) . (L∞F α r a (treq (α° α) (F α a) y (∞ α) (smeq (α° α) y (F α a) p5) p2))))))))
(λα:□ . λr:(α→α→*) . λtr:(Tr α r) . λx y z:(α° α) . λp:(map α r x y) . λp1:(∞̅ α y z) . (p (∞̅ α x z) (λa b:α . λp2:(r a b) . λp3
:(eq (α° α) x (F α a)) . λp4:(eq (α° α) y (F α b)) . (p1 (∞̅ α x z) (λp5:(eq (α° α) z (∞ α)) . λp6:(∃ α (λb1:α . (eq (α° α) y (F α
b1)))) . (&in (eq (α° α) z (∞ α)) (∃ α (λb1:α . (eq (α° α) x (F α b1)))) p5 (∃in α (λb1:α . (eq (α° α) x (F α b1))) a p3))))))))
(λα:□ . λr:(α→α→*) . λtr:(Tr α r) . λx y z:(α° α) . λp:(map α r x y) . λp1:(map α r y z) . λφ:* . λp2:Πa b:α . (r a b)⇒(eq (α° α
) x (F α a))⇒(eq (α° α) z (F α b))⇒φ . (p φ (λa b:α . λp3:(r a b) . λp4:(eq (α° α) x (F α a)) . λp5:(eq (α° α) y (F α b)) . (p1 φ
(λa1 b1:α . λp6:(r a1 b1) . λp7:(eq (α° α) y (F α a1)) . λp8:(eq (α° α) z (F α b1)) . (p2 a b1 (tr a a1 b1 (subeq α b a1 (injF α r
b a1 (treq (α° α) (F α b) y (F α a1) (smeq (α° α) y (F α b) p5) p7)) (r a) p3) p6) p4 p8))))))) (λα:□ . λr:(α→α→*) . λ
P:((α°α)→*) . λp:(ch (α° α) (r° α r) P) . λa:α . λp1:(MOD α r P a) . (p (F α a) p1 (∃ α (λb:α . (MOD α r P b)&(r b a))) (λ
z:(α° α) . λp2:(P z)&(r° α r z (F α a)) . (p2 (∃ α (λb:α . (MOD α r P b)&(r b a))) (λp3:(P z) . λp4:(r° α r z (F α a)) . (p4 (∃ α
(λb:α . (MOD α r P b)&(r b a))) (λp5:(map α r z (F α a)) . (p5 (∃ α (λb:α . (MOD α r P b)&(r b a))) (λa1 b:α . λp6:(r a1 b) . λ
p7:(eq (α° α) z (F α a1)) . λp8:(eq (α° α) (F α a) (F α b)) . (∃in α (λb1:α . (MOD α r P b1)&(r b1 a)) a1 (&in (MOD α r P a1)
(r a1 a) (p7 P p3) (subeq α b a (smeq α a b (injF α r a b p8)) (r a1) p6)))))) (λp5:(∞̅ α z (F α a)) . (p5 (∃ α (λb:α . (MOD α r P
b)&(r b a))) (λp6:(eq (α° α) (F α a) (∞ α)) . λp7:(∃ α (λb:α . (eq (α° α) z (F α b)))) . (exfalso (∃ α (λb:α . (MOD α r P b)&(r
b a))) (L∞F α r a p6)))))))))))) (λα:□ . λr:(α→α→*) . λP:((α°α)→*) . λa:α . (P (F α a)))) (λα:□ . λr:(α→α→*) . λa:α .
(∨inr (∞̅ α (F α a) (∞ α)) (map α r (F α a) (∞ α)) (&in (eq (α° α) (∞ α) (∞ α)) (∃ α (λb:α . (eq (α° α) (F α a) (F α b))))
(refleq (α° α) (∞ α)) (∃in α (λb:α . (eq (α° α) (F α a) (F α b))) a (refleq (α° α) (F α a))))))) (λα:□ . λr:(α→α→*) . λa:α . λ
p:(eq (α° α) (F α a) (∞ α)) . (p (λz:(α° α) . (z * ⊥ (λx:α . ⊤))) (λp1:⊥ . p1)))) (λα:□ . λr:(α→α→*) . λa b:α . λp:(eq (α° α)
(F α a) (F α b)) . λz:(α→*) . (p (λz′:(α° α) . (z′ * ⊥ z))))) (λα:□ . λr:(α→α→*) . λa b:α . λp:(r a b) . (∨inl (Πφ:* . (Πa1 b1:α .
(r a1 b1)⇒(eq (α° α) (F α a) (F α a1))⇒(eq (α° α) (F α b) (F α b1))⇒φ)⇒φ) ((eq (α° α) (F α b) (∞ α))&(∃ α (λb1:α . (eq
(α° α) (F α a) (F α b1))))) (λφ:* . λp1:Πa1 b1:α . (r a1 b1)⇒(eq (α° α) (F α a) (F α a1))⇒(eq (α° α) (F α b) (F α b1))⇒φ .
(p1 a b p (refleq (α° α) (F α a)) (refleq (α° α) (F α b))))))) (λα:□ . λr:(α→α→*) . λx:(α° α) . λy:(α° α) . (map α r x y)∨(∞̅ α
x y))) (λα:□ . λr:(α→α→*) . λx:(α° α) . λy:(α° α) . Πφ:* . (Πa b:α . (r a b)⇒(eq (α° α) x (F α a))⇒(eq (α° α) y (F α b))⇒φ)
⇒φ)) (λα:□ . λx:(α° α) . λy:(α° α) . (eq (α° α) y (∞ α))&(∃ α (λb:α . (eq (α° α) x (F α b)))))) (λα β:□ . λ∞:β . λf:α→β . ∞)
) (λα:□ . λx:α . λβ:□ . λ∞:β . λf:α→β . (f x))) (λα:□ . Πβ:□ . β→(α→β)→β)) (λA:□ . λR:(A→A→*) . λp:(Tr A R) . λp1:(SN<
A R) . λb:A . λP:Πα:□ . Πr:(α→α→*) . * . λp2:(ch_< P) . λp3:(P A (rst A b R)) . (L19iv A (rst A b R) (λa:A . λP1:(A→*) . λp4
:(ch A (rst A b R) P1) . λp5:(P1 a) . (SNel A R a P1 (L19ivaux A R p p1 a) (Lch A R b P1 p4) p5)) P p2 p3))) (λu:**U** . λ
P:(**U**→*) . λp:(ch**U**<i P) . λp1:(P u) . (ch-el **U** <i P p u p1 ⊥ (λb:**U** . λp2:(P b) . λp3:(<i b u) . (p3 ⊥ (λα:□ . λr:(α→α→*) . λ
α′:□ . λr′:(α′→α′→*) . λp4:b=(i α r) . λp5:(Tr α r) . λp6:(SN< α r) . λp7:u=(i α′ r′) . λp8:(Tr α′ r′) . λp9:(SN< α′ r′) . λp10
:(< α r α′ r′) . (SNel **U** <i (i α′ r′) P (L22ii α′ r′ p9) p (subeq **U** u (i α′ r′) p7 P p1)))))))) (λA:□ . λR:(A→A→*) . λp:(SN< A
R) . λP:(**U**→*) . λp1:(ch**U**<i P) . λp2:(P (i A R)) . (p (λα:□ . λr:(α→α→*) . (P (i α r))) (λα1:□ . λr1:(α1→α1→*) . λp3:(P (i
α1 r1)) . λβ:* . λp4:Πα2:□ . Πr2:(α2→α2→*) . (P (i α2 r2))⇒(< α2 r2 α1 r1)⇒β . (ch-el **U** <i P p1 (i α1 r1) p3 β (λb:**U** . λp5
:(P b) . λp6:(<i b (i α1 r1)) . (p6 β (λα:□ . λr:(α→α→*) . λα′:□ . λr′:(α′→α′→*) . λp7:b=(i α r) . λp8:(Tr α r) . λp9:(SN< α
r) . λp10:(i α1 r1)=(i α′ r′) . λp11:(Tr α′ r′) . λp12:(SN< α′ r′) . λp13:(< α r α′ r′) . (p4 α r (subeq **U** b (i α r) p7 P p5) (L22i α
r α1 r1 (subeq **U** b (i α r) p7 (λc:**U** . (<i c (i α1 r1))) p6))))))))) p2))) (λα:□ . λr:(α→α→*) . λα′:□ . λr′:(α′→α′→*) . λp:(<i
(i α r) (i α′ r′)) . (p (< α r α′ r′) (λα1:□ . λr1:(α1→α1→*) . λα′1:□ . λr′1:(α′1→α′1→*) . λp1:(i α r)=(i α1 r1) . λp2:(Tr α1 r1) .
λp3:(SN< α1 r1) . λp4:(i α′ r′)=(i α′1 r′1) . λp5:(Tr α′1 r′1) . λp6:(SN< α′1 r′1) . λp7:(< α1 r1 α′1 r′1) . (L3 α r α1 r1 α′ r′ (L20 α r
α1 r1 p1) (L5 α1 r1 α′1 r′1 α′ r′ p7 (L20 α′1 r′1 α′ r′ (smeq **U** (i α′ r′) (i α′1 r′1) p4))))))))) (λa b c:**U** . λp:(<i a b) . λp1:(<i b c) .
(p (<i a c) (λα:□ . λr:(α→α→*) . λα′:□ . λr′:(α′→α′→*) . λp2:a=(i α r) . λp3:(Tr α r) . λp4:(SN< α r) . λp5:b=(i α′ r′) . λp6
:(Tr α′ r′) . λp7:(SN< α′ r′) . λp8:(< α r α′ r′) . (p1 (<i a c) (λα1:□ . λr1:(α1→α1→*) . λα′1:□ . λr′1:(α′1→α′1→*) . λp9:b=(i
α1 r1) . λp10:(Tr α1 r1) . λp11:(SN< α1 r1) . λp12:c=(i α′1 r′1) . λp13:(Tr α′1 r′1) . λp14:(SN< α′1 r′1) . λp15:(< α1 r1 α′1 r′1) . λβ
:* . λp16:Πα2:□ . Πr2:(α2→α2→*) . Πα′2:□ . Πr′2:(α′2→α′2→*) . a=(i α2 r2)⇒(Tr α2 r2)⇒(SN< α2 r2)⇒c=(i α′2 r′2)⇒(Tr α′2
r′2)⇒(SN< α′2 r′2)⇒(< α2 r2 α′2 r′2)⇒β . (p16 α r α′1 r′1 p2 p3 p4 p12 p13 p14 (L4 α r α1 r1 α′1 r′1 (L5 α r α′ r′ α1 r1 p8 (L20 α′
r′ α1 r1 (treq **U** (i α′ r′) b (i α1 r1) (smeq **U** b (i α′ r′) p5) p9))) p15))))))))) (i **U** <i)) (λu:**U** . Πβ:* . (Πα:□ . Πr:(α→α→*) .
u=(i α r)⇒(Tr α r)⇒(SN< α r)⇒β)⇒β)) (λu u′:**U** . Πβ:* . (Πα:□ . Πr:(α→α→*) . Πα′:□ . Πr′:(α′→α′→*) . u=(i α r)⇒(Tr
α r)⇒(SN< α r)⇒u′=(i α′ r′)⇒(Tr α′ r′)⇒(SN< α′ r′)⇒(< α r α′ r′)⇒β)⇒β)) (λα:□ . λr:(α→α→*) . λα′:□ . λr′:(α′→α′
→*) . λp:(i α r)=(i α′ r′) . (p (λx:**U** . (x (<⁻ α r))) (refl<⁻ α r)))) (λx y:**U** . (eq **U** x y))) (λα:□ . λr:(α→α→*) . λh:H . (h α r))
) (Πh:H . *)) (Πα:□ . Πr:(α→α→*) . *)) (λA:□ . λR:(A→A→*) . λp:(Tr A R) . λp1:(SN< A R) . λa:A . λP:(A→*) . λp2:(chAR
P) . λp3:(P a) . (p1 (PP A R P) (λα1:□ . λr1:(α1→α1→*) . λp4:(PP A R P α1 r1) . λβ:* . λp5:Πα2:□ . Πr2:(α2→α2→*) . (PP
A R P α2 r2)⇒(< α2 r2 α1 r1)⇒β . (p4 β (λz:A . λp6:(P z)&(< A (rst A z R) α1 r1) . (p6 β (λp7:(P z) . λp8:(< A (rst A z R)
α1 r1) . (p2 z p7 β (λz1:A . λp9:(P z1)&(R z1 z) . (p9 β (λp10:(P z1) . λp11:(R z1 z) . (p5 A (rst A z R) (∃in A (λb:A . (P b)&(<
A (rst A b R) A (rst A z R))) z1 (&in (P z1) (< A (rst A z1 R) A (rst A z R)) p10 (L19ii A R p z1 z p11))) p8)))))))))) (p2 a
p3 (PP A R P A R) (λz:A . λp4:(P z)&(R z a) . (p4 (PP A R P A R) (λp5:(P z) . λp6:(R z a) . (∃in A (λb:A . (P b)&(< A (rst
A b R) A R)) z (&in (P z) (< A (rst A z R) A R) p5 (L19i A R z (∃in A (λb:A . (R z b)) a p6)))))))))))) (λA:□ . λR:(A→A→*)
. λP:(A→*) . λα:□ . λr:(α→α→*) . (∃ A (λb:A . (P b)&(< A (rst A b R) α r))))) (λA:□ . λR:(A→A→*) . λp:Πa:A . (SNAR a)
. λP:Πα:□ . Πr:(α→α→*) . * . λp1:(ch_< P) . λp2:(P A R) . (p1 A R p2 ⊥ (λα2:□ . λr2:(α2→α2→*) . λp3:(P α2 r2) . λp4:(<
α2 r2 A R) . (<_to_emb α2 r2 A R p4 ⊥ (λf:α2→A . λa′:A . λp5:(emb α2 r2 A R f a′) . (SNel A R a′ (Q A R P) (p a′) (L19iva
A R P p1) (λφ:* . λp6:ΠB:□ . ΠS:(B→B→*) . Πff:B→A . (P B S)⇒(emb B S A R ff a′)⇒φ . (p6 α2 r2 f p3 p5))))))))) (λA:□ . λ
R:(A→A→*) . λP:Πα:□ . Πr:(α→α→*) . * . λp:(ch_< P) . λa:A . λp1:(Q A R P a) . (p1 (∃ A (λb:A . (Q A R P b)&(R b a))) (λ
B:□ . λS:(B→B→*) . λff:B→A . λp2:(P B S) . λp3:(emb B S A R ff a) . (p B S p2 (∃ A (λb:A . (Q A R P b)&(R b a))) (λα2:□ .
λr2:(α2→α2→*) . λp4:(P α2 r2) . λp5:(< α2 r2 B S) . (<_to_emb α2 r2 B S p5 (∃ A (λb:A . (Q A R P b)&(R b a))) (λf:α2→
B . λa′:B . λp6:(emb α2 r2 B S f a′) . (∃in A (λb:A . (Q A R P b)&(R b a)) (ff a′) (&in (Q A R P (ff a′)) (R (ff a′) a) (λφ:* . λp7
:ΠB1:□ . ΠS1:(B1→B1→*) . Πff1:B1→A . (P B1 S1)⇒(emb B1 S1 A R ff1 (ff a′))⇒φ . (p7 α2 r2 (λc:α2 . (ff (f c))) p4 (tremb

α_2 r_2 B S A R f ff a′ a p_6 p_3))) (p_3 (R (ff a′) a) (λp_7 :($\mathrm{mor}_{<-}$ B S A R ff) . λp_8 :(dms B S A R ff a) . (p_8 (R (ff a′) a) (λp_9
:(Dom_{AR} a) . λp_{10} :Πa_1 :B . (Dom_{BS} a_1)⇒(R (ff a_1) a) . (p_6 (R (ff a′) a) (λp_{11} :($\mathrm{mor}_{<-}$ α_2 r_2 B S f) . λp_{12} :(dms α_2 r_2 B S f a′)
. (p_{12} (R (ff a′) a) (λp_{13} :(Dom_{BS} a′) . λp_{14} :Πa_1 :α_2 . ($\mathrm{Dom}_{\alpha_2 r_2}$ a_1)⇒(S (f a_1) a′) . (p_{10} a′ p_{13})))))))))))))))))))) (λA:□ . λ
R:(A→A→∗) . λP:Πα:□ . Πr:(α→α→∗) . ∗ . λa:A . Πφ:∗ . (ΠB:□ . ΠS:(B→B→∗) . Πff:B→A . (P B S)⇒(emb B S A R ff a)⇒φ)
⇒φ)) (λA:□ . λR:(A→A→∗) . λp:(Tr A R) . λa b:A . λp_1 :(R a b) . ($\exists_{in}$ (A→A) (λf:A→A . ($\mathrm{emb}_<$ A (rst A a R) A (rst A b R)
f)) (λx:A . x) ($\&_{in}$ ($\mathrm{mor}_{<-}$ A (rst A a R) A (rst A b R) (λx:A . x)) (bd A (rst A a R) A (rst A b R) (λx:A . x)) (L19ii$_a$ A R p a
b p_1) (L19ii$_b$ A R p a b p_1))))) (λA:□ . λR:(A→A→∗) . λp:(Tr A R) . λa b:A . λp_1 :(R a b) . (W_{bd} A (rst A a R) A (rst A b R)
(λx:A . x) a ($\&_{in}$ ($\mathrm{Dom}_{A(\mathrm{rstAbR})}$ a) (Πa_1 :A . ($\mathrm{Dom}_{A(\mathrm{rstAaR})}$ a_1)⇒(rst A b R a_1 a)) ($\exists_{in}$ A (λb_1 :A . (rst A b R a b_1)) b ($\&_{in}$
(R a b) (R a b) p_1 p_1)) (λa_1 :A . λp_2 :($\mathrm{Dom}_{A(\mathrm{rstAaR})}$ a_1) . (p_2 (rst A b R a_1 a) (λz:A . λp_3 :(rst A a R a_1 z) . (p_3 (rst A b R a_1 a)
(λp_4 :(R a_1 z) . λp_5 :(R a_1 a) . ($\&_{in}$ (R a_1 a) (R a_1 b) p_5 (p a_1 a b p_5 p_1))))))))))) (λA:□ . λR:(A→A→∗) . λp:(Tr A R) . λa
b:A . λp_1 :(R a b) . λa_1 b_1 :A . λp_2 :(rst A a R a_1 b_1) . (p_2 (rst A b R a_1 b_1) (λp_3 :(R a_1 b_1) . λp_4 :(R a_1 a) . ($\&_{in}$ (R a_1 b_1) (R a_1
b) p_3 (p a_1 a b p_4 p_1)))))) (λA:□ . λR:(A→A→∗) . λa:A . λp:(Dom_{AR} a) . ($W_<$ A (rst A a R) A R (λx:A . x) ($\&_{in}$ ($\mathrm{mor}_{<-}$ A
(rst A a R) A R (λx:A . x)) (bd A (rst A a R) A R (λx:A . x)) (λa_1 b:A . λp_1 :(rst A a R a_1 b) . (p_1 (R a_1 b) (λp_2 :(R a_1 b) . λp_3
:(R a_1 a) . p_2))) (W_{bd} A (rst A a R) A R (λx:A . x) a ($\&_{in}$ (Dom_{AR} a) (Πa_1 :A . ($\mathrm{Dom}_{A(\mathrm{rstAaR})}$ a_1)⇒(R a_1 a)) p (λa_1 :A . λp_1
:($\mathrm{Dom}_{A(\mathrm{rstAaR})}$ a_1) . (p_1 (R a_1 a) (λz:A . λp_2 :(rst A a R a_1 z) . (p_2 (R a_1 a) (λp_3 :(R a_1 z) . λp_4 :(R a_1 a) . p_4)))))))))) (λA:□ .
λR:(A→A→∗) . λa:A . λP:(A→∗) . λp:(ch A (rst A a R) P) . λa_1 :A . λp_1 :(P a_1) . (p a_1 p_1 (∃ A (λb:A . (P b)&(R b a_1))) (λ
z:A . λp_2 :(P z)&(rst A a R z a_1) . (p_2 (∃ A (λb:A . (P b)&(R b a_1))) (λp_3 :(P z) . λp_4 :(rst A a R z a_1) . ($\exists_{in}$ A (λb:A . (P b)&(R
b a_1)) z ($\&_{in}$ (P z) (R z a_1) p_3 (p_4 (R z a_1) (λp_5 :(R z a_1) . λp_6 :(R z a) . p_5)))))))))) (λA:□ . λa:A . λR:(A→A→∗) . λp:(Tr A
R) . λa_1 b c:A . λp_1 :(rst A a R a_1 b) . λp_2 :(rst A a R b c) . (p_1 (rst A a R a_1 c) (λp_3 :(R a_1 b) . λp_4 :(R a_1 a) . (p_2 (rst A a R a_1 c)
(λp_5 :(R b c) . λp_6 :(R b a) . ($\&_{in}$ (R a_1 c) (R a_1 a) (p a_1 b c p_3 p_5) p_4))))))) (λA:□ . λa:A . λR:(A→A→∗) . λb c:A . (R b c)&
(R b a))) (λα:□ . λr:(α→α→∗) . Πa b c:α . (r a b)⇒(r b c)⇒(r a c))) (λα:□ . λr:(α→α→∗) . ΠP:Πα_1 :□ . Πr_1 :(α_1 →α_1 →∗) . ∗ .
(ch_< P)⇒¬(P α r))) (λP:Πα:□ . Πr:(α→α→∗) . ∗ . Πα_1 :□ . Πr_1 :(α_1 →α_1 →∗) . (P α_1 r_1)⇒(Πβ:∗ . (Πα_2 :□ . Πr_2 :(α_2→α_2→∗)
. (P α_2 r_2)⇒(< α_2 r_2 α_1 r_1)⇒β)⇒β))) (λA:□ . λR:(A→A→∗) . λB:□ . λS:(B→B→∗) . λC:□ . λT:(C→C→∗) . λp:(< A R B
S) . λp_1 :($<^-$ B S C T) . (<_to_emb A R B S p (< A R C T) (λf:A→B . λa′:B . λp_2 :(emb A R B S f a′) . (p_1 (< A R C T) (λ
z:B→C . λp_3 :($\mathrm{mor}_{<-}$ B S C T z) . (emb_to_< A R C T (λa:A . (z (f a))) (z a′) (L1 A R B S C T f z a′ p_2 p_3)))))))) (λA:□ . λ
R:(A→A→∗) . λB:□ . λS:(B→B→∗) . λC:□ . λT:(C→C→∗) . λp:(< A R B S) . λp_1 :(< B S C T) . (L3 A R B S C T (p ($<^-$ A R
B S) (λz:A→B . λp_2 :($\mathrm{emb}_<$ A R B S z) . (p_2 ($<^-$ A R B S) (λp_3 :($\mathrm{mor}_{<-}$ A R B S z) . λp_4 :(bd A R B S z) . ($W_{<-}$ A R B S z
p_3))))) p_1))) (λA:□ . λR:(A→A→∗) . λB:□ . λS:(B→B→∗) . λC:□ . λT:(C→C→∗) . λp:($<^-$ A R B S) . λp_1 :(< B S C T) . (p
(< A R C T) (λz:A→B . λp_2 :($\mathrm{mor}_{<-}$ A R B S z) . (<_to_emb B S C T p_1 (< A R C T) (λf:B→C . λa′:C . λp_3 :(emb B S C T f
a′) . (emb_to_< A R C T (λa:A . (f (z a))) a′ (L2 A R B S C T z f a′ p_2 p_3)))))))) (λA:□ . λR:(A→A→∗) . λB:□ . λS:(B→B→∗)
. λC:□ . λT:(C→C→∗) . λf:A→B . λg:B→C . λb:B . λc:C . λp:(emb A R B S f b) . λp_1 :(emb B S C T g c) . (p_1 (emb A R C T (λ
a:A . (g (f a))) (g b)) (λp_2 :($\mathrm{mor}_{<-}$ B S C T g) . λp_3 :(dms B S C T g c) . (L1 A R B S C T f g b p p_2))))) (λA:□ . λR:(A→A→∗)
. λB:□ . λS:(B→B→∗) . λC:□ . λT:(C→C→∗) . λf:A→B . λg:B→C . λc:C . λp:($\mathrm{mor}_{<-}$ A R B S f) . λp_1 :(emb B S C T g c) . (p_1
(emb A R C T (λa:A . (g (f a))) c) (λp_2 :($\mathrm{mor}_{<-}$ B S C T g) . λp_3 :(dms B S C T g c) . ($\&_{in}$ ($\mathrm{mor}_{<-}$ A R C T (λa:A . (g (f a))))
(dms A R C T (λa:A . (g (f a))) c) (tr_{mor} A R B S C T f g p p_2) (p_3 (dms A R C T (λa:A . (g (f a))) c) (λp_4 :(Dom_{CT} c) . λp_5
:Πa:B . (Dom_{BS} a)⇒(T (g a) c) . ($\&_{in}$ (Dom_{CT} c) (Πa:A . (Dom_{AR} a)⇒(T (g (f a)) c)) p_4 (λa:A . λp_6 :(Dom_{AR} a) . (p_5 (f a)
(LDom A R B S f p a p_6))))))))))) (λA:□ . λR:(A→A→∗) . λB:□ . λS:(B→B→∗) . λC:□ . λT:(C→C→∗) . λf:A→B . λg:B→C .
λb:B . λp:(emb A R B S f b) . λp_1 :($\mathrm{mor}_{<-}$ B S C T g) . (p (emb A R C T (λa:A . (g (f a))) (g b)) (λp_2 :($\mathrm{mor}_{<-}$ A R B S f) . λp_3
:(dms A R B S f b) . ($\&_{in}$ ($\mathrm{mor}_{<-}$ A R C T (λa:A . (g (f a)))) (dms A R C T (λa:A . (g (f a))) (g b)) (tr_{mor} A R B S C T f g p_2
p_1) (p_3 (dms A R C T (λa:A . (g (f a))) (g b)) (λp_4 :(Dom_{BS} b) . λp_5 :Πa:A . (Dom_{AR} a)⇒(S (f a) b) . ($\&_{in}$ (Dom_{CT} (g b)) (Π
a:A . (Dom_{AR} a)⇒(T (g (f a)) (g b))) (LDom B S C T g p_1 b p_4) (λa:A . λp_6 :(Dom_{AR} a) . (p_1 (f a) b (p_5 a p_6))))))))))) (λ
A:□ . λR:(A→A→∗) . λB:□ . λS:(B→B→∗) . λC:□ . λT:(C→C→∗) . λf:A→B . λg:B→C . λp:($\mathrm{mor}_{<-}$ A R B S f) . λp_1 :($\mathrm{mor}_{<-}$
B S C T g) . λa b:A . λp_2 :(R a b) . (p_1 (f a) (f b) (p a b p_2)))) (λA:□ . λR:(A→A→∗) . ($\exists_{in}$ (A→A) (λf:A→A . ($\mathrm{mor}_{<-}$ A R A
R f)) (λx:A . x) (λa b:A . λp:(R a b) . p)))) (λA:□ . λR:(A→A→∗) . λA′:□ . λR′:(A′→A′→∗) . λf:A→A′ . λp:($\mathrm{mor}_{<-}$ A R A′
R′ f) . λa:A . λp_1 :(Dom_{AR} a) . (p_1 ($\mathrm{Dom}_{A'R'}$ (f a)) (λz:A . λp_2 :(R a z) . ($\exists_{in}$ A′ (λb:A′ . (R′ (f a) b)) (f z) (p a z p_2)))))) (λA:□
. λR:(A→A→∗) . λA′:□ . λR′:(A′→A′→∗) . λp:(< A R A′ R′) . (p (Πφ:∗ . (Πf:A→A′ . Πa′:A′ . (emb A R A′ R′ f a′)⇒φ)⇒φ)
(λz:A→A′ . λp_1 :($\mathrm{emb}_<$ A R A′ R′ z) . (p_1 (Πφ:∗ . (Πf:A→A′ . Πa′:A′ . (emb A R A′ R′ f a′)⇒φ)⇒φ) (λp_2 :($\mathrm{mor}_{<-}$ A R A′ R′
z) . λp_3 :(bd A R A′ R′ z) . (p_3 (Πφ:∗ . (Πf:A→A′ . Πa′:A′ . (emb A R A′ R′ f a′)⇒φ)⇒φ) (λz_1 :A′ . λp_4 :(dms A R A′ R′ z z_1) .
λφ:∗ . λp_5 :Πf:A→A′ . Πa′:A′ . (emb A R A′ R′ f a′)⇒φ . (p_5 z z_1 ($\&_{in}$ ($\mathrm{mor}_{<-}$ A R A′ R′ z) (dms A R A′ R′ z z_1) p_2 p_4)))))))
))) (λA:□ . λR:(A→A→∗) . λA′:□ . λR′:(A′→A′→∗) . λf:A→A′ . λa′:A′ . λp:(emb A R A′ R′ f a′) . (p (< A R A′ R′) (λp_1
:($\mathrm{mor}_{<-}$ A R A′ R′ f) . λp_2 :(dms A R A′ R′ f a′) . ($W_<$ A R A′ R′ f ($\&_{in}$ ($\mathrm{mor}_{<-}$ A R A′ R′ f) (bd A R A′ R′ f) p_1 ($\exists_{in}$ A′
(dms A R A′ R′ f) a′ p_2))))))) (λA:□ . λR:(A→A→∗) . λA′:□ . λR′:(A′→A′→∗) . λf:A→A′ . λa′:A′ . ($\mathrm{mor}_{<-}$ A R A′ R′ f)&
(dms A R A′ R′ f a′))) (λA:□ . λR:(A→A→∗) . λA′:□ . λR′:(A′→A′→∗) . λf:A→A′ . λp:($\mathrm{emb}_<$ A R A′ R′ f) . λβ:∗ . λp_1 :Πf_1
:A→A′ . ($\mathrm{emb}_<$ A R A′ R′ f_1)⇒β . (p_1 f p))) (λA:□ . λR:(A→A→∗) . λA′:□ . λR′:(A′→A′→∗) . (∃ (A→A′) ($\mathrm{emb}_<$ A R A′
R′)))) (λA:□ . λR:(A→A→∗) . λA′:□ . λR′:(A′→A′→∗) . λf:A→A′ . ($\mathrm{mor}_{<-}$ A R A′ R′ f)&(bd A R A′ R′ f))) (λA:□ . λR:(A
→A→∗) . λA′:□ . λR′:(A′→A′→∗) . λf:A→A′ . λa′:A′ . λp:(dms A R A′ R′ f a′) . ($\exists_{in}$ A′ (dms A R A′ R′ f) a′ p))) (λA:□ . λ
R:(A→A→∗) . λA′:□ . λR′:(A′→A′→∗) . λf:A→A′ . (∃ A′ (dms A R A′ R′ f)))) (λA:□ . λR:(A→A→∗) . λA′:□ . λR′:(A′→A′
→∗) . λf:A→A′ . λa′:A′ . ($\mathrm{Dom}_{A'R'}$ a′)&(Πa:A . (Dom_{AR} a)⇒(R′ (f a) a′)))) (λA:□ . λR:(A→A→∗) . λA′:□ . λR′:(A′→A′→
∗) . λf:A→A′ . λp:($\mathrm{mor}_{<-}$ A R A′ R′ f) . λβ:∗ . λp_1 :Πf_1 :A→A′ . ($\mathrm{mor}_{<-}$ A R A′ R′ f_1)⇒β . (p_1 f p))) (λA:□ . λR:(A→A→∗).
λA′:□ . λR′:(A′→A′→∗) . (∃ (A→A′) ($\mathrm{mor}_{<-}$ A R A′ R′)))) (λA:□ . λR:(A→A→∗) . λA′:□ . λR′:(A′→A′→∗) . λf:A→A′ . Π
a b:A . (R a b)⇒(R′ (f a) (f b)))) (λA:□ . λR:(A→A→∗) . λa:A . (∃ A (λb:A . (R a b))))) (λA:□ . λR:(A→A→∗) . λQ:(A→∗) .
λp:(cl_{AR} Q) . λp_1 :($\exists_{rel}$ A Q (λb:A . ($\forall_{rel}$ A Q (λa:A . (SN_{AR} a)⇔(R a b)))))) . (p_1 ⊥ (λz:A . λp_2 :(Q z)&($\forall_{rel}$ A Q (λa:A .
(SN_{AR} a)⇔(R a z))) . (p_2 ⊥ (λp_3 :(Q z) . λp_4 :($\forall_{rel}$ A Q (λa:A . (SN_{AR} a)⇔(R a z))) . ($L14_a$ A R z (p_4 z p_3 ((SN_{AR} z)⇒(R z
z)) (λp_5 :(SN_{AR} z)⇒(R z z) . λp_6 :(R z z)⇒(SN_{AR} z) . p_5)) ($L14_b$ A R z (λa:A . λp_5 :(R a z) . (p_4 a (p z a p_3 p_5) (SN_{AR} a) (λp_6
:(SN_{AR} a)⇒(R a z) . λp_7 :(R a z)⇒(SN_{AR} a) . (p_7 p_5))))))))))))) (λA:□ . λR:(A→A→∗) . λQ:(A→∗) . Πa b:A . (Q a)⇒(R b a)
⇒(Q b))) (λA:□ . λR:(A→A→∗) . λb:A . λp:Πa:A . (R a b)⇒(SN_{AR} a) . λP:(A→∗) . λp_1 :(ch_{AR} P) . λp_2 :(P b) . (p_1 b p_2 ⊥ (λ
z:A . λp_3 :(P z)&(R z b) . (p_3 ⊥ (λp_4 :(P z) . λp_5 :(R z b) . (p z p_5 P p_1 p_4)))))))) (λA:□ . λR:(A→A→∗) . λb:A . λp:(SN_{AR} b)⇒
(R b b) . λp_1 :(SN_{AR} b) . (p_1 (λy:A . (R y y)) (λa:A . λp_2 :(R a a) . ($\exists_{in}$ A (λb_1 :A . (R b_1 b_1)&(R b_1 a)) a ($\&_{in}$ (R a a) (R a a)
p_2 p_2))) (p p_1)))) (λA:□ . λR:(A→A→∗) . λa:A . λP:(A→∗) . λp:(SN_{AR} a) . λp_1 :(ch_{AR} P) . λp_2 :(P a) . (p_1 a p_2 ⊥ (λz:A . λp_3
:(P z)&(R z a) . (p_3 ⊥ (λp_4 :(P z) . λp_5 :(R z a) . (p P p_1 p_2)))))))) (λA:□ . λR:(A→A→∗) . λP:(A→∗) . λp:(ch_{AR} P) . λa:A . λp_1
:(P a) . λφ:∗ . λp_2 :Πb:A . (P b)⇒(R b a)⇒φ . (p a p_1 φ (λz:A . λp_3 :(P z)&(R z a) . (p_3 φ (λp_4 :(P z) . λp_5 :(R z a) . (p_2 z p_4 p_5)))
)))) (λA:□ . λR:(A→A→∗) . λa:A . ΠP:(A→∗) . (ch_{AR} P)⇒¬(P a))) (λA:□ . λR:(A→A→∗) . λP:(A→∗) . Πa:A . (P a)⇒(∃ A
(λb:A . (P b)&(R b a))))) (λA:□ . λQ B:(A→∗) . (∃ A (λa:A . (Q a)&(B a))))) (λA:□ . λQ B:(A→∗) . Πa:A . (Q a)⇒(B a))) (λ
t:□ . λx y z:t . λp:(eq t x y) . λp_1 :(eq t y z) . (p_1 (eq t x) p))) (λt:□ . λx y:t . λp:(eq t x y) . (p (λz:t . (eq t z x)) (refl_{eq} t x)))) (λ
t:□ . λx y:t . λp:(eq t x y) . λf:(t→∗) . λq:(f x) . (p f q))) (λt:□ . λc:t . λz:(t→∗) . λp:(z c) . p)) (λt:□ . λx y:t . Πz:(t→∗) . (z x)⇒(z
y))) (λa:□ . λp:(a→∗) . λx:a . λp_1 :(p x) . λβ:∗ . λp_2 :Πz:a . (p z)⇒β . (p_2 x p_1))) (λa:□ . λp:(a→∗) . Πβ:∗ . (Πz:a . (p z)⇒β)⇒β))
(λa b:∗ . λp:a . λα:∗ . λp_1 :b⇒α . λp_2 :a⇒α . (p_2 p))) (λa b:∗ . λp:a . λα:∗ . λp_1 :a⇒α . λp_2 :b⇒α . (p_1 p))) (λa b:∗ . Πα:∗ . (a⇒α)
⇒(b⇒α)⇒α)) (λa b:∗ . (a⇒b)&(b⇒a))) (λa b:∗ . λp:a . λp_1 :b . λα:∗ . λp_2 :a⇒b⇒α . (p_2 p p_1))) (λa b:∗ . Πα:∗ . (a⇒b⇒α)⇒
α)) (λa:∗ . a⇒⊥)) ⊥⇒⊥) (λa:∗ . λp:⊥ . (p a))) (Πa:∗ . a)) (λa b:∗ . Πp:a . b)

Acknowledgements

Two persons have been quite influential on the form and contents of this chapter. First of all, Mariangiola Dezani-Ciancaglini clarified to me the essential differences between the Curry and the Church typing systems. She provided a wealth of information on these systems (not all of which has been incorporated in this chapter; see the forthcoming [Barendregt and Dekkers, to appear] for more on the subject). Secondly, Bert van Benthem Jutting introduced me to the notion of type dependency as presented in the systems AUTOMATH and related calculi like the calculus of constructions. His intimate knowledge of these calculi—obtained after extensive mathematical texts in them—has been rather useful. In fact it helped me to introduce a fine structure of the calculus of constructions, the so called λ-cube. Contributions of other individuals—often important ones—will be clear form the contents of this chapter.

The following people gave interesting input or feedback for the contents of this chapter: Steffen van Bakel, Erik Barendsen, Stefano Berardi, Val Breazu-Tannen, Dick (N.G.) de Bruijn, Adriana Compagnoni, Mario Coppo, Thierry Coquand, Wil Dekkers, Ken-etsu Fujita, Herman Geuvers, Jean-Yves Girard, Susumu Hayashi, Leen Helmink, Kees Hemerik, Roger Hindley, Furio Honsell, Martin Hyland, Johan de Iongh, Bart Jacobs, Hidetaka Kondoh, Giuseppe Longo, Sophie Malecki, Gregory Mints, Albert Meyer, Reinhard Muskens, Mark-Jan Nederhof, Rob Nederpelt, Andy Pitts, Randy Pollack, Andre Scedrov, Richard Statman, Marco Swaen, Jan Terlouw, Hans Tonino, Yoshihito Toyama, Anne Troelstra and Roel de Vrijer.

Financial support came from several sources. Firstly, *Oxford University Press* gave the necessary momentum to write this chapter. The *Research Institute for Declarative Systems* at the *Department of Computer Science* of the *Catholic University Nijmegen* provided the daily environment where I had many discussions with colleagues and Ph.D. students. The EC Stimulation Project ST2J-0374-C (EDB) *lambda calcul typé* helped me to meet many of the people mentioned above, notably Berardi and Dezani-Ciancaglini. *Nippon Telephon and Telegraph (NTT)* made it possible to meet Fujita and Toyama. The most essential support came from *Philips Research Laboratories Eindhoven* where I had extensive discussions with van Benthem Jutting leading to the definition of the λ-cube.

Finally I would thank Mariëlle van der Zandt and Jane Spurr for typing and editing the never ending manuscript and Wil Dekkers for proofreading and suggesting improvements. Erik Barendsen was my guru for TEX. Use has been made of the macros of Paul Taylor for commutative diagrams and prooftrees. Erik Barendsen, Wil Dekkers and Herman Geuvers helped me with the production of the final manuscript.

References

[Barendregt and Dekkers, to appear] H. P. Barendregt and W. J. Dekkers. Typed lambda calculi, to appear.

[Barendregt and Hemerik, 1990] H. P. Barendregt and K. Hemerik. Types in lambda calculi and programming languages. In N. Jones, editor, *European Symposium on Programming*, volume 432 of *Lecture Notes in Computer Science*, pages 1–36. Springer, 1990.

[Barendregt and Rezus, 1983] H. P. Barendregt and A. Rezus. Semantics of classical AUTOMATH and related systems. *Information and Control*, 59:127–147, 1983.

[Barendregt *et al.*, 1983] H. P. Barendregt, M. Coppo, and M. Dezani-Ciancaglini. A filter lambda model and the completeness of type assignment. *J. Symbolic Logic*, 48(4):931–940, 1983.

[Barendregt, 1984] H. P. Barendregt. *The lambda calculus: its syntax and semantics.* Studies in Logic and the Foundations of Mathematics. North Holland, revised edition, 1984.

[Barendregt, 1990] H. P. Barendregt. Functional programming and lambda calulus. In J. van Leeuwen, editor, *Handbook of Theoretical Computer Science, Vol B, Formal Methods and Semantics*, pages 321–364. North Holland, 1990.

[Barendregt, 1991] H. P. Barendregt. Introduction to generalised type systems, 1991. To appear in *J. Functional Programming.*

[Barendsen and Geuvers, 1989] E. Barendsen and J. H. Geuvers. Conservativity of λP over PRED. Technical report, Dept. Computer Science, University of Nijmegen, Toernooiveld 1, 6525 ED Nijmegen, The Netherlands, 1989.

[Barendsen, 1989] E. Barendsen. Representation of Logic, Data Types and Recursive Functions in Typed Lambda Calculi. Master's thesis, Dept. Computer Science, Catholic University, Toernooiveld 1, 6525 ED Nijmegen, The Netherlands, 1989.

[Barwise, 1977] J. Barwise, editor. *Handbook of Mathematical Logic.* North-Holland, 1977.

[Berardi, 1988a] S. Berardi. Personal communication, 1988.

[Berardi, 1988b] S. Berardi. Towards a Mathematical Analysis of the Coquand-Huet Calculus of Constructions and the Other Systems in

Barendregt's Cube. Technical report, Dept. Computer Science, Carnegie-Mellon University and Dipartimento Matematica, Università di Torino, 1988.

[Berardi, 1989] S. Berardi. Personal communication, 1989.

[Berardi, 1990] S. Berardi. *Type Dependence and Constructive Mathematics*. PhD thesis, Dipartimento Matematica, Università di Torino, 1990.

[Böhm and Berarducci, 1985] C. Böhm and A. Berarducci. Automatic synthesis of typed λ-programs on term algebras. *Theor. Comput. Sci.*, 39:135–154, 1985.

[Cardelli and Wegner, 1985] L. Cardelli and P. Wegner. On understanding types, data abstraction and polymorphism. *ACM Comp. Surveys*, 17(4), 1985.

[Church, 193233] A. Church. A set of postulates for the foundation of logic. *Anals of Math.*, 2(33-34):346–366 and 839–864, 1932/33.

[Church, 1940] A. Church. A formulation of the simple theory of types. *J. Symbolic Logic*, 5:56–68, 1940.

[Church, 1941] A. Church. *The Calculi of Lambda Conversion*. Princeton University Press, 1941.

[Constable *et al.*, 1986] R. L. Constable, S. F. Allen, H. M. Bromley, W. R. C leveland, J. F. Cremer, R. W. Harper, D. J. Howe, T. B. Knoblock, N. P. Mendler, P. Panangaden, J. T. Sasaki, and S. F. Smith. *Implementing Mathematics with the Nuprl Proof Development Sys tem*. Prentice-Hall, New York, x+299pp, 1986.

[Coppo and Cardone, 1991] M. Coppo and F. Cardone. Type inference with recursive types: syntax and semantics. *Information and Computation*, 92(1):48–80, 1991.

[Coppo *et al.*, 1981] M. Coppo, M. Dezani-Ciancaglini, and B. Venneri. Functional characters of solvable terms. *Zeitschr. f. Math. Logik u. Grundlagen Math.*, 27:45–58, 1981.

[Coppo *et al.*, 1984] M. Coppo, M. Dezani-Ciancaglini, G. Longo, and F. Honsell. Extended type structures and filter lambda models. In G. Lolli, G. Longo, and A. Marcja, editors, *Logic Colloquium '82*, Studies in Logic and the Foundations of Mathematics, pages 241–262. North Holland, 1984.

[Coppo *et al.*, 1987] M. Coppo, M. Dezani-Ciancaglini, and M. Zacchi. Type Theories, normal forms and d_∞ lambda models. *Information and Computation*, 72:85–116, 1987.

[Coppo, 1985] M. Coppo. A completeness theorem for recursively defined types. In *Proc. of the 12th Int. Coll. on Automata and Programming*, volume 432 of *Lecture Notes in Computer Science*, pages 120–129. Springer, 1985.

[Coquand and Huet, 1988] Th. Coquand and G. Huet. The calculus of constructions. *Information and Computation*, 76:95–120, 1988.

[Coquand, 1985] Th. Coquand. Une théorie des constructions, 1985. Thèse de troisième cycle, Université Paris VII.

[Coquand, 1986] Th. Coquand. An analysis of girard's paradox. In *Proc. of the First Symposium of Logic in Computer Science*, pages 227–236. IEEE, 1986.

[Coquand, 1989a] Th. Coquand. Metamathematical investigation of a calculus of constructions, 1989. In [Odifreddi, 1990].

[Coquand, 1989b] Th. Coquand. Reynolds paradox with the Type : Type axiom. In *The calculus of constructions. Documentation and users's guide, version 4.10*, volume 110 of *Rapports Techniques*. INRIA, B.P. 105, 78153 Le Chesnay Cedex, France, 1989. (4 unnumbered pages at the end of the report).

[Curry and Feys, 1958] H. B. Curry and R. Feys. *Combinatory Logic, Vol. I*. Studies in Logic and the Foundations of Mathematics. North Holland, 1958.

[Curry *et al.*, 1972] H. B. Curry, J. R. Hindley, and J. P. Seldin. *Combinatory Logic, Vol. II*. Studies in Logic and the Foundations of Mathematics. North Holland, 1972.

[Curry, 1934] H. B. Curry. Functionality in combinatory logic. *Proc. Nat. Acad. Science USA*, 20:584–590, 1934.

[Curry, 1969] H. B. Curry. Modified basic functionality in combinatory logic. *Dialectica*, 23:83–92, 1969.

[Davis, 1958] M. Davis. *Computability and Unsolvability*. McGraw-Hill, 1958.

[de Bruijn, 1970] N. G. de Bruijn. The mathematical language AUTOMATH, its usage and some of its extensions. In *Symposium on automatic demonstration*, volume 125 of *Lecture Notes in Mathematics*, pages 29–61, IRIA, Versailles 1968, 1970. Springer.

[de Bruijn, 1980] N. G. de Bruijn. A survey of the AUTOMATH project, 1980. In [Hindley and Seldin, 1980].

[de Vrijer, 1975] R. de Vrijer. Big trees in a λ-calculus with λ-expressions as types. In C. Böhm, editor, *λ-Calculus and Computer Science Theory*, volume 37 of *Lecture Notes in Computer Science*, pages 252–271. Springer, 1975.

[Dezani-Ciancaglini and Margaria, 1987]
M. Dezani-Ciancaglini and I. Margaria. Polymorphic types, fixed-point combinators and continuous lambda models. In M. Wirsing, editor, *IFIP Conference on Formal Description of Programming Concepts III*, pages 425–450. North-Holland, 1987.

[Fitch, 1952] F. B. Fitch. *Symbolic Logic. An Introduction.* Ronald Press, New York, 1952.

[Fitch, 1974] F. B. Fitch. *Elements of Combinatory Logic.* Yale University Press, New Heaven, 1974.

[Fokkinga, 1987] M. M. Fokkinga. Programming languages concepts – the lambda calculus approach. In P. R. J. Asveld and A. Nijholt, editors, *Essays on concepts, formalism, and tools*, volume 42 of *CWI tracts*, pages 129–162. Centrum voor Wiskunde en Informatica, Box 4079, 1009 AB Amsterdam, The Netherlands, 1987.

[Fujita and Tonino, 1991] K. Fujita and H. Tonino. Logical systems are generalised type systems. Technical report, Technical University Delft, Faculty of Mathematics and Informatics, Julianalaan 132, 2628 BL Delft, The Netherlands, 1991.

[Gandy, 1980] R. O. Gandy. Proofs of strong normalisation, 1980. In [Hindley and Seldin, 1980].

[Geuvers and Nederhof, 1991] H. Geuvers and M. J. Nederhof. A modular proof of strong normalisation for the calculus of constructions. *J. Functional Programming*, 1(2):155–189, 1991.

[Geuvers, 1988] J. H. Geuvers. The interpretation of logics in type sstems. Master's thesis, Dept. Computer Science, Catholic University, Toernooiveld 1, 6525 ED Nijmegen, The Netherlands, 1988.

[Geuvers, 1989] J. H. Geuvers. Theory of constructions is not conservative over higher order logic. Technical report, Dept. Computer Science, Catholic University, Toernooiveld 1, 6525 ED Nijmegen, The Netherlands, 1989.

[Geuvers, 1990] J. H. Geuvers. Type systems for higher order logic. Technical report, Dept. Computer Science, Catholic University, Toernooiveld 1, 6525 ED Nijmegen, The Netherlands, 1990.

[Giannini and Ronchi della Roca, 1988] P. Giannini and S. Ronchi della Roca. Characterization of typings in polymorphic type discipline. In *Proc. Third Symposium of Logic in Computer Science*, pages 61–70. IEEE, 1988.

[Girard *et al.*, 1989] J.-Y. Girard, Y. Lafont, and P. Taylor. *Proofs and Types*, volume 7 of *Tracts in Theoretical Computer Science*. Cambridge University Press, 1989.

[Girard, 1972] J.-Y. Girard. *Interprétation fonctionelle et élimination des coupures dans l'arithmétique d'ordre supérieur*. PhD thesis, Université Paris VII, 1972.

[Harper *et al.*, 1987] R. Harper, F. Honsell, and G. Plotkin. A framework for defining logics. In *Proc. Second Symposium of Logic in Computer Science*, pages 194–204, Ithaca, N.Y., 1987. IEEE, Washington DC.

[Helmink, 1991] L. Helmink. Girard's paradox in λu. Technical report, Philips Research Laboratories, Box 80.000, 5600 JA Eindhoven, The Netherlands, 1991.

[Henglein, 1990] F. Henglein. A Lower Bound for Full Polymorphic Type Inference: Girard-Reynolds Typability is DEXPTIME-hard. Report RUU-CS-90-14, Dept. Computer Science, Utrecht University, The Netherlands, 1990.

[Hindley and Seldin, 1980] J. R. Hindley and J. P. Seldin, editors. *To H. B. Curry: Essays on Combinatory Logic, Lambda Calculus and Formalism*. Academic Press, 1980.

[Hindley and Seldin, 1986] J. R. Hindley and J. P. Seldin. *Introduction to Combinators and λ-calculus*, volume 1 of *London Mathematical Society Student Texts*. Cambridge University Press, 1986.

[Hindley, 1969] J. R. Hindley. The principal typescheme of an object in combinatory logic. *Trans. Amer. Math. Soc.*, 146:29–60, 1969.

[Hindley, 1983] J. R. Hindley. The simple semantics for Coppo-Dezani-Sallé types. In M. Dezani-Ciancaglini and H. Montanari, editors, *International Symposium on Programming*, volume 137 of *Lecture Notes in Computer Science*, pages 212–226, Berlin, 1983. Springer.

[Hofstadter, 1979] D. Hofstadter. *Gödel Escher Bach: An Eternal Golden Braid*. Harvester Press, 1979.

[Howard, 1980] W. A. Howard. The formulae-as-types notion of construction, 1980. In [Hindley and Seldin, 1980].

[Howe, 1987] D. Howe. The computational behaviour of girard's paradox. In *Proc. Second Symposium of Logic in Computer Science*, pages 205–214, Ithaca, N.Y., 1987. IEEE.

[Jacobs *et al.*, to appear] B. P. F Jacobs, I. Margaria, and M. Zacchi. Filter models with polymorphic types. *Theoretical Computer Science*, to appear.

[Jacobs, 1989] B. P. F. Jacobs. The inconsistency of higher order extensions of Martin-Löf's type theory. *J. Philosophical Logic*, 18:399–422, 1989.

[Jacobs, 1991] B. P. F. Jacobs. *Categorical type theory.* PhD thesis, Dept. Computer Science, Catholic University, Toernooiveld 1, 6525 ED Nijmegen, The Netherlands, 1991.

[Kfoury *et al.*, 1990] A. J. Kfoury, J. Tiuryn, and P. Urzcyzyn. ML typability is DEXPTIME-complete. In A. Arnold, editor, *CAAP '90*, volume 431 of *Lecture Notes in Computer Science*, pages 206–220. Springer, 1990.

[Kleene and Rosser, 1935] S. C. Kleene and J. B. Rosser. The inconsistency of certain formal logics. *Annals Math*, 2(36):630–636, 1935.

[Kleene, 1936] S. C. Kleene. λ-definability and recursiveness. *Duke Math. J.*, 2:340–353, 1936.

[Klop, 1980] J.-W. Klop. *Combinatory Reduction Systems.* PhD thesis, Utrecht University, Box 4079, 1009 AB Amsterdam, The Netherlands, 1980.

[Krivine, 1990] J. L. Krivine. *Lambda-calcul, Types et Modèles.* Masson, Paris, 1990.

[Lambek and Scott, 1986] J. Lambek and P. J. Scott. *Introduction to Higher Order Categorical Logic*, volume 7 of *Cambridge Studies in Advanced Mathematics.* Cambridge University Press, Cambridge, 1986.

[Läuchli, 1970] H. Läuchli. An abstract notion of realizability for which intuitionistic predicate calculus is complete. In A. Kino, J. Myhill, and R. E. Vesley, editors, *Intuitionism and Proof Theory*, Studies in Logic and The Foundations of Mathematics, pages 227–234. North-Holland, Amsterdam, vii+516pp, 1970. Proceedings of the *Summer Conference* at Buffalo, New York, 1968.

[Leivant, 1983] D. Leivant. Reasoning about functional programs and complexity classes associated with type disciplines. In *24th IEEE Symposium on Foundations of Computer Science*, pages 460–469, 1983.

[Leivant, 1990] D. Leivant. Contracting proofs to programs, 1990. In [Odifreddi, 1990].

[Löb, 1976] M. Löb. Embedding first order predicate logic in fragments of intuitionistic logic. *J. Symbolic Logic*, 41(4):705–718, 1976.

[Longo and Moggi, 1988] G. Longo and E. Moggi. Constructive natural deduction and its modest interpretation. Report CMU-CS-88-131, Carnegie Mellon University, Pittsburgh, USA, 1988.

[Luo, 1990] Z. Luo. *An Extended Calculus of Constructions.* PhD thesis, University of Edinburgh, 1990.

[MacQueen *et al.*, 1984] D. MacQueen, G. D. Plotkin, and R. Sethi. An ideal model for recursive polymorphic types. In *11th ACM Symposium on Principles of Programming Languages*, pages 165–174. ACM, 1984.

[Malecki, 1989] S. Malecki. Private communication, 1989.

[Martin-Löf, 1971] P. Martin-Löf. A construction of the provable wellorderings of the theory of species. Technical report, Mathematical Institute, University of Stockholm, Sweden, 1971. 14 pp.

[Martin-Löf, 1984] P. Martin-Löf. *Intuitionistic Type Theory.* Studies in Proof Theory. Bibliopolis, Naples, 1984.

[Mendelson, 1987] E. Mendelson. *Introduction to Mathematical Logic.* Wadsworth and Brooks/Cole, 3rd edition, 1987.

[Mendler, 1987] N. P. Mendler. Inductive types and type constraints in second-order lambda calculus. In *Proc. of the Second Symposium of Logic in Computer Science*, pages 30–36, Ithaca, N.Y., 1987. IEEE.

[Meyer, 1988] A. Meyer. Personal communication, 1988.

[Milner, 1978] R. Milner. A theory of type polymorphism in programming. *J. Computer and Systems Sciences*, 17:348–375, 1978.

[Milner, 1984] R. Milner. A proposal for standard ML. In *ACM Symposium on LISP and Functional Programming*, pages 184–197, Austin, 1984.

[Mirimanoff, 1917] D. Mirimanoff. Les antinomies de Russell et de Burali-Forti et le problème fondamental de la théorie des ensembles. *L'Enseignement Mathématique*, 19:37–52, 1917.

[Mitchell, 1984] J. C. Mitchell. Type inference and type containment. In G. Kahn, editor, *Proc. Internat. Symp. on Semantics of Data Types*, volume 173 of *Lecture Notes in Computer Science*, pages 257–277. Springer, 1984.

[Mitchell, 1988] J. C. Mitchell. Polymorphic type inference and containment. *Inform. and Comput.*, 76(2-3):211–249, 1988.

[Mitchell, 1990] J. C. Mitchell. Type systems for programming languages, 1990. In [van Leeuwen, 1990].

[Mostowski, 1951] A. Mostowski. On the rules of proof in the pure functional calculus of first order. *J. Symbolic Logic*, 16:107–111, 1951.

[Nederpelt, 1973] R. P. Nederpelt. *Strong Normalization in a Typed Lambda Calculus with Lambda Structured Types.* PhD thesis, Eindhoven Technological University, The Netherlands, 1973.

[Nerode and Odifreddi, to appear] A. Nerode and P. Odifreddi. *Lambda calculi and constructive logics.* to appear.

[Odifreddi, 1990] P. Odifreddi, editor. *Logic in Computer Science.* Academic Press, New York, 1990.

[Pavlović, 1990] D. Pavlović. *Predicates and Fibrations.* PhD thesis, Department of mathematics, University of Utrecht, Budapestlaan 6, 3508 TA Utrecht, The Netherlands, 1990.

[Peremans, 1949] W. Peremans. Een opmerking over intuitionistische logica. Report ZW-16, CWI, Box 4079, 1009 AB Amsterdam, The Netherlands, 1949.

[Pfenning, 1988] F. Pfenning. Partial polymorphic type inference and higher order unification. In *Proc. ACM LISP and Functional Programming Conference*, pages 153–163, 1988.

[Prawitz, 1965] D. Prawitz. *Natural Deduction: A Proof-theoretical Study.* Almqvist and Wiksell, Stockholm, 1965.

[Quine, 1963] W. V. O. Quine. *Set Theory and its Logic.* Belknap Press, Cambridge, Massachussetts, 1963.

[Renardel de Lavalette, 1991] G. R. Renardel de Lavalette. Strictness analysis via abstract interpretation for recursively defined types, 1991. To appear in *Information and Computation.*

[Reynolds, 1974] J. C. Reynolds. Towards a theory of type structure. In Ehring *et al.*, editor, *Mathematical Foundations of Software Development*, volume 19 of *Lecture Notes in Computer Science*, pages 408–425. Springer, 1974.

[Reynolds, 1984] J. C. Reynolds. Polymorphism is not settheoretic. In *Semantics of Data Types*, volume 173 of *Lecture Notes in Computer Science*, pages 145–156, Berlin, 1984. Springer.

[Reynolds, 1985] J. C. Reynolds. Three approaches to type theory. In *Colloquium on Trees in Algebra and Programming (CAAP'85)*, volume 185 of *Lecture Notes in Computer Science*, pages 145–146, Berlin, 1985. Springer.

[Robinson, 1965] J. A. Robinson. A machine oriented logic based on the resolution principle. *J. ACM.*, 12(1):23–41, 1965.

[Schönfinkel, 1924] M. Schönfinkel. Über die Bausteinen der mathematische Logik. *Math. Ann.*, 92:305–316, 1924.

[Schwichtenberg, 1977] H. Schwichtenberg. Proof theory: applications of cut-elimination. In J. Barwise, editor, *Handbook of Mathematical Logic*, pages 867–895. North-Holland, 1977.

[Scott, 1976] D. S. Scott. Data types as lattices. *SIAM J. Comput.*, 5:522–587, 1976.

[Smullyan, 1985] R. Smullyan. *To Mock a Mockngbird.* Knopf, New York, 1985.

[Stanford Report, 1963] Stanford Report. Unpublished notes by w. a. howard, g. kreisel, r. j. parikh and w. w. tait, 1963.

[Stenlund, 1972] S. Stenlund. *Combinators, λ-terms and Proof Theory.* D. Reidel, Dordrecht, 1972.

[Swaen, 1989] M. D. G. Swaen. *Weak and Strong Sum-elimination in Intuitionistic Type Theory.* PhD thesis, University of Amsterdam, 1989.

[Tait, 1967] W. W. Tait. Intensional interpretation of functionals of finite type I. *J. Symbolic Logic*, 32:198–212, 1967.

[Tait, 1975] W. W. Tait. A realizability interpretation of the theory of species. In R. Parikh, editor, *Logic Colloquium (Boston)*, volume 453 of *Lecture Notes in Mathematics*, pages 240–251. Springer, 1975.

[Terlouw, 1982] J. Terlouw. On definition trees of ordinal recursive functionals: reduction of the recursion orders by means of type level raising. *J. Symbolic Logic*, 47(2):395–402, 1982.

[Terlouw, 1989] J. Terlouw. Een nadere bewijstheoretische analyse van GSTT's. Technical report, Dept. Computer Science, University of Nijmegen, Toernooiveld 1, 6525 ED Nijmegen, The Netherlands, 1989.

[Troelstra, 1973] A. S. Troelstra. *Metamathematical Investigations of Intuitionistic Arithmetic and Analysis*, volume 344 of *Lecture Notes in Mathematics.* Springer, 1973.

[Turing, 1937] A. M. Turing. Computability and λ-definability. *J. Symbolic Logic*, 2:153–163, 1937.

[van Bakel, 1991] S. J. van Bakel. Complete restrictions of the intersection type discipline. Technical report 89-22, Dept. Computer Science, Catholic University, Toernooiveld 1, 6525 ED Nijmegen, The Netherlands, 1991. To appear in *Theoretical Computer Science.*

[van Benthem Jutting, 1989] L. S. van Benthem Jutting. Personal communication, 1989.

[van Benthem Jutting, 1990] L. S. van Benthem Jutting. Typing in pure type systems. Technical report, Dept. Computer Science, University of Nijmegen, Toernooiveld 1, 6525 ED Nijmegen, The Netherlands, 1990.

[van Daalen, 1980] D. T. van Daalen. *The Language Theory of AUTOMATH.* PhD thesis, Technical University Eindhoven, The Netherlands, 1980.

[van Dalen, 1983] D. van Dalen. *Logic and structure.* Springer, 2nd edition, 1983.

[van Leeuwen, 1990] J. van Leeuwen, editor. *Handbook of Theoretical Computer Science.* Elsevier/MIT Press, 1990.

[Wadsworth, 1971] C. P. Wadsworth. *Semantics and Pragmatics of Lambda Calculus.* PhD thesis, Oxford University, 1971.

[Wand, 1987] M. Wand. A simple algorithm and proof for type inference. *Fund. Informaticae*, X:115–122, 1987.

[Whitehead and Russell, 1910] A. N. Whitehead and B. Russell. *Principia Mathematica.* Cambridge University Press, 1910.

[Zwicker, 1987] W. Zwicker. Playing games with games: the hypergame paradox. *Amer. Math. Monthly*, pages 507–514, 1987.

Elements of Algorithmic Proof

D. M. Gabbay

Contents

1 The theme of the chapter

Imagine an expert system running on a personal computer, say the *Sinclair QL*. You put the data $\mathbf{P}$ into the system and ask it queries Q. We represent the situation schematically as

$$\mathbf{P}?Q = \text{yes/no}$$

depending on the answer. Assume further that the system has a natural language interface which puts on the screen together with the answer some annotated trace of its search for a solution. Of course, we can relate to the expert system because we know what it is supposed to be doing and we can judge whether its answers make reasonable sense. Suppose now that we spill coffee onto the keyboard. Most personal computers will stop working, but in the case of the *QL*, it may continue to work. Assume however, that it now responds only to symbol input and output, having lost its natural language interface. We want to know whether what we have is 'logical' or not. We do not expect that the original expert system still works but maybe we have a new system which is still a logic?

We are faced with the problem of:

'What is a logic?'

All we have is a series of responses

$$\mathbf{P}?Q_i = \text{yes/no}$$

How do we recognize whether we have a logic at all?

Let us denote the relation

$$\mathbf{P}?Q = \text{ yes by } \mathbf{P} \vdash Q$$

Chapter 1 (background logic) adopted the point of view that a *monotonic logical system* is a *consequence relation.*

A consequence relation $\vdash$ is a set theoretic relation among the syntactical well-formed formulae of the proposed logic which satisfies the following conditions, with **P Q** and **R** denoting sets of wffs:

1. *Reflexivity*: $\mathbf{P} \vdash \mathbf{Q}$ if $\mathbf{P} \cap \mathbf{Q} \neq \varnothing$
2. *Monotonicity*: $\mathbf{P} \vdash \mathbf{Q}$ implies $\mathbf{P} \cup \mathbf{R} \vdash \mathbf{Q}$
3. *Transitivity (cut)*: $\mathbf{P} \cup \{A\} \vdash \mathbf{Q}$ and $\mathbf{P} \vdash \mathbf{Q} \cup \{\mathrm{A}\}$ imply $\mathbf{P} \vdash \mathbf{Q}$

In many cases the consequence relation $\vdash$ is given in the form, $\mathbf{P} \vdash A$, where A is a single formula. In this case the conditions reduce to:

1. $\mathbf{P} \vdash A$ if $A \in \mathbf{P}$ (reflexivity)
2. $\mathbf{P} \vdash A$ implies $\mathbf{P} \cup \mathbf{Q} \vdash A$ (monotonicity)
3. $\mathbf{P} \vdash A$ and $\mathbf{P} \cup \{A\} \vdash B$ imply $\mathbf{P} \vdash B$ (transitivity or cut).

We mentioned above that the consequence relation is 'given' to us. What do we mean by that? We mean that we accept any mathematical definition of the relation $\vdash$ which defines $\vdash$ uniquely. It need not be computable.

Here is an example:

Example 1.0.1. Intuitionistic Implication
The propositional language contains a set of atomic letters $Q = \{q_1, q_2, \ldots\}$. Well-formed formulae are built from atoms and the implication symbol '$\to$' in the usual way. The relation $\mathbf{P} \vdash A$ is defined mathematically as the smallest (in the set theoretical sense) relation $\vdash$ on the above syntax which satisfies (1), (2) and (3) above (i.e. the conditions of a consequence relation) and also (4) below (the deduction theorem).

4. Deduction theorem $\mathbf{P} \cup A \vdash B$ iff $\mathbf{P} \vdash A \to B$.

Of course to show that the above definition is mathematically sound, we have to prove that the smallest consequence relation $\vdash$ satisfying (4) actually exists. This we can show by proving that the intersection of any family of consequence relations satisfying (4) is also a consequence relation satisfying (4).

Exercise 1.0.2. Prove the existence of the consequence relation of the previous example.

Exercise 1.0.3. Consider the language with $\to$ and $\neg$ and the many valued truth tables below. Define $A_1, \ldots, A_n \vdash B$ iff $A_1 \to (A_2 \to \cdots (A_n \to B) \cdots)$ always gets value 1 under all assignments. What consequence relations do we get for each table? What logics are they?

$\to$	1	$\frac{1}{2}$	0
1	1	$\frac{1}{2}$	0
$\frac{1}{2}$	1	1	$\frac{1}{2}$
0	1	1	1

	$\neg$
1	0
$\frac{1}{2}$	$\frac{1}{2}$
0	1

Table 1

$\to$	1	2	3	4
1	1	2	3	4
2	1	1	3	3
3	1	2	1	2
4	1	1	1	1

	$\neg$
1	4
2	3
3	2
4	1

Table 2

It is convenient to refer to the above considerations as the *mathematical stage* in defining a logic. We mean that $\vdash$ is defined *mathematically*, but not necessarily *algorithmically*. Given $\mathbf{P}$ and A, we do not necessarily give a computer program to check whether $\mathbf{P} \vdash A$ holds or not, nor can we necessarily recursively generate all pairs $(\mathbf{P}, Q)$ for which $\mathbf{P} \vdash Q$ holds. For example, how do we check, in the case of intuitionistic logic, whether:

$$\{A, ((B \to A) \to B) \to B\} \vdash ?B$$

We have no algorithm to use! Here the notation $\vdash ?$ means we do not know whether $\vdash$ holds or not.

We regard the second stage in the presentation of a logic as the *algorithmic proof* stage. This means that we actually have an algorithm for generating pairs $(\mathbf{P}, A)$ such that $\mathbf{P} \vdash A$ holds. We mean here an algorithm in the mathematical sense, i.e. some given procedure for checking whether $\mathbf{P} \vdash A$ holds. In logical terms this means that the set of pairs $(\mathbf{P}, Q)$ such that $\mathbf{P} \vdash Q$, is recursively enumerable. It need not be a practical automated algorithm which is actually implemented. So, for example, a recursive function generating the pairs $(\mathbf{P}, Q)$ such that $\mathbf{P} \vdash Q$, is a mathematical algorithm in our sense. On the other hand, a decision procedure in polynomial time for checking whether $\mathbf{P} \vdash ?Q$ holds could serve as an automated practical algorithm. It is quite possible that the set of pairs $(\mathbf{P}, Q)$ such that $\mathbf{P} \vdash Q$, is actually recursive. For reasons of convenience the system may initially be presented as an algorithmic proof system where it is not immediately clear that it is indeed recursive. In such a case we may obtain an effective decision procedure from the algorithmic proof system via optimization. Of course some logics can be presented directly in their algorithmic stage. We can give a recipe for checking whether $\mathbf{P} \vdash ?A$ holds or not, and provided we show that the relation: 'The procedure for checking $\mathbf{P} \vdash ?A$ terminates with answer yes' is a consequence relation, we have properly defined a logic.

For some logics $\vdash$ (i.e. consequence relations) which can be defined mathematically, there are no algorithms for enumerating the cases when $\mathbf{P} \vdash A$ holds. So, for these non-recursively enumerable (some are even not arithmetical) logics there is no algorithmic stage.

What about the automated stage? This stage is a practical implementation of an algorithmic stage. It should be sound (i.e. if the automated stage says that $\mathbf{P} \vdash A$ should hold then it does indeed hold) and possibly complete (i.e. if $\mathbf{P} \vdash A$ does hold then the automated stage can confirm that). We say 'possibly' complete because we do not necessarily require completeness. Most practical provers are not known to be complete. In practice we may have that the set of pairs $(\mathbf{P}, Q)$ such that $\mathbf{P} \vdash Q$, may be Σ_1 or Π_1 or even of some higher complexity. The automated stage may give us procedures which are sound (but not necessarily complete) for generating members of the sets and/or procedures for generating non-members of the set (non-theorem). In general the set of non-theorems of a logic is not well studied. There are no significant proof systems for non-theorems.

The relationship between the logic $\vdash$ and any of its automated stages will become more clear when we develop some examples in later sections. We can regard the algorithmic stage as a *proof checker* stage and the automated stage as a *proof finder* stage. The reason for this terminology is that an algorithmic proof system is generally RE and can effectively be used in general mainly to verify, for a given proof, if it is correct in the system. On the other hand, an effective (recursive in polynomial time on average) proof system can be used for finding proofs.

Meanwhile, here is how these stages might look for the case of classical logic.

Example 1.0.4 (Classical implication). The syntax is as in the previous example, i.e. is the same as intuitionistic implication.
Mathematical stage: $\mathbf{P} \vdash A$ is defined according to the classical truth tables, in the usual traditional manner.
Algorithmic stage: A Gentzen system for classical implication.
Automated stage: A machine implementation of the Gentzen system.

Note that in this example the truth table method can serve as the algorithmic stage as well. An automated stage for the truth table method would then be a (possibly incomplete but a sound) machine implementation of a truth table checker.

For any one consequence relation there can be more than one mathematical presentations and many algorithmic presentations. Each algorithmic presentation may have many machine implementations.

Thus there are many implementations of various logics around. The theme of the three-stage presentation of logics is important not only from the classification point of view but also from the theoretical point of view.

Consider an algorithmic proof system for a logic **L1**. Let us call it **S1**. Thus whenever $\mathbf{P} \vdash_{\mathbf{L1}} A$ holds, the algorithmic procedure **S1** would succeed when applied to $\mathbf{P} \vdash ?A$. **S1** contains manipulative rules. These rules can be tinkered with, changed, modified and made more efficient. It happens in many practical cases that by making *natural* changes in **S1** we get a new algorithmic system **S2** which defines a new logic **L2**. **L2** may be a well-known logic already mathematically defined, with completely different motivation and the insight that **S2** is an algorithmic system for **L2** can deepen our understanding of **L2**.

We thus can obtain a network of logics interconnected on many levels, mathematical and algorithmic, where different logics can be obtained in different ways from other logics in the network by making some *natural looking* local changes.

Thus our view of logic is also procedural. The declarative nature is only a component in the formulation of the logic. This is a radical departure from the traditional point of view. We thus intuitively define the notion of a recursively enumerable logical system $\mathbf{L}$ as a pair $\mathbf{L} = (\vdash, \mathbf{S})$, where $\vdash$ is a mathematically defined consequence relation and **S** is an algorithmic proof system for $\vdash$. The algorithmic system is sound and complete for $\vdash$. Thus different algorithmic systems for the same $\vdash$ give rise to different logics, according to our definition.

To make this new notion more intuitively acceptable to the reader consider the following example. Take a Gentzen style formulation for intuitionistic logic. A minor change in the rules will yield classical logic. Another minor change will yield linear logic. Thus from the point of view of the algorithmic proof system (i.e. Gentzen proof theory) intuitionistic logic and classical logic are neighbours or brother and sister.

Now consider classical logic from the point of view of the two-valued truth table. It is easy to generalize from two-values to Łukasiewicz n-valued logic L_n (see Exercise 1.0.3 for the three-valued table). From the truth table point of view, classical logic and L_n are neighbours. There is no nice Gentzen formulation for L_n and so it cannot be directly related to intuitionistic logic.

Now consider a Hilbert style presentation of classical logic, intuitionistic logic and Łukasiewicz n-valued logics. Such axiomatizations exist, at least for the implicational fragments. Through the Hilbert presentation, the relationship between the three systems is very clear. Some axioms are dropped and/or added from one to obtain the other.

Our view is that a different algorithmic proof presentation of a logic (in the old sense, i.e. the set of theorems) gives us different logics (in the new sense). Thus we have three distinct logics (all versions of classical logic) namely:

- Classical logic truth table formulation;
- Classical logic Hilbert system formulation;
- Classical logic Gentzen formulation.

These are different also from the point of view of the kind of information on the logic they highlight. Certainly a Gentzen system and a Hilbert system give us a completely different type and style of information about classical logic (old sense).

The reader may now ask again the question of why bother at all with the mathematical consequence relation as a logic and why not only talk of algorithmic proof. The answer is that we may still need the conceptual characterization residing in the mathematical definition.

Logics have meaning and intended interpretation and possible application areas and all these features usually manifest themselves in the mathematical definition of $\vdash$. We need **S** to compute, and we need $\vdash$ to understand and motivate. We need both!

The idea can be illustrated with the following example:

Example 1.0.5 (Modal logic S4).

1. We illustrate our point that even with the same $\mathbf{S}, (\Vdash, \mathbf{S})$ and $(\vDash, \mathbf{S})$, for different $\vDash$ and $\Vdash$ can be defined and perceived as *not the same logic!*

2. Consider a language with atoms $p, q, r, \ldots$ the classical connectives $\neg, \wedge$ and the unary connective $\Box$. Let h be a function assigning to each atom a set of points in the Euclidean plane $\mathcal{R}^2$. Let

$$\begin{array}{ll} h(A \wedge B) & = h(A) \cap h(B) \\ h(\neg A) & = \text{ complement of } h(A) \\ h(\Box A) & = \text{topological interior of } h(A). \end{array}$$

Let $\vDash A$ be defined as $\forall h[h(A) = \mathcal{R}^2]$
Let $A_1, \ldots, A_n \vDash B$ iff $\forall h[h(A_i) = \mathcal{R}^2$ for $i = 1, \ldots, n \Rightarrow h(B) = \mathcal{R}^2]$.
Then $\vDash$ is a consequence relation.
Let $A \to B$ be defined as $\neg(A \wedge \neg B)$ and let $A \leftrightarrow B$ be defined as $(A \to B) \wedge (B \to A)$. Then we have for example: $\vDash \Box(A \wedge B) \Leftrightarrow \Box A \wedge \Box B$.

3. Let $*$ be a translation from the previous language into classical logic. With each atom q associate a unary predicate $Q(t)$, with one free variable t. Let R be a binary relation symbol. Translate as follows (note that the translation function depends on t):

$$\begin{array}{ll} (q)^*_t & = Q(t). \\ (A \wedge B)^*_t & = A^*(t) \wedge B^*(t). \\ (\neg A)^*_t & = \neg A^*(t). \\ (\Box A)^*_t & = \forall s(tRs \to (A)^*_s). \end{array}$$

Let $A_1, \ldots, A_n \Vdash A$ hold iff in predicate logic one can prove in Classical logic
$\vdash [\forall x(xRx) \wedge \forall xyz(xRy \wedge yRz \to xRz)] \to \forall t(\bigwedge_i (A_i)^*_t \to (A)^*_t)$.

The two consequence relations $\vDash$ and $\Vdash$ are defined completely differently. They are the same, however, from the mathematical point of view. That is, $\mathbf{P} \Vdash A$ iff $\mathbf{P} \vDash A$ holds. Their meaning is not the same.

To define an algorithmic system for $\vDash$ or $\Vdash$ we can present a Hilbert style formulation. We can also use any theorem prover for classical logic, if we want, and obtain yet another algorithmic system.

4. The following is a Hilbert style axiomatization of our system:

   (a) Any instance of a truth functional tautology

(b) $\Box(A \to B) \to (\Box A \to \Box B)$

(c) $\Box A \to A$

(d) $\Box A \to \Box\Box A$

(e) $\dfrac{\vdash A, \vdash A \to B}{\vdash B}$ and $\dfrac{\vdash A}{\vdash \Box A.}$

Define $A_1, \ldots, A_n \vdash_{\mathbf{S4}} A$ iff $\vdash \bigwedge A_i \to A$.

There are further considerations in favour of viewing a logical system as a pair $(\vdash, \mathbf{S}_\vdash)$. We have considered monotonic consequence relations $\vdash$. There are many non-monotonic logics and consequence relations which have been studied in the area of logic and AI. These have essentially the property that $\mathbf{P} \vdash A$ depends on $\mathbf{P}$ in its entirety. So $\mathbf{P} \vdash A$ may hold but $\mathbf{P}, X \vdash A$ may not hold because the set of assumptions has changed.

Non-monotonic systems can be more easily presented as pairs $(\vdash, \mathbf{S}_\vdash)$. We cannot go into more details here.[1] We give an example of a non monotonic rule:

$\mathbf{P} \vdash \neg a$ iff a cannot be deduced from $\mathbf{P}$
(a is not the consequent of any rule in $\mathbf{P}$).

Clearly we can have $\mathbf{P} \vdash \neg a$ but $\mathbf{P}, a \not\vdash \neg a$.

What is the theme of the chapter? We have put forward the view that a logical system in the new sense is a pair $(\vdash, \mathbf{S}_\vdash)$ of a mathematically defined $\vdash$ and an algorithmic proof system $\mathbf{S}_\vdash$ for it. The family of logics (old sense) which this chapter is going to study is classical logic, intuitionistic logic, linear logic and some intermediate logic. The algorithmic proof system we want to present for these logics are all variations on a goal directed implication based deduction. This approach is new, and we introduce it in a natural way. We start with the mathematical formulation of intuitionistic implication as the smallest consequence relation satisfying the deduction theorem and ask ourselves, given the above definition of $\vdash$, how we find out whether $\mathbf{P} \vdash ?Q$ for a given $\mathbf{P}$ and Q.

The steps we take will be natural and will almost force us onto the goal directed algorithmic proof system of this chapter. Having defined the new system, we try to optimize it. The natural changes which suggest themselves will lead to variations in the algorithmic system which we will find (to our surprise) define neighbouring logics such as classical logic and linear logic.

There is another way of looking at the material of this chapter. We can start with the logic programming approach to Horn-clause computation in

[1] In the companion *Handbook of Logic in AI and Logic Programming*, an entire volume is devoted to non-monotonic reasoning.

intuitionistic or classical logic namely, the reading of any Horn-clause as a procedure

$$\Delta, a_1 \wedge a_2 \rightarrow c \quad ?c$$

reduces to

$$\Delta, a_1 \wedge a_2 \rightarrow c \quad ?a_1 \wedge a_2$$

This procedural way of looking at clauses is equivalent to the declarative way namely to $\vdash$ provability (which for Horn-clauses coincides for classical and for intuitionistic logics). We ask ourselves, can we extend this backward reasoning, goal directed paradigm to all of classical and neighbouring logics? In other words, can we have a logic programming (Prolog) like proof system presentation for full classical, intuitionistic linear and other logics? To achieve that, we have to extend our Prolog computation steps to handle implications, disjunctions, and quantifiers in the goal position. This can indeed be done, and we end up with the algorithmic proof system of this chapter.

To summarize, in this chapter we present a new algorithmic proof system for intuitionistic logic. This new system can be motivated in two ways. Either as an extension of the Prolog like computation of the Horn-clause fragment to the full logic or as an algorithmic system which we 'discover' through manipulating the deduction theorem. The chapter proceeds to discover the algorithmic system. We try to turn this algorithmic system into an implementable automated system. We obtain classical logic and other logics by making natural optimizing changes in the rules of the algorithmic system. Each new step will follow naturally from the previous steps. We conclude the chapter by describing a general algorithmic framework which unifies many known logics.

The next section starts with the mathematical definition of the intuitionistic implication via the deduction theorem. We develop an algorithmical proof system in a natural way by using only the means at our disposal. We further modify it and change it and get classical logic as well as other logics. Let's see how it's done!

2 Intuitionistic implication

The consequence relation for intuitionistic propositional implication is defined as the smallest consequence relation $\vdash$ satisfying the deduction theorem:

$$\mathbf{P}, A \vdash B \text{ iff } \mathbf{P} \vdash A \rightarrow B$$

The above is the mathematical stage for $\vdash$. We want to develop the algorithmic stage, i.e. given $\mathbf{P}$ and A, we want to find computation rules for deciding whether $\mathbf{P} \vdash A$ holds or not. We write $\mathbf{P}, A$ as an alternative notation for $\mathbf{P} \cup \{A\}$.

Let us use the terminology that $\mathbf{P}$ is the data and A is the goal. We want to know whether the goal follows from the data. What can we do?

The elements of $\mathbf{P}$ and A are all either atoms or implications of the form $B \to C$.

If A is of the form $A = A_1 \to A_2$, it is a sound policy to use the deduction theorem and try to show $\mathbf{P}, A_1 \vdash A_2$ instead of $\mathbf{P} \vdash A_1 \to A_2$. We do not have to be clever to figure this out. The deduction theorem is all that we have available.

The reason it is a good idea is because we simplify the goal to be proved and at the same time increase the data. This increases our chance of success, because the logic is monotonic. The more assumptions the better. This simplification is obviously natural.

We can adopt this as:

HR1: *Heuristic Rule 1*: (Simplification of goal)
Reduce any problem of the form $\mathbf{P} \vdash ?A_1 \to A_2$ to the problem $\mathbf{P}, A_1 \vdash ?A_2$.

Here we used the notation $\mathbf{P} \vdash ?A$ to represent the question 'does A follow from $\mathbf{P}$?'. We desperately need more insight. We turn our attention to $\mathbf{P}$. It contains elements of the form $B \to C$ or atoms; what can an element of the form $B \to C$ prove?

The formulae involved are $B, C, B \to C$, and $C \to B$. The possible provability combinations are listed below. (We can omit $C \to B$ for reasons of symmetry.)

1 a $B, C, B \to C \vdash ?B$
 b $B, C, B \to C \vdash ?C$
 c $B, C, B \to C \vdash ?B \to C$
2 a $C, B \to C \vdash ?B$
 b $C, B \to C \vdash ?C$
 c $C, B \to C \vdash ?B \to C$
3 a $B, B \to C \vdash ?B$
 b $B, B \to C \vdash ?C$
 c $B, B \to C \vdash ?B \to C$
4 a $B, C \vdash ?B$
 b $B, C \vdash ?C$
 c $B, C \vdash ?B \to C$
5 a $B \vdash ?B$
 b $B \vdash ?C$
 c $B \vdash ?B \to C$
6 a $C \vdash ?B$
 b $C \vdash ?C$
 c $C \vdash ?B \to C$
7 a $B \to C \vdash ?B$
 b $B \to C \vdash ?C$
 c $B \to C \vdash ?B \to C$

It is easy to see that the interesting cases are the ones which can immediately be seen to be true by the properties of the consequence relation. By 'immediately' we mean that we use the property of reflexivity, i.e. the right-hand side shows as a member of the left-hand side. These cases are 1a, 1b and 1c and also 2b, 2c, 3a, 3c, 4a, 4b, 5a, 6b, 7c.

We know that in the above cases the data does prove ($\vdash$) the goal by reflexivity. Since we have monotonicity, the above list of cases is generated by the sublist containing 5a, 6b, and 7c. The other cases in the list are obtained from the sublist by adding formulae on the left. We can take out the question mark since we know that $\vdash$ holds by reflexivity.

Cases like 5b and 6a are obviously hopeless because (since the consequence relation is assumed to be minimal for the deduction theorem to hold) one atom cannot logically imply another. We thus get the following reduction table. We wrote the currently irreducible cases explicitly in the table to enhance clarity. We also put ? for cases we do not yet know the answer to.

Case	**Case reduced to**	**Does it hold?**
1a	5a	yes
1b	6b	yes
1c	7c	yes
2a	$C, B \to C \vdash ?B$	?
2b	6b	yes
2c	7c	yes
3a	5a	yes
3b	$B, B \to C \vdash ?C$	?
3c	7c	yes
4a	5a	yes
4b	6b	yes
4c	$B, C, \vdash ?B \to C$	?
5a	$B \vdash ?B$	yes
5b	$B \vdash ?C$	no
5c	$B \vdash ?B \to C$	?
6a	$C \vdash ?B$	no
6b	$C \vdash ?C$	yes
6c	$C \vdash ?B \to C$	?
7a	$B \to C \vdash ?B$	?
7b	$B \to C \vdash ?C$	?
7c	$B \to C \vdash ?B \to C$	yes

Table 2.1

Note that in Table 2.1, case 4c reduces to case 6c if 6c does hold but we do not know that at this stage. Similarly 3b reduces to 7b in case 7b holds. 5b and 6a are essentially the same.

Thus we continue our search for more valid (yes) cases by considering 5a and 7c:

5a $B \vdash B$
7c $B \to C \vdash B \to C$

We have not yet used the deduction theorem and the transitivity for $\vdash$. Let us see what we can get.

Using the deduction theorem, the only means at our disposal, we get:

5a1 $\vdash B \to B$
7c1 $\vdash (B \to C) \to (B \to C)$
7c2 $B, B \to C \vdash C$

7c2 is case 3b.

Let us now consider 2b, 2c, 3a, 3c, 4a, 5b. These are obtained from 5a, 6b, 7c by adding a formula on the left. Let us examine generally what can happen when we put a new formula X on the left. Again we consider 5a and 7c. We remember that X can be B, C and $B \to C$. We get:

8 a $X, B \vdash B$
b $X, B \to C \vdash B \to C$
c $X \vdash B \to B$
d $B \vdash X \to B$
e $(B \to C) \vdash X \to (B \to C)$
f $X \vdash (B \to C) \to (B \to C)$
g $B, B \to C \vdash X \to C$

Case 8d for $X = B$ is case 6c with the letters B and C interchanged. Thus the answer is yes in the table for 6c and 4c.

The only cases left in the table are:

2a $C, B \to C \vdash ?B$
5c $B \vdash ?B \to C$
7a $B \to C \vdash ?B$
7b $B \to C \vdash ?C$

Let us use the deduction theorem again on the remaining cases. The only conclusive result we get is for case 5c.

$$B \vdash ?B \to C$$

becomes

$$B, B \vdash ?C$$

which is the same as

$$B \vdash ?C$$

and the answer is no.

This is as far as we can go using reflexivity, monotonicity and the deduction theorem. We have not used the cut rule yet. Can it help clarify the remaining cases?

To use the cut rule, we have to take each case of the form $X_1, X_2, X \vdash Y$ and try $X_1, X_2, \vdash ?X$. If the answer is yes, then we can get

$$X_1, X_2 \vdash Y$$

by cut. Thus since we already have some partial results we should try the cases 2a, 7a, 7b, which are the ones we do not know about and are of the form $X_1, X_2 \vdash ?Y$ and seek a case in the table of the form $X_1, X_2, X \vdash Y$ where the answer is yes and try for

$$X_1, X_2 \vdash ?Y.$$

We follow the above procedures and get the cases shown in Table 2.2:

Initial case	**Cases to check**	**Because the following holds**
2a: $C, B \rightarrow C \vdash ?B$	$C, B \rightarrow C \vdash ?B$	1a
7a:$B \rightarrow C \vdash ?B$	$B \rightarrow C \vdash ?C$	If 2a gets answer yes
7b: $B \rightarrow C \vdash ?C$	$B \rightarrow C \vdash B$	3b

Table 2.2

The above shows that the really interesting cases left are 7b and 7a. There is one more use of the cut rule which can help us. We used cut (positively) upwards, to get $X_1, X_2 \vdash ?Y$, we looked for cases where $X_1, X_2, X \vdash Y$ and tried $X_1, X_2 \vdash ?X$. We can use cut (negatively) downwards, namely to show that $X_1, X_2 \vdash ?Y$ is not possible, we assume in order to get a contradiction that the answer is yes and deduce a case to which we know the answer should not be yes.

Assume the answer to case 2a, namely; $C, B \rightarrow C \vdash ?B$, were yes. Then since $C \vdash B \rightarrow C$ (Case 6c) we get by cut $C \vdash B$ which should not hold.

Thus the answer to 2a and by monotonocity to 7a is no and we are left with 7b as the only open case in Table 2.1.

This is as far as we can go.

So far we have only one heuristic rule, HR1, which says we should simplify the goal. If we follow this rule throughout, we end up with atomic goals. We have also clarified all entries in Table 2.1 except 7c. Let us see which entries can give us atomic goals. These are:

5a $B \vdash B$
3b $B, B \to C$
7b $B \to C \vdash ?C$

The other cases either reduce to one of the above cases or are obviously hopeless (i.e. expected not to hold).

How can we make use of the above?

We have decided to use the deduction theorem to simplify. This is Heuristic Rule 1.

For the purpose of generating more true logical theorems the only other important rule we discovered is (3b). This is the well-known modus ponens. We thus adopt the following:

HR2 : *Heuristic Rule 2*: (Backward chaining heuristic) To show $\mathbf{P} \vdash ?C$ try and find whether there is a $B \to C \in \mathbf{P}$ and try to show $\mathbf{P} \vdash ?B$.

We need an immediate lemma, to assure us that this is a sound rule.

Lemma 2.0.1. *[Soundness of backward chaining]*
$\mathbf{P} \vdash B$ *and* $B \to C \in \mathbf{P}$ *imply* $\mathbf{P} \vdash C$

Proof. $\mathbf{P}, B \vdash C$ (modus ponens)
$\mathbf{P} \vdash B$ (given)
hence by cut $\mathbf{P} \vdash C$. ∎

We formulated two nice and useful rules, but we still have a minor problem. On the one hand we are reducing the goal to atomic form and on the other other hand we like to use modus ponens (Heuristic Rule 2). We would therefore like the items in the data to be of the form $B \to$ atom. Most data items will not be of this form. The general data item is of the form $C_0 \to C$, where C is not necesssarily atomic. If it is not, then it has the form $C_1 \to C_2$. Continuing to expand C_2 we find that the general form is $A = C_0 \to (C_1 \to \ldots \to (C_n \to q)\ldots)$, with q atomic. C_i may not be atomic. Thus when we try to check whether $\mathbf{P}?y$, y atomic, we may find that y is embedded in a formula A as above, either (1) as $y = q$ or (2) as an atom inside C_i.

Let us now explore the seemingly easier case, just to get a feel of what can happen. We check the case of $y = q$. The case where y shows up nested in some C_i seems difficult to us at this stage.

We are thus led naturally to initially explore what can be done in the case of the form

1. $\mathbf{P}, C_0 \to \ldots \to (C_n \to y)\ldots) \vdash ?y$

Heuristic Rule 2 can be extended to this case provided we use the rule:

$$C_0, \ldots, C_n, (C_0 \to (\ldots \to (C_n \to y))\ldots) \vdash y$$

Theorem 2.0.2. *[Generalized deduction]*

1. $x_1, \ldots, x_n, x_1 \to (x_2 \cdots \to ((x_n \to y)\ldots) \vdash y$
2. $x_1 \to (x_2 \to \ldots(x_m \to y)\ldots) \vdash z_1 \to (z_2 \to \ldots(z_m \to y)\ldots)$ *whenever* $\{x_1 \ldots x_m\} = \{z_1, \ldots, z_m\}$.

Proof. For (1) use MP, for (2), use the deduction theorem and then modus ponens. ∎

If we had conjunction in the language we would write $x_1 \to (x_2 \to y)$ as $x_1 \wedge x_2 \to y$ and this would allow us to reduce all data to the form $B \to$ atom. $x_1 \to (x_2 \to \ldots \to (x_n \to y)\ldots)$ would be equivalent to $x_1 \wedge \ldots \wedge x_n \to y$.

Without conjunctions, we need a rewrite representation.

In view of (2.0.2), any formula of the form $x_1 \to (x_2 \to \ldots \to (x_n \to y)\ldots)$ can be represented as

$$\{x_1, \ldots, x_n\} \to y$$

We can now modify Heuristic Rule 2 as follows:

HR2.1: *Heuristic Rule 2 (modified)*: To show $\mathbf{P} \vdash ?y$, for atomic y, show

$\mathbf{P} \vdash ?B_1$

$\vdots$

$\mathbf{P} \vdash ?B_n$

provided $B_1 \to (\ldots \to (B_n \to y) \in \mathbf{P}$.

We again must check soundness.

Lemma 2.0.3. *If* $\mathbf{P} \vdash B_i, i = 1 \ldots n$
and $B_1 \to (\ldots \to (B_n \to y)\ldots) \in \mathbf{P}$
then $\mathbf{P} \vdash y$.

Proof. Use modus ponens once, the deduction theorem $n - 1$ times and cut n times. ∎

We still have to check case 2, where we have $\mathbf{P}, C_1 \to (\ldots(C_n \to z)\ldots) \vdash ?y$ and y appears in some C_i or maybe $y = C_i$. To get a clue as to what to do in this case let us check a simplified case of two nested implications, with $y = C_i$.

(1.1) $\mathbf{P}, x \to (y \to z) \vdash ?y$

(1.2) $\mathbf{P}, x \to (y \to z) \vdash ?x$

The first case is new. The second case is the same as 7a (with $(y \to z)$ taken as a unit) of our table to which the answer was no. We further note that if $\mathbf{P}$ contains x, we can reduce (1.1) using modus ponens to (1.2). The impression is that for the case 2 of $y = C_i$ or y appears inside C_i, we should not hope for any results.

Let us stop here and consolidate what we have so far.

We find that we do have a candidate algorithmic proof system, consisting of Heuristic Rules 1 and 2.1. We know that it is sound but we don't know if it is complete.
Soundness means that:
If $\mathbf{P} \vdash ?A$ succeeds according to the computation rules then $\mathbf{P} \vdash A$
Completeness means that:
If $\mathbf{P} \vdash A$ then $\mathbf{P} \vdash ?A$ succeeds according to the computation rules.

How can we show completeness? Why should we expect to be able to show completeness? We were just playing with the mathematical definition of $\vdash$ (i.e. the deduction theorem) and we found some heuristic rules. Maybe there are more to be found? The answer is that we don't necessarily expect completeness. By trying to *prove* completeness, we may discover we need more rules and then try to adopt them. This is a sound policy. We can only gain. How do we attempt to prove completeness?

We must show that the algorithmic system is the same as the mathematically defined system. How was the intuitionistic implication system mathematically defined? It was defined as the smallest consequence relation satisfying the deduction theorem. We thus have an obvious way to attempt to show completeness. We show that the algorithmic system gives rise to a relation which is a consequence relation satisfying the deduction theorem.

In other words, we have to prove the deduction theorem and the conditions on the consequence relation for our Heuristic Rules 1 and 2.1. We summarize what we have to show in:

Theorem 2.0.4.

1. $\mathbf{P} \vdash ?A$ *succeeds if* $A \in \mathbf{P}$
2. *If* $\mathbf{P} \vdash ?A$ *succeeds then* $\mathbf{P} \cup \mathbf{P}' \vdash ?A$ *succeeds*
3. *If* $\mathbf{P} \vdash ?A$ *succeeds and* $\mathbf{P}, A \vdash ?B$ *succeeds then* $\mathbf{P} \vdash ?B$ *succeeds*
4. $\mathbf{P} \vdash ?(A \to B)$ *succeeds iff* $\mathbf{P}, A \vdash ?B$ *succeeds.*

We can expect to prove the above theorem by induction on the computation. We therefore need to present the computation rules rigorously and formulate them in a way which is convenient for the proof. This we do in the next section. Note that at this stage we are not at all sure that we can prove this theorem. We hope possibly to gain more insight from the attempt. The theorem will be proved in the next section. This theorem will yield completeness. Soundness is clear because the rules were discovered through manipulating the deduction theorem.

3 An algorithmic proof system for intuitionistic implication

We begin with a formal definition of the intuitionistic system.

Definition 3.0.1. Let $Q = \{q_1, q_2, \ldots\}$ be a set of atomic propositions and let $\rightarrow$ be implication. We recursively define the notions of a well-formed formula A, the set $\mathbf{B}[A]$ called the body of A, and the atom $\mathbf{H}[A]$ called the head of A.

(a) any atom q is a well-formed formula. $\mathbf{H}[q] = q$ and $\mathbf{B}[q] = \varnothing$.

(b) If A and B are formulae then also $A \rightarrow B$ is a formula, with

$$\mathbf{H}[A \rightarrow B] = \mathbf{H}[B]$$

and

$$\mathbf{B}[A \rightarrow B] = \{A\} \cup \mathbf{B}[B]$$

We can now give an algorithmic computation for deciding whether $\mathbf{P} \vdash ?A$ holds or not. $\mathbf{P}$ is the database and A is the goal. We define the computation in terms of a computation tree. The computation is based on the two Heuristic Rules **HR1** and **HR2**, which reflect our intuitive understanding of the computation.

HR1: $\mathbf{P} \vdash A \rightarrow B$ if $\mathbf{P}, A \vdash B$

HR2: $\mathbf{P} \vdash q$, for q atomic if for some $A \in \mathbf{P}, \mathbf{H}[A] = q$ and for all $B \in \mathbf{B}[A], \mathbf{P} \vdash B$.

In view of the relevance of the $\mathbf{B}$ function to computation, it is convenient to represent all formulae in a ready for computation form.

Definition 3.0.2. An RC-clause (ready for computation clause) is defined by induction as follows:

1. Any atomic q is an RC-clause, with head $\mathbf{H}[q] = q$ and body $\mathbf{B}[q] = \varnothing$.
2. If A_i are RC-clauses and q is atomic then $B = \{A_i\} \to q$ is an RC-clause with head $\mathbf{H}[B] = q$ and body $\mathbf{B}[B] = \{A_i\}$.

Note that if we had conjunctions in the language then any RC-clause A would be equivalent to $\wedge\mathbf{B}(A) \to \mathbf{H}(A)$.

Our computation procedure is defined on RC-clauses. $\mathbf{P}_0$ denotes a set of RC-clauses referred to as data and $\mathbf{G}_0$ denotes a set of RC-clauses referred to as goals.

We follow consistently our convention of writing A instead of the singleton $\{A\}$. $\mathbf{A}$ denotes $\{A_1, \ldots, A_n\}$. In the sequel we regard a formular $A_1 \to \ldots (\to (A_n \to q)$ as an *RC*-clause $\{A_1, \ldots, A_n\} \to q$ when convienient.

Definition 3.0.3. Let $\mathbf{P}_0$ be a database and let $\mathbf{G}_0$ be a goal. A quadruple $(T, \leq, 0, V)$ is said to be a successful computation tree of the goal $\mathbf{G}_0$ from $\mathbf{P}_0$ if the following conditions hold:

(a) $(T, \leq, 0)$ is a finite tree; T is its set of nodes, 0 is its root, and for s, t in $T, t \leq s$ means that $t = s$ or t lies closer to the root than s, on the same path.

(b) V is a labelling function on T. For each $t \in T, V(t)$ is a pair $(\mathbf{P}, \mathbf{G})$, where $\mathbf{P}$ is a database and $\mathbf{G}$ is a goal.

(c) $V(0) = (\mathbf{P}_0, \mathbf{G}_0)$. We say the clauses of $\mathbf{P}_0$ are *put in the data at node 0.*

(d) If $V(t) = (\mathbf{P}, \mathbf{G})$ and $\mathbf{G} = \{A_1, \ldots, A_n\}$, with A_i RC-clauses, then the node t has exactly n immediate successors in the tree, say $t_1, \ldots, t_n$ with $V(t_i) = (\mathbf{P}, A_i)$.

(e) If $V(t) = (\mathbf{P}, \mathbf{G})$, and $\mathbf{G} = \mathbf{A} \to q$, then t has exactly one immediate successor in the tree, say s, with $V(s) = (\mathbf{P} \cup \mathbf{A}, q)$. We say that the clauses in $\mathbf{A}$ were *put in the data at node* t.

(f) If $V(t) = (\mathbf{P}, q)$, with q atomic, then exactly one of the following holds.

 (f1) t has no immediate successors and $q \in \mathbf{P}$. We say that $q \in \mathbf{P}$ is *used at node* t.

(f2) t has exactly one immediate successor s in the tree with $V(s) = (\mathbf{P}, \mathbf{A})$ and with $(\mathbf{A} \rightarrow q) \in \mathbf{P}$. In this case we say that $\mathbf{A} \rightarrow q$ is *used at node* $t \in T$.

(g) Note that it is possible in case f2 that $q \in \mathbf{P}$. Nevertheless the computation goes through $\mathbf{A} \rightarrow q$. Further note that the databases involved need not be finite. In a successful computation tree only a finite number of clauses from the database will be used in the sense mentioned above.

Lemma 3.0.4. *Let* $\mathbf{Q}$ *be a database. Let* V_1 *be the function defined by* $V_1(t) = (\mathbf{P} \cup \mathbf{Q}, \mathbf{G})$ *if* $V(t) = (\mathbf{P}, \mathbf{G})$, *then* $(T, \leq, 0, V_1)$ *is a successful computation tree of* $\mathbf{G}_0$ *from* $\mathbf{P}_0 \cup \mathbf{Q}$.

Proof. Observe that 3.0.3 still holds for the new tree. Especially note remark (g) in 3.0.3.

We use the notation $\mathbf{P}?\mathbf{G} = 1$ to denote that there exists a successful computation tree for $(\mathbf{P}, \mathbf{G})$. (This suggests $\mathbf{P}?\mathbf{G} = 0$ for finite failure and $\mathbf{P}?\mathbf{G} = \perp$ for looping. We shall address these concepts at a later stage.) ∎

Theorem 3.0.5.

(a) $\mathbf{P}?G = 1$ *if* $G \in \mathbf{P}$

(b) $\mathbf{P}?G = 1$ *implies* $\mathbf{P} \cup \mathbf{Q}\ ?G = 1$

(c) $\mathbf{P}?(\mathbf{A} \rightarrow q) = 1$ *iff* $\mathbf{P} \cup \mathbf{A}\ ?q = 1$.

Proof. (a) is proved by induction on the complexity of G (defined in the usual way). If G is an atom q the result is obvious.

If G is $\mathbf{A} \rightarrow q$, with $\mathbf{A} = \{A_1, \ldots, A_n\}$, then we use the computation Rule **HR1** and check $\mathbf{P}, A_1, \ldots, A_n?q$.

Since $G \in \mathbf{P}$ using **HR2**, the problem reduces to the n computations.

$$\mathbf{P}, A_1, \ldots, A_n?A_i, i = 1 \ldots n,$$

which succeed by the induction hypothesis.

(b) follows from 3.0.4

(c) is obvious.

∎

In order to prove closure under cut we need the following:

Theorem 3.0.6. $\mathbf{P}?\mathbf{A} \to q = 1$ *and* $\mathbf{P}?\mathbf{A} = 1$ *imply* $\mathbf{P}?q = 1$.

To prove this theorem we need notions of complexity and depth.

Definition 3.0.7. (An inductive definition of the complexity of RC-clauses)

(a) We define the notion of the complexity of a database $\mathbf{P}$ and the notion of complexity (A),the complexity of an RC-clause by induction:

(a1) Complexity $(q) = 1$.

(a2) Complexity $(\mathbf{A} \to q)$ = complexity $(\mathbf{A}) + 1$.

(a3) Complexity $\{A_1, \ldots, A_n\} = 1+$ max (complexity (A_i))

(b) Let $\mathbf{P}$ be a finite nonempty set of RC-clauses. The complexity of $\mathbf{P}$ is defined as a function $f(n)$ on natural numbers giving for each n the number $f(n)$ of RC-clauses in $\mathbf{P}$ of complexity n. Let $\mid f \mid$ be the first natural number m such that $f(m) \neq 0$ and $(\forall m' > m) f(m') = 0$.

(b1) Since $\mathbf{P}$ is nonempty and finite, such an $\mid f \mid$ exists. For $\mathbf{P}$ empty f is undefined.

(c) Given two finite sets of clauses $\mathbf{P}_1$ and $\mathbf{P}_2$, let f_1, f_2 be their complexity functions.
Define an order $<$ on the functions as follows:$f_1 < f_2$ iff (definition) either

(1) $\mid f_1 \mid < \mid f_2 \mid$
or

(2) $\mid f_1 \mid = \mid f_2 \mid$ and for some k $f_1(k) < f_2(k)$, where k is the largest natural number k' such that $f_1(k') \neq f_2(k')$.
Note that the ordering on $\{f\}$ is well founded.

Theorem 3.0.8. *For any* $\mathbf{P}$, *any set* $\{\mathbf{A}_i \to x_i \mid i = 1, \ldots, r\}$ *and any atom* q, *conditions (a) and* $(b, i), i = 1, \ldots, r$ *below imply condition (c) below:*

(a) $\mathbf{P} \cup \{\mathbf{A}_i \to x_i \mid i \leq r\}?q = 1$

(b, i) $\mathbf{P} \cup \mathbf{A}_i?x_i = 1$

(c) $\mathbf{P}?q = 1$.

Proof. By induction on depth m of the success tree of (a) and the complexity of the set $\{\mathbf{A}_i \to x_i\}$. Let n_i be the complexity of $\mathbf{A}_i \to x_i$ and let f be the complexity function of the set $\{\mathbf{A}_i \to x_i\}$.

The induction is on the lexicographic ordering of the pairs (f, m).

Case 1

$m = 1, n_i$ arbitrary. In this case we must simply have $q \in \mathbf{P} \cup \{\mathbf{A}_i \to x_i\}$. So either $q \in \mathbf{P}$ or for some $i, \mathbf{A}_i = \varnothing$ (i.e. $\mathbf{A}_i$ does not exist) and $q = x_i$. In either case $\mathbf{P}?q = 1$.

Case 2

$n_i = 1, m$ arbitrary.

Subcase 2a

q succeeds because of $\{(\mathbf{B}_j \to y_j) \mid j = 1, \ldots, k\} \to q) \in \mathbf{P}$.
[Note: We shall not use the fact that $n_i = 1$ in this subcase]. Since we are dealing with a success tree of (a), we get that for each j

$$(a, j) : [\mathbf{P} \cup \mathbf{B}_j] \cup \{\mathbf{A}_i \to x_i\}?y_j = 1.$$

We also get (b, i, j) from (b, i) and 3.0.4, where
$(b, i, j) : \mathbf{P} \cup \mathbf{B}_j \cup \mathbf{A}_i?x_i = 1$
and the success tree of (a, j) has depth less than m, and the success tree of (b, i, j) has depth n_i.

Hence by the induction hypothesis:

$$(c, j) : \mathbf{P} \cup \mathbf{B}_j?y_j = 1$$

for each j, with a success tree $(0_j, T_j, V_j)$ of depth $\leq m$.

Thus $\mathbf{P}?q$ succeeds with a success tree of the form:

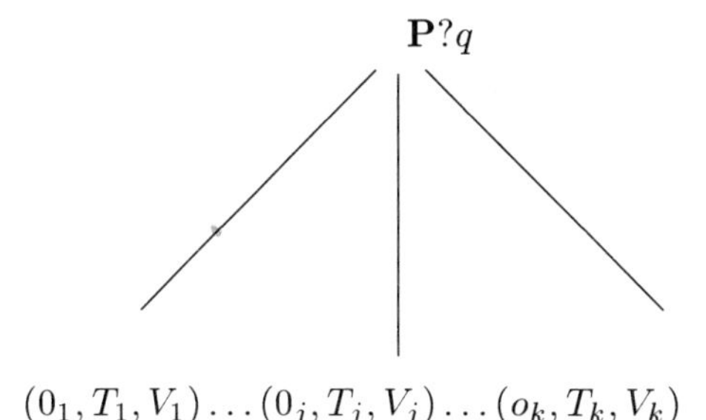

Subcase 2b

q succeeds because of $(\mathbf{A}_i \to x_i)$ for some i. This means $x_i = q$. Assume $i = 1$. Since for all $i, n_i = 1$, we have $\mathbf{P} \cup \mathbf{A}_i?x_i$ succeeds in one step. This means that $x_i \in \mathbf{P}$. Since $x_i = q$, we get $\mathbf{P}?q = 1$, with success tree of depth $n_i \leq 1 - -1+$ max (n_i).

Case 3a

$m > 1$ and some $n_i > 1$ and q succeeds because of $\{(\mathbf{B}_j \to y_j) \mid j = 1 \ldots k\} \to q \in \mathbf{P}$.

In this case the proof is the same as in subcase 2a; we have not used the fact that $n_i = 1$ in the proof of subcase 2a.

Case 3b

The $m > 1$, some $n_i > 1$ and q succeeds because of $\mathbf{A}_1 \to x_1$. This means that $x_1 = q$ and $\mathbf{A}_1 = \{(\mathbf{B}_j \to y_j) \mid j = 1, \ldots, k\}$ i.e. the clause $\mathbf{A}_1 \to x_1$ is $\{(\mathbf{B}_j \to y_j) \mid j = 1, \ldots, k\} \to q$.

The assumptions of the theorem are therefore:

(a) $\mathbf{P} \cup \{\{(\mathbf{B}_j \to y_j) \mid j = 1, \ldots, k\} \to q\} \cup \{\mathbf{A}_i \to x_i \mid i \geq 2\}?q = 1$

(b, 1) $\mathbf{P} \cup \{(\mathbf{B}_j \to y_j) \mid j = 1 \ldots k\}?q = 1$

(b, i) $\mathbf{P} \cup \mathbf{A}_i?x_i = 1, i = 2, \ldots, r.$

(a) succeeds with a tree of depth m and $(b, i)i = 1, \ldots, r$ have complexity n_i. Since q succeeds through $\{(\mathbf{B}_j \to y_j) \mid j = 1 \ldots k\} \to q$ in (a) and the success tree of (a) follows the computation Rule **HR2**, we get that the following holds with success trees of depth $m - -1$, for each $j = 1, \ldots, r$. (a,j) $[\mathbf{P} \cup \mathbf{B}_j] \cup \{\{(\mathbf{B}_j \to y_j) \mid j = 1 \ldots k\} \to q\} \cup \{\mathbf{A}_i \to x_i \mid i \geq 2\}?y_j = 1$.

The following also succeeds by 3.0.4

$(b, 1, j)$ $[\mathbf{P} \cup \mathbf{B}_j] \cup \{(\mathbf{B}_j \to y_j) \mid j = 1 \ldots k\}?q = 1$

(b, i, j) $[\mathbf{P} \cup \mathbf{B}_j] \cup \ \mathbf{A}_i?x_i = 1,$ for $i = 2, \ldots, r.$

Note that the complexity r remains unchanged. By the induction hypothesis we get

$$(c, j) : \mathbf{P} \cup \mathbf{B}_j?y_j = 1$$

we also have $(b, 1)$, namely

$$\mathbf{P} \cup \{(\mathbf{B}_j \to y_j) \mid j = 1 \ldots k\}?q = 1$$

with complexities $m_j \leq n_1 - 1$.

We can now use the induction hypothesis for the theorem. The case (f, m) is reduced to the case (f', m'), where f' is the complexity of the set $\{\mathbf{B}_j \to y_j\}$. f' is smaller than f since $f'(n_1) = 0$ and $f(n_1) \geq 1, n_1$ being the complexity of $\{(\mathbf{B}_j \to y_j) \mid j = 1 \ldots k\} \to q$.

From the induction hypothesis we get $\mathbf{P}?q = 1$.

This proves 3.0.8. ∎

Corollary 3.0.9. $\mathbf{P}?(\mathbf{A} \to q) = 1$ *and* $\mathbf{P}?\mathbf{A} = 1$ *imply* $\mathbf{P}?q = 1$.

Proof. 1. Let $\mathbf{A} = \{(\mathbf{B}_j \to y_j) \mid j = 1 \ldots m\}$
we have

(a) $\mathbf{P} \cup \{\mathbf{B}_j \to y_j\}?q = 1$,

(b) $\mathbf{P} \cup \mathbf{B}_j?y_j = 1$, for each j
and hence by 3.0.8 we get $\mathbf{P}?q = 1$.

■

Corollary 3.0.10.

(a) *For all* $\mathbf{P}$*, and all finite* $\mathbf{A}$, $\mathbf{G}$*:*
$\mathbf{P}?\mathbf{A} = 1$ *and* $\mathbf{P} \cup \mathbf{A}?\mathbf{G} = 1$ *imply* $\mathbf{P}?\mathbf{G} = 1$

(b) $\mathbf{P}$ *need not be finite in (a).*

Proof.

$\mathbf{G}$ has the form $\{\mathbf{B}_i \to q_i\}$. Hence we have $\mathbf{P}?\mathbf{A} = 1$ and $\mathbf{P} \cup \mathbf{A} \cup \mathbf{B}_i?q_i = 1$ implying by the previous corollary that $\mathbf{P} \cup \mathbf{B}_i?q_i = 1$ for each i and hence $\mathbf{P}?\mathbf{G} = 1$.

(b) Since all computations are finite, there exists a large enough finite subset $\mathbf{P}_0 \subseteq \mathbf{P}$ such that $\mathbf{P}_0?\mathbf{A} = 1$ and $\mathbf{P}_0 \cup \mathbf{A}?\mathbf{G} = 1$ and thus $\mathbf{P}_0?\mathbf{G} = 1$ and hence $\mathbf{P}?\mathbf{G} = 1$.

■

We now have to give the connection between our intuitionistic consequence relation and the computation.

Definition 3.0.11.

1. With every wff A of intuitionistic logic, we associate a unique RC-clause A^* as follows.

   (a) $q^* = q$, for q atomic

   (b) If A is not atomic, it has the form

   $$A_1 \to (A_2 \to \ldots \to (A_n \to q) \ldots)$$

   with q atomic. Then $A^* = \{A_1^*, \ldots, A_n^*\} \to q$.

2. Conversely, with every RC-clause A we associate a formula of intuitionistic logic $A\sharp$ as follows:

   (a) $q\sharp = q$, for q atomic.

(b) $(\{B_1, \ldots, B_n\} \to q)\sharp = B_1\sharp \to (\ldots \to (B_n\sharp \to q)\ldots)$.

Where the ordering $B_1 \ldots B_n$ is arbitrary. Notice that if $\{C_1, \ldots, C_n\} = \{B_1, \ldots, B_n\}$ is another listing of the set then $B_1\sharp \to (\ldots \to (B_n\sharp \to q)\ldots)$ is intuitionistically equivalent to $C_1\sharp \to (\ldots(C_n\sharp \to q)\ldots)$.

Further note that we can assume $A^*\sharp = A$ for all A.

Let $\mathbf{P}^*$ (respectively $\mathbf{P}^\sharp$) be the set of all A^* (respectively $A^\sharp$) in $\mathbf{P}$.

Theorem 3.0.12. $\mathbf{P} \vdash A$ *iff* $\mathbf{P}^*?A^* = 1$.

Proof. By induction on the length of computation. We show first that if $\mathbf{P}^*?A^* = 1$ then $\mathbf{P} \vdash A$.

A has the form

$$A_1 \to (A_2 \to \ldots (A_n \to q)\ldots).$$

and A^* is $\{A_i^*\} \to q$. The base of the induction is obvious.

1. $\mathbf{P}^*?A^* = 1$ iff $\mathbf{P}^* \cup \{A_i^*\}?q = 1$ therefore $\mathbf{P} \cup \{A_i\} \vdash q$ by the induction hypothesis, therefore by the deduction theorem $\mathbf{P} \vdash A$.

2. $\mathbf{P}^*?q = 1$ for q atomic if either $q \in \mathbf{P}^*$ or for some $\{B_i^*\} \to q \in \mathbf{P}^*, \mathbf{P}^*?B_i^* = 1$ for all i, iff by the induction hypothesis $\mathbf{P} \vdash B_i$. Since $\{B_i^*\} \to q \in \mathbf{P}^*, \mathbf{P}$ must contain some $A_1 \to (A_2 \to \ldots (A_n \to q)\ldots)$ with $\{A_i\} = \{B_i\}$. Hence $\mathbf{P} \vdash A_i$ and hence by modus ponens and cut, $\mathbf{P} \vdash q$.

This proves one direction.

To show that $\mathbf{P} \vdash A$ implies $\mathbf{P}^*?A^* = 1$, notice that the relation $\mathbf{P} \vdash_1 A$ iff (definition) $\mathbf{P}^*?A^* = 1$ was proved (3.0.5,3.0.10) to be a consequence relation satisfying the deduction theorem. Hence since $\vdash$ is the smallest such a relation we get that $\mathbf{P} \vdash A$ implies $\mathbf{P} \vdash_1 A$. ■

Theorem 3.0.13 (The cut rule for intuitionistic implication). *Assume* $\mathbf{P} \vdash q$, *for* q *atomic, then either* $q \in \mathbf{P}$ *or for some* $C_1 \to (C_2 \to \ldots \to (C_n \to q)\ldots)$ *in* $\mathbf{P}$, *we have* $\mathbf{P} \vdash C_i$ *for* $i = 1, \ldots, n$.

Proof. Follows from the previous theorem and the fact that if $\mathbf{P}?q = 1$ then the computation *has* to go through some clause in $\mathbf{P}$. Thus either $q \in \mathbf{P}$ or, in view of 3.0.11, for some $C_1 \to C_2 \ldots \to (C_n \to q)\ldots) \in \mathbf{P}?C_i = 1$ for $i - 1, \ldots, n$.

■

Examples 3.0.14. In the examples each line follows from the previous line by applying a rule. We use RC-clauses and formulas interchangeably.

1. $(a \to b) \to a?a$
   $(a \to b) \to a?a \to b$

$(a \to b) \to a, a?b$
fails

2. $(c \to a) \to c, c \to a?a$
   $(c \to a) \to c, c \to a?c$
   $(c \to a) \to c, c \to a?c \to a$
   $(c \to a) \to c, c \to a, c?a$
   $(c \to a) \to c, c \to a, c?c$
   succeeds

3. $(a \to b) \to b?(b \to a) \to a$
   $(a \to b) \to b, b \to a?a$
   $(a \to b) \to b, b \to a?b$
   $(a \to b) \to b, b \to a?a \to b$
   $(a \to b) \to b, b \to a, a?b$
   $(a \to b) \to b, b \to a, a?a \to b$
   $(a \to b) \to b, b \to a, a?b$
   loops

4. $(a \to x) \to a, (b \to x) \to b, (a \to (b \to x))?a$
   $(a \to x) \to a, (b \to x) \to b, a \to (b \to x)?a \to x$
   $(a \to x) \to a, (b \to x) \to b, a \to (b \to x), a?x$
   $(a \to x) \to a, (b \to x) \to b, a \to (b \to x), a?\{a, b\}$
   $?a$ succeeds so we continue with $?b$.
   $(a \to x) \to a, (b \to x) \to b, a \to (b \to x), a?b \to x$
   $(a \to x) \to a, (b \to x) \to b, a \to (b \to x), a, b?x$
   $(a \to x) \to a, (b \to x) \to b, a \to (b \to x), a, b?\{a, b\}$
   success

Theorem 3.0.15 (Interpolation property for databases P). *If* $\mathbf{P} \vdash B$ *then for some* $\mathbf{C}$ *in the common language* $\mathbf{P} \vdash \mathbf{C}$ *and* $\vdash \mathbf{C} \to B$.

Proof. To show interpolation we use (3.0.13) and induction on the complexity of the computation.
Length 1
Clearly if B is atomic and $B \in \mathbf{P}$ then the interpolant is B.
Length $n + 1$
Assume $\mathbf{P} = \{\mathbf{A}_j \to p_j\}$ and $B = \{(\mathbf{B}_k \to y_k)\} \to q$. Then we are given that $\mathbf{P} = \{\mathbf{A}_j \to p_j, \mathbf{B}_k \to y_k\} \vdash q$. The goal directed computation of q must succeed. We distinguish two cases:

1. q is equal to some y_m (and hence $y_m \vdash q$).
   In this case $\mathbf{P} \vdash \{\mathbf{B}_k \to y_k\} \to x$ for all $x \in \mathbf{B}_m$. Each x is proved

with a shorter computation. By the induction hypothesis there exists an interpolant $\mathbf{C}$ such that $\mathbf{P} \vdash \mathbf{C}$ and $\mathbf{C} \vdash \{(\mathbf{B}_k \to y_k)\} \to x$, for all $x \in \mathbf{B}_m$. Since $\mathbf{B}_m \to y_m$ is one of the antecedents and $y_m \vdash q$ we get that $\mathbf{C} \vdash B$.

2. q is equal to some p_m (and hence $p_m \vdash q$).
   In this case q is in the common language. We have

$$\{\mathbf{B}_k \to y_k\} \vdash \mathbf{P} \to A_m$$

Hence there exists an interpolant $\mathbf{I}$ such that $\vdash \{(\mathbf{B}_k \to y_k)\} \vdash \mathbf{I}$ and $\mathbf{I}, \mathbf{P} \vdash \mathbf{A}_m$. Then $\vdash (\mathbf{I} \to q) \vdash \{(\mathbf{B}_k \to y_k) \to q\}$ and $\mathbf{P}, \mathbf{I} \vdash \mathbf{A}_m$.

Since $\mathbf{P} \vdash A_m \to p_m$ and $p_m \vdash q$, we get $\mathbf{P}, I \vdash r$ and so $\mathbf{P} \vdash I \to r$. Thus our interpolant is $I \to r$.

If $\mathbf{B} = \{B_1, B_2\}$ and the interpolant for B_i is C_i then the interpolant for $\mathbf{B}$ is $\{C_1, C_2\}$.

This completes the induction and the theorem is proved. Notice that the interpolant can be constructed effectively from the computation and different computations may give rise to different interpolants. ∎

4 Automated deduction for intuitionistic implication; resource boundness

We have discovered an algorithmic proof method for the intuitionistic system with implication. We want now to look further into an automated implementation. We will be guided by key examples. The examples will show us difficulties to overcome in order to achieve tractability of computation. We will respond to the difficulties by proposing to do the most obvious optimizations at hand. Slowly the computation steps will evolve and we will most naturally be led to consider new logics, which correspond to various optimizations which ('unfortunately') are not complete. However, we will be happy to note that the new logics thus obtained are really old logics we already know, and we thus realize that we have stumbled on automated systems for other well-known logics. We are thus continuing in the same spirit of adventure and discovery as in Section 1.

Example 4.0.1. [Historical loop checking] Consider the data and query below:

$$q \to q?q.$$

Clearly the algorithm has to know it is looping. The simplest way of loop checking is to record the history of the computation. This can be done as follows: Let $\mathbf{P}?(G, \mathbf{H})$ represent the query of the goal G from data $\mathbf{P}$ and history $\mathbf{H}$. $\mathbf{H}$ is a list. The computation rules become:

Historical rule for $\to$

$\mathbf{P}?(A \to B, \mathbf{H}) = 1$
if $\mathbf{P} \cup \{A\}?(B, \mathbf{H} * ((\mathbf{P}, A \to B))) = 1$ and $(\mathbf{P}, A \to B)$ is not in $\mathbf{H}$.

where $*$ denote concatenation of lists. Thus $(\mathbf{P}, A \to B)$ is appended to $\mathbf{H}$.

Historical Rule for atoms

$\mathbf{P}?(q, \mathbf{H}) = 1$, for q atomic,
if for some $B = (x_1 \to (x_2 \to \ldots (x_n \to q) \ldots)$ in $\mathbf{P}$ we have that for all i
$\mathbf{P}?(x_i, \mathbf{H} * ((\mathbf{P}, q)) = 1$ and that $(\mathbf{P}, q)$ is not in $\mathbf{H}$.

Thus the computation for our example above becomes:

$$(q \to q)?(q, \varnothing)$$

$$(q \to q)?(q, ((q \to q, q)))$$

fail.

Note that the historical loop checking conjunct in *the rule for* $\to$ is redundant as the loop will be captured in *the rule for atoms.* Also note that in this case we made the decision that looping means failure. The most general case of loop checking may first detect the loop and then decide that under certain conditions looping implies success.

This type of loop checking, although effective, is very expensive on resources. Many copies of the database are required. One can optimize it a bit by listing in the history $\mathbf{H}$ only the additions to the original database, but this is expensive as well, as the additions to the data are of the same order of magnitude as the data.

Trying to think constructively, in order to make sure the algorithm terminates, let us ask ourselves what is involved in the computation. There are two parameters; the data and the goal. The goal is reduced to an atom via the rule for $\to$ and the looping occurs because a data item is being used by the rule for atoms again and again. Our aim in the historical loop checking is to stop that. Well, why don't we try a modified rule for atoms which can use each item of data only once? This way, we will certainly run out of data and the computation will terminate. We have to give a formal definition of the computation, where we keep track on how many times we use the data.

Let us adopt the point of view that each database item can be used at most once. Thus our rule for atoms becomes (**LLR** stands for locally linear rule):

LLR for atoms: $\mathbf{P}, \mathbf{A} \to q?q = 1$ if $\mathbf{P}?\mathbf{A} = 1$

The item $\mathbf{A} \to q$ is thus thrown out as soon as it is used.

Let us call such a computation *locally linear computation* (bounded resource computation where each formula can be used at most once in each path of the computation. That is why we are using the word 'locally'. One can also have the notion of (globally) linear computation, in which each formula can be used exactly once in the entire computation tree.

Before we proceed, we need to give a formal definition of these concepts. We give Definition 4.0.2 below and it should be compared with Definition 3.0.3 of the previous section. The goal directed computation of this Definition is the same as the one in 3.0.3.

Our computation procedure is defined on RC-clauses. $\mathbf{P}_0$ denotes a multiset of RC-clauses, referred to as data, and $\mathbf{G}_0$ denotes a multiset of RC-clauses referred to as goals.

We follow consistently our convention of writing A instead of the singleton $\{A\}$.

Definition 4.0.2. [Goal directed computation, locally linear goal directed computation and linear goal directed computation] We present three notions of computation by defining their computation trees. These are:

1. The goal directed computation for intuitionistic logic.
2. Locally linear goal directed computation
3. Linear goal directed computation.

The goal directed computation tree is defined by clauses (a)–(e), (f1), (f2) and (g) below. The locally linear computation is obtained by replacing clause (f2) by (f4). The linear goal directed computation is obtained by replacing clause (f1) by (f3), clause (f2) by (f4) and clause (d) by (d*).

Let $\mathbf{P}_0$ be a database and let $\mathbf{G}_0$ be a goal. A quadruple $(T, \leq, 0, V)$ is said to be a successful computation tree of the goal $\mathbf{G}_0$ from $\mathbf{P}_0$ if the following conditions hold:

(a) $(T, \leq, 0)$ is a finite tree; T is its set of nodes, 0 is its root, and for s, t in $T, t \leq s$ means that $t = s$ or t lies closer to the root than s, on the same path.

(b) V is a labelling function on T. For each $t \in T, V(t)$ is a pair $(\mathbf{P}, \mathbf{G})$, where $\mathbf{P}$ is a database and $\mathbf{G}$ is a goal.

(c) $V(0) = (\mathbf{P}_0, \mathbf{G}_0)$. We say the clauses of $\mathbf{P}_0$ are *put in the data at node 0.*

(d) If $V(t) = (\mathbf{P}, \mathbf{G})$ and $\mathbf{G} = \{A_1, \ldots, A_n\}$, with A_i RC-clauses then the node t has exactly n immediate successors in the tree, say $t_1, \ldots, t_n$ with $V(t_i) = (\mathbf{P}_i, A_i)$, where $\mathbf{P}_i = \mathbf{P}$.

(d*) For the case of linear computation we require that $V(t_i) = (\mathbf{P}_i, A_i)$, with $\cup \mathbf{P}_i = \mathbf{P}$.

(e) If $V(t) = (\mathbf{P}, \mathbf{G})$, and $\mathbf{G} = \mathbf{A} \to q$, then t has exactly one immediate successor in the tree, say s, with $V(s) = (\mathbf{P} \cup \mathbf{A}, q)$. We say that the clauses in $\mathbf{A}$ were *put in the data at node t.*

(f) If $V(t) = (\mathbf{P}, q)$, with q atomic, then exactly one of the following holds:

(f1) t has no immediate successors and $q \in \mathbf{P}$. We say $q \in \mathbf{P}$ is *used at node t.*

(f2) t has exactly one immediate successor s in the tree with $V(s) = (\mathbf{P}, \mathbf{A})$ and with $(\mathbf{A} \to q) \in \mathbf{P}$. In this case we say that $\mathbf{A} \to q$ is *used at node* $t \in T$.

(f3) For the case of linear computation we require that t has no immediate successors and $\{q\} = \mathbf{P}$.

(f4) For the case of locally linear computation we require that $V(s) = (\mathbf{P}', \mathbf{A})$, with $\mathbf{P} = \mathbf{P}' \cup \{\mathbf{A} \to q\}$.

(g) Note that it is possible in case (f2) or (f3) that $q \in \mathbf{P}$. Nevertheless the computation goes through $\mathbf{A} \to q$. Further note that the databases involved need not be finite. In a successful computation tree only a finite number of clauses from the database will be used in the sense mentioned above.

The question is now: Do we retain completeness? Are there examples for intuitionistic logic where items of data essentially need to be used locally more than once?

In other words, are there examples where no matter how we order our computation, some items of data have to be used more than once? We have to look at examples. What we have to do is run many examples and check.

It is reasonable to assume that if things go wrong, they do so with formulae with two nested implications, i.e. formulae with the structure $x \to (y \to z)$ or $(x \to y) \to z$. The reason is simply that any implication $A \to B$ can be renamed as $q = A \to B$, by a new atom q, and the data

$(A \to B) \to q$
$q \to (A \to B)$
define q to be $A \to B$. Thus, by adding more atoms and data we can reduce any database to an equivalent database with only two levels of nested implication.

We can now take four atomic letters a, b, c, d and check case by case all possible 'data ? query' computation cases of wffs built up from these letters and two nested implications.

Sooner or later we will discover the following examples: Note that it is easy to write a program which will generate all possible cases to be checked and see whether the two computation procedures — the one with the historical rules for $\to$ and for atoms of 4.0.1, and the second being the computation without history but with the rules for $\to$ and the linear rule for atoms — give the same results.

Examples 4.0.3.

1. $c \to a, (c \to a) \to c?a$
   The clause $(c \to a)$ has to be used twice in order for a to succeed.

   This example can be generalized.

2. Let $A_0 = c$
   $A_{n+1} = (A_n \to a) \to c.$

   Consider the following data and query:

$$\mathbf{P}_n = \{A_n, c \to a\}?a$$

   The clause $c \to a$ has to be used n times.

Example 4.0.4. Another example is

$$a \to (b \to c), a \to b, a?c$$

here a has to be used twice globally, but not locally on each branch of the computation. Thus the locally linear computation succeeds.

Let us do the full computation:

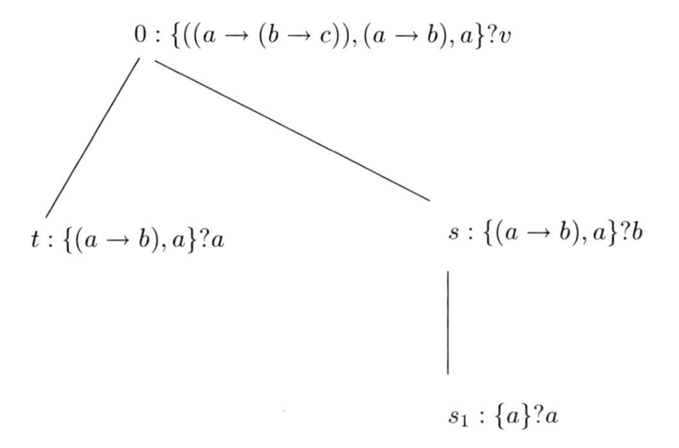

$0 : \{((a \to (b \to c)), (a \to b), a\}?v$
$t : \{(a \to b), a\}?a$
$s : \{(a \to b), a\}?b$
$s_1 : \{a\}?a$

It is obvious that 'a' is used twice 'globally' in the entire computation tree but not more than once 'locally', on each path.

Example 4.0.5. Note that the above examples show that linear computation does *not* give rise to a consequence relation. First monotonicity does not hold. The cut rule is also violated, if we understand cut as defined before.

In 4.0.4, a has to be used twice. Hence certainly

$$a, a \vdash (a \to b) \to [(a \to (b \to c)) \to c]$$

in globally linear logic where each assumption can be used only once. Also $a \vdash a$ holds. Therefore, by cut we should get

$$a \vdash (a \to b) \to [(a \to (b \to c)) \to c]$$

which, of course, does not hold. Thus, the cut rule

$$\frac{\mathbf{P} \vdash A; \mathbf{P}, A \vdash B}{\mathbf{P} \vdash B}$$

does not hold.

However, if we write the cut rule as

$$\frac{\mathbf{P}_1 \vdash A; \mathbf{P}_2, A \vdash B}{\mathbf{P}_1, \mathbf{P}_2 \vdash B}$$

The rule does hold. However, we need to restrict reflexivity to $A \vdash A$ (identity). For $\mathbf{P}_1 = \mathbf{P}_2 = \mathbf{P}$, we can understand $\mathbf{P}$, $\mathbf{P}$ as two copies of $\mathbf{P}$[2].

[2]The notion of a consequence relation can also be modified, so that the reading of union $\cup$ and intersection $\cap$ refers to multiset union and intersection. The axioms become:

Example 4.0.6. A simpler example is the following database:
$(A_1 \to a) \to c$
$(A_n \to a) \to c$
$A_1 \to (A_2 \to \ldots (A_n \to c) \ldots)$
$c \to a$
the query is '$?a$'.
$c \to a$ has to be used $n+1$ times globally to ensure success, but locally it is needed only twice.

Example 4.0.7. One can combine 4.0.6 and 4.0.3 to show a database and a query where a clause in the query needs to be used at least n times globally and at least m times locally. 4.0.6 is a case of $m = 2n = m$.

The above examples show that we do not have completeness for locally linear computations. We thus have to first check what we are getting, and second check whether we can compensate for the use of the locally linear rule (i.e. for throwing out the data) by some other means. We need to make our studies in a general framework where formulae can be 'used' a fixed number of times (e.g. only once). The appropriate notations and concepts must be developed. Such logics we call **BR**-Logics or logics of bounded resource. One needs an appropriate notation and an appropriate definition of the notion 'used'. In our computation above, we know intuitively what 'used' means, and our resource bounded principle was to allow each RC-clause to be 'used' at most once. The obvious generalization of the notion is to annotate a formula with a natural number which indicates how many times the formula can be used.

Volume 3 of this Handbook contains a chapter on Linear Logic. Linear logic has the implication connective $\multimap$ and $A_1, \ldots, A_n \vdash B$ in linear logic means that B can be proved from A_i using each A_i exactly once. A deduction theorem holds, namely that $A_1, \ldots, A_n \vdash B$ is equivalent to $\vdash A_1 \multimap (A_2 \multimap \ldots (A_n \multimap B) \ldots)$. Linear logic implication corresponds to the notion of linear computation of 4.0.2.

Linear logic also has the connective !. $!A$ means that A can be used as many times as required. Bounded linear logic also allows for the expression $!mA$, which reads that A can be used at most m times.

The reader is warned that the locally linear system of 4.0.2 is not the same as the linear system. First we do not require that all assumptions must be used, condition (f3), we only ask that they be used no more times than specified. A more serious difference is that we do our 'counting' of how many times a formula is used separately on each path of the computation and not globally for the entire computation. Linear logic is global, condition

---

Identity: $A \vdash A$
Monotonicity: $\mathbf{P} \vdash \mathbf{PR}$ implies $\mathbf{P} \cup \mathbf{Q} \vdash \mathbf{R}$
Cut: $\mathbf{P}_1 \vdash A, \mathbf{PR}_1$ and $\mathbf{P}_2, A \vdash \mathbf{R}_2$ imply $\mathbf{P}_1 \cup \mathbf{P}_2 \vdash \mathbf{R}_1 \cup \mathbf{R}_2$

(d*).

For example, the query $\{A, A \to (A \to B)\}?B$ will succeed in our locally linear computation because A is used once on each of two parallel paths. It will not be accepted in linear logic because A is used globally twice. This is ensured by condition (d*).

The difference in approach is rooted in our modest motivation which is the optimization of our computation procedures and not the development of a general conceptual resource allocation framework.

BR-logics, the logics of bounded resource, are extensively studied in [GAB92b]. Here we deal only with the aspects that have to do with our algorithmic proof system.

Let us begin with the basic definitions.

Example 4.0.8. This example shows that the notion of diminishing resource depends on the computation.

1. Consider

   (a) $(c \to a) \to c$.

   (b) $c \to a$.

   To show a either by forward modus ponens or by backward goal directed reasoning, we need to use $c \to a$ twice. We compare with resolution. The translated database is $\{c, \neg c \vee a, \neg a \vee c\}$.
   To show a we use clauses only once.

2. Consider the database

$$\{\neg a \vee d \vee \neg c, a, \neg a \vee c\}$$

   To show d using resolution we need to use a twice. The same database written with $\to$ is:

   (a) $a \to (c \to d)$

   (b) $a \to c$

   (c) a.

   To show d using backward reasoning, we use a once on each path, twice globally.

Let us now go back to the notion of locally linear computation. We saw that we do not have completeness. There are examples where formulae need to be used several times. Can we compensate? Can we at the same time throw data out once it has been used and retain completeness for intuitionistic logic by adding some other computation rule? The answer is yes. The rule is called the *(linear) bounded restart rule* and is used in the context of the notion of locally linear computation with history.

Let us examine more closely why we needed in Example 4.0.3 the clause $c \to a$ several times. The reason was that from other clauses, we got the query '$?a$' and we wanted to use $c \to a$ to continue to the query '$?c$'. Why was not $c \to a$ available ?; because $c \to a$ has already been used. In other words, $?a$ as a query, has already been asked and $c \to a$ was used. This means that the next query after '$?a$' in the history was '$?c$'.

If **H** is the history of the atomic queries asked, then somewhere in **H** there is '$?a$' and immediately afterwards '$?c$'.

We can therefore compensate for the re-use of $c \to a$ by allowing ourselves to go back in the history to where '$?a$' was, and allow ourselves to ask all queries that come afterwards. Let us see what happens to our example 4.0.8

$(c \to a) \to c$	[1]	$?a$
$c \to a$	[1]	
We use the second clause to get		
$(c \to a) \to c$	[1]	$?(c, (a))$
$(c \to a)$	[0]	
we continue		
$(c \to a) \to)c$	[0]	$?(c \to a, (a, c))$
$(c \to a)$	[0]	
we continue		
$(c \to a) \to c$	[0]	$?(a, (a, c))$
$(c \to a)$	[0]	
c	[1]	

The '1'('0') annotate the clause to indicate it is active (inactive) for use. The history can be seen as the right hand column of past queries.

We can now ask any query that comes after an 'a' in the history, hence

$(c \to a) \to c$	[0]	
$(c \to a)$	[0]	$?(c, (a, c, a))$
c	[1]	

Success.

The previous example suggests the following new computation with bounded restart rule.

Definition 4.0.9. [Locally linear computation with bounded restart; Locally linear computation with restart] Let $\mathbf{M}_0$ be a database and let $\mathbf{G}_0$ be a goal. We define two computations: *Locally linear computation with bounded restart, and locally linear computation with restart.* The first is defined with clauses (a)–(e), (f1)–(f3), (g) and the second with clauses (a)–(e), (f1), (f2), (f4) and (g). In the computation with bounded restart the history $\mathbf{H}_t$ is a sequence, while in the computation with restart $\mathbf{H}_t$ is a set. $\mathbf{M}_t$ and $\mathbf{G}_t$ are multisets in both computations.

A quadruple $(T, \leq, 0, V)$ is said to be a successful computation tree of the goal $\mathbf{G}_0$ from $\mathbf{M}_0$ with initial history $\mathbf{H}_0$ iff the following conditions hold.

(a) $(T, \leq, 0)$ is a finite tree; T is its set of nodes, 0 is its root and for $s, t \in T, t \leq s$ means $t = s$ or t lies closer to the root than s, on the same path.

(b) V is a labelling function on T. For each $t \in T, V(t)$ is a triple $(\mathbf{M}_t, \mathbf{G}_t, \mathbf{H}_t)$ where $\mathbf{M}_t$ is the current database at t, $\mathbf{G}_t$ is the current goal and $\mathbf{H}_t$ is the current history of previous goals.

(c) $V(0) = (\mathbf{M}_0, \mathbf{G}_0, \mathbf{H}_0)$. We say the clauses in $\mathbf{M}_0$ were put in the data at node 0.

(d) If $V(t) = (\mathbf{M}_t, \mathbf{G}_t, \mathbf{H}_t)$ with $\mathbf{G}_t = \{A_1, \ldots, A_n\}$ then the node t has exactly n immediate successors in the tree, say $t_1, \ldots, t_n$, with $V(t_i) = (\mathbf{M}_t, \{A_i\}, \mathbf{H}_t)$

(e) If $V(t) = (\mathbf{M}_t, \mathbf{G}_t, \mathbf{H}_t)$ and $\mathbf{G}_t = \{(\mathbf{A} \to q)\}$ then t has exactly one immediate successor s in the tree with $V(s) = (\mathbf{M}_t \cup \mathbf{A}, q, \mathbf{H}_t)$. We say that the new additional RC-clauses in $\mathbf{M}_t \cup \mathbf{A}$ were put in the data at node s.

(f) If $V(t) = (\mathbf{M}_t, \{q\}, \mathbf{H}_t)$, for q atomic then exactly one of the following holds:

(f1) t has no immediate successors and $q \in \mathbf{M}_t$. We say that the RC-clause q is used at this node t.

(f2) t has exactly one immediate successor s in the tree, and for some $(\mathbf{A} \to q) \in \mathbf{M}_t$ we have:

(a) $V(s) = (\mathbf{M}_s, \mathbf{A}, \mathbf{H}_t * (q))$, where $*$ is concatenation of sequences, or set union for the case $\mathbf{H}_t$ are sets.

(b) $\mathbf{M}_t = \mathbf{M}_s \cup \{(\mathbf{A} \to q)\}$

We say that the clause $(\mathbf{A} \to q)$ is used once at the node t.

(f3) *Bounded restart rule*
t has exactly one successor s in the tree, and $V(s) = (\mathbf{M}_t, \{q_1\}, \mathbf{H}_t*$

$(q))$, provided for some $\mathbf{H}_1, \mathbf{H}_2, \mathbf{H}_3$ $\mathbf{H}_t = \mathbf{H}_1 * (q) * \mathbf{H}_2 * (q_1) * \mathbf{H}_3$ where $\mathbf{H}_i$ can be empty.

(f4) *Restart rule*
If the proviso of (f3) is weakened, we get the restart rule, namely $V(s) = (\mathbf{M}_t, \{q_1\}, \mathbf{H}_t * (q))$, with $q_1 \in \mathbf{H}_t$. In this case we can simplify the entire definition and allow $\mathbf{H}_t$ to be a *set*, the history of previous goals. Thus $\mathbf{H}_t * (q)$ should be replaced by $\mathbf{H}_t \cup \{q\}$.

(g) We write $\mathbf{P}?(\mathbf{G}, \mathbf{H}) = 1$ iff there exists a successful computation tree of $\mathbf{G}$ from $\mathbf{P}$ with initial history $\mathbf{H}$. The computation involved will be specified in the context.

We still have the problem of completeness..

Consider the query: $\mathbf{P} = \mathbf{P}_0, x_1 \to (x_2 \to q)[1]?q$.

This continues as two parallel computations (a) and (b) which should both succeed where

(a) $\mathbf{P}_0, x_1 \to (x_2 \to q)[0]?x_1$ and

(b) $\mathbf{P}_0, x_1 \to (x_2 \to q)[0]?x_2$

Computation (a) may proceed and end up with the query $\mathbf{P}_1?q$ with history $(q, x_1, \ldots, q)$. Our rule allows us to continue to ask $\mathbf{P}_1?x_1$.

However, if we really had the clause itself available to us we would split the computation again into

$\mathbf{P}_1?x_1$ and $\mathbf{P}_1?x_2$

to be again continued in parallel.

So we are basically chopping out $\mathbf{P}_1?x_2$, in our present algorithm.

Does this affect the outcome? We do have the original branch (b), namely $\mathbf{P}_0, x_1 \to (x_2 \to q)?x_2$. If (b) succeeds, then we know $\mathbf{P}_1?x_2$ succeeds. If (b) fails, then $\mathbf{P}_1?x_2$ may still succeed because $\mathbf{P}_1 \supseteq \mathbf{P}_0$ may contain more data, but that makes no difference because the original $\mathbf{P}?q$ fails anyway, as (b) must succeed.

This requires proper study and we shall give the appropriate proof later on.

Example 4.0.10.

1. The following example shows the problem we might have. Consider schematically an original query $?c$ which splits to two queries as in the next Figure

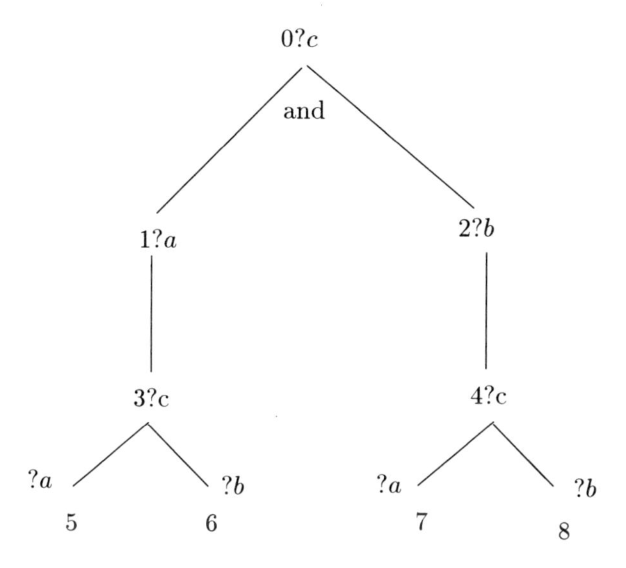

We numbered the end nodes 5, 6, 7, 8. We might have a situation where we do not pursue $?b$ at node 6 because it is already asked above at node 2 and at the same time we do not ask $?a$ at node 7 because $?a$ is already asked above at node 1. We might think that we never compute nodes 1 and 2 properly, and that we will get wrong results.

If we carry out the computation fully on the left branch (i.e. node 1) then at node 7 we can rely on the fact that $?a$ has already been computed at node 1.

2. Consider the following example:

$$(((a \to c) \to a) \to a) \to ((((b \to c) \to b) \to b) \to c)?c$$

The computation splits in two:

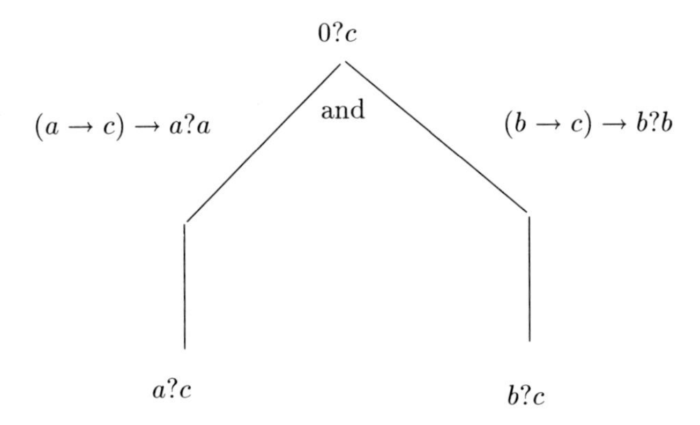

The figure shows only the data added at each node. If we follow the bounded restart rule we get success. Let us check what happens if we continue with the ordinary rule for atoms and try to succeed without bounded restart. From the rule for atoms, using the original data we get the following Figure:

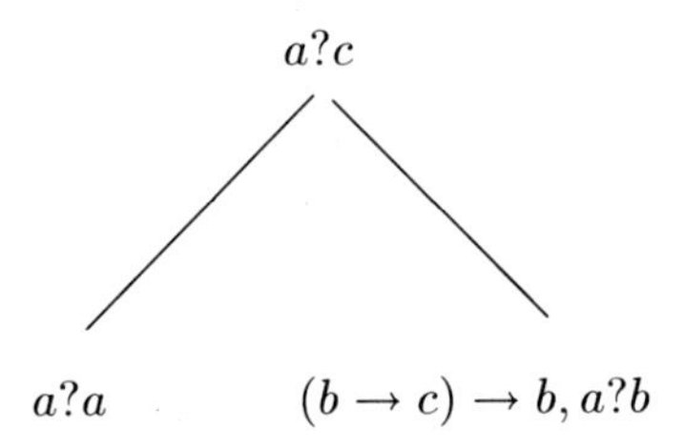

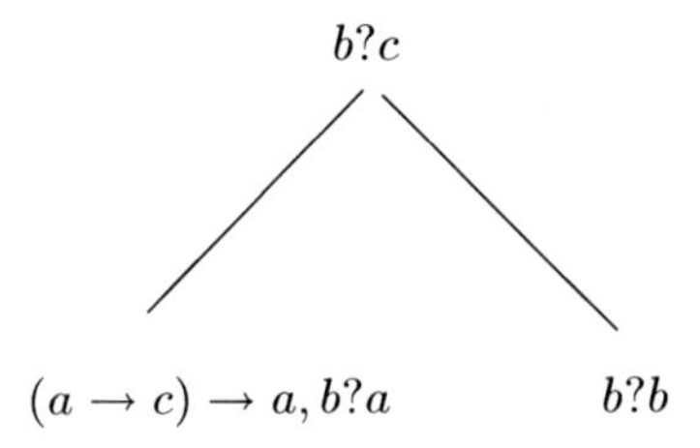

The nodes $a?b$ and $b?a$ can further be computed and they succeed.

We now have a rule which allows us to ask any previous query $?a$ instead of the current query $?q$ provided $?q$ was asked earlier than $?a$.

We now have two natural problems to consider, the problem of the efficiency of the proposed computation and the problem of the logical meaning of the computation.

We begin with the problem of the logical meaning and start with an example. Consider the following two databases:

$$\mathbf{P}_1 = \{(c \to a) \to b\} \text{ and } \mathbf{P}_2 = \{c, a \to b\}$$

If we ask the query $?b$ from each database, using the linear bounded restart rule, we get that the query is reduced to

$$\{c\}?(a, (b))$$

Thus we see that one cannot reconstruct the original database from the history. This problem has bearing upon soundness. Given a query $\mathbf{P}?(q, \mathbf{H})$, which succeeds, we can ask what is the logical meaning of the success of the computation, what is being proved? Can we say that for some intuitionistic wff $\varphi(\mathbf{P}, q, \mathbf{H})$, embodying in it the logical content of the computation, we have $\vdash \varphi(\mathbf{P}, q, \mathbf{H})$?

That is, we want to find a φ which satisfies the following:

$$\mathbf{P}?(q, \mathbf{H}) = 1 \text{ iff } \vdash \varphi(\mathbf{P}, q, \mathbf{H})$$

To achieve this, φ will have to satisfy:

1. $\vdash \varphi(\mathbf{P}, q, \varnothing)$ iff $\mathbf{P} \vdash q$
2. $\vdash \varphi(\mathbf{P} \cup \{\mathbf{A} \to q\}, q, \mathbf{H})$ if
   $\vdash \varphi(\mathbf{P}, \mathbf{A}, \mathbf{H} * (q))$
3. $\vdash \varphi(\mathbf{P} \cup \{x\}, q, \mathbf{H})$
   if $x = q$ or x is in $\mathbf{H}$, bounded by q.
4. $\vdash \varphi(\mathbf{P}, \mathbf{A} \to q, \mathbf{H})$ iff $\vdash \varphi(\mathbf{P} \cup \mathbf{A}, q, \mathbf{H})$
5. $\vdash \varphi(\mathbf{P}, \{A, B\}\mathbf{H})$ iff $\vdash \varphi(\mathbf{P}, A, \mathbf{H})$ and $\vdash \varphi(\mathbf{P}, B, \mathbf{H})$

Lemma 4.0.11. *The following hold in intuitionistic logic:*

1. *If* $\mathbf{P}, A, q \to x \vdash q$
   Then $\mathbf{P}, (A \to q) \to x \vdash A \to q$
2. $(A \to x) \to A, (B \to x) \to B \vdash (A \wedge B \to x) \to (A \wedge B)$.

Proof.

Note that with A in the data, $A \to q$ is equivalent to q and hence $\mathbf{P}, A, q \to x \vdash q$ implies $\mathbf{P}, A, (A \to q) \to x \vdash q$, which implies $\mathbf{P}, (A \to q) \to x \vdash A \to q$.

2. We use the completeness Theorem 3.0.12 and Example 3.0.14, part 4.

■

We now introduce a new rule, the restart rule, which is a natural more convenient rule. It is a variation of the bounded restart rule obtained by cancelling any restrictions and simply allowing us to ask any earlier atomic query. If we allow that, we will be simplifying our algorithm a lot. We need not keep history as a sequence but only as a *set* of previous queries. The rule becomes

Restart rule:

$\mathbf{P}?(q, \mathbf{H}) = 1$ if $\mathbf{P}?(a, \mathbf{H} \cup \{q\}) = 1$, for any $a \in \mathbf{H}$.

The formal definition of *locally linear computation with restart* is Definition 4.0.2

Remark 4.0.12. Note that in Definition 4.0.2, the history is that of atomic queries only. This is sufficient for completeness. There are logics where restart cannot be restricted to the atomic case, see Section 7.

Example 4.0.13. [Computation using the restart rule]

$$\{(a \to b) \to)a\}?(a, \varnothing)$$

use the clause and throw it out to get:

$$\varnothing?((a \to b), \{a\})$$

and

$$a?(b, \{a, a \to b\})$$

restart

$$a?(a, \{a, a \to b, b\})$$

success.

This example shows that we are getting a stronger 'logic'? (we don't know that we get a logic here yet) than intuitionistic logic. The above should fail in the intuitionistic computation. What are we getting?

The surprising answer is that we are getting classical logic. This claim has to be properly proved, of course.

5 Completeness theorems for the restart rules

We will now prove completeness of the restart rule for classical logic for the computation where we do not cancel any data formulae, as described in 3.0.3.

As the argument is involved, we would like to state the computation again explicitly in terms of computation trees.

Definition 5.0.1. $(T, \leq, 0, V)$ is said to be a goal directed computation tree with the restart rule and no cancellation of data if all the conditions (a)–(e), (f1), (f2) of 3.0.3 are satisfied together with the following extra clause:
(g3) t has exactly one immediate successor s in the tree and $V(s) = (\mathbf{P}, \mathbf{G}_0)$.

Theorem 5.0.2. $\mathbf{P} \vdash A$ *in classical implicational logic iff* $(\mathbf{P}^*, A^*)$ *has a successful computation tree with the restart rule (as defined in 5.0.1 above).*

For the definition of P^*, A^*, *see 3.0.11. For the definition of classical logic, take truth table tautological validity.*

Definition 5.0.3. Let $\mathbf{A}$ be a goal. Then the complement of $\mathbf{A}$, denoted by Cop($\mathbf{A}$) is the following set of clauses:

Cop $(\mathbf{A}) = \{\mathbf{A} \to x \mid x \text{ any atom of the language}\}$

Proof. To prove this theorem we need a series of definitions and lemmas, 5.0.3–5.0.6 Note that $\mathbf{P}?\mathbf{G} = 1$ is understood according to 3.0.3 in the proofs below, in 5.0.4 and 5.0.5.

Note that from 5.0.3 and 5.0.5 we get that $\mathbf{P} \vdash A$ in classical logic iff $\mathbf{P}^* \cup Cop(A^*)?A^* = 1$. However $\mathbf{P}^*?A^* = 1$ with restart iff $\mathbf{P}^* \cup$ Cop$(A^*)?A = 1$. ∎

Lemma 5.0.4. *For any database* $\mathbf{P}$ *and goal* $\mathbf{G}$ *such that* $\mathbf{P} \supseteq$ *Cop* $(\mathbf{G})$, *and for any goal* $\mathbf{A}$, *conditions (a) and (b) below imply condition (c):*

(a) $\mathbf{P} \cup \mathbf{A}?\mathbf{G} = 1$
(b) $(\mathbf{P} \cup \text{ Cop } (\mathbf{A}))?\mathbf{G} = 1$
(c) $\mathbf{P}?\mathbf{G} = 1$

Proof. Since $\mathbf{P} \cup$ Cop $(\mathbf{A})?\mathbf{G} = 1$ and computations are finite, only a finite number of the elements of Cop $(\mathbf{A})$ are used in the computation. Assume then that

(b1) $\mathbf{P}, (\mathbf{A} \to x_1), \ldots, (\mathbf{A} \to x_n)?\mathbf{G} = 1$

We use the cut rule. Since $\mathbf{P} \supseteq Cop(\mathbf{G})$ we have $\mathbf{G} \to x_i \in \mathbf{P}$ and hence by the computation rules $\mathbf{P} \cup \mathbf{A}?x_i = 1$. Now by cut on (b1) we get $\mathbf{P}?\mathbf{G} = 1$. ∎

Theorem 5.0.5. *For any* $\mathbf{P}$ *and any* A*, (a) is equivalent to (b) below:*

(a) $\mathbf{P} \vdash A$ *in classical logic*

(b) $(\mathbf{P}^* \cup \ Cop\ (A^*))?A^* = 1$

Proof. 1. Show (b) implies (a):
Assume $(\mathbf{P}^* \cup Cop(A^*))?A^* = 1$

Then by the soundness of our computation procedure we get that $\mathbf{P}^* \cup$ Cop $(A^*\sharp) \vdash A$ in intuitionistic logic, and hence in classical logic, where $A^*\sharp$ are defined in 3.0.11.

Since the *proof* is *finite* there is a finite set of the form $\{A \to x_i, \ldots, A \to x_n\}$ (note that $A^*\sharp = A$) such that

(a1) $\mathbf{P}, (A \to x_1), \ldots (A \to x_n) \vdash A$ (in intuitionistic logic).

We must also have that $\mathbf{P} \vdash A$, in classical logic, because if there were an assignment h making $\mathbf{P}$ true and A false, it would also make $A \to x_i$ all true, contradicting (a1).

The above concludes the proof that (b) implies (a).

2. Show that (a) implies (b).
We prove that if $\mathbf{P}^* \cup$ Cop $(A^*)?A^* \neq 1$, then $\mathbf{P} \not\vdash A$ in classical logic. Let $\mathbf{P}_0 = \mathbf{P}^* \cup$ Cop (A^*). We define a sequence of databases $\mathbf{P}_n, n = 1, 2 \ldots$ as follows:
Let $\mathbf{B}_1, \mathbf{B}_2, \mathbf{B}_3, \ldots$ be an enumeration of all goals of the language.
Assume $\mathbf{P}_{n-1}$ has been defined and assume that $\mathbf{P}_{n-1}?A^* \neq 1$. We define $\mathbf{P}_n$:
If $\mathbf{P}_{n-1} \cup \mathbf{B}_n?A^* \neq 1$, let $\mathbf{P}_n = \mathbf{P}_{n-1} \cup \mathbf{B}_n$. Otherwise from 5.0.4 we must have:
$\mathbf{P}_{n-1} \cup$ Cop $(\mathbf{B}_n)?\mathbf{A}^* \neq 1$.
and so let $\mathbf{P}_n = \mathbf{P}_{n-1} \cup$ Cop $(\mathbf{B}_n)$.

Let $\mathbf{P}' = \bigcup_n \mathbf{P}_n$
Clearly $\mathbf{P}'?A^* \neq 1$.

Define an assignment of truth values h on the atoms of the language by
$h(x) = \mathbf{true}$ iff $\mathbf{P}'?x = 1$.

Lemma 5.0.6. *For any* $B, h(B) = \mathbf{true}$ *iff* $\mathbf{P}'?B^* = 1$

Proof. By induction on B.

(a) For atoms this is the definition

(b) Let $B = B_1 \to (B_2 \to \ldots (B_n \to q)\ldots)$ and let $B^* = \mathbf{C} \to q$. We thus have to check the case of $(\mathbf{C} \to q), q$ atomic, with $\mathbf{C} = \{B_1, \ldots B_n\}$.

(b1) If $\mathbf{P}'?(\mathbf{C} \to q) = 1$, then if $\mathbf{P}'?\mathbf{C} = 1$ then by 5.0.4 also $\mathbf{P}'?q = 1$. This means, by the induction hypothesis, that if $h(B_i) = \mathbf{true}$ for all i then also $h(q) = \mathbf{true}$, hence $h(B) = \mathbf{true}$.

(b2) If $\mathbf{P}'?(\mathbf{C} \to q) \neq 1$, then $\mathbf{P}' \cup \mathbf{C}?q \neq 1$. Hence by definition $h(q) =$ **false**, since certainly $\mathbf{P}'?q \neq 1$.

If $h(B_i) = \mathbf{true}$ for all i, then we are finished, since this makes $h(B)$ $= \mathbf{false}$. We now show that indeed $h(B_i) = \mathbf{true}$ for all i by showing that $h(B_i) = \mathbf{false}$ leads to a contradiction.

Assume that $h(B_i) = \mathbf{false}$.

Then, by the induction hypothesis, $\mathbf{P}'?\mathbf{C} \neq 1$.

Thus certainly $\mathbf{C} \not\subseteq \mathbf{P}'$ (if $\mathbf{C} \subseteq \mathbf{P}'$ then $\mathbf{P}'?\mathbf{C} = 1$). We have that $\mathbf{C} = \mathbf{B}_n$, for some n in the enumeration of the goals and so since $\mathbf{C}\neg \subseteq \mathbf{P}'$, by construction Cop $(\mathbf{C}) \subseteq \mathbf{P}'$, and especially $(\mathbf{C} \to q) \in \mathbf{P}'$. Thus $\mathbf{P}'?(\mathbf{C} \to q) = 1$, which contradicts the assumption of our case (b2).

Thus case (b) is proved and 5.0.6 is proved.

∎

We can now prove direction 2 of 5.0.5. Since $\mathbf{P}'?A^* \neq 1$, we get $h(A) =$ **false**. Thus h is an assignment of truth values such that for any $B^* \in \mathbf{P}$, and for any $B^* \in \mathbf{P} \cup Cop(A^*), h(B) = \mathbf{true}$ (since $B^* \in \mathbf{P}'$ implies $\mathbf{P}'?B^* = 1$) and $h(A) = \mathbf{false}$. This means that $\mathbf{P} \cup \mathrm{Cop}(A^*)\sharp \not\vdash A$ in classical logic. Thus (a) of 5.0.5 implies (b), as we showed that not (b) implies not (a).

This proves 5.0.5. ∎

We now examine completeness for locally linear computation.

Lemma 5.0.7. *[Soundness and completeness for classical logic of the notion of locally linear computation with restart, defined in 4.0.2]* $\mathbf{P}?(G, \mathbf{H}) = 1$ *iff* $\mathbf{P} \vdash G \vee \bigvee \mathbf{H}$ *in classical logic.*

Proof. *Soundness.* We prove soundness by induction on the length of the computation.

1. *Length 1*
   In this case $G = q$ is atomic and $q \in \mathbf{P}$.
   Thus $\mathbf{P} \vdash q \vee \bigvee \mathbf{H}$.

2. *Length* $k+1$

   (a) $G = A_1 \rightarrow (A_2 \rightarrow \ldots \rightarrow (A_n \rightarrow q)\ldots)$
   Then $\mathbf{P}?(G, \mathbf{H}) = 1$ if $\mathbf{P} \cup \{A_i\}?(q, \mathbf{H}) = 1$ and hence $\mathbf{P} \cup \{A_i\} \vdash q \vee \bigvee \mathbf{H}$ by the induction hypothesis and hence $\mathbf{P} \vdash G \vee \bigvee \mathbf{H}$.

   (b) $G = q$ and for some $B = B_1 \rightarrow (\ldots \rightarrow (B_n \rightarrow q)\ldots) \in \mathbf{P}$, $(\mathbf{P} - \{B\})?(B_i, \mathbf{H} \cup \{q\}) = 1$ for $i = 1, \ldots, n$.
   By the induction hypothesis $\mathbf{P} - \{B\} \vdash B_i \vee q \vee \bigvee \mathbf{H} i = 1 \ldots n$.
   However in classical logic $\bigwedge_{i=1}^{n} (B_i \vee q) \equiv (B_1 \rightarrow (B_2) \rightarrow (B_n \rightarrow q)\ldots) \rightarrow q$. Hence $\mathbf{P} - \{B\} \vdash (B \rightarrow q) \vee \bigvee \mathbf{H}$ and by the deduction theorem $\mathbf{P} \vdash q \vee \bigvee \mathbf{H}$

   (c) The restart rule was used, i.e. for some $a \in \mathbf{H}$

   $$\mathbf{P}?(a, \mathbf{H} \cup \{q\}) = 1$$

   Hence $\mathbf{P} \vdash a \vee q \vee \bigvee \mathbf{H}$ and since $a \in \mathbf{H}$ we get $\mathbf{P} \vdash q \vee \bigvee \mathbf{H}$

Completeness. We prove completeness by induction on the structure of the goal and the size and complexity of the database.

1. The case of G atomic and the database $\mathbf{P}$ are all atoms is clear, because $\mathbf{P} \cap (\{G\} \cup \mathbf{H}) \neq \varnothing$.

2. For the case G not atomic of the form $\mathbf{P} \rightarrow q$ we use the deduction theorem for classical logic and the induction hypothesis.

3. For the case $G = A \wedge B$, we have $\mathbf{P} \vdash (A \wedge B) \vee \bigvee \mathbf{H}$
   iff $\mathbf{P} \vdash (A \vee \bigvee \mathbf{H}) \wedge (B \vee \bigvee \mathbf{H})$

iff $\mathbf{P} \vdash A \vee \bigvee \mathbf{H}$ and $\mathbf{P} \vdash B \vee \bigvee \mathbf{H}$
and again we use the induction hypothesis.

4. Assume $\{\mathbf{A}_i \rightarrow x_i\} \vdash q \vee \bigvee \mathbf{H}, q$ atomic. Clearly $\{x_i\}$ and $\{q\} \cup \mathbf{H}$ must have an element in common, otherwise we can define a countermodel. Assume it is x_1. Thus $x_1 \in \mathbf{H}$. If A_1 is non-existent, then the computation succeeds by the restart rule. Otherwise,

$$\{A_i \rightarrow x_i\} \vdash q \vee \bigvee \mathbf{H}$$

iff in classical logic

$$\{A_2 \rightarrow x_2, A_3 \rightarrow x_3, \ldots\} \vdash A_1 \vee q \vee \bigvee \mathbf{H}.$$

By the induction hypothesis,

$$\{A_2 \rightarrow x_2, \ldots\}?(A_1, \mathbf{H} \cup \{q\}) = 1$$

We can now show that

$$\{A_1 \rightarrow x_1, A_2 \rightarrow x_2, \ldots\}?(q, \mathbf{H}) = 1$$

as follows:

Use restart with $x_1 \in \mathbf{H}$ and ask

$$\{A_1 \rightarrow x_1, A_2 \rightarrow x_2, \ldots\}?(x_1, \mathbf{H} \cup \{q\})$$

Unify with $A_1 \rightarrow x_1$ and ask

$$\{A_2 \rightarrow x_2, \ldots\}?(A_1, \mathbf{H} \cup \{q\} \cup \{x_1\})$$

which succeeds by the induction hypothesis (remember that $x_1 \in \mathbf{H}$).

∎

Lemma 5.0.8 (Soundness and completeness of locally linear computation with bounded restart for intuitionistic logic). *For the computation of 4.0.2 we have (1) if and only if (2):*

1. $\mathbf{P}?(G, (x_n, \ldots, x_1)) = 1$

2. $\mathbf{P}, G \rightarrow x_1, x_1 \rightarrow x_2, \ldots, x_{n-1} \rightarrow x_n \vdash G$

Proof. [Soundness, (1) implies (2)] By induction on the length of the computation, leading to success.

1. If $G \in \mathbf{P}, G$ atomic, then clearly (1) holds.
2. If $G = \{A_1, A_2\}$, then the computation succeeds with A_1 and succeeds with A_2. By the induction hypothesis, we have:

   $$\mathbf{P}, A_i \to x_1, x_1 \to x_2, \ldots, x_{n-1} \to x_n \vdash A_i$$

   for $i = 1, 2$.
   We want to show:

   $$\mathbf{P}, \{A_1, A_2\} \to x_1, x_1 \to x_2, \ldots, x_{n-1} \to x_n \vdash \{A_1, A_2\}$$

   The above holds because of lemma 4.0.11, namely

   $$((A \to x) \to A) \wedge ((B \to x) \to B) \vdash ((A \wedge B \to x) \to A \wedge B).$$

3. Case $G = A \to q$
   We need to show that

   $$\mathbf{P}, A, q \to x_1, \ldots, x_{n-1} \to x_n \vdash q$$

   implies

   $$\mathbf{P}, (A \to q) \to x_1, x_1 \to x_2, \ldots, x_{n-1} \to x_n \vdash A \to q$$

   This follows from Lemma 4.0.11 applied to the pair $A, q \to x$.
4. Case of bounded restart: We have to show that if

   $$\mathbf{P}, x_i \to q, q \to x_i, \ldots, x_{i-1} \to x_i, \ldots, x_{i+k} \to q, \ldots, \vdash x_i$$

   then

   $$\mathbf{P}, q \to x_1, \ldots, x_{i-1} \to x_i, \ldots, x_{i+1} \to q, \ldots, \vdash q$$

   however the two are equivalent since $x_i \to q$ is in the data, as x_i is bounded by q.

Completeness. We first prove that

$$\text{if } \mathbf{P} \vdash G \text{ then } \mathbf{P}?(G, \varnothing) = 1.$$

We shall later use this fact to show that (2) implies (1).

It is sufficient, in view of the deduction theorem, to assume that $G = q$ is atomic.

Assume that $\mathbf{P} \vdash q$, then by Theorem 3.0.12.

$(*)$ $\mathbf{P}?q = 1$
where the computation is the goal directed computation of 3.0.3.

We prove from $(*)$ that

$(**)$ $\mathbf{P}?(q, \varnothing) = 1.$

We do this by transforming a computation tree of $(*)$ into a computation tree of $(**)$.

First note that if $\mathbf{P}'$ is any database such that $\mathbf{P}'$? G=1 in the goal directed computation of (4.0.2) then some RC-clauses may be used ('used' is defined in 4.0.2,f1 and 4.0.2,f2) more than once. We can let $\mathbf{P}''$ be like $\mathbf{P}'$ except that some clauses are duplicated according to the number of times they are used in the successful computation of $\mathbf{P}'?G = 1$. For this $\mathbf{P}''$, we have $\mathbf{P}''?G = 1$, through a computation which uses each clause at most once. Furthermore, $\mathbf{P}' \equiv \mathbf{P}''$ in intuitionistic logic.

We can regard $\mathbf{P}''$ as a multiset and this will allow for several copies of the same clause B to be members or we can label the various copies of the clause B in some manner.

Thus, for example, $\mathbf{P}' = \{c \to a, (c \to a) \to c\}?a = 1$ in intuitionistic logic. The clause $c \to a$ is used twice. $\mathbf{P}''$ will be the multiset $\{c \to a, c \to a, (c \to a) \to c\}$.

The query $?a$ will succeed through a computation which uses every clause just once. However, it does use two copies of $c \to a$, each copy is used once. $\mathbf{P}''$ however, is obtained only by duplicating elements of $\mathbf{P}'$. This is not sufficient for our purpose. It may be the case that we have a database of the form $B = [(c \to a) \to [((c \to a) \to c) \to a)] \to q]$ and the query is $?q$.

We have that the query $?q$ reduces to the query $\{c \to a, (c \to a) \to c\}?a$ and now we have the case that $c \to a$ needs to be duplicated.

Duplicating B does not help. We have to duplicate inside B itself, i.e. $c \to a$ can be duplicated inside B by writing B as $(c \to a) \to ((c \to a) \to ((c \to a) \to c) \to a)))$.

Assume now that $\mathbf{P}'?G = 1$, through a tree $(T, \leq, 0, V')$ in the sense of 4.0.2. Consider the multiset $\mathbf{P}''$ which duplicates clauses in $\mathbf{P}'$ as needed. We can transform the labelling function V' into a labelling function V'' in the sense of 4.0.2 for a linear computation of $\mathbf{P}''?G = 1$.

The transformation is straightforward. The duplication has to be done more carefully, however. Consider $(T, \leq, 0, V')$. Part of the 3.0.3 and 4.0.2 is the notion of a wff A being *put into the database at a node t*. We also have a notion of the wff A being *used at a node s*. It is therefore possible to count for any A put in the database at a node t, how many times it has been used at nodes s below t. (i.e. at nodes s with $t \leq s$). Let m be the maximal number that any A was used in the entire tree. This means that if we duplicate any Am times whenever it was first put in, then no copy of any A needs to be used more than once. We duplicate m times systematically in the manner described above. We thus can get a computation $(T, \leq, 0, V'')$ that has the additional property that the maximal number of copies are put in right at the start and these copies are the ones used at the nodes. So if at lower nodes more copies are put in, they are not needed and not used. Call such a V'' 'rich'. Of course, since V'' represents a linear computation, each time a copy of a clause is used, it is thrown out, and a history is recorded. Note that in the tree $(T, \leq, 0, V'')$, the restart rule is not used, since it is not originally used in $(T, \leq, 0, V')$.

Coming back to our successful computation $\mathbf{P}?q$, we can assume there exists a $\mathbf{P}^*$ which is a duplicate extension of $\mathbf{P}$ such that $\mathbf{P}^*?q = 1$ through a tree $(T, \leq, 0, V^*)$ according to 4.0.2. Our aim is to transform this tree to a tree $(T_0, \leq\restriction T_0, 0, V_0)$ with $T_0 \subseteq$ T which is also a linear computation tree (4.0.2), which uses only clauses from $\mathbf{P}$.

This will prove the theorem. The proof is by induction on the number of 'bad' pairs of nodes in the tree, namely, nodes that 'use' copies of the 'same' formulae. We drop some nodes out of T and modify V^* and change it to V_0 and thus obtain the new tree.

Take a node $t \in T$ in the computation tree of $\mathbf{P}^*?(q, \varnothing)$, namely in $(T, \leq, 0, V^*)$.

This node is t and the tree label is $V^*(t) = (\mathbf{P}''_t, \{x\}, \mathbf{H}_t)$.

The original computation tree continues through the use of a clause of the form $B = (C_1 \to (C_2 \to, \ldots, (C_k \to x) \in \mathbf{P}$ with $C_i = C_1^i \to (C_2^i \to, \ldots, (C_{f(i)}^i \to y_i)$.

There are, therefore, successor points to t in the tree $t_1, \ldots, t_k$ and with $t \leq t_i, i = 1 \ldots k$ and successor points to t_i (if C_j^i indeed exist) of the form $t_i \leq s_i$ such that the following holds;

$V^*(t_i) = (\mathbf{P}''_t - \{B\}, \{C_i\}, \mathbf{H}_t \cup \{x\})$

$V^*(s_i) = ((\mathbf{P}''_t - \{B\}) \cup \{C_1^i, \ldots, C_{f(i)}^i\}, \{y_i\}, \mathbf{H}_t \cup \{x\})$

We distinguish several cases:

1. $B \in \mathbf{P}$ and this node t is the first node where a copy of B is used. In this case we do nothing.

2. $B \in \mathbf{P}$ and at some higher node $t^* \not\leq t$ another copy B' of B was used. In this case t^* will have as its immediate successors nodes $t_1^*, \ldots, t_k^*; s_1^*, \ldots, s_k^*$ and the node t is below one of the s_i^*, say below s_1^*. We thus have: $V^*(t_i^*) = (\mathbf{P}''_t - \{B'\}, \{C_i\}, \mathbf{H}_t \cup \{x\})$

   $V^*(s_i^*) = ((\mathbf{P}''_{t^*} - \{B'\} \cup \{C_1^i, \ldots, c_{f(i)}^i\}, \mathbf{H}_t \cup \{x\})$. See the following figure.

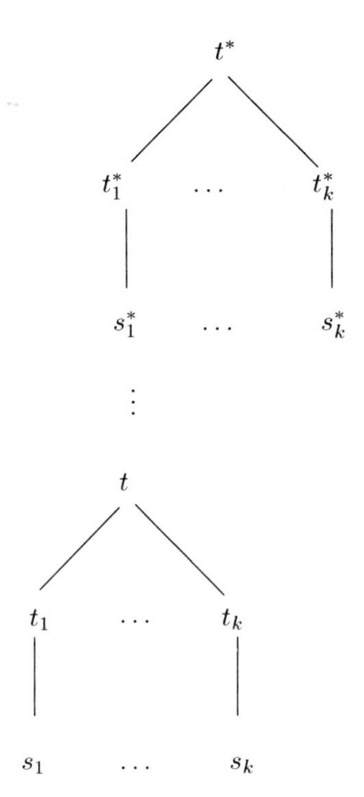

Notice two important facts:

Fact 1: The clauses $C_1^i, \ldots, C_{f(i)}^i$ are put in $\mathbf{P}_{s_1^*}$ and therefore are redundantly put into $\mathbf{P}_{s_1}$. They are already there. Note that we assume our tree is 'rich' and any clause (such as C_k^i) is put in with enough copies 'first time'.

Fact 2: y_1 is put in the history $\mathbf{H}_s$ at all points s which are immediate successors of s_1^*. Therefore $y_1 \in \mathbf{H}_t$.

In view of the above two facts, we can drop the point t_1 from the tree and also drop all points $t_2, \ldots, t_k$ and all subtrees below $t_1, \ldots, t_k$ respectively including $s_2, \ldots, s_k$. We modify $V^*(s_1)$ and $V^*(s)$ for all s such that $s_1 \leq s$ by *taking out* from $\mathbf{P}_s$ the extra copies of $C_1^i, \ldots, c_{f(i)}^i$ which we put into $\mathbf{P}_{s_1}$. We justify the new junction $t \leq s_1$ by the bounded restart rule in view of fact 2.

We thus get a correct locally linear computation tree with a smaller number of 'bad' pairs of nodes.

This inductive proof shows that there exists a tree with no 'bad' pairs at all. It follows from the construction that only wffs arising from subformulae of $\mathbf{P}$ are used and these are used at most once. We can therefore take V_0 to be the following function

$$V_0(t) = (\mathbf{P}_t^0, \mathbf{G}_t^0, \mathbf{H}_t^0)$$

where $\mathbf{P}_t^0, \mathbf{G}_t^0, \mathbf{H}_t^0$ are obtained from $\mathbf{P}_t^*, \mathbf{G}_t^*, \mathbf{H}_t^*$ respectively by substituting 'truth' for any duplicate not used in the transformed computation.

It is clear, since there are no 'bad' pairs that $\mathbf{P}_t^0 \subseteq \mathbf{P}$ for all t. This means that $\mathbf{P}?(q, \varnothing) = 1$.

We now prove completeness, namely show that (2) implies (1).

Let $\mathbf{P}' = \mathbf{P} \cup \{q \to x_1, (x_1 \to x_2), \ldots, x_{n-1} \to x_n\}$ then if $\mathbf{P}' \vdash q$ then $\mathbf{P}?(q, (x_n, \ldots, x_1)) = 1$.

By (1) above, we have that

$$\mathbf{P}, q \to x_1, x_1 \to x_2, \ldots, x_{n-1} \to x_n?(q, \varnothing) = 1$$

Let $(T, \leq, 0, V)$ be the computation tree of the above computation as in definition 3.8. For each node $t \in T$ we have $V(t) = (\mathbf{M}_t, \mathbf{G}_t, \mathbf{H}_t)$. Let $\mathbf{X}$ be the sequence $(x_m, \ldots, x_1)$. Let $\mathbf{H}_t' = \mathbf{X} * \mathbf{H}_t$. Let $V'(t) = (\mathbf{M}_t, \mathbf{G}_t, \mathbf{H}_t')$. Then $(T, \leq, 0, V')$ is a success tree for $\mathbf{P} \cup \{q \to x_1, \ldots, x_{n-1} \to x_n\}?(q, \mathbf{X}) = 1$.

All uses of the bounded restart rule in $(T, \leq, 0, V')$ are still valid because we have appended $\mathbf{X}$ at the beginning of $\mathbf{H}_t$.

Observe that we can use the bounded restart rule to justify any node of the form as in 5.

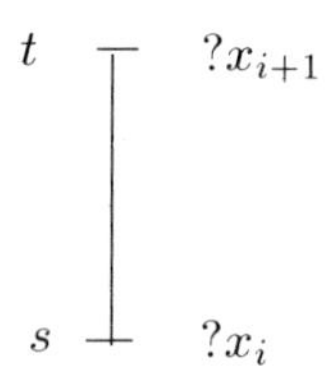

Because $\mathbf{X}$ is appended first in $\mathbf{H}_t'$. Thus if we let $\mathbf{M}_t' = \mathbf{M}_t \cup \{q \to x_1, x_1 \to x_2, \ldots, x_{n-1} \to x_n\}$ for $t \in T$, we get that $(T, \leq, 0, (\mathbf{M}', \mathbf{G}, \mathbf{H}'))$ is also a correct computation tree for $\mathbf{P}, \{q \to x_1, q \to x_1, \ldots, x_{n-1} \to x_n, x_{n-1} \to x_n\}?(q, \mathbf{X})$.

In this computation tree the clauses of $\{q \to x_1, \ldots, x_{n-1} \to x_n\}$ are *never* used. Thus these can be taken out of the database and the computation tree above justifies $\mathbf{P}?(q, \mathbf{X}) = 1$. ∎

Lemma 5.0.9. *In the notation of 5.0.7, for the case of classical logic, let*

$$A = A_1 \to (A_2 \to \ldots \to (A_n \to q) \ldots)$$

and

$$B = B_1 \to (B_2 \to \ldots \to (B_m \to q) \ldots).$$

Then (a) is equivalent to (b):

(a) $\mathbf{P} \cup \{A\}?(B_i, \mathbf{H} \cup \{q\}) = 1$ *for* $i = 1, \ldots m$.

(b) $\mathbf{P} \cup \{B\}?(A_i, \mathbf{H} \cup \{q\}) = 1$ *for* $i = 1, \ldots, n$.

Proof. From 5.0.7 and conditions (a) and (b) are equivalent, respectively, to (a') and (b') below:

(a') $\mathbf{P}, A \vdash B_i \vee q \vee \bigvee \mathbf{H}$, for $i = 1, \ldots, n$.

(b') $\mathbf{P}, B \vdash A_i \vee q \vee \bigvee \mathbf{H}$, for $i = 1, \ldots, n$.

By classical logic rules (a') and (b') are equivalent to (a'') and (b'') respectively:

(a'') $\mathbf{P}, A \vdash (\bigwedge_{i=1}^m B_i) \vee q \vee \bigvee \mathbf{H}$

(b'') $\mathbf{P}, B \vdash (\bigwedge_{i=1}^n A_i) \vee q \vee \bigvee \mathbf{H}$

Which are equivalent to (a''') and (b''') respectively:

(a''') $\mathbf{P}, A \vdash ((\bigwedge_{i=1}^m B_i \to q) \to q) \vee \bigvee \mathbf{H}$

(b''') $\mathbf{P}, B \vdash ((\bigwedge_{i=1}^n A_i \to q) \to q) \vee \bigvee \mathbf{H}$

Both (a'') and (b'') are equivalent to (c) below by the deduction theorem for classical logic.

(c) $\mathbf{P}, A, B \vdash q \vee \bigvee \mathbf{H}$

By 5.0.7 (c) is equivalent to

$$\mathbf{P}, A, B?(q, \mathbf{H}).$$

This proves 5.0.9. ∎

Lemma 5.0.10. *In the computation* $\mathbf{P}?(q, \mathbf{H})$ *with restart, no backtracking is necessary. The atom* q *can unify with any clause* $(A_1 \to \ldots \to (A_n \to q) \ldots) \in \mathbf{P}$ *and success or failure does not depend on the choice of the clause.*

Proof. Follows from 5.0.9 above. ∎

Example 5.0.11. The parallel to 5.0.9, 5.0.10 does not hold for the intuitionistic case. In the notation of 5.0.8, for the case of intuitionistic logic, let $A = A_1 \to \ldots \to (A_n \to q)\ldots)$, $B = B_1 \to \ldots \to (B_m \to q)\ldots)$ Then (a) is *not necessarily* equivalent to (b):

(a) $\mathbf{P} \cup \{A\}?(B_i, \mathbf{H} * (q)) = 1$
for $i = 1, \ldots, m$

(b) $\mathbf{P} \cup \{B\}?(A_i, \mathbf{H} * q) = 1$
for $i = 1, \ldots, n$.

Let

$$\mathbf{P} = \{a\}$$

$$A = a \to q$$

$$B = (c \to b) \to q$$

Then

$$\mathbf{P} \cup \{A\}?(b, (q)) \text{ is } \{c, a, a \to q\}?(b, (q))$$

while

$$\mathbf{P} \cup \{B\}?(a, (q)) \text{ is } \{a, (c \to b) \to q\}?(a, (q))$$

The first computation fails (we cannot restart here) and the second computation succeeds. The soundness direction of 4.8 does give us that $\{c, a, a \to q, b \to q\}$ does not prove b in the first case and it does prove a in the second case.

We thus see that in the intuitionistic computation $\mathbf{P}?(q, \mathbf{H})$, with bounded restart, backtracking is certainly necessary. The atom q can unify with any clause $(A_1 \to \ldots \to (A_n \to q)\ldots)$ and success or failure may depend on the choice of clause.

6 Conjunctions and negations

The addition of conjunction to the propositional language does not change the system much. Conjunction, $\wedge$, can be fully characterized by the following two conditions on the consequence relation:

1. $\wedge$-Elimination rule
   $A \wedge B \vdash A$
   $A \wedge B \vdash B$

2. $\wedge$-Introduction rule
   $\{A, B\} \vdash A \wedge B$.

It is easy to show that $A \wedge B \vdash B \wedge A$.

Let $\vdash_\wedge$ be the smallest consequence relation for the language with $\{\to, \wedge\}$ closed under the deduction theorem and the $\wedge$ elimination and introduction rules. In the future we shall omit the subscript $\wedge$ from $\vdash_\wedge$.

We want to characterize $\vdash_\wedge$ computationally. This we do using the following lemmas.

Lemma 6.0.1.

1. $A \to (B \to C) \vdash A \wedge B \to C$
2. $A \wedge B \to C \vdash A \to (B \to C)$
3. $(A \to B \wedge C) \vdash (A \to B) \wedge (A \to C)$
4. $(A \to B) \wedge (A \to C) \vdash A \to (B \wedge C)$.

Proof. Exercise. ■

Lemma 6.0.2. *Every formula A with conjunctions is equivalent in intuitionistic logic to a conjunction of formulae which contain no conjunctions.*

Proof. Use the equivalences of 6.0.1 to pull the conjunctions out. ■

Definition 6.0.3.

1. With any formula A with conjunctions we associate a unique (up to equivalence) set $\mathbf{H}(A)$ of RC-clauses as follows: (compare with 3.0.11). Given A, use 6.0.2 to present it as $\wedge A_i$, where each A_i contains no conjunctions. Let $\mathbf{H}(A) = \{A_i^*\}$.
2. Let $\mathbf{P}$ be a set of formulae. Define $\mathbf{H}(\mathbf{P}) = \bigcup_{A \in \mathbf{P}} \mathbf{H}(A)$.
3. We can now define $\mathbf{P}?A$, for $\mathbf{P}$ and A containing conjunctions. We simply compute $\mathbf{H}(\mathbf{P})?\mathbf{H}(A)$ according to 3.0.3.
4. The computation rule for conjunction can be stated directly: $\mathbf{P}?A \wedge B = 1$ iff $\mathbf{P}?A = 1$ and $\mathbf{P}?B = 1$.

We now turn to negation. It is well known that negation can be added to many systems of logic (including classical logic, intuitionistic logic, relevance logic) by adding a constant symbol $\bot$ for falsity and defining the new connective $\neg A$ for negation as $A \to \bot$.

For different logical systems, $\neg$ satisfies different properties. In intuitionistic logic, negation satisfies the axiom schemas

$$A, \neg A \vdash B$$

and

$$B, A \to \neg B \vdash \neg A.$$

Note that classical logic is obtained by adding

$$\neg\neg A \vdash A.$$

If we let $\neg A \equiv A \to \bot$ then the first property becomes

$$A, A \to \bot \vdash B$$

and the second becomes

$$B, A \to (B \to \bot) \vdash A \to \bot.$$

The second property holds in intuitionistic logic for any q (not only for $\bot$) i.e. $B, A \to (B \to q) \vdash A \to q$.

However, to have the first property we need the following property of $\bot$:

$$\bot \vdash B$$

For classical logic the third property becomes

$$(A \to \bot) \to \bot \vdash A.$$

It is convenient for us, in the case of intuitionistic logic, to add negation into the system by adding a falsity symbol $\bot$, which is considered as atomic. It has the further property that $\bot \vdash A$, for any A.

Thus the notion of RC-clause remains the same since $\bot$ can be considered as just another atom.

What we have to modify are the computation rules for RC-clauses, because we have to allow for the special nature of $\bot$, namely that $\bot \vdash A$ holds for any A.

Definition 6.0.4. [Computation tree for RC-clause data and goal containing $\bot$] The definition is the same as 3.0.3 except for the following modifications:

1. Modify (f1) to read: t has no immediate successors and $q \in \mathbf{P}$ or $\bot \in \mathbf{P}$ or both.

2. Modify (f2) to read: t has exactly one immediate successor s in the tree with $V(s) = (\mathbf{P}, \mathbf{A})$ and with $(\mathbf{A} \to q) \in \mathbf{P}$ or $(\mathbf{A} \to \bot) \in \mathbf{P}$.

3. Note that classical logic with $\bot$ will be obtained if the restart rule is added, namely clause (f3) of 5.0.1.

We now have two computations, as defined in 6.0.4. One for intuitionistic logic with $\bot$, corresponding to computation without the restart rule (f3) and the other for classical logic, which corresponds to computation with the restart rule. We have to prove that indeed the above statements are true. This is easy to see. The rule $\bot \vdash A$ is built into the computation via the modifications in (a) and (b) of 6.0.4 and hence we know we are getting intuitionistic logic. To show that the restart rule yields classical logic, it is sufficient to show that the computation

$$(A \to \bot) \to \bot ? A$$

always succeeds with the restart rule. This can also be easily checked.

To complete the picture we prove 6.0.5 below which essentially shows that the computation of $\mathbf{P}?A$ with restart is the same as the computation of $\mathbf{P}?(A \to \bot) \to A$ without restart. This means that the restart rule (with original goal A) can be effectively implemented by adding $A \to \bot$ to the database and using the $A \to \bot$ clause and the $\bot$ rules to replace uses of the restart rule. The above considerations correspond to the known translation from classical logic to intuitionistic logic, namely:
$\mathbf{P} \vdash A$ in classical logic
iff $\mathbf{P} \vdash \neg A \to A$ in intuitionistic logic.

Lemma 6.0.5. *For any database* $\mathbf{P}$, *and original goal* G_0:

$$\mathbf{P}?G_0 = 1 \text{ with restart iff } \mathbf{P} \cup \{G_0 \to \bot\}?G_0 = 1 \text{ without restart.}$$

Proof. Given a computation tree for $(\mathbf{P}?G_0)$, we can construct an isomorphic tree for $(\mathbf{P} \cup \{G_0 \to \bot\}?G_0)$, which employs the same computation rules at corresponding nodes. We shall then transform it into a tree for $(\mathbf{P} \cup \{G_0 \to \bot\}?G_0)$ which is restart-free.

Consider a node n of the tree with $(\mathbf{P} \cup \{G_0 \to \bot\}, q)$ that has been expanded into a successor node, using the restart rule. Since the database may only be augmented through computation, never diminished, we can write the node n as $(\mathbf{P}_n \cup \{G_0 \to \bot\}, A)$ where $\mathbf{P}_n$ and A are the current database and goal at that node, and its successor as $(\mathbf{P}_n \cup \{G_0 \to \bot\}, G_0)$. $\mathbf{P}_n$ will be a superset of $\mathbf{P}$. We employ rule 6.0.4,b (with $G_0 \to \bot$) in place of the restart rule.

In this way, we can remove all uses of the restart rule from the tree, thus obtaining a computation tree $\mathbf{P} \cup \{G_0 \to \bot\}?G_0 = 1$, without restart.

Conversely, if we have a computation tree for $(\mathbf{P} \cup \{G_0 \to \bot\}?G_0$ without restart, then the clause $G_0 \to \bot$ in the database could only have been employed at node $(\mathbf{P}_n \cup \{G_0 \to \bot\}, G_n)$ in connection with rule 6.0.4,a, if the current goal G_n was $\bot$, or in connection with 6.0.4,b if G_n was atom q. Either way, the successor node $(\mathbf{P}_n \cup \{G_0 \to \bot\}, G_0)$ could have been obtained without reference to the clause $G_0 \to \bot$ if we had had the use of the restart rule.

In this way, we can remove all uses of the clause $G_0 \to \bot$ from the computation tree for $(\mathbf{P} \cup \{G_0 \to \bot\}?G_0 = 1)$ and instead introduce uses of the classical restart rule thus obtaining a computation tree for $(\mathbf{P}?G_0) = 1$.

∎

Remark 6.0.6. The above lemma can be used to prove that the restart rule can be modified. Our restart rule allows us to restart when the current query is atomic, i.e.

$$\mathbf{P}?q = 1 \text{ if } \mathbf{P}?G_0 = 1$$

where G_0 is the original goal.

The more general restart rule is when we can restart at any time, i.e.

$$\mathbf{P}?\mathbf{A} = 1 \text{ if } \mathbf{P}?G_0 = 1$$

for any A.

The proof is simple and follows from 6.0.5. First observe that

(*) $\mathbf{P}?\mathbf{A} = 1$ (with restart in classical logic) iff $\mathbf{P} \cup \{G_0 \to \bot\}?\mathbf{A} = 1$ in intuitionistic logic. By 6.0.5.
Second observe that

(**) $\mathbf{P}?G_0 = 1$ in classical logic iff $\mathbf{P} \cup \{G_0 \to \bot\}?G_0 = 1$ in intuitionistic logic.

Now assume $\mathbf{P}?G_0 = 1$ in classical logic. We want to show $\mathbf{P}?A = 1$ in classical logic. From (**) we get $\mathbf{P} \cup \{G_0 \to \bot\}?G_0 = 1$ in intuitionistic logic. Hence by soundness $\mathbf{P} \cup \{G_0 \to \bot\} \vdash G_0$ in intuitionistic logic. Hence $\mathbf{P} \cup \{G_0 \to \bot\} \vdash \bot$ in intuitionistic logic.

Hence $\mathbf{P} \cup \{G_0 \to \bot\} \vdash \mathbf{A}$ in intuitionistic logic. Hence $\mathbf{P} \cup \{G_0 \to \bot\}?\mathbf{A} = 1$ in intuitionistic logic and hence by (**) $\mathbf{P}?\mathbf{A} = 1$ in classical logic.

We therefore saw that the general restart rule

$$\mathbf{P}?\mathbf{A} = 1 \text{ if } \mathbf{P}?G_0 = 1$$

is a sound one. It is of course complete since the ordinary (weaker) restart rule is complete.

We shall see in Section 8 that for certain intermediate logics, the restart rule for atoms does not give completeness, and the general restart rule, for any **A** is needed.

We best give examples of the computation in practice.

Example 6.0.7.

$(a \to b) \to b \quad ? \quad (a \to \bot) \to b$
We use rule for $\to$
$(a \to b) \to b, a \to \bot \quad ? \quad b.$

we have two choices here. One is to use the rule for atoms with $a \to \bot$ and the second to use the rule for atoms with $(a \to b) \to b$. You can guess that the first case loops, so we use the second case:

$(a \to b) \to b, a \to \bot \quad ? \quad a \to b$
$(a \to b) \to b, a \to \bot, a \quad ? \quad b$
We use the rule for atoms with $a \to \bot$

$(a \to b) \to b, a \to \bot, a \quad ? \quad a$
success.

Example 6.0.8.
$(q \to \bot) \to q \quad ? \quad q$
rule for atoms
$(q \to \bot) \to q \quad ? \quad (q \to \bot)$
rule for $\to$
$(q \to \bot) \to q, q \quad ? \quad \bot$

Note that the rule for atoms involving $\bot$ can be used only when $\bot$ is in the database, i.e. in $(q \to \bot)?a$ we can ask for q but *not* in the case of $(q \to a)? \bot$. We cannot use the rule for atoms here. So, we fail in intuitionistic logic. In classical logic we can use restart to obtain:
$(q \to \bot) \to q, q?q$
and terminate successfully.

Example 6.0.9.
$a \to b \quad ? \quad ((x \to \bot) \to a) \to ((x \to \bot) \to b))$
rule for $\to$
$a \to b, (x \to \bot) \to a \quad ? \quad (x \to \bot) \to b$
rule for $\to$
$a \to b, (x \to \bot) \to a, x \to \bot \quad ? \quad b$
rule for atoms using $a \to b$
$a \to b, (x \to \bot) \to a, x \to \bot \quad ? \quad a$

rule for atoms using $(x \to \bot) \to a$

$a \to b, (x \to \bot) \to a, x \to \bot \quad ? \quad x \to \bot$

rule for $\to$

$a \to b, (x \to \bot) \to a, x \to \bot, x \quad ? \quad \bot$

Note that you cannot say 'we have $x \to \bot$ in the database hence *success*', since the rules are mechanical. Success can be obtained only in the rule for atoms. But $x \to \bot$ is *not* an atom. So

rule for atoms with $x \to \bot$

$a \to b, (x \to \bot) \to a, x \to \bot, x \quad ? \quad x$

success.

Example 6.0.10.

$a \quad ? \quad (a \to \bot) \to b$

rule for $\to$

$a, a \to \bot \quad ? \quad b$

rule for atoms using $a \to \bot$

$a, a \to \bot \quad ? \quad a$

success.

Example 6.0.11.

$a \to b, b \to \bot \quad ? \quad a \to \bot$

rule for $\to$

$a \to b, b \to \bot, a \quad ? \quad \bot$

rule for atoms using $b \to \bot$

$a \to b, b \to \bot, a \quad ? \quad b$

rule for atoms using $a \to b$

$a \to b, b \to \bot, a \quad ? \quad a$

success.

Example 6.0.12.

$\varnothing \quad ? \quad (a \to \bot) \to (a \to b)$

rule for $\to$

$a \to \bot \quad ? \quad a \to b$

rule for $\to$

$a \to \bot, a \quad ? \quad b$

rule for atoms using $a \to \bot$

$a \to \bot, a \quad ? \quad b$

success.

Example 6.0.13.

$(((a \to \bot) \to b) \to \bot) \to c \quad ? \quad (a \to \bot) \to [(b \to \bot) \to c$
rule for $\to$
$(((a \to \bot) \to b) \to \bot) \to c, a \to \bot \quad ? \quad (b \to \bot) \to c$
rule for $\to$
$(((a \to \bot) \to b) \to \bot) \to c, a \to \bot, b \to \bot \quad ? \quad c$

The rule for atoms can be used with each of the three assumptions. If you want to use the system automatically try all three. Otherwise try the first one because it will make you *add* to the data and thus increase the chances of success.

$((a \to \bot) \to b) \to \bot) \to c, a \to \bot, b \to \bot \ ? \ ((a \to \bot) \to b) \to \bot$
rule for $\to$
$(((a \to \bot) \to b) \to \bot) \to c, a \to \bot, b \to \bot, (a \to \bot) \to b \ ? \ \bot$
rule for atoms with $b \to \bot$
$(((a \to \bot) \to b) \to \bot) \to c, a \to \bot, b \to \bot, (a \to \bot) \to b \ ? \ b$
rule for atoms with $(a \to \bot) \to b$
$(((a \to \bot) \to b) \to \bot) \to c, a \to \bot, b \to \bot, (a \to \bot) \to b \ ? \ a \to \bot$
rule for $rightarrow$
$(((a \to \bot) \to b) \to \bot) \to c, a \to \bot, b \to \bot, (a \to \bot) \to b, a \ ? \ \bot$
rule for atoms using $a \to \bot$
$(((a \to \bot) \to b) \to \bot) \to c, a \to \bot, b \to \bot), (a \to \bot) \to b, a \ ? \ a$
success.

7 Disjunction

To describe how we handle disjunctions in intuitionistic and other logics, we need a background definition.

Definition 7.0.1. Consider a language with the connectives $\{\wedge, \vee, \to, \bot\}$. Let $\vdash$ be the smallest consequence relation on the wffs of this language satisfying the following:

1. The deduction theorem for $\to$:

$$\mathbf{P} \vdash A \to B \text{ iff } \mathbf{P}, A \vdash B.$$

2. Conjunction rules

   (a) $A \wedge B \vdash A$

   (b) $A \wedge B \vdash B$

   (c) $A, B \vdash A \wedge B$.

3. Negation Rule

$$\bot \vdash B.$$

4. Disjunction rules

   (a) $A \vdash A \vee B$

   (b) $B \vdash A \vee B$

   (c) $\mathbf{P}, A \vdash C$ and $\mathbf{P}, B \vdash C$ imply $\mathbf{P}, A \vee B \vdash C$.

The above closure rules define the intuitionistic propositional consequence relation. In the fragment without $\bot$, the other rules (1), (2), and (4) suffice to define intuitionistic logic for that fragment.

Classical logic can be obtained as the smallest consequence relation satisfying (1)–(4) and (5) below:

5. Strong deduction theorem

$$\mathbf{P}, A \vdash B \vee C \text{ iff } \mathbf{P} \vdash (A \to B) \vee C.$$

The logic known as Dummett's **LC** is defined as the smallest consequence relation satisfying (1)–(4) and (6)

6. $A \to (B \vee C) \vdash (A \to B) \vee (A \to C)$.

The handling of disjunction is more difficult than the handling of conjunction and negation. Consider the formula $a \to (b \vee (c \to d))$.

We cannot rewrite this formula in intuitionistic logic to anything of the form $B \to q$, where q is atomic (or $\bot$).

We therefore have to change our computation procedures to accommodate the general form of an intuitionistic formula with disjunction.

In classical logic disjunctions can be pulled out to the outside of formulas using the following rules:

1. $(A \vee B \to C) \equiv (A \to C) \wedge (B \to C)$

2. $(C \to A \vee B) \equiv (C \to A) \vee (C \to B)$.

Where $\equiv$ denotes logical equivalence (in our case logical equivalence in classical logic). (1) is valid in intuitionistic logic but (2) is not valid. In fact, if we add (2) as an axiom schema to intuitionistic logic we get the logical system known as Dummett's **LC**.

The pure implication fragment of Dummett's **LC** is also stronger than intuitionistic logic. For example

$$((A \to B) \to C) \to (((B \to A) \to C) \to C)$$

is a theorem of this fragment but is not a theorem of intuitionistic logic.

In intuitionistic logic **I** we have the disjunction property, namely $\vdash_{\mathbf{I}} A \vee B$ iff $\vdash_{\mathbf{I}} A$ or $\vdash_{\mathbf{I}} B$. This is not true in classical logic, **C**. Thus for example $\vdash A \vee (A \rightarrow B)$ but $\nvdash_{\mathbf{C}} A$ and $\nvdash_{\mathbf{C}} A \rightarrow B$.

In view of the above we may want to adopt the computation rule below for disjunction in the goal.

HR3 $\mathbf{P}?A \vee B = 1$ if $\mathbf{P}?A = 1$ or $\mathbf{P}?B = 1$.

This corresponds to the consequence relation rules $A \vdash A \vee B$ and $B \vdash A \vee B$.

In case we have disjunction in the data, the rule is clear:

HR4 $\mathbf{P} \cup \{A \vee B\}?C = 1$ if $\mathbf{P} \cup \{A\}?C = 1$ and $\mathbf{P} \cup \{B\}?C = 1$.

This corresponds to the consequence relation rule

$$\frac{\mathbf{P}, A \vdash C \quad \mathbf{P}, B \vdash C}{\mathbf{P}, A \vee B \vdash C}$$

Let us adopt the above two rules for computation.

Example 7.0.2. $A \vee B?A \vee B$. Using **HR3** we get

$$A \vee B?A$$

or

$$A \vee B?B$$

which fail. However using **HR4**, we get

$$A?A \vee B$$

and

$$B?A \vee B$$

which succeed using **HR3**.

Definition 7.0.3. Computation rules for full intuitionistic logic with disjunction.

1. The propositional language contains the connectives $\wedge, \vee, \rightarrow, \bot$. Formulae are defined inductively as usual.
2. We define the operation $\mathbf{P} + A$, for any formula $A = \bigwedge_i A_i$, as follows: $\mathbf{P} + A = \mathbf{P} \cup \{A_i\}$ provided A_i are not conjunctions.
3. We define the computation rules by induction on the formula structure.

(a) $\mathbf{P}?A \wedge B = 1$ if $\mathbf{P}?A = 1$ and $\mathbf{P}?B = 1$

(b) $\mathbf{P}?A \vee B = 1$ if $\mathbf{P}?A = 1$ or $\mathbf{P}?B = 1$

(c) $\mathbf{P}?A \vee B = 1$ if for some $C_1 \to \ldots (C_n \to D) \ldots) \in P$, we have

   i. $\mathbf{P}?C_i = 1, fori = 1, \ldots, n$, and

   ii. $\mathbf{P} + D?A \vee B = 1$

(d) $\mathbf{P}?A \to B = 1$ if $\mathbf{P} + A?B = 1$

(e) $\mathbf{P}?q = 1$ if $q \in P$ or $\bot \in \mathbf{P}$ or for some $(A_1 \to \ldots (A_n \to B) \ldots) \in \mathbf{P}$ we have that

   i. $\mathbf{P}?A_i = 1$ for $i = 1, \ldots, n$, and

   ii. $\mathbf{P} + B?q = 1$

Notice that rule (3e) does not require B to be atomic $B = q$. This is because we cannot rewrite all formulae to the form $A \to$ atom.

(f) $\mathbf{P} \cup \{A \vee B\}?C = 1$ if $\mathbf{P} + A?C = 1$ $\mathbf{P} + B?C = 1$

The computation described above is not efficient, especially because of rule (3f). It is therefore good policy to apply rule (3f) and then rule (3e) forward as much as possible and then apply rule rule (3e) for atomic heads $B = q$. In order to do that effectively we must rewrite the formulae in a ready for computation form.

Lemma 7.0.4. *Any formula A is equivalent in intuitionistic logic to a conjunction of formulae of the form $\bigwedge A_i$, containing no '$\wedge$' and no '$\vee$' in the body of implications.*

Proof. We use the following equivalences to pull conjunctions out:

$$
\begin{aligned}
A \wedge (B \vee C) &\equiv (A \vee B) \wedge (A \vee C) \\
(A \to B \wedge C) &\equiv (A \to B) \wedge (A \to C) \\
(A \wedge B \to C) &\equiv A \to (B \to C) \\
(A \vee B \to C) &\equiv (A \to C) \wedge (B \to C).
\end{aligned}
$$

The previous lemma is the best we can do for eliminating disjunctions. Basically disjunctions in the heads of implications cannot be eliminated by rewriting the formula. Thus nothing can be done to a formula of the form $a \to b \vee c$

There is one thing we could do, however. Suppose we regard $b \vee c$ as an atom $q = b \vee c$. Thus we can write $a \to q$ instead of $a \to b \vee c$. However, we have to say that $q = b \vee c$. What are the logical properties characterizing the above equation? These are:

- $b \to q$
- $c \to q$
- $(b \to x) \to [(c \to x) \to (q \to x)]$, where x ranges over arbitrary formulae.

Thus if **P** is a database containing $a \to b \vee c$ as an item we can replace this item by $a \to q$ and all instances of the •-items. ∎

Example 7.0.5. The problem in (1) is replaced by the problem in (2)

1. $a \to b \vee c, a, b \to d, c \to d \ ? \ d$
2. $a \to q, a, b \to d, c \to d, b \to q, c \to q, (a \to x) \to ((b \to x) \to (q \to x))$ $? \ d$
   where x ranges over all subformulae of the data and query i.e. $x = a, b, c, d$; etc.

Basically we are using the second-order functional equation for disjunction.

Dis $(a, b, q) \equiv$ def. $\forall x[(a \to x) \to ((b \to x) \to (q \to x))]$

Let us proceed to do the above systematically:

Definition 7.0.6. We want to eliminate disjunctions from our computations. Let us consider the language $\mathbf{L_1}$, with $\to$ and $\vee$ only, and consider a new language, $\mathbf{L_2}$, with a pairing operator $\mathbf{v}(x, y)$. Define a formula and an **v**-atom in the new language as follows:

1. any atom is a **v**-atom and a formula
2. If A, B are formulae then $A \to B$ is a formula and $\mathbf{v}(A, B)$ is a **v**-atom.

Let **P** be a database in $\mathbf{L_1}$ (the language with $(\to, \vee)$. It can be considered a database in the language $\mathbf{L_2}$ (with $\to$, **v**) by translating any formula as follows (T_1 is the translation):

$T_1 q = q.$
$T_1(A \to B) = T_1 A \to T_1 B$
$T_1(A \vee B) = \mathbf{v}(T_1 A, T_1 B)$

Note that the reverse translation $T_2 : \mathbf{L_2} \mapsto \mathbf{L_1}$ can also be defined:

$$T_2 q = q$$
$$T_2(A \to B) = (T_2 A \to T_2 B)$$
$$T_2 \mathbf{v}(A, B) = T_2 A \vee T_2 B.$$

We have for $A \in \mathbf{L}_2, B \in \mathbf{L}_1$

$$T_1 T_2 A = A$$
$$T_2 T_1 B = B$$

Let $\mathbf{P}_1$ be a finite database and let A be a goal in $\mathbf{L_1}$. Let $\mathbf{Q}$ be the set of all subformulae of $\mathbf{P} \cup \{A\}$ and let $T_1\mathbf{Q}$ be $\{T_1 B \mid B \in \mathbf{Q}.\}$.

Let $\mathbf{P}_2$ be $T_1\mathbf{P}$ $\cup$ $\{T_1 x \to)\mathbf{v}(T_1 x, T_1 y) \mid x, y \in \mathbf{Q}\}$
$\cup$ $\{T_1 y \to \mathbf{v}(T_1 x, T_1 y) \mid x, y \in \mathbf{Q}\}$
$\cup$ $\{(T_1 x \to z) \to ((T_1 y \to z) \to (\mathbf{v}(T_1 x, T_1 y) \to z))$
$\mid x, y \in \mathbf{Q}, \in T_1\mathbf{Q}\}$.

Clearly $\mathbf{P}_2$ is finite.

Lemma 7.0.7. $\mathbf{P}_1?A = 1$ *iff* $\mathbf{P}_2?T_1A = 1$ *where the* $\mathbf{P}_1?A$ *computation is carried within* $\mathbf{L}_1$ *(with disjunction) and* $\mathbf{P}_2?T_1A$ *is carried out in* $\mathbf{L}_2$ *(the implicational fragment with* $\mathbf{v}$*).*

Proof. By induction on the length of the proof.

(a) $\mathbf{P}_1?A \to B = 1$ iff $\mathbf{P}_1 + A?B = 1$ iff $\mathbf{P}_1 + T_1A?T_1B = 1$ iff $\mathbf{P}_2?T_1A \to T_1B = 1$ iff $\mathbf{P}_2?T_1(A \to B) = 1$.

(b) Assume $\mathbf{P}_1?q = 1$; then either (b1) $q \in \mathbf{P}_1$ or (b2) for some $(B_1 \to \cdots (B_n \to C) \cdots) \in \mathbf{P}_1, \mathbf{P}_1?B_i = 1$ for $i = 1, \ldots, n$, and $\mathbf{P}_1 + C?q = 1$.

(b1) If $q \in \mathbf{P}_1$ then $T_1 q \in \mathbf{P}_2$ and hence $\mathbf{P}_2?T_1 q = 1$

(b2) If $(B_1 \to \ldots (B_n \to C) \ldots) \in \mathbf{P}_1$, then $T_1(B_1 \to \ldots (B_n \to C) \ldots) \in \mathbf{P}_2$ and since $\mathbf{P}_2?T_1B_i = 1$ for $i = 1, \ldots, n$, by the induction hypothesis, we get $\mathbf{P}_2?T_1C = 1$, by the deduction theorem and cut for the implicational language $\mathbf{L}_2$.
We also have that $\mathbf{P}_2 + T_1C?q = 1$, hence again by cut, $\mathbf{P}_2?q = 1$.

(c) Assume $\mathbf{P}_2?q = 1$ for q atomic. If $q \in \mathbf{P}_2$ then $q \in \mathbf{P}_1$ and hence $\mathbf{P}_1?q = 1$. If for some $D = D_1 \to \ldots \to (D_n \to q) \in \mathbf{P}_2, \mathbf{P}_2?D_i = 1$ for $i = 1, \ldots, n$, then there are two possibilities.

(c1) $T_2D \in \mathbf{P}_1$, in which case, since $T_1T_2D = D$, we get $\mathbf{P}_1?T_2D_i = 1$ for $i = 1, \ldots, n$, and hence $\mathbf{P}_1?q = 1$.

(c2) $D = (T_1 A \to q) \to ((T_1 B(\to q) \to (\mathbf{v}(T_1 A, T_1 B) \to q)))$, and $\mathbf{P}_2?(T_1 A \to q) = 1$, and $\mathbf{P}_2?(T_1 B \to q) = 1$, and $\mathbf{P}_2?\mathbf{v}(T_1 A, T_1 B) = 1$ all hold. By the induction hypothesis, $\mathbf{P}_1?(A \to q) = 1$ and $\mathbf{P}_1?(B \to q) = 1$ hold.

How can $\mathbf{P}_2?\mathbf{v}(T_1 A, T_1 B) = 1$ hold ? Either because $\mathbf{v}(T_1 A, T_1 B) \in \mathbf{P}2$, in which case $A \vee B \in \mathbf{P}_1$, and hence $\mathbf{P}_1?q = 1$ by the disjunction rule; or because some clause having $\mathbf{v}(T_1 A, T_1 B)$ in its head succeeds from $\mathbf{P}_2$. The only clauses with such a head are of the form $T_1 C_1 \to \cdots (T_1 C_n \to \mathbf{v}(T_1 A, T_1 B)) \cdots)$ and we have $\mathbf{P}_2?T_1 C_i = 1, i = 1, \ldots, n$.
We thus have by the induction hypothesis

1. $C_1 \to \ldots \to ((C_n \to A \vee B) \ldots) \in \mathbf{P}_1$
2. $\mathbf{P}_1?C_i = 1, i = 1, \ldots, n$
3. $\mathbf{P}_1 + A?q = 1$
4. $\mathbf{P}_1 + B?q = 1$
5. Hence by the definition of the calculation with $\mathbf{P}_1$ we have $\mathbf{P}_1?q = 1$.

(d) Assume $\mathbf{P}_1?A_1 \vee A_2 = 1$. Then if $\mathbf{P}_1?A_i = 1$, for $i = 1$ or $i = 2$. Then, by the induction hypothesis, $\mathbf{P}_2?T_1 A_i = 1$ and since $T_1 A_i \to \mathbf{v}(T_1 A_1, T_1 A_2)$, we get $P_2?\mathbf{v}(T_1 A_1 \vee T_1 A_2) = 1$, which is $\mathbf{P}_2?T_1(A_1 \vee A_2) = 1$.
The other way for a disjunction to succeed is through a

$$(C_1 \to \ldots (C_n \to D) \ldots) \in \mathbf{P}_1$$

with $\mathbf{P}_1?C_i = 1$, for $i = 1, \ldots, n$ and $\mathbf{P}_1 + D?A_1 \vee A_2 = 1$. Using the induction hypothesis we get $\mathbf{P}_2?T_1 C_i = 1$, and $T_1 C_1 \to \ldots \to (T_1 C_n \to T_1 D) \ldots) \in \mathbf{P}_2$ and $\mathbf{P}_2 + T_1 D?\mathbf{v}(T_1 A_1, T_1 A_2) = 1$.
We therefore get by the deduction theorem for $\mathbf{P}_2$ that

$$\mathbf{P}_2?\mathbf{v}(T_1 A_1, T_1 A_2) = 1.$$

This completes the proof of 7.0.7. ∎

Theorem 7.0.8. *Let* $\mathbf{I}v$ *be the intuitionistic fragment with disjunction. Let* $\mathbf{P}?A = 1$ *be the computation of 7.0.3. Then* $\mathbf{P} \vdash_{\mathbf{I}v} A$ *if* $\mathbf{P}?A = 1$.

Proof. From 7.0.7 and the fact that $\mathbf{P} \vdash_{\mathbf{I}v} A$ iff $T_1 \mathbf{P}_1 \vdash_{\mathbf{I}} T_1 A$ iff $T_1 \mathbf{P}?T_1 A = 1$ iff $\mathbf{P}?A = 1$. ∎

8 Intermediate logics

This section treats the sequence of intermediate logics between intuitionistic logic and classical logic based on the weakening of the restart rule, for the fragment with $\{\wedge, \rightarrow, \perp\}$.

Definition 8.0.1. Let **I** be intuitionistic logic. Consider the following axioms:

$\pi_1 = ((a_1 \rightarrow a_0) \rightarrow a_1) \rightarrow a_1$

$\vdots$

$\pi_{n+1} = ((a_{n+1} \rightarrow \pi_n) \rightarrow a_{n+1} \rightarrow a_{n+1}$

Let C_n be the extension of intuitionistic logic with the axiom schema π_n. This means that $\vdash_{\mathbf{C}n}$ is defined as the smallest consequence relation $\vdash$ containing intuitionistic logic which satisfies $\vdash \pi_{n'}$, for any substitution instance π'_n of π_n. Then $\mathbf{I} \subseteq \cdots \subseteq C_{n+1} \subseteq C_n \subseteq \cdots \subseteq C_1$. C_1 is classical logic and intuitionistic logic is $\cap C_n$, which can also be denoted by C^∞.

Definition 8.0.2. Let $\mathbf{S}(\mathbf{P}, G, G_1, C_n)$ mean that the computation for the goal G from data $\mathbf{P}$(with original goal G_1) in the logic C_n succeeds. We now define by induction on n the notion of: $\mathbf{S}(\mathbf{P}, G, G_1, C_n)$

1. $\mathbf{P}?G = 1$ in C_n if $\mathbf{S}(\mathbf{P}, G, G, C_n)$
2. $\mathbf{S}(\mathbf{P}, A_1 \wedge A_2, G, C_n)$ if both $\mathbf{S}(\mathbf{P}, A_1, G, C_n)$ and $\mathbf{S}(\mathbf{P}, A_2, G, C_n)$.
3. $\mathbf{S}(\mathbf{P}, A \rightarrow q, G, C_n)$ holds if $\mathbf{S}(\mathbf{P} + A, q, G, C_n)$ holds, where $\mathbf{P} + A$ is the result of adding to $\mathbf{P}$ all the conjuncts of A.
4. $\mathbf{S}(\mathbf{P}, q, G, C_n)$ holds for q atomic if either of the following holds:
   (a) $q \in \mathbf{P}$
   (b) $\perp \in \mathbf{P}$
   (c) Some $C \rightarrow q \in \mathbf{P}$ and $\mathbf{S}(P, C, G, C_n)$ holds.
   (d) Some $C \rightarrow \perp \in \mathbf{P}$ and $\mathbf{S}(\mathbf{P}, C, G, C_n)$ holds, this rule is correct because if $\mathbf{S}(\mathbf{P}, C, G, C_n)$ holds then $\mathbf{S}(\mathbf{P}, \perp, G, C_n)$ holds and $\perp$ implies anything.

Rule (5n): $\mathbf{S}(\mathbf{P}, A, G, C_n)$ holds ($n \geq 2$) if both $\mathbf{S}(\mathbf{P}, G, G, C_n)$ holds and $\mathbf{S}(\mathbf{P}, A, A, C_{n-1})$ holds

Remark 8.0.3. Rule (5) of 8.0.1 is the restart rule. Note that we can restart with a current goal which is not atomic. By 6.0.6, this general restart rule is sound for classical logic.

Lemma 8.0.4. $\mathbf{S}(\varnothing, \pi_n, \pi_n, C_n)$

Proof. By induction on n.
$n = 1$: This is the case of classical logic. The result was proved in 3.0.14.

Assume that the result holds for n.

$\mathbf{S}(\varnothing, \pi_{n+1}, \pi_{n+1}, C_{n+1})$,	i.e. $\mathbf{S}(\varnothing, (((a_{n+1}) \to \pi_{n+1}) \to a_{n+1}) \to a_{n+1}, \pi_{n+1}, C_{n+1})$
if, by rule 3:	$\mathbf{S}(\{((a_{n+1} \to \pi_n) \to a_{n+1})\}, a_{n+1}, \pi_{n+1}, C_{n+1})$,
if, by rule 4(c):	$\mathbf{S}(\{((a_{n+1} \to \pi_n) \to a_{n+1})\}, a_{n+1} \to \pi_n, \pi_{n+1}, C_{n+1})$,
if, by rule 3:	$\mathbf{S}(\{a_{n+1}, ((a_{n+1} \to \pi_n) \to a_{n+1})\}, \pi_n, \pi_{n+1}, C_{n+1})$,
if, by rule 5_{n+1}:	both $\mathbf{S}(\{a_{n+1}, ((a_{n+1} \to \pi_n) \to a_{n+1})\}, \pi_{n+1}, \pi_{n+1}, C_{n+1})$, and $\mathbf{S}(\{a_{n+1}, ((a_{n+1} \to \pi_n) \to a_{n+1})\}, \pi_n, \pi_n, C_n)$.

Now, $\mathbf{S}(\{a_{n+1}, ((a_{n+1}, \to \pi_n) \to a_{n+1})\}, \pi_{n+1}, \pi_{n+1}, C_{n+1})$ that is

$\mathbf{S}(\{a_{n+1}, ((a_{n+1} \to \pi_n) \to a_{n+1})\}, ((a_{n+1} \to \pi_n) \to a_{n+1}) \to a_{n+1}, \pi_{n+1}, C_{n+1})$

If, by rule 3:

$$\mathbf{S}(\{a_{n+1}, ((a_{n+1} \to \pi_n) \to a_{n+1})\}, a_{n+1}, \pi_{n+1}, C_{n+1})$$

which is true, by rule 4(a).

Also, since $\mathbf{S}(\varnothing, \pi_n, \pi_n, C_n)$ is true by inductive hypothesis, it follows that:

$$\mathbf{S}(\{a_{n+1}, ((a_{n+1} \to \pi_n) \to a_{n+1})\}, \pi_n, \pi_n, C_n)$$

is true. ∎

Lemma 8.0.5. *For any $n \geq 1$, if $\mathbf{S}(\mathbf{P}, A, G_0, C_n)$, then*

$$P \cup \{G_0 \to \alpha_{n-1} \mid \alpha_{n-1} \text{ is a substitution instance of } \pi_{n-1}\} \vdash_{C_n} A.$$

Proof. We prove the result by induction on the height h of the subtree below $\mathbf{S}(\mathbf{P}, A, G_0, C_n)$.
$h = 1$: In this case, there is a single step, using rules 4(a) or 4(b) to success, and A is an atom q. If rule 4(a) was employed, then $q \in \mathbf{P}$ and so $\mathbf{P} \vdash_{C_n} q$. If rule 4(b) was used, then $\bot \in \mathbf{P}$, and so $\mathbf{P} \vdash_{C_n} \bot$. Hence $\mathbf{P} \vdash_{C_n} q$.

We assume the result for subtrees of height $< h$, and that $\mathbf{S}(\mathbf{P}, A, G_0, C_n)$ has a subtree of height h.

If one of rules 2, 3, 4(a) to 4(d) was applied at node $\mathbf{S}(\mathbf{P}, A, G_0, C_n)$, then the required result follows using arguments analogous to those given in the soundness theorem for the intuitionistic case, 3.0.6. Now let us assume that the restart rule 5.n was applied at node $\mathbf{S}(\mathbf{P}, A, G_0, C_n)$. If $n = 1$, then this is the case of classical logic, whose soundness has already been proved. We can therefore assume that $n > 1$. There are two nodes immediately below $\mathbf{S}(\mathbf{P}, A, G_0, C_n)$, namely $\mathbf{S}(\mathbf{P}, A, G_0, C_n)$ and $\mathbf{S}(\mathbf{P}, A, G_0, C_{n-1})$. By inductive hypothesis:

(C1) $\mathbf{P} \cup \{G_0 \to \alpha_{n-1} \mid \alpha_{n-1}$ is a substitution instance of $\pi_{n-1}\} \vdash_{C_n} G_0$

and

(C2) $\mathbf{P} \cup \{G_0 \to \alpha_{n-2} \mid \alpha_{n-2}$ is a substitution instance of $\pi_{n-2}\} \vdash_{C_{n-1}} A$

By the finiteness of the proof procedures of C_n, it follows from (C2) and the deduction theorem that for some finite set $\{\alpha^j_{n-2}\}$ of substitution instances of π_{n-2}:

$$\mathbf{P} \vdash_{C_{n-1}} \bigwedge_j (A \to \alpha^j_{n-2}) \to A.$$

Since $\vdash_{C_{n-1}} \bigwedge_j (A \to \alpha^j_{n-2}) \to A) \to A$, for each j (the formulae being substitution instances of π_{n-1}), it follows by induction on the number of a^j_{n-2} involved that $\mathbf{P} \vdash_{C_{n-1}} A$. Moreover, it follows from $\vdash_{C_{n-1}} A$ that:

$$\mathbf{P} \cup \{\alpha_{n-1} \mid \alpha_{n-1} \text{ is a substitution instance of } \pi_{n-1}\} \vdash_I A$$

Therefore, since $\mathbf{I} \subseteq C_n$:

$$\mathbf{P} \cup \{\alpha_{n-1} \mid \alpha_{n-1} \text{ is a substitution instance of } \pi_{n-1}\} \vdash_{C_n} A$$

Thus for some finite set $\{\alpha^j_{n-1}\}$:

(C3) $\mathbf{P} \vdash_{C_n} \bigwedge_j \alpha^j_{n-1} \to A$

Clearly

$P \cup \{G_0 \to \alpha_{n-1} \mid \alpha_{n-1}$ is a substitution instance of $\pi_{n-1}\} \vdash_{C_n} G_0 \to a^j_{n-1}$

where α^j_{n-1} is any substitution instance of π_{n-1}. It therefore follows from(C1) and modus ponens that:

(C4) $\mathbf{P}\cup\{G_0 \rightarrow \alpha_{n-1} \mid \alpha_{n-1}\text{is a substitution instance of } \pi_{n-1}\} \vdash_{C_n} \alpha^j_{n-1}$.

Therefore, from (C3), (C4) and cut, we obtain:

$$P \cup \{G_0 \rightarrow \alpha_{n-1} : \alpha_{n-1}\text{is a substitution instance of } \pi_{n-1}\} \vdash_{C_n} A.$$

■

Lemma 8.0.6. *[Soundness for intermediate logics] For each $n \geq 1$, if $\mathbf{S}(\mathbf{P}, G, G, C_n)$ then $\mathbf{P} \vdash_{C_n} G$.*

Proof. Assume that $\mathbf{S}(\mathbf{P}, G, G, C_n)$. By 8.0.4:

$$\mathbf{P} \cup \{G \rightarrow \alpha_{n-1} \mid \alpha_{n-1} \text{ is a substitution instance of } \pi_{n-1}\} \vdash_{C_n} G.$$

By the finiteness of the proof procedures for C_n and the deduction theorem it follows that for some finite set $\{\alpha^j_{n-1}\}$ of substitution instances of π_{n-1}:

$$P \vdash_{C_n} \bigwedge_j (G \rightarrow \alpha^j_{n-1}) \rightarrow G.$$

Since $\vdash_{C_n} ((G \rightarrow \alpha^j_{n-1}) \rightarrow G) \rightarrow G$, for each j, (the formulae being substitution instances of π_n), it follows by induction on the number of α^j_{n-1} involved that: $P \vdash_{C_n} G$. ■

Example 8.0.7. The restart rule $5n$, for $n > 1$ cannot be strengthened with the restriction that the current goal, G be atomic.

Let us assume that rule 5.2 has been strengthened in this way, and consider $\mathbf{S}(\varnothing, \pi_2, \pi_2, C_2)$. This holds if $\mathbf{S}(\varnothing, ((a_2, \rightarrow \pi_1) \rightarrow a_2) \rightarrow a_2, \pi_2, C_2)$, for atomic a_2, which holds if, by rule 3,

(†) $\mathbf{S}((a_2 \rightarrow \pi_1) \rightarrow a_2, a_2, \pi_2, C_2)$.

Since a_2 is atomic, either rule 5.2 or rule 4(c) is applicable here. Using rule 5.2 at this point leads to a loop. For applying this rule, query (†) holds if

$$\mathbf{S}((a_2 \rightarrow \pi_1) \rightarrow a_2, \pi_2, \pi_2, C_2) \text{ and } \mathbf{S}((a_2 \rightarrow \pi_1) \rightarrow a_2, a_2, a_2, C_1).$$

Although the second of these is true, the first one can only be computed by making π_2 explicit and using rule 3 again, leading us straight back to

$\mathbf{S}((a_2 \to \pi_1) \to a_2, a_2, \pi_2, C_2)$. Hence, employing rule 5.2 at this point gets us into a loop.

We shall employ rule 4(c) instead. Query (†) holds if

$$\mathbf{S}((a_2 \to \pi_1) \to a_2, a_2 \to \pi_1, \pi_2, C_2)$$

if, by rule 3,

$$\mathbf{S}(\{a_2, (a_2 \to \pi_1) \to a_2\}, \pi_1, \pi_2, C_2),$$

if

$$\mathbf{S}(\{a_2, (a_2, \to \pi_1) \to a_2\}, ((a_1 \to a_0) \to a_1, \pi_2, C_2)$$

if, by rule 3,

$$(\dagger\dagger)\ \mathbf{S}(\{((a_1 \to a_0) \to a_1), a_2, (a_2, \to \pi_1) \to a_2\}, a_1, \pi_2, C_2).$$

Again, since a_1 is atomic, either rule 5.2 or rule 4(c) is applicable here. As in the case of query (†), employing rule 5.2 would get us into a loop. Trying 4(c) instead, query (††) holds if

$$\mathbf{S}(\{((a_1 \to a_0) \to a_1), a_2, (a_2 \to \pi_1) \to a_2\}, a_1 \to a_0, \pi_2, C_2)$$

if, by rule 3,

$$\mathbf{S}(\{((a_1 \to a_0) \to a_1), a_2, (a_2 \to \pi_1) \to a_2\}, a_0, \pi_2, C_2)$$

Only rule 5.2 is applicable here, yielding two subqueries:

$$\mathbf{S}(\{a_1, (a_1 \to a_0) \to a_1), a_2, (a_2 \to \pi_1) \to a_2\}, \pi_2, \pi_2, C_2)$$

and

$$\mathbf{S}(\{a_1, (a_1 \to a_0) \to a_1), a_2, (a_2 \to \pi_1) \to a_2\}, a_0, a_0, C_1).$$

By the completeness for classical logic, the second of these is true if

$$\{a_1, (a_1 \to a_0) \to a_1), a_2, (a_2 \to \pi_1) \to a_2\}, \vdash_C a_0$$

But this is *not* the case, as can be seen by giving a_0, a_1, a_2 the truth values F, T, T respectively.

Hence $S(\varnothing, \pi_2, \pi_2, C_2)$ is not true, unless the restart rule 5.2 applies to arbitrary current goals.

Lemma 8.0.8. *$S(\varnothing, \pi_n, \pi_n, C_m)$ is false for $m > n$.*

Proof. The result follows immediately from Lemma 8.5 (soundness), together with the well-known fact that $\vdash_{C_m} \pi_n$ is false, for $m > n$.

However, it is instructive to see explicitly how the computation fares, given a loop checker. The following lemma is central to the direct proof of the result. ∎

Lemma 8.0.9. *Let $1 \leq i \leq j \leq m$ and assume that database* $\mathbf{P}$ *contains no a_k, for $0 \leq k \leq i$ and no implications with consequent a_k, for $0 \leq k \leq i$. Then*

$$\mathbf{S}(\mathbf{P}, \pi_i, \pi_j, C_m), \mathbf{S}(\mathbf{P}, \pi_i, a_j, C_m)$$

and

$$\mathbf{S}(\mathbf{P}, \pi_i, a_j \rightarrow \pi_{j-1}, C_m)$$

are all false.

We want to give a direct rule for handling disjunction in the goal. The rule is (for $\mathbf{P}$ without disjunctions in case of intuitionistic logic):

> $\mathbf{S}(\mathbf{P}, A_1 \vee A_2, G, \mathbf{L})$ succeeds if $\mathbf{S}(\mathbf{P}, A_i, G, \mathbf{L})$ succeeds either for $i = 1$ or for $i = 2$

where $\mathbf{L}$ is either classical logic or intuitionistic logic. In the latter logic, this rule must be restricted to databases without disjunction. Thus first eliminate all disjunctions from the data and only then we can use the rule for disjunction in the goal.

Example 8.0.10. $\varnothing ? A \vee \neg A$
translate
$\varnothing ? A \vee (A \rightarrow \bot)$
either $\varnothing ? A$ or $\varnothing ? A \rightarrow \bot$
Try: $\varnothing ? A \rightarrow \bot$
ask
$A ? \bot$

The above fails in intuitionistic logic. In classical logic we can restart.

The original goal is $A \vee (A \rightarrow \bot)$
restart
$A ? A \vee (A \rightarrow \bot)$
choose the disjunct A and succeed.

Example 8.0.11. Let us try in the logic C_2.
$\varnothing ? A \vee (A \rightarrow \bot)$
choose $(A \rightarrow \bot)$
$\varnothing ?(A \rightarrow \bot)$
$A ? \bot$

Use rule (5,2). We must succeed in $A?A \vee (A \rightarrow \bot)$ in intuitionistic logic and also in $A?\ \bot$ in classical logic with original goal $\bot$. This second query fails! Here $A \vee \neg A$ is not a theorem of C_2, as should be the case.

Example 8.0.12. [intuitionistic logic] $A \vee B?A \vee B$
We cannot use the disjunction in the goal rule, first because we will get $A \vee B?A$ and $A \vee B?B$
which fails in intuitionistic logic. In classical logic we can always restart.

We saw the two rules:

$$\begin{array}{lcl} A \rightarrow (x \vee y) & = & (A \rightarrow x) \vee (A \rightarrow y) \\ x \vee y \rightarrow A & = & (x \rightarrow A) \wedge (y \rightarrow A) \end{array}$$

allowed us to pull disjunctions out from inside a formula. This enabled us to give in the case of classical logic direct computation rules for disjunction. We also gave rules for $\vee$ for intuitionistic logic but if we have data of the form $A \rightarrow x \vee y$, we cannot apply the disjunction rules, because we cannot prepare the data for computation by writing

$$(A \rightarrow x) \vee (A \rightarrow y).$$

If we adopt this equivalence as an additional axiom to intuitionistic logic, we do not get classical logic but a weaker logic, known as Dummett's **LC**. Thus

Definition 8.0.13. Let Dummett's **LC** be the smallest consequence relation $\vdash$ containing intuitionistic logic and satisfying the following rule (see Definition 6.1):

$$A \rightarrow (B \vee C) \vdash (A \rightarrow B) \vee (A \rightarrow C)$$

In Dummett's **LC** we can pull all disjunctions outside a formula. Thus an item of data A containing $\vee$ is equivalent to $\vee A_i$ where A_i contain no disjunctions and are ready for computation. Thus if G is a goal,

$$A?G = 1 \text{ if for all } \ i, A_i?G = 1.$$

In case of classical logic computation the computation $A_i?\ G$ proceeds using the rules for classical logic. In case of **LC**, what are the computation rules for $A_i?G$ in **LC** ?

Do we go on as in intuitionistic logic and the effect of the **LC** axiom is only in the translation from A to the equivalent $\vee A_i$? Let us check. Our guess is negative, since **LC** can be axiomatized by the pure implicational formula $((A \to B) \to C) \to (((B \to A) \to C) \to C)$.

Example 8.0.14.

Data	**original goal**
$(A \to B) \to C$	C
$(B \to A) \to C$	

The above is a theorem of Dummett's **LC**. It contains no $\vee$. The rules of intuitionistic logic cannot make it succeed. Obviously the rules for $\to$ have to be adapted to **LC**, to capture the implicational fragment of **LC**.

We will not pursue this topic any further.

8.1 Appendix to Section 8

Classical logic, intuitionistic logic and intermediate logics Consider the propositional language with $\wedge, \vee, \to, \neg$. The following is a Hilbert style axiom system for intuitionistic propositional logic, **I**.

1. $A \to (B \to A)$
2. $(A \to (B \to C)) \to ((A \to B) \to (A \to C))$
3. $A \to (B \to A \wedge B)$
4. $A \wedge B \to A; A \wedge B \to B$
5. $(A \to C) \to ((B \to C) \to (A \vee B \to C))$
6. $A \to A \vee B; B \to A \vee B$
7. $A \to (\neg A \to B)$
8. $(A \to \neg B) \to (B \to \neg A)$

Inference rule:

$$\frac{\vdash A \quad \vdash A \to B}{\vdash B}$$

To obtain classical logic C we can add the axiom

9. $\neg\neg A \to A$

Remark 8.1.1. One can prove in intuitionistic logic that $A \wedge \neg A \vdash B \wedge \neg B$ and hence by calling $\bot = A \wedge \neg A$ we can define $\neg A$ as $A \to \bot$.

To obtain intermediate logics consider the following additional axioms.

$$\pi_1 = ((A_1 \to A_0) \to A_1) \to A_1$$
$$\vdots$$
$$\pi_n = ((A_n \to \pi_{n-1}) \to A_n) \to A_n.$$

The axiom π_n (Peirce rule of depth n) contains all the different atoms $A_0, \ldots, A_n$. If we add the axiom schema π_1 to **I** we get **C**.

The axiom π_{n+1} is strictly weaker than π_n, i.e. we have $(\mathbf{I} + \pi_{n+1}) \subsetneq \mathbf{I} + \pi_n$.

We also have:

Theorem 8.1.2.

$$\mathbf{I} = \cap(\mathbf{I} + \pi_n)$$

where $(\mathbf{I} + \pi_n)$ *is the logic obtained by adding to* **I** *the schema* π_n. *Call this logic* C_n.

There are other well known intermediate logics, one of them is Dummett's **LC**. It is obtained by adding to **I** the schema:

$$\text{(lc1):} \quad (A \to B) \vee (B \to A),$$

or equivalently the schema:

$$\text{(lc2)} \quad ((A \to B) \to C) \to [((B \to A) \to C) \to C].$$

Its significance is as follows: In classical logic one can pull disjunctions out of formulae to the front, i.e.

$$(*) \quad A \wedge (B \vee C) = (A \wedge B) \vee (A \wedge C)$$
$$(**) \quad A \to (B \vee C) = (A \to B) \vee (A \to C)$$

In intuitionistic logic (**) is not valid. So we cannot get normal forms in intuitionistic logic by pulling out $\vee$ from the inside of a formula. Dummett's **LC** allows us to do that. In other words it is the smallest logic in which (**) is valid. In fact (**) can be taken as an axiom schema for **LC**. **LC** turns out to be weaker than **C** itself. We do not need full classical logic for pulling disjunctions out.

The meaning of π_n will become apparent in the next sections. It suffices to say that it is connected with various weakenings of ancestral resolution.

9 The universal quantifier and the fragment without disjunctions

This section assumes we are dealing with the fragment without disjunction, i.e. predicate logic with atomic predicate $Q(x_1, \ldots, x_n)$, variables $\{x_1, x_2, \ldots\}$, the connectives $\wedge, \rightarrow, \perp$ and the quantifiers $\forall$ and $\exists$.

We build the set of formulae in the usual way but our backward computation is given for data and goals of a special form which we call *clauses*. (Compare with Section 6).

Definition 9.0.1.

1. An atomic formula $Q(x_1, \ldots, x_n)$ is both a clause and a goal. Q is the head of the clause.

2. If A and B are goals so is $A \wedge B$.

3. If A_i are clauses and Q is atomic formula then $\bigwedge A_i \rightarrow Q$ and $\bigwedge A_i \rightarrow \perp$ are clauses. $\bigwedge A_i$ is the body of the clause and Q and $\perp$ are heads of the clause.

4. A database $\mathbf{P}$ is a set of clauses.

5. When a clause $A(x)$ appears in the database its intended meaning is $\forall x A(x)$. When it appears as a goal its intended meaning is $\exists x A(x)$.

Given a set of formulae intended to serve as a database $\mathbf{P}$ and given a goal G, in predicate logic, we have first to prepare it for computation.

This involves skolemizing and translating. Thus we pull quantifiers out and skolemize and then translate into clauses.

We can therefore assume that the database is written as a set of universal clauses and the goal is an existential clause. We do not write the quantifiers explicitly but use two types of variables.

$$\begin{aligned} \text{VAR 1} &= \{u_1, u_2, \ldots v_1, v_2, \ldots\} \qquad \text{and} \\ \text{VAR 2} &= \{x_1, x_2, \ldots y_1, y_2, \ldots z_1, z_2, \ldots\} \end{aligned}$$

VAR 1 are variables to be quantified universally and VAR 2 are to be quantified existentially.

Note that in any clause only one type of variable occurs throughout. We start the computation with a single database and original goal

$$\mathbf{P}?G \text{ (with original goal } G).$$

The variables of **P** are from VAR 1 and the variables of G are from VAR 2. In the course of the computation, the database will increase to other databases $\mathbf{P}_i \supseteq \mathbf{P}$, where the additional clauses in $\mathbf{P}_i$ are clauses containing VAR 2, and various current goals G_i will be asked. G_i are also written with VAR 2. Thus in the middle of the computation we have a list of databases and goals

$$\mathbf{L} = (\mathbf{P}_1?G_1, \ldots, \mathbf{P}_i?G_i, \ldots, \mathbf{P}_n?G_n)$$

to be jointly made to succeed. Success in the computation means that

(Existential closure of VAR 2) $\bigwedge_i$ [(Universal closure of VAR 1) $\wedge \mathbf{P}_i) \rightarrow G_i$]

Definition 9.0.2. The following is a description of the computation for the original query $\mathbf{P}?G$:

P is written in a VAR 1 variables and G in VAR 2.

During the course of the computation we get a list of goals and databases

$$\mathbf{L} = (\mathbf{P}_i?G_i) \text{ (with original goal G)}$$

$\mathbf{P}_i$ contains clauses totally using VAR 1 or totally using VAR 2. G_i are goals totally using VAR 2. Thus formally we are describing **S (L, G, name of logic)**. Where **L** is $\{\mathbf{P}_i?G_i\}, G$ is the original goal, and **name of logic** is the logic of the theorem prover.

Let $\Theta = (\Theta_1, \Theta_2)$ be a notation of a substitution Θ_1 for VAR 1 and Θ_2 for VAR 2. The substitution gives either ground names as values or terms of VAR 2. (*Never do we* substitute a term with VAR 1 as value.)

The substitution is performed in parallel and simultaneously. The unit computation step is done by picking a goal and database, say

$$\mathbf{P}_i?G_i$$

and replacing it by other queries and possibly performing substitution on the other queries. Thus $\mathbf{L} = (\mathbf{P}_1?G_1, \ldots \mathbf{P}_i?G_i, \ldots \mathbf{P}_n?G_n)$ is replaced by

$$\ldots \mathbf{P}_{i-1}\Theta_2?G_{i-1}\Theta_2$$

replacement of

$$\mathbf{P}_i?G_i, \mathbf{P}_{i+1}\Theta_2?G_{i+1}\Theta_2, \ldots$$

Notice that Θ_2 is used on the other databases and goals.

We now give the computation rules: These have the form:

$$\textbf{S (L, G, name of logic) if } S(L_1, G, \textbf{name of logic})$$

Where $\mathbf{L}_1$ is obtained as follows: We choose $\mathbf{P}_i?G_i$ and consider several cases and replace $\mathbf{P}_i?G_i$ according to those cases:

(a) If $G_i = A_i \wedge B_i$
then replace
$\mathbf{L} = (\ldots, \mathbf{P}_i?G_i, \ldots)$ by
$\mathbf{L}_1 = (\ldots; \mathbf{P}_i?A_i, \mathbf{P}_i?B_i; \ldots)$
and continue

(b) If $G_i = A_i \rightarrow B_i$
then replace
$(\ldots, \mathbf{P}_i?G_i, \ldots)$
by
$(\ldots, (\mathbf{P}_i + A_i)?B_i, \ldots)$
and continue

(c) If $G_i = Q, Q$ atomic
then proceed by replacing $\mathbf{P}_i?Q$ according to the following cases.

(1) If for some substitution (Θ_1, Θ_2) and some $B \in \mathbf{P}_i$, we have
$B\Theta = Q\Theta_2, \Theta = \Theta_1\Theta_2$
Then *delete* $\mathbf{P}_i?Q$ from the list and continue with the new list *after* substituting Θ_2 in all VAR 2 variables in all wffs and appearing in the list.

(2) If $\bot \in \mathbf{P}_i$ then proceed as in case 1 above with Θ = the identity substitution.

(3) If for some $A \rightarrow B \in \mathbf{P}_i$ and some $(\Theta_1, \Theta_2), \Theta = \Theta_1\Theta_2$
$B\Theta = Q\Theta_2$, then
replace
$(\ldots, \mathbf{P}_i?Q, \ldots)$
by
$(\ldots, \mathbf{P}_i?A\Theta_1 \ldots,)\Theta_2$

(Notice we use $A\Theta_1$ because we unified with the $(A \rightarrow B)\Theta_1$ copy of the VAR 1 universally quantified $(A \rightarrow B) \in \mathbf{P}_i$, where $(\ldots)\Theta_2$ means the list obtained by substituting Θ_2 in all VAR 2 variables appearing in the list $(\ldots)$.

(4) If some $(A \rightarrow \bot) \in \mathbf{P}_i$ proceed with the list
$(\ldots, \mathbf{P}_i?A, \ldots)$

(5) The restart rule
Replace
$(\ldots, \mathbf{P}_i?G_i, \ldots)$
by $(\ldots, \mathbf{P}_i?G, \ldots)$

Where G is the same as the original goal of the computation with completely new variables in it.

(d) The empty list always succeeds.

Theorem 9.0.3. *[Completeness] A list* $\mathbf{L}$ *of databases and goals of the form*

$\mathbf{L} = \mathbf{P}_i?G_i$ *succeeds if and only if in classical logic (Existential closure of VAR 2)* $\bigwedge$ *[(universal closure of VAR 1)* $\wedge \mathbf{P}_i \to G_i$*].*

The above holds for intuitionistic logic if we do not use the restart rule in the computation.

Remark 9.0.4. The above is a full theorem prover for classical logic but not for intuitionistic logic. In the latter logic we deal only with $\{\wedge, \to, \bot\}$ fragment. Furthermore in classical logic we can pull all quantifiers out in front of the formula and skolemize, thus leaving our database in a universal form ready for computation. This cannot be done in intuitionistic logic. Thus to obtain a theorem prover for full predicate intuitionistic logic we must:

1. Deal with disjunctions along the lines already indicated
2. Skolemize at run time (i.e. do not skolemize but compute directly on the data given).

This will be done in the next section.

10 Full predicate system

The previous section dealt with a computation with clauses written without quantifiers in the fragment with $\{\wedge, \to, \bot\}$.

The clauses in the data were understood as quantified universally and the goal was understood as quantified existentially.

In classical logic, this fragment is sufficiently strong to describe the full classical system.

The connectives $\neg$ and $\vee$ can be eliminated by, for example,

$$\neg A \equiv A \to \bot$$

$$A \vee B \equiv (A \rightarrow \bot) \rightarrow B.$$

An arbitrary formula of classical logic can be skolemized into a universal or existential form as required.

Given therefore an arbitrary set of data and an arbitrary goal in classical logic, the data and goal can be skolemized and re-written in a form ready for the computation procedures of the previous section.

Thus we see that in classical logic, the question of when and how to skolemize is a practical question and not a logical one. In the case of modal logic or intuitionistic logic, we cannot always skolemize at the beginning of the computation because the logic may not allow it.

The result of skolemizing may not be logically equivalent to the original formula. Thus we are faced here with a logical problem. To illustrate, note that in modal logic $C = \Diamond\exists x A(x)$ is not equivalent to $B = \exists x \Diamond A(x)$ and so we cannot skolemize $C = \Diamond\exists x A(x)$ by putting a constant c and obtaining $C_1 = \Diamond A(c)$. $\Diamond A(c)$ is logically equivalent to $\exists x \Diamond A(x)$.

In intuitionistic logic we have a similar problem. The wff $\neg\neg\exists x A(x)$ in intuitionistic logic is not logically equivalent to $\exists x \neg\neg A(x)$.

Furthermore, while $\Diamond\exists x A(x)$ implies the existence of a Skolem constant c_1 in some possible world, for which $A(c_1)$ is true, in intuitionistic logic it is wrong to think of the existence of any unique c_1 for $\neg\neg\exists x A(x)$. We therefore conclude that we must find a way to skolemize at 'run time', whatever that is supposed to mean. We must understand the workings and logical import of skolemizing and we must develop it systematically and incorporate it into the computation scheme of the previous section.

We begin with some examples in intuitionistic logic which illustrate our difficulties.

Example 10.0.1.

(a) We know that in intuitionistic logic, $\neg\neg\exists x A(x) \not\vdash \exists x A(x)$. Thus given the problem: $\neg\neg\exists x A(x)?\exists x\neg\neg A(x)$ we cannot skolemize the data. Let us compute with run time skolemization: Rewriting and eliminating the existential quantifier in the goal, we get:

$$(\exists x A(x) \rightarrow \bot) \rightarrow \bot ?(A(u) \rightarrow \bot) \rightarrow \bot$$

where u is a value to be chosen so that the computation succeeds. Notice that the database is not pure clause database because it has an existential quantifier in the data. However, we can continue to compute in the spirit of the previous section.

We therefore ask:

$$(\exists x A(x) \rightarrow \bot) \rightarrow \bot, A(u) \rightarrow \bot ?\ \bot$$

Unifying with the first clause we get

$$?\exists x A(x) \to \bot$$

and hence we get:

$$(\exists x A(x) \to \bot) \to \bot, A(u) \to \bot, \exists x A(x)?\ \bot$$

If we skolemize now in the data and put a constant a for the $\exists$ in the third clause of the data we get:

$$(\exists x A(x) \to \bot) \to \bot, A(u) \to \bot, A(a)?\ \bot$$

We unify with the second clause and get:

$$?A(u).$$

Since u is to be chosen, we would like to take $u = a$ and succeed. Something is wrong, because we should not succeed. The only way out is to say that the constant a depends on u, i.e. we should skolemize with $a(u)$ and get: $A(a(u))?A(u)$ which cannot unify because of the occur check. What is the justification of that in intuitionistic logic? Notice that the constant a was introduced after u was introduced. This may be of importance. Namely we may restrict unification of u only to constants introduced before u was introduced. We shall explore this restriction later.

(b) Let us see what happens with the other direction, which should succeed.

$\exists x \neg\neg A(x)$	?	$\neg\neg\exists x A(x)$
becomes		
$\exists x((A(x) \to \bot) \to \bot)$	?	$(\exists x A(x) \to \bot) \to \bot$
which becomes		
$\exists x((A(x) \to \bot) \to \bot), \exists x A(x) \to \bot$	?	$\bot.$
Unify with the second clause and ask		
	?	$\exists x A(x)$
i.e. we are to look for a u		
	?	$A(u)$

Skolemize clause 1 of the data and make the Skolem function dependent on u, as we agreed:

$(A(a(u)) \to\bot) \to\bot, \exists x A(x) \to\bot$	?	$A(u)$
unify $A(u)$ with clause 1 and get		
	?	$A(a(u)) \to\bot$
which becomes		
$(A(a(u)) \to\bot) \to\bot, \exists x A(x) \to\bot, A(a(u))$	?	$\bot$
unify with the second clause		
	?	$\exists x A(x)$
Find u_1		
	?	$A(u_1)$
$u_1 = a(u)$.		

(c) Let us try (b) again. This time suppose we skolemize the data right at the beginning; we get:

$(A(a) \to\bot) \to\bot$	?	$(\exists x A(x) \to\bot) \to\bot$
Hence		
$(A(a) \to\bot) \to\bot, \exists x A(x) \to\bot$	?	$\bot$.
Unify with clause 1		
	?	$A(a) \to\bot$.
Hence		
$A(a), (A(a) \to\bot) \to\bot, \exists x A(x) \to\bot$	?	$\bot$.
Unify with clause 2		
	?	$\exists x A(x)$
	?	$A(u)$.
Succeed with $u = a$.		

(d) Thus the rule of making any skolem function $\mathbf{f}$ dependent also on all the 'u' (the variables to be chosen) in the database, seems to work for this example. Is it sound?
Let $\mathbf{P}$ be a database with $\exists x A(x)$ and $B(u)$ and suppose the goal is $G(u)$. Success means that in intuitionistic logic

$$\vdash \exists u[\exists x A(x) \wedge B(u) \to G(u)].$$

In intuitionistic logic we have the equivalence:

$$\vdash \forall x[A(x) \wedge q \to r] \leftrightarrow [\exists x A(x) \wedge q \to r]$$

for q and not containing x. Therefore, success in the above computation means that

$$\vdash \exists u \forall x(A(x) \wedge B(u) \to G(u)).$$

If we ask the above formula as a goal and skolemize on the x, then the Skolem function will depend on u, which is exactly what we proposed to do.

This argument shows that our skolemising rule is sound relative to the other computation rules.

However, for the case of classical logic, we lose completeness if we insist on making the Skolem functions depend on all the variables U around even if we allow for restart from the original goal.

Consider the following:

$\neg\forall x A(x)$	?	$\exists x \neg A(x)$
$\forall x A(x) \to \bot$	?	$\exists x (A(x) \to \bot)$.
Choose a u:		
	?	$A(u) \to \bot$
by the rule for $\to$:		
$A(u)$	?	$\bot$
Unify with the first clause:		
	?	$\forall x A(x)$
Skolemize		
	?	$A(\mathbf{f}(u))$

Intuitionistically we fail because of the occur check. If we restart, we ask:

	?	$\exists x (A(x) \to \bot)$.
Choose u_1:		
	?	$A(u_1) \to \bot$
$A(u_1)$	?	$\bot$
	?	$\forall x A(x)$

Again we cannot succeed because of the occur check.

The only way to succeed is either to allow us to restart not from the original goal but from any previous goal or to allow in the classical case to skolemize with functions dependent only on the variables in the formula itself.

In the first case we can restart with

$$?A(\mathbf{f}(u))$$

and succeed with

$$u_1 = \mathbf{f}(u).$$

In the second case we need not make $\mathbf{f}(u)$ dependent on u in the computation and hence the occur check will not stop our unification $u = \mathbf{f}$.

Let us look at some more examples.

Example 10.0.2. Let us check the computation:

$\neg\neg\forall x A(x)$? $\forall x A(x)$
This should fail.
Rewriting we get:
$(\forall x A(x) \rightarrow \perp) \rightarrow \perp$? $\forall x A(x)$.
Skolemize and get:
$(\forall x A(x) \rightarrow \perp) \rightarrow \perp$? $A(c)$.
Unify with $\perp$ and get:
? $\forall x A(x) \rightarrow \perp$
Hence:
$\forall x A(x), (\forall x A(x) \rightarrow \perp) \rightarrow \perp$? $\perp$.

In intuitionistic logic we fail. But in classical logic we can restart:

$$\forall x A(x), (\forall x A(x) \rightarrow \perp) \rightarrow \perp ? \forall x A(x)$$

and succeed.

Example 10.0.3. Check the computation:
$\forall x \exists y B(x, y)$? $\exists y \forall x B(x, y)$.
This should fail.
Rewrite:
$\exists y, B(x, y)$? $\forall x B(x, u)$
Skolemize
$B(x, g(x, u))$? $B(f(u), u)$

Which fails because of the occur check.

Example 10.0.4. Let us check the following non-theorem of intuitionistic logic:

? $\exists x(A(x) \rightarrow \forall y A(y))$
We ask:
? $A(u) \rightarrow \forall y A(y)$
Hence:
$A(u)$? $\forall y A(y)$
Skolemize
? $A(a(u))$

If a is not dependent on u we will succeed. Therefore we must make $a(u)$ dependent on u, and we fail because of the occur check.

Notice that if we do not make a depend on the u but do impose the restriction that u cannot unify with any a which is introduced later. We still fail. We will study this restriction later.

The above examples show that whenever we skolemize we must make the Skolem function dependent on all existential variables u appearing anywhere in the same branch of the computation, even though these variables may not appear in the actual formula we are skolemizing.

We are now ready to define our clauses and computation rules. We call them *RS*-clauses (runtime skolemization clauses). First another example:

Example 10.0.5. Consider the clause

$$\forall x A(x, z) \to \exists y \forall u [B(u, y \to C(z)]$$

In intuitionistic logic the quantifiers cannot be moved and we are forced to compute with this clause as it is. In classical logic we can write the equivalent clause

$$\exists x \exists y \forall u [A(x, z) \wedge B(u, y) \to C(z)].$$

Skolemizing we get:

$$A(a, z) \wedge B(u, b) \to C(z)$$

Where a and b are constants.

So classical logic allows us not only to skolemize but also to rewrite the clause in such a way that $C(z)$ is the head of the clause. Thus if our goal is $D(z)$, we know we should not attempt using the clause with head $C(z)$. In intuitionistic logic we compute with the original clause but then it is advisable to annotate it, indicating that its 'output' head is $C(z)$, which may be buried inside it. Our definition of clauses will also define the notion of output.

Definition 10.0.6. Definition of *RS-clauses*, *RS-goals*, *RS-heads*, *RS-outputs* and *RS-databases*.

1. (a) An atomic formula $Q(x_1, \ldots, x_n)$ is a *clause*, a *head* and a *goal*. Its free variables are $x_1, \ldots, x_n$. Its *output* set is Q.

   (b) **truth** is an atomic formula. Its output set is empty $\varnothing$.

   (c) **Falsity** $\bot$ is an atomic formula. Its output set is the set of all atomic formulae.

2. Let $C_i(y_1, \ldots, y_m, x_{ij}, z_{ik})$ be clauses with free variables as indicated and output sets O_i.

Then the following expression H is a *head* with free variables $\{z_{ik} \mid i = 1, \ldots, j = 1 \ldots\}$ and output set $\bigcup_i O_i$.

$$H = (\exists y_1, \ldots, y_m)[\bigwedge_i [(\forall x_{i1} x_{i2} \ldots) C_i] \ldots)$$

3. Let C_i be clauses with free variables V_i, (the output sets are not relevant here) then $\bigwedge C_i$ is a goal with free variables $\bigcup_i V_i$.

4. Let G be a goal with free variables V and let H be a head with free variables V_1 and output set O. Then $G \rightarrow H$ is a *clause* with free variables $V \cup V_1$ and output set O.

5. A *database* is a set of clauses.

Lemma 10.0.7.

1. *In classical logic, every wff A is equivalent to an RS-Clause.*

2. *In intuitionistic logic every wff without disjunction is equivalent to an RS-clause.*

Note: disjunction will be discussed later.

Proof.

(a) Write A in a conjunctive prenex normal form B as below:

$$B = \text{(quantifiers) [quantifier free matrix]}$$

The matrix can be written in an *RS*-clause form with $\wedge$, $\rightarrow$, $\bot$.

For a wff of the form QxA, where Q is a quantifier, let Q^*xA be $Qx(\mathbf{truth} \rightarrow A)$. Let B^* be the result of replacing each quantifier Q in B by Q^*.
The entire formula B can be regarded as a Head and B is equivalent to $\mathbf{truth} \rightarrow B^*$, which is a clause.

In intuitionistic logic we do not have this lemma, as disjunctions are not definable in terms of the other connectives.

(b) Proof by induction is left to the reader as an exercise.

∎

We are ready to describe the computation procedure with run time skolemization. The basic situation is a database $\mathbf{P}$ which is a set of clauses, and a current goal A, and the original goal G. Each clause in the database contains free variables drawn from two sets of variables:

$$\text{VAR1} = \{x_1, x_2, \ldots y_1, \ldots y_2, \ldots\}$$

and

$$\text{VAR2} = \{u_1, u_2, \ldots, v_1, v_2, \ldots\}$$

The goals contain variables from VAR2 only. The variables in VAR1 are universally quantified and the variables from VAR2 are existentially quantified.

Success in the computation of the current goal A from the database $\mathbf{P}$ with original goal G means

$$\vdash (\exists \text{VAR2})[(\forall \text{VAR1}) \bigwedge \mathbf{P} \to A \vee G]$$

where $(\exists \text{VAR}i)B, (\forall \text{VAR}i)B$, (for $i = 1, 2$) are existential or universal closure on all VARi variables in B. $\bigwedge \mathbf{P}$ denotes the conjunction of all clauses in $\mathbf{P}$. The relation $\vdash$ is that of intuitionistic logic.

Let TERM$_i$ be the set of all terms built up using function symbols constants and variables from VAR$_i$ (for $i = 1, 2$). Let TERM be the set of all terms containing any variables either from VAR1 or from VAR2.

The basic computational state is a family of predicates of the form $\mathbf{T} = \{\mathbf{S}(\mathbf{P}_i, G_i, A_i, U_i)\}$ and a substitution Θ: VAR2 $\to$ TERM2. Where U_i is the set of variables from VAR2 free in $\mathbf{P}_i \cup \{A_i; G_i\}, A_i$ is a goal, called the current goal, G_i is the original goal and $\mathbf{P}_i$ is the database. $\mathbf{S}(\mathbf{P}_i, G_i, A_i, U_i)$ holds for a substitution Θ for VAR2 if the computation of $A_i\Theta$ succeeds from $\mathbf{P}_i\Theta$, with original goal $G_i\Theta$. The computational state $(\mathbf{T}, \Theta)$ succeeds if all $\mathbf{S}(\mathbf{P}, G, A, U) \in \mathbf{T}$ succeed with substitution Θ.

Note below that whenever we skolemize in the computation the Skolem function in the intutionistic case must be dependent on all the VAR2 variables u_i appearing in the computation and not only on those variables from u_i which actually appear in the skolemized formula.

The computation for classical logic does not require this condition. It is sufficient to make Skolem functions dependent only on the variables appearing in the formula itself.

Definition 10.0.8. We now define by induction the simultaneous success of $(\mathbf{T}, \Theta)$. This is done by giving reduction rules of the form $(\mathbf{T}, \Theta)$ succeeds if $(\mathbf{T}', \Theta')$ succeeds and $(\mathbf{T}', \Theta')$ is related to $(\mathbf{T}, \Theta)$ by one of the following cases:

Case 1: $\mathbf{T}$ is empty

Then $(\mathbf{T}, \Theta)$ succeeds

Case 2: For some $\mathbf{S}(\mathbf{P}, G, A, U)$ in $\mathbf{T}$ either (1) or (2) holds:

1. $\perp \in \mathbf{P}$

2. For some Q atomic, $Q \in \mathbf{P}$ and some substitution Θ_1 to the VAR1 variables of Q to TERM2 we have:
   $Q\Theta_1\Theta = A\Theta$.
   and $\mathbf{T}' = \mathbf{T} - \{\mathbf{S}(\mathbf{P}, \Theta, A, U)\}$, and $\Theta' = \Theta$.

Case 3: For some $\mathbf{S}(\mathbf{P}, G, A, U) \in \mathbf{T}$,
$A = A_1 \wedge A_2$
and
$\mathbf{T}' = (\mathbf{T} - \{\mathbf{S}(\mathbf{P}, G, A, U)\}) \cup \{\mathbf{S}(\mathbf{P}, G, A_1, U), \mathbf{S}(\mathbf{P}, G, A_2, U)\}$ and
$\Theta' = \Theta$

Case 4: For some $\mathbf{S}(\mathbf{P}, G, A, U) \in \mathbf{T}$
$A = \exists z B(z)$
and
$\mathbf{T}' = (\mathbf{T} - \{\mathbf{S}(\mathbf{P}, G, A, U)\}) \cup \{\mathbf{S}(\mathbf{P}, G, B(w), U \cup \{w\})\}$
where w is completely new variable form VAR2 and Θ' is defined as

$$\Theta'(x) = \Theta(x) \text{ for } x \neq z \text{ and } \Theta'(x) = w \text{ for } x = z.$$

Case 5: For some $\mathbf{S}(\mathbf{P}, G, A, U) \in \mathbf{T}$
$A = \bigwedge C_i \to H$ and $\mathbf{T}' = (\mathbf{T} - \{\mathbf{S}(\mathbf{P}, G, A, U)\}) \cup \{\mathbf{S}(\mathbf{P} \cup \{C_i\}, G, H, U)\}$
and $\Theta' = \Theta$.

Case 6: For some $\mathbf{S}(\mathbf{P}, G, A, U) \in \mathbf{T}$ such that $A = Q(v_i), Q$ atomic, and for some $\bigwedge C_i \to H \in \mathbf{P}$, and some substitution Θ_1 to the free VAR1 variables of $\bigwedge C_i \to H$ to TERM2, such that *output* (H) contains a non-empty subset of *output* (Q) we have

$$\begin{aligned} \mathbf{T}' = \quad & \mathbf{T} - \{\mathbf{S}(\mathbf{P}, G, A, U)\} \cup \{\mathbf{S}(\mathbf{P}, G, \textstyle\bigwedge C_i*, U*)\} \cup \\ & \cup \{\mathbf{S}(\mathbf{P} \cup \{B_j*(\mathbf{f}_1(U*), \ldots, \mathbf{f}_m(U*))\}, G, A, U*)\} \end{aligned}$$

and $H = \exists y_1, \ldots, y_m \bigwedge B_j$ for some B_j and $\mathbf{f}_k(U*)$ is a Skolem function dependent on *all* the variables of $U*$, and $\Theta' = \Theta$, and $C_i* = C_i\Theta_1\Theta, B_j* = B_j\Theta_1\Theta$, and $U* = U \cup$ {all the VAR2 free variables of C_i* and B_i*}. What case 6 basically does is that given the query

$$\mathbf{Data}, \textstyle\bigwedge c_i \to (\exists y_1 \ldots y_m \bigwedge B_i?Q$$

we ask the two queries:

$$\textbf{Data} \ ? \wedge C_i$$

and

$$\textbf{Data}, (\exists y_1, \ldots, y_m \bigwedge B_i)?Q$$

The functions $\mathbf{f}_i$ arise because we skolemize. Note that the main external connective of $\bigwedge C_i \to H$ is '$\to$'. Also note that in the case of classical logic it is enough to make the Skolem functions dependent only on the variables U' of C_i^* and B_i^* and not on U. In fact we lose completeness if we do not dispense with the dependence on U.

Case 6a: Like case 6, with $H = \perp, \Theta' = \Theta$ and

$$\mathbf{T}' = (\mathbf{T} - \{\mathbf{S}(\mathbf{P}, G, A, U\}) \cup \{\mathbf{S}(\mathbf{P}, G, \bigwedge C_i*, U*)\}$$

where C_i* are obtained from C_i by replacing all free VAR1 variables by new VAR2 variables, respectively, and $U*$ is U together with the new VAR2 variables of C_i*.

Case 7: For some $\mathbf{S}(\mathbf{P}, G, A, U) \in \mathbf{T}$ and some B, $A = \forall y\ B(y)$ and $\mathbf{T}' = (\mathbf{T} - \{\mathbf{S}(\mathbf{P}, G, A, U)\}) \cup \{\mathbf{S}(\mathbf{P}, G, B(\mathbf{f}_A(U)), U)\}$ where $\mathbf{f}_A$ is a Skolem function (associated with $\forall y B(y)$) which is dependent on all elements of U (*whether they appear in B or not*, see Example 10.0.1), and $\Theta' = \Theta$. In classical logic we do not make $\mathbf{f}_A$ dependent on U but only on the variables actually appearing in A.

Case 8: For some $\mathbf{S}(\mathbf{P}, G, A, U) \in \mathbf{T}$ there exists $D = \forall y B(y) \in \mathbf{P}$ and $\mathbf{P}'$ is obtained from $\mathbf{P}$ by adding to $\mathbf{P}$ the additional formula $B(z)$, where z is a new VAR1 variables and $\mathbf{T}'$ is obtained from $\mathbf{T}$ by replacing $\mathbf{S}(\mathbf{P}, G, A, U)$ by $\mathbf{S}(\mathbf{P}', G, A, U)$ and $\Theta' = \Theta$.

Case 9: For some $\mathbf{S}(\mathbf{P}, G, A, U) \in \mathbf{T}$ and some $\mathbf{P}'$

$$\mathbf{T}' = (\mathbf{T} - \{\mathbf{S}(\mathbf{P}, G, A, U)\}) \cup \{\mathbf{S}(\mathbf{P}', G, A, U)\}$$

and $\mathbf{P}'$ is obtained from $\mathbf{P}$ by replacing some $\exists y B(y) \in \mathbf{P}$ by the expression $B(\mathbf{f}_{\exists y B(y)}(x_i, U))$, where x_i are all free VAR1 variables in B and U are all the VAR2 variables of U, *irrespective of whether they appear in B or not* and $\Theta' = \Theta$. In the case of classical logic $\mathbf{f}$ depends only on those variables from U which appear in B and other VAR1 free variables of B.

Case 10: Restart rule.

$\mathbf{T}' = (\mathbf{T} - \{\mathbf{S}(\mathbf{P}, G, A, U)\}) \cup \{\mathbf{S}(\mathbf{P}, G, G*, U*)\}$ for some $\mathbf{S}(\mathbf{P}, G, A, U) \in \mathbf{T}$

where $G*$ is obtained from G by replacing all free VAR2 variables of G by completely new set of VAR2 variables and $U*$ is the union of the set of these variables with U.

Theorem 10.0.9. *[Soundness for classical logic] Let* $\mathbf{T} = \{\mathbf{S}(\mathbf{P}_i, G_i, A_i, U_i)\}$ *be a computation state and assume that* $(\mathbf{T}, \Theta)$ *succeeds. Then in classical logic*

$$\vdash (\exists VAR2)(\bigwedge_i(\forall VAR1 \bigwedge \mathbf{P}_i \rightarrow (\neg G_i \rightarrow A_i)))$$

where $(\exists VAR2)B$ *is the existential closure of* B *over all VAR2 variables and* $(\forall\ VAR1)B$ *is the universal closure of* B *over all VAR1 variables. Note that the subformulae* $\neg G_i \rightarrow A_i$ *arise to accommodate the restart rule. Moreover,* $\neg A$ *is* $A \rightarrow \bot$.

Proof. By induction on the computation steps (the 'cases' of the previous definition). The only significant cases to check are case 6 and case 10.

Case 6:
We have $\mathbf{S}(\mathbf{P}, G, Q, U)$ and $D \in \mathbf{P}$ for some $D =$

$$\bigwedge C_i \rightarrow \exists y_1, \ldots, y_m \bigwedge B_i.$$

In case 6 we replace $\mathbf{S}(\mathbf{P}, G, Q, U)$ by

$$\mathbf{S}(\mathbf{P}, G, \bigwedge C_i, U) \text{ and } \mathbf{S}(\mathbf{P} \cup \{B_i(\mathbf{f}_j(U'))\}, G, Q, U)$$

By the induction hypothesis success means that for some Θ,

1. $\vdash [(\forall\text{VAR1}) \bigwedge \mathbf{P} \wedge \bigwedge B_i(\mathbf{f}_j(U')) \rightarrow (\neg G \rightarrow Q)]\Theta$ and
2. $\vdash [\forall\ \text{VAR1} \bigwedge \mathbf{P} \rightarrow (\neg G \rightarrow \bigwedge C_i)]\Theta$.
   Since $D = \bigwedge C_i \rightarrow (\exists y_1 \ldots y_m) \bigwedge B_i$ is a conjunct in $\bigwedge \mathbf{P}$ we get:
3. $\vdash [(\forall\ \text{VAR1}) \bigwedge \mathbf{P} \rightarrow (\forall\ \text{VAR1})D]\Theta$, and from (2) and (3) we get
4. $\vdash [(\forall\ \text{VAR1}\ ) \bigwedge \mathbf{P} \rightarrow D]\Theta$, and from (2) we get
5. $\vdash [(\forall\ \text{VAR1})\mathbf{P} \rightarrow (\neg G \rightarrow (\exists y_1 \ldots y_m) \bigwedge B_i)]\Theta$. From (1) and (5) we get $\vdash [(\forall\ \text{VAR1}) \bigwedge \mathbf{P} \rightarrow Q]\Theta$, which is the formula to prove for $\mathbf{S}(\mathbf{P}, G, Q, U)$.

Case 10: We have to show that if $\mathbf{S}(\mathbf{P}, G, G, U)$ holds then $\mathbf{S}(\mathbf{P}, G^*, A, U^*)$ holds, where G^*, U^* are like G, U with different names for the variables..

By the induction hypothesis we have that for some Θ,

$$\vdash (\exists \text{VAR2})[\forall \text{VAR1} \bigwedge \mathbf{P} \to (\neg G \to G)]\Theta.$$

We want to show that

$$\vdash (\exists \text{VAR2})[\forall \text{VAR1} \bigwedge \mathbf{P} \to (\neg G \to A)]\Theta$$

This is obviously true since in classical logic

$$\vdash (\neg G \to G^*) \to (\neg G \to A).$$

■

Theorem 10.0.10. *(Soundness for intuitionistic logic) Let* $(\mathbf{T}, \Theta)$ *be as in Theorem 10.0.9 and assume that* $(\mathbf{T}, \Theta)$ *succeeds without the use of the restart rule, then in intuitionistic logic*

$$\vee(\exists \mathit{VAR2}) \bigwedge_i (\forall \mathit{VAR1} \bigwedge \mathbf{P}_i \to A_i).$$

Proof. It is sufficient to consider case 6. The proof for this case is the same as the proof in 10.0.9 with G not appearing, i.e. taken as **truth**. ■

Example 10.0.11.
Data
If everybody buys Jane Fonda's Quick Slimming Book, then someone is bound to follow the program successfully, and be liked by all her friends, envied by her neighbours and generally feel more self-confident and loving towards her children.

Anyone liked by all her friends must be good natured.
Goal
Therefore if everybody buys Jane Fonda's book then some one is good natured.

Let us translate:
Data

(1) $\forall x \, \text{Buy}(x, J) \quad \to \quad \exists y, [\text{Follow}(y) \wedge$
$\forall z \, [\text{Friend}(z, y) \to \text{Like}(z, y)] \wedge$
$\forall z \, [\text{Neighbour}(z, y) \to \text{Envy}(z, y)] \wedge$
$\text{Confident}(y) \wedge$
$\forall z \, [\text{Child}(z, y) \to \text{Love}\ (y, z)]\ ]$

(2) $\forall x[\forall y[\text{Friend}(y, x) \rightarrow \text{Like}(y, x)] \rightarrow \text{Good}(x)]$

Goal

(3) $\forall x \text{Buy}(x, J) \rightarrow \exists x \text{Good}(x)$

This problem can be solved entirely in the computation of the previous section. We pull the Θ quantifiers out and get the (*) formulation as follows:

$$\textbf{(1*)} \quad \exists x \exists y \forall z_1 \forall z_2 \forall z_3 \ \text{Buy}(x, J) \rightarrow \begin{array}{l} (\text{Follow}(y) \wedge \\ [\text{Friend}(z_1, y) \rightarrow \text{Like}(z_1, y)] \wedge \\ [\text{Neighbour}(z_2, y) \rightarrow \text{Envy}(z_2, y)] \wedge \\ \text{Confident}(y) \wedge \\ [\text{Child}(z_3, y) \rightarrow \text{Love}(y, z_3)]) \end{array}$$

(2*) $\forall x \exists y[(\text{Friend}(y, x) \rightarrow \text{Like}(y, x)) \rightarrow \text{Good}(x)]$

and the Goal is:

(3*) $\exists x \exists y[\text{Buy}(x, J) \rightarrow \text{Good}(y)]$.

The above equivalences are valid in classical logic. In intuitionistic logic we cannot rewrite as we did. Both clause (2*) and the goal require the use of the computation of last section.

Skolemizing and decomposing (1*) into several clauses we get the final (#) formulation:

Data

(1#)
1. $\text{Buy}(c_1, J) \rightarrow \text{Follow}(c_2)$
2. $\text{Buy}\ (c_1, J) \rightarrow (\text{Friend}(x, c_2) \rightarrow \text{Likes}(x, c_2))$
3. $\text{Buy}\ (c_1, J) \rightarrow (\text{Neighbour}(x, c_2) \rightarrow \text{Envy}(x, c_2))$
4. $\text{Buy}\ (c_1, J) \rightarrow \text{Confident}(c_2)$
5. $\text{Buy}\ (c_1, J) \rightarrow (\text{Child}(x, c_2) \rightarrow \text{Love}(c_2, x))$.

(2#) $[\text{Friend}(\mathbf{f}(x), x) \rightarrow \text{Like}(\mathbf{f}(x), x)] \rightarrow \text{Good}(x)$

Goal

(3♯) $\text{Buy}(x, J) \rightarrow \text{Good}(y)$.

The above is ready for computation. Notice that after skolemizing and rewriting we lost a bit of structure.

Example 10.0.12. Let us perform the computation for 10.0.11 first as in Section 9, and then, in 10.0.13 below, in *RS*-clause computation.

The Computation according to Section 9:

Data$\sharp$	?	**Goal$\sharp$**
which reduces to		
$(1\sharp), (2\sharp)$	?	$(3\sharp)$
which reduces to		
$(1\sharp), (2\sharp)$	?	$\text{Buy}(u, J) \to \text{Good}(v)$
where $u, v \in \text{VAR2}$		
$(4\sharp), (1\sharp), (2\sharp)$	?	$\text{Good}(v)$
Where $(4\sharp) = \text{Buy}(u, J)$		
Unify with $(2\sharp)$ and get		
	?	$\text{Friend}(\mathbf{f}(v), v) \to \text{Like}(\mathbf{f}(v), v))$
which reduces to		
$(5\sharp)\text{Friend}(\mathbf{f}(v), v)$	?	$\text{Like}(\mathbf{f}(v), v))$.

Where $(5\sharp)$ was added to the database.
Unify with $(1\sharp2)$. Choose $c_2 = v$. Thus everywhere where v appears it becomes c_2, including the database.

We get now

Current data		**Current goal**
$(1\sharp)$	?	$\text{Friend}(\mathbf{f}(c_2), c_2)$
$(2\sharp)$		
$(4\sharp)$ $\text{Buy}(u, J)$		
$(5\sharp)$ $\text{Friend}(\mathbf{f}(v), v))$, for $v = c_2$		
i.e. $\text{Friend}(\mathbf{f}(c_2)$, c_2		
Therefore success.		

Example 10.0.13. Let us now run the *RS*-computation for the previous example, with skolemizing at run time. We will choose the wrong branch to compute. We will succeed, but will be forced to use restart. The next example will do the computation better. We will omit the outermost brackets.

Data		**Goal**
(1), (2)	?	(3)
	$\downarrow$	
(1),(2)	?	$\forall x\ \text{Buy}(x, J) \to \exists x\ \text{Good}(x)$
	$\downarrow$	
(1), (2), (4), $\forall x\ \text{Buy}(x, J)$	?	$\exists x\ \text{Good}(x)$

We can strip $\forall x$ from clauses (2) and (4) in the data. This is case 8 of the computation. We get

Data		**Goal**
(1)		
$(2')\forall y\ [\text{Friend}(y,x) \to \text{Like}(y,x)] \to \text{Good}(x)$	?	$\exists x\ \text{Good}(x)$
$(4')\ \text{Buy}(x,J)$		

We now strip $\exists x$ from the goal, creating a set U of variables to be chosen with $w \in U$. This is case 4 of the computation rule.

Data		**Goal**
as before		$\text{Good}(w)$.
Unify with $(2')$ and ask		
	?	$\forall y[\text{Friend}(y,u_1) \to \text{Like}(y,w)]$

We now skolemize $\forall y$ at run time according to case 7.
The skolem function $\mathbf{f}_1$ depends on $U = \{w\}$.

$$? \ \text{Friend}(\mathbf{f}_1(w), w) \to \text{Like}(\mathbf{f}_1(w), w).$$

Add the antecedent to the database, and continue:

Data		**Goal**
$(1), (2'), (4')$	?	$\text{Like}\ (\mathbf{f}_1(w), w)$
$(5) = \text{Friend}(\mathbf{f}_1(w), w)$		

We now use (1) of the data. This is case 6 of the *RS*-computation. We have to check two subcomputations, **A** and **B**. Both subcomputations carry $U = \{w\}$ to choose. The subcomputations are identified as **Data A**? **Goal A** and **Data B** ? **Goal B**.

Data A	**Goal A**
	(The antecedent of (1))
(1)	$\forall x \text{Buy}(x, J)$
(2′)	
(4′)	
(5)	

Data B	**Goal B**
(1)	
(2′)	
(4′)	
(5)	
(6a)Follow $(\mathbf{f}_2(w))$	
(6b)$\forall z[\text{Friend}(z, \mathbf{f}_2(w)) \rightarrow \text{Like}(z, \mathbf{f}_2(w))]$	
(6c)$\forall z[\text{Neighbour}(z, \mathbf{f}_2(w) \rightarrow \text{Envy}(z, \mathbf{f}_2(w))]$	
(6d)Confident$(\mathbf{f}_2(w))$	
(6e)$\forall z[\text{Child}(z, \mathbf{f}_2(w)) \rightarrow \text{Love}(\mathbf{f}_2(w), z)]$	

Where $\mathbf{f}_2$ is the result of skolemizing on the head of (1).

$\text{Like}(\mathbf{f}_1(w), w)$

We continue with subcomputation **A** first. In this case we skolemize on $\forall x$ in **Goal A**. We substitute $\mathbf{f}_0(w)$ and get the goal to be Buy $(\mathbf{f}_0(w), J)$. Notice that whenever we skolemize the Skolem function depends on all elements of U. The goal Buy $(\mathbf{f}_0(w), J)$ succeeds by unifying with clause (4′) in **Data A**. We do not have to choose the w yet.

We continue with subcomputation **B**. If we fail with subcomputation **B** then the entire original computation fails.

Computation B:
First get rid of $\forall z$ in the various clauses of (6).
Second consider **Goal** B. We try unifying with 6b, but we cannot because of the occur check. Thus we conclude that we probably chose the wrong computation path. The sensible thing to do now is to backtrack to a better computation path. Since this is only an example to illustrate the use of our computation rules, let us restart. (Case 10 of the *RS*-computation). When we restart we can continue in any way we want. However, we choose to retrace our computation steps right form the beginning to this point using a new variable w'. We get the structure shown in the following figure.

Note that when you restart you *don't* have to follow the *same* compu-

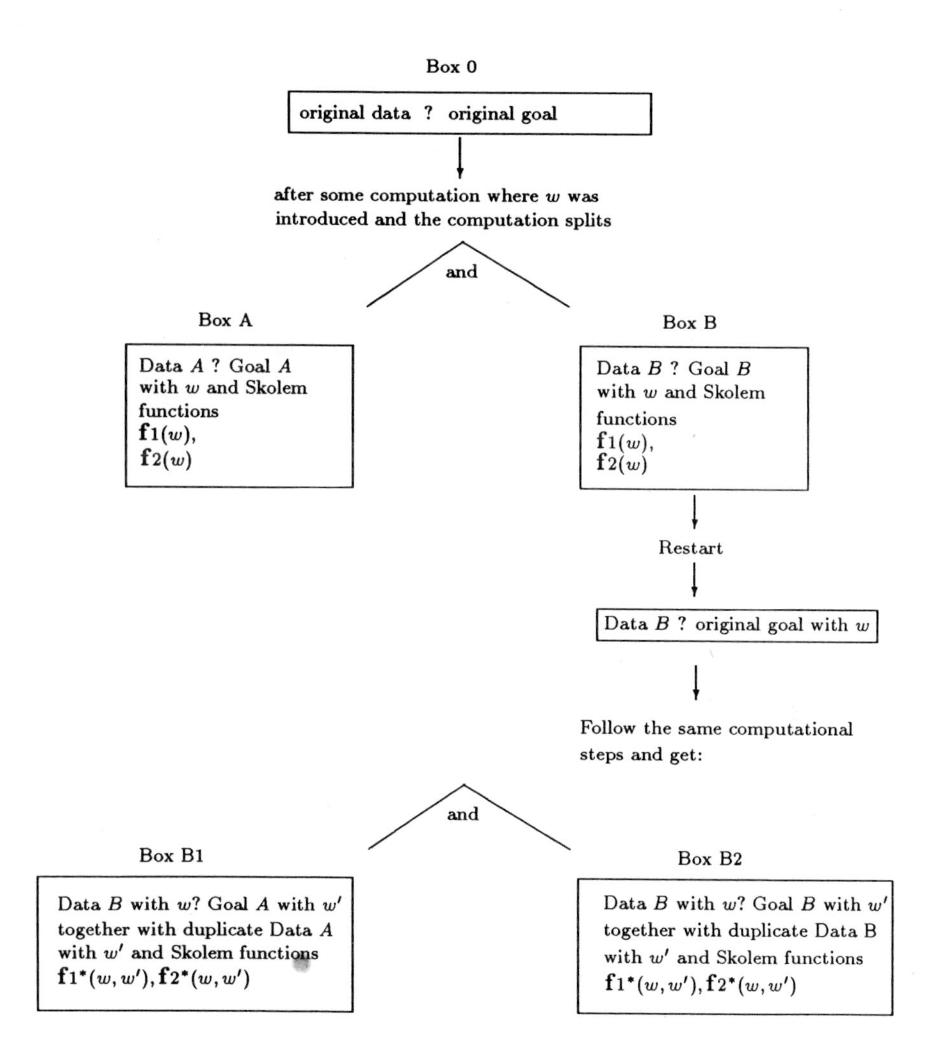

Box 0
original data ? original goal
after some computation where w was introduced and the computation splits
and
Box A
Data A ? Goal A with w and Skolem functions f1(w), f2(w)
Box B
Data B ? Goal B with w and Skolem functions f1(w), f2(w)
Restart
Data B ? original goal with w
Follow the same computational steps and get:
and
Box B1
Data B with w? Goal A with w' together with duplicate Data A with w' and Skolem functions f1*(w, w'), f2*(w, w')
Box B2
Data B with w? Goal B with w' together with duplicate Data B with w' and Skolem functions f1*(w, w'), f2*(w, w')

Fig. 1.

tational steps again. Any steps are allowed. In this case **Goal** B with w will succeed because the goal is: 'Like $(\mathbf{f}_1(w, w'), w')$' and it can be unified with (6b) of the original data **B** which is:

(6b) Friend$(z, \mathbf{f}_2(w)) \rightarrow$ Like$(z, \mathbf{f}_2(w))$.

The second copy of (6b) is

(new 6b) Friend$(z, \mathbf{f}_{2,*}(w, w')) \rightarrow$ Like$(z, \mathbf{f}_{2,*}(w, w'))$.

Note the new Skolem functions are dependent on both w and w'.

Now choose $z = \mathbf{f}_{2,*}(w, w')$ and $w' = \mathbf{f}_{2,*}(w)$ and ask for the body of (new 6b). Note that the same choice substitution must be made also in other computations, i.e. the old computation box A and the new computations Box B1 and Box B2.

We now ask for the body of the (new 6b). The goal is

? Friend$(\mathbf{f}_{1,*}(w, \mathbf{f}_2(w)), \mathbf{f}_2(w))$

In the database of Box B2 we have also another copy of $(5')$. It is:

(new $5'$): Friend$(\mathbf{f}_{1,*}(w, w',), w')$

which after the above choice of $w' = \mathbf{f}_2(w)$, becomes

(new $5'$): Friend$(\mathbf{f}_{1,*}(w, \mathbf{f}_2(w)), f_2(w)))$
and hence the goal succeeds. Notice again the use of the new Skolem function $\mathbf{f}_{1,*}(w, w',)$.

Box B1 will also succeed and the entire computation succeeds.
We made the wrong choice of branch when we computed and so the computation had to use restart. Let us take a better computation branch, where we do not need to use restart. This is the next example.

Example 10.0.14.

Data	**Goal**
Same as previous 10.0.13.	Same as previous 10.0.13.

Proceed as in the previous example to get

Data	**Goal**
(1)	$\exists z$Good(x)
(2′)	
(4′)	

In the previous computation our next step was to get rid of $\exists x$ in the goal; we will not do that now, but take another branch of the computation and use instead case 6 of the RS-computation applied to item (1) of the data. We therefore split to two subcomputation $A*$ and $B*$.

Data A*	**Goal A***
(1)	$\forall x$Buy(x, J)
(2′)	
(4′)	
Data B*	**Goal B***
(1)	$\exists x$Good(x)
(2′)	
(4′)	
(6a*) Follow(c_1)	
(6b*) $\forall z$[Friend$(z, c_1)(\rightarrow$Like(z, c_1)]	
(6c*) $\forall)z$[Neighbour$(z, c_1) \rightarrow$ Envy(z, c_1)]	
(6d*) Confident(c_1)	
(6e*) $\forall z$[Child$(z, c_1) \rightarrow$ Love(c_1, z)]	

The reason we skolemize in the data as a c_1 is because the set of variables $U \subseteq$ VAR2 to be chosen is still empty. This computation will succeed because it is essentially the same as the one, in 10.0.12. We now turn to computation with disjunctions.

In intuitionistic logic disjunctions are not eliminable in favour of other connectives and so direct computation rules for disjunctions must be given. Thus10.0.6 (the notion of a clause) must be modified to allow for disjunctions and also 10.0.8 (the computation rules on clauses) must be extended to deal with disjunctions.

Before we do that formally, let us give informally the two disjunction rules, numbered (11) and (12) (as they will be cases 11 and 12 added to 10.0.8):

(11)	$\mathbf{P}, A \vee B?C$	Succeeds
	if both	
	$\mathbf{P}, A?C$ and $\mathbf{P}, B?C$	succeed.
(12)	$\mathbf{P}?A \vee B$	succeeds
	if either $\mathbf{P}?B$	succeeds
	or $\mathbf{P}?B$	succeeds.

In our formal notation.

(11) $\mathbf{S}(\mathbf{P}, \cup\{A \vee B\}, G, C, U)$ if
$\mathbf{S}(\mathbf{P} \cup \{A\}, G, C, U)$ and $\mathbf{S}(\mathbf{P} \cup \{B\}, G, C, U)$

(12) $\mathbf{S}(\mathbf{P}, G, A \vee B, U)$ if
either $\mathbf{S}(\mathbf{P}, G, A, U)$ or $\mathbf{S}(P, G, B, U)$.

Example 10.0.15. $A \vee B?A \vee B$
Using rule (12) we try either $A \vee B?A$ or $A \vee B?B$. Neither succeeds, so we backtrack and use rule (11) and ask for both $A?A \vee B$ and $B?A \vee B$ and both succeed. It is advisable to use rule (11) first when possible.

Notion of a clause with disjunction. We modify 10.0.6 to allow for disjunctions by adding

(6) If A_i are goals then $\bigvee_i A_i$ is a goal and if B_i are clauses then $\bigvee_i B_i$ is a clause. The free variable of the disjunction is the union of the free variable of the disjuncts.

Notion of computation with disjunctions. We modify 10.0.8 by adding two more cases:

Case 11: *Disjunction in the data*
For some $\mathbf{S}(P \cup \{A \vee B\}, G, C, U) \in \mathbf{T}$
we have:
$\mathbf{T}' = (\mathbf{T} - \mathbf{S}(\mathbf{P} \cup \{A \vee B\}, G, C, U))$
$\cup \mathbf{S}(\mathbf{P} \cup \{A\}, G, C, U), \mathbf{S}(\mathbf{P} \cup \{B\}, G, C, U)$
and $q' = q$.

Case 12: *Disjunction in the goal*
(a) For some $\mathbf{S}(\mathbf{P}, G, A \vee B, U) \in \mathbf{T}$
we have:
$\mathbf{T}' = (\mathbf{T} - \mathbf{S}(\mathbf{P}, G, A \vee B, U)) \cup \mathbf{S}(\mathbf{P}, G, D, U)$ where $D = A$, and $q' = q$.
(b) Similar to (a) with $D = B$.

11 Conclusion

This chapter has four objectives:

1. To show how an algorithmic proof system can arise naturally from the original presentation of a logic, and various natural optimization ideas (the diminished resource theme);

2. To provide an algorithmic proof system (a theorem prover) for intuitionistic predicate logic, classical logic and neighbouring systems;

3. To promote the methodology of *human oriented algorithmic proof* (as opposed to machine oriented);

4. To motivate the need for developing the *logic of Skolem functions.*

(1) and (2) are the main objectives of the chapter. The algorithmic proof system which we proposed followed the methodology of (3) and was achieved by solving the logical problems of (4) for the particular case of intuitionistic logic, via the device of *run time skolemization.*

The idea of a more human oriented algorithmic proof system (3) was introduced in and developed in [Gabbay, 1984], now appearing as [Gabbay and Owens, 1991], and developed in [Gabbay and Reyle, 1984; Gabbay and Reyle, 1985]. In [Gabbay and Kriwaczek, 1991] and [Gabbay and Reyle, 1992] a family of such algorithmic proof systems, based on conjunctions and implication, was introduced. These results were reproduced in Section 8. The terminology of *human oriented* algorithmic proof system, as opposed to *machine oriented* algorithmic proof system, was coined following . To explain informally and intuitively what we mean here, we consider the following basic problem of algorithmic proof systems. We assume we have a database $\mathbf{P}$ and a query Q, and we want to know whether $\mathbf{P} \vdash Q$. We denote this situation by $\mathbf{P} \vdash ?Q$, (or just $\mathbf{P}?Q$). The relation $\vdash$ is the consequence relation of some logic, say classical logic. Most algorithmic proof systems will operate in the two stages. First they would rewrite $\mathbf{P}$ and Q into a normal form $\mathbf{P}^N, Q^N$ and then consider the problem of $\mathbf{P}^N \vdash ?Q^N$. This rewrite may even be a translation into another language and logic.

The algorithmic proof system available for the normalized language will offer computation rules for the solution of the above normalized problem. If we take a snapshot of what the machine is doing in the middle of the computation, we will probably find it solving several subproblems which we can schematically denote by $\mathbf{P}_i^* \vdash ?Q_i^*$.

Finally when (and if) the machine stops, it may come out with an answer 'yes' or 'no' to the question $\mathbf{P}^N?Q^N$ and put forward a possible output which we denote by A^*.

Generally the original problem $\mathbf{P} \vdash ?Q$ will be represented in a humanly intuitive and meaningful form, or at least in a form natural to the original representation language. In machine oriented algorithmic proof system, neither $\mathbf{P}^N \vdash ?Q^N$ nor any intermediate problems $\mathbf{P}_i^* \vdash ?Q_i^*$ are required to be transparent or mean anything (to the user) in terms of the original representation. All we want is to get the final answer (yes/no) and possibly have a tolerable understanding of the output A^*. The representations $\mathbf{P}^N \vdash ?Q^N$ and $\mathbf{P}_i \vdash ?Q_i^*$ are machine oriented only.

In human oriented algorithmic proof systems we require each stage $\mathbf{P}^N \vdash Q^N$ and $\mathbf{P}_i^* \vdash ?Q_i^*$ to be meaningful and humanly intuitive and to naturally relate to $\mathbf{P} \vdash ?Q$. Furthermore the computation rules must be intuitively meaningful in terms of the language of $\mathbf{P} \vdash ?Q$ and be close to the way a human would reason. This human oriented requirement is a severe restriction.

Further thought along these lines would rule out, for example, resolution based methods for classical logic and classify resolution as machine oriented only. Further thought along these lines would also rule out, in many cases, algorithmic proof systems for application areas through translation into classical logic. The human oriented methodology would be in favour of a direct algorithmic proof system on the natural representations in the application area itself (see [Gabbay and Reyle, 1992]). It is for this reason that we chose our original presentation of intuitionistic logic in terms of implication $\to$.

Turning to (4), recall that Skolem functions are used extensively in theorem proving in classical logic. The question of how and when to skolemize is considered in the community as a practical question and not as a logical one. This view is based on the observation that, although a database $\mathbf{P}$ may not be logically equivalent (in classical logic) to its skolemized version $\mathbf{P}^*$, we do have the theorem that, for any query $Q, \mathbf{P} \vdash Q$ iff $\mathbf{P}^* \vdash Q^*$.

Thus for finding out whether Q follows from $\mathbf{P}$, we can safely ask the query Q^* from $\mathbf{P}^*$.

Although in classical logic skolemizing is safe and leads to improved algorithmic performance, there are practical difficulties associated with their use. Chief among them are:

1. Natural structural information in $\mathbf{P}$ gets lost or buried when we turn to the skolemized version $\mathbf{P}^*$. In other words, skolemizing is a machine oriented tool.

2. Answers to queries may contain Skolem functions whose natural meaning and role is not transparent intuitively to the user and in many cases is also meaningless computationally.

3. There are cases where Skolem functionals dependencies do exist naturally in the database and the difficulty is how to allow the querying

mechanism to extract this information. (This is exactly the opposite of (2) above.)

The above are practical problems and not logical problems. In classical logic, we can always skolemize in the beginning of the computation and give our computation rules for universal or existential formulae only. Unfortunately, in non-classical logics we may have logical problems. In the case of modal logic or intutitionistic logic, we cannot always skolemize at the beginning of the computation because the logic may not allow it. The result of skolemizing may not be logically equivalent to the original problem. That is why we had to resort to run time skolemization.

We conclude the chapter with some remarks about the literature.

The algorithmic proof point of view presented in this chapter is novel, as well as the idea of diminishing resource, see [Gabbay, 1991] and compare with [Girard, 1987]. It is goal directed and implication based, treating the various connectives as naturally as possible. There are other approaches, most central among them being resolution. In the companion *Handbook of Logic in Artificial Intelligence and Logic Programming*, [Gabbay, 1992] an entire volume is devoted to theorem proving methods and especially to resolution.

Our approach was introduced originally in [Gabbay, 1984] and further developed in subsequent papers. L T McCarty and D Miller have later and independently put forward similar approaches [McCarty, 1988a; McCarty, 1988b; Miller, 1989; Bonner, 1991].

A. W. Bollen in his thesis [Bollen, 1988] extended this approach to relevance logic. We can extend this approach to other logics including many valued logics and modal and temporal logics. We hope to present the material in the forthcoming [Gabbay, forthcoming]. A general proof methodology for monotonic and non-monotonic logics is now being developed in [Gabbay, to appear]. Decision procedures for intuitionisitc logic based on this approach can be found in [Hudelmaier, 1990].

Our chapter does not prove completeness in the predicate case, but only soundness. Completeness proofs can be found in the forthcoming [Gabbay, 1992].

Acknowledgements

I am grateful to Marcello D'Agostino, Robin Milner, Jörg Hudelmaier and Uwe Reyle for valuable criticism.

References

[Bollen, 1988] A. W. Bollen. *Relevant Conditional Logic Programming.* PhD thesis, Australian National University, 1988.

[Bonner, 1991] A. J. Bonner. *Hypothetical reasoning in deductive databases.* PhD thesis, State University of New Jersey, Rutgers, 1991.

[Gabbay and Kriwaczek, 1991] D. M. Gabbay and F. Kriwaczek. A family of goal directed theorem provers based on conjunction and implication. *Journal of Automated Reasoning*, 7:511–536, 1991.

[Gabbay and Owens, 1991] D. M. Gabbay and R. Owens. *Elementary Logic, a Procedural Perspective.* E Horwood, 1991.

[Gabbay and Reyle, 1984] D. M. Gabbay and U. Reyle. N-Prolog I. *Journal of Logic Programming*, 1:319–355, 1984.

[Gabbay and Reyle, 1985] D. M. Gabbay and U. Reyle. N-Prolog II. *Journal of Logic Programming*, 2:251–283, 1985.

[Gabbay and Reyle, 1992] D. M. Gabbay and U. Reyle. Computation with run time skolemization. *Journal of Applied Non-Classical Logics*, 1992. To appear.

[Gabbay, 1984] D. M. Gabbay. Elementary logic – a procedural perspective. Lecture Notes, Imperial College, 1984.

[Gabbay, 1991] D. M. Gabbay. Algorithmic proof with diminishing resources. In E. Börger, H. Kleine Büning, M. M. Richter, and W. Schönfeld, editors, *Proceedings CSL '90*, volume 533 of *Lecture Notes in Computer Science*, pages 156–173. Springer-Verlag, 1991.

[Gabbay, 1992] D. M. Gabbay. Classical vs non-classical logic. In D. M. Gabbay, C. J. Hogger, and J. A. Robinson, editors, *Handbook of Logic in Artificial Intelligence and Logic Programming. Vol. 1.* Oxford University Press, 1992.

[Gabbay, forthcoming] D. M. Gabbay. *Elements of Algorithmic Proof.* Oxford University Press, forthcoming.

[Gabbay, to appear] D. M. Gabbay. *Labelled Deductive Systems.* Oxford University Press, to appear.

[Girard, 1987] J.-Y. Girard. Linear Logic. *Theoretical Computer Science*, 50:1–102, 1987.

[Hudelmaier, 1990] J. Hudelmaier. Decision procedure for propositional N-Prolog. In P. Schroeder-Heister, editor, *Extensions of Logic Programming*, pages 245–251. Springer Verlag, 1990.

[McCarty, 1988a] L. T. McCarty. Clausal Intuitionistic Logic I: Fixed-Point Semantics. *Journal of Logic Programming*, 5(1):1–31, 1988.

[McCarty, 1988b] L. T. McCarty. Clausal Intuitionistic Logic II: Tableau Proof Procedures. *Journal of Logic Programming*, 5(2):93–132, 1988.

[Miller, 1989] D. Miller. A logical analysis of modules in logic programming. *Journal of Logic Programming*, pages 79–108, 1989.

Designing a Theorem Prover

Lawrence C. Paulson

Contents

1 Folderol: a simple theorem prover

Because many different forms of logic are applicable to computer science, a common question is — *How do I write a theorem prover?* This question can be answered with general advice. For instance, first do enough paper proofs to show that automation of your logic is both necessary and feasible. The question can also be answered with a survey of existing provers, as will be done in this chapter. But automatic theorem proving involves a combination of theoretical and coding skills that is best illustrated by a case study. So this chapter presents a toy theorem prover, called *Folderol*, highlighting the key design issues. Code fragments are discussed in the text; a full program listing appears at the end of the chapter.

Folderol works in classical first-order logic. It follows an automatic strategy but is interactive. You can enter a conjecture, let Folderol work with it for a while, and finally modify or abandon the conjecture if it cannot be proved. There is no practical automatic proof procedure, even for most complete theories. Even if there were, interaction with the machine would still be necessary for exploring mathematics.

A theorem prover should offer some evidence that its proofs are valid. The [Boyer and Moore, 1979] theorem prover prints an English summary of its reasoning, while Folderol prints a trace of the rules. Most LCF-style systems offer no evidence of correctness other than an obstinate insistence on playing by the rules [Paulson, 1987]. If correctness is a matter of life and death, then a prover can be designed to output its proof for checking by a separate program.

Absolute correctness can never be obtained, even with a computer-checked proof. There are fundamental reasons for this. Any program may contain errors, including the one that checks the proofs; we have no absolutely reliable means by which to verify the verifier. In addition, a proof of correctness of a program relies on assumptions about the real world; it assumes that the computer works correctly, and usually assumes that the program is used properly. Hardware correctness proofs depend upon similar assumptions [Cohn, 1989b]. Even in pure mathematics, the premises of a theorem are subject to revision [Lakatos, 1976].

Although Folderol performs well on certain examples, its proof strategy suffers inherent limitations. The strategy would be even worse if we adopted modal or intuitionistic logic, and cannot easily be remedied. My hope is that, once you have studied this chapter, you will gain the confidence to implement more sophisticated strategies.

Folderol exploits many of the concepts of functional programming, although it is not pure. It is written in Standard ML, which is increasingly popular for theorem proving. Several recent books teach this language.

Remark on quantifiers. The usual notation for quantifiers, seen elsewhere in this volume, gives the quantified variable the smallest possible scope. To save on parentheses, quantifiers in this chapter employ a dot convention, extending the scope of quantification as far as possible. So $\forall x.P \rightarrow Q$ abbreviates $\forall x.(P \rightarrow Q)$, and

$$\exists y.P \wedge \exists z.Q \vee R \text{ abbreviates } \exists y.(P \wedge (\exists z.(Q \vee R))).$$

1.1 Representation of rules

Given that Folderol will handle classical first-order logic, what formal system is best suited for automation? Gentzen's sequent calculus LK [Takeuti, 1987] supports backwards proof in a natural way. A naïve process of working upwards from the desired conclusion yields many proofs.

Most rules act on one formula, and they come in pairs: one operating on the left and one on the right. We must inspect the rules carefully before choosing data structures. The quantifier rules, especially, constrain the representation of terms.

The classical sequent calculus deals with sequents of the form $\Gamma \vdash \Delta$. Here Γ is the left part and Δ is the right part, and $\Gamma \vdash \Delta$ means 'if every formula in Γ is true then some formula in Δ is true.' The sequent $A \vdash A$ (called a *basic* sequent) is trivially true. You may prefer to think in terms of refutation. Then $\Gamma \vdash \Delta$ is false if every formula in Γ is true and every formula in Δ is false. If these conditions are contradictory then the sequent is true.

Structural rules, namely exchange, thinning, and contraction, make sequents behave like a consequence relation.

The *thinning* rules, in backwards proof, delete a formula from the goal. Since a formula should not be deleted unless it is known to be redundant, let us postpone all deletions. A goal is trivially true if it has the form $\Gamma \vdash \Delta$ where there exists a common formula $A \in \Gamma \cap \Delta$. Accepting these as basic sequents makes thinning rules unnecessary; the other formulae are simply thrown away.

The *exchange* rules swap two adjacent formulae, for traditionally Γ and Δ are lists, not sets. Lists are also convenient in programming. We can do without exchange rules by ignoring the order of formulae in a sequent. In the rule

$$\frac{\Gamma \vdash \Delta, A \qquad \Gamma \vdash \Delta, B}{\Gamma \vdash \Delta, A \land B} \quad \land\text{:right}.$$

There is no reason why $A \land B$ needs to be last. It can appear anywhere in the right part of the conclusion. For backwards proof: if the goal contains $A \land B$ anywhere in the right part then we can produce two subgoals, replacing $A \land B$ by A and B respectively. We can write the rule more concisely and clearly as follows, showing only formulae that change:

$$\frac{\vdash A \qquad \vdash B}{\vdash A \land B}. \quad \land\text{:right}.$$

The *contraction* rules, in backwards proof, duplicate a formula. Duplicating the $A \land B$, then applying the conjunction rule above, makes subgoals $\vdash A, A \land B$ and $\vdash B, A \land B$. These are equivalent to $\vdash A$ and $\vdash B$, so the $A \land B$ is redundant.

A case-by-case inspection of the rules reveals that the only formulae worth duplicating are $\forall x.A$ on the left and $\exists x.A$ on the right. Let us add contraction to the rules $\forall$:left and $\exists$:right. The rule $\forall$:left takes a goal containing $\forall x.A$ on the left and makes one subgoal by adding the formula $A[t/x]$ for some term t. The subgoal retains a copy of $\forall x.A$ so that the rule can be applied again for some other term. This example requires n repeated uses of the quantified formula on terms a, $f(a)$, ...:

$$\forall x\,.\,P(x) \to P(f(x)) \ \vdash\ P(a) \to P(\underbrace{f(f(\cdots f}_{n\text{ times}}(a)\cdots))).$$

The rule $\exists$:right similarly retains the quantified formula in its subgoal.

Folderol uses these quantified formulae in rotation. It never throws them away. Thus even

$$\forall x.P(x) \vdash Q$$

makes Folderol run forever. If not for the re-use of quantified formulae, the search space would be finite. A theorem prover should only instantiate a quantifier when strictly necessary — but there is no effective test. First-order logic is undecidable.

1.2 Propositional logic

Propositional logic concerns the connectives $\land$, $\lor$, $\to$, $\leftrightarrow$, and $\neg$. We take negation as primitive rather than defining $\neg A$ as $A \to \bot$. Although $A \leftrightarrow B$ means $(A \to B) \land (B \to A)$, performing this expansion could cause exponential blowup! The rules for $\leftrightarrow$ permit natural reasoning.

$$
\begin{array}{ccc}
 & \textit{left} & \textit{right} \\[2ex]
\wedge & \dfrac{A, B \vdash}{A \wedge B \vdash} & \dfrac{\vdash A \qquad \vdash B}{\vdash A \wedge B} \\[3ex]
\vee & \dfrac{A \vdash \qquad B \vdash}{A \vee B \vdash} & \dfrac{\vdash A, B}{\vdash A \vee B} \\[3ex]
\rightarrow & \dfrac{\vdash A \qquad B \vdash}{A \rightarrow B \vdash} & \dfrac{A \vdash B}{\vdash A \rightarrow B} \\[3ex]
\leftrightarrow & \dfrac{A, B \vdash \qquad \vdash A, B}{A \leftrightarrow B \vdash} & \dfrac{A \vdash B \qquad B \vdash A}{\vdash A \leftrightarrow B} \\[3ex]
\neg & \dfrac{\vdash A}{\neg A \vdash} & \dfrac{A \vdash}{\vdash \neg A}
\end{array}
$$

Fig. 1. Propositional logic

$$
\begin{array}{ccc}
 & \textit{left} & \textit{right} \\[2ex]
\forall & \dfrac{\forall x.A, A[t/x] \vdash}{\forall x.A \vdash} & \dfrac{\vdash A[a/x]}{\vdash \forall x.A}\,* \\[3ex]
\exists & \dfrac{A[a/x] \vdash}{\exists x.A \vdash}\,* & \dfrac{\vdash \exists x.A, A[t/x]}{\vdash \exists x.A}
\end{array}
$$

* Proviso: the parameter a must not appear in the conclusion

Fig. 2. Quantifier rules

Figure 1 shows the rules for each connective. In backwards proof each rule breaks down a non-atomic formula in the conclusion. If more than one rule is applicable, as in $A \wedge B \vdash B \wedge A$, which should be chosen? Some choices give shorter proofs than others. This proof of $A \wedge B \vdash B \wedge A$ uses $\wedge$:left before $\wedge$:right (working upwards):

$$\dfrac{\dfrac{A, B \vdash B \qquad A, B \vdash A}{A, B \vdash B \wedge A}\ \wedge\text{:right}}{A \wedge B \vdash B \wedge A}\ \wedge\text{:left.}$$

If $\wedge$:right is used first then $\wedge$:left must be used twice. In larger examples the difference can be exponential.

$$\dfrac{\dfrac{A, B \vdash B}{A \wedge B \vdash B}\ \wedge\text{:left} \qquad \dfrac{A, B \vdash A}{A \wedge B \vdash A}\ \wedge\text{:left}}{A \wedge B \vdash B \wedge A}\ \wedge\text{:right.}$$

Rules can be chosen to minimize the proliferation of subgoals. If a goal is a basic sequent then trying other rules seems pointless.[1] Let us say that the *cost* of a rule is the number of premises it has. A rule with one premise is cheaper than a rule with two premises; $\wedge$:left is cheaper than $\wedge$:right.

The obvious representation of the goal $\Gamma \vdash \Delta$, a pair of lists, is awkward for choosing the cheapest rule. A Folderol goal is a list of triples ordered by cost. Each triple contains a formula, a 'side' (either left or right), and a cost.

1.3 Quantifiers and unification

First-order logic extends propositional logic with the quantifiers $\forall$ and $\exists$, as well as variables and other terms. Examination of the rules (Figure 2) reveals several difficulties involving terms.

In backwards proof, $\forall$:left and $\exists$:right, the term t is unspecified. It could be any combination of variables, constants, and functions. The possibilities are infinite. Why not defer the choice? At some future time, perhaps the correct choice will be obvious. Folderol uses a special kind of variable, really a meta variable, to stand for an unspecified term. Such variables are written with a question mark: $?a$, $?b$, $?c$, ... A backwards $\forall$:left or $\exists$:right inserts a fresh meta variable $?b$ in place of t in the subgoal.

Whenever a new subgoal is produced, Folderol tries to change it to a basic sequent. It looks for a left-formula A_1 and right-formula A_2 such

[1] But once we introduce unification, we have to be careful. Solving a goal by unification may instantiate variables in other goals, possibly rendering them unprovable.

that replacing meta variables by properly chosen terms turns both into the same formula A. We say A is a *common instance* of A_1 and A_2.

The process of making such choices is called *unification*. For example, $R(?a, f(x))$ and $R(g(?b), ?b)$ both become $R(g(f(x)), f(x))$ replacing $?a$ by $g(f(x))$ and $?b$ by $f(x)$. This assignment is written $?a \mapsto g(f(x))$, $?b \mapsto f(x)$. Similarly, $R(?a, f(?c))$ and $R(g(?d), ?b)$ have $R(g(?d), f(?c))$ as a common instance. The resulting formula contains meta variables $?c$ and $?d$ which can be replaced later.

No formula is a common instance of $P(?a)$ and $Q(f(y))$ if P and Q are distinct. More subtly, $P(?a)$ and $P(f(?a))$ have no common instance: no term t is identical to $f(t)$ unless we admit the infinite term $f(f(f(\cdots)))$. Cycles can arise indirectly, as in unifying $R(?a, f(?a))$ and $R(?b, ?b)$.

1.4 Parameters in quantifier rules

Substitution should never cause a free variable to become bound. This error, called *variable capture*, permits unsound inferences such as the following:

$$\frac{\vdash \forall x.\exists y.y \neq x}{\vdash \exists y.y \neq y}\ \forall\text{:right.}$$

While substituting y for x in the subformula $\exists y.y \neq x$, the free variable y becomes bound by the quantifier $\exists y$. In any model with two distinct individuals, the premise of the inference is true while the conclusion is clearly false. Renaming the bound variable y to z yields a correct conclusion, $\vdash \exists z.z \neq y$.

Variable capture can be prevented by renaming bound variables during substitution, but the algorithms to do this are complicated and liable to obscure errors. It is simpler to abandon the idea that a free variable is a variable that happens not to be bound. Instead have disjoint sets of parameters a, b, c, ..., and variables x, y, z, ..., where parameters may not be bound and variables must be bound.

Many logicians maintain this distinction between bound variables and parameters [Prawitz, 1965]. Observe that a subformula may, under this distinction, not be a legal formula by itself. For instance, $\forall x.\exists y.y \neq x$ has the subformula $\exists y.y \neq x$, where x appears unbound. We must replace the bound variable x by a parameter, say a. Applying $\forall$:right to $\vdash \forall x.\exists y.y \neq x$ produces the conclusion $\vdash \exists y.y \neq a$.

1.4.1 Enforcement of provisos of quantifier rules

The proviso of $\forall$:right and $\exists$:left — that a must not appear in the conclusion — ensures that a can denote an arbitrary value. It may seem that if we choose a fresh parameter every time we use these rules, there is no danger of its appearing in the conclusion. But instantiation of meta variables can change the conclusion, adding new parameters.

For example, $\forall x.R(x,x) \vdash \exists y.\forall x.R(x,y)$ is not valid. (To see this, let $R(x,y)$ mean $x = y$.) A derivation using meta variables might be (deleting some quantified formulae)

$$\cfrac{\cfrac{\cfrac{R(?c,?c) \vdash R(b,?a)}{\forall x.R(x,x) \vdash R(b,?a)}\ \forall\text{:left}}{\forall x.R(x,x) \vdash \forall x.R(x,?a)}\ \forall\text{:right}}{\forall x.R(x,x) \vdash \exists y.\forall x.R(x,y)}\ \exists\text{:right.}$$

It appears that replacing both $?c$ and $?a$ by b completes the proof, with top sequent $R(b,b) \vdash R(b,b)$. But then the second inference is nonsense:

$$\frac{\cdots \vdash R(b,b)}{\cdots \vdash \forall x.R(x,b)}\ \forall\text{:right.}$$

Assigning b to $?a$ sneaks b into the conclusion of the rule $\forall$:right, violating its proviso. Let us say 'b depends on $?a$', which means b must differ from the parameters in any term substituted for $?a$.

To apply $\forall$:right and $\exists$:left, choose a fresh parameter b that depends on all the meta variables in the goal, say $?a_1, \ldots, ?a_n$. To emphasize the dependence we write the parameter as $b[?a_1, \ldots, ?a_n]$. Compare with the function application $f(?a_1, \ldots, ?a_n)$ — parameters resemble Skolem terms, but do not use fictitious functions. Logically, $b[?a_1, \ldots, ?a_n]$ is like a Henkin constant ([Barwise, 1977], page 30).

Variable $?a$ is unifiable with term t just if $?a$ does not occur in t. This *occurs check* can be extended to prevent invalid assignments to meta variables. Folderol associates with every parameter the list of meta variables it depends on: in the derivation above, the parameter is $b[?a]$. Assigning $b[?a]$ to $?a$ creates an obvious circularity. If t contains $b[?a]$ then the occurs check will find that it depends on $?a$. The assignment $?a \mapsto t$, which would make b appear in the conclusion, is forbidden.

For an exercise, verify that other possible proofs of $\forall x.R(x,x) \vdash \exists y.\forall x.R(x,y$ fail.

Compare with a derivation of the valid sequent $\forall x.R(x,x) \vdash \forall x.\exists y.R(x,y)$:

$$\cfrac{\cfrac{\cfrac{R(?c,?c) \vdash R(a,?b)}{\forall x.R(x,x) \vdash R(a,?b)}\ \forall\text{:left}}{\forall x.R(x,x) \vdash \exists y.R(a,y)}\ \exists\text{:right}}{\forall x.R(x,x) \vdash \forall x.\exists y.R(x,y)}\ \forall\text{:right.}$$

Here the parameter a does not depend on meta variables $?b$ and $?c$ since these appear above it. Assigning $?c \mapsto a$ and $?b \mapsto a$ produces a valid proof:

$$\cfrac{\cfrac{\cfrac{R(a,a) \vdash R(a,a)}{\forall x.R(x,x) \vdash R(a,a)}\ \forall\text{:left}}{\forall x.R(x,x) \vdash \exists y.R(a,y)}\ \exists\text{:right}}{\forall x.R(x,x) \vdash \forall x.\,\exists y.R(x,y)}\ \forall\text{:right.}$$

1.4.2 No second-order dependence

So each new parameter depends on all the meta variables in the goal. But if the goal contains some other parameter $b[?a]$ this does not mean it contains $?a$. Consider this proof:

$$\cfrac{\cfrac{\vdash P(?a, b[?a]) \qquad \cfrac{\vdash Q(b[?a], c)}{\vdash \forall y.Q(b[?a], y)}\ \forall\text{:right}}{\vdash P(?a, b[?a]) \land (\forall y.Q(b[?a], y))}\ \land\text{:right}}{\vdash \forall x.\,P(?a, x) \land (\forall y.Q(x, y))}\ \forall\text{:right.}$$

Here b depends on $?a$, sequent $\vdash \forall y.Q(b[?a], y)$ contains $b[?a]$ but not $?a$, and c does not depend on $?a$. The assignment $?a \mapsto c$ is unlikely to occur, for it takes c outside of its natural scope. But this assignment would not violate the proviso of any rule. Only variables actually present in the conclusion affect the proviso. Thus Folderol does not make c depend on $?a$.

Stricter conditions on the use of meta variables can keep parameters within their scope. Folderol generates distinct meta variables and only assigns $?a \mapsto t$ when all the symbols in $?a$ and t are present in a single goal.

1.4.3 Summary

Let us restate the procedure for enforcing provisos of the rules $\forall$:right and $\exists$:left.

- When applying either rule, choose a fresh parameter — one that appears nowhere else in the proof — and make it depend on all meta variables present in the conclusion.
- Allow the assignment $?a \mapsto t$ only if t does not depend on $?a$. This ensures that each parameter b in t does not depend on $?a$, so the assignment respects the proviso of the rule that created b.
- To perform the assignment $?a \mapsto t$, replace $?a$ by t throughout the proof. Replace each parameter depending on $?a$ by one depending on the meta variables in t.

A lemma about LK justifies the substitution of terms for meta variables under suitable conditions, ([Takeuti, 1987], Lemma 2.11). There is no logical need to distinguish meta variables from parameters. But the distinction helps us — and Folderol — remember which variables are candidates for substitution.

2 Basic data structures and operations

Only now, having studied proof construction, can we choose a representation of terms and formulae. We will start to look at ML code including type definitions and substitution functions.

2.1 Terms

The function application $f(t_1, \ldots, t_n)$, where f is an n-place function symbol and the t_i are terms, is represented by the name of the function paired with the list of its arguments. There are n-place function symbols for all $n \geq 0$, where 0-place function symbols are constant symbols.

The three kinds of variables — bound variables, parameters, and meta variables — require a system of names. In many-sorted logic, variables would also have a sort.

Meta-variables (henceforth called just 'variables') have a name, a character string. Names could be more complex: an integer subscript would allow quick renaming of variables.

Each parameter has a name and is paired with a list of variables (possibly empty) representing provisos of quantifier rules. So a parameter has the form $b[?a_1, \ldots, ?a_n]$. Alternatively we could maintain a table to pair each parameter b with a list $?a_1, \ldots, ?a_n$.

Bound variables are distinguished from parameters using an approach [de Bruijn, 1972] that also identifies expressions that are equivalent up to bound variable renaming. For example, $\forall x.\forall y.P(x)$ is equivalent to $\forall y.\forall x.P(y)$ but differs from $\forall x.\forall y.P(y)$, $\forall x.\forall x.P(x)$, and $\forall x.\forall y.P(a)$.

De Bruijn eliminates all bound variable names. The binding occurrence (after a quantifier in first-order logic) of a variable is dropped. Every other occurrence is represented by a non-negative integer, namely the number of enclosing quantifiers between the variable occurrence and its quantifier. These numbers are called de Bruijn indices and are written $\underline{0}$, $\underline{1}$, etc. Different occurrences of a variable may have different indices, and vice versa. Examples:

$\forall x.\forall y.P(x)$	$\forall\forall P(\underline{1})$	two equivalent formulae
$\forall y.\forall x.P(y)$	$\forall\forall P(\underline{1})$	
$\forall x.\forall y.P(y)$	$\forall\forall P(\underline{0})$	two equivalent formulae
$\forall x.\forall x.P(x)$	$\forall\forall P(\underline{0})$	
$\forall x.\forall y.P(a)$	$\forall\forall P(a)$	
$\exists x.((\exists y.Q(y)) \wedge S(x))$	$\exists((\exists Q(\underline{0})) \wedge S(\underline{0}))$	different variables, same index
$\forall x.(Q(x) \vee \exists z.R(z,x))$	$\forall(Q(\underline{0}) \vee \exists R(\underline{0},\underline{1}))$	same variables, different indices

De Bruijn developed this representation for the λ-calculus, where λ-notation can bind variables in terms. A β-reduction may move a subterm into the scope of another λ. For example, $\lambda z.(\lambda x.\lambda y.x)(az)$ goes by β-conversion to $\lambda z.(\lambda y.az)$. The variable z is free in (az), which is substituted for x in $\lambda y.x$. We must adjust the index in $(a\underline{0})$ as it goes inside the λy:

$$\lambda z.(\lambda x.\lambda y.x)(az) \qquad \lambda(\lambda\lambda\underline{1})(a\underline{0})$$
$$\lambda z.(\lambda y.az) \qquad \lambda(\lambda a\underline{1}).$$

[de Bruijn, 1972] gives simple algorithms for substitution, etc. They are especially simple for first-order logic, where terms cannot bind variables.

2.2 Formulae

There are three kinds of formula.

An atomic formula $P(t_1, \ldots, t_n)$, where P is an n-place predicate symbol and the t_i are terms, is represented by the name of the predicate and the list of its arguments. There are n-place predicate symbols for all $n \geq 0$.

A formula $A \wedge B$, $A \vee B$, $A \rightarrow B$, $A \leftrightarrow B$, or $\neg A$, where A and B are formulae, is represented by the connective and the list of subformulae: $[A, B]$ or $[A]$. Other connectives, like modal operators $\Box$ and $\Diamond$, can be represented similarly. This gives easy access to the subformulae. Most formula operations do not have a separate case for each connective.

A quantified formula $\forall x.A$ or $\exists x.A$, where the body A is a formula and x is a bound variable, is represented by the type of quantifier and the body. De Bruijn's notation does not require the name of the bound variable, but Folderol keeps it for printing results.

The discussion leads to the ML type definitions:

```
datatype term =
    Var   of string
  | Param of string * string list
  | Bound of int
  | Fun   of string * term list;
```

```
datatype form =
    Pred  of string * term list
  | Conn  of string * form list
  | Quant of string * string * form;
```

2.3 Abstraction and substitution

Two operations involving bound variables in formulae are abstraction and substitution.

- Abstraction maps A to $\forall x.A[x/t]$ (or $\exists x.A[x/t]$), replacing all occurrences of the term t by the bound variable x.
- Substitution maps $\forall x.A$ (or $\exists x.A$) to $A[t/x]$, replacing all occurrences of the bound variable x by the term t.

Why is abstraction important? Recall that free variables are forbidden under de Bruijn notation. In $\forall x.A$ and $\exists x.A$, if x is free in A then the formula A standing alone is not well-formed. So we cannot make a quantified formula by attaching $\forall x$ to the illegal formula A. Instead we use abstraction: if A is a formula, t is a term, and x is a bound variable not present in A, then $\forall x.A[x/t]$ and $\exists x.A[x/t]$ are formulae.

Both abstraction and substitution start with bound variable index $\underline{0}$. This is incremented whenever a quantifier is encountered.

Abstraction replaces occurrences of t by a bound variable. It calls the operation $\text{abs}(i)$ for index $i \geq 0$, and $\text{abs}(i)$ of a quantified formula involves $\text{abs}(i+1)$ of the body. Clearly $\text{abs}(i)$ of a conjunction, disjunction, ... involves $\text{abs}(i)$ of each subformula. For predicates, $\text{abs}(i)$ involves replacing t by $\underline{i}$ in the arguments.

Example: abstract $(\forall z.R(z,a)) \leftrightarrow P(a)$ over a to get $\exists x.\,(\forall z.R(z,x)) \leftrightarrow P(x)$:

$$\begin{aligned} \text{abs}(0)[(\forall R(\underline{0},a)) \leftrightarrow P(a)] &= \text{abs}(0)[\forall R(\underline{0},a)] \leftrightarrow \text{abs}(0)[P(a)] \\ &= (\forall\,\text{abs}(1)[R(\underline{0},a)] \leftrightarrow P(\underline{0})) \\ &= (\forall R(\underline{0},\underline{1})) \leftrightarrow P(\underline{0}). \end{aligned}$$

Having computed $\text{abs}(0)$ we attach the quantifier, getting the de Bruijn representation of the result:

$$\exists((\forall R(\underline{0},\underline{1})) \leftrightarrow P(\underline{0})).$$

Substitution replaces occurrences of the bound variable by t, having detached the outer quantifier. It calls the operation $\text{subst}(i)$ for index $i \geq 0$. As above, $\text{subst}(i)$ of a quantifier involves $\text{subst}(i+1)$, while connectives do not require incrementing i and predicates require replacing $\underline{i}$ by t in the arguments. Substituting a for x in the body of $\exists x.(\forall z.R(z,x)) \leftrightarrow P(x)$ produces a computation almost identical to the previous example.

For the arguments of predicates both abstraction and substitution replace one term by another. This suggests a separate replacement operation on terms. This need not adjust indices since there is no λ-binding. The code for replacement, abstraction, and substitution is simple:

```
fun replace_term (u,new) t =
    if t=u then new else
    case t of Fun(a,ts) => Fun(a, map (replace_term(u,new)) ts)
            | _ => t;

fun abstract t =
    let fun abs i (Pred(a,ts)) =
                  Pred(a, map (replace_term (t, Bound i)) ts)
          | abs i (Conn(b,As)) = Conn(b, map (abs i) As)
          | abs i (Quant(q,b,A)) = Quant(q, b, abs (i+1) A)
    in  abs 0  end;

fun subst_bound t =
    let fun subst i (Pred(a,ts)) =
                    Pred(a, map (replace_term (Bound i, t)) ts)
          | subst i (Conn(b,As)) = Conn(b, map (subst i) As)
          | subst i (Quant(q,b,A)) = Quant(q, b, subst (i+1) A)
    in  subst 0  end;
```

Observe the use of the functional `map` to apply a function over a list, getting a list of results. This is used to handle the arguments of functions and predicates and the subformulae of connectives.

2.4 Parsing and printing

A good quarter of Folderol is concerned with parsing and printing of formulae. Let us pass over this quickly.

Abstraction is used only in the parser: given an input string for $\forall x.A$ it parses A treating x as a constant, then abstracts over x. This is hidden in the function

```
fun makeQuant q b A = Quant(q, b, abstract (Fun(b,[])) A);
```

Recall that a constant is a 0-place function.

Similarly the printer, given the formula $\forall x.A$, substitutes a constant named x for the bound variable in A. The output is misleading if the body already contains a constant x. A better printer would make sure the name was unique.

Identifiers are sequences of letters or digits. Examples of terms include

`r 12 banana`	constants
`?s ?12 ?apple`	variables
`f(x,?y) succ(succ(0))`	function applications

The parser is crude. It accepts `f(f(f),f(f,f),f)`, for there is no table of function names. Also parameters cannot be expressed: an identifier by itself is taken for a constant.[2] There is no notation for bound variables, but none is needed.

Logical symbols are written as follows using computer characters:

`~`	$\neg$
`&`	$\wedge$
`|`	$\vee$
`--> <->`	$\rightarrow \leftrightarrow$
`ALL EXISTS`	$\forall \; \exists$
`|-`	$\vdash$

They appear in order of decreasing precedence; if precedence is equal, infixes associate to the right. Because quantifiers incorporate the dot notation, their scope extends as far as possible to the right. Enclose a quantified formula in parentheses if it is an operand of a connective.

For example, these theorems are provable by Folderol:

$$(P \vee (Q \wedge R)) \leftrightarrow ((P \vee Q) \wedge (P \vee R))$$

$$((P \rightarrow Q) \rightarrow P) \rightarrow P$$

$$\neg(\exists x.\forall y.F(x,y) \leftrightarrow \neg F(y,y))$$

$$\exists xy.P(x,y) \rightarrow \forall xy.P(x,y)$$

$$\exists x.\forall yz.(P(y) \rightarrow Q(z)) \rightarrow (P(x) \rightarrow Q(x)).$$

Here they are in computer syntax:

```
P | (Q & R)  <-> (P | Q) & (P | R)
((P-->Q) --> P)  -->  P
~ (EXISTS x. ALL y. F(x,y) <-> ~ F(y,y))
EXISTS x. EXISTS y. P (x,y) -->  (ALL x. ALL y. P(x,y))
EXISTS x. ALL y. ALL z. (P(y)-->Q(z)) --> (P(x)-->Q(x))
```

3 Unification

The unification of terms t and u amounts to solving the equation $t = u$ over the (meta) variables in the terms. In the standard situation, all parameters and functions are distinct — the only equalities that hold are reflexivity ($t = t$) and the substitution of equals for equals. Thus $f(?a) = b$, $a = b$,

[2]This limitation happily keeps the original goal free of parameters; these could otherwise clash with parameters created for quantifier rules.

and $f(?c) = g(?a, ?b)$ are each unsolvable, while each solution of $g(t_1, t_2) = g(u_1, u_2)$ solves $t_1 = u_1$ and $t_2 = u_2$ simultaneously.

In general we must solve a set of equations $\{t_1 = u_1, \ldots, t_n = u_n\}$. Equations are considered one at a time. Given an equation, there are nine cases: each term may be a function application, a parameter, or a variable. (Standard unification does not permit bound variables.) Most cases are unsolvable. If one term is a parameter then the other term must be the same parameter. If one term is a function application then the other must be an application of the same function, with the same number of arguments. The equation

$$f(t'_1, \ldots, t'_m) = f(u'_1, \ldots, u'_m)$$

is replaced by the equations

$$t'_1 = u'_1 \quad \ldots \quad t'_m = u'_m.$$

The crucial case is an equation between a variable and a term: $?a = t$ or $t = ?a$. If t is identical to $?a$ then we can drop the equation. Otherwise we must perform the *occurs check*. If $?a$ occurs in t then the equation has no solution, for no term can properly contain itself. If $?a$ does not occur in t then setting $?a \mapsto t$ solves the equation. In $?a = ?b$ either variable may be set to the other.

An equation is solved when it has been simplified to the form variable=term. Each solution must be substituted in the other equations, since we are solving them simultaneously. Then another equation is chosen. The process fails if an unsolvable equation is found and finishes when the entire set is solved. A solution set (or *unifier*) has the form $\{?a_1 = u_1, \ldots, ?a_k = u_k\}$, where the $?a_i$ are distinct and appear in none of the u_j. A unifier amounts to a substitution for $\{?a, \ldots, ?a_k\}$.

3.1 Examples

Here is an unsolvable example. The solutions of $g(a, c) = g(?b, ?b)$ are precisely solutions of the set of equations

$$a = ?b \qquad c = ?b.$$

Substitution for $?b$ gives

$$?b = a \qquad c = a.$$

and the second equation is unsolvable (two distinct constants).

Similarly $g(?a, f(?a)) = g(?b, ?b)$ reduces to

$$?a = ?b \qquad f(?a) = ?b.$$

Substitution for $?a$ in the second equation makes it unsolvable (occurs check):

$$?a = ?b \qquad f(?b) = ?b.$$

The equation $h(?a, f(?a), ?d) = h(g(0, ?d), ?b, ?c)$ reduces to

$$?a = g(0, ?d) \qquad f(?a) = ?b \qquad ?d = ?c.$$

The first equation is solved; substituting it elsewhere gives

$$?a = g(0, ?d) \qquad f(g(0, ?d)) = ?b \qquad ?d = ?c.$$

The second equation is solved:

$$?a = g(0, ?d) \qquad ?b = f(g(0, ?d)) \qquad ?d = ?c.$$

Success! Solving the third equation gives the unifier

$$?a = g(0, ?c) \qquad ?b = f(g(0, ?c)) \qquad ?d = ?c.$$

Infinitely many unifiers are instances of this, replacing $?c$ by any term.

Reversing the third equation to $?c = ?d$ above gives an equivalent unifier:

$$?a = g(0, ?d) \qquad ?b = f(g(0, ?d)) \qquad ?c = ?d.$$

Since $?c = ?d$ exchanging the variables has no significance.

The method sketched above finds the *most general* unifier, one that includes all other unifiers as special cases. The equations may be attempted in any order without significantly affecting the outcome. If a unifier exists then a most general unifier will be found. Two most general unifiers can differ up to variable renaming, as with $?c$ and $?d$ above.

3.2 Parameter dependencies in unification

Recall that a parameter b generated in a quantifier rule has the form $b[?a_1, \ldots, ?a_n]$, where the $?a_i$ are all the variables in the conclusion. The occurs check (now a dependency check) finds that every $?a_i$ occurs in $b[?a_1, \ldots, ?a_n]$. In a parameter, assigning $?a_i \mapsto t$ replaces $?a_i$ by the variables present in t.

For example, the set

$$?a = g(?c) \qquad ?c = b[?a]$$

reduces to the unsolvable

$$?a = g(?c) \qquad ?c = b[?c]$$

since $?c$ appears in $g(?c)$.

Contrast with this example, replacing $g(?c)$ by the parameter $d[?c]$. The set

$$?a = d[?c] \qquad ?c = b[?a]$$

is solvable since $?c$ does not actually appear in d (thus $b[d[?c]]$ is just b):

$$?a = d[?c] \qquad ?c = b.$$

This strange situation cannot happen in a real proof. If $?a$ and $?c$ are present then one, say $?a$, must have appeared first. Parameters $b[?a], d[?c]$ could never arise at once, instead perhaps $b[?c], d[?a, ?c]$ or $b[?a], d$.

The following set is also unifiable:

$$?a = d \qquad ?c = b[?a].$$

It corresponds to a proof where (going upwards) d, $?a$, $b[?a]$, and finally $?c$ appear.

3.3 The environment

It is inefficient to substitute throughout the equations every time a variable is assigned. Instead, the algorithm maintains an environment

$$[(?a_k, t_k), \ldots, (?a_1, t_1)],$$

where $?a_i \neq t_i$ for all i. It interprets every term with respect to the environment, replacing $?a_i$ by t_i on the fly. Whenever the algorithm encounters one of the $?a_i$ it follows the assignment, recursively operating on t_i. This terminates: the occurs check prevents cycles like $[(?b, f(?a)), (?a, g(?b))]$.

Most implementations represent variables by pointers for quick updating. To be different, we present a non-destructive version. The environment is represented by a list of assignments: (variable, term) pairs.

Calling `lookup(a,env)` returns the empty list if `a` is not assigned in `env`, and otherwise returns this assignment in a list.

```
fun lookup (X, []) = []
  | lookup (X, (Y,z)::env) = if X = (Y:string) then [z]
                             else  lookup(X,env);
```

Updating means just adding pairs to the list.

3.4 The ML code for unification

The unification code has a lot of nested functions. These refer to global variables to minimize parameter passing.

The main function is `unify_terms`. Calling `unify_terms(ts,us,env)` tackles a set of equations given by two lists of terms `ts` and `us`. It fails if their lengths differ. Given two non-empty lists, it calls `unify_term` to unify their heads, then calls itself using the updated environment.

Calling `chasevar` repeatedly replaces its argument, if a variable, by its assignment. For example, if `env` contains $?a \mapsto ?b$ and $?b \mapsto ?c$ then `chasevar` will map $?a$ to $?c$. Doing this 'variable chasing' elsewhere may let the occurs check falsely report that $?c$ occurs in $?a$. Early versions of Folderol contained this error!

Calling `unify_var` unifies a variable with a term. Local functions `occs` and `occsl` (for lists of terms) search for occurrences of the variable. If found, exception `UNIFY` signals the failure, aborting the entire unification. Otherwise `unify_var` returns an updated environment.

Calling `unify_term(t,u)` attempts to unify two terms within the global environment `env`.

```
exception UNIFY;

fun unify_terms ([],[], env) = env
  | unify_terms (t::ts, u::us, env) =
    let fun chasevar (Var a) =  (*Chase variable assignments*)
             (case  lookup(a,env)  of
                 u::_ => chasevar u  |  [] => Var a)
          | chasevar t = t;
        fun unify_var (Var a, t) = (*unification with var*)
             let fun occs (Fun(_,ts)) = occsl ts
                   | occs (Param(_,bs)) = occsl(map Var bs)
                   | occs (Var b) =  a=b
                                orelse occsl(lookup(b,env))
                   | occs _ = false
                 and occsl [] = false
                   | occsl(t::ts) = occs t  orelse  occsl ts
             in  if t = Var a  then  env
                 else if occs t then  raise UNIFY else (a,t)::env
             end
          | unify_var (t,u) = unify_term(t,u)
        and unify_term (Var a, t) =
               unify_var (chasevar (Var a), chasevar t)
          | unify_term (t, Var a) =
               unify_var (chasevar (Var a), chasevar t)
          | unify_term (Param(a,_), Param(b,_)) =
               if a=b then env  else  raise UNIFY
          | unify_term (Fun(a,ts), Fun(b,us)) =
               if a=b then unify_terms(ts,us,env) else raise UNIFY
          | unify_term _ =  raise UNIFY
    in  unify_terms (ts, us, unify_term (t,u))  end
  | unify_terms _ =  raise UNIFY;
```

Finally, `unify` handles atomic formulae:

$$P(t_1, \ldots, t_m) \text{ and } Q(u_1, \ldots, u_n)$$

are unifiable precisely when $P = Q$, $m = n$, and all the pairs of arguments are unifiable.

```
fun unify (Pred(a,ts), Pred(b,us), env) =
        if a=b then unify_terms(ts,us,env)  else  raise UNIFY
  | unify _ =  raise UNIFY;
```

3.5 Extensions and omissions

Folderol unifies only atomic formulae. Could we make unification handle quantifiers? We should not 'unify' $\exists x.P(x)$ with $\exists x.P(?a)$ by setting $?a$ to x. It is easy to make the occurs check reject terms containing 'loose' bound variables. It is much harder to make unification take account of β-conversion and find instantiations of function variables. This *higher-order unification* has many interesting applications, but the general problem is undecidable [Huet, 1975].

The occurs check is essential in theorem proving for correct quantifier reasoning. Most Prolog implementations omit the check to gain speed; the price can be circular data structures and looping.

Folderol's unification algorithm is naïve. Though it usually performs well, it requires exponential time in rare cases. There is an efficient algorithm [Martelli and Montanari, 1982] that safely omits the occurs check by a sophisticated sorting of the equations. The Martelli/Montanari algorithm is mainly of theoretical importance, but their analysis of unification has had a profound effect on the literature.

3.6 Instantiation by the environment

The environment speeds unification by delaying the substitutions. Substitutions can be delayed forever: the environment can be passed from one unification to the next, accumulating ever more assignments. The technique of *structure sharing* even handles variable renaming [Boyer and Moore, 1972]. This technique is used in resolution theorem provers and some Prolog systems.

Folderol uses environments only in unification. After a successful unification, it copies out (or *instantiates*) the entire proof, performing all substitutions indicated in the environment. There are two reasons for this. Environments complicate coding, and lookups can be slow.

To instantiate parameters we need to gather all the variables in a term. Folderol uses some general-purpose gathering functionals.

```
fun accumulate f ([], y) = y
  | accumulate f (x::xs, y) = accumulate f (xs, f(x,y));

fun accum_form f (Pred(_,ts),bs) = accumulate f (ts, bs)
  | accum_form f (Conn(_,As),bs) = accumulate(accum_form f)(As,bs)
  | accum_form f (Quant(_,_,A),bs) = accum_form f (A,bs);
```

The function `accumulate` turns a 'gathering function' $f : (\alpha \times \beta) \to \beta$ into one of type $(\alpha\, list \times \beta) \to \beta$: one that, for $n \geq 0$, maps

$$([x_1, x_2, \ldots, x_n], y) \quad \longmapsto \quad f(x_n, \ldots, f(x_2, f(x_1, y)) \ldots).$$

Similarly, `accum_form` turns a gathering function $f : (term \times \beta) \to \beta$ into one of type $(form \times \beta) \to \beta$: one that maps

$$(A, y) \quad \longmapsto \quad f(t_n, \ldots, f(t_2, f(t_1, y)) \ldots).$$

where the terms $[t_1, t_2, \ldots, t_n]$ are all the arguments of predicates in the formula A. Gathering functionals uniformly extend a term operation to handle term lists and formulae. They promote brevity and clarity, and are typical of functional programming.

The function `vars_in_term` accumulates the distinct variable names in a term. For a variable it calls `ins` to add the name to the list. For a function application it calls `accumulate` to process the argument list.

```
infix ins;  (*insertion into list if not already there*)
fun x ins xs = if x mem xs then  xs   else  x::xs;

fun vars_in_term (Var a, bs) = a ins bs
  | vars_in_term (Fun(_,ts), bs) = accumulate vars_in_term (ts,bs)
  | vars_in_term (_, bs) = bs;
```

Calling `inst_term env t` instantiates term `t` using environment `env`. Observe how it instantiates the variable $?a$. If the environment has an assignment $?a \mapsto u$ then a recursive call on u is necessary; otherwise the result is $?a$. When `inst_term` receives a parameter $a[?b_1, \ldots, ?b_n]$, the `map(inst_term...)bs` converts the variables into terms. Their variables are gathered into a new list.

```
fun inst_term env (Fun(a,ts)) = Fun(a, map (inst_term env) ts)
  | inst_term env (Param(a,bs)) =
        Param(a, accumulate vars_in_term
                    (map (inst_term env o Var) bs, [])  )
  | inst_term env (Var a) =
      (case  lookup(a,env)  of
           u::_ =>  inst_term env u
         | []    =>  Var a)
  | inst_term env t = t;
```

4 Inference in Folderol

Folderol builds a proof upwards from the desired goal. Each inference rule reduces some goal to zero or more subgoals. The proof is complete when no subgoals remain. Each proof step involves several tasks:

- selection of a goal
- selection of an inference rule
- construction of the subgoals
- observing if the new goals are immediately solvable

We have already discussed these tasks. Recall that the goal $\Gamma \vdash \Delta$ is a list of entries, each containing a cost, a side (`Left` or `Right`), and a formula. A proof state, or `goaltable`, is simply a list of goals, though other information could be stored there.

```
datatype side = Left | Right;
type entry = int * side * form;
type goal = entry list;
type goaltable = goal list;
```

4.1 Solving a goal

The goal $A_1, \ldots, A_m \vdash B_1, \ldots, B_n$ is solved by unifying some A_i and B_j — there are $m \times n$ possible combinations. To save time, Folderol considers only atomic formulae; two complicated formulae are unlikely to unify.[3]

The goal is represented as a list of triples, so `split_goal` has the job of producing the two lists $A_1, \ldots, A_m$ and $B_1, \ldots, B_n$. Reversing the input list makes the output lists come out in the correct order. Thus Folderol prefers new formulae to old and is less prone to looping. If Folderol's analysis of formulae were less superficial the order would not matter.

```
fun split_goal G =
  let fun split (As,Bs, []: goal) = (As,Bs)
        | split (As,Bs, (_,Left,A)::H) = split (A::As,Bs, H)
        | split (As,Bs, (_,Right,B)::H) = split (As, B::Bs, H)
  in  split([], [], rev G)  end;
```

In `solve_goal` two nested loops compare every atomic A_i and B_j. If unifiable then `findB` returns a 1-element list containing A_i paired with the unifier; these together determine the goal's 'success formula'. The usual outcome is exception `UNIFY` and then trying B_{j+1}. After trying all pairs without success, `findA` returns the empty list. If there are several ways of solving a goal then `solve_goal` returns the first.

```
fun filter p [] = []
  | filter p (x::xs) = if p(x) then  x :: filter p xs
                       else  filter p xs;

fun is_pred (Pred _) = true  |  is_pred _ = false;

fun solve_goal G =
    let fun findA ([], _) = []    (*failure*)
          | findA (A::As, Bs) =
              let fun findB [] = findA (As,Bs)
                    | findB (B::Bs) = [ (A, unify(A,B,[])) ]
                      handle UNIFY => findB Bs
              in  findB Bs  end
        val (As,Bs) = split_goal G
    in  findA(filter is_pred As, filter is_pred Bs)  end;
```

The function `insert_goals` takes a list of new goals, a list of success formulae (initially empty), and a goaltable. It tries to solve each new goal rather than simply adding it to the goaltable. After solving a goal, `insert_goals` instantiates all the other goals with the resulting environment, since its variables may appear in other goals. If `solve_goal` succeeds, its success formula is accumulated for printing the proof trace.

[3]Classifying the formulae, say by predicate name, could speed the process further. Testing a goal with no repeated predicates on either side would require $\min\{m,n\}$ unifications.

```
fun insert_goals ([], As, tab) = (As,tab)
  | insert_goals (G::Gs, As, tab) =
      case  solve_goal G  of
          (A,env)::_ =>
             insert_goals (inst_goals env Gs,
                           (inst_form env A) :: As,
                           inst_goals env tab)
        | [] =>  insert_goals (Gs, As, G::tab);
```

4.2 Selecting a rule

Folderol selects a rule by looking at the outermost connective of each formula in the selected goal. A rule that produces the fewest subgoals is chosen, but ∀:left and ∃:right are used only if no other rules apply.

Function `cost` does a case analysis on the formula's connective and side (`Left` or `Right`). Function `paircost` attaches a cost to a (side, formula) pair. The cost of ∀:left and ∃:right is three and the cost of other rules is the number of premises.

```
fun cost (_,     Conn("~", _))             = 1   (*a single subgoal*)
  | cost (Left,  Conn("&", _))             = 1
  | cost (Right, Conn("|", _))             = 1
  | cost (Right, Conn("-->", _))           = 1
  | cost (Right, Quant("ALL",_,_))         = 1
  | cost (Left,  Quant("EXISTS",_,_))      = 1
  | cost (Right, Conn("&", _))             = 2   (*2 subgoals*)
  | cost (Left,  Conn("|", _))             = 2
  | cost (Left,  Conn("-->", _))           = 2
  | cost (_    , Conn("<->", _))           = 2
  | cost (Left,  Quant("ALL",_,_))         = 3   (*quant expansion*)
  | cost (Right, Quant("EXISTS",_,_))      = 3   (*quant expansion*)
  | cost _ = 4 ;                                 (*no reductions*)

fun paircost (si,A) = (cost(si,A), si, A);
```

The entries in a goal are ordered by cost — the first entry is cheapest. The function `insert` maintains an ordered list given a comparison function `less` for sort keys. If the comparison is $<$ then `insert` places the new entry first among entries of equal cost; if $\leq$ then the entry goes last. Thus `insert_early` puts the entry where it may be chosen earlier, while `insert_late`'s effect is the opposite.

```
fun insert less =
  let fun insr (x,[]) = [x]
        | insr (x,y::ys) = if less(y,x) then y::insr(x,ys)
                                         else x::y::ys
  in  insr  end;

fun entry_less ((m,_,_): entry, (n,_,_): entry) = m<n;
val insert_early = insert entry_less;

fun entry_lesseq ((m,_,_): entry, (n,_,_): entry) = m<=n;
val insert_late  = insert entry_lesseq;
```

The quantified formula in ∀:left or ∃:right is put last among its fellows so that they will get a turn.

4.3 Constructing the subgoals

The sequent calculus LK is suited for backwards proof because it has the *subformula property* — every formula in a proof is a subformula of the original goal. True, quantifier rules ∀:left and ∃:right introduce unknown terms (requiring an unusual notion of subformula), but these are just meta variables. The key point is this: once we have chosen a rule and a formula from the goal, the subgoals are completely determined.

A goal is a list of triples. A rule is applied to the head of this list. The tail holds the remaining formulae, which must be included in each subgoal. Each subgoal is made from the tail by adding new (side, formula) pairs. Calling `new_goal G pairs` copies the `pairs` into goal `G`, which is the tail of the goal. It calls `paircost` to attach a cost to each new formula.

Since a rule may make more than one subgoal, `new_goals` forms a list of subgoals from a goal and a list of new (side, formula) pairs.

```
fun new_goal G pairs =
    accumulate insert_early (map paircost pairs, G);

fun new_goals G pairslist = map (new_goal G) pairslist;
```

The function `reduce_goal` handles all the rules. Given a formula and its side (`Left` or `Right`), it uses the immediate subformulae to build subgoals. Function `goals` permits a concise description of each subgoal.

For rules ∀:right and ∃:left it generates a fresh parameter and attaches all the variables in the goal. For ∀:left and ∃:right it generates a fresh variable; the subgoal contains the original entry inserted 'late' and the new entry inserted 'early'. Exception `REDUCE` indicates that no reductions are possible, indicating that all the formulae are atomic.

```
exception REDUCE;

fun reduce_goal (pair, G) =
 let val goals = new_goals G;
  fun vars_in A = vars_in_goal (G, vars_in_form(A,[]));
  fun subparam A = subst_bound (Param(gensym(), vars_in A)) A;
  fun subvar A   = subst_bound (Var(gensym())) A;
  fun red(_,Right,Conn("~",[A]))    = goals[[(Left,A)]]
    | red(_,Left, Conn("~",[A]))    = goals[[(Right,A)]]
    | red(_,Right,Conn("&",[A,B])) = goals[[(Right,A)],[(Right,B)]]
    | red(_,Left, Conn("&",[A,B])) = goals[[(Left,A),(Left,B)]]
    | red(_,Right,Conn("|",[A,B])) = goals[[(Right,A),(Right,B)]]
    | red(_,Left, Conn("|",[A,B])) = goals[[(Left,A)],[(Left,B)]]
    | red(_,Right,Conn("-->",[A,B]))=goals[[(Left,A),(Right,B)]]
    | red(_,Left, Conn("-->",[A,B]))=goals[[(Right,A)],[(Left,B)]]
    | red(_,Right,Conn("<->",[A,B])) =
          goals[[(Left,A),(Right,B)],[(Right,A),(Left,B)]]
    | red(_,Left, Conn("<->",[A,B])) =
          goals[[(Left,A),(Left,B)],[(Right,A),(Right,B)]]
    | red(_,Right,Quant("ALL",_,A)) = goals[[(Right, subparam A)]]
    | red(_,Left, Quant("ALL",_,A)) =
         [ insert_early (paircost(Left, subvar A),
                         insert_late(pair,G)) ]
    | red(_,Right,Quant("EXISTS",_,A)) =
         [ insert_early (paircost(Right, subvar A),
                         insert_late(pair,G)) ]
    | red(_,Left,Quant("EXISTS",_,A)) = goals[[(Left, subparam A)]]
    | red _ = raise REDUCE
 in  red pair  end;
```

The function gensym, like its LISP namesake, generates unique variable names. Functional programmers may hear with dismay that gensym increments a counter. We could do without the reference variable varcount by keeping the count with the goal list, but why? Side-effects are more dangerous in programmable theorem provers like LCF and Isabelle, where a proof strategy may spawn subproofs that must run independently. Yet LCF's simplifier uses a form of gensym.

Up to this point Folderol is largely applicative. As we approach the top-level commands it becomes more and more imperative. Applying a rule prints tracing information as a side effect, and the proof state is kept in reference variables.

4.4 Goal selection

A proof fails if some goal is unprovable, so a theorem prover should choose the goal that seems most likely to fail. Folderol is not intended to detect unprovability, so it always chooses the next goal using 'last in first out': like a stack. Folderol keeps a list of goals (the goaltable). At each step it replaces the first goal by its subgoals. This simple structure makes proofs easier to follow.

The function `proof_step` gives the head of the goal list to `reduce_goal`, and then `insert_goals` creates a new goaltable. Calling `proof_steps` with $n \geq 0$ performs up to n steps; negative n allows unbounded repetition. These functions print a proof trace.

```
fun proof_step [] = [] : goaltable
  | proof_step ([]::tab) = raise ERROR "Empty goal"
  | proof_step ((ent::G)::tab) =
      let val (As,newtab) = insert_goals(reduce_goal(ent,G),[],tab)
      in  print_step(ent,tab,As);     newtab   end;

fun proof_steps (_,[]) = []     (*success -- no goals*)
  | proof_steps (0,tab) = tab
  | proof_steps (n,tab) = proof_steps (n-1, proof_step tab)
      handle REDUCE => (prints"\n**No proof rules applicable**\n";
                        tab);
```

Let us skip the code for reading and printing goaltables. At the end of the program are Folderol's commands:

- to read a goal, a sequent $\Gamma \vdash \Delta$ or formula $\vdash B$
- to perform one step, or n steps, or run without bound
- to read a goal and immediately run

Folderol has a top-level proof state, and this requires a reference variable, `the_goaltable`. The only other reference is the variable counter for `gensym`.

```
val the_goaltable = ref ([] : goaltable);

fun set_tab tab = (the_goaltable := tab;  print_tab tab);

fun read_goalseq (Astrs,Bstrs) =
    (init_gensym();  set_tab(read_tab (Astrs,Bstrs)));

fun read_goal Bstr = read_goalseq([],[Bstr]);

fun step()  = set_tab (proof_step(!the_goaltable));
fun steps n = set_tab (proof_steps (max(n,0), !the_goaltable));
fun run()   = set_tab (proof_steps (~1, !the_goaltable));

fun run_goalseq (Astrs,Bstrs) = (read_goalseq(Astrs,Bstrs); run());
fun run_goal b = run_goalseq([],[b]);
```

Note that Folderol may reorder the formulae in your original goal, so you may not recognize it.

5 Folderol in action

The computer sessions below were run using D. C. J. Matthews's Poly/ML, a compiler for Standard ML. Input lines to Folderol begin with the Poly/ML prompt characters (> or #). All other lines are output. I have edited the output to make it more compact and readable.

5.1 Propositional examples

Pelletier has published a list of graded problems in classical first-order logic for testing theorem provers [Pelletier, 1986]. Folderol, running on a Sun-3,[4] can prove any of the propositional ones in 0.1 seconds. Folderol is complete for propositional logic.

5.1.1 A distributive law

Here is part of a distributive law:

$$(P \vee Q) \wedge (P \vee R) \rightarrow P \vee (Q \wedge R).$$

The command `read_goal` accepts this formula; then `step()` performs the only possible rule. Observe how Folderol reports its choice of rule, here $\rightarrow$:right.

```
> read_goal "(P | Q) & (P | R)  -->  P | (Q & R)";
empty  |-  (P | Q) & (P | R) --> P | Q & R

> step();
-->:right
(P | Q) & (P | R)  |-  P | (Q & R)
```

Reducing the conjunction on the left or the disjunction on the right will produce one subgoal. A goal is a single ordered list but Folderol prints it as two lists, the left and right formulae. We can only be sure that Folderol will reduce the first formula on the left or the right. It happens that Folderol first reduces the disjunction. Next it ignores the new conjunction on the right (which would produce two subgoals) and reduces the conjunction on the left.

```
> step();
|:right
(P | Q) & (P | R)  |-  Q & R, P

> step();
&:left
P | R, P | Q  |-  Q & R, P
```

Now all three possible reductions will make two subgoals. Arbitrarily the $P \vee R$ is reduced first. The P subgoal is solved (hence the `P` in the

[4]Sun-3 is a trade mark of Sun Microsystems, Inc.

trace) while the R subgoal remains. Next $P \vee Q$ behaves similarly. Finally $Q \wedge R$, on the right, is split when Q and R are both assumed true. Thus both subgoals are solved and the proof is complete.

```
> step();
|:left   P
P | Q, R  |-  Q & R, P

> step();
|:left   P
Q, R  |-  Q & R, P

> step();
&:right   Q   R
No more goals: proof finished
```

5.1.2 An associative law for $\leftrightarrow$

The classical identity

$$((P \leftrightarrow Q) \leftrightarrow R) \leftrightarrow (P \leftrightarrow (Q \leftrightarrow R)),$$

one of Pelletier's sample problems, is excellent for illustrating the $\leftrightarrow$ rules.

To shorten the proof let us consider only one direction. The command `read_goalseq` accepts this as a sequent. Since both $\leftrightarrow$ rules have two premises, Folderol's initial choice of $\leftrightarrow$:right is arbitrary. The next step removes $Q \leftrightarrow R$ on the left.

```
> read_goalseq (["((P <-> Q) <-> R)"],  ["(P <-> (Q <-> R))"]);
(P <-> Q) <-> R  |-  P <-> (Q <-> R)

> step();
<->:right
Q <-> R, (P <-> Q) <-> R  |-  P
(P <-> Q) <-> R, P  |-  Q <-> R

> step();
 <->:left
(P <-> Q) <-> R  |-  R, Q, P
(P <-> Q) <-> R, R, Q  |-  P
(P <-> Q) <-> R, P  |-  Q <-> R
```

Reducing $(P \leftrightarrow Q) \leftrightarrow R$ has the effect of replacing R by $P \leftrightarrow Q$; the nontrivial subgoal has $P \leftrightarrow Q$, Q, and P on the right.[5] Note that if Q and P are both false then $P \leftrightarrow Q$ is true. So applying $\leftrightarrow$:right completely solves this subgoal.

---

[5] It also has two copies of R; Folderol ought to remove duplicate formulae and other redundancies.

```
> step();
  <->:left   R
empty  |-  P <-> Q, R, R, Q, P
(P <-> Q) <-> R, R, Q  |-  P
(P <-> Q) <-> R, P  |-  Q <-> R

> step();
  <->:right   P   Q
(P <-> Q) <-> R, R, Q  |-  P
(P <-> Q) <-> R, P  |-  Q <-> R
```

Here we informally see that assuming $(P \leftrightarrow Q) \leftrightarrow R$ and R amounts to assuming $P \leftrightarrow Q$, as indeed happens. In the next step, assuming $P \leftrightarrow Q$ and Q amounts to assuming P. Impatience now suggests typing `run()` to finish.

```
> step();
 <->:left   R
P <-> Q, R, R, Q  |-  P
(P <-> Q) <-> R, P  |-  Q <-> R

> step();
 <->:left   P   Q
(P <-> Q) <-> R, P  |-  Q <-> R

> run();
<->:right
 <->:left   R
 <->:left   Q   P
<->:left   R
<->:right   Q   P
No more goals: proof finished
```

Observe how the indentation of the proof trace varies. Folderol prints additional space before the name of a rule to indicate the number of subgoals. Often the indentation will increase for a time and then decrease; if it gets bigger and bigger, look out!

5.1.3 The completeness of propositional logic

Folderol is complete for propositional logic. For a formula A, if A is valid then it constructs a proof; if A is invalid then it constructs a model that falsifies A ([Gallier, 1986], page 71).

Is this formula valid?

$$(P \to (Q \to R)) \to (P \vee Q \to R).$$

Folderol answers in no time.

```
> run_goal "(P --> (Q-->R))  -->  (P | Q --> R)";
empty  |-  (P --> (Q --> R)) --> (P | Q --> R)

-->:right
-->:right
|:left
 -->:left
  -->:left   Q   R

**No proof rules applicable**
Q  |-  P, R
P --> (Q --> R), P  |-  R
```

The first goal is not provable: if Q is true while P and R are false then the goal is false, as is the original goal.

This session demonstrates the power of decidability: every question can be answered.

5.2 Quantifier examples

Most of the data structures were designed around quantifiers. Let us verify that parameters and variables really work for the examples we discussed originally. Then we shall see a complicated theorem Folderol can prove — and a simple one it cannot prove.

5.2.1 Valid reasoning permitted

Here is one of our quantifier examples:

$$\forall x.R(x,x) \vdash \forall x.\exists y.R(x,y).$$

We enter the goal. The first step is $\forall$:right since the alternative, $\forall$:left, has high cost. Folderol prints a table of parameters showing the associated variables; the parameter a has none.

```
> read_goalseq ( ["ALL x.R(x,x)"],  ["ALL x. EXISTS y. R(x,y)"] ) ;
ALL x. R(x,x)  |-  ALL x. EXISTS y. R(x,y)

> step();
ALL:right
ALL x. R(x,x)  |-  EXISTS y. R(a,y)

Param     Not allowed in
a
```

Now $\exists$:right is arbitrarily chosen, introducing the variable ?b. The quantified formula $\exists y.R(a,y)$ is put far back in the queue. So the other quantifier is expanded next; $\forall$:left adds the assumption $R(?c,?c)$, which immediately unifies with $R(a,?b)$ giving $R(a,a)$.

```
> step();
EXISTS:right
ALL x. R(x,x)  |-  EXISTS y. R(a,y), R(a,?b)

> step();
ALL:left   R(a,a)
No more goals: proof finished
```

5.2.2 Invalid reasoning forbidden

Reversing the quantifiers turns the last example into an invalid sequent:

$$\forall x.R(x,x) \vdash \exists y.\, \forall x.R(x,y).$$

Given this goal Folderol arbitrarily chooses $\exists$:right, introducing ?a.

```
> read_goalseq (["ALL x.R(x,x)"],  ["EXISTS y. ALL x. R(x,y)"]) ;
ALL x. R(x,x)  |-  EXISTS y. ALL x. R(x,y)

> step();
EXISTS:right
ALL x. R(x,x)  |-  ALL x. R(x,?a), EXISTS y. ALL x. R(x,y)
```

The new formula has the least cost; $\forall$:right introduces the parameter b, depending on ?a. Next it is time to expand $\forall x.R(x,x)$.

```
> step();
ALL:right
ALL x. R(x,x)  |-  EXISTS y. ALL x. R(x,y), R(b,?a)

Param      Not allowed in
b          (?a)

> step();
ALL:left
ALL x. R(x,x), R(?c,?c)  |-  EXISTS y. ALL x. R(x,y), R(b,?a)

Param      Not allowed in
b          (?a)
```

Folderol has left this subgoal because $R(?c, ?c)$ and $R(b, ?a)$ are not unifiable. They may look unifiable, but assigning $?a \mapsto b[?a]$ would be circular. Instead we expand the quantifiers again. The next application of $\forall$:right adds $R(e, ?d)$, and $?d \mapsto e[?a, ?c, ?d]$ is also circular. Thus $R(e, ?d)$ is not unifiable with $R(?c, ?c)$, nor with the new assumption $R(?f, ?f)$.

```
> step();
EXISTS:right
ALL x. R(x,x), R(?c,?c)
|-  ALL x. R(x,?d), EXISTS y. ALL x. R(x,y), R(b,?a)

Param     Not allowed in
b         (?a)

> step();
ALL:right
ALL x. R(x,x), R(?c,?c)
|-  EXISTS y. ALL x. R(x,y), R(e,?d), R(b,?a)

Param     Not allowed in
b         (?a)
e         (?a,?c,?d)

> step();
ALL:left
ALL x. R(x,x), R(?f,?f), R(?c,?c)
|-  EXISTS y. ALL x. R(x,y), R(e,?d), R(b,?a)

Param     Not allowed in
b         (?a)
e         (?a,?c,?d)
```

Obviously we are getting nowhere. But this is less obvious to Folderol.

```
> steps 9;
EXISTS:right
ALL:right
ALL:left
EXISTS:right
ALL:right
ALL:left
EXISTS:right
ALL:right
ALL:left


ALL x. R(x,x), R(?o,?o), R(?l,?l), R(?i,?i), R(?f,?f), R(?c,?c)
|-  EXISTS y. ALL x. R(x,y), R(n,?m), R(k,?j),
    R(h,?g), R(e,?d), R(b,?a)

Param     Not allowed in
b         (?a)
e         (?a,?c,?d)
h         (?a,?c,?d,?f,?g)
k         (?a,?c,?d,?f,?g,?i,?j)
n         (?a,?c,?d,?f,?g,?i,?j,?l,?m)
```

Folderol will never quit. The general problem of when to quit is undecidable.

5.2.3 A complicated proof

Pelletier's problem 29 dates back to *Principia Mathematica* (*11.71):

$$(\exists x.P(x)) \wedge (\exists x.Q(x)) \vdash (\forall x.P(x) \rightarrow R(x)) \wedge (\forall x.Q(x) \rightarrow S(x)) \leftrightarrow (\forall xy.P(x) \wedge Q(y) \rightarrow R(x) \wedge S(y))$$

Let us enter this sequent to Folderol:

```
> read_goalseq (["(EXISTS x. P(x)) & (EXISTS x. Q(x))"],
#             ["(ALL x. P(x)-->R(x)) & (ALL x. Q(x)-->S(x)) <->  \
#\              (ALL x. ALL y. P(x) & Q(y) --> R(x) & S(y))"]);

(EXISTS x. P(x)) & (EXISTS x. Q(x))
|-  (ALL x. P(x) --> R(x)) & (ALL x. Q(x) --> S(x))
    <-> (ALL x. ALL y. P(x) & Q(y) --> R(x) & S(y))
```

The proof begins with routine reductions on the left followed by analysis of one direction of the equivalence. The parameters a, b, c depend on no variables; redundant parameter listings are omitted.

```
> steps 7;
&:left
EXISTS:left
EXISTS:left
<->:right
 &:right
  ALL:right
  -->:right

ALL x. ALL y. P(x) & Q(y) --> R(x) & S(y), Q(c), P(b), Q(a)
|-  S(c)

ALL x. ALL y. P(x) & Q(y) --> R(x) & S(y), P(b), Q(a)
|-  ALL x. P(x) --> R(x)

(ALL x. P(x) --> R(x)) & (ALL x. Q(x) --> S(x)), P(b), Q(a)
|-  ALL x. ALL y. P(x) & Q(y) --> R(x) & S(y)
```

The first subgoal involves proving $S(c)$ from $Q(c)$ and $P(b)$ using the quantified formula. This takes five steps.

```
> steps 5;
  ALL:left
  ALL:left
  -->:left
   &:left   S(c)
  &:right   P(b)   Q(c)

ALL x. ALL y. P(x) & Q(y) --> R(x) & S(y), P(b), Q(a)
|-  ALL x. P(x) --> R(x)

(ALL x. P(x) --> R(x)) & (ALL x. Q(x) --> S(x)), P(b), Q(a)
|-  ALL x. ALL y. P(x) & Q(y) --> R(x) & S(y)
```

Two reductions on the right produce an analogous situation.

```
> steps 2;
 ALL:right
 -->:right

ALL x. ALL y. P(x) & Q(y) --> R(x) & S(y), P(f), P(b), Q(a)
|-  R(f)

(ALL x. P(x) --> R(x)) & (ALL x. Q(x) --> S(x)), P(b), Q(a)
|-  ALL x. ALL y. P(x) & Q(y) --> R(x) & S(y)
```

We now prove $R(f)$ from $P(f)$ and $Q(a)$:

```
> steps 5;
 ALL:left
 ALL:left
 -->:left
  &:left   R(f)
 &:right   P(f)    Q(a)

(ALL x. P(x) --> R(x)) & (ALL x. Q(x) --> S(x)), P(b), Q(a)
|-  ALL x. ALL y. P(x) & Q(y) --> R(x) & S(y)
```

One direction of the original goal is proved. Now we tackle the other direction.

```
> steps 6;
ALL:right
ALL:right
-->:right
&:left
&:left
&:right

ALL x. Q(x) --> S(x), ALL x. P(x) --> R(x), Q(j), P(i), P(b), Q(a)
|-  S(j)

ALL x. Q(x) --> S(x), ALL x. P(x) --> R(x), Q(j), P(i), P(b), Q(a)
|-  R(i)
```

The two goals are similar. The first Folderol proves directly.

```
> steps 2;
 ALL:left
 -->:left   Q(j)   S(j)

ALL x. Q(x) --> S(x), ALL x. P(x) --> R(x), Q(j), P(i), P(b), Q(a)
|-  R(i)
```

But here Folderol fails to see that $\forall x.Q(x) \rightarrow S(x)$ is irrelevant. Luckily the proof succeeds when the correct formula is picked.

```
> steps 2;
ALL:left
-->:left   Q(j)

ALL x. P(x) --> R(x), ALL x. Q(x) --> S(x),
              S(j), Q(j), P(i), P(b), Q(a)   |-  R(i)

> steps 2;
ALL:left
-->:left   P(i)   R(i)
No more goals: proof finished
```

5.2.4 Folderol fooled

In the last example, reducing the wrong quantifier did no harm. But needless quantifier expansions can cause subgoals to multiply: reducing $\forall z.A \vee B$ on the left causes a case split. Folderol expands quantifiers and instantiates variables according to routines that never consider the proof as a whole.

Folderol easily proves the following contrapositive:

$$\forall x.P(x) \to Q(x) \vdash \forall x.\neg Q(x) \to \neg P(x)$$

Adding $\exists x.P(x)$ to this yields a more complicated theorem:

$$\exists x.P(x), \forall x.P(x) \to Q(x) \vdash \forall x.\neg Q(x) \to \neg P(x)$$

The extra formula distracts Folderol from the correct instantiation.

```
> read_goalseq (["EXISTS x. P(x)", "ALL x. P(x)-->Q(x)"],
#               ["ALL x. ~Q(x) --> ~P(x)"]);

EXISTS x. P(x), ALL x. P(x) --> Q(x)  |-  ALL x. ~Q(x) --> ~P(x)

> steps 5;
ALL:right
-->:right
~:right
~:left
EXISTS:left

ALL x. P(x) --> Q(x), P(b), P(a)  |-  Q(a)
```

The proof should follow by putting a into $\forall x.P(x) \to Q(x)$ and using $P(a)$. The $P(b)$ is simply noise.

```
> steps 6;
ALL:left
-->:left   P(b)
ALL:left
-->:left   P(b)
ALL:left
-->:left   P(b)

ALL x. P(x) --> Q(x), Q(b), Q(b), Q(b), P(b), P(a)  |-  Q(a)
```

Reducing $\forall x.P(x) \to Q(x)$ produces the subgoal $P(b), P(a) \vdash P(?c)$. Folderol always chooses the first solution, b, instead of a, and gets nowhere.

In another version of Folderol, `solve_goal` chooses among multiple solutions randomly. When lucky (!) it works well, but its performance is not reliable.

5.3 Beyond Folderol: advanced automatic methods

Folderol is a toy. Its purpose is to illustrate coding techniques; its main strength is its simplicity. Naïve proof methods have surprising power but obvious limitations. How can we do better?

Function `solve_goal` always takes the first solution it finds, though this may block the proof of other goals. Sometimes the prover should choose another solution or even ignore them all (thus leaving the goal open to further proof steps). Backtracking is the obvious way to search these possibilities. I have written such a prover in Prolog.

The predicate `proof(As,Bs,N,P)` succeeds if it proves the sequent $As \vdash Bs$, where `N` limits quantifier expansions and `P` is the proof tree. The limit on quantifier expansion (applications of $\forall$:left and $\exists$:right) makes the search space finite so that backtracking can explore it. The program returns a proof tree instead of tracing its search.

The Prolog prover is 2.5 times smaller than the ML one. It does not need a parser because of Prolog operator declarations. Within a goal, sorting the formulae by cost is no longer necessary. Instead the rules are tried in order of cost. Here are the clauses for the rules $\neg$:right, $\wedge$:left, and $\wedge$:right. Predicate `delmem` searches for a given element in a list and deletes it. The cuts prevent backtracking over the choice of rule.

```
delmem(X, [X|Xs], Xs).
delmem(X, [Y|Ys], [Y|Zs]) :- delmem(X, Ys, Zs).

proof(As, Bs, N, notr(P)) :- delmem(~B, Bs, Ds),
        !, proof([B|As], Ds, N, P).

proof(As, Bs, N, andl(P)) :- delmem(A1&A2, As, Cs),
        !, proof([A1,A2|Cs], Bs, N, P).

proof(As, Bs, N, andr(P1,P2)) :- delmem(B1&B2, Bs, Ds),
        !, proof(As, [B1|Ds], N, P1), proof(As, [B2|Ds], N, P2).
```

Predicates `abstract` and `subst` handle abstraction and substitution in the de Bruijn representation. The rule $\forall$:right is

```
proof(As, Bs, N, allr(abs(Id,P))) :-
        delmem(all(abs(Id,B1)), Bs, Ds),
        make_param((As,Bs), X), !, subst(X,B1,BX),
        proof(As, [BX|Ds], N, P1), abstract(X,P1,P).
```

Finally, if no other rules apply and `N` is positive, then all top-level quantifiers are expanded.

Prolog can be extremely useful for experiments with theorem proving. But the time may come when you are constantly fighting Prolog's view of data and control. To check whether some left side formula is unifiable with some right side formula requires a proper unification predicate, with the occurs check and de Bruijn indices. The code for this predicate is a collection of Prolog hacks — not logic programming.

The Prolog version is complete. Given a large enough value of `N` it should find a proof if there is one. Yet on hard problems it is little better than Folderol. Even with `N`=2, the 'finite' search space is astronomical.[6] Both provers are weak because they choose a formula simply by its outer connective, not for its contents or relevance.

The links in a *connection graph* help to decide which formula to reduce next. Kowalski [Kowalski, 1975] invented connections for resolution theorem provers (see also [Eisinger, 1986]. The graph links pairs of atomic formulae that are potentially *complementary*: unifiable and of opposite signs. With resolution's clause form, the sign of an atomic formula is obvious. With sequents, the sign is determined by counting the surrounding negations (including $\rightarrow$ and $\leftrightarrow$). Observe that applying sequent calculus rules to a formula breaks it apart, bringing its subformulae to the surface; a subformula's sign indicates whether it will end up on the left or the right. Unification must allow for quantified variables using methods such as Folderol's.

The theorem prover HARP [Oppacher and Suen, 1988] resembles Folderol in its logical formalism. It uses semantic tableaux, which are equivalent to sequents. HARP is much more powerful than Folderol by virtue of its heuristics and connection methods. But a collection of heuristics is hard to analyse scientifically.

The matrix methods of [Bibel, 1987] define a notion of *path* in a formula. A formula is a theorem if all paths within it contain a connection. The number of paths is exponential but each connection rules out a whole class of paths. Matrix methods can determine that a proof can be constructed without constructing one, avoiding certain redundancies in the search.

A specialized but established method is classical *resolution* [Chang and Lee, 1973]. To prove A, translate $\neg A$ into a set of clauses, each a disjunction of atomic formulae or their negations. Each resolution step takes two clauses and yields a new one. The method succeeds if it produces the empty clause (a contradiction), thus refuting $\neg A$. Because resolution is the only inference rule, the method is easy to analyse, and many refinements have been found. One such refinement led to the language Prolog. Conversely, Prolog systems have been used to make fast resolution provers [Stickel, 1988]. Resolution's chief drawback is its clause form, which renders

[6] Of Pelletier's problems 1–45, Folderol failed on 34, 38, and 41–44, while the Prolog version failed on 34, 37, 38, 43, and 45.

a formula unintelligible.

What about non-classical logics? Each must be treated individually. Intuitionistic logic differs from classical logic by the lack of the one rule $\frac{\neg\neg A}{A}$, but it requires a completely different approach. TPS proves theorems in higher-order logic [Andrews *et al.*, 1984]. It uses general matings (essentially Bibel's method) and higher-order unification. Lincoln Wallen has developed matrix methods for several modal logics and intuitionistic logic through a careful analysis of their semantics [Wallen, 1990].

A remarkable system exploits an efficient decision procedure for a propositional temporal logic [Clarke *et al.*, 1986]. Statements are verified by checking a small number of cases. This is really model checking, not theorem proving, but such an effective method must come under the heading of algorithmic proof. They chose their temporal logic mainly for its fast decision procedure: expressiveness had to be secondary.

Powerful automatic techniques are often brittle, unable to accept the slightest change in the logic. Adding an induction rule would count as a revolutionary change. So we have to direct the proof. We next shall see how interactive systems are organized and controlled.

6 Interactive theorem proving

Suppose we want to prove something from the transitivity axiom

$$\forall xyz\,.\, x = y \land y = z \rightarrow x = z.$$

Folderol will apply $\forall$:left to get

$$\forall yz\,.\, ?a = y \land y = z \rightarrow ?a = z.$$

At the next round, Folderol will apply $\forall$:left to *both* quantified formulae, producing

$$\forall yz\,.\, ?a_1 = y \land y = z \rightarrow ?a_1 = z$$

$$\forall z\,.\, ?a = ?b \land ?b = z \rightarrow ?a = z.$$

Folderol keeps all of these; the next round produces

$$\forall yz\,.\, ?a_2 = y \land y = z \rightarrow ?a_2 = z$$

$$\forall z\,.\, ?a_1 = ?b_1 \land ?b_1 = z \rightarrow ?a_1 = z$$

$$?a = ?b \land ?b = ?c \rightarrow ?a = ?c.$$

The last formula may be useful; the others are rapidly multiplying junk.

It is not hard to improve the treatment of nested quantifiers. But the improved prover will still flounder because of transitivity itself. Given the goal

$$a = b, b = a, b = c \vdash a = c$$

unguided use of transitivity could generate $a = a$, $b = b$, and other useless facts before succeeding. Effective reasoning about equality requires an algorithm specific to the problem at hand. *Rewriting* reduces an expression to normal form. *Equational unification* solves a set of equations in the presence of equational laws. *Congruence closure*, given a set of equations, efficiently tests whether certain other equations hold [Gallier, 1986].

The ideal interactive theorem prover would provide all useful algorithms known. The Boyer/Moore theorem prover knows a good many algorithms and how to use them. But new algorithms are constantly being developed and some users would like to invent their own. Equality is just one example of the limitations of general algorithms. Knowledge of the problem domain may suggest effective specialized algorithms. *Tactics* and *tacticals* are a flexible language for describing proofs at a high level.

6.1 The Boyer/Moore theorem prover

The control language of the [Boyer and Moore, 1979] theorem prover is extremely simple. You can define new data structures and functions, or ask it to prove a theorem. It applies a vast battery of heuristics to theorems it already has. You guide this process by carefully planning a sequence of lemmas, leading to the main theorem. The prover should be told what each lemma is for — rewriting, generalization, induction — or, sometimes, to 'forget' a lemma.

Its success is due to an effective combination of quantifier-free logic and well-founded induction. No quantifiers means no worries about bound variables and unification. Well-founded induction permits proofs that would otherwise involve quantifiers. Consider proving $\forall n . P(m, n)$ by mathematical induction on m. The inductive step $(m > 0)$ is to prove $\forall n . P(m, n)$ from $\forall n . P(m-1, n)$. If the proof uses this induction hypothesis for several values of n, then the $\forall n$ seems essential. But it is equivalent to prove $P(m, n)$ by well-founded induction on (m, n) under the following well-founded relation:

$$(m', n') \prec (m, n) \quad \text{if and only if} \quad m' < m.$$

Then the inductive step is to prove $P(m, n)$ assuming $P(m', n')$ for all $(m', n') \prec (m, n)$. Argue by cases. If $m = 0$ the argument is the same as before; if $m > 0$ then $(m - 1, n') \prec (m, n)$ so we may assume $P(m - 1, n')$ for all n'. Thus the previous proof goes through without quantifiers.

Boyer and Moore's treatment of induction is particularly impressive. A well-founded relation is used to prove termination for each recursive function definition. The prover exploits this information to choose a form of induction appropriate for a goal involving several recursive functions. It also knows that proving something by induction may require proving something stronger. It can strengthen a goal by generalizing it or discarding useless information.

One drawback is that the user needs to understand the heuristics and their many interactions. The lack of quantifiers impairs the expressiveness of the logic, despite recent work on bounded quantification [Boyer and Moore, 1988].

The prover has done many proofs in pure mathematics, including Gödel's Incompleteness Theorem. A complete computer system has been verified, both software and hardware, from a compiler down to gate level [Bevier *et al.*, 1989].

6.2 The Automath languages

The Automath project [de Bruijn, 1980] has tackled a different problem: that of expressing mathematical concepts formally. First-order logic is a rich language for expressing statements, but it includes nothing to make statements about. Defining even the natural numbers in first-order logic is not easy. The induction axiom is not first-order unless it is given as an axiom scheme (an infinite set of axioms). While the Boyer/Moore logic includes induction, it is extremely constructive and seems to rule out many forms of classical mathematical reasoning: say, defining the real numbers as certain sets of rationals.

Automath introduced a formal language in which mathematical notions could be assumed or constructed, and even the proofs formalized. The language (actually several were developed) was an extension of the typed λ-calculus. It provided just enough structure to permit assumptions to be made or discharged. Through this could be defined the basic connectives of logic — then perhaps the natural numbers, the integers, the rationals, and the real numbers. The translation into Automath of Landau's textbook *The Foundations of Analysis* was a triumph that has seldom been surpassed [van Benthem Jutting, 1977].

Automath did not stress interaction; a mathematician would write a 'book' in the language, then submit it to be checked. In another sense, however, Automath was revolutionary. It viewed the introduction of an assumption as the introduction of a variable, and viewed the discharge of an assumption as the creation of a function. It accomplished this using Π types (sometimes called 'dependent types'), interpreting propositions as types. These concepts may be familiar now, but Automath was hardly appreciated in its day.

The *Calculus of Constructions*, by Coquand and Huet, continues this work [Formel Project, 1989]. The Calculus is closely related to the Automath languages. Coquand has investigated its formal properties. Huet and others have implemented the calculus and formalized large pieces of mathematics: the Schroeder–Bernstein Theorem,[7] to name one example. The calculus is also being applied towards the synthesis of correct programs by proof.

6.3 LCF, a programmable theorem prover

Edinburgh LCF was developed during the 1970s by Robin Milner and his colleagues [Gordon *et al.*, 1979]. Its techniques have been adopted in numerous theorem provers.

In order to be extensible, Edinburgh LCF was programmable. (Its Meta Language, called ML, was the predecessor of Standard ML.) The user could write ML functions to process terms, formulae, and theorems. Theorems were not simply created, but proved; they belonged to an *abstract type* called `thm`, which provided the inference rules as functions. Type checking ensured that theorems were only proved by applying rules to axioms and other theorems.

This collection of rule functions is best viewed as a virtual machine code. Like machine instructions they are hard to use directly; they should be used to implement higher levels of abstraction. LCF uses various 'blocks' — *conversions* for rewriting[8] and *tactics* for backwards proof — together with 'mortar' for putting the blocks together. The blocks are typically functions and they are combined by functionals (higher-order functions). Tactics are combined by *tacticals*.

Each tactic specifies a backwards proof step, reducing a goal to subgoals. Most tactics only accept a certain set of goals and *fail* on all goals outside this domain. A tactic succeeds on a goal if it returns any number of subgoals, and proves it if this number is zero. Tactics may also be applied to subgoals, their subgoals, etc., and once they have all been proved, some mechanism returns the desired theorem. Tactics include primitive tactics and compound tactics built using tacticals such as `THEN`, `ORELSE`, `REPEAT`.

- Every rule that may be useful in backwards proof has a corresponding primitive tactic.
- The tactic `tac1 THEN tac2` applies `tac1` to a goal then applies `tac2` to the result. The effect is that of applying both tactics in succession.
- The tactic `tac1 ORELSE tac2` applies `tac1` to a goal. If `tac1` fails (because the goal is outside its domain) then it tries `tac2` as an

[7] If $|A| \leq |B|$ and $|B| \leq |A|$ then $|A| = |B|$, where $|\cdots|$ denotes the cardinality of a set.

[8] Conversions were introduced in Cambridge LCF, a derivative of Edinburgh LCF.

alternative. If both fail then `ORELSE` fails. Its domain is the union of the domains of `tac1` and `tac2`.

- The tactic `REPEAT tac` applies `tac` repeatedly to a goal.

Ideally, tactics should capture the control structures people use when describing proofs. In practice, tactics do not always work at such a high level. But through tacticals like `REPEAT`, a single user command can perform hundreds of inferences.

Many different conceptions of tactic exist, including those of Edinburgh LCF and Isabelle. They are all consistent with the general ideas above.

6.4 Validation-based tactics

An LCF goal is a description of the desired theorem, possibly with additional information.[9] A tactic maps a goal to a list of subgoals and a proof function, which will be used to map a theorem list to a theorem.

```
type proof = thm list -> thm;
type goal = form list * form;
type tactic = goal -> ((goal list) * proof);
```

The proof function is also called a *validation.* It is not the name of a rule but an arbitrary function from theorems to a theorem. Likewise the tactic may use an arbitrary function from the goal to the subgoals. Subgoal construction and proof construction are completely separate.

Relating these operations are the concepts of *achievement* and *validity* [Milner, 1985]. Each goal defines some set of theorems that achieve it. If the goal is false then this set is empty. A tactic is *valid* provided: whenever it reduces goal G to subgoals G_1, ..., G_n and proof P, and theorems T_1, ..., T_n achieve G_1, ..., G_n, then theorem $P[T_1, \ldots, T_n]$ achieves G.

In this model, tactical proof has two phases. In the top-down phase, the original goal is decomposed into subgoals, and all are ultimately solved. Then the bottom-up phase, which should be automatic, applies validations to theorems. When a subgoal is solved outright (the tactic returns an empty goal list) the validation is applied to the empty theorem list and returns a theorem. These theorems are given to the validations one level up, and so forth until we reach the root.

Below is a goal tree and the corresponding tree of theorems. We must keep track of the validations and use them to make the T_i. Cambridge LCF has a 'subgoal package' that stores validations on a stack and applies them automatically. This package constrains somewhat the selection of the next subgoal.

---

[9] In Edinburgh LCF each goal contained a *simpset*, consisting of simplification data; these were dropped in Cambridge LCF.

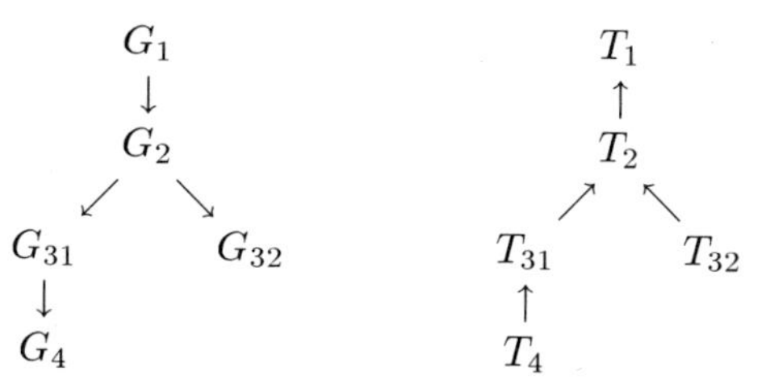

If all the tactics are primitive, this might be the goal tree for the following proof:

$$\dfrac{\dfrac{\dfrac{A, B \vdash B}{A \vdash B \to B}\ \to\text{:right} \qquad A \vdash A}{A \vdash (B \to B) \wedge A}\ \wedge\text{:right}}{\vdash A \to (B \to B) \wedge A}\ \to\text{:right}$$

There should be primitive tactics for all the inference rules. If the rule maps premises $T_1, \ldots, T_n$ to conclusion T, the tactic recognizes a goal corresponding to T and returns subgoals corresponding to $T_1, \ldots, T_n$, along with a validation that invokes the rule. Sometimes a rule function depends on extra arguments, which the validation must supply. The tactic can usually obtain this information from the goal. If construction of the subgoals or validation requires extra information then the tactic will have extra arguments.

The simplest tactical is `ORELSE`. It tries `tac1` and tests whether it fails by catching the corresponding exception (say `tactic`):

```
fun ORELSE (tac1,tac2) g =
    (tac1 g)  handle  tactic => (tac2 g);
```

The tactical `THEN` keeps track of many lists. It applies `tac1` to the goal, getting a list of subgoals $G_1, \ldots, G_n$ and validation P. It applies `tac2` to $G_1, \ldots, G_n$, getting a list of lists and a list of validations $P_1, \ldots, P_n$. Combining the validations involves tedious code. The final validation takes a list of theorems and partitions them into a list of lists $L_1, \ldots, L_n$, each of correct length for its corresponding validation. It applies each P_i to L_i and applies P to the resulting theorems.

The following trivial tactic succeeds on all goals, mapping a goal to itself. It is an identify for `THEN`. The validation maps a one-element list to its sole element.

```
fun ALL_TAC g =  ([g],  fn [th] => th);
```

Tactical `REPEAT` is a recursive function that calls `ALL_TAC`.[10]

```
fun REPEAT tac g =
    ((tac THEN REPEAT tac) ORELSE ALL_TAC) g;
```

[10] `REPEAT` mentions goal `g` just to delay evaluation. Otherwise `REPEAT tac` would loop immediately, due to ML's strict semantics.

Validation-based tactics are flexible because subgoals and proofs are generated by arbitrary functions, but this flexibility has a cost. There is no way of detecting an invalid tactic until it is too late. When we attempt to use the validation it may fail, diverge, or return something unwanted. Each primitive tactic must be written individually.

The validation model above does not handle unification. Goals may not contain unknowns to be instantiated later. As a consequence, the LCF user must supply an explicit term at each $\exists$:right step. For $\forall$:left there are tactics that try to use universally quantified assumptions by matching. Sokołowski wrote a set of Edinburgh LCF tactics permitting unification [Sokołowski, 1987]. They maintain an environment of variable instantiations.

My recent book on LCF describes rules and tactics, as well as some theory and applications [Paulson, 1987]. The hHigher-order logic (HOL) prover, which is based on LCF, is coming into widespread use for hardware verification [Gordon, 1988]. Several complicated chips have been verified using HOL. One of the largest HOL proofs concerns the Viper microprocessor [Cohn, 1989a].

Nuprl, which is another relative of LCF, has unusual tactics that manipulate proof objects [Constable *et al.*, 1986]. Nuprl implements a constructive logic based on Martin-Löf Type Theory, and has performed many proofs; in hardware verification, for example, [Basin and Del Vecchio, 1990] have verified part of a floating point processor.

The next section describes the theorem prover Isabelle, which takes LCF's ideas in a different direction. Isabelle has been used in several laboratories for program verification and synthesis. Philippe Noël (1989) has formalized large pieces of Zermelo–Fraenkel set theory. Tobias Nipkow, in a case study in data type refinement, has verified both sequential and distributed implementations of a memory system [Nipkow, 1989].

6.5 State-based tactics

Isabelle is a *generic* theorem prover: it supports reasoning in various logics [Paulson, 1990]. It aims to minimize the amount of effort involved in adding a new logic. Neither rules nor their corresponding tactics require programming.

Isabelle represents rules as assertions, not as functions. The rule that takes $\phi_1, \ldots, \phi_n$ to ϕ, written

$$[\phi_1, \ldots, \phi_n] \Rightarrow \phi$$

is a syntactic object. Its structure can be examined, which is impossible when rules are represented by functions. For instance, the conjunction rules might be represented as follows:

$$[?A, ?B] \Rightarrow ?A \wedge ?B \qquad [?A \wedge ?B] \Rightarrow ?A \qquad [?A \wedge ?B] \Rightarrow ?B$$

Meta-variables $?A$ and $?B$ can be replaced by formulae, producing instances of the rules.

What about rules with provisos, such as quantifier rules? An LCF rule can do any computation to check syntactic conditions. Isabelle has ways of handling provisos like 'x not free in A', but other provisos may become extra premises — and must be proved rather than checked.

A rule also represents the state of a backwards proof. Thus $[\phi_1, \ldots, \phi_n] \Rightarrow \phi$ represents the proof where the final goal is ϕ and the current subgoals are $\phi_1, \ldots, \phi_n$. The initial proof state is the trivial rule $[\phi] \Rightarrow \phi$. A typical backwards step replaces some ϕ_i by new subgoals $\psi_1, \ldots, \psi_m$. When $m = 0$, the total number of subgoals decreases. A successful proof terminates with simply ϕ; this proof state is itself the desired theorem.

For example, the proof sketched in the previous section might produce the following sequence of states:

$$\begin{array}{r} [G_1] \Rightarrow G_1 \\ [G_2] \Rightarrow G_1 \\ [G_{31}, G_{32}] \Rightarrow G_1 \quad (*) \\ [G_4, G_{32}] \Rightarrow G_1 \\ [G_{32}] \Rightarrow G_1 \\ G_1. \end{array}$$

Here we have always chosen the first subgoal. Choosing G_{32} before G_{31} at state $(*)$ would produce $[G_{31}] \Rightarrow G_1$ as the next state.

A backwards step using the rule $[\psi_1, \ldots, \psi_m] \Rightarrow \psi$ matches its conclusion, ψ, with the chosen subgoal, ϕ_i. The new subgoals are the corresponding instances of the rule's premises $\psi_1, \ldots, \psi_m$. If s is a substitution such that $\psi s = \phi_i$ then Isabelle permits the following meta-level inference:

$$\frac{[\psi_1, \ldots, \psi_m] \Rightarrow \psi \qquad [\phi_1, \ldots, \phi_n] \Rightarrow \phi}{[\phi_1, \ldots, \phi_{i-1}, \psi_1 s, \ldots, \psi_m s, \phi_{i+1}, \ldots, \phi_n] \Rightarrow \phi.}$$

Note that $\Rightarrow$ is essentially implication, so (object) rules are Horn clauses and the above inference is a form of resolution. It is a small step from matching to unification. If the proof state contains meta variables then resolution involves unifying ψ with ϕ_i. If $\psi s = \phi_i s$ then resolution makes a new proof state by applying s throughout:

$$[\phi_1 s, \ldots, \phi_{i-1} s, \psi_1 s, \ldots, \psi_m s, \phi_{i+1} s, \ldots, \phi_n s] \Rightarrow \phi s$$

Thus variables in the proof state can be instantiated, even if they are shared between several subgoals.

An Isabelle tactic is a function that maps one proof state to another. It takes not one goal but the entire proof state, and may change it in any way. Updating variables in the state can alter other subgoals and even the final goal. By starting with a goal that contains variables, we can use an Isabelle proof to compute answers. The proof state is a meta-theorem stating that the subgoals imply the goal: no validations are necessary.

Tacticals are implemented differently from LCFs. The tactic `tac1 THEN tac2` applies `tac1` to a proof state, and then applies `tac2` to the result. Tactic `ALL_TAC` returns an unchanged proof state. Tacticals `ORELSE` and `REPEAT` are as in LCF. Resolution provides all the primitive tactics free.

6.6 Technical aspects of Isabelle

Some technical points about nondeterminism and quantifiers were omitted from the previous section for simplicity.

Tactical `ORELSE` does not permit backtracking. Consider the tactic

```
(tac1 ORELSE tac2)  THEN  tac3
```

If `tac1` succeeds then the `ORELSE` will choose it. If `tac3` then fails, the `ORELSE` cannot try `tac2`; instead, the entire tactic fails. To take account of the success of `tac3`, use the tactic

```
(tac1 THEN tac3)  ORELSE  (tac2 THEN tac3)
```

To solve this problem more generally, Isabelle tactics incorporate nondeterminism. A tactic returns a list of next states. An empty list means the tactic has failed. The tactic `tac1 THEN tac2` returns all states that could result by applying `tac1` followed by `tac2`. A new tactical, `APPEND`, is a nondeterministic `ORELSE`. Calling `tac1 APPEND tac2` returns all states that could result by applying `tac1` or `tac2`.

Since a tactic can return a list of outcomes, repetition of a tactic can produce a tree of states. Tactical `DEPTH_FIRST` performs a depth-first search of this tree, giving Prolog-style backtracking. Other strategies are available, including breadth-first and best-first (search guided by a distance function). The next state list must be lazy,[11] for it could be infinite, and only a few elements will be needed.

Complex techniques are required for quantifier rules:

$$[\forall x \,.\, ?F(x)] \Rightarrow ?F(?t)$$

Here $?F$ is a function variable. If it gets instantiated with the λ-abstraction $\lambda x.A$, then $?F(?t)$ causes the substitution of $?t$ into A. Ordinary unification cannot instantiate function variables or perform substitutions. Isabelle uses higher-order unification [Huet, 1975], which is powerful but sometimes

[11] Standard ML uses strict evaluation, but lazy lists can be implemented using closures.

ill-behaved. Perhaps something simpler should be adopted; second-order matching is decidable [Huet and Lang, 1978].

Originally Isabelle enforced quantifier provisos using parameters resembling Folderol's, and took resolution as a primitive meta-rule. Now Isabelle takes higher-order logic as its meta-logic [Paulson, 1989]. This permits provisos to be enforced using meta-quantifiers and function variables, a dual of skolemization. Derived forms of meta-reasoning include resolution and methods for natural deduction.

7 Conclusion

Folderol has achieved its purpose if it has illustrated the prospects, hazards, and techniques of writing a theorem prover. Although Folderol can prove some complex theorems, there is much that it cannot do. If you have a particular verification task in mind, you will probably see at once that Folderol is not up to the job.

A real theorem prover must include numbers, functions, pairs, and other mathematical concepts. It must provide flexible methods of proof discovery. It must maintain a database of symbols, axioms, theorems, and maybe proofs. We have surveyed other systems to see how they meet these requirements.

You may now recognize that writing a theorem prover is a mammoth task. My final advice is this. Don't write a theorem prover. Try to use someone else's.

Acknowledgement

Thomas Forster, Mike Fourman, and Robin Milner commented on this chapter. LCF, ML, and Isabelle were all developed by funding from the Science and Engineering Research Council (grants GR/B67766, GRT/D 30235, and GR/E0355.7, among others).

8 Program listing

```
(*BASIC FUNCTIONS*)

(*Length of a list*)
local fun length1 (n, [ ])  = n
        | length1 (n, x::l) = length1 (n+1, l)
in  fun length l = length1 (0,l) end;
```

```
(*The elements of a list satisfying the predicate p.*)
fun filter p [] = []
  | filter p (x::xs) = if p(x) then  x :: filter p xs  else  filter p xs;

infix mem;  (*membership in a list*)
fun x mem []  =  false
  | x mem (y::l)  =  (x=y) orelse (x mem l);

infix ins;  (*insertion into list if not already there*)
fun x ins xs = if x mem xs then  xs   else  x::xs;

fun repeat x 0 = []
  | repeat x n = x :: (repeat x (n-1));

fun accumulate f ([], y) = y
  | accumulate f (x::xs, y) = accumulate f (xs, f(x,y));

(*Look for a pair (X,z) in environment, return [z] if found, else [] *)
fun lookup (X, []) = []
  | lookup (X, (Y,z)::env) = if X = (Y:string) then [z]  else  lookup(X,env);

exception ERROR of string;


(*TERMS AND FORMULAE*)

datatype term =
    Var   of string
  | Param of string * string list
  | Bound of int
  | Fun   of string * term list;

datatype form =
    Pred  of string * term list
  | Conn  of string * form list
  | Quant of string * string * form;

(*variables
    a,b,c: string     q,r: string (quantifier names)
    i,j: int     (Bound indexes)
    t,u: term     A,B: form
    x,y: any      f,g: functions
*)


(*Operations on terms and formulae*)

(*Replace the atomic term u by new throughout a term*)
fun replace_term (u,new) t =
    if t=u then new else
    case t of Fun(a,ts) => Fun(a, map (replace_term(u,new)) ts)
            | _ => t;
```

```
(*Abstraction of a formula over u (containing no bound vars).*)
fun abstract t =
    let fun abs i (Pred(a,ts)) = Pred(a, map (replace_term (t, Bound i)) ts)
          | abs i (Conn(b,As)) = Conn(b, map (abs i) As)
          | abs i (Quant(q,b,A)) = Quant(q, b, abs (i+1) A)
    in  abs 0  end;

(*Replace (Bound 0) in formula with t (containing no bound vars).*)
fun subst_bound t =
    let fun subst i (Pred(a,ts)) = Pred(a, map (replace_term (Bound i, t)) ts)
          | subst i (Conn(b,As)) = Conn(b, map (subst i) As)
          | subst i (Quant(q,b,A)) = Quant(q, b, subst (i+1) A)
    in  subst 0  end;



(*SYNTAX: SCANNING, PARSING, AND DISPLAY*)

(*Scanning a list of characters into a list of tokens*)

datatype token = Key of string  |  Id of string;

fun is_char(l,c,u) = ord l <= ord c  andalso  ord c <= ord u;

fun is_letter_or_digit c =
    is_char("A",c,"Z") orelse is_char("a",c,"z") orelse is_char("0",c,"9");

(*Scanning of identifiers and keywords*)

fun token_of a = if a mem ["ALL","EXISTS"]  then  Key(a)  else  Id(a);

fun scan_ident (front, c::cs) =
      if is_letter_or_digit c
      then  scan_ident (c::front, cs)
      else  (token_of (implode(rev front)), c::cs)
  | scan_ident (front, []) = (token_of (implode(rev front)), []);

(*Scanning, recognizing --> and <->, skipping blanks, etc.*)
fun scan (front_toks, []) = rev front_toks    (*end of char list*)
            (*long infix operators*)
  | scan (front_toks, "-"::"-"::">"::cs) = scan (Key"-->" ::front_toks,  cs)
  | scan (front_toks, "<"::"-"::">"::cs) = scan (Key"<->" ::front_toks,  cs)
            (*blanks, tabs, newlines*)
  | scan (front_toks, " "::cs) = scan (front_toks,  cs)
  | scan (front_toks, "\t"::cs) = scan (front_toks,  cs)
  | scan (front_toks, "\n"::cs) = scan (front_toks,  cs)
  | scan (front_toks, c::cs) =
      if is_letter_or_digit c then scannext(front_toks, scan_ident([c], cs))
      else  scan (Key(c)::front_toks,  cs)
and scannext (front_toks, (tok, cs)) = scan (tok::front_toks,  cs);
```

```
(*Parsing a list of tokens*)

fun apfst f (x,toks) = (f x, toks);

(*Functions for constructing results*)
fun cons x xs = x::xs;
fun makeFun fu ts = Fun(fu,ts);
fun makePred id ts = Pred(id,ts);
fun makeNeg A = Conn("~", [A]);
fun makeConn a A B = Conn(a, [A,B]);
fun makeQuant q b A = Quant(q, b, abstract (Fun(b,[])) A);


(*Repeated parsing, returning the list of results  *)
fun parse_repeat (a,parsefn) (Key(b)::toks) =  (*    a<phrase>...a<phrase>  *)
          if a=b then parse_repeat1 (a,parsefn) toks
          else ([], Key(b)::toks)
  | parse_repeat (a, parsefn) toks = ([], toks)
and parse_repeat1 (a,parsefn) toks =             (*    <phrase>a...a<phrase>  *)
      let val (u,toks2) = parsefn toks
      in  apfst (cons u) (parse_repeat (a, parsefn) toks2)  end;


fun rightparen (x, Key")"::toks) = (x, toks)
  | rightparen _ = raise ERROR "Symbol ) expected";


fun parse_term (Id(a)::Key"("::toks) =
        apfst (makeFun a) (rightparen (parse_repeat1 (",", parse_term) toks))
  | parse_term (Id(a)::toks) = (Fun(a,[]), toks)
  | parse_term (Key"?"::Id(a)::toks) = (Var a, toks)
  | parse_term _ = raise ERROR "Syntax of term";


(*Precedence table*)
fun prec_of "~"   = 4
  | prec_of "&"   = 3
  | prec_of "|"   = 2
  | prec_of "<->" = 1
  | prec_of "-->" = 1
  | prec_of _     = ~1    (*means not an infix*);


(*Parsing of formulae;  prec is the precedence of the operator to the left;
    parsing stops at an operator with lower precedence*)
fun parse (Key"ALL"   ::Id(a)::Key"."::toks) =
      apfst (makeQuant "ALL" a) (parse toks)
  | parse (Key"EXISTS"::Id(a)::Key"."::toks) =
      apfst (makeQuant "EXISTS" a) (parse toks)
  | parse toks = parsefix 0 (parse_atom toks)
and parsefix prec (A, Key(co)::toks) =
```

```
      if prec_of co < prec then (A, Key(co)::toks)
      else parsefix prec
              (apfst (makeConn co A)
                 (parsefix (prec_of co) (parse_atom toks)))
  | parsefix prec (A, toks) = (A, toks)
and parse_atom (Key"~"::toks) = apfst makeNeg (parse_atom toks)
  | parse_atom (Key"("::toks) = rightparen (parse toks)
  | parse_atom (Id(pr)::Key"("::toks) =
        apfst (makePred pr) (rightparen (parse_repeat1 (",", parse_term) toks))
  | parse_atom (Id(pr)::toks) = (Pred(pr,[]), toks)
  | parse_atom _ = raise ERROR "Syntax of formula";


(*check that no tokens remain*)
fun parse_end (x, []) = x
  | parse_end (_, _::_) = raise ERROR "Extra characters in formula";

fun read a = parse_end (parse (scan([], explode a)));



(*Printing: conversion of terms/formulae to strings*)

fun enclose a = "(" ^ a ^ ")";

fun conc_list sep [] = ""
  | conc_list sep (b::bs) = (sep ^ b) ^ (conc_list sep bs);

fun conc_list1 sep (b::bs) = b ^ (conc_list sep bs);


fun stringof_term (Param(a,_)) = a
  | stringof_term (Var a) = "?"^a
  | stringof_term (Bound i) = "B." ^ makestring i
  | stringof_term (Fun (a,ts)) =  a ^ stringof_args ts
and stringof_args [] = ""
  | stringof_args ts = enclose (conc_list1 "," (map stringof_term ts));



fun max(m,n) : int = if m>n then m else n;

fun stringof_form prec (Pred (a,ts)) =  a ^ stringof_args ts
  | stringof_form prec (Conn("~", [A])) =  "~" ^ stringof_form (prec_of "~") A
  | stringof_form prec (Conn(C, [A,B])) =
        let val stringf = stringof_form (max(prec_of C, prec));
            val Z = stringf A ^ " " ^ C ^ " " ^ stringf B
        in  if (prec_of C <= prec)  then  (enclose Z)  else Z
        end
  | stringof_form prec (Quant(q,b,A)) =
        let val B = subst_bound (Fun(b,[])) A
            val Z = q^" "^b ^ ". " ^ stringof_form 0 B
```

```
        in  if  prec>0  then  (enclose Z)  else Z
        end
  | stringof_form prec _ = raise ERROR "stringof_form: Bad formula";

val stringof = stringof_form 0;


(*UNIFICATION*)

exception UNIFY;

(*Naive unification of terms containing no bound variables*)
fun unify_terms ([],[], env) = env
  | unify_terms (t::ts, u::us, env) =
      let fun chasevar (Var a) =  (*Chase variable assignments*)
(case  lookup(a,env)  of
    u::_ => chasevar u  |  [] => Var a)
    | chasevar t = t;
  fun unify_var (a, t) = (*unification with var*)
let fun occs (Fun(_,ts)) = occsl ts
      | occs (Param(_,bs)) = occsl(map Var bs)
      | occs (Var b) =  a=b  orelse occsl(lookup(b,env))
      | occs _ = false
    and occsl [] = false
      | occsl(t::ts) = occs t  orelse  occsl ts
in  if t = Var a  then  env
    else if occs t then  raise UNIFY  else  (a,t)::env
end
  and unify_term (Var a, t) = unify_var (a, t)
    | unify_term (t, Var a) = unify_var (a, t)
    | unify_term (Param(a,_), Param(b,_)) =
  if a=b then env  else  raise UNIFY
    | unify_term (Fun(a,ts), Fun(b,us)) =
  if a=b then unify_terms (ts,us,env)  else  raise UNIFY
    | unify_term _ =  raise UNIFY
    in  unify_terms (ts, us, unify_term (chasevar t, chasevar u))  end
  | unify_terms _ =  raise UNIFY;



(*Unification of atomic formulae*)
fun unify (Pred(a,ts), Pred(b,us), env) =
        if a=b then unify_terms(ts,us,env)  else  raise UNIFY
  | unify _ =  raise UNIFY;


(*Accumulate all Vars in the term (not Vars attached to a Param).*)
fun vars_in_term (Var a, bs) = a ins bs
  | vars_in_term (Fun(_,ts), bs) = accumulate vars_in_term (ts,bs)
  | vars_in_term (_, bs) = bs;
```

```
(*Instantiate a term by an environment*)
fun inst_term env (Fun(a,ts)) = Fun(a, map (inst_term env) ts)
  | inst_term env (Param(a,bs)) =
        Param(a, accumulate vars_in_term (map (inst_term env o Var) bs, []))
  | inst_term env (Var a) =
      (case  lookup(a,env)  of
          u::_ =>  inst_term env u
        | []   =>  Var a)
  | inst_term env t = t;


(*INFERENCE: GOALS AND PROOF STATES: GOALS AND PROOF STATES*)

datatype side = Left | Right;

type entry = int * side * form;
type goal = entry list;
type goaltable = goal list;


fun inst_form [] A = A
  | inst_form env (Pred(a,ts))    = Pred(a, map (inst_term env) ts)
  | inst_form env (Conn(b,As))    = Conn(b, map (inst_form env) As)
  | inst_form env (Quant(q,b,A)) = Quant(q, b, inst_form env A);

fun inst_goal env [] = []
  | inst_goal env ((m,si,A)::G) = (m, si, inst_form env A) :: inst_goal env G;

fun inst_goals [] Gs = Gs
  | inst_goals env Gs = map (inst_goal env) Gs : goaltable;


(*Accumulate over all terms in a formula*)
fun accum_form f (Pred(_,ts), bs) = accumulate f (ts, bs)
  | accum_form f (Conn(_,As), bs) = accumulate (accum_form f) (As, bs)
  | accum_form f (Quant(_,_,A), bs) = accum_form f (A,bs);

(*Accumulate over all formulae in a goal*)
fun accum_goal f ([], bs) = bs
  | accum_goal f ((_,_,A)::G, bs) = accum_goal f (G, f(A,bs));

val vars_in_form = accum_form vars_in_term;
val vars_in_goal = accum_goal vars_in_form;


(*Accumulate all Params*)
fun params_in_term (Param (a,bs), pairs) = (a,bs) ins pairs
  | params_in_term (Fun(_,ts), pairs) = accumulate params_in_term (ts, pairs)
  | params_in_term (_, pairs) = pairs;

val params_in_form = accum_form params_in_term;
val params_in_goal = accum_goal params_in_form;
```

```
(*Returns (As,Bs),preserving order of elements
  As = Left entries,  Bs = Right entries *)
fun split_goal G =
    let fun split (As,Bs, []: goal) = (As,Bs)
          | split (As,Bs, (_,Left,A)::H) = split (A::As,Bs, H)
          | split (As,Bs, (_,Right,B)::H) = split (As, B::Bs, H)
    in  split([], [], rev G)  end;


fun is_pred (Pred _) = true
  | is_pred _ = false;

(*Solve the goal (A|-A') by unifying A with A', Left and Right atomic formulae.
  Returns list [ (A,env) ] if successful, otherwise []. *)
fun solve_goal G =
    let fun findA ([], _) = []    (*failure*)
          | findA (A::As, Bs) =
              let fun findB [] = findA (As,Bs)
                    | findB (B::Bs) = [ (A, unify(A,B,[])) ]
                      handle UNIFY => findB Bs
              in  findB Bs  end
        val (As,Bs) = split_goal G
    in  findA(filter is_pred As, filter is_pred Bs)  end;


(*Insert goals into a goaltable.  For each solved goal (A,env),
  accumulates the formula (in reverse) and instantiates all other goals.*)
fun insert_goals ([], As, tab) = (As,tab)
  | insert_goals (G::Gs, As, tab) =
      case  solve_goal G  of
          (A,env)::_ =>         (*instantiate other goals*)
             insert_goals (inst_goals env Gs,
                           (inst_form env A) :: As,
                           inst_goals env tab)
        | [] =>  insert_goals (Gs, As, G::tab);


fun stringof_sy (Pred(a,_)) = a
  | stringof_sy (Conn(a,_)) = a
  | stringof_sy (Quant(q,_,_)) = q;

fun stringof_side Right = ":right"
  | stringof_side Left = ":left";


(*Generation of new variable names*)
local
  fun make_letter n = chr(ord("a")+n);
  fun make_varname (n,tail) =
     if n<26 then make_letter n ^ tail
```

```
    else make_varname (n div 26, make_letter(n mod 26) ^ tail);
  val varcount = ref ~1
in
fun gensym() = (varcount := !varcount+1;  make_varname (!varcount,""))
and init_gensym() = varcount := ~1
end;


(*The "cost" of reducing a connective*)
fun cost (_,     Conn("~", _))          = 1      (*a single subgoal*)
  | cost (Left,  Conn("&", _))          = 1
  | cost (Right, Conn("|", _))          = 1
  | cost (Right, Conn("-->", _))        = 1
  | cost (Right, Quant("ALL",_,_))      = 1
  | cost (Left,  Quant("EXISTS",_,_))   = 1
  | cost (Right, Conn("&", _))          = 2      (*case split: 2 subgoals*)
  | cost (Left,  Conn("|", _))          = 2
  | cost (Left,  Conn("-->", _))        = 2
  | cost (_    , Conn("<->", _))        = 2
  | cost (Left,  Quant("ALL",_,_))      = 3      (*quantifier expansion*)
  | cost (Right, Quant("EXISTS",_,_))   = 3      (*quantifier expansion*)
  | cost _ = 4 ;                                 (*no reductions possible*)

fun paircost (si,A) = (cost(si,A), si, A);


(*Insertion into a list, ordered by sort keys. *)
fun insert less =
  let fun insr (x, []) = [x]
        | insr (x, y::ys) = if less(y,x) then y :: insr (x,ys) else x::y::ys
  in  insr  end;

(*Insert an entry into a goal, in correct order *)
fun entry_less ((m,_,_): entry, (n,_,_): entry) = m<n;
val insert_early = insert entry_less;

(*Quantified formulae are put back at end -- they are used in a cycle*)
fun entry_lesseq ((m,_,_): entry, (n,_,_): entry) = m<=n;
val insert_late  = insert entry_lesseq;

(*Extend the goal G by inserting a list of (side,form) pairs*)
fun new_goal G pairs = accumulate insert_early (map paircost pairs, G);

(*Extend the goal G, making a list of goals*)
fun new_goals G pairslist = map (new_goal G) pairslist;


exception REDUCE;

(*Reduce the pair using the rest of the goal (G) to make new goals*)
fun reduce_goal (pair, G) =
  let val goals = new_goals G;
```

```
      fun vars_in A = vars_in_goal (G, vars_in_form(A,[]));
      fun subparam A = subst_bound (Param(gensym(), vars_in A)) A;
      fun subvar A   = subst_bound (Var(gensym())) A;
      fun red(_,Right,Conn("~", [A]))   = goals[[(Left,A)]]
        | red(_,Left, Conn("~", [A]))   = goals[[(Right,A)]]
        | red(_,Right,Conn("&", [A,B])) = goals[[(Right,A)], [(Right,B)]]
        | red(_,Left, Conn("&", [A,B])) = goals[[(Left,A),(Left,B)]]
        | red(_,Right,Conn("|", [A,B])) = goals[[(Right,A),(Right,B)]]
        | red(_,Left, Conn("|", [A,B])) = goals[[(Left,A)], [(Left,B)]]
        | red(_,Right,Conn("-->", [A,B])) = goals[[(Left,A),(Right,B)]]
        | red(_,Left, Conn("-->", [A,B])) = goals[[(Right,A)], [(Left,B)]]
        | red(_,Right,Conn("<->", [A,B])) =
                goals[[(Left,A),(Right,B)], [(Right,A),(Left,B)]]
        | red(_,Left, Conn("<->", [A,B])) =
                goals[[(Left,A),(Left,B)], [(Right,A),(Right,B)]]
        | red(_,Right,Quant("ALL",_,A)) = goals[[(Right, subparam A)]]
        | red(_,Left, Quant("ALL",_,A)) =
              [ insert_early (paircost(Left, subvar A), insert_late(pair,G)) ]
        | red(_,Right,Quant("EXISTS",_,A)) =
              [ insert_early (paircost(Right, subvar A), insert_late(pair,G)) ]
        | red(_,Left, Quant("EXISTS",_,A)) = goals[[(Left, subparam A)]]
        | red _ = raise REDUCE
  in  red pair  end;


(*Print the string a*)
fun prints a = output(std_out,a);

(*Print the rule used, with each formula found by unification,
    indenting by number of goals left.*)
fun print_step ((_,si,C), ngoals, As) =
   (prints (implode(repeat " " ngoals) ^
                stringof_sy C ^ stringof_side si);
    prints (conc_list "   " (map stringof (rev As)));  prints"\n");

(*A single inference in the goaltable*)
fun proof_step [] = [] : goaltable
  | proof_step ([]::tab) = raise ERROR "Empty goal"
  | proof_step ((ent::G)::tab) =
      let val (As,newtab) = insert_goals (reduce_goal(ent,G), [], tab)
      in  print_step(ent, length tab, As);    newtab   end;

(*Perform n proof steps, no limit if n<0.  Stops if impossible to continue.*)
fun proof_steps (_,[]) = []    (*success -- no goals*)
  | proof_steps (0,tab) = tab
  | proof_steps (n,tab) = proof_steps (n-1, proof_step tab)
      handle REDUCE => (prints"\n**No proof rules applicable**\n";  tab);

fun pair si A = (si,A);

(*Make a goal from lists of formulae: As|-Bs*)
fun make_goal (As,Bs) : goal =
```

```
    new_goal [] (map (pair Left) As   @   map (pair Right) Bs);


(*Reading of goals: Astrs|-Bstrs *)
fun read_tab (Astrs,Bstrs) : goaltable =
    let val As = rev(map read Astrs)
        and Bs = rev(map read Bstrs);
val G = make_goal(As,Bs);
        val (_, tab) = insert_goals ([G],  [],  [])
    in  tab  end;

fun stringof_sequent [] = "empty"
  | stringof_sequent As = conc_list1 ", " (map stringof As);

fun print_goal G =
    let val (As,Bs) = split_goal G
    in  prints (stringof_sequent As ^ "  |-  " ^ stringof_sequent Bs ^ "\n\n")
    end;

fun print_param (a,ts) =
      prints (a ^ "          " ^ stringof_args (map Var ts) ^ "\n");

fun print_params [] = ()
  | print_params pairs =
      (prints "Param     Not allowed in\n";
       map print_param pairs;  prints "\n");

fun print_count 1 = ()
  | print_count n = prints (makestring n ^ " goals\n");

fun print_tab [] = prints"No more goals: proof finished\n"
  | print_tab Gs =
     (prints"\n";   map print_goal Gs;  print_count (length Gs);
      print_params (accumulate params_in_goal (Gs,[])));


(*Top-level commands: interaction with proof state*)

val the_goaltable = ref ([] : goaltable);

fun set_tab tab = (the_goaltable := tab;  print_tab tab);

(*Read a goal: the sequent As|-Bs *)
fun read_goalseq (Astrs,Bstrs) =
    (init_gensym();  set_tab(read_tab (Astrs,Bstrs)));

(*Read the goal |-B *)
fun read_goal Bstr = read_goalseq([],[Bstr]);

fun step()  = set_tab (proof_step(!the_goaltable));
fun steps n = set_tab (proof_steps (max(n,0), !the_goaltable));
fun run()   = set_tab (proof_steps (~1, !the_goaltable));
```

```
fun run_goalseq (Astrs,Bstrs) = (read_goalseq (Astrs,Bstrs);  run());
fun run_goal b = run_goalseq([],[b]);


(*Raises exception unless some goals are left unsolved after n proof steps*)
fun fail_goal n A =
   (read_goal A;
    steps n;
    (case !the_goaltable of
        [] => raise ERROR "This proof should have failed!"
      | _::_ => prints"Failed, as expected\n"));
```

References

[Andrews *et al.*, 1984] P. B. Andrews, D. A. Miller, E. L. Cohen, and F. Pfenning. Automating higher-order logic. In W. W. Bledsoe and D. W. Loveland, editors, *Automated Theorem Proving: After 25 Years*, pages 169–192. American Mathematical Society, 1984.

[Barwise, 1977] J. Barwise. An introduction to first-order logic. In J. Barwise, editor, *Handbook of Mathematical Logic*, pages 5–46. North-Holland, 1977.

[Basin and Del Vecchio, 1990] D. A. Basin and P. Del Vecchio. Verification of combinational logic in nuprl. In M. Leeser and G. Brown, editors, *Hardware Specification, Verification and Synthesis: Mathematical Aspects*, volume 408 of *Lecture Notes in Computer Science*, pages 333–357. Springer-Verlag, 1990.

[Bevier *et al.*, 1989] W. R. Bevier, W. A. Hunt Jr., J. S. Moore, and W. D. Young. An approach to systems verification. *Journal of Automated Reasoning*, 5:411–428, 1989.

[Bibel, 1987] W. Bibel. *Automated Theorem Proving.* Friedr. Vieweg & Sohn, 1987.

[Boyer and Moore, 1972] R. S. Boyer and J. S. Moore. The sharing of structure in theorem proving programs. In B. Meltzer and D. Michie, editors, *Machine Intelligence 7*, pages 101–116. Edinburgh University Press, 1972.

[Boyer and Moore, 1979] R. S. Boyer and J. S. Moore. *A Computational Logic.* Academic Press, 1979.

[Boyer and Moore, 1988] R. S. Boyer and J. S. Moore. The addition of bounded quantification and partial functions to a computational logic and its theorem prover. *Journal of Automated Reasoning*, 4:117–172, 1988.

[Chang and Lee, 1973] C.-L. Chang and R. C.-T. Lee. *Symbolic Logic and Mechanical Theorem Proving.* Academic Press, 1973.

[Clarke *et al.*, 1986] E. M. Clarke, E. A. Emerson, and A. P. Sistla. Automatic verification of finite-state concurrent systems using temporal logic specifications. *ACM Transactions on Programming Languages and Systems*, 8:244–263, 1986.

[Cohn, 1989a] A. Cohn. Correctness properties of the Viper block model: the second level. In G. Birtwistle and P. A. Subrahmanyam, editors, *Current Trends in Hardware Verification and Automated Theorem Proving*, pages 1–91. Springer-Verlag, 1989.

[Cohn, 1989b] A. Cohn. The notion of proof in hardware verification. *Journal of Automated Reasoning*, 5:127–139, 1989.

[Constable *et al.*, 1986] R. L. Constable, S. F. Allen, H. M. Bromley, W. R. Cleaveland, J. F. Cremer, R. W. Harper, D. J. Howe, T. B. Knoblock, N. P. Mendler, P. Panagaden, J. T. Sasaki, and S. F. Smith. *Implementing Mathematics with the Nuprl Proof Development System.* Prentice-Hall International, 1986.

[de Bruijn, 1972] N. G. de Bruijn. Lambda calculus notation with nameless dummies, a tool for automatic formula manipulation, with application to the Church-Rosser Theorem. *Indagationes Mathematicae*, 34:381–392, 1972.

[de Bruijn, 1980] N. G. de Bruijn. A survey of the project Automath. In J. P. Seldin and J. R. Hindley, editors, *To H. B. Curry: Essays on Combinatory Logic, Lambda Calculus and Formalism*, pages 579–606. Academic Press, 1980.

[Eisinger, 1986] N. Eisinger. What you always wanted to know about clause graph resolution. In J. H. Siekmann, editor, *Proc. 8th International Conference on Automated Deduction*, volume 230 of *Lecture Notes in Computer Science*, pages 316–335. Springer-Verlag, 1986.

[Formel Project, 1989] Formel Project. The calculus of constructions: documentation and user's guide. Technical report 110, INRIA-Rocquencourt, 1989.

[Gallier, 1986] J. H. Gallier. *Logic for Computer Science: Foundations of Automatic Theorem Proving.* Harper & Row, 1986.

[Gordon *et al.*, 1979] M. J. C. Gordon, R. Milner, and C. P. Wadsworth. *Edinburgh LCF: A Mechanised Logic of Computation*, volume 78 of *Lecture Notes in Computer Science*. Springer-Verlag, 1979.

[Gordon, 1988] M. J. C. Gordon. HOL: a proof generating system for higher-order logic. In G. Birtwistle and P. A. Subrahmanyam, editors, *VLSI Specification, Verification and Synthesis*, pages 73–128. Kluwer Academic Publishers, 1988.

[Huet and Lang, 1978] G. P. Huet and B. Lang. Proving and applying program transformations expressed with second-order patterns. *Acta Informatica*, 11:31–55, 1978.

[Huet, 1975] G. P. Huet. A unification algorithm for typed λ-calculus. *Theoretical Computer Science*, 1:27–57, 1975.

[Kowalski, 1975] R. Kowalski. A proof procedure using connection graphs. *Journal of the ACM*, 22:572–595, 1975.

[Lakatos, 1976] I. Lakatos. *Proofs and Refutations: The logic of Mathematical Discovery*. Cambridge University Press, 1976.

[Martelli and Montanari, 1982] A. Martelli and U. Montanari. An efficient unification algorithm. *ACM Trans. on Programming Languages and Systems*, 4(2):258–282, 1982.

[Milner, 1985] Robin Milner. The use of machines to assist in rigorous proof. In C. A. R. Hoare and J. C. Shepherdson, editors, *Mathematical Logic and Programming Languages*, pages 77–88. Prentice-Hall International, 1985.

[Nipkow, 1989] T. Nipkow. Formal verification of data type refinement — theory and practice. In *REX Workshop on Refinement of Distributed Systems*, volume 430 of *Lecture Notes in Computer Science*, pages 561–591. Springer-Verlag, 1989.

[Oppacher and Suen, 1988] F. Oppacher and E. Suen. HARP: a tableau-based theorem prover. *Journal of Automated Reasoning*, 4:69–100, 1988.

[Paulson, 1987] L. C. Paulson. *Logic and Computation: Interactive proof with Cambridge LCF*. Cambridge University Press, 1987.

[Paulson, 1989] L. C. Paulson. The foundation of a generic theorem prover. *Journal of Automated Reasoning*, 5:363–397, 1989.

[Paulson, 1990] L. C. Paulson. Isabelle: The next 700 theorem provers. In P. Odifreddi, editor, *Logic and Computer Science*, pages 361–385. Academic Press, 1990.

[Pelletier, 1986] F. J. Pelletier. Seventy-five problems for testing automatic theorem provers. *Journal of Automated Reasoning*, 2:191–216, 1986. Errata in 4(1988):236–236.

[Prawitz, 1965] D. Prawitz. *Natural Deduction: A Proof-theoretical Study.* Almqvist and Wiksell, 1965.

[Sokołowski, 1987] S. Sokołowski. Soundness of Hoare's logic: an automatic proof using LCF. *ACM Trans. on Programming Languages and Systems*, 9:100–120, 1987.

[Stickel, 1988] M. E. Stickel. A Prolog technology theorem prover: implementation by an extended Prolog compiler. *Journal of Automated Reasoning*, 4:353–380, 1988.

[Takeuti, 1987] G. Takeuti. *Proof Theory.* North Holland, 2nd edition, 1987.

[van Benthem Jutting, 1977] L. S. van Benthem Jutting. *Checking Landau's 'Grundlagen' in the Automath system.* PhD thesis, Eindhoven University of Technology, The Netherlands, 1977.

[Wallen, 1990] L. A. Wallen. *Automated Deduction in Nonclassical Logics.* MIT Press, 1990.

Modal and Temporal Logics

Colin Stirling

Contents

1 Introduction

1.1 Transition systems

In achieving their goals, programs manipulate data and thereby may change th state of the computer. Regarded as a dynamic system, the computer responds to program instructions and in so doing may change state. Activity and change are formalized by the operational semantics of programs and systems. Modal and temporal logics can directly express activity with their paradigm operators such as $[a]$ (*box* a) when a is an action, and F. Where Φ is a proposition, $[a]\Phi$ expresses *after every* a *action* Φ *holds* while $F\Phi$ expresses *eventually* Φ *holds.* The *modal* operator $[a]$ highlights the action that may provoke change of state whereas the *temporal* operator F focuses on the resulting changes. In both cases these operators may express properties of events that happen during a run of a system, events that may be crucial to understanding its overall behaviour. It is no accident that these logics can be used to express such notions. For their models comprehend structures that are encountered in operational semantics of programs and systems. These structures, (labelled) transition systems, are pivotal to this chapter.

Definition 1.1.1. A *transition system* is a pair $\mathcal{T} = (\mathcal{S}, \{\xrightarrow{a} \mid a \in \mathcal{L}\})$ where $\mathcal{S}$ is a non-empty set (of states or configurations), $\mathcal{L}$ is a non-empty set (of labels), and for each $a \in \mathcal{L}$, $\xrightarrow{a} \subseteq \mathcal{S} \times \mathcal{S}$.

Transition systems may be presented diagrammatically: figure 1 pictures the transition system with state set $\{s_0, s_1, s_2\}$, label set $\{a, b, c, d\}$, and where, for instance, $\xrightarrow{a} = \{(s_0, s_1), (s_0, s_2)\}$ (and $\xrightarrow{d} = \emptyset$). Usually we write $s \xrightarrow{a} s'$ instead of $(s, s') \in \xrightarrow{a}$.

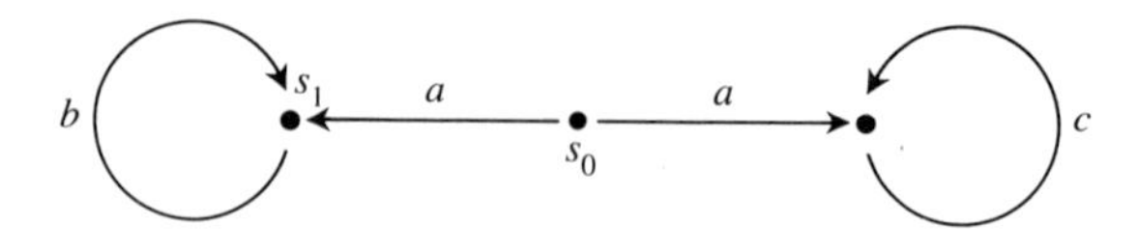

Fig. 1. A transition system where $\mathcal{L} = \{a, b, c, d\}$

Typically S is a set of states or configurations: states of a database, program states, states of knowledge, configurations of a machine and so on. Each relation $\xrightarrow{a}$ is a *transition* relation: $s \xrightarrow{a} s'$ represents that state s may become s' due to, or under the influence of, a which could be an action, a period of time, a person, or whatever. A transition system with label set $\mathcal{L}$ is said to have *sort* $\mathcal{L}$. Transition systems may carry further structure, as we note below. A useful extension is the inclusion of an initial state, commonly called a *rooted* transition system.

Figure 2 embodies the behaviour of a very elementary vending machine V. In state V either a 2p or 1p coin can be accepted, resulting in one of the states V_1 or V_2. Depending on which coin is accepted a *big* or *little* button may be depressed, and then an item may be collected. (Explicit representation of sort is omitted when it just consists of all the labels mentioned.)

Pictures of transition systems can become very large and unwieldy. It is therefore useful to have succinct presentations of them. A general technique for doing this is to have a language of expressions for states, together with rules for generating transitions. For instance, for the vending machine of Fig. 2 we could appeal to the language of CCS [Milner, 1989]:

$$V \stackrel{def}{=} 2p.V_1 + 1p.V_2 \qquad V_1 \stackrel{def}{=} big.V_3$$
$$V_2 \stackrel{def}{=} little.V_3 \qquad V_3 \stackrel{def}{=} collect.V$$

Employed here are some state constructors: $W \stackrel{def}{=} E$ declares the state constant W to be E; $a.E$ names a state whenever $a \in \mathcal{L}$ and E is a state; and $+$ is a binary state combinator. Their meanings are given by the following rules for generating transitions:

$$\frac{}{a.E \xrightarrow{a} E} \qquad \frac{E \xrightarrow{a} F}{W \xrightarrow{a} F}\ W \stackrel{def}{=} E \qquad \frac{E \xrightarrow{a} E'}{E + F \xrightarrow{a} E'} \qquad \frac{F \xrightarrow{a} F'}{E + F \xrightarrow{a} F'}$$

The definition rule, for instance, is to be understood as: if $E \xrightarrow{a} F$ and $W \stackrel{def}{=} E$ then also $W \xrightarrow{a} F$. These rules underpin the illustrated vending machine, justifying transitions such as $V \xrightarrow{2p} V_1$. A second example,

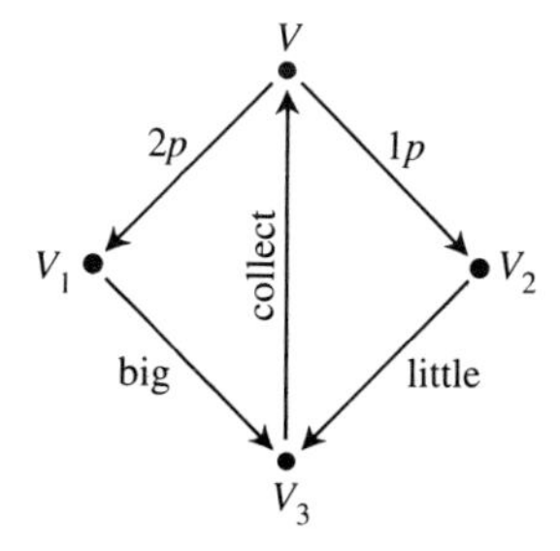

Fig. 2. A simple vending machine

presented in this expression and rule format, is an unbounded stack where $i \in \mathbb{N}$:

$$St_0 \stackrel{def}{=} empty.St_0 + push.St_1 \qquad St_{i+1} \stackrel{def}{=} pop.St_i + push.St_{i+2}$$

The previous examples appeal to a language of states together with rules for transitions. An alternative approach is to have a language of labels, and transition rules. Consider the family of while programs, defined by:

$$p ::= c \mid p_1; p_2 \mid \texttt{if}\ b\ \texttt{then}\ p_1\ \texttt{else}\ p_2 \mid \texttt{while}\ b\ \texttt{do}\ p$$

where c ranges over members of a family of elementary programs (such as assignments) and b over a family of boolean expressions. The meaning of these programs can be defined as a transition system whose states are memories, finite associations of program variables with values. The family of labels consists of the boolean expressions and all the programs. The transition relations are defined by rules, assuming first that the relations $\stackrel{c}{\longrightarrow}$ are given, and that $\stackrel{b}{\longrightarrow} = \{(M, M) \mid b \text{ is true at memory } M\}$. For instance we would expect that $M \stackrel{x:=x+1}{\longrightarrow} M'$ when M is the memory state $\{(x, 3), (y, 4)\}$ and M' is $\{(x, 4), (y, 4)\}$, and that $M' \stackrel{x=y}{\longrightarrow} M'$ whereas $M \stackrel{x \neq y}{\longrightarrow} M$. So $M \stackrel{c}{\longrightarrow} M'$ represents that an execution of basic command c in memory state M may terminate in the (possibly new) state M', and $M \stackrel{b}{\longrightarrow} M$ that the boolean expression may evaluate successfully to true in the program state M. Rules for the remaining labels (programs) are structurally defined:

$$\frac{M \stackrel{p}{\longrightarrow} M_1 \quad M_1 \stackrel{q}{\longrightarrow} M_2}{M \stackrel{p;q}{\longrightarrow} M_2}$$

$$\frac{M \stackrel{b}{\longrightarrow} M \quad M \stackrel{p_1}{\longrightarrow} M'}{M \stackrel{q}{\longrightarrow} M'} \; q = \texttt{if}\ b\ \texttt{then}\ p_1\ \texttt{else}\ p_2 \; \frac{M \stackrel{\neg b}{\longrightarrow} M \quad M \stackrel{p_2}{\longrightarrow} M'}{M \stackrel{q}{\longrightarrow} M'}$$

$$\frac{M \stackrel{b}{\longrightarrow} M \quad M \stackrel{p;q}{\longrightarrow} M'}{M \stackrel{q}{\longrightarrow} M'} \; q = \texttt{while}\ b\ \texttt{do}\ p \; \frac{M \stackrel{\neg b}{\longrightarrow} M}{M \stackrel{q}{\longrightarrow} M}$$

These rules capture the intended meaning of the constructors when $M \stackrel{p}{\longrightarrow} M'$ is understood as *an execution of program p in state M may terminate in state M'*.

Assume that the formulae Φ and Ψ express properties of memory states. The *modal* formula $[p]\Psi$ also describes a property: *Ψ holds after every execution of p*. This is true at state M if Ψ is true at each M' in the set

$\{M' \mid M \xrightarrow{p} M'\}$. More significantly, if $\Phi \rightarrow [p]\Psi$ (where $\rightarrow$ is implication) is true at every memory then program p is *partially correct* with respect to the precondition Φ and postcondition Ψ. This explicit association between the semantics of modal logic and the meaning of while programs was made by Pratt [Pratt, 1976]. Related work includes *algorithmic logic* [Salwicki, 1977], as well as the Floyd–Hoare *logic of partial correctness*, [Floyd, 1967; Hoare, 1969], and the *weakest precondition calculus* [Dijkstra, 1976]. Alternatively, if Φ expresses properties of states of the vending machine then the modal formula $[2p]\Phi$ expresses that Φ holds after every acceptance of $2p$: for instance, V_2 trivially has this property whereas V has it if V_1 has Φ. Modal formulae in this way can describe local capabilities of systems, a use of modal logic due to Hennessy and Milner [Hennessy and Milner, 1980; Hennessy and Milner, 1985].

Transition systems generalize Kripke structures introduced in the late 1950s [Kripke, 1959; Kripke, 1963], for interpreting modal, intuitionistic and later temporal logics. An important extension is *polymodal logics*, consisting of families of modalities $[a]$ for each $a \in \mathcal{L}$ instead of a single modality $[\ ]$. Polymodal logics are traditionally associated with logics of knowledge and belief, where $[a]\Phi$ is understood as *a knows or believes* Φ [Hintikka, 1962]: in a transition system representing belief or knowledge $s \xrightarrow{a} t$ symbolizes that a's knowledge or belief at state s is of t. The examples above suggest that polymodal logic can be applied naturally to understand (computational) activity and change. They also reveal the potential use of extra (computational) structure even at the level of propositional modal logics either in the set of labels, as an algebra of programs, or in the set of states, via a structured language of behaviours. In one case there is interest in the formal relationships between modalities such as $[p; q]$ and the modalities $[p]$ and $[q]$. In the other case there are questions about the relationship between modal properties of a structured state such as $E + F$ and the properties of its components, E and F.

1.2 Runs

For many crucial programs (including operating systems) termination is a catastrophe rather than an intended virtue. When p is such a program, the modality $[p]$ is ineffectual since there should not be memory states M and M' with the feature $M \xrightarrow{p} M'$. The vending machine provides another instance where termination is undesirable. More generally these are examples of *reactive* systems, whose behaviours may essentially depend on concurrent interaction with other systems (such as their users). Concurrency as a binary parallel operator $\|$ may be added to the language of states and also to the while language of labels. For instance, when E and F are states assume that $E \| F$ is their concurrent composition. Transition rules for $\|$ include the following interleaving rules:

$$\frac{E \xrightarrow{a} E'}{E \| F \xrightarrow{a} E' \| F} \qquad \frac{F \xrightarrow{a} F'}{E \| F \xrightarrow{a} E \| F'}.$$

There may also be synchronization rules. For instance, [Milner, 1989] associates with each label a a partner $\overline{a}$, and the performances of a and $\overline{a}$ together constitute a handshake synchronization.

The previous relational semantics of while programs as labels cannot cope with either perpetual programs that are not intended to terminate or with parallel programs: the relation $\xrightarrow{p\|q}$ is not definable solely from the relations $\xrightarrow{p}$ and $\xrightarrow{q}$. Knowledge of intermediate memory states is needed as the components may interact either by interfering or by cooperating with each other. As with the vending machine, a transition system semantics for these programs may be presented which only involves transitions for elementary actions instead of whole structured programs. By single stepping the transition relations in this way programs that are not intended to terminate are covered as is concurrent interaction.

Assume that $\|$ is added to the while language earlier. Again let c range over elementary programs which may now also include synchronization or communication primitives (such as await or channel input and output commands). The states of the transition system are now program and memory pairs (p, M), as well as pairs (ε, M) where ε is a new symbol representing the empty (or terminated) program. Labels are restricted to booleans and elementary programs. Initially part of the relations $\xrightarrow{c}$ and $\xrightarrow{b}$ are given. The assumed part of $\xrightarrow{c}$ relates pairs (c, M), (ε, M'): for instance we would expect that $(x := x + 1, M) \xrightarrow{x:=x+1} (\varepsilon, M')$ whenever $(x, n) \in M$ and $(x, n + 1) \in M'$. The given part of $\xrightarrow{b}$ is for `if` and `while` programs: if $p =$ `if` b `then` q_1 `else` q_2 and b is true at M then $(p, M) \xrightarrow{b} (q_1, M)$, otherwise $(p, M) \xrightarrow{\neg b} (q_2, M)$; similarly if $p =$ `while` b `do` q and b is true at M then $(p, M) \xrightarrow{b} (q; p, M)$, otherwise $(p, M) \xrightarrow{\neg b} (\varepsilon, M)$. Transitions from other composite programs and memories are defined by rules as follows assuming $\varepsilon; p = p$ and $\varepsilon \| p = p = p \| \varepsilon$, and that a ranges over b or c labels:

$$\frac{(p, M) \xrightarrow{a} (p', M')}{(p; q, M) \xrightarrow{a} (p'; q, M')}$$

$$\frac{(p, M) \xrightarrow{a} (p', M')}{(p \| q, M) \xrightarrow{a} (p' \| q, M')} \qquad \frac{(q, M) \xrightarrow{a} (q', M')}{(p \| q, M) \xrightarrow{a} (p \| q', M')}.$$

Again there may be extra synchronization or communication rules for $\|$.

Modal formulae such as $[c]\Phi$ and $[2p]\Psi$ express local properties of program memory pairs, or of structured states such as those of the vending machine. Less local properties expressing features of eventual evolution such as that a program may eventually terminate (reach ε) when initially at a memory state are also salient. A similar example is the following *responsiveness* property of the vending machine that whenever a 2p is accepted then eventually *collect* must happen. Crucial for both the while language and the vending machine is a *run* of a program or system, as a maximal length path through its transition system. For instance, a run of the concurrent program $p \parallel q$ when p is $\texttt{while}\ y \neq 0\ \texttt{do}\ x := x + 1$, and q is $y := 0$, and where (n, m) represents the memory $\{(x, n), (y, m)\}$, is

$$(p \parallel q, (0,1)) \stackrel{y\neq 0}{\longrightarrow} \ldots \stackrel{x:=x+1}{\longrightarrow} (p \parallel q, (n,1)) \stackrel{y:=0}{\longrightarrow} (p, (n,0)) \stackrel{\neg y\neq 0}{\longrightarrow} (\varepsilon, (n,0)).$$

And the following is a run of the vending machine: $V \stackrel{2p}{\longrightarrow} V_1 \stackrel{big}{\longrightarrow} V_3 \stackrel{collect}{\longrightarrow} V \stackrel{2p}{\longrightarrow} \ldots$.

Petri nets provide another kind of example. Associated with the net of figure 3 is a transition system whose state space is the set of markings, vectors of the form (k, m, n) representing that condition A has k tokens, B has m, and C has n. The transition relations (assuming that only one event happens at a time) are given by

$$\begin{aligned}(k+1, m, n) &\stackrel{a}{\longrightarrow} (k+1, m+1, n)\\ (k+1, m, n) &\stackrel{b}{\longrightarrow} (k, m, n+1)\\ (k, m+1, n+1) &\stackrel{c}{\longrightarrow} (k, m, n+1).\end{aligned}$$

A feature of any run from the initial state, the marking $(1,0,0)$, is that event c can happen only finitely often.

These properties of runs are expressible in temporal logics as developed by Prior, thereby providing a formal framework for describing and reasoning about change through time [Prior, 1957; Prior, 1967]. A variety of temporal operators (such as the eventually operator) specify how the truth of a formula at one time depends on the truth of subformulae at other times. Pnueli pioneered this use of temporal logics for describing and

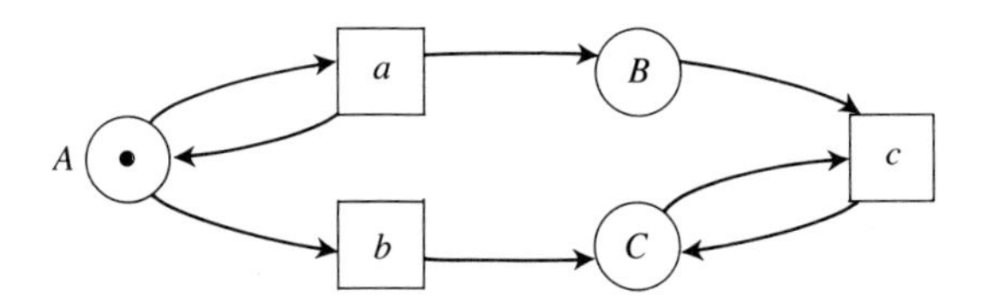

Fig. 3. A small Petri net

reasoning about the behaviour of concurrent, non-deterministic, or cyclic systems by linking the semantics of temporal logics and the semantics of such systems [Pnueli, 1977]. Precursors include uses of transition systems such as [Keller, 1976], the work on understanding cyclic programs, and applications of Büchi's sequential calculus.

Not every maximal length path through a transition system may count as a run. Fairness, or liveness assumptions, may preclude some. For instance, the following ω length run for the parallel program $p \parallel q$ defined earlier may be excluded on the ground that the component q does not contribute:

$$(p \parallel q, (0, 1)) \stackrel{y \neq 0}{\longrightarrow} \ldots \stackrel{x:=x+1}{\longrightarrow} (p \parallel q, (n, 1)) \stackrel{y \neq 0}{\longrightarrow} \ldots.$$

Focal structures for the temporal logics examined later are *extended* transition systems, containing an extra constituent which is a non-empty set of runs through its underlying transition system. For simplicity it is assumed that all paths in this constituent have ω length. This is guaranteed when the underlying transition system is *total*, in the sense that for every state s there is an s' and an a such that $s \stackrel{a}{\longrightarrow} s'$. Loops with an imaginary label can be grafted onto states with no transitions emanating from them to make a transition system total such as that for the concurrent while language.

Definition 1.2.1. An *extended* transition system is a pair $(\mathcal{T}, \mathcal{R})$ where $\mathcal{T}$ is a total transition system, and $\mathcal{R}$ is a non-empty set of runs through $\mathcal{T}$ with the property that every $s \in \mathcal{S}_{\mathcal{T}}$ occurs in some run.

Included here, for technical reasons, is that every state of the underlying transition system belongs to some run. More generally, the presupposition that a run has an initial state may be lifted, allowing it to take the form $\ldots s_i \stackrel{a_i}{\longrightarrow} s_{i+1} \stackrel{a_{i+1}}{\longrightarrow} \ldots$ with indices drawn from the integers—useful for interpreting *reverse* temporal operators such as *previously*. Extended transition systems may be presented diagrammatically, with a statement about which are the admissible runs, as in figure 4.

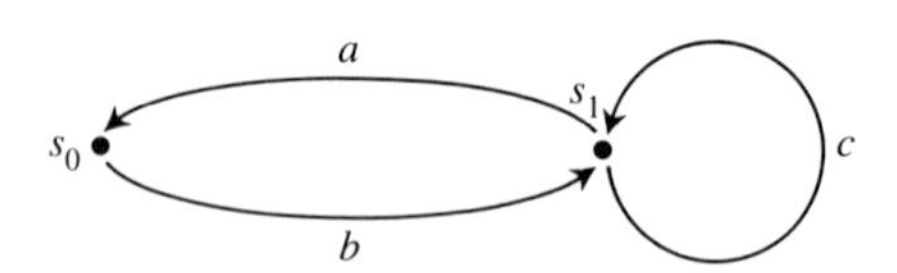

Fig. 4. Every run contains a finite number of c labels

1.3 Computational concerns

Transition systems model the behaviour of programs, and at the same time are models for modal and temporal logics. Showing that a program meets its specification expressed as a modal or temporal formula amounts to proving that the formula is true at a state (or set of states) or a set of runs in the transition system model of the program. One approach, advocated by Manna and Pnueli, is proof-theoretic [Manna and Pnueli, 1981]. They propose that the program via its model be coded as a theory (a set of temporal formulae) Γ. The required property should then follow from, be a temporal logic consequence of, Γ. A sound and complete axiomatization of valid formulae provides a framework wherein such deductions may be presented. This method views the transition system model of a program as secondary, to be dispensed with in favour of the theory Γ.

More direct methods of establishing relative truth, that a family of states or runs has a property, can be formalized using tableau techniques. Logically, these underpin *model checkers*, algorithms that automatically establish whether properties hold in finite state systems, as pioneered by [Clarke *et al.*, 1983], and [Quielle and Sifakis, 1981]. Deriving a program from a modal or temporal specification is more difficult. Formally it amounts to producing a transition system model wherein the formula is true at a state or a set of runs and then extracting a program from it. This is intimately related to the *satisfiability* problem of deciding whether a formula has a model. This approach to program synthesis is discussed in [Clarke and Emerson, 1981; Manna and Wolper, 1984]. An alternative, proposed in [Gabbay, 1989; Moszkowski, 1986], is to view temporal formulae not only as specifications but also as being executable. For instance the formula $F\Phi$ can be understood as the command *make* Φ *true in the future.*

Transition systems are also naturally rooted in language and automata theory. In this circumstance think of the relation $s \stackrel{a}{\longrightarrow} t$ as representing that s *accepts* a (and becomes t). Any grammar determines a transition system. For instance, in figure 5 any finite length run from the state labelled X contains a string of labels $a^n cb^n$. The language accepted by X is the set of these strings. Extended transition systems are produts of automata on infinite strings or infinite trees. Their runs, either as sets or

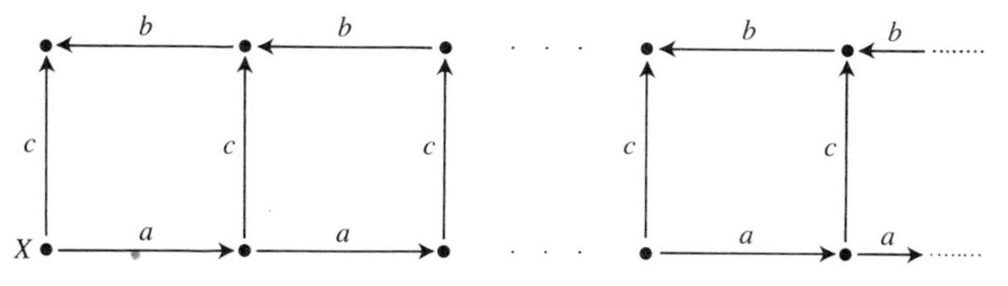

Fig. 5. The transition system generated by $X \Rightarrow aXb \quad X \Rightarrow c$

assembled instead into computation trees, fulfill the automata acceptance condition. Explicitly relating finite automata to modal and temporal logics has proved to be very fruitful, offering new insights into, and extensions of, these logics. As regular sequences of events are not first-order definable, and consequently not definable within traditional modal and temporal logics, this has provoked second-order propositional versions of these logics including extended temporal logic [Wolper, 1983], and the modal mu-calculus [Kozen, 1983]. Automata-theoretic methods for satisfiability and model checking have been employed. These appeal to translations of formulae into automata which are then tested for non-emptiness [Streett, 1982; Wolper *et al.*, 1983; Streett and Emerson, 1989].

A key feature of modal and temporal logics is that their basic definition of truth is *relativized* to a state or a run (of a transition system model). Less local notions of truth are then abstractions: for example, that program p has the temporal property Φ can be captured by the stipulation that Φ is true of every admissible run starting from p (in the model for p). So questions of verification and program synthesis raise new issues about exposing structure in these models. A clear example is compositionality : can techniques be developed that, for instance, associate properties of $p \parallel q$ with properties of its components? Such questions take seriously the binary structures involved: program structure and logical structure.

Transition system models of programs are overly concrete. Useful abstractions are therefore of interest. Especially relevant here is the work on process algebras [Bergstra and Klop, 1989; Hennessy, 1988; Milner, 1989] whose models are transition systems quotiented by equivalences (or preorders). Paramount is *bisimulation* equivalence [Park, 1981] which is much finer than language equivalence: not only is it a congruence for a very large class of process combinators, but also it is decidable on general families of infinite state transition systems generated from context free grammars [Baeten *et al.*, 1987]. This equivalence also has a simple modal (and temporal) logic *characterization*: two states of an image finite [1] transition system are equivalent iff they have the same modal properties [Hennessy and Milner, 1980].

Expressive power is a foundational logical concern bearing on practical issues. One immediate interest is whether a logic is able to (succinctly) capture a particular crucial property of a program. However notions of relevant program properties can themselves be guided by perspicuous formalisms. One very successful application of temporal logics is a general classification of program properties covering both concurrent and perpetual systems, see [Manna and Pnueli, 1989] for a survey.

This chapter presents a brief view of (classical) propositional modal

[1] A transition system is image finite if for each state s and label a the set $\{t \mid s \stackrel{a}{\longrightarrow} t\}$ is finite.

and temporal logics (and their second-order versions with fixed point operators). I have concentrated on those logics that have been used to describe properties of computational systems presented as transition systems, and the results outlined are just a selection from this active research area. For a more general perspective see [van Benthem, 1989; van Benthem, 1990], and for more details of the application of temporal logics to Computer Science see Kuiper [Barringer and Kuiper, 1991]. Besides the editors, I would like to thank Johan van Benthem, Julian Bradfield, Ed Clarke, Rance Cleaveland, Mads Dam, Hans Hüttel, Kim Larsen, Angelika Mader, Pawel Paczkowski, Amir Pnueli, Michael Siegel, Bernhard Steffen, Martin Steffen, Terry Stroup, Dirk Taubner, Wolfgang Thomas, David Walker, and Jeff Zucker for comments on previous versions of this survey, or discussions about topics covered in this work.

2 Propositional Modal Logics

2.1 Basics

The basic propositional modal language in abstract syntax form is

$$\Phi ::= Q \mid \neg\Phi \mid \Phi_1 \wedge \Phi_2 \mid [a]\Phi$$

where Q ranges over members of a family of atomic sentences, and a over labels belonging to a set $\mathcal{L}$. This definition just means that a formula is either an atomic sentence Q; a negated formula $\neg\Phi$; a conjunction of formulae $\Phi \wedge \Psi$; or a modalized formula $[a]\Phi$. Really the syntax specifies a family of languages parameterized by atomic sentences and labels. A modal language with labels drawn from $\mathcal{L}$ is said to have *sort* $\mathcal{L}$. This term is extended to formulae: the formula Φ has sort $\mathcal{L}$ if it belongs to a language of sort $\mathcal{L}$. Each modal language is an extension of classical propositional logic. Usual classical abbreviations for disjunction and implication apply: $\Phi \vee \Psi \stackrel{def}{=} \neg(\neg\Phi \wedge \neg\Psi)$; and $\Phi \rightarrow \Psi \stackrel{def}{=} \neg\Phi \vee \Psi$. Moreover, for each $a \in \mathcal{L}$ the dual of $[a]$ is the modal operator $\langle a \rangle$ (*diamond* a): that is, $\langle a \rangle\Phi \stackrel{def}{=} \neg[a]\neg\Phi$.

A modal language with sort $\mathcal{L}$ is interpreted on *transition systems* of sort $\mathcal{L}$. Recall from the Introduction, Definition 1.1.1, that these are structures $\mathcal{T}$ that are pairs $(\mathcal{S}, \{\stackrel{a}{\longrightarrow} \mid a \in \mathcal{L}\})$ where $\mathcal{S}$ is a set of states, $\mathcal{L}$ (the sort of $\mathcal{T}$) a set of labels, and $\stackrel{a}{\longrightarrow}$ for each $a \in \mathcal{L}$ is a binary relation on $\mathcal{S}$. As with propositional logic we also need to interpret the atomic sentences. So a *modal model* on the transition system $\mathcal{T}$ is a pair $\mathcal{M} = (\mathcal{T}, \mathcal{V})$ where $\mathcal{V}$ is a valuation which assigns to each atomic sentence Q a subset of the states of $\mathcal{T}$: the sentence Q is deemed to be true at each state $s \in \mathcal{V}(Q)$ under $\mathcal{M}$. Truth at state s of an arbitrary formula Φ under $\mathcal{M}$ is inductively defined using the notation $s \models_{\mathcal{M}} \Phi$. When Φ is not true at s under $\mathcal{M}$ we write $s \not\models_{\mathcal{M}} \Phi$:

$$\begin{array}{lll} s \models_{\mathcal{M}} Q & \text{iff} & s \in \mathcal{V}(Q) \\ s \models_{\mathcal{M}} \neg\Phi & \text{iff} & s \not\models_{\mathcal{M}} \Phi \\ s \models_{\mathcal{M}} \Phi \wedge \Psi & \text{iff} & s \models_{\mathcal{M}} \Phi \text{ and } s \models_{\mathcal{M}} \Psi \\ s \models_{\mathcal{M}} [a]\Phi & \text{iff} & \forall\, s'.\ \text{if } s \xrightarrow{a} s' \text{ then } s' \models_{\mathcal{M}} \Phi. \end{array}$$

In the final clause the quantifier $\forall s'$ ranges over $\mathcal{S}_{\mathcal{M}}$, the states of the model. (Commonly in the sequel this kind of implicit understanding is assumed to avoid burdensome notation.) The derived semantic clause for $\langle a \rangle$ is

$$s \models_{\mathcal{M}} \langle a \rangle \Phi \;\text{ iff }\; \exists s'.\ s \xrightarrow{a} s' \text{ and } s' \models_{\mathcal{M}} \Phi$$

The major difference with traditional modal logic as presented in [Hughes and Cresswell, 1973; Chellas, 1980; Bull and Segerberg, 1984] is the generalization to *families* of modalities, a feature exploited in some of the intended interpretations mentioned in the Introduction.

Example 2.1.1. Consider the transition system for the vending machine V presented in Section 1.1. Assume $\mathtt{tt}$ is an atomic formula expressing true, and $\mathcal{M}$ a modal model for V. Now $V \models_{\mathcal{M}} \langle 2p \rangle \mathtt{tt}$, that is V *can accept* $2p$. But a button can not yet be depressed (before money is deposited), so $V \models_{\mathcal{M}} [big]\neg\mathtt{tt} \wedge [little]\neg\mathtt{tt}$. V has more interesting properties too:

- $V \models_{\mathcal{M}} [2p]([little]\neg\mathtt{tt} \wedge \langle big \rangle \mathtt{tt})$: after $2p$ is deposited the *little* button can not be depressed whereas the *big* one can.
- $V \models_{\mathcal{M}} [1p][little]\langle collect \rangle \mathtt{tt}$: after $1p$ is entrusted, and then the *little* button is depressed, an item can be collected.

Similar properties could be defined for the stack of Section 1.1.

Example 2.1.2. The application of modal logic to the transition system for while programs in Section 1.1 has structured programs as labels. Transitions have the form $M \xrightarrow{p} M'$, representing that an execution of p in memory state M may terminate in state M'. The modal logic now contains modalities of the the form $[p]$, $\langle p \rangle$. Consider a family of atomic formulae of the form $x \leq t$ and $x \geq t$ where x is a variable and t an arithmetic term. Let $\mathcal{V}$ be a valuation which assigns to each atomic formula the set of memories (finite associations of variables and numbers) at which it is true. For instance $\mathcal{V}(x \leq 3) = \{M \mid (x, n) \in M \text{ and } n \leq 3\}$. In this case $\mathcal{V}$ is the *intended* valuation, and the resulting modal model the *intended* model.

An important kind of modal formula is $\Phi \rightarrow [p]\Psi$, called a *partial correctness* formula: M has this property (in $\mathcal{M}$) provided that if $M \models_{\mathcal{M}} \Phi$ and $M \xrightarrow{p} M'$ then $M' \models_{\mathcal{M}} \Psi$.

Verifying that the vending machine above has a modal property is a straightforward application of the inductive definition of truth at a state under a model. It is more difficult for partial correctness formulae where additional induction (on the data) may also be necessary: for instance, consider showing $M \models_{\mathcal{M}} z = n \wedge y = 1 \rightarrow [q]y = n!$, for any M when q is the program `while` $z \geq 0$ `do` $(y := z \times y; z := z - 1)$.

Expressiveness of the basic modal language can be increased by additional modalities. Natural candidates are the *reverse* operators $\overline{[a]}$ (and their duals $\overline{\langle a \rangle}$) for any label a.

$$s \models_{\mathcal{M}} \overline{[a]}\Phi \text{ iff } \forall s'. \text{ if } s' \xrightarrow{a} s \text{ then } s' \models_{\mathcal{M}} \Phi.$$

In the case of a while program p the formula $\overline{\langle p \rangle}\Phi$ expresses a property of running p backwards. Another useful extension when the label set $\mathcal{L}$ is infinite is to permit modalities $[J]$ for $J \subseteq \mathcal{L}$: $s \models_{\mathcal{M}} [J]\Phi$ iff for each s' and $a \in J$, if $s \xrightarrow{a} s'$ then $s' \models_{\mathcal{M}} \Phi$. In which case the unrelativized modality $[\,]$, which pays no attention to the labels, abbreviates $[\mathcal{L}]$.

Some standard notation and terminology which abstracts from truth at a state under a model is

Definition 2.1.3.

(a) Φ is $\mathcal{M}$-true, written $\models_{\mathcal{M}} \Phi$, if for all states s, $s \models_{\mathcal{M}} \Phi$,

(b) Φ is $\mathcal{T}$-valid, written $\models_{\mathcal{T}} \Phi$, if for all models $\mathcal{M}$ on $\mathcal{T}$, $\models_{\mathcal{M}} \Phi$,

(c) Φ is $\mathcal{T}$-satisfiable if for some $\mathcal{M}$ on $\mathcal{T}$ and state s, $s \models_{\mathcal{M}} \Phi$.

Implicit here is that formulae and transition systems have common sorts. There are numerous generalizations of these notions. One extension is the notion that Φ is $\mathcal{T}$*-valid at* s: $s \models_{\mathcal{T}} \Phi$ if for all models $\mathcal{M}$ on $\mathcal{T}$, $s \models_{\mathcal{M}} \Phi$. Another is the extension to sets of formulae Γ. The set Γ is $\mathcal{M}$*-true*, written either as $\models_{\mathcal{M}} \Gamma$ or $\mathcal{M} \models \Gamma$, if for every $\Phi \in \Gamma$, $\models_{\mathcal{M}} \Phi$. Similarly, Γ is $\mathcal{T}$*-valid*, again written as either $\mathcal{T} \models \Gamma$ or $\models_{\mathcal{T}} \Gamma$, if every formula in Γ is $\mathcal{T}$-valid. Moreover, we say that Γ is $\mathcal{T}$*-satisfiable* if every formula in Γ is simultaneously true at a state under a model on $\mathcal{T}$. A third generalization is to sets of models, or sets of transition systems Λ (of the appropriate sort). For instance, Φ is Λ-true if for all $\mathcal{M} \in \Lambda$, $\mathcal{M} \models \Phi$. These extensions may be taken together. An example is: Γ is Λ-valid (which holds if every formula in Γ is $\mathcal{T}$-valid for every $\mathcal{T} \in \Lambda$). Finally, when Λ is the family of all transition systems of an appropriate sort, it is dropped as an index from the terms Λ-valid and Λ-satisfiable: Φ of sort $\mathcal{L}$ is *valid* if it is $\mathcal{T}$-valid for every $\mathcal{T}$ of sort $\mathcal{L}$.

Example 2.1.4. When $\mathcal{M}$ is the intended modal model for while programs, $\models_{\mathcal{M}} \Phi \rightarrow [p]\Psi$ expresses that p is partially correct with respect to Φ and Ψ.

Example 2.1.5. Suppose $\mathcal{T}$ is the transition system for the vending machine V and $\mathcal{M}$ is the model $(\mathcal{T}, \mathcal{V})$ with $\mathcal{V}(Q) = \{V, V_3\}$. Then

$$\begin{array}{ll} V \models_{\mathcal{M}} [2p][big]Q \wedge [1p]\langle little\rangle Q & \models_{\mathcal{M}} [big]Q \\ V \models_{\mathcal{T}} Q \rightarrow [1p]\langle little\rangle[collect]Q & \models_{\mathcal{T}} \langle collect\rangle Q \rightarrow [collect]Q. \end{array}$$

It is usual to define semantic consequence relations between sets of formulae Γ and individual formulae Φ as $\Gamma \models \Phi$ meaning Φ *follows from* Γ. Various definitions of $\models$ are possible. Especially important, when Λ is a family of models, is the *global* consequence relation $\Vdash_{\Lambda}$ and its *local* version $\models_{\Lambda}$:

$$\begin{array}{lll} \Gamma \Vdash_{\Lambda} \Phi & \text{if} & \forall \mathcal{M} \in \Lambda.\ \text{if } \mathcal{M} \models \Gamma \text{ then } \mathcal{M} \models \Phi \\ \Gamma \models_{\Lambda} \Phi & \text{if} & \forall \mathcal{M} \in \Lambda.\ \forall s \in \mathcal{S}_{\mathcal{M}}.\ \text{if } s \models_{\mathcal{M}} \Gamma \text{ then } s \models_{\mathcal{M}} \Phi. \end{array}$$

(A similar pair can be defined when instead Λ is a family of transition systems.) Clearly, if $\Gamma \models_{\Lambda} \Phi$ then $\Gamma \Vdash_{\Lambda} \Phi$. But the converse fails. For instance let Λ be the family of models on the vending machine example above. Then $Q \Vdash_{\Lambda} [2p]Q$, but under the model $\mathcal{M}$ of the example $V \models_{\mathcal{M}} Q$ and $V \not\models_{\mathcal{M}} [2p]Q$.

2.2 Minimal modal logic

For each sort $\mathcal{L}$ the smallest modal logic, called $K_{\mathcal{L}}$, is the set of *valid* formulae (of sort $\mathcal{L}$):

$$K_{\mathcal{L}} \stackrel{def}{=} \{\Phi \mid \Phi \text{ has sort } \mathcal{L} \text{ and } \models \Phi\}.$$

$K_{\mathcal{L}}$ consists of all those formulae that are true at every state under every model on every transition system (of sort $\mathcal{L}$). An alternative characterization of $K_{\mathcal{L}}$ is the set of theorems of the following axiom system where a ranges over members of $\mathcal{L}$ (and Φ, Ψ over modal formulae):

Axioms	1. Any tautology instance
	2. $[a](\Phi \rightarrow \Psi) \rightarrow ([a]\Phi \rightarrow [a]\Psi)$
Rules	MP if Φ and $\Phi \rightarrow \Psi$ then Ψ
	Nec if Φ then $[a]\Phi$.

The rule Nec (necessitation) states that if Φ, the premise, then $[a]\Phi$, the conclusion. Φ is a *theorem* of this axiom system, written $\vdash \Phi$, if there is a *proof* of Φ, a finite sequence of formulae $\Phi_1, \ldots, \Phi_n$ where $\Phi = \Phi_n$ and Φ_i for all $i : 1 \leq i \leq n$ is either an axiom instance or the result of an application of a rule instance to premises contained in the set $\{\Phi_1, \ldots, \Phi_{i-1}\}$.

Example 2.2.1. $\vdash [2p](Q \wedge R) \rightarrow [2p]Q$

1. $Q \wedge R \rightarrow Q$	tautology instance
2. $[2p](Q \wedge R \rightarrow Q)$	Nec applied to 1
3. $[2p](Q \wedge R \rightarrow Q) \rightarrow ([2p](Q \wedge R) \rightarrow [2p]Q)$	axiom 2 instance
4. $[2p](Q \wedge R) \rightarrow [2p]Q$	MP applied to 2, 3.

For each sort, this axiom system is both sound and complete:

$$\begin{array}{ll} \text{Soundness :} & \text{if } \vdash \Phi \text{ then } \models \Phi \\ \text{Completeness :} & \text{if } \models \Phi \text{ then } \vdash \Phi. \end{array}$$

Soundness states that every provable formula is valid, and completeness that every valid formula is provable. So the set of theorems of this axiom system provide an alternative characterization of $K_{\mathcal{L}}$. Techniques for showing soundness and completeness of axiom systems are the topics of Section 6.

The axiom system for $K_{\mathcal{L}}$ supports local and global proof-theoretic consequence relations (correlates of $\models$ and $\Vert\!\models$). The formula Φ follows from the set of *assumptions* Γ, written $\Gamma \vdash \Phi$, if there is a finite sequence of formulae $\Phi_1, \ldots, \Phi_n$ with $\Phi = \Phi_n$, and where each Φ_i is either an axiom instance; or a member of Γ; or the result of MP applied to premises contained in $\{\Phi_1, \ldots, \Phi_{i-1}\}$; or, finally, the result of an application of Nec to a *theorem* in $\{\Phi_1, \ldots, \Phi_{i-1}\}$. Restricting the permissible application of Nec precludes derivations of $\Phi \vdash [a]\Phi$ (when Φ is not a theorem). This constraint on the application of Nec is relaxed in the definition of $\Gamma \Vdash \Phi$ which otherwise is the same. For $\Gamma \Vdash \Phi$ is to be understood differently as: Φ follows from the (extra) family of *axiom instances* Γ. As Φ is an extra axiom instance, $\Phi \Vdash [a]\Phi$. A consequence of this is that the deduction theorem holds for the local, but not the global, relation:

$$\Gamma, \Phi \vdash \Psi \quad \text{iff} \quad \Gamma \vdash \Phi \rightarrow \Psi.$$

Strong soundness and completeness of the axiom system for $K_{\mathcal{L}}$ is given by the next result, which is proved in Section 6.2.

Proposition 2.2.2. $\Gamma \vdash \Phi$ *iff* $\Gamma \models \Phi$

In general, this proposition fails for the global relations $\Vdash$ and $\Vert\!\models$, an example is presented later.

An alternative presentation of the local consequence relation for $K_{\mathcal{L}}$ is as a Gentzen system. Assume the usual Gentzen rules for classical propositional logic centred on the sequent $\Gamma \vdash \Phi$. There is just one extra rule for modalities:

$$\frac{\Gamma \vdash \Phi}{\{[a]\Psi \mid \Psi \in \Gamma\} \vdash [a]\Phi}.$$

Surprisingly, there is no elimination rule for $[a]$. This is also a strongly sound and complete presentation of $K_{\mathcal{L}}$.

Wherever possible in the sequel the notion of sort is dropped, so we speak of the logic K rather than the family $K_{\mathcal{L}}$. Also we shall often index $\vdash$ with the name of a particular axiom system: $\vdash_J \Phi$ or $J \vdash \Phi$ abbreviates that Φ is a theorem of the system J.

Let $\overline{K}$ be the richer family of valid formulae drawn from the modal language which also includes the reverse modalities $\overline{[a]}$. A simple extension of the axiom system for K, employing the following extra axioms and rules completely characterizes this set:

$$\begin{array}{ll} \text{Axioms}: & 3.\ \overline{[a]}(\Phi \rightarrow \Psi) \rightarrow (\overline{[a]}\Phi \rightarrow \overline{[a]}\Psi) \\ & 4.\ \Phi \rightarrow [a]\overline{\langle a \rangle}\Phi \\ & 5.\ \Phi \rightarrow \overline{[a]}\langle a \rangle\Phi \\ \text{Rule} & \overline{\text{Nec}}\ \text{if}\ \Phi\ \text{then}\ \overline{[a]}\Phi. \end{array}$$

The two schemas 4 and 5 relate the forwards and backwards modalities. The notion of a proof of Φ is suitably amended to take account of the additional axioms and rule.

2.3 Correspondence and incompleteness

Families of transition systems can be classified by the properties of their transition relations. A notable case is the transition system for while programs where, for instance, the relation $\stackrel{p;q}{\longrightarrow}$ is defined from the pair $\stackrel{p}{\longrightarrow}$ and $\stackrel{q}{\longrightarrow}$. Other cases include (traditional) temporal structures whose transition relations are orderings. A simpler example is the following family: $\Lambda_0 \stackrel{def}{=} \{\mathcal{T} \mid \stackrel{2p}{\longrightarrow}$ is transitive in $\mathcal{T}\}$. That is, each $\mathcal{T}$ in Λ_0 has the feature that if $s \stackrel{2p}{\longrightarrow} s_1$ and $s_1 \stackrel{2p}{\longrightarrow} s_2$ then also $s \stackrel{2p}{\longrightarrow} s_2$. One task is to examine the resultant logics, the sets of Λ-valid formulae for such families Λ. These sets always contain K, minimal modal logic (of the appropriate sort). Sometimes these logics can also be characterized by the theorems of a finite axiom system. It is then usual to name them as $KA_1 \ldots A_n$, where $A_1 \ldots A_n$ are the additional axiom schemas.

Transition systems can also be categorized by the individual modal schemas that they validate. A straightforward instance is the family

$$\Lambda_1 \stackrel{def}{=} \{\mathcal{T} \mid \mathcal{T} \models [2p]\Phi \rightarrow [2p][2p]\Phi\}.$$

So a transition system $\mathcal{T}$ belongs to Λ_1 if $[2p]\Phi \rightarrow [2p][2p]\Phi$ is $\mathcal{T}$-valid (for every instance of Φ).

A pertinent inquiry is to discover how far these two classification methods coincide. For example, the two sets Λ_0 and Λ_1 are the *same* despite their very distinct definitions. That is, for any transition system $\mathcal{T}$ (whose sort includes $2p$):

$$\mathcal{T} \models [2p]\Phi \rightarrow [2p][2p]\Phi \text{ iff } \stackrel{2p}{\longrightarrow} \text{ is transitive in } \mathcal{T}.$$

A proof of this follows from the general *correspondence* theorem below relating validity of schemas and conditions on transition relations.

Derived transition relations labelled by words belonging to the language $\mathcal{L}^*$ can be simply defined. Assuming ε is the empty word and aw is the word whose first letter is a (in $\mathcal{L}$) and $w \in \mathcal{L}^*$ is the remainder, then

$$\begin{array}{l} s \stackrel{\varepsilon}{\longrightarrow} s \\ s \stackrel{aw}{\longrightarrow} s' \text{ iff } \exists\, s_1.\ s \stackrel{a}{\longrightarrow} s_1 \text{ and } s_1 \stackrel{w}{\longrightarrow} s'. \end{array}$$

Let $C(v, w', w, v')$ be the following condition on a transition system of sort $\mathcal{L}$ (where $v, w', w, v' \in \mathcal{L}^*$):

$$\text{if } s \stackrel{v}{\longrightarrow} s_1 \text{ and } s \stackrel{w}{\longrightarrow} s_2 \text{ then } \exists s'.\ s_1 \stackrel{w'}{\longrightarrow} s' \text{ and } s_2 \stackrel{v'}{\longrightarrow} s'.$$

This is a convergence (or Church–Rosser) condition on transition systems. Here are four examples:

- $C(\varepsilon, 2p, 2p2p, \varepsilon)$: $\stackrel{2p}{\longrightarrow}$ is transitive
- $C(a, \varepsilon, a, \varepsilon)$: $\stackrel{a}{\longrightarrow}$ is *monogenic*, if $s \stackrel{a}{\longrightarrow} s_1$ and $s \stackrel{a}{\longrightarrow} s_2$ then $s_1 = s_2$
- $C(\varepsilon, a, \varepsilon, \varepsilon)$: $\stackrel{a}{\longrightarrow}$ is reflexive
- $C(a, a, \varepsilon, \varepsilon)$: $\stackrel{a}{\longrightarrow}$ is symmetric.

An interesting case arising in concurrency is $C(a, b, b, a)$, a diamond property when events a and b are causally independent. More complex conditions such as $C(a^k, b^l, c^m, d^n)$ for $k, l, m, n \in \mathbb{N}$ are covered too.

Derived modalities, indexed by words in $\mathcal{L}^*$, are definable as expected: $[\varepsilon]\Phi \stackrel{def}{=} \Phi$; $[aw]\Phi \stackrel{def}{=} [a][w]\Phi$; $\langle\varepsilon\rangle\Phi \stackrel{def}{=} \Phi$; and $\langle aw\rangle\Phi \stackrel{def}{=} \langle a\rangle\langle w\rangle\Phi$. Clearly, the modalities $[w]$, $\langle w\rangle$ receive their intended interpretation relative to the derived transition relations $\stackrel{w}{\longrightarrow}$:

$$s \models_{\mathcal{M}} [w]\Phi \quad \text{iff} \quad \forall\, s'.\ \text{if } s \xrightarrow{w} s' \text{ then } s' \models_{\mathcal{M}} \Phi$$
$$s \models_{\mathcal{M}} \langle w\rangle\Phi \quad \text{iff} \quad \exists s'.\ s \xrightarrow{w} s' \text{ and } s' \models_{\mathcal{M}} \Phi.$$

The following is a general correspondence result, based on [Lemmon, 1977].

Theorem 2.3.1. *$\mathcal{T} \models \langle v\rangle[w']\Phi \to [w]\langle v'\rangle\Phi$ iff $\mathcal{T}$ satisfies the condition $C(v, w', w, v')$.*

Proof. Suppose $\langle v\rangle[w']\Phi \to [w]\langle v'\rangle\Phi$ for every Φ is $\mathcal{T}$-valid. Assume $s \xrightarrow{v} s_1$ and $s \xrightarrow{w} s_2$. So we need to show $s_1 \xrightarrow{w'} s'$ and $s_2 \xrightarrow{v'} s'$ for some s'. Let $\mathcal{M}$ be a modal model on $\mathcal{T}$ with valuation $\mathcal{V}$ having the feature $\mathcal{V}(Q) = \{t \mid s_1 \xrightarrow{w'} t\}$. We know $s \models_{\mathcal{M}} \langle v\rangle[w']Q \to [w]\langle v'\rangle Q$. By definition of $\mathcal{V}$, $s_1 \models_{\mathcal{M}} [w']Q$. Since $s \xrightarrow{v} s_1$, $s \models_{\mathcal{M}} \langle v\rangle[w']Q$. Therefore s also has the property $[w]\langle v'\rangle Q$ under $\mathcal{M}$. But $s \xrightarrow{w} s_2$ and so $s_2 \models_{\mathcal{M}} \langle v'\rangle Q$. That is, for some s', $s_2 \xrightarrow{v'} s'$ and $s' \models_{\mathcal{M}} Q$: but then by definition of $\mathcal{V}(Q)$, $s_1 \xrightarrow{w'} s'$. Suppose $\mathcal{T}$ has the property $C(v, w', w, v')$. To show $\mathcal{T} \models \langle v\rangle[w']\Phi \to [w]\langle v'\rangle\Phi$ consider any model $\mathcal{M}$ on $\mathcal{T}$ and any state s. Suppose $s \models_{\mathcal{M}} \langle v\rangle[w']\Phi$, then we need to show $s \models_{\mathcal{M}} [w]\langle v'\rangle\Phi$. Assume $s \xrightarrow{w} s_2$. Because $s \models_{\mathcal{M}} \langle v\rangle[w']\Phi$ for some s_1, $s \xrightarrow{v} s_1$ and $s_1 \models_{\mathcal{M}} [w']\Phi$. However, by the condition $C(v, w', w, v')$ there is an s' with the features $s_1 \xrightarrow{w'} s'$ and $s_2 \xrightarrow{v'} s'$. As $s_1 \models_{\mathcal{M}} [w']\Phi$ then $s' \models_{\mathcal{M}} \Phi$. Finally because $s_2 \xrightarrow{v'} s'$, $s_2 \models_{\mathcal{M}} \langle v'\rangle\Phi$. ∎

Consider the four examples earlier:

- $[2p]\Phi \to [2p][2p]\Phi$ corresponds to transitivity of $\xrightarrow{2p}$
- $\langle a\rangle\Phi \to [a]\Phi$ corresponds to monogenicity of $\xrightarrow{a}$
- $[a]\Phi \to \Phi$ corresponds to reflexivity of $\xrightarrow{a}$
- $\langle a\rangle[a]\Phi \to \Phi$ corresponds to symmetry of $\xrightarrow{a}$

The concurrency case is given by $\langle a\rangle[b]\Phi \to [b]\langle a\rangle\Phi$.

There are many examples of correspondence results that are not covered by the previous theorem. The relation $\xrightarrow{a}$ is *connected* (in $\mathcal{T}$) if whenever $s \xrightarrow{a} s_1$ and $s \xrightarrow{a} s_2$ then either $s_1 \xrightarrow{a} s_2$ or $s_2 \xrightarrow{a} s_1$. The modal schema that corresponds to this condition is

$$[a]([a]\Phi \to \Psi) \vee [a]([a]\Psi \to \Phi).$$

A further example, this time of a property which is not definable within the first-order theory of transition systems, is (a relativized version of) Löb's axiom, $[a]([a]\Phi \to \Phi) \to [a]\Phi$. This corresponds to the condition that $\xrightarrow{a}$ is transitive and that there are no a^ω paths, sequences of the form $s_0 \xrightarrow{a} s_1 \xrightarrow{a} \dots \xrightarrow{a} s_i \xrightarrow{a} \dots$. Another interesting second-order case is that the relation $\xrightarrow{a}$ is the *reflexive* and *transitive* closure of $\xrightarrow{b}$:

$$s \xrightarrow{a} s' \text{ iff } \exists w \in \{b\}^*.\ s \xrightarrow{w} s'$$

which corresponds to the following schema Ψ:

$$([a]\Phi \to (\Phi \wedge [b][a]\Phi)) \wedge ([a](\Phi \to [b]\Phi) \to (\Phi \to [a]\Phi))$$

Lemma 2.3.2. *$\mathcal{T} \models \Psi$ iff $\xrightarrow{a}$ is the reflexive and transitive closure of $\xrightarrow{b}$ in $\mathcal{T}$.*

Proof. Suppose $\mathcal{T} \models \Psi$ and $s \xrightarrow{a} s'$. Then we need to show $s \xrightarrow{w} s'$ for some $w \in \{b\}^*$. Let $\mathcal{M}$ be the model on $\mathcal{T}$ with $\mathcal{V}(Q) = \{t \mid s \xrightarrow{w} t \text{ and } w \in \{b\}^*\}$. By validity of Ψ, $s \models_{\mathcal{M}} [a](Q \to [b]Q) \to (Q \to [a]Q)$. A small argument shows $s \models_{\mathcal{M}} [a](Q \to [b]Q)$. Consequently $s \models_{\mathcal{M}} Q \to [a]Q$. Since $s \xrightarrow{\varepsilon} s$ it follows that $s \models_{\mathcal{M}} Q$, and so also $s \models_{\mathcal{M}} [a]Q$. Since $s \xrightarrow{a} s'$ this means $s' \models_{\mathcal{M}} Q$, but then $s \xrightarrow{w} s'$ for some $w \in \{b\}^*$ as required. Again suppose $\mathcal{T} \models \Psi$ and now $s \xrightarrow{w} s'$ for some $w \in \{b\}^*$. Then we need to show $s \xrightarrow{a} s'$. Let $\mathcal{M}$ be the model on $\mathcal{T}$ with $\mathcal{V}(Q) = \{t \mid s \xrightarrow{a} t\}$. By definition $s \models_{\mathcal{M}} [a]Q$. From the validity of Ψ, $s \models_{\mathcal{M}} [a]Q \to (Q \wedge [b][a]Q)$. So $s \models_{\mathcal{M}} Q \wedge [b][a]Q$. A simple argument shows that if $s \xrightarrow{b} s_1 \xrightarrow{b} \dots \xrightarrow{b} s_n$ then for each $i : 1 \leq i \leq n$, $s_i \models_{\mathcal{M}} Q \wedge [b][a]Q$. But we know that $s \xrightarrow{w} s'$ for some $w \in \{b\}^*$. Hence $s' \models_{\mathcal{M}} Q$, and so $s \xrightarrow{a} s'$. The other half of the proof is left as an exercise. ∎

This example has applications in epistemic logic when [a] means *it is common knowledge that* and [b] *it is known that*; in dynamic logic when the labels are programs and a is just b^*, in temporal logic when [a] means *now or later (eventually)* and [b] means *at the very next moment*. Many other cases of correspondence (for the unrelativized) modalities can be found in [van Benthem, 1984].

Sound and complete axiom systems are also supported by Theorem 2.3.1. Let $G(v, w', w, v')$ be the schema $\langle v\rangle[w']\Phi \rightarrow [w]\langle v'\rangle\Phi$. The axiom system $KG(v, w', w, v')$ characterizes the set of formulae that are $\Lambda(v, w', w, v')$-valid when $\Lambda(v, w', w, v')$ is the family of transition systems with the property $C(v, w', w, v')$. This result, Proposition 2.3.3, is proved in Section 6.2.

Proposition 2.3.3. $\Lambda(v, w', w, v') \models \Phi$ *iff* $KG(v, w', w, v') \vdash \Phi$.

Strong soundness and completeness hold here too. A similar result (but not for strong completeness) is also supported by Lemma 2.3.2, as we note later when examining dynamic logic.

A sound and complete axiom system for Λ-validity does not imply that the family is modally definable. For instance, the axiom system K is also a sound and complete axiomatization of Λ-validity when Λ is restricted to the family of models with irreflexive transition relations, or when Λ is restricted to the set of image finite transition systems. This shows that irreflexivity and image finiteness are not by themselves modally definable: see [van Benthem, 1983; van Benthem, 1984] for details of which conditions are so definable, and [Koymans, 1989] for a slight extension of modal logic with a difference operator which permits irreflexivity (and other conditions) to be defined.

More surprising is that if Φ corresponds to the condition C then this does not guarantee that $K\Phi$ completely axiomatizes Λ-validity, when Λ consists of just the transition systems with the property C. An example from [van Benthem, 1984] is provided by the following schema Ψ:

$$([a]\Phi \rightarrow \Phi) \wedge ([a]\langle a\rangle\Phi \rightarrow \langle a\rangle[a]\Phi) \wedge (((\langle a\rangle\Phi \wedge [a](\Phi \rightarrow [a]\Phi)) \rightarrow \Phi)$$

which defines the condition: $s \xrightarrow{a} s'$ iff $s = s'$. Let Λ be the family of transition systems having this property. At a first glance it would seem reasonable to conclude that the axiom system $K\Psi$ characterizes the set of Λ-valid formulae. But the formula $\Phi \leftrightarrow [a]\Phi$ which also corresponds to this condition is not derivable in $K\Psi$. The system $K\Psi$ is, therefore, *incomplete.* The problem is the second-order nature of the global consequence relation, $\Vdash$. For a sound and completeness axiomatization of Λ-validity must be able to deliver as theorems all formulae in the set $\{\Phi \mid \Gamma \Vdash \Phi\}$, where Γ is the set of all instances of Ψ.

2.4 Dynamic logic

Dynamic logic, introduced by [Pratt, 1976] was the first explicitly developed modal logic of programs. Our interest is *propositional* dynamic logic due to [Fischer and Ladner, 1979]. A *dynamic* transition system has as label set a Kleene algebra of the form $\mathcal{L} = (\mathcal{L}, ; , \cup, ^*)$. The labels are closed under the binary operations ; (sequential composition) and $\cup$ (choice), and under the unary operation * (iteration). Their intended meanings are given by imposing closure conditions on the transition relations of a dynamic system. Sequentially composed labels obey the condition: $s \stackrel{a;b}{\longrightarrow} t$ iff $s \stackrel{ab}{\longrightarrow} t$. Corresponding to this condition (in the sense of the previous section) is the schema D1 below. Labels combined by choice satisfy the following requirement: $s \stackrel{a\cup b}{\longrightarrow} t$ iff $s \stackrel{a}{\longrightarrow} t$ or $s \stackrel{b}{\longrightarrow} t$ which corresponds to D2. Thirdly, $\stackrel{a^*}{\longrightarrow}$ is the reflexive and transitive closure of $\stackrel{a}{\longrightarrow}$, a condition we have met before. We divide the corresponding schema (Lemma 2.3.2) into two, D3 and D4. The second of these is an induction schema. Dynamic logic is usually presented with a further set of labels (programs), tests: programs of the form $\Phi?$ where Φ is a formula (which may be restricted so as not to involve modalities). The transition relation $\stackrel{\Phi?}{\longrightarrow}$ is model dependent: $s \stackrel{\Phi?}{\longrightarrow} s$ iff $s \models_{\mathcal{M}} \Phi$ (where $\mathcal{M}$ is the dynamic model). Nevertheless D5 corresponds to this condition.

$$\begin{array}{ll}
\text{D1.} & [a;b]\Phi \leftrightarrow [a][b]\Phi \\
\text{D2.} & [a\cup b]\Phi \leftrightarrow [a]\Phi \wedge [b]\Phi \\
\text{D3.} & [a^*]\Phi \rightarrow (\Phi \wedge [a][a^*]\Phi) \\
\text{D4.} & [a^*](\Phi \rightarrow [a]\Phi) \rightarrow (\Phi \rightarrow [a^*]\Phi) \\
\text{D5.} & [\Phi?]\Psi \leftrightarrow (\Phi \rightarrow \Psi).
\end{array}$$

Propositional dynamic logic, PDL, is the set of formulae which are true in every dynamic model (of the appropriate sort). When arbitrary modal formulae can be tests then the notion of sort is defined by mutual recursion (on formulae and labels). Let Λ be the family of dynamic models. The axiom system KD1–D5 is a sound and complete axiomatization of PDL.

Proposition 2.4.1. $KD1 - D5 \vdash \Phi$ *iff* $\Lambda \models \Phi$

A proof of this result, due to [Kozen and Parikh, 1981], is presented in Section 6.2. Strong completeness fails because of the second-order nature of the axioms D3 and D4. For instance, let Γ be the set of formulae $\{[a]^n Q \mid n \geq 0\}$. Although $\Gamma \models [a^*]Q$ it is not the case that $\Gamma \vdash [a^*]Q$.

The set of labels in a dynamic model can be thought of as the set of regular expressions generated by the atomic labels (and the tests $\Phi?$). They correspond to iterative or flowchart program schemes. For instance, the conditional and while schemes are expressed as

$$\begin{array}{lcl}
\texttt{if } \Phi \texttt{ then } a \texttt{ else } b & \stackrel{def}{=} & (\Phi?;a)\cup(\neg\Phi?;b) \\
\texttt{while } \Phi \texttt{ do } a & \stackrel{def}{=} & (\Phi?;a)^*;\neg\Phi?
\end{array}$$

One use is to show soundness of Hoare logic rules for while programs, as the following are derived rules of dynamic logic:

if $\Phi \rightarrow [a]\Phi'$ and $\Phi' \rightarrow [b]\Psi$ then $\Phi \rightarrow [a;b]\Psi$
if $\Phi \wedge \Psi \rightarrow [a]\Phi'$ and $\Phi \wedge \neg\Psi \rightarrow [b]\Phi'$ then $\Phi \rightarrow [\texttt{if}\ \Psi\ \texttt{then}\ a\ \texttt{else}\ b]\Phi'$
if $\Phi \wedge \Psi \rightarrow [a]\Phi$ then $\Phi \rightarrow [\texttt{while}\ \Psi\ \texttt{do}\ a](\Phi \wedge \neg\Psi)$

Using Theorem 2.3.1 further model conditions can be imposed. One example is deterministic dynamic logic, where each $\xrightarrow{a}$, when a is atomic, is monogenic. This condition, as we saw, corresponds to the schema $\langle a\rangle\Phi \rightarrow [a]\Phi$ (with a atomic). Moreover adding it to KD1–D5 results in an axiom system which characterizes validity with respect to deterministic dynamic systems [Ben-Ari *et al.*, 1982].

Various enrichments of the label set have been studied. A curious example is the inclusion of the binary operator $\cap$ obeying the condition:

$$s \xrightarrow{a \cap b} t \text{ iff } s \xrightarrow{a} t \text{ and } s \xrightarrow{b} t$$

Now irreflexivity of $\xrightarrow{a}$ is definable by the formula $[a \cap \texttt{tt}?]\texttt{ff}$. Moreover, the following formula

$$[a^*](\langle a\rangle\texttt{tt} \wedge [(a^*; a) \cap \texttt{tt}?]\texttt{ff})$$

is only satisfiable in an infinite dynamic model—if there is an a^ω run passing through distinct states. This modal logic, therefore, fails to have the small model property (see Section 2.6).

Other enrichments of the label sets are known to yield undecidable dynamic logics. One such example is the addition of complement, $-$, fulfilling the requirement: $s \xrightarrow{-a} t$ iff not$(s \xrightarrow{a} t)$. Alternatively, the label set can be expanded to correspond to recursive procedures involving mutual calls of each other, given by the context-free languages over the atomic labels and tests. For a detailed survey of dynamic logics see [Harel, 1984].

2.5 Modal algebras

Useful in the case of a while program p and a postcondition Ψ is the set of memories $\{M \mid M \models_{\mathcal{M}} [p]\Psi\}$ when $\mathcal{M}$ is the intended model. This consists of all those memories with respect to which if p is executed then it can not terminate at a memory failing Ψ. More generally, for any modal model $\mathcal{M}$ and formula Φ we can define the set $\{s \mid s \models_{\mathcal{M}} \Phi\}$ containing all the states at which Φ is true.

An alternative presentation of the meaning of modal formulas is to define the sets $\{s \mid s \models_{\mathcal{M}} \Phi\}$ directly by induction on the structure of Φ. This we now do, using the notation $\| \Phi \|_{\mathcal{V}}^{\mathcal{T}}$ to denote this set when $(\mathcal{T}, \mathcal{V})$ is the model. We drop the index $\mathcal{T}$ which we may assume is fixed:

$$
\begin{array}{lcl}
\| Q \|_{\mathcal{V}} & = & \mathcal{V}(Q) \\
\| \neg\Phi \|_{\mathcal{V}} & = & \mathcal{S}_{\mathcal{T}} - \| \Phi \|_{\mathcal{V}} \\
\| \Phi \wedge \Psi \|_{\mathcal{V}} & = & \| \Phi \|_{\mathcal{V}} \cap \| \Psi \|_{\mathcal{V}} \\
\| [a]\Phi \|_{\mathcal{V}} & = & \| [a] \|^{\mathcal{T}} \; \| \Phi \|_{\mathcal{V}} .
\end{array}
$$

Here $\| [a] \|^{\mathcal{T}}$ transforms any set $\mathcal{S}' \subseteq \mathcal{S}_{\mathcal{T}}$ into the set $\| [a] \|^{\mathcal{T}} \; \mathcal{S}' = \{s \mid \forall s' \in \mathcal{S}_{\mathcal{T}}.$ if $s \stackrel{a}{\longrightarrow} s'$ then $s' \in \mathcal{S}'\}$, the *weakest liberal precondition* of $\mathcal{S}'$ with respect to a. Derived operators have their expected meanings. In particular associated with $\langle a \rangle$ is the state transformer $\| \langle a \rangle \|^{\mathcal{T}}$ defined by $\| \langle a \rangle \|^{\mathcal{T}} \; \mathcal{S}' = \{s \mid \exists s' \in \mathcal{S}'. \; s \stackrel{a}{\longrightarrow} s'\}$. Clearly, the two semantic definitions of the modal language agree, $s \models_{\mathcal{M}} \Phi$ iff $s \in \| \Phi \|^{\mathcal{T}}_{\mathcal{V}}$ when $\mathcal{M}$ is $(\mathcal{T}, \mathcal{V})$. A simple consequence is that Φ is $\mathcal{M}$-true when the set $\| \Phi \|^{\mathcal{T}}_{\mathcal{V}}$ is the full state space $\mathcal{S}_{\mathcal{T}}$.

A set of states $\| \Phi \|^{\mathcal{T}}_{\mathcal{V}}$ can be regarded as a *modal property*, a demarcation of the state space into two, those with and those without the property Φ. Modal properties form a boolean algebra, as they are closed under the operations of complementation and intersection, and obey the usual boolean axioms. The unit is the full state space while its complement, the zero, is the empty set. However, properties are also closed under the operations $\| [a] \|^{\mathcal{T}}$ which obey the healthiness conditions:

$$
\| [a] \|^{\mathcal{T}} \; \mathcal{S}_{\mathcal{T}} = \mathcal{S}_{\mathcal{T}} \qquad \| [a] \|^{\mathcal{T}} \; (\mathcal{S}_1 \cap \mathcal{S}_2) = \| [a] \|^{\mathcal{T}} \; \mathcal{S}_1 \cap \| [a] \|^{\mathcal{T}} \; \mathcal{S}_2
$$

In turn $\| \langle a \rangle \|^{\mathcal{T}}$ complies with the dual conditions: $\| \langle a \rangle \|^{\mathcal{T}} \; \emptyset = \emptyset$ and $\| \langle a \rangle \|^{\mathcal{T}} \; (\mathcal{S}_1 \cup \mathcal{S}_2) = \| \langle a \rangle \|^{\mathcal{T}} \; \mathcal{S}_1 \cup \| \langle a \rangle \|^{\mathcal{T}} \; \mathcal{S}_2$.

Moreover, the state transformers $\| [a] \|^{\mathcal{T}}$ (and $\| \langle a \rangle \|^{\mathcal{T}}$) are *monotonic* with respect to the subset ordering on state sets: if $\mathcal{S}_1 \subseteq \mathcal{S}_2$ then $\| [a] \|^{\mathcal{T}} \; \mathcal{S}_1 \subseteq \| [a] \|^{\mathcal{T}} \; \mathcal{S}_2$. Also pertinent is under what conditions these transformers are continuous. An indexed non-empty family of state sets $\{\mathcal{S}_i \mid i \in I\}$ is *directed* if for every $j, k \in I$ $\mathcal{S}_j \cup \mathcal{S}_k \subseteq \mathcal{S}_i$ for some $i \in I$. Then $\| [a] \|^{\mathcal{T}}$ is *continuous* if for any directed family of subsets of $\mathcal{S}_{\mathcal{T}}$: $\| [a] \|^{\mathcal{T}} \bigcup \mathcal{S}_i = \bigcup \mid \| [a] \|^{\mathcal{T}} \; \mathcal{S}_i$. Continuity of $\| [a] \|^{\mathcal{T}}$ corresponds to the condition that $\stackrel{a}{\longrightarrow}$ is image finite in $\mathcal{T}$.

Lemma 2.5.1. *$\| [a] \|^{\mathcal{T}}$ is continuous iff $\stackrel{a}{\longrightarrow}$ is image finite in $\mathcal{T}$.*

Proof. Suppose $\| [a] \|^{\mathcal{T}}$ is continuous but $\stackrel{a}{\longrightarrow}$ is not image finite. Then for some state s the set $\mathcal{S}' = \{s' \mid s \stackrel{a}{\longrightarrow} s'\}$ is not finite. Let $\mathcal{S}''$ be a countable subset of $\mathcal{S}'$. Consider the family of sets $\{\mathcal{S}^{fin} \mid \mathcal{S}^{fin} = (\mathcal{S}' - \mathcal{S}'') \cup \mathcal{S}_1$ where $\mathcal{S}_1$ is a finite subset of $\mathcal{S}''\}$. Clearly this family is directed. But for each member $\mathcal{S}^{fin}$ we have that $s \notin \| [a] \|^{\mathcal{T}} \; \mathcal{S}^{fin}$ but $s \in \| [a] \|^{\mathcal{T}} \; \mathcal{S}'$. Assume that $\stackrel{a}{\longrightarrow}$ is image finite. Suppose $\{\mathcal{S}_i \mid i \in I\}$ is a directed family of state sets. By monotonicity if $s \in \| [a] \|^{\mathcal{T}} \mathcal{S}_j$ for $j \in I$ then $s \in \| [a] \|^{\mathcal{T}} \bigcup \mathcal{S}_i$. If instead $s \in \| [a] \|^{\mathcal{T}} \bigcup \mathcal{S}_i$ then because of image finiteness $s \in \| [a] \|^{\mathcal{T}} \mathcal{S}'$ for some finite subset of $\bigcup \mathcal{S}_i$. But then there is an $\mathcal{S}_j$ with $j \in I$ such that $s \in \| [a] \|^{\mathcal{T}} \mathcal{S}_j$. ∎

Notice that image finiteness holds when a ranges over standard while programs, but fails for constructs permitting countable nondeterminism such as random assignment.

Viewed as abstract objects subject to equational laws, rather than as sets of states, modal properties become *modal algebras*.

Definition 2.5.2. A *modal algebra* is a quintuple $(\mathcal{U}, 1, \sqcap, -, \{[\![a]\!] \mid a \in \mathcal{L}\})$ where $(\mathcal{U}, 1, \sqcap, -)$ is a boolean algebra; and $[\![a]\!] : \mathcal{U} \to \mathcal{U}$ for each $a \in \mathcal{L}$ satisfies $[\![a]\!]\, 1 = 1$ and $[\![a]\!]\,(x \sqcap y) = [\![a]\!]\, x \sqcap [\![a]\!]\, y$.

The unit of the boolean algebra is 1, its product is $\sqcap$, and $-$ is complementation. The sum, $\sqcup$, the dual of $\sqcap$, is defined as expected: $x \sqcup y = -(-x \sqcap -y)$. Similarly, $\langle\!\langle a \rangle\!\rangle$ is the dual, $-[\![a]\!]-$, of $[\![a]\!]$. The *sort* of a modal algebra $\mathcal{U}$ is its label set $\mathcal{L}$.

Modal algebras were historically the first models of modal logics. For each modal formula Φ determines a modal equation $\Phi^+ = 1$. Suppose Φ contains at most the atomic sentences $Q_1, \ldots, Q_n$ then Φ^+ is an n-ary polynomial with free variables $z_1, \ldots, z_n$ which is defined inductively as follows: $Q_i^+ = z_i$; $(\neg\Phi)^+ = -\Phi^+$; $(\Phi \wedge \Psi)^+ = \Phi^+ \sqcap \Psi^+$; and $([a]\Phi)^+ = [\![a]\!]\, \Phi^+$. A modal formula Φ of sort $\mathcal{L}$ is $\mathcal{U}$-valid (where $\mathcal{U}$ has the same sort) when $\mathcal{U} \models \Phi^+ = 1$: that is, when all instances of the equation $\Phi^+ = 1$ are true in $\mathcal{U}$. Φ is *algebraically* valid, written $\models \Phi^+ = 1$, if it is $\mathcal{U}$-valid for every modal algebra $\mathcal{U}$ of the appropriate sort. Algebraic validity coincides with validity (on transition systems).

Theorem 2.5.3. $\models \Phi$ *iff* $\models \Phi^+ = 1$.

Proof. Suppose $\models \Phi$ then Φ is a theorem of the axiom system for K (of Section 2.2). But the axioms of K are algebraically valid, and the rules preserve algebraic validity. Hence $\models \Phi^+ = 1$. For the other direction, suppose $\not\models \Phi$. Therefore $\mathcal{T} \not\models \Phi$ for some transition system $\mathcal{T}$. But each $\mathcal{T}$ determines a powerset modal algebra $\mathcal{U}(\mathcal{T}) = (2^{\mathcal{S}_{\mathcal{T}}}, \mathcal{S}_{\mathcal{T}}, \cap, -, \{\| [a] \|^{\mathcal{T}} \mid a \in \mathcal{L}\})$. A small exercise shows that for every formula Ψ, $\mathcal{T} \models \Psi$ iff $\mathcal{U}(\mathcal{T}) \models \Psi^+ = 1$. ∎

Associated with any transition system $\mathcal{T}$, as shown in the proof of the previous theorem, is its powerset modal algebra $\mathcal{U}(\mathcal{T})$ which validates the same modal formulae. Consequently, modal algebras provide a more general class of structures for interpreting modal languages than transition systems. As with transition systems, modal algebras can be classified in terms of conditions that they obey. Sometimes these requirements may be presented as sets of equations. A notable case is dynamic algebras which fulfill the equational versions of the axioms of dynamic logic of the previous section [Pratt, 1980a]. A variant is to define the ω-continuous dynamic algebras which comply with the stronger requirement: $\langle\!\langle a^* \rangle\!\rangle x = \bigsqcup\{\langle\!\langle a^n \rangle\!\rangle x \mid n \geq 0\}$ [Kozen, 1981].

Modal algebras also determine transition systems via a construction similar to the Stone representation theorem for boolean algebras. Think of elements of a modal algebra as modal properties or formulae. From these we need to construct a transition system. A state, therefore, will be an assembly of properties. As a strong indicator consider first the set $\| s \|^{\mathcal{T}}_{\mathcal{V}}$ of modal properties true at state s in a model $(\mathcal{T}, \mathcal{V})$. Clearly $\mathtt{tt} \in \| s \|^{\mathcal{T}}_{\mathcal{V}}$; $\neg\Phi \in \| s \|^{\mathcal{T}}_{\mathcal{V}}$ iff $\Phi \notin \| s \|^{\mathcal{T}}_{\mathcal{V}}$; and $\Phi \wedge \Psi \in \| s \|^{\mathcal{T}}_{\mathcal{V}}$ iff $\Phi \in \| s \|^{\mathcal{T}}_{\mathcal{V}}$ and $\Psi \in \| s \|^{\mathcal{T}}_{\mathcal{V}}$. Consequently, we can identify as a state of a modal algebra $\mathcal{U}$ any set $X \subseteq \mathcal{U}$ obeying these conditions (when 1 replaces $\mathtt{tt}$, $-$ replaces $\neg$, and $\sqcap$ replaces $\wedge$). Such a set is an *ultrafilter* in $\mathcal{U}$. For the transition relations again consider a modal model: if $s \stackrel{a}{\longrightarrow} s'$ then whenever $[a]\Phi \in \| s \|^{\mathcal{T}}_{\mathcal{V}}$, $\Phi \in \| s' \|^{\mathcal{T}}_{\mathcal{V}}$. This is the criterion used for defining $\stackrel{a}{\longrightarrow}$ between ultrafilters in $\mathcal{U}$ (when $[\![a]\!]$ replaces $[a]$). Hence, a modal algebra $\mathcal{U}$ of sort $\mathcal{L}$ determines the transition system $\mathcal{T}(\mathcal{U}) = (\mathcal{S}(\mathcal{U}), \{\stackrel{a}{\longrightarrow} \mid a \in \mathcal{L}\})$ where $\mathcal{S}(\mathcal{U})$ is the set of ultrafilters in $\mathcal{U}$. The Stone representation theorem for modal algebras states that $\mathcal{U}$ is isomorphic to a subalgebra of $\mathcal{U}(\mathcal{T}(\mathcal{U}))$ (given by the morphism $\lambda x \in \mathcal{U}.\ \{\{X \in \mathcal{S}(\mathcal{U}) \mid x \in X\}\}$).

But $\mathcal{U}$ and $\mathcal{T}(\mathcal{U})$ need not validate the same formulae. Although from the Stone representation result (and the proof of Theorem 2.5.3) if $\mathcal{T}(\mathcal{U}) \models \Phi$ then $\mathcal{U} \models \Phi^+ = 1$, the converse may fail. The problem is that $\mathcal{S}(\mathcal{U})$ may contain non-standard states (given by non-principal ultrafilters). For instance, if $\mathcal{U}$ is a non-finite dynamic algebra then there are ultrafilters containing as subsets $\{[\![a^n]\!]\,x \mid n \geq 0\} \cup \{-\,[\![a^*]\!]\,x\}$. But in this circumstance $\mathcal{T}(\mathcal{U})$ fails the dynamic axiom schema D3$\wedge$D4 (of the previous section). This mismatch between $\mathcal{U}$ and $\mathcal{T}(\mathcal{U})$ prompted the introduction of descriptive frames [Goldblatt, 1976] and dynamic spaces [Kozen, 1981]. Further restrictions provide dualites between modal algebras and spaces. For details see [Sambin and Vaccaro, 1988]. A general account of the significance of Stone duality to computation is contained in [Abramsky, 1989].

2.6 Decision procedures

Besides having sound and complete axiom systems, the logics K, PDL, and $KG(v, w', w, v')$ are *decidable*: that is, there are algorithms for determining whether or not a formula is Λ-valid (or, what amounts to the same thing, Λ-satisfiable) when Λ is the appropriate set of models. There are various techniques available for showing this (besides exhibiting the particular algorithm) which we now briefly mention.

An important feature of minimal modal logic K is its possession of the small model property *small model property*: each satisfiable formula Φ is satisfiable in a finite model whose size (the number of states) is bounded by the number of connectives in Φ. A simple proof of this follows from the modal collapse of a modal model with respect to a set of formulae. Suppose Γ is a non-empty set of formulae and $\mathcal{M}$ a modal model (both of the same sort). Two states s and t of $\mathcal{S}_{\mathcal{M}}$ are Γ-equivalent in $\mathcal{M}$, written as $s \equiv_{\Gamma}^{\mathcal{M}} t$, if they have the same properties drawn from Γ: that is, if $\{\Phi \in \Gamma \mid s \models_{\mathcal{M}} \Phi\} = \{\Phi \in \Gamma \mid t \models_{\mathcal{M}} \Phi\}$. Let $|s|_{\Gamma}^{\mathcal{M}}$ be the equivalence class induced on $\mathcal{S}_{\mathcal{M}}$, the set $\{t \mid s \equiv_{\Gamma}^{\mathcal{M}} t\}$. The modal collapse is defined by filtering $\mathcal{M}$ through $\equiv_{\Gamma}^{\mathcal{M}}$.

Definition 2.6.1. The modal collapse of $\mathcal{M}$ with respect to Γ is the model $\mathcal{M}_{\Gamma}$ where

(a) $\mathcal{S}_{\Gamma} = \{|s|_{\Gamma}^{\mathcal{M}} \mid s \in \mathcal{S}_{\mathcal{M}}\}$,

(b) $\mathcal{L}_{\Gamma} = \mathcal{L}_{\mathcal{M}} \cap \{a \mid a \text{ occurs in } \Gamma\}$,

(c) $x \xrightarrow{a}_{\Gamma} y$ iff $\exists s \in x.\ \exists t \in y.\ s \xrightarrow{a} t$,

(d) $x \in \mathcal{V}_{\Gamma}(Q)$ iff $\exists s \in x.\ s \in \mathcal{V}_{\mathcal{M}}(Q)$.

By definition $\mathcal{M}_{\Gamma}$ is a modal model. Moreover, irrespective of the size of $\mathcal{M}$, the model $\mathcal{M}_{\Gamma}$ only contains a finite number of states (and labels) whenever Γ is a finite set. If Γ is closed under subformulae then $\mathcal{M}_{\Gamma}$ inherits important semantic properties of $\mathcal{M}$. A set Γ is *closed under subformulas* if whenever $\neg\Phi \in \Gamma$ or $[a]\Phi \in \Gamma$ then also $\Phi \in \Gamma$, and if $\Phi \wedge \Psi \in \Gamma$ then also $\Phi \in \Gamma$ and $\Psi \in \Gamma$.

Lemma 2.6.2. *If Γ is closed under subformulae and $\Phi \in \Gamma$ then, $s \models_{\mathcal{M}} \Phi$ iff $|s|_{\Gamma}^{\mathcal{M}} \models_{\mathcal{M}_{\Gamma}} \Phi$.*

Proof. For $\Phi \in \Gamma$, $\Phi \in |s|_{\Gamma}^{\mathcal{M}}$ iff $\forall t \in |s|_{\Gamma}^{\mathcal{M}}.\ \Phi \in |t|_{\Gamma}^{\mathcal{M}}$. By definition if $\Phi \in \Gamma$ then $s \models_{\mathcal{M}} \Phi$ iff $\Phi \in |s|_{\Gamma}^{\mathcal{M}}$. So we need to show that $\Phi \in |s|_{\Gamma}^{\mathcal{M}}$ iff $|s|_{\Gamma}^{\mathcal{M}} \models_{\mathcal{M}_{\Gamma}} \Phi$ (for $\Phi \in \Gamma$). This follows by induction on the structure of Φ. The base case is by definition. The only interesting case in the induction step is $\Phi = [a]\Psi$. Suppose $[a]\Psi \in |s|_{\Gamma}^{\mathcal{M}}$. Consider any $|t|_{\Gamma}^{\mathcal{M}}$ such that $|s|_{\Gamma}^{\mathcal{M}} \xrightarrow{a}_{\Gamma} |t|_{\Gamma}^{\mathcal{M}}$. Clearly, as $s' \xrightarrow{a} t'$ for some $s' \in |s|_{\Gamma}^{\mathcal{M}}$ and $t' \in |t|_{\Gamma}^{\mathcal{M}}$ $\Psi \in |t|_{\Gamma}^{\mathcal{M}}$. The other direction is similar. ∎

The small model property for K is now a consequence of this lemma. Suppose Φ is true at s in $\mathcal{M}$; then $|s|_{\Gamma}^{\mathcal{M}} \models_{\mathcal{M}_{\Gamma}} \Phi$ for any Γ closed under subformulae containing Φ. In particular, there is the smallest such Γ consisting of Φ and its subformulae. The size of $\mathcal{M}_\Gamma$ is at most 2^n where n is the number of connectives in Φ. This property guarantees that satisfiability (and hence validity) is decidable.

Lemma 2.6.2 does not imply that other modal logics have the small model property. Although $\mathcal{M}_\Gamma$ is always a modal model, there is no assurance, for instance in the case of PDL and $KG(v, w', w, v')$, that it obeys the requisite model conditions, the dynamic model conditions or the condition $C(v, w', w, v')$. Sometimes extra closure conditions on Γ suffice. Alternatively, it may be possible to show that $\mathcal{M}_\Gamma$ can be extended into a finite model fulfilling the appropriate reqirements. A mixture of these two is sufficient for dynamic logic (compare Section 6.2). However, as the formula $[a^*](\langle a\rangle \mathtt{tt} \wedge [(a^*; a) \cap \mathtt{tt}?]\mathtt{ff})$, from Section 2.4, shows it is not assured that a logic does have the small model property. More powerful techniques for proving decidability include [Bull, 1966], as well as reduction to a known decidability result [Gabbay, 1976; Streett, 1982].

Proofs of complete axiomatizations can also provide decidability results, as we illustrate in Section 6.2 for K and PDL. Simple algorithms for deciding Λ-satisfiability are given by tableau techniques, as described, for example, in [Hughes and Cresswell, 1973; Fitting, 1983], and for PDL by [Pratt, 1980b].

Another arena for decision procedures is proving properties *within* a given model and, in particular, of verifying modal properties of systems or programs structurally. For instance, suppose we are presented with a description of a transition system (such as the vending machine of Section 1.1) just in terms of the state constructors ., +, and $\stackrel{def}{=}$: for simplicity it is assumed that all state constants on the right-hand side of $\stackrel{def}{=}$ occur within the scope of a . constructor. Assume $\mathcal{M}$ is a modal model on this transition system whose valuation is $\mathcal{V}$. The following tableau system is an effective decision procedure for determining whether state E has the modal property Φ (under $\mathcal{M}$) which does not appeal to the transition relations, but instead to the state constructors. The rules, built from sequents of the form $E \vdash_\mathcal{M} \Phi$ (proof-theoretic analogues of $E \models_\mathcal{M} \Phi$), are goal directed: the premise sequent represents the goal to be achieved, the conclusions the subgoals:

$$\frac{E \vdash_\mathcal{M} \neg\neg\Phi}{E \vdash_\mathcal{M} \Phi} \qquad \frac{E \vdash_\mathcal{M} \Phi \wedge \Psi}{E \vdash_\mathcal{M} \Phi \quad E \vdash_\mathcal{M} \Psi} \qquad \frac{E \vdash_\mathcal{M} \neg(\Phi \wedge \Psi)}{E \vdash_\mathcal{M} \neg\Phi}$$

$$\frac{E \vdash_\mathcal{M} \neg(\Phi \wedge \Psi)}{E \vdash_\mathcal{M} \neg\Psi} \qquad \frac{a.E \vdash_\mathcal{M} [a]\Phi}{E \vdash_\mathcal{M} \Phi} \qquad \frac{a.E \vdash_\mathcal{M} \neg[a]\Phi}{E \vdash_\mathcal{M} \neg\Phi}$$

$$\frac{E + F \vdash_\mathcal{M} [a]\Phi}{E \vdash_\mathcal{M} [a]\Phi \quad F \vdash_\mathcal{M} [a]\Phi} \qquad \frac{U \vdash_\mathcal{M} \Phi}{E \vdash_\mathcal{M} \Phi}\ U \stackrel{def}{=} E$$

$$\frac{E + F \vdash_{\mathcal{M}} \neg[a]\Phi}{E \vdash_{\mathcal{M}} \neg[a]\Phi} \qquad \frac{E + F \vdash_{\mathcal{M}} \neg[a]\Phi}{F \vdash_{\mathcal{M}} \neg[a]\Phi}.$$

A tableau for $E \vdash_{\mathcal{M}} \Phi$ is a maximal proof tree whose root is labelled with this sequent. Sequents labelling the immediate successors of a node are determined by an application of one of the rules. Maximality means that no rules apply to a sequent labelling a leaf of a tableau. These rules are straightforward. A tableau is *successful* if all its leaves are successful. A leaf labelled $F \vdash_{\mathcal{M}} \Psi$ is *successful* if one of the following conditions applies: $\Psi = Q$ and $F \in \mathcal{V}(Q)$; $\Psi = \neg Q$ and $F \notin \mathcal{V}(Q)$; $\Psi = [b]\Psi'$ and $F = a.G$. A simple consequence is that $E \models_{\mathcal{M}} \Phi$ iff $E \vdash_{\mathcal{M}} \Phi$ has a successful tableau. This system provides an instance of *structured* model checking. For extensions to concurrency see [Winskel, 1985; Stirling, 1987].

3 Propositional Temporal Logics

3.1 Between modal and temporal logics

Transition systems, as emphasized in the Introduction, are suitable vehicles for defining the meanings of programs. They are also primary structures for interpreting modal logics, carrying through that fundamental idea of an action as a state transformer. However, for many computational systems, especially when they involve concurrency, their on-going behaviour as sequences of actions or state changes is more important. Temporal logics are designed to reason about such behaviour. Initially, temporal logics were modal logics on unlabelled transition systems, whose transition relations are orderings [Prior, 1957]. Viewing these orderings as temporal, and the state set as consisting of times, the modality $\langle\ \rangle$ expresses a form of *eventually*, and $[\ ]$ expresses *invariantly*. A richer framework, for computational purposes, due to [Pratt, 1976; Pnueli, 1977; Abrahamson, 1979; Lamport, 1980; Emerson and Clarke, 1980] amongst others, is to discern these temporal structures within transition systems themselves by extracting appropriate paths through them representing (partial) runs of a program, a net or whatever.

A *path* σ through a transition system is a finite or ω length sequence of the form $s_0 \xrightarrow{a_1} s_1 \xrightarrow{a_2} \ldots$ representing (part of) an ongoing behaviour from the state s_0. The length of a path is its number of transitions (so a shortest path of zero length is a singleton state). For instance, $St_i \xrightarrow{push} St_{i+1} \xrightarrow{pop} St_i$ is a path through the transition system for the stack of Section 1.1.

Suppose $\sigma = s_0 \xrightarrow{a_1} s_1 \xrightarrow{a_2} \ldots$ has length at least n, then for $i \leq n$:

- $\sigma(i)$ is the ith state, s_i, of σ
- σ^i is the ith suffix of σ, the subpath $s_i \xrightarrow{a_{i+1}} \ldots$ starting from s_i
- $\mathcal{L}(\sigma, i)$ is the ith label a_i of σ when $i > 0$.

When σ has finite length let $\sigma(*)$ be its final state. Two paths can be concatenated if the final state of one is the initial state of the other. Let $\sigma \cdot \pi$ represent the *concatenation* of σ and π (which is only defined when $\sigma(*) = \pi(0)$).

Modal formulae can be interpreted on paths by *unravelling* transition systems. If $\mathcal{T}$ is $(\mathcal{S}, \{\xrightarrow{a} \mid a \in \mathcal{L}\})$ then $\mathcal{T}^+$ is the transition system $(\mathcal{S}^+, \{\xrightarrow{a}_+ \mid a \in \mathcal{L}\})$ where $\mathcal{S}^+$ is the set of all *finite* length paths through $\mathcal{T}$ and for any any $a \in \mathcal{L}$, $\sigma \xrightarrow{a}_+ \pi$ iff $\pi = \sigma \cdot s \xrightarrow{a} t$. When $\mathcal{M}$ is the modal model $(\mathcal{T}, \mathcal{V})$ let $\mathcal{M}^+$ be the model $(\mathcal{T}^+, \mathcal{V}^+)$ whose valuation stipulates that $\mathcal{V}^+(Q)$ for any atomic Q is the set $\{\sigma \in \mathcal{S}^+ \mid \sigma(*) \in \mathcal{V}(Q)\}$. A straightforward consequence of unravelling models is the following preservation result (justified by a routine induction on modal formulae Φ): $s \models_{\mathcal{M}} \Phi$ iff $\forall \sigma$. if $s = \sigma(*)$ then $\sigma \models_{\mathcal{M}^+} \Phi$. When the label set has structure as in dynamic systems, it is more natural to assume that $\xrightarrow{a}_+$ is only defined as above in the case that a is non-composite. Such a label represents an *uninterruptable* state change, while composite labels name sequences of such changes. For instance, the operations of dynamic systems naturally extend to (finite or ω length) paths:

$$
\begin{array}{lll}
\sigma \xrightarrow{a;b}_+ \pi & \text{iff} & \exists \sigma_1.\ \sigma \xrightarrow{a}_+ \sigma_1 \text{ and } \sigma_1 \xrightarrow{b}_+ \pi \\
\sigma \xrightarrow{a \cup b}_+ \pi & \text{iff} & \sigma \xrightarrow{a}_+ \pi \text{ or } \sigma \xrightarrow{b}_+ \pi \\
\sigma \xrightarrow{a^*}_+ \pi & \text{iff} & \exists w \in \{a\}^*.\ \sigma \xrightarrow{w}_+ \pi.
\end{array}
$$

A small exercise shows that the preservation result above is invariant under this redefinition of the transition relations for composite labels in dynamic systems.

Unravelled models are richer in structure than their modal counterparts. New operators, expressing path features, which are not naturally modally interpretable can be assigned meanings. An example is an extension of dynamic logic called process logic [Pratt, 1979; Harel *et al.*, 1982] which includes the extra path operators *f*, *chop* and *suf* whose meanings on unravelled dynamic models are

$$
\begin{array}{lll}
\sigma \models_{\mathcal{M}^+} f(\Phi) & \text{iff} & \sigma(0) \models_{\mathcal{M}^+} \Phi \\
\sigma \models_{\mathcal{M}^+} \Phi\, chop\, \Psi & \text{iff} & \exists \sigma_1. \exists \sigma_2.\ \sigma = \sigma_1 \cdot \sigma_2,\ \sigma_1 \models_{\mathcal{M}^+} \Phi \text{ and } \sigma_2 \models_{\mathcal{M}^+} \Psi \\
\sigma \models_{\mathcal{M}^+} \Phi\, suf\, \Psi & \text{iff} & \exists\, i > 0.\ \sigma^i \models_{\mathcal{M}^+} \Psi \text{ and } \forall k : 0 < k < i. \sigma^k \models_{\mathcal{M}^+} \Phi.
\end{array}
$$

So *eventually* Φ can be expressed in this logic by the formula $\Phi \vee (\mathtt{tt}\, suf\, \Phi)$: for σ has this property if some suffix σ^i has the property Φ.

Runs have a special status amongst paths, as they represent complete computations. It is therefore common to interpret temporal logics on this distinguished set. Modal logics can also be interpreted on these maximal length paths. When $\mathcal{T}$ is the transition system $(\mathcal{S}, \{\stackrel{a}{\longrightarrow} \mid a \in \mathcal{L}\})$ let $\mathcal{T}^\times$ be the system $(\mathcal{S}^\times, \{\stackrel{a}{\longrightarrow}_\times \mid a \in \mathcal{L}\})$ whose state set consists of *all* runs through $\mathcal{T}$ and where $\sigma \stackrel{a}{\longrightarrow}_\times \pi$ iff $\sigma(0) \stackrel{a}{\longrightarrow} \pi(0)$. When $\mathcal{M}$ is the modal model $(\mathcal{T}, \mathcal{V})$ let $\mathcal{M}^\times$ be the model $(\mathcal{T}^\times, \mathcal{V}^\times)$ where $\mathcal{V}^\times(Q)$ for any atomic Q is the set $\{\sigma \mid \sigma(0) \in V(Q)\}$. A consequence of this unravelling is a similar preservation result (again proved by a routine induction on Φ): $s \models_\mathcal{M} \Phi$ iff $\forall\sigma$. if $\sigma(0) = s$ then $\sigma \models_{\mathcal{M}^\times} \Phi$. As before, operators expressing path properties can be naturally interpreted on unravelled systems. A sample collection is

$$
\begin{array}{lll}
\sigma \models_{\mathcal{M}^\times} (a)\Phi & \text{iff} & \sigma^1 \models_{\mathcal{M}^\times} \Phi \text{ and } \mathcal{L}(\sigma, 1) = a \\
\sigma \models_{\mathcal{M}^\times} \Phi U' \Psi & \text{iff} & \exists j > 0.\ \sigma^j \models_{\mathcal{M}^\times} \Psi \text{ and } \forall k : 0 < k < j.\ \sigma^k \models_{\mathcal{M}^\times} \Phi \\
\sigma \models_{\mathcal{M}^\times} \forall F \Phi & \text{iff} & \forall \pi.\ \text{if } \pi(0) = \sigma(0) \text{ then } \exists i \geq 0.\ \pi^i \models_{\mathcal{M}^\times} \Phi \\
\sigma \models_{\mathcal{M}^\times} E_a \Phi & \text{iff} & \exists\ \pi.\ \mathcal{L}(\pi, 1) = a \text{ and } \pi^1 \models_{\mathcal{M}^\times} \Phi \\
\sigma \models_{\mathcal{M}^\times} G_f \Phi & \text{iff} & \forall j \geq 0.\ \sigma^{f(j)} \models_{\mathcal{M}^\times} \Phi.
\end{array}
$$

The first example is a *relativized next* operator expressing that the initial action is a and after it Φ holds. The second is an *until* operator: $\Phi U' \Psi$ holds if eventually Ψ holds and until then Φ is true. $\forall F$ expresses a *strong eventuality.* $E_a \Phi$ expresses *somewhen* a and after it Φ. The final example defines a family of operators indexed by functions $f : \mathbb{N} \to \mathbb{N}$. For instance, $G_{\lambda n.2n}$ expresses *at every even point* Φ is true, and $G_{\lambda n.n}$ expresses *now and always.*

Example 3.1.1. Consider the transition system which is the union of the vending machine and the stack of Section 1.1. Let $\mathcal{M}$ be any model on this transition system and let σ and π be the following cyclic runs:

$$
\begin{array}{lll}
\sigma & = & (V \stackrel{2p}{\longrightarrow} V_1 \stackrel{big}{\longrightarrow} V_3 \stackrel{collect}{\longrightarrow} V)^\omega \\
\pi & = & (St_{i+1} \stackrel{pop}{\longrightarrow} \dots \stackrel{pop}{\longrightarrow} St_0 \stackrel{empty}{\longrightarrow} St_0 \stackrel{push}{\longrightarrow} \dots \stackrel{push}{\longrightarrow} St_{i+1})^\omega.
\end{array}
$$

The following temporal properties are true of these runs:

$$
\begin{array}{ll}
\sigma \models_{\mathcal{M}^\times} (2p)\mathtt{tt} & \pi \models_{\mathcal{M}^\times} (pop)\mathtt{tt}U'(empty)\mathtt{tt} \\
\sigma \models_{\mathcal{M}^\times} \forall F(collect)\mathtt{tt} & \pi \not\models_{\mathcal{M}^\times} \forall F(pop)\mathtt{tt} \\
\sigma \models_{\mathcal{M}^\times} G_{\lambda n.3n}(2p)\mathtt{tt} & \pi \models_{\mathcal{M}^\times} E_{2p}\mathtt{tt}.
\end{array}
$$

Reverse operators are common to temporal logics. A more general notion of path through a transition system does not assume an initial state: a path may now have the form $\dots \stackrel{a_{-1}}{\longrightarrow} s_{-1} \stackrel{a_0}{\longrightarrow} s_0 \stackrel{a_1}{\longrightarrow} \dots$. The notion of run is also generalized to those paths that are maximal in both forwards and backwards directions. Instead of employing runs and their suffixes an alternative semantics appeals to pairs (σ, i) where σ is a run and $i \in \mathbb{N}$ (or $\mathbb{Z}$) is an index. The pair σ, i (we drop the brackets) should be read as *σ at its ith point.* This is different from $\sigma(i)$, the ith state of σ, and σ^i, its ith suffix. Both forward and reverse operators can now be interpreted in the same framework, as the following examples illustrate:

$$\begin{array}{lll}
\sigma, i \models_{\mathcal{M}} \overline{(a)}\Phi & \text{iff} & \mathcal{L}(\sigma, i) = a \text{ and } \sigma, i-1 \models_{\mathcal{M}} \Phi \\
\sigma, i \models_{\mathcal{M}} \forall\overline{G}\Phi & \text{iff} & \forall\pi.\text{ if } \pi(j) = \sigma(i) \text{ then } \forall k \leq j.\ \pi, k \models_{\mathcal{M}} \Phi \\
\sigma, i \models_{\mathcal{M}} \Phi U' \Psi & \text{iff} & \exists j > i.\ \sigma, j \models_{\mathcal{M}} \Psi \text{ and } \forall k : i < k < j.\ \sigma, k \models_{\mathcal{M}} \Phi.
\end{array}$$

3.2 Basics

Unravelling focuses on paths or runs through a transition system. More explicitly, they are an ingredient of *temporal* structures, extended transition systems, Definition 1.2.1. These are pairs $(\mathcal{T}, \mathcal{R})$ where $\mathcal{T}$ is a total transition system while $\mathcal{R}$ is a non-empty set of runs through $\mathcal{T}$. We let $\mathcal{T}$ range over extended transition systems as well as transition systems. The *sort* of an extended transition system is its label set. The definition allows $\mathcal{R}$ to consist of an arbitrary set of runs. In applications it could consist of the admissible computations relative to some fairness assumptions. Such a set could for instance be generated by an automaton (see Section 3.5).

A propositional temporal language has the form:

$$\Phi ::= Q \mid \neg\Phi \mid \Phi_1 \wedge \Phi_2 \mid Op(\Phi_1, \ldots, \Phi_n).$$

where Q ranges over members of a family of atomic formulae and Op over n-ary temporal operators. The sort of a temporal language is given by the labels that the meanings of temporal operators may depend on. A temporal model for a language with sort $\mathcal{L}$ is a pair $\mathcal{M} = (\mathcal{T}, \mathcal{V})$, where $\mathcal{T}$ is an extended transition system with sort $\mathcal{L}$ and $\mathcal{V}$, as in the modal case, assigns to each atomic formula a subset of $\mathcal{S}_{\mathcal{T}}$. The satisfaction relation representing truth of a formula Φ at the index i of a run $\sigma \in \mathcal{R}$ is defined inductively using the notation $\sigma, i \models_{\mathcal{M}} \Phi$. When Φ is not true at i of σ we write $\sigma, i \not\models_{\mathcal{M}} \Phi$. We assume the general case here when there may be reverse operators. The clauses are:

$$\begin{array}{lll}
\sigma, i \models_{\mathcal{M}} Q & \text{iff} & \sigma(i) \in \mathcal{V}(Q) \\
\sigma, i \models_{\mathcal{M}} \neg\Phi & \text{iff} & \sigma, i \not\models_{\mathcal{M}} \Phi \\
\sigma, i \models_{\mathcal{M}} \Phi \wedge \Psi & \text{iff} & \sigma, i \models_{\mathcal{M}} \Phi \text{ and } \sigma, i \models_{\mathcal{M}} \Psi \\
\sigma, i \models_{\mathcal{M}} Op(\Phi_1, \ldots \Phi_n) & \text{iff} & \ldots
\end{array}$$

Example temporal operators were given in the previous section.

In the circumstance that a temporal language does not contain reverse operators the semantic clauses can be simplified by employing suffixes σ^i of a run σ instead of the pair σ, i. Hence we pick out as a special class of structures *future time extended transition systems* whose sets of runs $\mathcal{R}$ have the two features that first every member run has an initial state, and that secondly they are *suffix closed*: whenever $\sigma \in \mathcal{R}$ then the ith suffix $\sigma^i \in \mathcal{R}$ for each i. Now $\models_{\mathcal{M}}$ can be defined directly between runs and formulae:

$$
\begin{array}{lll}
\sigma \models_{\mathcal{M}} Q & \text{iff} & \sigma(0) \in \mathcal{V}(Q) \\
\sigma \models_{\mathcal{M}} \neg\Phi & \text{iff} & \sigma \not\models_{\mathcal{M}} \Phi \\
\sigma \models_{\mathcal{M}} \Phi \wedge \Psi & \text{iff} & \sigma \models_{\mathcal{M}} \Phi \text{ and } \sigma \models_{\mathcal{M}} \Psi \\
\sigma \models_{\mathcal{M}} Op(\Phi_1, \ldots, \Phi_n) & \text{iff} & \ldots
\end{array}
$$

Notation for truth and validity follows that for modal logic, Definition 2.1.3.

Definition 3.2.1.

(a) Φ is $\mathcal{M}$-true, $\models_{\mathcal{M}} \Phi$, if for all pairs σ, i. $\sigma, i \models_{\mathcal{M}} \Phi$,

(b) Φ is $\mathcal{T}$-valid, $\models_{\mathcal{T}} \Phi$, if for all models $\mathcal{M}$ on $\mathcal{T}$, $\models_{\mathcal{M}} \Phi$,

(c) Φ is $\mathcal{T}$-satisfiable if for some $\mathcal{M}$ on $\mathcal{T}$ and pair σ, i. $\sigma, i \models_{\mathcal{M}} \Phi$.

Implicit here is that the sorts of formulae and extended transition systems correspond and that quantification of runs is over the set $\mathcal{R}_{\mathcal{M}}$. As with the modal case (see Section 2.1) there are numerous extensions of these notions. First is the generalization to sets of formulae: for instance, Γ is $\mathcal{T}$-satisfiable if every formula in Γ is simultaneously true at an index of a run in some model on $\mathcal{T}$. Second is the extension to sets of models, or extended transition systems: for instance, Φ is Λ-valid if for every $\mathcal{T} \in \Lambda$ Φ is $\mathcal{T}$-valid. Moreover, semantic consequence relations between sets of formulas Γ and individual formulas Φ can also be defined. As in Section 2.1, these divide into *global* and *local* relations. For instance, when Λ is a family of models:

$$
\begin{array}{lll}
\Gamma \Vdash_{\Lambda} \Phi & \text{iff} & \forall \mathcal{M} \in \Lambda.\ \text{if } \mathcal{M} \models \Gamma \text{ then } \mathcal{M} \models \Phi \\
\Gamma \models_{\Lambda} \Phi & \text{iff} & \forall \mathcal{M} \in \Lambda.\ \forall \sigma \in \mathcal{R}_{\mathcal{M}}. \forall i.\ \text{if } \sigma, i \models_{\mathcal{M}} \Gamma \text{ then } \sigma, i \models_{\mathcal{M}} \Phi.
\end{array}
$$

Similar but simpler definitions can be given for truth, validity and consequence with respect to future time structures and their models. When Λ is the family of all (possibly future) extended transition systems of the appropriate sort it is dropped as an index from the terms Λ-valid and Λ-satisfiable: Φ of sort $\mathcal{L}$ is *valid* if it is $\mathcal{T}$-valid for every (future) $\mathcal{T}$ of sort $\mathcal{L}$.

A useful additional generalization is that of a temporal formula being *true at a state* s under a model $\mathcal{M}$:

$$s \models_{\mathcal{M}} \Phi \text{ iff } \forall \sigma \in \mathcal{R}_{\mathcal{M}}. \forall i. \text{ if } \sigma(i) = s \text{ then } \sigma, i \models_{\mathcal{M}} \Phi$$

When $\mathcal{M}$ is future time the right-hand side can be simplified to: $\forall \sigma$. if $\sigma(0) = s$ then $\sigma \models_{\mathcal{M}} \Phi$. This abstraction permits contrasts between modal and temporal logics. As every state in $\mathcal{S}_{\mathcal{M}}$ appears in some run in $\mathcal{R}_{\mathcal{M}}$, Φ is $\mathcal{M}$-true just in case Φ is true at every state under $\mathcal{M}$. (In the case of a rooted extended transition system, validity may be defined in terms of truth at the root state.)

Example 3.2.2. Consider the stack again defined by the equations $St_0 \stackrel{def}{=} empty.St_0 + push.St_1$; $St_{i+1} \stackrel{def}{=} pop.St_i + push.St_{i+2}$. Let $\mathcal{T}$ be the future time extended transition system, representing an *active* stack, whose set of runs consists of those where *pop* happens infinitely often. Assume $\mathcal{M}$ is a model on $\mathcal{T}$ where $\mathcal{V}(Q) = \{St_{2i} \mid i \geq 0\}$. Finally, let Λ be the family of all models on this transition system.

$$\begin{array}{ll} St_{2i} \models_{\mathcal{M}} \neg(pop)Q & \models_{\mathcal{M}} \forall FQ \\ St_0 \models_{\mathcal{T}} \neg(pop)Q & \models_{\mathcal{T}} \forall F(pop)\mathtt{tt} \\ \{Q\} \Vdash_{\Lambda} G_{\lambda n.n} Q & \{Q\} \not\models_{\Lambda} G_{\lambda n.n} Q. \end{array}$$

Propositional temporal languages are identified by their temporal operators. The expressive power of formulae and languages (of the same sort) can therefore be compared over families of models. The following definition encompasses standard stipulations.

Definition 3.2.3.

(a) $\Phi \equiv_{\mathcal{M}} \Psi$ iff $\forall \sigma. \forall i.\ \sigma, i \models_{\mathcal{M}} \Phi$ iff $\sigma, i \models_{\mathcal{M}} \Psi$,

(b) $\Phi \equiv_{\Lambda} \Psi$ iff $\forall \mathcal{M} \in \Lambda.\ \Phi \equiv_{\mathcal{M}} \Psi$,

(c) $TL \leq_{\Lambda} TL'$ iff $\forall \Phi \in TL.\ \exists \Psi \in TL'.\ \Phi \equiv_{\Lambda} \Psi$.

First is the definition of when two temporal formulae are *equi-expressive* with respect to a model. A variant of this is to define $\equiv_{\mathcal{M}}$ with respect to *states* instead of run index pairs. Part ii. of the definition generalizes equi-expressiveness to families of models. The final stipulation defines when one temporal language is no more Λ-expressive than another: it is assumed that TL and TL$'$ have the same sort and share atomic sentences. When Λ is the set of all models of the appropriate sort it is dropped as an index from $\equiv_\Lambda$ and $\leq_\Lambda$. Moreover, if TL and TL$'$ are no more Λ-expressive than each other we write TL $=_\Lambda$ TL$'$. And, finally, if TL $\leq_\Lambda$TL$'$ but TL$'$ $\not\leq_\Lambda$ TL then TL is strictly less Λ-expressive than TL$'$, and we denote this by TL $<_\Lambda$ TL$'$.

Example 3.2.4. Consider a very simple clock $Cl \stackrel{def}{=} tick.Cl$ and let Λ be the family of models on this transition system. Then $G_{\lambda n.n}\Phi \equiv_\Lambda G_{\lambda n.2n}\Phi$; as temporal distinctions collapse on such a simple structure. Assume TL contains as sole operator $G_{\lambda n.n}$, while TL$'$ has the single until operator U'. Then TL $\leq$ TL$'$ as $G_{\lambda n.n}\Phi \equiv \Phi \wedge \neg(\mathtt{tt}U'\neg\Phi)$. In fact, TL $<$ TL$'$ as is shown below.

3.3 Linear and branching time

The meaning of the modality $[a]$ in an unravelled modal model based on runs is

$$\sigma \models_{\mathcal{M}^\times} [a]\Phi \ \text{ iff } \ \forall\, \pi.\text{ if } \pi(0) = \sigma(0) \text{ and } \mathcal{L}(\pi, 1) = a \text{ then } \pi^1 \models_{\mathcal{M}^\times} \Phi.$$

Two general concepts are intertwined here: first is the idea that a run *branches* into all those runs with the same initial state and second is the notion of the subsequent *point* of a run. These aspects can be separated into the following two operators (generalizing to arbitrary temporal models):

$$\begin{array}{lll} \sigma, i \models_{\mathcal{M}} \forall\Phi & \text{iff} & \forall\pi.\forall j.\text{ if } \pi(j) = \sigma(i) \text{ then } \pi, j \models_{\mathcal{M}} \Phi \\ \sigma, i \models_{\mathcal{M}} (a)\Phi & \text{iff} & \mathcal{L}(\sigma, i+1) = a \text{ and } \sigma, i+1 \models_{\mathcal{M}} \Phi. \end{array}$$

So $[a]$ can be dissected into the combination $\forall\neg(a)\neg$ and $\langle a\rangle$, its dual, into $\exists(a)$, where $\exists$ is $\neg\forall\neg$, the dual of $\forall$. Similarly the reverse modality $\overline{[a]}$ becomes the combination $\forall\neg\overline{(a)}\neg$, where $\overline{(a)}$ is the reverse of (a). Under this analysis modal logic can be viewed as a *relativized next* temporal logic (where there are two modes of next).

The operator $\forall$ [Emerson and Clarke, 1980; Ben-Ari *et al.*, 1983] expresses constrained path switching. It is a quantifier over all paths passing through a particular state. In contrast (a) does not involve path switching. This contrast is the basis for an important division of temporal logics used for describing program properties into *linear* and *branching* time. Although a traditional division of temporal logics [Prior, 1967; Rescher and Urquhart, 1971], its relevance to computation was primarily due to [Lamport, 1980]. When $\mathcal{R}$ captures the potential computational behaviour of a program, linear time temporal logics reason about it in terms of the properties of these runs. However, runs in $\mathcal{R}$ can be organized into computation trees or graphs with choice points at a state s representing the different ways that computation may proceed from s. Branching time logics reason about the program in terms of the properties of these trees (with their choice points). Logically the difference between a linear and a branching time operator resides with the possibility of path switching: the semantic clause for a branching time operator may involve the constrained path switching that $\forall$ expresses.

Example 3.3.1. Consider the difference between the two vending machines V_1 and V_2: $V_1 \stackrel{def}{=} 2p.big.collect.V_1 + 2p.little.collect.little.collect.V_1$ and $V_2 \stackrel{def}{=} 2p.(big.collect.V_2 + little.collect.little.collect.V_2)$. Although their runs involve the same sequences of actions, V_2, unlike V_1, has the property $\forall(2p)\exists(little)\mathtt{tt}$.

A more syntactic criterion for linearity appeals to the following infinitary language L_∞:

$$\Phi ::= Q \mid \neg\Phi \mid \bigwedge\{\Phi_j \mid j \in J\} \mid (a)\Phi \mid \overline{(a)}\Phi.$$

where J is a possibly infinite (indexed) set. The semantic clause for conjunction is as expected: $\sigma, i \models_{\mathcal{M}} \bigwedge\{\Phi_j \mid j \in J\}$ iff $\forall k \in J.\ \sigma, i \models_{\mathcal{M}} \Phi_k$. We say that a temporal language TL is *linear* if $TL \leq L_\infty$.

Example 3.3.2. The temporal language TL whose operators are $G_{\lambda n.2n}$ and O, the unrelativized next operator, is less expressive than L_∞: $O\Phi \equiv \bigvee\{(a)\Phi \mid a \in \mathcal{L}\}$ (where $\mathcal{L}$ is the sort) while $G_{\lambda n.2n}\Phi \equiv \bigwedge\{O^{2i}\Phi \mid i \in \mathbb{N}\}$ (where $O^0\Psi = \Psi$ and $O^{n+1}\Psi = OO^n\Psi$). On the other hand if TL has as sole operator $\exists(a)$ then TL $\not\leq \mathrm{L}_\infty$.

Moreover, TL is said to be a *future* (*past*) linear time language if it is less expressive than the sublanguage of L_∞ without the reverse operators $\overline{(a)}$ (without the (a) operators). Not every linear language is either future or past: an example is the language whose sole operator expresses the future perfect, *will have been*, $F\overline{F}$:

$$\sigma, i \models_{\mathcal{M}} F\overline{F}\Phi \quad \text{iff} \quad \exists j \geq i.\ \exists k \leq j.\ \ \sigma, k \models_{\mathcal{M}} \Phi.$$

We use the notation $L(Op_1, \ldots, Op_n)$ to name the linear time temporal language whose temporal operators are $Op_1, \ldots, Op_n$. An important future instance is $L(O, U)$ where O is the unrelativized *next* operator and U is a binary *until* operator:

$$\begin{array}{lll} \sigma \models_{\mathcal{M}} O\Phi & \text{iff} & \sigma^1 \models_{\mathcal{M}} \Phi \\ \sigma \models_{\mathcal{M}} \Phi U \Psi & \text{iff} & \exists j \geq 0.\ \sigma^j \models_{\mathcal{M}} \Psi \text{ and } \forall k : 0 \leq k < j.\ \sigma^k \models_{\mathcal{M}} \Phi. \end{array}$$

A useful derived operator is F expressing *now or eventually*: $F\Phi \stackrel{def}{=} ttU\Phi$. Its dual ($\neg F \neg$), written as G, expresses *now and always*. Unlike U' the operator U includes the moment of evaluation as a possible point for Ψ to be true at. The logic $L(U')$ is a more succinct version of $L(O, U)$, as they are equi-expressive: for instance, $O\Phi$ is just $\mathtt{ff}U'\Phi$. A reason for choosing U rather than U' is that the operator O is not definable in terms of U (as shown by the following lemma) a virtue according to [Lamport, 1983] who argues against the presence of O in temporal logics for programs.

Lemma 3.3.3. *$L(U) < L(O, U)$ and $L(O, F) < L(O, U)$.*

Proof. Let $\mathcal{T}$ be the transition system for W given by: $W \stackrel{def}{=} down.D$; $D \stackrel{def}{=} down.R$; $R \stackrel{def}{=} round.R$. Assume $\mathcal{M}$ is a model whose valuation stipulates that $\mathcal{V}(Q) = \{W, D\}$. Consider the run $\sigma = W \stackrel{down}{\longrightarrow} D \stackrel{down}{\longrightarrow} (R \stackrel{round}{\longrightarrow} R)^\omega$ and its initial suffix σ^1. A small induction on formulae $\Phi \in L(U)$ shows $\sigma \models_{\mathcal{M}} \Phi$ iff $\sigma^1 \models_{\mathcal{M}} \Phi$. But $\sigma \models_{\mathcal{M}} OQ$ and $\sigma^1 \not\models_{\mathcal{M}} OQ$. For the second half assume $Q_1 U Q_2 \equiv \Psi$ for $\Psi \in L(O, F)$. Suppose Ψ contains less than m occurrences of the operator O. Let $\mathcal{T}$ be the transition system generated from the following: $T_i \stackrel{def}{=} up.T_{i+1}$ for $i : 0 \leq i \leq 4m - 1$; and $T_{4m} \stackrel{def}{=} down.T_{2m}$. Let $\mathcal{M}$ be a model that stipulates that $\mathcal{V}(Q_1) = \{T_i \mid i \neq 3m\}$ and $\mathcal{V}(Q_2) = \{T_{2m-1}, T_{4m}\}$. Now consider the paths $\sigma = (T_{2m} \stackrel{up}{\longrightarrow} \ldots \stackrel{up}{\longrightarrow} T_{4m} \stackrel{down}{\longrightarrow} T_{2m})^\omega$ and $\pi = T_0 \stackrel{up}{\longrightarrow} \ldots \stackrel{up}{\longrightarrow} T_{2m} \cdot \sigma$. When $\Phi \in L(O, F)$ contains less than m occurrences of O, $\sigma \models_{\mathcal{M}} \Phi$ iff $\pi \models_{\mathcal{M}} \Phi$. But $\pi \models_{\mathcal{M}} Q_1 U Q_2$ even though $\sigma \not\models_{\mathcal{M}} Q_1 U Q_2$. ∎

The reverses of the operators O and U are $\overline{O}$ and $\overline{U}$:

$$\begin{array}{lll} \sigma, i \models_{\mathcal{M}} \overline{O}\Phi & \text{iff} & \sigma, i - 1 \models_{\mathcal{M}} \Phi \\ \sigma, i \models_{\mathcal{M}} \Phi \overline{U} \Psi & \text{iff} & \exists j \leq i.\ \sigma, j \models_{\mathcal{M}} \Psi \text{ and } \forall k : j < k \leq i.\ \sigma, k \models_{\mathcal{M}} \Phi. \end{array}$$

$\overline{O}$ expresses *at the previous moment* while $\Phi \overline{U} \Psi$ expresses Φ *has been true since* Ψ. The reverse of F *now or previously* is $\overline{F}$ defined by $\mathtt{tt}\overline{U}Q_1$. The previous lemma holds when these reverse operators are substituted for their forward versions. Reverse operators are a hallmark of traditional temporal logics where $\overline{O}\,\overline{F}$ is written as P and $\overline{U'}$ as S, *since*, Prior [Prior, 1967].

As testified by the previous lemma, showing that an operator is *not* definable in a temporal language is generally much harder than showing that it is. General techniques for showing non-definability spring from Section 5 where relationships between temporal languages and other formalisms are considered. One reason that $L(O, U)$ is an interesting logic is because it is *expressively complete.* A natural question to ask is whether there are other future linear time operators (whose meanings are independent of labels) that are not definable in $L(O, U)$. [Gabbay *et al.*, 1980] extending [Kamp, 1968] showed that $L(O, U)$ is as expressive as the first-order language the semantics these temporal formulas is couched in—a result discussed in Section 5. However, as pointed out by [Wolper, 1983] if attention is shifted from the metalanguage of $L(O,U)$ to ω-regular expressions as expressions of path properties, then there are natural future linear time operators that are not definable in $L(O,U)$. This turns out to be equivalent, as noted in Section 5.2, to considering operators whose semantics are given in a second-order metalanguage. Wolper proved the following result.

Proposition 3.3.4. $L(O,U) < L(O,U,G_{\lambda n.2n})$.

Instead Wolper proposed generating (unrelativized) future linear time operators from grammars. Transition systems with finite label sets would do instead. Suppose $\mathcal{T}$ is a transition system whose label set is of size n. Each state X of $\mathcal{T}$ determines an n-ary future linear time operator $X_{\mathcal{T}}$ as follows, where σ ranges over all the runs through $\mathcal{T}$, and π over those runs whose initial state is X:

$$\sigma \models_{\mathcal{M}} X_{\mathcal{T}}(\Phi_1,\ldots,\Phi_n) \text{ iff } \exists\pi.\ \forall i>0.\ \text{if } \mathcal{L}(\pi,i)=a_k \text{ then } \sigma^{i-1} \models_{\mathcal{M}} \Phi_k.$$

In general, satisfiability of formulae of the resulting temporal logics is undecidable. However, Wolper just considered a decidable subfamily of such logics, generated from regular grammars, or in this case finite state transition systems.

Example 3.3.5. Assume that $\mathbf{0}$ is a state which has no transitions emanating from it. Consider the transition system $\mathcal{T}$ given by: $X \stackrel{def}{=} a_1.a_2.\mathbf{0}$; $Y \stackrel{def}{=} a_1.Y$; and $Z \stackrel{def}{=} a_1.Z + a_2.\mathbf{0}$. Then $O\Phi$ is $X_{\mathcal{T}}(\mathtt{tt},\Phi)$; $G\Phi$ is given by $Y_{\mathcal{T}}(\Phi,\mathtt{tt})$ and $\Phi U \Psi$ is $F\Psi \wedge Z_{\mathcal{T}}(\Phi,\Psi)$. If instead $X \stackrel{def}{=} a_1.a_2.X$ then $X_{\mathcal{T}}(\Phi,\mathtt{tt}) \equiv G_{\lambda n.2n}\Phi$.

Let EL, for *extended* temporal logic [Wolper, 1983], be the future time linear temporal logic $L(Op_1,\ldots,Op_n,\ldots)$ where $Op_1,\ldots$ consists of all the regular grammar definable temporal operators. We will return to EL in Section 4.2 in a much more succinct form, as a finitary temporal language, a fixed point extension of $L(O)$. There are, of course, future linear time operators (definable in L_∞) that are not definable in EL. An example is $G_{\lambda n.2^n}$, as can be shown by the pumping lemma.

Associated with any linear time operator Op is the pair of *pure* branching time operators $\forall Op$ and $\exists Op$. For instance $\forall F$ is a strong eventually operator in contrast to $\exists F$:

$$\begin{array}{lll} \sigma \models_{\mathcal{M}} \forall F\Phi & \text{iff} & \forall\pi.\ \text{if } \pi(0)=\sigma(0) \text{ then } \exists k\geq 0.\ \pi^k \models_{\mathcal{M}} \Phi \\ \sigma \models_{\mathcal{M}} \exists F\Phi & \text{iff} & \exists\pi.\ \pi(0)=\sigma(0) \text{ and } \exists k\geq 0.\ \pi^k \models_{\mathcal{M}} \Phi. \end{array}$$

When $L(Op_1,\ldots,Op_n)$ is a linear time language then $B(Op_1,\ldots,Op_n)$ is its *pure* branching time version containing the temporal operators $\forall Op_i$ and

$\exists Op_i$. With respect to models on unravelled total transition systems, modal logic is merely a sublogic of $B(\langle a\rangle, \neg\langle a\rangle\neg)$, a branching time next logic. Pure branching time formulae cannot distinguish paths passing through the same state at those points. That is, any such formula Φ obeys the following condition: if $\sigma(i) = \pi(j)$ then $\sigma, i \models_{\mathcal{M}} \Phi$ iff $\pi, j \models_{\mathcal{M}} \Phi$. This property generally has the consequence that a linear time logic and its branching time version are incomparable. For instance the following result is proved by [Emerson and Halpern, 1986].

Proposition 3.3.6. *$L(O,U) \not\leq B(O,U)$, and $L(O,U) \not\geq B(O,U)$.*

The future branching time language $B(O,U)$ introduced by [Clarke and Emerson, 1981] is called CTL (standing for *computation tree logic*—as it naturally expresses tree properties). There are numerous pure branching time extensions of CTL. A very general extension is the language EB which is the pure branching version of EL. That Op is a derived operator of a linear time language does not mean that $\exists Op$ or $\forall Op$ are derivable from its pure branching time version. As pointed out by [Emerson and Halpern, 1986] the operator $\overset{\infty}{F}$ is definable in $L(O,U)$ as FGQ_1 (meaning *almost always*) but $B(O,U,\overset{\infty}{F})$ is strictly more expressive than $B(O,U)$.

A more general temporal logic encompassing $L(Op_1, \ldots, Op_n)$ and its pure branching time version is its *full* branching time version $\forall L(Op_1, \ldots, Op_n)$. This temporal logic contains the linear operators together with the branching operator $\forall$. Such logics are very expressive, allowing arbitrary embedding of linear time and branching operators. For instance, $\forall L(O,U)$ includes formulas such as $\exists FG\Phi$ as well as $\exists(F\Phi \wedge O\forall(\Phi_1 U \Psi))$: the reader is invited to work out the intuitive meaning of the latter formula. The language $\forall L(O,U)$ is called CTL* and was introduced by Clarke, Emerson, Halpern and Sistla in various papers. Standard presentations of CTL* involve a slightly unwieldy syntactic and semantics definition, distinguishing between path and state formulae—a state formula is a boolean combination of formulae of the form $\forall\Phi$ and $\exists\Phi$. The important semantic property enjoyed by a state formula was given above: a state formula cannot distinguish paths passing through the same state at those points. This property could be used instead to provide a more general distinction between these two kinds of formulae. More expressive than $\forall L(O,U)$ is the language $\forall EL$, the full branching time version of EL—this is examined in a more succinct form in Section 4.2. All full branching time languages are sublanguages of $\forall L_\infty$. There are various branching time logics between $B(O,U)$ and $\forall L(O,U)$, see [Emerson and Halpern, 1986]. These authors also show equi-expressiveness of various temporal languages—however, their definition of a temporal model is more restricted than here as they assume that sets of paths are both fusion and limit closed, terms explained in Section 3.5.

Starting with a linear time language there is a systematic method of generating pure branching and full branching time languages. The merits of using these languages for specification and verification have been widely discussed by a number of authors, initiated by [Lamport, 1980]. Increasingly, technical criteria are adduced for preferring one kind of language over another. These include expressiveness of the particular system properties that are of interest, as well as the complexity of model checking. The consequence has been a rich set of results, some of which we will encounter later. Finally, it should be pointed out that there are temporal languages that are neither linear nor branching. An example is the language whose sole operator is the *somewhen a* operator, E_a, defined earlier.

Proposition 3.3.7. *If TL contains the operator E_a then $TL \not\leq \forall L_\infty$.*

The proof of this is left as an exercise for the reader.

3.4 Minimal temporal logics

For each temporal language its associated minimal temporal logic is its set of *valid* formulae, consisting of those formulae that are true at every point in every run in every model (of the appropriate sort). We use the same notation for naming minimal temporal logics as for naming temporal languages. So $L(Op_1, \ldots, Op_n)$ now names the minimal linear time temporal logic whose operators are $Op_1, \ldots, Op_n$. Similarly, $B(Op_1, \ldots, Op_n)$ and $\forall L(Op_1, \ldots, Op_n)$ name the minimal pure and full branching time logics associated with $L(Op_1, \ldots, Op_n)$.

A characterization of $L(O, U)$ is the set of theorems of the following axiom system:

Axioms	L1.	Any tautology instance
	L2.	$G(\Phi \to \Psi) \to (G\Phi \to G\Psi)$
	L3.	$O\neg\Phi \leftrightarrow \neg O\Phi$
	L4.	$O(\Phi \to \Psi) \to (O\Phi \to O\Psi)$
	L5.	$G\Phi \to \Phi \wedge OG\Phi$
	L6.	$G(\Phi \to O\Phi) \to (\Phi \to G\Phi)$
	L7.	$\Phi U \Psi \to F\Psi$
	L8.	$\Phi U \Psi \leftrightarrow \Psi \vee (\Phi \wedge O(\Phi U \Psi))$
Rules	MP	if Φ and $\Phi \to \Psi$ then Ψ
	RG	if Φ then $G\Phi$.

As in Section 2.2 Φ is a *theorem* of this axiom system, written $\vdash \Phi$, if there is a *proof* of Φ. As with modal logics a proof of Φ is a finite sequence of formulae $\Phi_1, \ldots, \Phi_n$ with $\Phi = \Phi_n$ and where each Φ_i is either an axiom instance or the result of an application of a rule instance to premises belonging to the set $\{\Phi_1, \ldots, \Phi_{i-1}\}$. The rule RG is reminiscent of the modal rule Nec. Moreover the relationship between G and O is similar to that between $[a^*]$ and $[a]$ in dynamic logic: hence the correspondence schemas L5 and L6 (the induction schema). We call this axiom system LT. It is a sound and complete characterization of $L(O, U)$, a result due to [Gabbay *et al.*, 1980], which is also proved in Section 6.3.

Proposition 3.4.1. $LT \vdash \Phi$ *iff* $\models \Phi$

LT also supports local and global proof-theoretic consequence relations. The formula Φ follows from the set of *assumptions* Γ, written $\Gamma \vdash \Phi$, if there is a finite sequence of formulas $\Phi_1, \ldots, \Phi_n$ with $\Phi = \Phi_n$, and where each Φ_i is an instance of an axiom; or the result of an application of MP to premises in $\{\Phi_1, \ldots, \Phi_{i-1}\}$; or the result of an application of RG to a *theorem* in $\{\Phi_1, \ldots, \Phi_{i-1}\}$. As with the similar restriction on the application of the rule Nec, derivations of the form $\Phi \vdash G\Phi$ are precluded except when Φ is a theorem. The same relaxation of the application of RG distinguishes the local from the global relation as $\Phi \Vdash G\Phi$. Again the deduction theorem holds for the local but not the global relation (which as before is to be understood as Φ *follows from the additional axioms* Γ). Although LT is strongly sound (whenever $\Gamma \vdash \Phi$ then also $\Gamma \models \Phi$) the converse, strong completeness, fails for the same reason as dynamic logic. A simple counterexample is that although $\Gamma \models GQ$ when $\Gamma = \{O^n Q \mid n \geq 0\}$, we do not have that $\Gamma \vdash GQ$: for any purported proof, being finite, can only depend on a finite subset of Γ, and clearly no such subset could deliver GQ as a consequence without being inconsistent.

A characterization of the sublogic $L(O, F)$ is given by the theorems of the axiom system LT without the two axioms L7 and L8 for until. And the logic $L(O)$ is completely axiomatized by L1, L3, L4, MP and the rule RO:

$$\text{RO} \quad \text{if } \Phi \text{ then } O\Phi.$$

This axiom system is also strongly sound and complete.

The reverse logics can also be characterized by axiom systems. But there is a question as to their models. If runs do not have initial states then the axiom system for $L(\overline{O}, \overline{U})$ is just the *reverse* of LT: where each temporal operator in each axiom and rule is replaced by its reverse. And similarly for sublogics. However, if runs have initial states then changes are necessary: only one half of the reverse of L3 remains, namely $\overline{O}\neg\Phi \to \neg\overline{O}\Phi$; and in the reverses of L5 and L6 the operator $\overline{O}$ should be replaced by its dual $\neg\overline{O}\neg$.

In the case of $L(O, U, \overline{O}, \overline{U})$ with respect to models with runs lacking an initial state instead of adding reverse axioms and rules we can just add a reverse, or a *mirror image*, rule. Let $\overline{\Phi}$ be the formula Φ when all its temporal operators are reversed (assuming that $\overline{\overline{O}}$ is O and $\overline{\overline{U}}$ is U). The reverse rule is

$$\text{R}^- \text{ if } \Phi \text{ then } \overline{\Phi}.$$

Also needed are axioms which interrelate temporal operators and their reverses:

$$\begin{array}{ll} \text{L9.} & \Phi \leftrightarrow O\overline{O}\Phi \\ \text{L10.} & \Phi \rightarrow F\overline{F}\Phi. \end{array}$$

By R^- we also have: $\Phi \leftrightarrow \overline{O}O\Phi$ and $\Phi \rightarrow \overline{F}F\Phi$. A complete axiom system for $L(O, U, \overline{O}, \overline{U})$ is given by LT together with L9, L10, and R$^-$. Sublogics are determined by the appropriate subsystems.

A richer logic incorporates the relativized next operators (a). An axiomatic characterization of $L(O, U, \{(a) \mid a \in \mathcal{L}\})$ includes the following extra axiom schemas:

$$\begin{array}{ll} \text{L11.} & (a)(\Phi \rightarrow \Psi) \rightarrow ((a)\Phi \rightarrow (a)\Psi) \\ \text{L12.} & (a)\neg\Phi \rightarrow \neg(a)\Phi \\ \text{L13.} & (a)\Phi \rightarrow O\Phi. \end{array}$$

(A complete axiomatization depends on further axioms relating O and (a): in the case of a finite label set $\mathcal{L}$ the extra axiom is $O\Phi \rightarrow \bigvee\{(a)\Phi \mid a \in \mathcal{L}\}$).

All the full branching time logics for any of the linear time systems above are completely axiomatized by adding the following axioms and rules to their linear time axiom system:

$$\begin{array}{lll} \text{Axioms} & \text{B1.} & Q \rightarrow \forall Q \quad Q \text{ atomic} \\ & \text{B2.} & \exists Q \rightarrow Q \quad Q \text{ atomic} \\ & \text{B3.} & \forall\Phi \rightarrow \Phi \\ & \text{B4.} & \forall(\Phi \rightarrow \Psi) \rightarrow (\forall\Phi \rightarrow \forall\Psi) \\ & \text{B5.} & \forall\Phi \rightarrow \forall\forall\Phi \\ & \text{B6.} & \exists\Phi \rightarrow \forall\exists\Phi \\ \text{Rule} & \text{R}\forall & \text{if } \Phi \text{ then } \forall\Phi. \end{array}$$

In particular, the full branching time logic $\forall L(O, U)$ is completely characterized by LT together with these additional axioms and rule. We call this logic $\forall LT$. The following result [Stirling, 1989] is proved in Section 6.3.

Proposition 3.4.2. $\forall LT \vdash \Phi$ *iff* $\models \Phi$.

The pure branching time logic $B(O, U)$ is $\forall LT$ restricted to pure branching time formulae.

The axiom system consisting of the axioms L1,B1-B6 and the two rules MP, R$\forall$ can be viewed as a *modal* logic with the operator $\forall$ as an unrelativized modality [ ]. Let Λ consist of all modal models (of any sort) $\mathcal{M} = (\mathcal{T}, \mathcal{V})$ obeying the conditions:

i. *$\mathcal{L}$ is a singleton set.*

ii. $\xrightarrow{a}$ *is an equivalence relation.*

iii. *if* $s \in \mathcal{V}(Q)$ *and* $s \xrightarrow{a} s'$ *then* $s' \in \mathcal{V}(Q)$.

The family of theorems of this modal logic then coincides with the set of Λ-true formulae. Hence the logics $\forall L(Op_1, \ldots, Op_n)$ can be thought of as *modalized* linear time temporal logics with $\forall$ expressing *must* and $\exists$ *may*, see [Thomason, 1984] for a different perspective on such logics, and [Zanardo, 1991] for an axiom system. No special axioms are needed to interrelate the $\forall$ operator and the linear time operators: we can completely separate out their independent inferential contributions. However, this is no longer true when we restrict attention to families of models satisfying various conditions.

3.5 Classes of models, automata, and correspondence

We now examine canonical representatives for future time structures. Initially attention is restricted to future time logics without temporal operators whose meanings depend on the transition labels. Let L^+_∞ be the following sublogic of L_∞:

$$\Phi ::= Q \mid \neg\Phi \mid \bigwedge\{\Phi_j \mid j \in J\} \mid O\Phi.$$

A general future time structure for L^+_∞ is the extended transition system $\mathcal{T}_0 = (\{0\}^*, \{\xrightarrow{0}\}, \mathcal{R})$ whose set of states is the set of words on $\{0\}^*$, and where $w \xrightarrow{0} w0$ for any state w, and whose set of runs $\mathcal{R}$ comprises all runs of the form: $w \xrightarrow{0} w0 \xrightarrow{0} w00 \xrightarrow{0} \ldots$. Consequently $\mathcal{R}$ is suffix closed, and so $\mathcal{T}_0$ is a future time structure (and is just the unravelling of its underlying transition system). The next result shows that it is a *canonical* future time structure for L^+_∞:

Lemma 3.5.1. *If* $\Phi \in L^+_\infty$ *and* $\mathcal{T}_0 \models \Phi$ *then* $\models \Phi$.

Proof. Suppose $\not\models \Phi$. So there is a model $\mathcal{M} = (\mathcal{T}, \mathcal{V})$ and a run $\sigma \in \mathcal{R}_\mathcal{T}$ and an index i such that $\sigma, i \not\models_\mathcal{M} \Phi$. Let $\mathcal{M}' = (\mathcal{T}_0, \mathcal{V}')$ whose valuation has the property that $0^n \in \mathcal{V}'(Q)$ iff $\sigma(n) \in \mathcal{V}(Q)$. Let π be the run $\varepsilon \xrightarrow{0} 0 \xrightarrow{0} 00 \xrightarrow{0} \ldots$. A small induction on the structure of $\Psi \in L^+_\infty$ shows that $\pi^j \models_\mathcal{M} \Psi$ iff $\sigma, j \models_\mathcal{M} \Psi$. ∎

A small consequence of this result is that the minimal logics $L(O, U)$ and EL are characterized either as the sets of valid formulae or as the sets of formulae that are valid on all future time structures, thus justifying the dual semantics of previous sections which appeal at one time to pairs, runs and indices, and at other times to runs and their suffixes.

A natural generalization for branching time logics subsumed by $\forall L^+_\infty$ is the structure $\mathcal{T}_\omega = (\mathbb{N}^*, \{\stackrel{i}{\longrightarrow} \mid i \in \mathbb{N}\}, \mathcal{R})$ whose states are finite sequences of numerals and where $w \stackrel{i}{\longrightarrow} wi$, and $\mathcal{R}$ consists of all ω length sequences of the form $w \stackrel{i_1}{\longrightarrow} wi_1 \stackrel{i_2}{\longrightarrow} wi_1i_2 \stackrel{i_3}{\longrightarrow} \ldots$. But Lemma 3.5.1 fails to generalize to $\forall L^+_\infty$ formulae. The problem is that $\mathcal{T}_\omega$-validity is too permissive. For example the following two formulae, interrelating branching and linear time operators, are $\mathcal{T}_\omega$-valid but not valid

$$\forall O\Phi \rightarrow O\forall\Phi$$
$$\forall G(\forall\Phi \rightarrow \exists O\forall\Phi) \rightarrow (\forall\Phi \rightarrow \exists G\forall\Phi).$$

$\mathcal{T}_\omega$ contains every run through its underlying transition system $(\mathbb{N}^*, \{\stackrel{i}{\longrightarrow} \mid i \in \mathbb{N}\})$. A future time structure with this feature is said to be $\mathcal{R}$*-generable* (as $\mathcal{R}$ commonly names the transition relation of a Kripke structure). Such structures are just the unravelled transition systems described in Section 3.1. Let Λ be the family of all $\mathcal{R}$-generable structures. $\mathcal{T}_\omega$ is a canonical representative of Λ for branching time formulae.

Theorem 3.5.2. *If* $\Phi \in \forall L^+_\omega$ *and* $\mathcal{T}_\omega \models \Phi$ *then* $\Lambda \models \Phi$.

Proof. By similar techniques to those used in Lemma 3.5.1. ∎

This result can be refined. For any $n \in \mathbb{N}$, consider $\mathcal{T}_n = (\{0, \ldots, n\}^*, \{\stackrel{i}{\longrightarrow} \mid i \leq n\}, \mathcal{R})$, mediating between $\mathcal{T}_0$ and $\mathcal{T}_\omega$, where $w \stackrel{i}{\longrightarrow} wi$ and again $\mathcal{R}$ is all the generable runs. Let the branching degree of a formula $\Phi \in \forall L^+_\infty$ be the number of occurrences of $\forall$ in Φ. Now $\mathcal{T}_n$ is canonical with respect to Λ for any formula whose degree is no more than n.

Extended transition systems can be classified in terms of conditions on their label sets and their transition relations. But they can also be catalogued according to the properties of their run sets. The $\mathcal{R}$-generable structures constitute one family. In fact this family Λ can also be characterized in terms of closure conditions. A little extra notation: the ith prefix, for $i \geq 0$, of a run $\sigma = s_0 \stackrel{a_1}{\longrightarrow} s_1 \ldots$ is the finite length path $\sigma[i] = s_0 \stackrel{a_1}{\longrightarrow} \ldots \stackrel{a_i}{\longrightarrow} s_i$. We say:

- $\mathcal{R}$ is fusion closed if $\sigma(i) = \pi(j)$ (for σ and $\pi \in \mathcal{R}$) then $\sigma[i] \cdot \pi^j \in \mathcal{R}$
- $\mathcal{R}$ is limit closed if $\forall i \geq 0.\ \exists \pi_i.$ such that $\sigma[i] \cdot \pi_i \in \mathcal{R}$ then $\sigma \in \mathcal{R}$.

Limit closure states that if every finite prefix of σ is a prefix of some run in $\mathcal{R}$ then σ is in $\mathcal{R}$. The next result is due to [Emerson, 1983].

Lemma 3.5.3.

(a) *If $\mathcal{T} \in \Lambda$ then $\mathcal{R}_{\mathcal{T}}$ is suffix, fusion and limit closed,*

(b) *if $\mathcal{R}$ is suffix, fusion and limit closed then $\exists \mathcal{T} \in \Lambda.\ \mathcal{R} = \mathcal{R}_{\mathcal{T}}$.*

Proof. Part (a) is straightforward. For (b) suppose $\mathcal{R}$ is suffix, fusion and limit closed. Let $\mathcal{S} = \{\sigma[i] \mid \sigma \in \mathcal{R}\}$ and let $\mathcal{L}$ be the set of labels appearing in $\mathcal{R}$. For $a \in \mathcal{L}$ let $w \xrightarrow{a} w'$ when $w' = w \cdot (s \xrightarrow{a} s')$ for $w, w' \in \mathcal{S}$ and where $s \xrightarrow{a} s'$ appears within a run in $\mathcal{R}$. Clearly, $\mathcal{R}$ consists of all runs through $(\mathcal{S}, \{\xrightarrow{a} \mid a \in \mathcal{L}\})$. ∎

Notice, however, if $\mathcal{R}_{\mathcal{T}}$ is suffix, fusion, and limit closed this does not guarantee that $\mathcal{T}$ itself is in Λ. For instance, let $\mathcal{T} = (\{s, s_1, s_2\}, \{\xrightarrow{a}\}, \mathcal{R})$ with $s \xrightarrow{a} s_1$, $s \xrightarrow{a} s_2$, $s_1 \xrightarrow{a} s$, and $s_2 \xrightarrow{a} s$, and where $\mathcal{R}$ consists of the suffixes of $s_1 \xrightarrow{a} (s \xrightarrow{a} s_2 \xrightarrow{a} s)^\omega$. Clearly, $\mathcal{R}$ is also fusion and limit closed, but does not contain the run $(s \xrightarrow{a} s_1 \xrightarrow{a} s)^\omega$. The set $\mathcal{R}_{\mathcal{T}}$ should also be *prefix* closed: if $s \xrightarrow{a} t$ and $\sigma \in \mathcal{R}_{\mathcal{T}}$ with $\sigma(0) = t$ then $(s \xrightarrow{a} t) \cdot \sigma \in \mathcal{R}_{\mathcal{T}}$.

Consequently, we can define families of future time extended transition systems Σ_X denoting the family fulfilling conditions X where F is fusion closure, L limit closure, and P prefix closure as in figure 6. So Σ_{FLP} is Λ and Σ the family of all future time extended transition systems. One enterprise is to axiomatize Σ'-validity for particular future temporal logics. Some results are collected in Proposition 3.5.4 below. First, the condition P makes no difference: so any axiomatization of Σ_X-validity also characterizes Σ_{XP}-validity (for formulae definable in $\forall L^{+}_{\infty}$). Second, the different closure conditions are not reflected within linear time logics (and so they cannot contain formulae that correspond to them, in the sense of Section 2.3). One immediate consequence of this is that the axiom system LT is sound and complete for Λ-validity. For branching time logics the additional axiom for fusion closure is FC:

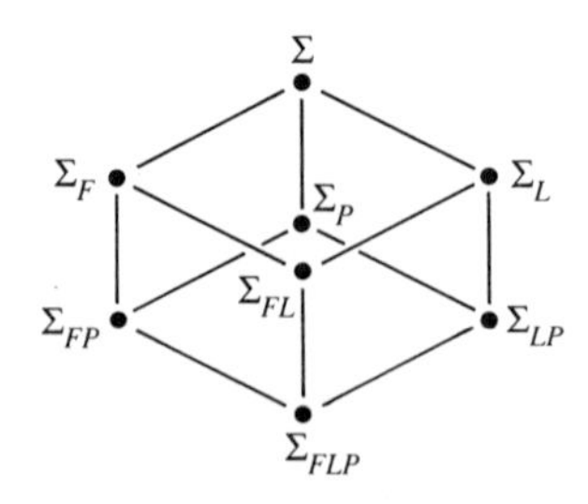

Fig. 6. Families of extended transition systems

$$\text{FC} \quad \forall O\Phi \to O\forall\Phi.$$

The axiom system ∀LT + FC characterizes Σ_F-validity of ∀L(O,U) formulae. Part (d) states that limit closure without fusion closure is uninteresting. Finally, part (e) offers an axiomatic characterization of Λ-validity of the pure branching time logic B(O,U) employing the added axiom LC:

$$\text{LC} \quad \forall G(\forall\Phi \to \exists O\forall\Phi) \to (\forall\Phi \to \exists G\forall\Phi).$$

A somewhat different axiomatization is given in [Emerson and Halpern, 1982]. Most of these results are proved later in Section 6.3. Missing, however, as an open problem, is the crucial axiomatization of Λ-validity of the full branching language ∀L(O,U) formulae, known as CTL*. For instance, the following extra induction schema is also valid:

$$\forall G(\forall\Phi \to \exists OF\forall\Phi) \to (\forall\Phi \to \exists GF\forall\Phi).$$

Notice that $\forall G(\Phi \to \exists O\Phi) \to (\Phi \to \exists G\Phi)$ is *not* Λ-valid.

Proposition 3.5.4.

(a) *If* $\Phi \in \forall L^+_\infty$ *then* $\Sigma_X \models \Phi$ *iff* $\Sigma_{XP} \models \Phi$,

(b) *If* $\Phi \in L^+_\infty$ *then* $\Sigma \models \Phi$ *iff* $\Sigma_X \models \Phi$,

(c) *If* $\Phi \in \forall L(O,U)$ *then* $\forall LT + FC \vdash \Phi$ *iff* $\Sigma_F \models \Phi$,

(d) *If* $\Phi \in \forall L(O,U)$ *then* $\forall LT \vdash \Phi$ *iff* $\Sigma_L \models \Phi$,

(e) *If* $\Phi \in B(O,U)$ *then* $\forall LT + FC + LC \vdash \Phi$ *iff* $\Sigma_{FL} \models \Phi$.

Computationally, the family Σ_{FP} (or Σ_F) is important, as members naturally model computations relative to fairness assumptions. Not every run through the underlying transition system may count as admissible. Standard definitions of fairness produce fusion closed families of admissible computations. A small amendment to the definition of $\mathcal{T}_\omega$-validity, see [Courcoubetis *et al.*, 1986] transforms $\mathcal{T}_\omega$ into a canonical structure for Σ_{FP}-validity. A *leftist* path σ has the property that almost all its labels are 0: $\exists i \geq 0.\ \mathcal{L}(\sigma^i) = 0^\omega$. If the meaning of $\forall$ on models $\mathcal{M} = (\mathcal{T}_\omega, V)$ is reinterpreted as

$$\sigma \models_{\mathcal{M}} \forall\Phi \quad \text{iff} \quad \forall \text{ leftist } \sigma'.\ \text{if } \sigma'(0) = \sigma(0) \text{ then } \sigma' \models_{\mathcal{M}} \Phi$$

and the definition of $\mathcal{M}$-true is similarly changed, $\mathcal{M} \models \Phi$ if for all leftist σ. $\sigma \models_{\mathcal{M}} \Phi$, then $\mathcal{T}_\omega$ is canonical for Σ_{FP}. This result can also be refined by introducing the meditors $\mathcal{T}_n$, as in [Courcoubetis *et al.*, 1986].

Automata generate future time temporal structures from transition systems. Consider them as pairs $(\mathcal{T}, \mathcal{A})$ where $\mathcal{T}$ is a total transition system, and $\mathcal{A}$ an *acceptance* condition which an admissible run must fulfill. As with Büchi and Rabin acceptance, $\mathcal{A}$ could constrain the states that runs may pass through, or instead it could limit their associated labels. Another possibility is that $\mathcal{A}$ could be a formula of some logic (such as a temporal formula) that admissible runs must satisfy. In all these cases one can ask if the condition $\mathcal{A}$ corresponds, in the sense of Section 2.3, to a formula of the temporal logic $(\mathcal{T}, \mathcal{A})$ is a structure for. More specifically, correspondence can be relativized to states of $\mathcal{S}_{\mathcal{T}}$. Let $\mathcal{R}(s)$ be the set of all generable runs through $\mathcal{T}$ starting at s, and $\mathcal{R}_{\mathcal{A}}(s)$ the admissible subset of $\mathcal{R}(s)$ according to $\mathcal{A}$. The condition $\mathcal{A}$ *corresponds* to the temporal formula Φ at state $s \in \mathcal{S}_{\mathcal{T}}$ if $\forall \sigma \in \mathcal{R}(s)$, $\sigma \models_{\mathcal{T}} \Phi$ iff $\sigma \in \mathcal{R}_{\mathcal{A}}(s)$.

A concrete case is Büchi automata where the acceptance condition $\mathcal{A} \subseteq \mathcal{S}_{\mathcal{T}}$ and where $\mathcal{S}_{\mathcal{T}}$ is finite. Let $\sigma(*)$ be the set of states that occur infinitely often in σ. Büchi acceptance requires that any admissible run σ has the feature that $\sigma(*) \cap \mathcal{A} \neq \emptyset$. An appropriate linear time logic for such structures is $L(\{(a) \mid a \in \mathcal{L}\}, U)$ with sole atomic sentence $\mathtt{tt}$. This logic can be directly interpreted on Büchi automata without recourse to valuations.

Example 3.5.5. Consider the Büchi automaton $(\mathcal{T}, \{X\})$ where $\mathcal{T}$ is given by: $X \stackrel{def}{=} c.X + b.X + a.Y$ and $Y \stackrel{def}{=} a.Y + c.Y + b.X$. This acceptance condition corresponds to the temporal formula $G((a)\mathtt{tt} \rightarrow F(b)\mathtt{tt})$ at state X or Y.

An alternative notion of correspondence for Büchi automata is based on the ω-language, the set of ω length words on $\mathcal{L}$, recognized by a state s in $(\mathcal{T}, \mathcal{R})$. For each $s \in \mathcal{S}_{\mathcal{T}}$ let $\mathcal{L}(s)$ be the language $\{\mathcal{L}(\sigma) \mid \sigma \in \mathcal{R}_{\mathcal{A}}(s)\}$, where $\mathcal{L}(\sigma)$ is the ω length sequence of labels in σ.

Example 3.5.6. Consider the example above $(\mathcal{T}, X)$. The languages $\mathcal{L}(X)$ and $\mathcal{L}(Y)$ consist of ω length words on $\{a, b, c\}$ with the property that after any occurrence of a there is some occurrence of b which corresponds to the formula: $G((a)\mathtt{tt} \vee (b)\mathtt{tt} \vee (c)\mathtt{tt}) \wedge G((a)\mathtt{tt} \rightarrow F(b)\mathtt{tt})$.

However, Proposition 3.3.4 shows that there are sets $\mathcal{L}(s)$ that do not correspond to $L(\{(a) \mid a \in \mathcal{L}\}, U)$ formulas. More will be said on this topic in Section 5.

3.6 Families of runs and temporal properties

An alternative presentation of the meaning of temporal formulae is to directly define the set of runs (or of pairs σ, i) at which a formula is true in a model— compare Section 2.5 for the appropriate abstraction in the case of modal formulae. We use the notation $\| \Phi \|_{\mathcal{V}}^{\mathcal{T}}$ to denote this set when $(\mathcal{T}, \mathcal{V})$ is the model. For instance, the meanings of formulae drawn from $\forall L(O, U)$ with respect to future time models are defined as follows (where the fixed index $\mathcal{T}$ is omitted from $\| \Phi \|_{\mathcal{V}}^{\mathcal{T}}$):

$$\begin{array}{lcl} \| Q \|_{\mathcal{V}} & = & \{\sigma \mid \sigma(0) \in \mathcal{V}(Q)\} \\ \| \neg\Phi \|_{\mathcal{V}} & = & \mathcal{R}_{\mathcal{T}} - \| \Phi \|_{\mathcal{V}} \\ \| \Phi \wedge \Psi \|_{\mathcal{V}} & = & \| \Phi \|_{\mathcal{V}} \cap \| \Psi \|_{\mathcal{V}} \\ \| O\Phi \|_{\mathcal{V}} & = & \| O \|^{\mathcal{T}} \| \Phi \|_{\mathcal{V}} \\ \| \Phi U \Psi \|_{\mathcal{V}} & = & \| U \|^{\mathcal{T}} (\| \Phi \|_{\mathcal{V}}, \| \Psi \|_{\mathcal{V}}) \\ \| \forall\Phi \|_{\mathcal{V}} & = & \| \forall \|^{\mathcal{T}} \| \Phi \|_{\mathcal{V}} . \end{array}$$

Here, $\| O \|^{\mathcal{T}}$, $\| U \|^{\mathcal{T}}$, and $\| \forall \|^{\mathcal{T}}$ are the following expected run transformers where $\mathcal{R}_1, \mathcal{R}_2 \subseteq \mathcal{R}_{\mathcal{T}}$:

$$\begin{array}{lcl} \| O \|^{\mathcal{T}} \mathcal{R}_1 & = & \{\sigma \in \mathcal{R}_{\mathcal{T}} \mid \sigma^1 \in \mathcal{R}_1\} \\ \| U \|^{\mathcal{T}} (\mathcal{R}_1, \mathcal{R}_2) & = & \{\sigma \in \mathcal{R}_{\mathcal{T}} \mid \exists i \geq 0.\ \sigma^i \in \mathcal{R}_2 \text{ and } \forall j : 0 \leq j < i.\ \sigma^j \in \mathcal{R}_1\} \\ \| \forall \|^{\mathcal{T}} \mathcal{R}_1 & = & \{\sigma \in \mathcal{R}_{\mathcal{T}} \mid \forall \pi \in \mathcal{R}_{\mathcal{T}}.\ \text{if } \pi(0) = \sigma(0) \text{ then } \pi \in \mathcal{R}_1\}. \end{array}$$

Derived operators induce corresponding transformers: for example, $\| G \|^{\mathcal{T}} \mathcal{R}_1 = \{\sigma \in \mathcal{R}_{\mathcal{T}} \mid \forall i \geq 0.\ \sigma^i \in \mathcal{R}_1\}$. Clearly the two semantic definitions of $\forall L(O, U)$ formulae agree: $\sigma \models_{\mathcal{M}} \Phi$ iff $\sigma \in \| \Phi \|_{\mathcal{V}}^{\mathcal{T}}$ when $\mathcal{M} = (\mathcal{T}, \mathcal{V})$. Consequently, Φ is $\mathcal{M}$-true if it determines the admissible run space $\mathcal{R}_{\mathcal{T}}$.

The run transformers are monotonic with respect to the subset ordering on run sets: if $\mathcal{R} \subseteq \mathcal{R}'$ then, for instance, $\| \forall \|^{\mathcal{T}} \mathcal{R} \subseteq \| \forall \|^{\mathcal{T}} \mathcal{R}'$, and $\| U \|^{\mathcal{T}} (\mathcal{R}, \mathcal{R}_1) \subseteq \| U \|^{\mathcal{T}} (\mathcal{R}', \mathcal{R}_1)$. Continuity with respect to an extended transition system $\mathcal{T}$ is a further issue. A monadic temporal operator Op is *continuous* if $\| Op \|^{\mathcal{T}} \bigcup \mathcal{R}_i = \bigcup \| Op \|^{\mathcal{T}} \mathcal{R}_i$ for any directed family $\bigcup \mathcal{R}_i$ of subsets of $\mathcal{R}_{\mathcal{T}}$ (see Section 2.5): for polyadic operators continuity is defined componentwise. The next lemma relates continuity to other notions: $\mathcal{R}_{\mathcal{T}}$ is finitary branching if for all $\sigma \in \mathcal{R}_{\mathcal{T}}$ the set $\{\pi \in \mathcal{R}_{\mathcal{T}} \mid \pi(0) = \sigma(0)\}$ is finite, and $\sigma \in \mathcal{R}_{\mathcal{T}}$ is *eventually cyclic* if the set $\{\sigma^i \mid i \geq 0\}$ is finite.

Lemma 3.6.1.

(a) $\| O \|^{\mathcal{T}}$ *is continuous,*

(b) $\| \forall \|^{\mathcal{T}}$ *is continuous iff* $\mathcal{R}_{\mathcal{T}}$ *is finitary branching,*

(c) $\| G \|^{\mathcal{T}}$ *is continuous iff every* $\sigma \in \mathcal{R}_{\mathcal{T}}$ *is eventually cyclic.*

Proof. Similar to the proof of Lemma 2.5.1. ■

Just as we viewed a set of states $\| \Phi \|_{\mathcal{V}}^{\mathcal{T}}$ as a modal property when Φ is a modal formula, we can regard a set of runs (or pairs) $\| \Phi \|_{\mathcal{V}}^{\mathcal{T}}$ as a temporal property here. Temporal properties also form a boolean algebra whose unit is $\mathcal{R}_{\mathcal{T}}$. Moreover they are closed under the operations $\| Op \|^{\mathcal{T}}$ when Op is a temporal operator. These obey healthiness conditions corresponding to the axioms of minimal temporal logics (such as $\| O \|^{\mathcal{T}} - \mathcal{R} = - \| O \|^{\mathcal{T}} \mathcal{R}$ where $-$ is complementation). From these ingredients, linear and branching time temporal algebras can be defined when temporal properties are viewed as abstract objects subject to equational laws. The reader is invited to fill out details such as the relevant Stone representation theorems.

An attractive application of temporal logics is the classification of program properties. Lamport proposed a distinction between *safety* and *liveness* properties: intuitively, a safety property expresses that something bad *never* happens (expressed as a formula $\forall G \neg \Phi$) while a liveness property states that something good does *eventually* happen (expressed as a formula $\forall F \Phi$). There are various more abstract accounts of these properties as sets of runs [Alpern and Schneider, 1985; Sistla, 1985] as well as an alternative classification [Manna and Pnueli, 1989].

3.7 Decision procedures

The linear and branching time logics $L(O, U)$, EL, $B(O, U)$, and $\forall L(O, U)$, even when restricted to R-generable or fusion closed (future time) models are decidable. However techniques for proving decidability are more intricate than for similar results for modal logics as outlined in Section 2.6.

A useful criterion for indicating that a modal logic is decidable is its possession of the small model property , given by a function $f : \mathbb{N} \rightarrow \mathbb{N}$, and a proof that any Λ-satisfiable formula of size n is true somewhere in a Λ-model whose size is no more than $f(n)$. An immediate question in the temporal case, because of the extra run component, is what counts as the size of a model. The simplest proposal is to identify it with the size of its underlying transition system. Definition 2.6.1 shows how an arbitrary modal model may be collapsed by filtering it through a set of formulae Γ: when Γ is finite so is the filtered model. Similarly, we can define the *temporal* collapse of a model.

Assume that $\mathcal{M}$ is a future time model, and Γ is a non-empty set of temporal formulae. Two states s and t of $\mathcal{S}_{\mathcal{M}}$ are Γ-equivalent in $\mathcal{M}$, $s \equiv_{\Gamma}^{\mathcal{M}} t$, if they have the same properties drawn from Γ: that is, if $\{\Phi \in \Gamma \mid s \models_{\mathcal{M}} \Phi\} = \{\Phi \in \Gamma \mid t \models_{\mathcal{M}} \Phi\}$. Let $|s|_{\Gamma}^{\mathcal{M}}$ be the equivalence class induced on $\mathcal{S}_{\mathcal{M}}$ by s with respect to $\equiv_{\Gamma}^{\mathcal{M}}$. As with the modal case, the temporal collapse of $\mathcal{M}$ is defined by filtering it through $\equiv_{\Gamma}^{\mathcal{M}}$.

Definition 3.7.1. The *temporal* collapse of $\mathcal{M}$ with respect to Γ is the model $\mathcal{M}_{\Gamma}$ where (assuming the index Γ abbreviates $\mathcal{M}_{\Gamma}$)

(a) $\mathcal{S}_{\Gamma} = \{|s|_{\Gamma}^{\mathcal{M}} \mid s \in \mathcal{S}_{\mathcal{M}}\}$,

(b) $\mathcal{L}_\Gamma = \mathcal{L}_\mathcal{M} \cap \{a \mid a \text{ occurs in } \Gamma\}$,

(c) $x \xrightarrow{a}_\Gamma y$ iff $\exists s \in x.\ \exists t \in y.\ s \xrightarrow{a} t$,

(d) $\mathcal{R}_\Gamma = \{x_0 \xrightarrow{a_0} x_1 \xrightarrow{a_1} \dots \mid$
$\exists \sigma \in \mathcal{R}_\mathcal{M}.\ \forall i \geq 0.\ \sigma(i) \in x_i$ and $L(\sigma, i) = a_i\}$,

(e) $x \in \mathcal{V}_\Gamma(Q)$ iff $\exists s \in x.\ s \in \mathcal{V}_\mathcal{M}(Q)$.

By definition $\mathcal{M}_\Gamma$ is a future time model (as $\mathcal{R}_\Gamma$ is suffix closed). Moreover, whenever Γ is finite so is the underlying transition system of $\mathcal{M}_\Gamma$. The essential difference between this definition and that of the modal collapse is condition (d), which stipulates that every run in $\mathcal{R}_\Gamma$ is represented in $\mathcal{R}_\mathcal{M}$, and vice versa. As with the modal case, if Γ is closed under subformulae then $\mathcal{M}_\Gamma$ inherits important semantic properties of $\mathcal{M}$. When σ is a run of $\mathcal{R}_\mathcal{M}$ let $|\sigma|_\Gamma$ be its representative in $\mathcal{M}_\Gamma$. The following result holds for future formulae of $\forall L_\infty$.

Lemma 3.7.2. *If Γ is closed under subformulae and $\Phi \in \Gamma$, then $\sigma \models_\mathcal{M} \Phi$ iff $|\sigma|_\Gamma \models_{\mathcal{M}_\Gamma} \Phi$.*

Proof. By induction on $\Phi \in \Gamma$ we show the stronger: $\sigma^i \models_\mathcal{M} \Phi$ iff $|\sigma|^i_\Gamma \models_{\mathcal{M}_\Gamma} \Phi$. The only interesting case is the $\forall$ operator which depends on the definition of $\mathcal{R}_\Gamma$. ∎

The role of condition (d) in Definition 3.7.1 is illustrated in the following example.

Example 3.7.3. Let $\mathcal{T}$ be the transition system determined by $S_i \stackrel{def}{=} up.S_{i+1}$ for $i \geq 0$, and assume that $\mathcal{R}$ is the set of all runs through $\mathcal{T}$. Moreover, let $\mathcal{M}_j$ be the model $(\mathcal{T}, \mathcal{V}_j)$ where $\mathcal{V}_j(Q) = \{S_j\}$. Clearly, for any j $S_0 \models_{\mathcal{M}_j} \forall FQ$. But consider a temporal collapse of $\mathcal{M}_j$ with respect to a finite set Γ containing $\forall FQ$ closed under subformulae. For sufficiently large j, $|S_k|^{\mathcal{M}_j}_\Gamma = |S_n|^{\mathcal{M}_j}_\Gamma$ for some k and n such that $k < n < j$. However, the run $(|S_k|^{\mathcal{M}_j}_\Gamma \xrightarrow{up} \dots \xrightarrow{up} |S_n|^{\mathcal{M}_j}_\Gamma)^\omega$ does not belong to $\mathcal{R}_\Gamma$.

In this example the temporal collapse of an R-generable model is not itself R-generable. Lemma 3.7.2 shows, for instance, that $\forall EL$ and its sublogics (such as $\forall LT$) have the small model property (assuming that the size of a model is the size of its underlying transition system). But it does not imply that $\forall LTFC$ or CTL^* (valid $\forall L(O, U)$ formulae with respect to R-generable models) also has this property. Again extra closure conditions on the set Γ may suffice (as it does in the case of $\forall LTFC$ — this follows from Section 6.3). Alternatively, it may be possible to show that $\mathcal{M}_\Gamma$ can be extended into a finite model fulfilling the required model conditions.

Tableau methods may be used instead to prove decidability of a temporal logic. [Emerson and Sistla, 1984] use automata to guide the construction of tableaux in their proof that CTL^* is decidable. Reduction to SnS ($S1S$ or Büchi automata in the case of linear time logics) provides another technique for establishing decidability of temporal logics [Gabbay, 1976; Harel *et al.*, 1982; Sistla *et al.*, 1987]. Also see [Gurevitch and Shelah, 1985].

Another important arena for decision procedures is proving that a temporal formula is true somewhere in a given finite (and usually R-generable model). Algorithms that decide this are known as *model checkers* : see [Clarke *et al.*, 1983] for a model checker for $B(O,U)$ formulas, and [Lichtenstein and Pnueli, 1984] for $L(O,U)$ formulae.

4 Modal and Temporal Mu-Calculi

4.1 Modal and temporal equations

Consider appealing to definitional equality, $\stackrel{def}{=}$, when defining modal or temporal properties. For instance, the modal equation $Z \stackrel{def}{=} \langle tick \rangle \mathtt{tt}$ stipulates that Z expresses the same property, of having a *tick* transition, as $\langle tick \rangle \mathtt{tt}$. In any modal model $(\mathcal{T}, \mathcal{V})$, whose sort includes *tick*, this property is given by the set $\| \langle tick \rangle \mathtt{tt} \|^{\mathcal{T}}_{\mathcal{V}}$, see Section 2.5 for notation. Suppose recursive equations are also permitted such as $Z \stackrel{def}{=} \langle tick \rangle Z$. Now Z can be viewed as expressing (various) properties on a model, each of which is a subset $\mathcal{S}'$ of the state set $\mathcal{S}_{\mathcal{T}}$ with the feature:

$$\mathcal{S}' \;=\; \| \langle tick \rangle \|^{\mathcal{T}} \; \mathcal{S}' \;=\; \{ s \in \mathcal{S}_{\mathcal{T}} \mid \exists s' \in \mathcal{S}'.\; s \stackrel{tick}{\longrightarrow} s' \}.$$

Any such set $\mathcal{S}'$ is a *fixed point* of the function $f = \lambda \mathcal{S}_1 \subseteq \mathcal{S}_{\mathcal{T}}.\; \| \langle tick \rangle \|^{\mathcal{T}} \; \mathcal{S}_1$, as $f(\mathcal{S}') = \mathcal{S}'$.

Example 4.1.1. Both subsets, $\emptyset$ and $\{Cl\}$, of any modal model on the simple transition system generated by $Cl \stackrel{def}{=} tick.Cl$ solve $Z \stackrel{def}{=} \langle tick \rangle Z$. In the case of $Cl' \stackrel{def}{=} tick.tock.Cl'$ there is just one solution, $\emptyset$. If instead we consider this modal equation on any model for the following, $Co_0 \stackrel{def}{=} tick.Co_0 + up.Co_1$; $Co_{2i+1} \stackrel{def}{=} up.Co_{2i+2} + down.Co_{2i}$; $Co_{2i+2} \stackrel{def}{=} tick.Co_{2i+2} + up.Co_{2i+3} + down.Co_{2i+1}$ then every subset of $\{Co_{2i} \mid i \in \mathbb{N}\}$ is a solution.

On any modal model (of the appropriate sort) $Z \stackrel{def}{=} \langle tick \rangle Z$ not only has solutions, but also has a *smallest* and a *largest* with respect to the subset ordering on state sets (which may coincide as for Cl' above) suggesting that we can select these as the prominent solutions. The general theorem that guarantees this is due to Tarski.

Proposition 4.1.2. *Let $\mathcal{P}$ be any set and assume $f : 2^{\mathcal{P}} \to 2^{\mathcal{P}}$ is monotonic (with respect to $\subseteq$). Then f has*

(a) a least fixed point given by $\bigcap\{\mathcal{P}' \subseteq \mathcal{P} \mid f(\mathcal{P}') \subseteq \mathcal{P}'\}$,

(b) a greatest fixed point given by $\bigcup\{\mathcal{P}' \subseteq \mathcal{P} \mid \mathcal{P}' \subseteq f(\mathcal{P}')\}$.

This proposition applies to $Z \stackrel{def}{=} \langle tick \rangle Z$ on any modal model as $\| \langle tick \rangle \|^{\mathcal{T}}$ is a monotonic state transformer (see Section 2.5). But what properties are expressed by these two solutions? The least case is of little import as it expresses the same property as $\mathtt{ff}$: irrespective of the state set $\mathcal{S}$, clearly $\emptyset = \{s \in \mathcal{S} \mid \exists t \in \emptyset.\ s \stackrel{tick}{\longrightarrow} t\}$. More stimulating is the maximal solution, as it expresses an ability to endlessly perform the *tick* transition. A state $s_0 \in \mathcal{S}$ has this property if there is an ω length run from s_0 of the form $s_0 \stackrel{tick}{\longrightarrow} s_1 \stackrel{tick}{\longrightarrow} \ldots$. Consequently, allowing recursive modal equations blurs the distinction between modal and temporal logics. For the maximal solution here on any modal model $\mathcal{M}$ expresses the same property as the temporal formula $\exists G(tick)\mathtt{tt}$ on the R-generable or unravelled future time model associated with $\mathcal{M}$.

A slightly more composite equation schema (where Φ does not contain Z free) is $Z \stackrel{def}{=} \Phi \vee \langle a \rangle Z$. As before the function $\lambda \mathcal{S}' \subseteq \mathcal{S}_{\mathcal{T}}.\ \| \Phi \|^{\mathcal{T}}_{\mathcal{V}} \cup \| \langle a \rangle \|^{\mathcal{T}}\ \mathcal{S}'$ is monotonic. On any dynamic model the least solution expresses the property $\langle a^* \rangle \Phi$ and, mixing formalisms, the maximal solution expresses $\langle a^* \rangle \Phi \vee \exists G(a)\mathtt{tt}$.

Not every modal equation has a solution. For instance, $Z \stackrel{def}{=} \Phi \wedge [a]\neg Z$ may not, depending on the model: the problem is that the function $\lambda \mathcal{S}' \subseteq \mathcal{S}_{\mathcal{T}}.\ \| \Phi \|^{\mathcal{T}}_{\mathcal{V}} \cap \| [a] \|^{\mathcal{T}}\ (\mathcal{S}_{\mathcal{T}} - \mathcal{S}')$ is not in general monotonic, and so Proposition 4.1.2 does not apply. Such equations can be ruled out, by only permitting those of the form $Z \stackrel{def}{=} \Psi$ where all occurrences of Z in Ψ lie within an even number of negations.

Proposition 4.1.2 also applies to recursive temporal equations, when $\mathcal{P}$ is the set of runs of a temporal model. For instance, the equation $Z \stackrel{def}{=} \Phi \wedge OZ$ (when Φ does not contain Z free) determines the monotonic function $\lambda \mathcal{R} \subseteq \mathcal{R}_{\mathcal{T}}.\ \| \Phi \|^{\mathcal{T}}_{\mathcal{V}} \cap \| O \|^{\mathcal{T}}\ \mathcal{R}$ on any future time model $(\mathcal{T}, \mathcal{V})$— see Section 3.5 for notation. Its maximal solution expresses $G\Phi$. Evidence for this is the *LT* theorem $\vdash G\Phi \leftrightarrow \Phi \wedge OG\Phi$. Another example is that the least solution to $Z \stackrel{def}{=} Q \vee (R \wedge \exists OZ)$ is just $\exists(RUQ)$ when R and Q are atomic. Moreover such equations can yield operators which are not definable in $\forall L(O,U)$: a simple case is that the maximal solution to $Z \stackrel{def}{=} Q \wedge OOOZ$ on any future time model defines the operator $G_{\lambda n.3n}$ (compare Proposition 3.3.4). Equations can also be used to capture families of runs in terms of their label sequences. An example is the maximal solution to $Z \stackrel{def}{=} (a)(b)(c)Z$ which defines the set of runs whose sequence of labels is $(abc)^\omega$.

Combinations of $L(O,U)$ definable operators are not given by individual temporal equations. Instead, families of equations are needed. For instance, $F(Q_1UQ_2)$ is determined by the pair $Z_1 \stackrel{def}{=} Z_2 \vee OZ_1$ and $Z_2 \stackrel{def}{=} Q_2 \vee (Q_1 \vee OZ_2)$, both of which must be solved as least solutions. But other combinations depend on families of equations whose solutions are mixtures of least and greatest: a simple case is FGQ defined by the pair $Z_1 \stackrel{def}{=} Z_2 \vee OZ_1$ and $Z_2 \stackrel{def}{=} Q \wedge OZ_2$ where the second is to be the greatest, while the first is the least, solution. Quickly the equational format becomes cumbersome. Instead modal and temporal languages can be extended with fixed point operators $\mu Z.$ (and their duals $\nu Z.$) which bind free occurrences of Z in Φ in the formula $\mu Z.\,\Phi$. It expresses the minimal solution to the equation $Z \stackrel{def}{=} \Phi$ where Φ may contain further fixed point operators. For instance, $F(Q_1UQ_2)$ is given by the single formula $\mu Z.\,(\mu Y.\,Q_2 \vee (Q_1 \wedge OY)) \vee OZ$. Semantics of such languages are now examined.

4.2 The mu-calculi

Formulas of the modal and temporal mu-calculi are defined by the following abstract syntax:

$$\Phi ::= Q \mid Z \mid \neg\Phi \mid \Phi_1 \wedge \Phi_2 \mid Op\Phi \mid \mu Z.\Phi,$$

where Q ranges over atomic sentences; Z over a denumerable family of propositional variables; and Op over a family of monotonic one place modal or temporal operators.[2] One syntactic restriction on $\mu Z.\,\Phi$, motivated earlier through Proposition 4.1.2, is that all free occurrences of Z in Φ lie within the scope of an even number of negations. As with $\exists Z$ and λZ, the operator $\mu Z.$ is a binder. Consequently usual terminology applies, such as that of a *closed formula* containing no free propositional variables. The dual binder $\nu Z.$ is definable:

$$\nu Z.\,\Phi \quad \stackrel{def}{=} \quad \neg\mu Z.\,\neg(\Phi[Z := \neg Z])$$

where $\Phi[Z := \neg Z]$ is the result of replacing all free occurrences of Z in Φ with $\neg Z$. For instance, $\nu Z.\,Q \wedge OZ$ abbreviates $\neg\mu Z.\,\neg(Q \wedge O\neg Z)$ which is

[2]The restriction to single place operators could be relaxed—but in the sequel we only appeal to mu-calculi built from such operators.

equivalent to $\neg\mu Z.\neg Q \vee OZ$: the former defines GQ while the latter defines its equivalent $\neg F\neg Q$. Depending on the range of Op, various mu-calculi are determined, each of which is identified by its family of *closed* formulae:

$$\begin{array}{rl} \text{modal}: & \{[a] \mid a \in \mathcal{L}\} \\ \text{linear time}: & \{(a), O \mid a \in \mathcal{L}\} \\ \text{pure branching time}: & \{\exists O, \exists(a), \forall(a) \mid a \in \mathcal{L}\} \\ \text{full branching time}: & \{O, (a), \forall \mid a \in \mathcal{L}\}. \end{array}$$

Often the relativized operators are omitted from the temporal mu-calculi. The modal mu-calculus was introduced by [Kozen, 1983], and in a different form by [Pratt, 1982] who interprets $\mu Z.$ as a least root, as in recursive function theory, instead of as a least fixed point. The temporal mu-calculi are due to [Emerson and Clarke, 1980], and [Barringer *et al.*, 1984]. Mention should also be made of the mu-calculus, first-order logic extended with fixed point operators, studied by de Bakker, de Roever, and Park. The notion of sort of a modal or temporal mu-calculus is, as previously, the label set $\mathcal{L}$ appealed to in its definition.

A model for both kinds of mu-calculi is a pair $\mathcal{M} = (\mathcal{T}, \mathcal{V})$ where $\mathcal{T}$ is a transition system or a future time structure. In the case of a modal model the valuation $\mathcal{V}$ assigns to each atomic formula Q and propositional variable Z a set of states (a subset of $\mathcal{S}_\mathcal{T}$). But when the model is temporal $\mathcal{V}$ assigns a set of *runs* (a subset of $\mathcal{R}_\mathcal{T}$) to each propositional variable (and, as before, sets of states to atomic sentences). The standard updating notation $\mathcal{V}[\mathcal{W}/Z]$ is assumed where $\mathcal{W}$ is either a set of runs or a set of states: $\mathcal{V}[\mathcal{W}/Z]$ is the valuation $\mathcal{V}'$ which agrees with $\mathcal{V}$ everywhere except on Z when $\mathcal{V}'(Z) = \mathcal{W}$. The set of runs (states) Φ is true as in the temporal (modal) model $(\mathcal{T}, \mathcal{V})$ is defined inductively as the set $\| \Phi \|_\mathcal{V}^\mathcal{T}$. First for atomic sentences:

$$\begin{array}{lrcl} \text{modal}: & \| Q \|_\mathcal{V}^\mathcal{T} & = & \mathcal{V}(Q) \\ \text{temporal}: & \| Q \|_\mathcal{V}^\mathcal{T} & = & \{\sigma \in \mathcal{R}_\mathcal{T} \mid \sigma(0) \in \mathcal{V}(Q)\}. \end{array}$$

The rest of the clauses are given jointly, assuming that $\mathcal{W}_\mathcal{T}$ is $\mathcal{S}_\mathcal{T}$ in the modal case and $\mathcal{R}_\mathcal{T}$ in the temporal case:

$$\begin{array}{lcl} \| Z \|_\mathcal{V}^\mathcal{T} & = & \mathcal{V}(Z) \\ \| \neg\Phi \|_\mathcal{V}^\mathcal{T} & = & \mathcal{W}_\mathcal{T} - \| \Phi \|_\mathcal{V}^\mathcal{T} \\ \| \Phi \wedge \Psi \|_\mathcal{V}^\mathcal{T} & = & \| \Phi \|_\mathcal{V}^\mathcal{T} \cap \| \Psi \|_\mathcal{V}^\mathcal{T} \\ \| Op\Phi \|_\mathcal{V}^\mathcal{T} & = & \| Op \|^\mathcal{T} \| \Phi \|_\mathcal{V}^\mathcal{T} \\ \| \mu Z.\, \Phi \|_\mathcal{V}^\mathcal{T} & = & \bigcap\{\mathcal{W}' \subseteq \mathcal{W}_\mathcal{T} \mid \| \Phi \|_{\mathcal{V}[\mathcal{W}'/Z]}^\mathcal{T} \subseteq \mathcal{W}'\}. \end{array}$$

The clause for the least fixed point operator is directly determined from Proposition 4.1.2 as is the derived clause for $\nu Z.$:

$$\| \nu Z.\, \Phi \|_{\mathcal{V}}^{\mathcal{T}} \;=\; \bigcup \{\mathcal{W}' \subseteq \mathcal{W}_{\mathcal{T}} \mid \mathcal{W}' \subseteq \| \Phi \|_{\mathcal{V}[\mathcal{W}'/Z]}^{\mathcal{T}}\}$$

Notice that the meaning of a formula in a model may depend on the meanings of its subformulae in other models.

The derived notion of satisfaction, that Φ is true at a state or a run w in a model $\mathcal{M} = (\mathcal{T}, \mathcal{V})$ is defined as expected: $w \models_{\mathcal{M}} \Phi$ if $w \in\| \Phi \|_{\mathcal{V}}^{\mathcal{T}}$. A more direct definition of $\models_{\mathcal{M}}$ is possible using ordinal approximants. Let $\mu^0 Z.\Phi = \mathtt{ff}$ and for any ordinal κ let $\mu^{\kappa+1} Z.\Phi = \Phi[Z := \mu^{\kappa} Z.\Phi]$, and for any limit ordinal ξ let $\mu^{\xi} Z.\Phi = \bigvee\{\mu^{\kappa} Z.\Phi \mid \kappa < \xi\}$. Now it follows that $w \in\| \mu Z.\, \Phi \|_{\mathcal{V}}^{\mathcal{T}}$ iff $w \models_{\mathcal{M}} \bigvee\{\mu^{\kappa} Z.\Phi \mid \kappa \in \alpha\}$ when α is the family of ordinals whose cardinality is that of $\mathcal{S}_{\mathcal{T}}$ or $\mathcal{R}_{\mathcal{T}}$ according to whether $\mathcal{M}$ is modal or temporal. Consequently, this shows that the linear time mu-calculus is a future time linear logic in the sense of Section 3.3 as every formula of it is equivalent to a formula of the future fragment of L_{∞} (of the same sort).

The usual semantic abstractions, Definition 2.1.3 and Definition 3.2.1, of truth and validity apply to the mu-calculi. An example of a valid formula is an unrolling of a fixed point, $\mu Z.\, \Phi \rightarrow \Phi[Z := \mu Z.\, \Phi]$. Global and local consequence relations can also be defined, as before. Richer mu-calculi employing reverse operators $\overline{[a]}$, $\overline{O}$, and $\overline{(a)}$ can also be introduced. Then in the temporal case $\| \Phi \|_{\mathcal{V}}^{\mathcal{T}}$ is defined as a set of run index pairs, instead of as future runs.

Definition 3.2.3 stipulated when one temporal language is as expressive as another relative to a family of models. A similar definition also applies to modal languages. First Φ and Ψ are equally expressive with respect to Λ, $\Phi \equiv_{\Lambda} \Psi$, if for every model $(\mathcal{T}, \mathcal{V}) \in \Lambda$. $\| \Phi \|_{\mathcal{V}}^{\mathcal{T}} = \| \Psi \|_{\mathcal{V}}^{\mathcal{T}}$. So $M_1 \leq_{\Lambda} M_2$ when $\forall \Phi \in M_1.\, \exists \Psi \in M_2.$ such that $\Phi \equiv_{\Lambda} \Psi$. Suppose M is the standard modal language of Section 2.1 and μM the modal mu-calculus (both of the appropriate sort). The next lemma (from [Kozen, 1983]) states that μM is more expressive than M, and that it is more expressive than PDL (see Section 2.4) relative to the family Λ of dynamic models (of the appropriate sort).

Lemma 4.2.1. *$M < \mu M$, and $PDL <_{\Lambda} \mu M$.*

Proof. Clearly every $\Phi \in M$ also belongs to μM. Below we show that $\mu Z.\, [a] Z$ is not equivalent to any modal formula. For the second part, every formula $\Phi \in PDL$ can be translated into an equivalent μM formula Φ^t as follows: $Q^t = Q$; $Z^t = Z$; $(\neg\Phi)^t = \neg\Phi^t$; $(\Phi \wedge \Psi)^t = \Phi^t \wedge \Psi^t$; if a is atomic then $([a]\Phi)^t = [a]\Phi^t$; $([a \cup b]\Phi)^t = ([a]\Phi)^t \wedge ([b]\Phi)^t$; $([\Psi ?]\Phi)^t = \Psi^t \rightarrow \Phi^t$; $([a; b]\Phi)^t = ([a][b]\Phi)^t$; and the final important case $([a^*]\Phi)^t = \nu Z.\, \Phi^t \wedge ([a]Z)^t$ where Z is a new propositional variable. For all models $(\mathcal{T}, \mathcal{V}) \in \Lambda$. $\| \Phi \|_{\mathcal{V}}^{\mathcal{T}} = \| \Phi^t \|_{\mathcal{V}}^{\mathcal{T}}$. So $PDL \leq_{\Lambda} \mu M$. To show μM is strictly more expressive than PDL (and M) consider the formula $\mu Z.[a]Z$ when a is an atomic label. This formula is true at a state s if there are no a^ω runs emanating from s. But consider any (dynamic) model $\mathcal{M}$ generable from the following transition system where $\mathbf{0}$ is a state with no transitions emanating from it: $St_0 \stackrel{def}{=} \mathbf{0}$; $St_{i+1} \stackrel{def}{=} a.St_i$. Suppose $\Phi \in PDL$ (or in M) is equivalent to $\mu Z.[a]Z$. Let Γ be the smallest set of formulae containing Φ which is closed under subformulae. Now consider the modal collapse of $\mathcal{M}$ with respect to Γ, the model $\mathcal{M}_\Gamma$. By Lemma 2.6.2 $St_i \models_{\mathcal{M}} \Phi$ iff $|St_i|_\Gamma^{\mathcal{M}} \models_{\mathcal{M}_\Gamma} \Phi$. But as Γ is finite, $|St_i|_\Gamma^{\mathcal{M}} = |St_j|_\Gamma^{\mathcal{M}}$ for some j and $i > j$. But then $|St_i|_\Gamma^{\mathcal{M}} \not\models_{\mathcal{M}_\Gamma} \mu Z.[a]Z$ as $|St_i|_\Gamma^{\mathcal{M}} \stackrel{a}{\longrightarrow} \ldots \stackrel{a}{\longrightarrow} |St_j|_\Gamma^{\mathcal{M}}$. ■

Let $\mu L(O)$, and $\mu\forall L(O)$ be the future linear and full branching time mu-calculi without the relativized next operators. The next lemma states expressibility results for these mu-calculi. The most noticeable is that $\mu L(O)$ and Wolper's extended temporal logic EL, Section 3.3, are equi-expressive, despite the appeal to an infinite family of temporal operators in EL. Thus $\mu L(O)$ is a very succinct version of EL.

Lemma 4.2.2.

(a) $L(O,U) < \mu L(O) = EL$,

(b) $\forall L(O,U) < \mu\forall L(O)\forall EL$.

Proof. (sketch) Part (b) follows from (a). First $EL \leq \mu L(O)$ is straightforward to establish as every regular grammar temporal operator is definable in $\mu L(O)$. To show $\mu L(O) \leq EL$ is much more delicate. The proof proceeds by establishing that every formula of $\mu L(O)$ is equivalent to an $S1S$ formula with one free variable (see Section 5.1). But every such $S1S$ formula is equivalent to an EL formula. ■

Elegant expressibility results relating the mu-calculi to automata and language theory can also be given. When $\mathcal{L}$ is a finite set of labels consider the following mu-calculi of sort $\mathcal{L}$: the closed formulae of μM, $\mu L((a))$, and $\mu\forall L((a))$, built from the empty set of atomic sentences. These logics can be directly interpreted on ω-words of, and ω-trees on, $\mathcal{L}$. For instance the meaning of $\mu L((a))$ formulae is given as follows, where $\mathcal{V}$ assigns to each variable a subset of $\mathcal{L}^\omega$.

$$\begin{array}{lcl} \| Z \|_{\mathcal{V}} & = & \mathcal{V}(Z) \\ \| \neg\Phi \|_{\mathcal{V}} & = & \mathcal{L}^\omega - \| \Phi \|_{\mathcal{V}} \\ \| \Phi \wedge \Psi \|_{\mathcal{V}} & = & \| \Phi \|_{\mathcal{V}} \cap \| \Psi \|_{\mathcal{V}} \\ \| (a)\Phi \|_{\mathcal{V}} & = & \{aw \mid w \in \| \Phi \|_{\mathcal{V}}\} \\ \| \mu Z.\,\Phi \|_{\mathcal{V}} & = & \bigcap\{\mathcal{L}' \subseteq \mathcal{L}^\omega \mid \| \Phi \|_{\mathcal{V}[\mathcal{L}'/Z]} \subseteq \mathcal{L}'\}. \end{array}$$

For any closed formula let $\| \Phi \|$ be the language $\| \Phi \|_{\mathcal{V}}$ for some $\mathcal{V}$. Each formula determines an ω-language on $\mathcal{L}$. An interesting result is that each such language is ω-regular (see Section 5.2), and that every ω-regular language is determined by some formula. Less is known about the tree languages determined by $\mu\forall L((a))$ and its sublanguages.

4.3 Monotonicity and continuity

Every closed formula of a modal or temporal mu-calculus from the previous section is equivalent to a formula in *positive* form. Positive forms are defined as follows:

$$\Phi ::= Q \mid \neg Q \mid Z \mid \Phi_1 \vee \Phi_2 \mid \Phi_1 \wedge \Phi_2 \mid Op\Phi \mid \mu Z.\, \Phi \mid \nu Z.\, \Phi,$$

where Op ranges over appropriate subsets and combinations of the following: $\{[a], \langle a\rangle, \forall, \exists, O, (a), \neg(a)\neg\}$. The dual of each connective is included in this stipulation: for instance,the dual of $\wedge$ is $\vee$; the dual of $[a]$ is $\langle a\rangle$; and the dual of O is itself. The equivalence follows easily by moving negations inwards and invoking dual connectives.

As in the previous section, the interpretation of a positive form Φ in a model $(\mathcal{T}, \mathcal{V})$ is the set $\| \Phi \|_{\mathcal{V}}^{\mathcal{T}}$ where dual operators receive their intended meanings. Valuations $\mathcal{V}$ form a partial order under the ordering $\sqsubseteq$:

$$\mathcal{V} \sqsubseteq \mathcal{V}' \quad \text{iff} \quad \begin{array}{l} \text{(a) for all atomic } Q.\ \mathcal{V}(Q) = \mathcal{V}'(Q) \text{ and} \\ \text{(b) for all variables } Z.\ \mathcal{V}(Z) \subseteq \mathcal{V}'(Z). \end{array}$$

A benefit of positive forms is the following monotonicity property, showing that syntactic restrictions on $\mu Z.\, \Phi$ and $\nu Z.\, \Phi$ are no longer necessary for Proposition 4.1.2 to apply.

Lemma 4.3.1. *If* $\mathcal{V} \sqsubseteq \mathcal{V}'$ *then* $\| \Phi \|_{\mathcal{V}}^{\mathcal{T}} \subseteq \| \Phi \|_{\mathcal{V}'}^{\mathcal{T}}$.

Proof. By induction on positive forms Φ. Just one case is examined, $\Phi = \mu Z.\, \Psi$. Assume that $w \in \| \Phi \|_{\mathcal{V}}^{\mathcal{T}}$ but $w \notin \| \Phi \|_{\mathcal{V}'}^{\mathcal{T}}$. But then there is a set $\mathcal{W}$ where $w \notin \mathcal{W}$ and $\| \Psi \|_{\mathcal{V}'[\mathcal{W}/Z]}^{\mathcal{T}} \subseteq \mathcal{W}$. But by the induction hypothesis $\| \Psi \|_{\mathcal{V}[\mathcal{W}/Z]}^{\mathcal{T}} \subseteq \| \Psi \|_{\mathcal{V}'[\mathcal{W}/Z]}^{\mathcal{T}}$ which contradicts that $w \in \| \Phi \|_{\mathcal{V}}^{\mathcal{T}}$. ∎

A non-empty set of valuations $\{\mathcal{V}_i \mid i \in I\}$ is directed if for every $\mathcal{V}_j$, $\mathcal{V}_k$ $(j, k \in I)$ there is a $\mathcal{V}_m$, $m \in I$, such that $\mathcal{V}_j \sqsubseteq \mathcal{V}_m$ and $\mathcal{V}_k \sqsubseteq \mathcal{V}_m$. Every valuation in a directed family agrees on atomic sentences, but may differ on propositional variables. Clearly, any directed set $X = \{\mathcal{V}_i \mid i \in I\}$ has a least upper bound (relative to $\sqsubseteq$), the valuation $\bigsqcup X$ defined as $\bigsqcup X(Q) = \mathcal{V}(Q)$ for any $\mathcal{V} \in X$; and $\bigsqcup X(Z) = \bigcup\{\mathcal{V}(Z) \mid \mathcal{V} \in X\}$. Given this, we can stipulate that a modal or temporal mu-calculus of positive forms, μC, is *continuous* on a structure $\mathcal{T}$ if for all non-empty directed families X and $\Phi \in \mu C$. $\| \Phi \|_{\bigsqcup X}^{\mathcal{T}} = \bigcup\{\| \Phi \|_{\mathcal{V}}^{\mathcal{T}} \mid \mathcal{V} \in X\}$.

Lemma 2.5.1 and Lemma 3.6.1 provide criteria for when modal and temporal operators are continuous. However, the presence of fixed points presents further possibilities for failing continuity as the next example illustrates.

Example 4.3.2. Let $\mathcal{T}$ be the structure determined by $St_i \xrightarrow{a} St_{i+1}$ for $i \in \mathbb{N}$. When viewed as a temporal structure let $\sigma_i = St_i \xrightarrow{a} \ldots$ and $\mathcal{R} = \{\sigma_i \mid i \geq 0\}$. For the modal case let $\mathcal{V}_i$ be the valuation with the property $\mathcal{V}_i(Y) = \{St_0, \ldots, St_i\}$, and in the temporal case let $\mathcal{V}_i(Y) = \{\sigma_0, \ldots, \sigma_i\}$, and assume $\mathcal{V}_i = \mathcal{V}_j$ otherwise. Clearly $X = \{\mathcal{V}_i \mid i \geq 0\}$ is directed. When Φ is the formula $\nu Z. Y \wedge OZ$ or $\nu Z. Y \wedge [a]Z$ continuity fails (even though $\mathcal{T}$ is image finite and O is continuous) as $\| \Phi \|^{\mathcal{T}}_{\bigsqcup X} \neq \emptyset$, whereas $\| \Phi \|^{\mathcal{T}}_{\mathcal{V}} = \emptyset$ for each $\mathcal{V} \in X$.

The next result provides a *compactness* compactness criterion for when μC is continuous on $\mathcal{T}$, which appeals to finite valuations: $\mathcal{V}$ is *finite* if for each variable Z the set $\mathcal{V}(Z)$ is finite.

Lemma 4.3.3. *μC is continuous on $\mathcal{T}$ iff for all $\Phi \in \mu C$ if $w \in \| \Phi \|^{\mathcal{T}}_{\mathcal{V}}$ then $w \in \| \Phi \|^{\mathcal{T}}_{\mathcal{V}'}$ for some finite $\mathcal{V}' \sqsubseteq \mathcal{V}$.*

Proof. Suppose μC is continuous on $\mathcal{T}$, but $w \in \| \Phi \|^{\mathcal{T}}_{\mathcal{V}}$ and $w \notin \| \Phi \|^{\mathcal{T}}_{\mathcal{V}'}$ for all finite $\mathcal{V}' \sqsubseteq \mathcal{V}$. Consider $X = \{\mathcal{V}' \mid \mathcal{V}' \sqsubseteq \mathcal{V}$ and $\mathcal{V}'$ finite$\}$. Clearly, $\mathcal{V} = \bigsqcup X$ which contradicts continuity. Suppose μC is not continuous on $\mathcal{T}$. Then for some directed X and Φ, $\| \Phi \|^{\mathcal{T}}_{\sqcup X} \neq \bigcup\{\| \Phi \|^{\mathcal{T}}_{\mathcal{V}} \mid \mathcal{V} \in X\}$. But this can only happen if for some w, $w \in \| \Phi \|^{\mathcal{T}}_{\sqcup X}$ and $w \notin \| \Phi \|^{\mathcal{T}}_{\mathcal{V}}$ for each $\mathcal{V} \in X$. Let $\{Z_1, \ldots, Z_k\}$ be the free variables of Φ. Then it follows that $\bigsqcup X$ must associate a non-finite set to at least one Z_j, otherwise $w \in \| \Phi \|^{\mathcal{T}}_{\mathcal{V}}$ for some finite $\mathcal{V} \sqsubseteq \bigsqcup X$. So the result follows. ∎

When μC is continuous on $\mathcal{T}$, the meaning of a fixed point formula in a model $(\mathcal{T}, \mathcal{V})$ can be *computed* iteratively via the approximants as then the only limit ordinal required is ω. In the previous section a syntactic approach was described. Instead, the iterations could be done semantically as follows: $\| \mu Z. \Phi \|^{\mathcal{T}}_{\mathcal{V}} = \bigcup\{\mathcal{W}_n \mid n \geq 0\}$ where $\mathcal{W}_0 = \emptyset$ and $\mathcal{W}_{n+1} = \| \Phi \|^{\mathcal{T}}_{\mathcal{V}[\mathcal{W}_n/Z]}$.

4.4 Minimal mu-calculi

Minimal modal and temporal mu-calculi consist of their valid formulae, those that are true at every state (run) in every model (of the appropriate sort). We call the minimal modal mu-calculus μK , an extension of the logic K of Section 2.2. Similarly, $\mu L(O)$ is minimal linear time logic, an extension of $L(O, U)$ of Section 3.4 (when U is defined as $\mu Y. Q_2 \vee (Q_1 \wedge OY)$). Associated with $\mu L(O)$ are its pure and full branching time minimal logics $\mu B(O)$ and $\mu \forall L(O)$. Although some of these logics are known to be decidable, the techniques for showing this which appeal to automata have not yielded axiomatic characterizations.

However, [Kozen, 1983] produced a sound and complete axiomatization of a sublogic of μK (when formulae are aconjunctive, a technical notion we will not expand on) using a tableau method. From this a clear indication of sound and complete axiom systems may be gleaned:

Axioms	1. All tautology instances
	2. Axioms for the basis operators $([a], O, \forall)$
	3. $\Phi[Z := \mu Z.\, \Phi] \rightarrow \mu Z.\, \Phi$
Rules	MP if Φ and $\Phi \rightarrow \Psi$ then Ψ
	ROp if Φ then $Op\Phi$ (for $Op \in \{[a], O, \forall\}$)
	Rμ if $\Phi[Z := \Psi] \rightarrow \Psi$ then $(\mu Z.\, \Phi) \rightarrow \Psi$.

The axioms for the basis operators are those provided in Section 2.2 and Section 3.4 such as the K axiom $[a](\Phi \rightarrow \Psi) \rightarrow ([a]\Phi \rightarrow [a]\Psi)$. The third axiom is the fixed point unfolding (whose converse is a derived theorem). The rules include modus ponens, MP, and those for the basis operators. Finally there is a fixed point induction rule Rμ. Soundness of the respective systems is straightforward. But it is not known if all the resources necessary to prove valid fixed point formulae are provided here.

4.5 Decision procedures

The logics μK and $\mu L(O)$ are decidable as they can be embedded within Rabin's SnS. But this reduction does not yield proofs of their elementary decidability. [Streett and Emerson, 1989] appeal to a tableau method which is guided by an automaton for showing elementary decidability of μK. A tableau technique for a similar result for $\mu L(O)$ is employed in [Banieqbal and Barringer, 1989].

Another concern is proving properties within a given model. Consider, for example, the question of how to extend the model checker of Section 2.6 for modal formulae to μK formulae. The tableau system presented there verified modal properties of states structurally by appealing to the state constructors ., $\stackrel{def}{=}$, and +, instead of the transition relations. The goal directed rules were built from sequents of the form $E \vdash_{\mathcal{M}} \Phi$, analogues of $E \models_{\mathcal{M}} \Phi$, where E is a state term. A tableau for $E \vdash_{\mathcal{M}} \Phi$ is a maximal proof tree whose root is labelled with this sequent. Sequents labelling the immediate successors of a node are determined by an application of one of the rules. A tableau was said to be successful if all its leaves are successful.

Assume all the rules from Section 2.6. The only question is how to deal with fixed point formulae (and their negations). One proposal, inspired by [Larsen, 1988], is to invoke fixed point induction . However, for this to work in the presence of alternating fixed points we need an auxiliary family of propositional constants, ranged over by A. The two rules for fixed point formulae introduce new constants:

$$\frac{E \vdash_{\mathcal{M}} \mu Z.\,\Phi}{E \vdash_{\mathcal{M}} A}\ A \text{ new} \qquad \frac{E \vdash_{\mathcal{M}} \neg\mu Z.\,\Phi}{E \vdash_{\mathcal{M}} A}\ A \text{ new.}$$

Consequently, extra rules are now needed for these constants. Assume that $A \stackrel{def}{=} \mu Z.\,\Phi$ ($A \stackrel{def}{=} \neg\mu Z.\,\Phi$) represents that the constant A was introduced for the fixed point formula $\mu Z.\,\Phi$ ($\neg\mu Z.\,\Phi$). Then the rules for constants are, in effect, fixed point unrolling rules:

$$\frac{E \vdash_{\mathcal{M}} A}{E \vdash_{\mathcal{M}} \Phi[Z := A]}\ A \stackrel{def}{=} \mu Z.\,\Phi \qquad \frac{E \vdash_{\mathcal{M}} A}{E \vdash_{\mathcal{M}} \neg\Phi[Z := \neg A]}\ A \stackrel{def}{=} \neg\mu Z.\,\Phi.$$

To test if E has the property Φ in the model $\mathcal{M}$, one tries to achieve the goal $E \vdash_{\mathcal{M}} \Phi$ by building a successful tableau, a maximal proof tree containing only successful leaves and whose root is labelled with this sequent. An extension of the modal case here is to count as a leaf any node labelled with a sequent $F \vdash_{\mathcal{M}} A$ if the very same sequent appears above it in the proof tree: thus, the constant rules above only apply to nodes that are not leaves. A leaf labelled $F \vdash_{\mathcal{M}} \Psi$ is *successful* if one of the following conditions applies: $\Psi = Q$ and $F \in \mathcal{V}_{\mathcal{M}}(Q)$; $\Psi = \neg Q$ and $F \notin \mathcal{V}_{\mathcal{M}}(Q)$; $\Psi = A$ and $A \stackrel{def}{=} \neg\mu Z.\,\Phi$; and finally $\Psi = [b]\Phi$ and $F = a.E$ (with $a \neq b$). Therefore, a leaf of the form $F \vdash_{\mathcal{M}} A$ when $A \stackrel{def}{=} \mu Z.\,\Phi$ is unsuccessful.

The next result, a consequence of [Stirling and Walker, 1989], affirms the soundness, completeness, and decidability of this tableau method with respect to finite models.

Proposition 4.5.1. *If E (built from ., $\stackrel{def}{=}$, and +)*[3] *generates the finite transition system $\mathcal{T}$, and $\mathcal{M} = (\mathcal{T}, \mathcal{V})$, then for each $\Phi \in \mu K$*

(a) *every tableau for $E \vdash_{\mathcal{M}} \Phi$ is finite,*

(b) *$E \vdash_{\mathcal{M}} \Phi$ has a successful tableau iff $E \in \| \Phi \|_{\mathcal{V}}^{\mathcal{T}}$.*

The propositional constants are essential to this method: if instead, fixed point formulae were syntactically unfolded, and a node labelled $E \vdash_{\mathcal{M}} \neg\mu Z.\,\Phi$ ($E \vdash_{\mathcal{M}} \mu Z.\,\Phi$) counted as a successful (unsuccessful) leaf when the very same sequent appeared above it in the proof tree, then the resulting method would be neither sound nor complete. A semantic analysis explaining this can be found in [Cleaveland, 1990; Winskel, 1989]. Moreover,

[3] As in Section 2.6 we assume that all state occurrences of variables on the right-hand side of $\stackrel{def}{=}$ occur within the scope of the . operator.

this local model checking technique can be extended to arbitrary infinite state transition systems at the expense of losing decidability [Bradfield and Stirling, 1990].

An alternative approach to model checking fixed point formulae is to employ finite approximations. But although this can be done for μK with respect to finite models, unlike the fixed point method, it may fail whenever the mu-logic is not continuous with respect to the model such as in the case of infinite state models and for $\mu L(O)$ formulae with respect to finite models, as the next example shows.

Example 4.5.2. Let $\mathcal{T}$ be the extended transition system determined by $U \stackrel{def}{=} a.U + a.V$ and $V \stackrel{def}{=} a.V$ where $\mathcal{R}_\mathcal{T}$ is the set of runs passing through V almost always. Let $\mathcal{V}(Q) = \{V\}$. Although U has the property FQ, given by $\mu Z.\, Q \vee OZ$, it fails to have the properties $\mu^n Z.\, Q \vee OZ$ for all $n \in \mathbb{N}$.

5 Expressiveness

5.1 Expressive completeness

Temporal logics are identified by their families of operators. In previous sections special attention has been accorded to the linear time logics $L(O, U)$ and $\mu L(O)$ possibly augmented with the relativized operators (a) and reverse operators, as well as their branching time versions. There are good reasons for this. First, these logics are able to express properties of elements (states and runs) of transition systems, properties such as liveness and safety that are crucial to computational systems. Secondly, they support verification methods for showing that systems have these properties either via decision procedures for, or axiomatizations of, validity or via effective model checkers. A further question about expressiveness is: are there families of temporal operators that are *completely expressive*, i.e. the addition of further operators adds nothing to their expressive power? Complete truth functional expressiveness and combinator completeness provide two relevant analogies. However, unlike these two there is not a sufficiently rounded, or agreed upon, notion of a temporal operator. Instead we can consider expressive completeness relative to particular formal prescriptions of what a temporal operator is. Natural formalisms for describing such operators are the metalanguages within which the semantics of temporal languages are couched. An appropriate starting point is to examine canonical models.

Recall the canonical structures $\mathcal{T}_0 = (\{0\}^*, \{\stackrel{0}{\longrightarrow}\}, \mathcal{R})$ from Section 3.6 for future linear time logics. Members of $\mathcal{R}$ can be represented as natural numbers: n symbolizing the run starting from 0^n. With this understanding $>$ on $\mathbb{N}$ is the suffix ordering. Consequently, the ω-structure $(\mathbb{N}, >)$ is also a canonical structure for future linear time logics. As our interest is with sets of models individual formulae define, let Q range over a fixed finite family of atomic sentences $\{Q_1, \ldots, Q_n\}$. A temporal model on $(\mathbb{N}, >)$, called an *ω-model*, includes the extra information as to which elements of $\mathbb{N}$ each Q_i is true at. An ω-model can itself be viewed as a structure $\Omega = (\mathbb{N}, >, q_1, \ldots, q_n)$ where each q_i, the interpretation of Q_i, is a subset of $\mathbb{N}$. However, to interpret $\mu L(O)$ subformulae with free variables valuation extensions of ω-models are required. These are pairs $(\Omega, \mathcal{V})$ where $\mathcal{V}$ maps each propositional variable into a subset of $\mathbb{N}$. For uniformity, redundant valuation extensions are also assumed when interpreting $L(O, U)$ formulae. Each formula of these future time logics determines a subset of $\mathbb{N}$ in any model $(\Omega, \mathcal{V})$: we write $\| \Phi \|^{\Omega}_{\mathcal{V}}$ for this set. Some sample clauses of the expected inductive definition are

$$\begin{array}{lcl}
\| Q_j \|^{\Omega}_{\mathcal{V}} & = & q_j \\
\| \neg\Phi \|^{\Omega}_{\mathcal{V}} & = & \mathbb{N} - \| \Phi \|^{\Omega}_{\mathcal{V}} \\
\| O\Phi \|^{\Omega}_{\mathcal{V}} & = & \{n \mid n+1 \in \| \Phi \|^{\Omega}_{\mathcal{V}}\} \\
\| \mu Z.\, \Phi \|^{\Omega}_{\mathcal{V}} & = & \bigcap\{I \subseteq \mathbb{N} \mid \ \| \Phi \|^{\Omega}_{\mathcal{V}[I/Z]} \subseteq I\}.
\end{array}$$

Clearly, if $\| \Phi \|^{\Omega}_{\mathcal{V}} = \mathbb{N}$ for every valuation $\mathcal{V}$ then Φ is valid. Moreover, since we are dealing with future time logics, this result may be sharpened:

Lemma 5.1.1. *If $0 \in \| \Phi \|^{\Omega}_{\mathcal{V}}$ for every $\mathcal{V}$ then Φ is valid.*

Proof. Suppose $0 \in \| \Phi \|^{\Omega}_{\mathcal{V}}$ for every $\mathcal{V}$, but Φ is not valid. Then there is a model $(\Omega, \mathcal{V})$ and an n such that $n \not\in \| \Phi \|^{\Omega}_{\mathcal{V}}$, as ω-models are canonical. But then consider the model $(\Omega', \mathcal{V}')$ where Ω' is $(\mathbb{N}, >, q'_1, \ldots, q'_n)$ with $q'_i = \{m - n \mid m \geq n \text{ and } m \in q_i\}$ (where q_i is in Ω). Similarly for $\mathcal{V}'$. An easy induction shows that for $m \geq n$, $m \in \| \Phi \|^{\Omega}_{\mathcal{V}}$ iff $m - n \in \| \Phi \|^{\Omega'}_{\mathcal{V}'}$. ∎

Assume that the set of ω-models defined by a closed temporal formula is $\{\Omega \mid \text{ for some } \mathcal{V}.\ 0 \in \| \Phi \|^{\Omega}_{\mathcal{V}}\}$, and that this set is denoted by $\| \Phi \|$. For instance $\| FQ_i \| = \{\Omega \mid q_i \neq \emptyset\}$ and $\| \nu Z.\, Q_i \wedge OOZ \| = \{\Omega \mid \{2m \mid m \geq 0\} \subseteq \{q_i\}\}$.

The expressive power of individual formulae can be revealed by comparing and contrasting the sets of models they define as in Section 3.3. But we can also examine expressiveness by identifying the ω-models formulae define. Assume that α ranges over sets of ω-models. When L is either $L(O, U)$ or $\mu L(O)$, we say that α is *L-definable* if for some $\Phi \in L$, $\| \Phi \| = \alpha$. But are there independent characterizations of these L-definable sets? To explore this, further notations for defining ω-models are needed.

The interpretation of $L(O, U)$ formulae in an ω-model is described using the following first-order language L_1 with identity:

$$\Phi ::= q(x) \mid x_1 > x_2 \mid x_1 = x_2 \mid \neg\Phi \mid \Phi_1 \wedge \Phi_2 \mid \forall x.\Phi.$$

Here q ranges over the family $\{q_1, \ldots, q_n\}$ viewed now as monadic predicates; x ranges over individual variables; and $>$ is a binary relation. The interpretation of $\mu L(O)$ formulae goes beyond the resources of L_1, requiring quantification over subsets of $\mathbb{N}$ to describe the meaning of $\mu Z.\, \Phi$. The natural language for describing the meaning of such formulae is L_2 , the monadic second-order extension of L_1. This involves the following two extra constructors:

$$\Phi ::= Z(x) \mid \ldots \mid \forall Z.\Phi$$

where Z ranges over monadic predicate variables.[4] Formulas of L_1 and L_2 can be interpreted on ω-models. As before we need valuation extensions to interpret variables. Now let $(\Omega, \mathcal{V})$ be a model where $\mathcal{V}$ maps individual variables into $\mathbb{N}$, and predicate variables into subsets of $\mathbb{N}$. We use the notation $(\Omega, \mathcal{V}) \models \Phi$ to denote that Φ is true in the model $(\Omega, \mathcal{V})$, which is inductively defined in the expected way. Some sample clauses are

$$\begin{array}{lll} (\Omega, \mathcal{V}) \models q_j(x) & \text{iff} & \mathcal{V}(x) \in q_j^{\Omega} \\ (\Omega, \mathcal{V}) \models Z(x) & \text{iff} & \mathcal{V}(x) \in \mathcal{V}(Z) \\ (\Omega, \mathcal{V}) \models x > y & \text{iff} & \mathcal{V}(x) >_{\Omega} \mathcal{V}(y) \\ (\Omega, \mathcal{V}) \models \forall Z.\Phi & \text{iff} & \forall I \subseteq \mathbb{N}.\ (\Omega, \mathcal{V}[I/Z]) \models \Phi. \end{array}$$

Assume that $\Phi(x)$ represents an L_1 or L_2 formula containing one free variable x. Let the set of ω-models defined by this formula be $\parallel \Phi(x) \parallel$ $= \{\Omega \mid \text{for some } \mathcal{V}.\ (\Omega, \mathcal{V}[0/x]) \models \Phi(x)\}$. As with the temporal case, 0 receives special treatment because we are dealing with future time logics: consequently, the formula $\exists y.x \geq y \wedge q_i(y)$ picks out the same models as $q_i(x)$ instead of defining $\overline{F} q_i$. We say that a set of ω-models α is L_1-*definable* (L_2-definable) if for some $\Phi(x) \in L_1$ (L_2) $\parallel \Phi(x) \parallel = \alpha$. Clearly, this invites comparisons between $L(O, U)$ and L_1, and $\mu L(O)$ and L_2-definability. First

Lemma 5.1.2. *i. If α is $L(O, U)$-definable then α is L_1-definable,*
ii. If α is $\mu L(O)$-definable then α is L_2-definable.

Proof. For both parts there is a straightforward translation from closed temporal formulae into L_1 and L_2 formulae with one free variable, preserving definability. For each closed temporal formula Φ and individual variable

[4] L_2 is equivalent to the second-order theory of one successor, $S1S_q$, with predicate symbols in q.

y, define (Φ, y) inductively as follows: $(Q_i, y) = q_i(y)$; $(\neg\Phi, y) = \neg(\Phi, y)$; $(\Phi \wedge \Psi, y) = (\Phi, y) \wedge (\Psi, y)$; $(O\Phi, y) = \exists z > y.\forall u > y.u \geq z \wedge (\Phi, z)$; $(\Phi U \Psi, y) = \exists z \geq y.(\Psi, z) \wedge \forall u.(z > u \wedge u \geq y) \rightarrow (\Phi, u)$; $(\mu Z.\, \Phi, y) = \forall Z.(\forall u.(\Phi, u) \rightarrow Z(u)) \rightarrow Z(y)$. Clearly, $\| \Phi \| = \| (\Phi, x) \|$. ∎

This result is hardly surprising, given that the semantics of temporal formulae is defined in L_1 and L_2.

What is surprising is that the converses of Lemma 5.1.2 also hold.

Proposition 5.1.3.

(a) *If α is L_1-definable then α is $L(O, U)$-definable,*

(b) *If α is L_2-definable then α is $\mu L(O)$-definable.*

The proofs of these are extremely difficult, and depend on providing suitable normal forms for L_1 and L_2 formulas $\Phi(x)$. The proof of (a) is due to [Gabbay *et al.*, 1980] where details of the normal form are provided. The proof of (b) is more indirect. First L_2 formulae $\Phi(x)$ can be reduced to a normal form via Büchi automata on the alphabet 2^q [Büchi, 1962]. And, secondly, Büchi automata define the ω-regular languages (see the next section) which turn out to be equivalent to Wolper's EL [Wolper *et al.*, 1983], which is a sublogic of $\mu L(O)$.

A consequence of Proposition 5.1.3 is that the temporal languages $L(O, U)$ and $\mu L(O)$ are expressively complete relative to L_1 and L_2: adding additional future time operators whose meaning is definable as formulas $\Phi(x)$ from L_1 or L_2 does not increase their expressiveness. Extensions to L_1 and L_2 are needed if similar results are to be obtained for temporal languages employing the relativized operators (a). Decidable extensions of L_2 permit more expressive temporal logics such as $\mu L(O, G_{\lambda n.2^n})$.

Part (a) of Proposition 5.1.3 is a particularization of a more general result due to [Kamp, 1968], that the temporal logic $L(U', \overline{U}')$ (where U' is the until operator of Section 3.1) is expressively complete with respect to the first-order logic of complete linear orders. A linear order $(\mathcal{C}, >)$ is complete if every non-empty bounded subset of $\mathcal{C}$ has both a least upper bound and a greatest lower bound with respect to $>$: so $(\mathbb{N}, >)$ and $(\mathbb{R}, >)$ are complete, unlike $(\mathbb{Q}, >)$ where $\mathbb{Q}$ is the rationals. Given a structure $(\mathcal{C}, >)$ each L_1 formula $\Phi(x)$ defines an n-ary temporal operator:

$$\| Op^n_\Phi \| \;=\; \lambda q_1 \ldots \lambda q_n \subseteq \mathcal{C}.\{c_i \in \mathcal{C} \mid (\mathcal{C}, >, q_1, \ldots, q_n, \mathcal{V}[c_i/x]) \models \Phi(x)\}.$$

Kamp showed that each such operator is definable in $L(U', \overline{U}')$. Stavi, in unpublished work, extended this result to all linear orders by introducing a further until operator and its inverse (see [Gabbay, 1981] for their description). A more general technique for proving expressive completeness is given in [Gabbay, 1981]. Moreover, [Amir and Gabbay, 1987] have extended Proposition 5.1.3 (a) to multi-dimensional linear time logics whose temporal formulae may depend on more than one time index for their truth value—such temporal formulas are associated with L_1 formulas containing more than one free variable.

Generalizing Proposition 5.1.3 to branching time logics is problematic. One issue is the choice of a suitable metalanguage. A natural candidate at the second-order level is SkS_Q, the second-order theory of k successors [Rabin, 1969]. This is given by the monadic second-order logic over structures constructed from $\mathcal{T}_k$ of the form

$$\Omega_k = (\{0,\ldots,k\}^*, \{\stackrel{i}{\longrightarrow} \mid i \in \{0,\ldots,k\}\}, >, q_1, \ldots, q_n),$$

where again $>$ is the suffix ordering. Runs are definable as appropriate sets of elements. However, this language is too rich for expressive completeness of $\mu\forall L(O)$ because incomparable elements can be counted. For instance, the formula $\exists x_1, \ldots, x_i. \bigwedge(x \not\leq x_i \wedge x_i \not\leq x)$ has no branching time correlate. A natural candidate temporal logic for expressive completeness here is $\mu B(\{(i) \mid 0 \leq i \leq k\})$ when (i) have their expected meaning (see [Hüttel, 1990]. At the first-order level the notion of run is not definable, making it impossible to relate it to $\forall L(O, U)$. For more details together with positive results for theories of the binary tree see [Amir, 1985; Thomas, 1987; Hafer and Thomas, 1987; Schlingloff, 1990].

5.2 ω-regular expressions

Language theory offers another framework for defining families of ω-models. Assume, as in the previous section, a fixed finite set of atomic sentences $\{Q_1, \ldots, Q_n\}$. The alphabet of interest consists of all subsets of these atomic sentences. Consequently, a word is a finite sequence $u_0 u_1 \ldots u_m$ where each $u_i \subseteq \{Q_1, \ldots, Q_n\}$ such as $\{Q_1\}\emptyset\{Q_2, Q_n\}$. An ω-*word* is an ω length sequence $u_0 u_1 \ldots u_m \ldots$, and an ω-*language* is a set of such words.

Each ω-model $\Omega = (\mathbb{N}, >, q_1, \ldots, q_n)$ determines a unique ω-word, which we denote by $w(\Omega)$, defined as the sequence $u_0 u_1 \ldots u_m \ldots$ where the sets u_i consist of those atomic sentences that are true at i in Ω: $u_i = \{Q_j \mid i \in q_j\}$. Conversely, associated with any ω-word σ is the unique model Ω with the property that $\sigma = w(\Omega)$. These notions can be generalized to languages and sets of models. Any family of ω-models uniquely determines an ω-language. And conversely, any ω-language L defines a unique set of ω-models: we let $\| L \|$ denote this set:

$$\| L \| \stackrel{def}{=} \{\Omega \mid w(\Omega) \in L\}.$$

This offers the potential for a further classification of ω-models: a set α of ω-models is language definable just in case $\alpha = \| L \|$ for some ω-language L.

By restricting to particular notations for defining languages, we can obtain a result analogous to Proposition 5.1.3 and its converse.

Regular expressions have proved to be extremely useful for defining languages. They define languages whose words have finite length. The *star-free* regular languages on an alphabet ranged over by u is defined as follows:

$$Sf ::= \{u\} \mid Sf_1 \cup Sf_2 \mid -Sf \mid Sf_1; Sf_2.$$

Here $\cup$ is language union; $-$ is complementation, so $-Sf$ defines the set of finite length words which are not in Sf; and $Sf_1; Sf_2$ is the set $\{w_1 w_2 \mid w_1 \in Sf_1 \text{ and } w_2 \in Sf_2\}$. The regular languages are similarly defined:

$$Re ::= \{u\} \mid Re_1 \cup Re_2 \mid -Re \mid Re_1; Re_2 \mid Re^*.$$

Included is the extra * operator: the language Re^* is $\{w_0 \dots w_m \mid m \geq 0 \wedge w_i \in Re\}$. A regular language L is said to be concatenation closed if $L; L \subseteq L$.

These definitions are now extended to ω-languages. A simple enhancement is to permit the operation $^\omega$. However, assume that it is only defined for concatenation closed languages containing at least one word other than the empty word ε: L^ω is then the ω-language $\{w_0 \dots w_n \dots \mid \varepsilon \neq w_i \text{ and } w_i \in L\}$. The star-free ω-regular languages, ranged over by S, have the following syntax:

$$S ::= \emptyset \mid Sf_1; Sf_2^\omega \mid S_1 \cup S_2$$

and the ω-regular languages, ranged over by R, are defined similarly:

$$R ::= \emptyset \mid Re_1; Re_2^\omega \mid R_1 \cup R_2.$$

A set of ω-models α is R-definable (S- definable) if there is a (star-free) ω-regular language L with the feature that $\alpha = \| L \|$. The main result is that these language definable models coincide with those definable in L_2 and L_1, of the previous section.

Proposition 5.2.1.

(a) α is S-definable iff α is L_1-definable,

(b) α is R-definable iff α is L_2-definable.

For discussion and details of these results see [Thomas, 1989].

5.3 Zig-zags, bisimulations, and histories

Various expressibility issues stem from modal and temporal logics. At the micro-level there is interest in the particular way that individual formulae express properties and delimit models. Pertinent to this, as we have seen, is the extent to which the metalanguage itself is reflected in the underlying modal or temporal logic. Instead, our concern here is at the macro-level, with the totality of modal or temporal formulae of a logic. We examine when two states of a model satisfy exactly the same formulae. This is of special interest in the context of program or process equivalence, as transition systems are widely used as models of processes: $s \xrightarrow{a} s'$ is to be understood as process s may perform action a and become the process s'. Usually as noted in the Introduction, the state set is structured algebraically. A variety of behavioural equivalences between processes have been proposed, see [De Nicola, 1987] for a discussion. Often these are also congruences with respect to the algebraic operators. Some of these equivalences appeal to the path behaviour of processes, how they perform under sequences of actions. Modal and temporal logics offer another kind of equivalence: two processes are equivalent if they are not distinguishable by formulas of the logical language under investigation [Hennessy and Milner, 1980; Brookes and Rounds, 1983].

Given a modal (or modal mu-calculus) model $\mathcal{M} = (\mathcal{T}, \mathcal{V})$ when do two states in $\mathcal{S}_\mathcal{T}$ satisfy the same formulae? Equally, the question could be asked of two states from different models. The answer appeals to zig-zag relations as introduced in the 1960s, see the survey [van Benthem, 1984].

Definition 5.3.1. A *zig-zag* on $\mathcal{M}$ is a binary relation Z on $\mathcal{S}_\mathcal{M}$ such that if sZs' then for all labels a and atomic Q

(a) $s \in V(Q)$ iff $s' \in V(Q)$,

(b) $\forall s_1.$ if $s \xrightarrow{a} s_1$ then $\exists s_1'.\ s' \xrightarrow{a} s_1'$ and $s_1 Z s_1'$,

(c) $\forall s_1'$ if $s' \xrightarrow{a} s_1'$ then $\exists s_1.\ s \xrightarrow{a} s_1$ and $s_1 Z s_1'$.

Notice that a zig-zag is just a relation with the hereditary property in the final two clauses and only relating states satisfying the same atomic formulas. Without clause (a). the definition is of a bisimulation relation due to [Park, 1981], and used by [Hennessy and Milner, 1985]. Alternatively, a bisimulation is a zig-zag for modal logics whose sole atomic sentence is `tt`. Zig-zags are closed under various operations: if Z_1 and Z_2 are zig-zags on $\mathcal{M}$ then so are $Z_1 \cup Z_2$, and $Z_1 \circ Z_2$. When there is a zig-zag on $\mathcal{M}$ relating s and s', we say s and s' are *zig-zag equivalent* in $\mathcal{M}$ and we write $s \rightleftharpoons_\mathcal{M} s'$.

Clearly, $\rightleftharpoons_{\mathcal{M}}$ is an equivalence relation on $\mathcal{M}$ (and is itself a zig-zag, being the union of all zig-zags on $\mathcal{M}$). When the set of atomic sentences and the model are finite, then there is a natural decision procedure for deciding which states of $\mathcal{S}_{\mathcal{M}}$ are zig-zag equivalent [Kannellakis and Smolka, 1990]. Let $\| s \|^{\mathcal{M}}$ be the set of modal formulas or (closed) modal mu-calculus formulas that are true at the state s.

Theorem 5.3.2. *If* $s \rightleftharpoons_{\mathcal{M}} s'$ *then* $\| s \|^{\mathcal{M}} = \| s' \|^{\mathcal{M}}$.

Proof. By routine structural induction on modal formulae and in the case of the modal mu-calculus by induction on formulae of infinitary modal propositional logic. ∎

Note that this theorem fails if the modal logics include the reverse operators $\overline{[a]}$. However, by extending the definition of zig-zag to include inverse transitions then a corresponding theorem holds: for an interesting application see [De Nicola and Vaandrager, 1990].

The converse of Theorem 5.3.2 holds if infinitary conjunction is allowed in the modal languages. Alternatively, it holds for modal logic and the modal mu-calculus if the model $\mathcal{M}$ is image finite [Hennessy and Milner, 1985].

Theorem 5.3.3. *If* $\mathcal{M}$ *is image finite and* $\| s \|^{\mathcal{M}} = \| s' \|^{\mathcal{M}}$ *then* $s \rightleftharpoons_{\mathcal{M}} s'$.

Proof. It suffices to show that the relation Z defined by $s_1 Z s_2$ whenever $\| s \|^{\mathcal{M}} = \| s' \|^{\mathcal{M}}$ is a zig-zag. Suppose not. If $s_1 \in V(Q)$ and $s_2 \notin V(Q)$ then this contradicts $\| s \|^{\mathcal{M}} = \| s' \|^{\mathcal{M}}$. Otherwise, suppose $s_1 \xrightarrow{a} s_1'$ and for all s_2'. $s_2 \xrightarrow{a} s_2'$, $\| s_1' \|^{\mathcal{M}} \neq \| s_2' \|^{\mathcal{M}}$. Let $\{t_1, \ldots, t_n\} = \{s_2' \mid s_2 \xrightarrow{a} s_2'\}$. If this set is empty then $s_2 \models_{\mathcal{M}} [a]\mathtt{ff}$ unlike s_1 which contradicts that $s_1 Z s_2$. Hence, there are formulas $\Phi_i, 1 \leq i \leq n$, such that $s_1' \models_{\mathcal{M}} \Phi_i$ and $t_i \models_{\mathcal{M}} \neg\Phi_i$. Let $\Psi = \Phi_1 \wedge \ldots \wedge \Phi_n$. But $s_1 \models_{\mathcal{M}} \langle a \rangle \Psi$ whereas $s_2 \models_{\mathcal{M}} \neg\langle a \rangle \Psi$ which contradicts that $s_1 Z s_2$. ∎

Let $\mathcal{M}$ now be a future time temporal model. We are interested when two states satisfy the same future linear or branching time formulas (including the mu-calculi). First, we define a history equivalence relation $\simeq_{\mathcal{M}}$ on the sets of runs $\Sigma_{\mathcal{M}}$ where $\mathcal{L}(\sigma)$ is the ω sequence of labels of σ.

Definition 5.3.4. Two runs σ and π of $\mathcal{R}_{\mathcal{M}}$ are *history equivalent*, written $\sigma \simeq_{\mathcal{M}} \pi$ iff

(a) $\mathcal{L}(\sigma) = \mathcal{L}(\pi)$,

(b) for all i, and atomic Q. $\sigma(i) \in V(Q)$ iff $\pi(i) \in V(Q)$.

Condition (a) is dropped when the temporal logic doesn't involve indexed temporal operators like (a). When the only atomic sentence is $\mathtt{tt}$ then condition (b) is redundant. A general lemma for any future linear time logic (where $\| \sigma \|^{\mathcal{M}}$ is the set $\{\Phi \mid \sigma \models_{\mathcal{M}} \Phi\}$) is as follows:

Lemma 5.3.5. *If* $\sigma \simeq_{\mathcal{M}} \pi$ *then* $\| \sigma \|^{\mathcal{M}} = \| \pi \|^{\mathcal{M}}$.

Proof. By routine structural induction on formulae Φ from the future fragment of the infinitary linear time language L_∞ of Section 3.3. ∎

A suitable amendment to Definition 5.3.4 caters for linear time logic with reverse operators. For future linear logics which don't include the next operator there is a notion of a stuttering history equivalence [Lamport, 1983].

The converse of Lemma 5.3.5 is guaranteed when the linear time logic can express the relative next operators (a). We now generalize the history equivalence to states, the linear time version of zig-zags. Let $\mathcal{R}_{\mathcal{M}}(s)$ be the set of runs in $\mathcal{R}_{\mathcal{M}}$ whose initial state is s.

Definition 5.3.6. Two states s, s' of $\mathcal{S}_{\mathcal{M}}$ are *history* equivalent, written $s \downarrow_{\mathcal{M}} s'$, iff

(a) $\forall \sigma \in \mathcal{R}_{\mathcal{M}}(s).\ \exists \sigma' \in \mathcal{R}_{\mathcal{M}}(s').\ \sigma \simeq_{\mathcal{M}} \sigma'$,

(b) $\forall \sigma' \in \mathcal{R}_{\mathcal{M}}(s').\ \exists \sigma \in \mathcal{R}_{\mathcal{M}}(s).\ \sigma \simeq_{\mathcal{M}} \sigma'$.

The following is almost a corollary of Lemma 5.3.5, where $\| s \|^{\mathcal{M}}$ is now the family of linear time formulae true at s: if $s \downarrow_{\mathcal{M}} s'$ then $\| s \|^{\mathcal{M}} = \| s' \|^{\mathcal{M}}$. The converse of this holds if infinitary conjunction is allowed in the linear time logic (or, for finitary logics, if one of the sets $\mathcal{R}_{\mathcal{M}}(s)$ or $\mathcal{R}_{\mathcal{M}}(s')$ is finite) and if it expresses the operators (a). In the particular case that these relative operators are expressible, and `tt` is the only atomic sentence, then we can think of $\downarrow_{\mathcal{M}}$ as ω-language equivalence: if $s \downarrow_{\mathcal{M}} s'$ then these states (in the machine $\mathcal{M}$) accept the same ω-words on the alphabet $\mathcal{L}$. But the associated branching time logics distinguishes states which are not bisimulation equivalent as the modalities $[a]$ are expressible. So there is an enormous chasm in state distinguishability between, for instance, the linear time mu-calculus with sole atomic sentence `tt` and its associated branching time versions.

The notion of zig-zag needs to be extended when we examine states satisfying the same sets of future branching time formulae. First, we extend zig-zags to be relations on runs. Assume $\mathcal{M}$ is a future time model.

Definition 5.3.7. A *run* zig-zag on $\mathcal{M}$ is a binary relation Z on $\mathcal{R}_{\mathcal{M}}$ such that if $\sigma Z \pi$ then for all $i \geq 0$

(a) $\sigma \simeq_{\mathcal{M}} \pi$,

(b) $\forall \sigma_1 \in \mathcal{R}(\sigma(i)).\ \exists \pi_1 \in \mathcal{R}(\pi(i)).\ \sigma_1 Z \pi_1$,

(c) $\forall \pi_1 \in \mathcal{R}(\pi(i)).\ \exists \sigma_1 \in \mathcal{R}(\sigma(i)).\ \sigma_1 Z \pi_1$.

Two runs σ and π are zig-zag equivalent on $\mathcal{M}$, written as $\sigma \rightleftharpoons_{\mathcal{M}} \pi$, if there is a run zig-zag on $\mathcal{M}$ between them. The correlate of Lemma 5.3.5 for future branching time logics is: if $\sigma \rightleftharpoons_{\mathcal{M}} \pi$ then $\| \sigma \|^{\mathcal{M}} = \| \pi \|^{\mathcal{M}}$. Run zig-zags can be extended to states.

Definition 5.3.8. An *extended* zig-zag on $\mathcal{M}$ is a binary relation Z on $\mathcal{S}_{\mathcal{M}}$ such that if sZs' then $\exists \sigma \in \mathcal{R}(s).\ \exists \pi \in \mathcal{R}(s').\sigma \rightleftharpoons_{\mathcal{M}} \pi$.

We write $s \rightleftharpoons^{+}_{\mathcal{M}} s'$ if s and s' are related by an extended zig-zag. The correlate for branching future time logics is: if $s \rightleftharpoons^{+}_{\mathcal{M}} s'$ then $\| s \|^{\mathcal{M}} = \| s' \|^{\mathcal{M}}$. Extended zig-zag equivalence is associated with branching time temporal logics. If these logics don't contain the next operator then there is a stuttering variant [Browne *et al.*, 1988]. In the case of the branching time mu-calculus with `tt` as sole atomic formula the associated equivalence is extended bisimulation equivalence [Hennessy, 1984]. Generally, extended zig-zag equivalence is finer than zig-zag equivalence. However, in the particular case that $\mathcal{R}_{\mathcal{M}}$ consists of all runs through the underlying transition system then they coincide—a slight variant of this result is proved in [Hennessy and Stirling, 1985].

6 Sound and Complete Axiom Systems

6.1 Soundness

In previous sections a variety of modal and temporal logics have been introduced. Typically these are sets of Λ-valid formulae when Λ is a general claes of models. In some cases axiom systems were also provided, yielding an alternative characterization of Λ-validity (given by their sets of theorems). Examples include the axiom systems for K (Section 2.2) and PDL (Section 2.4), and the systems $KG(v, w, w', v')$ (Section 2.3); LT, $\forall LT$ (Section 3.4); and $\forall LTFC$ (Section 3.5). An axiom system J consists of a finite set of axiom schemas, and a finite set of rules. A proof of Φ in J (written $J \vdash \Phi$ or $\vdash_J \Phi$) is a finite sequence of formulae $\Phi_1, \ldots, \Phi_n$, with $\Phi = \Phi_n$ and where each Φ_i, $1 \leq i \leq n$, is either an axiom instance, or the result of an application of a rule to formulas in the set $\{\Phi_1, \ldots, \Phi_{i-1}\}$.

One half of the axiomatic characterization of validity is *soundness*: if $J \vdash \Phi$ then $\Lambda \models \Phi$. The usual technique for showing this is straightforward: first prove that every axiom instance of J is Λ-valid, and then show that the rules of J preserve Λ-validity. Similarly, proving that J is *not* sound is also clear, by exhibiting a counterexample to an axiom instance or an application of a rule. The following lemma offers samples from axiom systems scattered throughout previous sections.

Lemma 6.1.1.

(a) *If Λ is the family of dynamic models then* $\Lambda \models (\Phi \wedge [a^*](\Phi \rightarrow [a]\Phi)) \rightarrow [a^*]\Phi$;

(b) *If Λ is all temporal models then* $\Lambda \models \Phi U \Psi \leftrightarrow \Psi \vee (\Phi \wedge O(\Phi U \Psi))$;

(c) *If Λ is all fusion closed future models then* $\Lambda \models \forall O \Phi \rightarrow O \forall \Phi$;

(d) *If Λ is all modal models (with a in its sort) and $\Lambda \models \Phi$ then $\Lambda \models [a]\Phi$.*

Proof. (a) Suppose $\mathcal{M}$ is a dynamic model and $s \models_{\mathcal{M}} \Phi \wedge [a^*](\Phi \rightarrow [a]\Phi)$. We show that for all $w \in \{a\}^*$ if $s \xrightarrow{w} s'$ then $s' \models_{\mathcal{M}} \Phi$ by induction on the length of w. The base case is given as $s \models_{\mathcal{M}} \Phi$. Assume $s \xrightarrow{w} s_1 \xrightarrow{a} s'$. Since $s \xrightarrow{w} s_1$, $s_1 \models_{\mathcal{M}} \Phi \rightarrow [a]\Phi$. And by the induction hypothesis $s_1 \models_{\mathcal{M}} \Phi$. Consequently $s' \models_{\mathcal{M}} \Phi$ as $s_1 \models_{\mathcal{M}} [a]\Phi$.

(b) Suppose $\mathcal{M}$ is a temporal model and $\sigma, i \models_{\mathcal{M}} \Phi U \Psi$. Then $\exists j \geq i.\ \sigma, j \models_{\mathcal{M}} \Psi$ and $\forall k : i \leq k < j.\ \sigma, k \models_{\mathcal{M}} \Phi$. If $j = i$ then $\sigma, i \models_{\mathcal{M}} \Psi$. Otherwise $j > i$ and clearly $\sigma, i \models_{\mathcal{M}} \Phi \wedge O(\Phi U \Psi)$. The other direction is similar.

(c) Suppose $\mathcal{M}$ is a fusion closed future time model with $\sigma \models_{\mathcal{M}} \forall O \Phi$. So $\forall \pi.$ if $\pi(0) = \sigma(0)$ then $\pi^1 \models_{\mathcal{M}} \Phi$. On the other hand if $\sigma \not\models_{\mathcal{M}} O \forall \Phi$ then $\sigma^1 \not\models_{\mathcal{M}} \forall \Phi$. But then there is a run π_1 with $\pi_1(0) = \sigma^1(0)$ and $\pi_1 \not\models_{\mathcal{M}} \Phi$. However, by fusion closure there is the run $(\sigma(0) \xrightarrow{a} \pi_1(0)) \cdot \pi_1$ (for some label a). But then $\sigma \not\models_{\mathcal{M}} \forall O \Phi$.

(d) Suppose $\Lambda \models \Phi$. Then for any modal model $\mathcal{M}$ whose sort includes a and state $s \in \mathcal{S}_{\mathcal{M}}$, we have that $s \models_{\mathcal{M}} \Phi$. But then also $s \models_{\mathcal{M}} [a]\Phi$. So $\Lambda \models [a]\Phi$.

∎

Moreover the axiom systems mentioned above are *strongly* sound with respect to validity: if $\Gamma \vdash_J \Phi$ then $\Gamma \models_\Lambda \Phi$ when $\models_\Lambda$ is the *local* consequence relation (and $\Gamma \vdash_J \Phi$ means that there is a proof of Φ in J from the set of assumptions Γ as in Section 2.2). This follows from the deduction theorem for these logics: $\Gamma, \Phi \vdash_J \Psi$ iff $\Gamma \vdash_J \Phi \rightarrow \Psi$, and from the observation that $\Gamma \vdash_J \Phi$ iff $\Gamma_0 \vdash_J \Phi$ for some finite $\Gamma_0 \subseteq \Gamma$.

6.2 Canonical models

The other half of the axiomatic characterization of validity is *completeness*: if $\Lambda \models \Phi$ then $J \vdash \Phi$. Techniques for a direct proof of this property are not known, as sets of valid formulae can not be described in terms of simple inductive features. Instead the standard approach for proving completeness (called the *Henkin method*) is indirect. First, as every formula can be rewritten as a negated formula, by contraposition completeness is equivalent to: if $J \nvdash \neg\Phi$ then $\Lambda \not\models \neg\Phi$. Clearly, $\neg\Phi$ is *not* Λ-valid when Φ is Λ-satisfiable. A formula Φ is said to be *J-consistent* if $J \nvdash \neg\Phi$, which is equivalent to the statement that there is not a proof of `ff` in J from the assumption Φ. Consequently, an alternative statement of completeness is: *if Φ is J-consistent then Φ is Λ-satisfiable.* The notion of J-consistency can be extended to arbitrary sets of formulae: Γ is J-consistent if there is not a proof of `ff` in J from the set of assumptions Γ, that is if $\Gamma \nvdash_J$ `ff`. *Strong* completeness of J (with respect to Λ-validity) is therefore equivalent to: if Γ is J-consistent then Γ is Λ-satisfiable.

The Henkin method for showing an axiom system is complete, as presented for instance in [Hughes and Cresswell, 1973], involves building a modal or temporal model $(\mathcal{T}, \mathcal{V})$ with $\mathcal{T} \in \Lambda$ from sets of J-consistent formulae. The simplest technique, when it applies, is to build the *canonical model* with respect to a set of formulas. This approach is now illustrated for modal axiom systems.

A set of formulae $\Gamma \subseteq \alpha$ is a *maximal* J-consistent set of α formulas if Γ is J-consistent and $\Gamma \vdash_J \neg\Phi$ for any $\Phi \in \Gamma - \alpha$. No additional formulas belonging to α can be added to Γ without incurring inconsistency. Let Jmc_α be the set of all maximal J-consistent sets of α formulae. Every J-consistent subset of α formulae can be extended to a maximal J-consistent set of α formulae.

Lemma 6.2.1. *If $\beta \subseteq \alpha$ is J-consistent then $\exists\Gamma \in Jmc_\alpha.\ \beta \subseteq \Gamma$.*

Proof. By construction. Let $\alpha - \beta$ be the set $\{\Phi_1, \ldots, \Phi_n, \ldots\}$. Let Γ_0 be the set β. For each $i > 0$ let $\Gamma_i = \Gamma_{i-1}$ if $\Gamma_{i-1} \vdash_J \neg\Phi_i$, otherwise let $\Gamma_i = \Gamma_{i-1} \cup \{\Phi_i\}$. A small exercise shows that $\bigcup\{\Gamma_i \mid i \geq 0\} \in \mathrm{Jmc}_\alpha$. ∎

In the sequel attention is restricted to non-empty sets of formulae α subject to closure conditions. The set α is closed under *subformulae* and *negation* if whenever $\Phi \in \alpha$ and Ψ is a subformula of Φ then $\Psi \in \alpha$; and, whenever $\Phi \in \alpha$ and $\Phi \neq \neg\Psi$ for some Ψ then $\neg\Phi \in \alpha$. The second condition ensures that there are finite closed sets of formulae. A finite set of formulae $\beta = \{\Phi_1, \ldots, \Phi_n\}$ is J-consistent just in case the single conjunction $\Phi_1 \wedge \ldots \wedge \Phi_n$ is J-consistent. Hence in the following, we often let a finite set such as β stand for the single formula $\Phi_1 \wedge \ldots \wedge \Phi_n$.

Assume that J is a modal axiom system (which, at least, contains the axioms and rules for minimal modal logic of Section 2.2), and let α be a non-empty set of modal formulae closed under subformulae and negation. Uniquely associated with α and J is its canonical modal model.

Definition 6.2.2. The *canonical* modal model with respect to α and J is $\mathcal{M}_J^\alpha = (\mathcal{T}, \mathcal{V})$ where:

(a) $\mathcal{S}_\mathcal{T} = \mathrm{Jmc}_\alpha$,

(b) $\mathcal{L}_\mathcal{T} = \{a \mid a \text{ occurs in some formula in } \alpha\}$,

(c) $s \xrightarrow{a} s'$ iff $\forall$ finite $\beta \subseteq s'$. $s \cup \{\langle a \rangle \beta\}$ is J-consistent,

(d) $\mathcal{V}(Q) = \{s \mid Q \in s\}$.

By definition $\mathcal{M}_J^\alpha$ is a modal model. Moreover because of the closure conditions on α and because J contains those axioms and rules presented for minimal modal logic, this model has the following crucial property:

Theorem 6.2.3. *For all $\Phi \in \alpha$. $s \models_{\mathcal{M}_J^\alpha} \Phi$ iff $\Phi \in s$.*

Proof. By induction on the structure of Φ. The base case when Φ is atomic follows from the definition of the valuation $\mathcal{V}$. The only interesting case in the inductive step is $\Phi = [a]\Psi$. Suppose first $[a]\Psi \in s$. Then $\Psi \in s'$ for all s' such that $s \xrightarrow{a} s'$. So via the induction hypothesis $s \models_{\mathcal{M}_J^\alpha} [a]\Psi$. Instead suppose $s \models_{\mathcal{M}_J^\alpha} [a]\Psi$ but $[a]\Psi \notin s$. We show that if $[a]\Psi \notin s$ then $\Psi \notin s'$ for some s' such that $s \xrightarrow{a} s'$ which contradicts $s \models_{\mathcal{M}_J^\alpha} [a]\Psi$. This we do by construction. Let $\Gamma_0 = \{\neg\Psi\} \cup \Delta$ where $\Delta = \{\Phi \mid s \vdash_J [a]\Phi\}$ where these formulae need not all be in α. First Γ_0 is J-consistent. For otherwise for some finite $\beta \subseteq \Delta$ we would have $J \vdash \beta \to \Psi$ and so by the axioms and the rule Nec $J \vdash [a]\beta \to [a]\Psi$. But $\beta \in \Delta$ (as this set is closed under $\wedge$). So $s \vdash_J [a]\Psi$ which contradicts J-consistency of s. By Lemma 6.2.1 there is a $\Gamma \supseteq \Gamma_0$ such that $\Gamma \in Jmc_{\alpha'}$ where α' is the full modal language (of the appropriate sort). Now consider $s' = \Gamma \cap \alpha$. Clearly $s' \in Jmc_\alpha$ and $s \xrightarrow{a} s'$. But $\Psi \notin s'$. ∎

Let J be the axiom system for minimal modal logic. Strong completeness of J follows from Lemma 6.2.1 and Theorem 6.2.3. Any J-consistent set Γ is satisfiable, as witnessed by any model $\mathcal{M}_J^\alpha$ with $\Gamma \subseteq \alpha$. Two important models stand out for each Γ. First is the minimal model when α is the smallest closed set containing Γ. If Γ is finite then so is this model. Second is the largest model when α is the set of all modal formulae (of the appropriate sort). This model, abbreviated to $\mathcal{M}_J$, is known as the *canonical* J-model, as every J-consistent set Γ is satisfiable within it.

Theorem 6.2.3 does not deliver, by itself, completeness of those extensions of the axiom system for K such as the systems $KG(v, w', w, v)$ and the axiom system for PDL. A further condition is required in these cases, that the resulting model $\mathcal{M}_J^\alpha$ is of the appropriate kind. In the case of the system for $KG(v, w', w, v')$ the model $\mathcal{M}_J^\alpha$ should obey the condition $C(v, w', w, v')$:

$$\text{if } s \xrightarrow{v} s_1 \text{ and } s \xrightarrow{w} s_2 \text{ then } \exists s'.\ s_1 \xrightarrow{w'} s' \text{ and } s_2 \xrightarrow{v'} s'.$$

Strong completeness of this family of axiom systems follows from the next result which states that the canonical model has this property.

Theorem 6.2.4. *If J is $KG(v, w', w, v')$ then $\mathcal{M}_J$ satisfies the model condition $C(v, w', w, v')$.*

Proof. Suppose $s \xrightarrow{v} s_1$ and $s \xrightarrow{w} s_2$ within $\mathcal{M}_J$. Let $\beta = \beta_1 \cup \beta_2$ where $\beta_1 = \{\Phi \mid [w']\Phi \in s_1\}$ and $\beta_2 = \{\Psi \mid [v']\Psi \in s_2\}$. These sets are not empty as they at least contain $\mathtt{tt}$. We show that β is J-consistent. Suppose not. Then $\vdash_J \Phi \rightarrow \neg\Psi$ (where $\Phi \in \beta_1$ and $\Psi \in \beta_2$, as these sets are closed under $\wedge$). So $\vdash_J [w']\Phi \rightarrow [w']\neg\Psi$ via axioms and rules of J. Consequently, $[w']\neg\Psi \in s_1$. Because $s \xrightarrow{v} s_1$, $\langle v\rangle[w']\neg\Psi \in s$. Therefore, by the $\mathrm{G}(v, w', w, v')$ schema $[w]\langle v'\rangle\neg\Psi \in s$ too. But then $\langle v'\rangle\neg\Psi \in s_2$ as $s \xrightarrow{w} s_2$. But this is a contradiction because $[v']\Psi \in s_2$. The proof is completed by showing that any maximal J-consistent set $\Gamma \supseteq \beta$ has the property $s_1 \xrightarrow{w'} \Gamma$ and $s_2 \xrightarrow{v'} \Gamma$ which is clear from the definition of β. ∎

In general the minimal modal model $\mathcal{M}_J^\alpha$, when J is $KG(v, w', w, v')$, does not obey the condition $C(v, w', w, v')$. Imposing extra closure conditions on α rectifies this but at the expense of its finiteness. However, for particular instances of v, w', w and v', when Γ is finite, there is a finite subset β of α (containing Γ) with the property that $\forall\Phi \in \alpha.\ \exists\Psi \in \beta.\ \vdash_J \Phi \leftrightarrow \Psi$. In which case the finite model $\mathcal{M}_J^\beta$ is sufficient for proving completeness.

Unlike the axiom system $KG(v, w', w, v')$, the axiom system J for PDL (of Section 2.4) does not have a canonical model. The problem, as noted in Section 2.3, is the second-order condition that $\xrightarrow{a^*}$ is the reflexive and transitive closure of $\xrightarrow{a}$. The model $\mathcal{M}_J$ contains strange states. For instance the set $\Gamma = \{[w]Q \mid w \in \{a\}^*\} \cup \{\neg[a^*]Q\}$ is J-consistent (because every finite subset of it is). So there is a state s in $\mathcal{M}_J$ with $\Gamma \subseteq s$. By Theorem 6.2.4 there is an s' with $\neg Q \in s'$ and where $s \xrightarrow{a^*} s'$. But for all $w \in \{a\}^*$ not $s \xrightarrow{w} s'$. Moreover this shows that the axiom system for PDL is not strongly complete because although Γ is J-consistent it is not satisfiable in a dynamic model.

At the other extreme the minimal model $\mathcal{M}_J^\alpha$ is also not a dynamic model (where α is the smallest closed set containing the J-consistent Φ). However by imposing further closure conditions on α the model $\mathcal{M}_J^\alpha$ becomes *almost* a dynamic model. A set α is *Fischer-Ladner closed* , after [Fischer and Ladner, 1979] if it is closed under subformulas, negation and the following: if $[a \cup b]\Psi \in \alpha$ then $[a]\Psi, [b]\Psi \in \alpha$; if $[a;b]\Psi \in \alpha$ then $[a][b]\Psi \in \alpha$; if $[\Psi?]\Psi' \in \alpha$ then $\Psi \in \alpha$; and, if $[a^*]\Psi \in \alpha$ then $[a][a^*]\Psi \in \alpha$. The smallest closed set α containing Φ is finite. For such an α the model $\mathcal{M}_J^\alpha$ is not quite a dynamic model because its label set is not a Kleene algebra. Shadowing $\mathcal{M}_J^\alpha$ is the dynamic model $\mathcal{N}_J^\alpha$ whose state set and valuation is the same as $\mathcal{M}_J^\alpha$. But its label set $\mathcal{L}'$ and its transition relations $\stackrel{a}{\Longrightarrow}$ differ from $\mathcal{L}$ and $\stackrel{a}{\longrightarrow}$ of $\mathcal{M}_J^\alpha$. Let $\mathcal{L}_0 \subseteq \mathcal{L}$ be the atomic labels of $\mathcal{L}$. For $a \in \mathcal{L}_0$ let $\stackrel{a}{\Longrightarrow}=\stackrel{a}{\longrightarrow}$. Now assume $\mathcal{L}'$ is the full Kleene algebra generated from $\mathcal{L}_0$ (and arbitrary tests). The transition relations for $\stackrel{a}{\Longrightarrow}\in \mathcal{L}' - \mathcal{L}_0$ are defined as for dynamic models (with $s \stackrel{\Phi?}{\Longrightarrow} s$ just in case $s \wedge \Phi$ is J-consistent). By definition $\mathcal{N}_J^\alpha$ *is* a dynamic model. So completeness of the axiom system for PDL follows if Theorem 6.2.3 holds for this model. This is guaranteed by the next result as the theorem does hold for $\mathcal{M}_J^\alpha$.

Theorem 6.2.5.

(a) *For* $a \in \mathcal{L}$. $\stackrel{a}{\longrightarrow}\subseteq\stackrel{a}{\Longrightarrow}$,

(b) *If* $[a]\Phi \in s$ *and* $s \stackrel{a}{\Longrightarrow} s'$ *then* $\Phi \in s'$.

Proof. Both results follow by induction on the structure of a. We just consider (a). The base case when a is atomic or a test holds by definition. Let $S = \{s_1, \ldots, s_n\}$ be the finite state set of $\mathcal{M}_J^\alpha$ and $\mathcal{N}_J^\alpha$. Because α is closed under subformulae and negation then $J \vdash s_1 \vee \ldots \vee s_n$. Assume that $a = b;c$ and $s \stackrel{a}{\longrightarrow} s'$. So $s \wedge \langle b;c\rangle s'$ is J-consistent. Consequently, so are $s \wedge \langle b\rangle\langle c\rangle s'$ and $s \wedge (\bigvee S \wedge \langle c\rangle s')$ via J axioms and rules. So for some s_i, $s \wedge \langle b\rangle(s_i \wedge \langle c\rangle s')$ is J-consistent. Hence $s \stackrel{b}{\longrightarrow} s_i \stackrel{c}{\longrightarrow} s'$. So by the induction hypothesis $s \stackrel{b}{\Longrightarrow} s_i \stackrel{c}{\Longrightarrow} s'$, and therefore $s \stackrel{b;c}{\Longrightarrow} s'$. Suppose $a = b \cup c$ and $s \stackrel{a}{\longrightarrow} s'$. Then $s \wedge \langle b \cup c\rangle s'$ is J-consistent. But then either $s \wedge \langle b\rangle s'$ or $s \wedge \langle c\rangle s'$ is J-consistent. Now the result follows that $s \stackrel{a}{\Longrightarrow} s'$. Finally, assume $a = b^*$ and $s \stackrel{a}{\longrightarrow} s'$. Hence $s \wedge \langle a\rangle s'$ is J-consistent. Let $S' \subseteq S$ be the smallest set containing s such that if $t \in S'$ and $t \wedge \langle b\rangle t'$ is J-consistent then $t' \in S'$. If $s' \in S'$ then via the induction hypothesis $s \stackrel{a}{\Longrightarrow} s'$. So instead suppose $s' \notin S'$. Assume $S' = \{s_1, .., s_k\}$. For all $t \in S - S'$, $J \vdash \bigvee S' \rightarrow [b]\neg t$. Therefore $J \vdash \bigvee S' \rightarrow [b]\bigvee S'$. By the Nec rule and the induction axiom $J \vdash \bigvee S' \rightarrow [a]\bigvee S'$. But $J \vdash s \rightarrow \bigvee S'$ and

$J \vdash \bigvee S' \rightarrow \neg s'$. So if $s' \notin S'$ then $J \vdash s \rightarrow [a]\neg s'$ which contradicts that $s \xrightarrow{a} s'$. ∎

A decision procedure for determining whether a *PDL* formula is satisfiable can be extracted from this completeness result by appealing to tableau methods.

6.3 Points and schedulers

The building blocks of completeness proofs are maximal J-consistent sets, as we have seen in the case of modal logics. Members of Jmc_α were regarded as states, and transition system models were constructed from them. Here we prove parts of Propositions 3.4.1, 3.4.2, and 3.5.4; that the temporal axiom systems LT, $\forall LT$, and $\forall LTFC$ are complete. The additional complication, not present in the modal case, is that we need to build both runs and states from members of Jmc_α, when J is a temporal axiom system. We now call members of Jmc_α *points* .

A future run will just be an ω length sequence of points. Typically we use σ and π to range over such sequences of sets: $\pi = \Gamma_0\Gamma_1 \ldots$. Here the transition labels are omitted as the temporal operators of these logics do not appeal to them. We use the notation $\sigma(i)$ to represent the ith point in σ, and σ^i to be the ith suffix. First, we isolate an acceptable subset of ω length sequences of points.

Definition 6.3.1.
An ω length sequence σ of Jmc_α points is *admissible* if for all $i \geq 0$:

(a) if $O\Phi \in \alpha$ then $O\Phi \in \sigma(i)$ iff $\Phi \in \sigma(i+1)$,

(b) if $F\Phi \in \alpha$ then $F\Phi \in \sigma(i)$ iff $\exists j \geq i.\ \Phi \in \sigma(j)$,

(c) if $\Phi U \Psi \in \alpha$ then $\Phi U \Psi \in \sigma(i)$ iff $\exists j \geq i.\ \Psi \in \sigma(j)$ and $\forall k : i \leq k < j.$ $\Phi \in \sigma(k)$.

Notice that σ is admissible iff every suffix σ^i is also admissible.

A first attempt at building admissible sequences is to define a next (or suffix) relation $\mathcal{X}$ on Jmc_α:

$$\Gamma \mathcal{X} \Delta \quad \text{iff} \quad \Gamma \cup \{O\Psi \mid \Psi \in \Delta\} \text{ is } J-\text{consistent}$$

with the intention that if $\Gamma_0 \mathcal{X} \Gamma_1 \mathcal{X} \ldots$ then the sequence $\Gamma_0\Gamma_1 \ldots$ is admissible. Certainly, as the next lemma shows, each $\Gamma_0 \in Jmc_\alpha$ gives rise to at least one ω length sequence for any logic J which extends the axiom system for $L(O)$ of Section 3.4.

Lemma 6.3.2. $\forall \Gamma \in Jmc_\alpha .\ \exists \Gamma' \in Jmc_\alpha .\ \Gamma \mathcal{X} \Gamma'$.

Proof. Let β be the full temporal language under consideration so $\alpha \subseteq \beta$. Suppose $\Gamma \in Jmc_\alpha$. Then by Lemma 6.2.1 there is a $\Delta \in Jmc_\beta$ such that $\Gamma \subseteq \Delta$. Let $\Delta^1 = \{\Phi | O\Phi \in \Delta\}$. By the axioms and rules for O it follows that $\Delta \in Jmc_\beta$ too, and by definition $\Delta \mathcal{X} \Delta^1$. Let Γ' be $\Delta^1 \cap \alpha$. It follows that $\Gamma \mathcal{X} \Gamma'$. ∎

If O is the sole linear time operator of J then any ω length sequence generated by $\mathcal{X}$ is admissible. But this is not true for temporal logics involving F (or U) as well. Here we face a major problem. If the set α is closed under the operator O (so $O\Phi \in \alpha$ whenever $\Phi \in \alpha$) then inadmissible sequences can be explicitly generated. Consider the J-consistent set $\beta = \{O^n Q \mid n \geq 0\} \cup \{F\neg Q\}$. So $\beta \subseteq \Gamma \in Jmc_\alpha$ for some Γ. But any ω sequence from Γ must be inadmissible. This is similar to the non-existence of the canonical model for PDL, which here shows that LT, $\forall LT$, and $\forall LTFC$ are not strongly complete. The problem was overcome in the case of PDL by restricting to finite sets of formulae. But if α is finite (and, therefore not closed under O) then the relation $\mathcal{X}$ on Jmc_α is not functional. This means that, in general, inadmissible sequences can also be generated by $\mathcal{X}$, merely by making inappropriate choices of $\mathcal{X}$ successors which do not fulfill formulae of the form $F\Phi$ and $\Phi U \Psi$. To overcome this problem we add one additional closure condition on α, that if $\Phi U \Psi \in \alpha$ then $F\Psi \in \alpha$ (or $\mathtt{tt} U \Psi$ when F is not a primitive operator), and we also introduce some extra structure.

The extra structure comes in the guise of simple schedulers which control generation of runs under $\mathcal{X}$. Suppose α is finite. For each $\Gamma \in Jmc_\alpha$ let Γ^+ be the possible $\mathcal{X}$ successors of Γ, the set $\{\Delta \mid \Gamma \mathcal{X} \Delta\}$. Lemma 6.3.2 guarantees that Γ^+ is not empty. A permutation of Γ^+ is any sequence $\Gamma_0 \ldots \Gamma_n$ where each Γ_i is distinct, and $\{\Gamma_0, \ldots, \Gamma_n\} = \Gamma^+$. A *scheduler* for Jmc_α is a function which associates a permutation of Γ^+ with each $\Gamma \in Jmc_\alpha$. We let f_Γ be the sequence associated with Γ: so $f_\Gamma(0)$ is its initial member and f^1_Γ its initial suffix. Moreover, if f is a scheduler and σ a permutation of Γ^+ then $f[\sigma/\Gamma]$ is the scheduler like f except that it associates σ with Γ. An *extended* is a pair (Γ, f) where $\Gamma \in Jmc_\alpha$ and f is a scheduler on Jmc_α. The $\mathcal{X}$ relation is redefined for extended points: $(\Gamma, f)\mathcal{X}(f_\Gamma(0), f[f^1_\Gamma f_\Gamma(0)/\Gamma])$. The relation $\mathcal{X}$ is now functional since f determinises the $\mathcal{X}$ successor for Γ (which is then placed at the end of the permutation). Now $\mathcal{X}$ only generates admissible sequences on extended points when J contains the axiom system for LT of Section 3.4.

Lemma 6.3.3. *If* $(\Gamma_0, f_0)\mathcal{X}(\Gamma_1, f_1)\mathcal{X} \ldots$ *then* $\Gamma_0\Gamma_1 \ldots$ *is admissible.*

Proof. Let $(\Gamma_0, f_0)\mathcal{X}(\Gamma_1, f_1) \ldots$, and let $\sigma = \Gamma_0\Gamma_1 \ldots$. By induction on Φ we show that σ is admissible. If Φ is $O\Psi$ then this follows as $\Gamma_i \mathcal{X} \Gamma_{i+1}$ for all i. Suppose $F\Psi \in \alpha$ and $\Psi \in \Gamma_j$ then $F\Psi \in \Gamma_j$. And as $J \vdash OF\Psi \rightarrow F\Psi$ then also $F\Psi \in \Gamma_k$ for any $k < j$. Suppose $F\Psi \in \Gamma_i$. We need to show that $\Psi \in \Gamma_j$ for some $j \geq i$. Suppose not. Then for all $j \geq i$ $\neg\Psi \in \Gamma_j$. But as $J \vdash F\Psi \rightarrow \Psi \vee OF\Psi$ consequently $F\Psi \in \Gamma_j$ for all $j \geq i$. Consider any suffix of σ^i such that each Γ in it occurs infinitely often. There is such a suffix σ^k as Jmc_α is finite. Let $\{\Gamma_1, \ldots, \Gamma_m\}$ be all the points occurring in σ^k. By definition of the scheduler, for each i, $\Gamma_i^+ \subseteq \{\Gamma_1, \ldots, \Gamma_m\}$. Let $\Phi' = \Gamma_1 \vee \ldots \vee \Gamma_m$. It therefore follows that $J \vdash \Gamma_i \rightarrow O\Phi'$. So $J \vdash \Phi' \rightarrow O\Phi'$. By the rule RG and the induction axiom it follows that $J \vdash \Phi' \rightarrow G\Phi'$. But $J \vdash \Phi' \rightarrow F\Psi \wedge \neg\Psi$. So we get the contradiction $J \vdash \Phi' \rightarrow G(F\Psi \wedge \neg\Psi)$. A similar argument holds for $\Phi U \Psi$ given the extra closure condition on α. ∎

Lemma 6.3.3 is the crucial step in the proof of completeness of the axiom system LT. Suppose J is this axiom system and α is a *finite* closed set. We now construct a canonical finite model $\mathcal{M}_J^\alpha$. Its set of states is the family of extended points (Γ, f) where $\Gamma \in Jmc_\alpha$ and f is a scheduler for Jmc_α. The transition relation $\xrightarrow{a}$ is just $\mathcal{X}$, and the set of runs $\mathcal{R}$ contains *all* future runs through the underlying transition system: so $\mathcal{R}$ is suffix (fusion, limit, and prefix) closed. Finally, the valuation $\mathcal{V}$ decrees that $\mathcal{V}(Q) = \{(\Gamma, f) \mid Q \in \Gamma\}$. A little piece of notation: we write $\Psi \in (\Gamma, f)$ just in case $\Psi \in \Gamma$. An important consequence of the definition of $\mathcal{M}_J^\alpha$ is the following.

Theorem 6.3.4. *If $\Psi \in \alpha$ and $\sigma \in \mathcal{R}_{\mathcal{M}_J^\alpha}$ then for all $i \geq 0$. $\sigma^i \models_{\mathcal{M}_J^\alpha} \Psi$ iff $\Psi \in \sigma(i)$.*

Proof. By induction on Ψ, utilizing Lemma 6.3.3 for formulae whose main connective is a temporal operator. ∎

This theorem proves completeness of LT. Suppose Φ is LT-consistent, then let α be the smallest closed set containing Φ. By Lemma 6.2.1 there is a point Γ containing Φ. Consider any state (Γ, f) of $\mathcal{M}_{LT}^\alpha$ and unique run from it: by Theorem 6.3.4 Φ is true of σ.

The proofs of completeness of the axiom systems $\forall LT$ and $\forall LTFC$ require us to distinguish between points and states, a separation that is essential for interpreting the path modality $\forall$. One idea is to construct states from equivalence classes of points. A formula Φ is a *state* formula iff $J \vdash \Phi \leftrightarrow \forall\Phi$ or $J \vdash \Phi \leftrightarrow \exists\Phi$ (compare Section 3.3). Notice that Φ is a state formula provided that $\neg\Phi$ is too. Let ST_α be the state formulae of α. Two points in Jmc_α are *state equivalent*, denoted by $\equiv$, if they contain the same state formulae: $\Gamma \equiv \Delta$ iff $\Gamma \cap ST_\alpha = \Delta \cap ST_\alpha$. The axioms and rules for $\forall$ of $\forall LT$ guarantee the next property.

Lemma 6.3.5. *If $\exists\Phi \in \Gamma$ then for some $\Delta \equiv \Gamma$. $\Phi \in \Delta$.*

Proof. It suffices to show that the set $\Delta_0 = (\Gamma \cap ST_\alpha) \cup \{\Phi\}$ is J-consistent. If it is, then by Lemma 6.2.1 Δ_0 can be extended into a point $\Delta \in Jmc_\alpha$, and for any such Δ, $\Delta \equiv \Gamma$. Suppose Δ_0 is not consistent. Then for some $\Phi_1, \ldots, \Phi_n \in \Gamma \cap ST_\alpha$, $J \vdash \Phi_1 \wedge \ldots \wedge \Phi_n \rightarrow \neg\Phi$. Since $J \vdash \Phi_i \leftrightarrow C_i\Phi_i$ where C_i is either $\forall$ or $\exists$, also $J \vdash C_1\Phi_1 \wedge \ldots \wedge C_n\Phi_n \rightarrow \neg\Phi$. By the rules and axioms for $\forall$ and $\exists$ we can then derive $J \vdash C_1\Phi_1 \wedge \ldots \wedge C_n\Phi_n \rightarrow \forall\neg\Phi$. But then $\forall\neg\Phi \in \Gamma$ which contradicts that $\exists\Phi \in \Gamma$. ∎

For each $\Gamma \in Jmc_\alpha$ let $|\Gamma|$ be the set $\{\Delta \mid \Gamma \equiv \Delta\}$. We now construct a finite canonical transition system $\mathcal{T}_J^\alpha$ when J is any of the branching time logics, and α is finite. Its set of states consists of pairs of the form $(|\Gamma|, f)$ where $\Gamma \in Jmc_\alpha$ and f is a scheduler, and the transition relation $\stackrel{a}{\longrightarrow}$ is defined as follows: $(|\Gamma|, f) \stackrel{a}{\longrightarrow} (|\Delta|, g)$ iff $\exists\Gamma' \in |\Gamma|$ and $\Delta' \in |\Delta|$. $(\Gamma', f) \stackrel{a}{\longrightarrow} (\Delta', g)$. Moreover, for any of the models constructed below we assume the expected valuation $\mathcal{V}$ which stipulates that $\mathcal{V}(Q) = \{(|\Gamma|, f) \mid Q \in \Gamma\}$, which is well defined as Q is a state formula.

Missing are the definitions of the families of runs. These will consist of a subset of all the possible runs through $\mathcal{T}_J^\alpha$ (which is total by Lemma 6.3.2). The required runs should generate admissible sequences of Jmc_α points. The following useful result shows that there can be at most one such sequence of points associated with any run.

Lemma 6.3.6. *If* $(|\Gamma_0|, f_0) \stackrel{a}{\longrightarrow} (|\Gamma_1|, f_1) \stackrel{a}{\longrightarrow} \ldots$ *is a run through* $\mathcal{T}_J^\alpha$ *then there is at most one admissible sequence of points* $\Gamma_0'\Gamma_1' \ldots$ *with* $\Gamma_j' \in |\Gamma_j|$, *for all* $j \geq 0$.

Proof. A simple induction shows that if $\Gamma_0'\Gamma_1' \ldots$ and $\Delta_0'\Delta_1' \ldots$ are both admissible when Γ_j' and Δ_j' belong to $|\Gamma_j|$ then $\Gamma_j' = \Delta_j'$, for any $j \geq 0$. ∎

In the case of $\forall LT$ we assume that $(|\Gamma_0|, f_0) \stackrel{a}{\longrightarrow} (|\Gamma_1|, f_1) \stackrel{a}{\longrightarrow} \ldots$ belongs to the set of runs $\mathcal{R}$ provided

$$\exists\Gamma_0' \in |\Gamma_0|.\ (\Gamma_0', f_0)\mathcal{X}(\Gamma_1', f_1)\mathcal{X} \ldots \text{and } \forall j > 0.\ \Gamma_j' \in |\Gamma_j|.$$

Clearly, $\mathcal{R}$ is suffix closed (but need not be fusion closed). Moreover, it is also limit closed. By definition there is at least one admissible sequence of points associated with any such run σ, and therefore by the previous lemma there is exactly one: we let $Ad(\sigma)$ be this unique sequence of points. Let $\mathcal{M}_J^\alpha$ be the future time model built on $\mathcal{T}_J^\alpha$ with the run set $\mathcal{R}$, and the valuation $\mathcal{V}$ described above. The following result amounts to completeness of $\forall LT$ both with respect to arbitrary models and limit closed models.

Theorem 6.3.7. *If* $\Psi \in \alpha$ *and* $\sigma \in \mathcal{R}$ *then for all* $i \geq 0$. $\sigma^i \models_{\mathcal{M}_J^\alpha} \Psi$ *iff* $\Psi \in (Ad(\sigma))(i)$.

Proof. This merely extends Theorem 6.3.4. There is only one new case when Ψ is $\forall\Psi'$, which follows from Lemma 6.3.5 and the definition of $Ad(\sigma)$. ∎

The proof of completeness of $\forall LTFC$ is similar. However extra closure conditions need to be imposed on the set α: if Φ, $\Psi \in \alpha$ then $\Phi \wedge \Psi \in \alpha$; and if $\Phi \in \alpha$ then $\forall\Phi \in \alpha$. Now the smallest closed set containing Φ is not finite. However, there is a finite subset $\beta \subseteq \alpha$ with the property: $\forall\Psi \in \alpha.\exists\Psi' \in \beta.\ \forall LTFC \vdash \Psi \leftrightarrow \Psi'$. Assume that α now ranges over such finite representatives. The following extra result is needed for showing that the set of runs below is fusion closed.

Lemma 6.3.8. *If* $\Gamma\mathcal{X}\Delta$ *then* $\forall\Delta' \in |\Delta|.\exists\Gamma' \in |\Gamma|.\ \Gamma'\mathcal{X}\Delta'$.

Proof. Suppose $\Gamma\mathcal{X}\Delta$ and $\Delta' \in |\Delta|$. We show $\Gamma'\mathcal{X}\Delta'$ for some $\Gamma' \in |\Gamma|$. It suffices to prove that the set $\Gamma'_0 = (\Gamma \cap ST_\alpha) \cup \{O\Psi \mid \Psi \in \Delta'\}$ is $\forall LTFC$-consistent. Suppose not. Then $(\Gamma \cap ST_\alpha) \vdash \neg(O\Psi_1 \wedge \ldots \wedge O\Psi_k)$ for some $\Psi_1, \ldots, \Psi_k \in \Delta'$. But then by O and $\forall$ axioms and rule, $(\Gamma \cap ST_\alpha) \vdash \forall O\neg(\Psi_1 \wedge \ldots \wedge \Psi_k)$. Consequently, by the axiom FC and closure conditions above, $\Delta \vdash \forall\neg(\Psi_1 \wedge \ldots \wedge \Psi_k)$ which is impossible as $\Delta' \equiv \Delta$. ∎

Now $(|\Gamma_0|, f_0) \stackrel{a}{\longrightarrow} (|\Gamma_1|, f_1) \stackrel{a}{\longrightarrow} \ldots$ counts as a run in $\mathcal{R}$ through $\mathcal{T}^\alpha_J$ if the following holds:

$$\exists i \geq 0.\ \exists\Gamma'_i \in |\Gamma_i|.\ (\Gamma'_i, f_i)\mathcal{X}(\Gamma'_{i+1}, f_{i+1})\mathcal{X} \ldots \text{and } \forall j > i.\ \Gamma'_j \in |\Gamma_j|\}$$

$\mathcal{R}$ is both suffix and fusion closed: the latter follows from Lemma 6.3.8. Moreover there is exactly one admissible sequence of points associated with any run $\sigma \in \mathcal{R}$. Theorem 6.3.7 also applies to the model $\mathcal{M}^\alpha_J$ built on $\mathcal{T}^\alpha_J$ with this new run set and the valuation as before, and thereby shows completeness of $\forall LTFC$ with respect to fusion closed models.

References

[Abrahamson, 1979] K. Abrahamson. Modal logic of concurrent nondeterministic programs. volume 70 of *Lecture Notes in Computer Science*, pages 21–33. Springer Verlag, 1979.

[Abramsky, 1989] S. Abramsky. Domain theory in logical form. *Annals of Pure and Applied Logic*, 51:1–77, 1989.

[Alpern and Schneider, 1985] A. Alpern and F. Schneider. Defining liveness. *Information Processing Letters*, 21:181–185, 1985.

[Amir and Gabbay, 1987] A. Amir and D. Gabbay. Preservation of expressive completeness in temporal models. *Information and Control*, 72:66–83, 1987.

[Amir, 1985] A. Amir. Separation in nonlinear time models. *Information and Control*, 66:177–203, 1985.

[Baeten *et al.*, 1987] J. Baeten, J. Bergstra, and J. Klop. Decidability of bisimulation equivalence for processes generating context-free languages. volume 259 of *Lecture Notes in Computer Science*, pages 94–113. Springer Verlag, 1987.

[Banieqbal and Barringer, 1989] B. Banieqbal and H. Barringer. Temporal logic with fixed points. volume 398 of *Lecture Notes in Computer Science*, pages 62–74. Springer Verlag, 1989.

[Barringer and Kuiper, 1991] H. Barringer and R. Kuiper. Temporal logic and concurrency, 1991. To appear in Volume VI of this *Handbook*.

[Barringer *et al.*, 1984] H. Barringer, R. Kuiper, and A. Pnueli. Now you may compose temporal logic specifications. In *Proc. 16th ACM Symp. on Theory of Computing*, pages 51–63, 1984.

[Ben-Ari *et al.*, 1982] M. Ben-Ari, J. Halpern, and A. Pnueli. Deterministic propositional dynamic logic: finite models, complexity, and completeness. *J. Comput. System Sci.*, 25:402–417, 1982.

[Ben-Ari *et al.*, 1983] M. Ben-Ari, Z. Manna, and A. Pnueli. The temporal logic of branching time. *Acta Informatica*, 20:207–226, 1983.

[Bergstra and Klop, 1989] J. Bergstra and J. Klop. Process theory based on bisimulation semantics. volume 354 of *Lecture Notes in Computer Science*, pages 50–122. Springer Verlag, 1989.

[Bradfield and Stirling, 1990] J. Bradfield and C. Stirling. Verifying temporal properties of processes. volume 458 of *Lecture Notes in Computer Science*, pages 115–125. Springer Verlag, 1990.

[Brookes and Rounds, 1983] S. Brookes and W. Rounds. Behavioural equivalence relations induced by programming logics. volume 154 of *Lecture Notes in Computer Science*, pages 97–108. Springer Verlag, 1983.

[Browne *et al.*, 1988] M. Browne, E. Clarke, and O. Grumberg. Characterizing finite Kripke structures in propositional temporal logic. *Theoretical Computer Science*, 59:115–131, 1988.

[Büchi, 1962] J. Büchi. On a decision method in restricted second order arithmetic. In *Logic, Methodology, and Philosophy of Science: Proc. 1960 Int. Congress*, pages 1–11. Stanford University Press, 1962.

[Bull and Segerberg, 1984] R. Bull and K. Segerberg. Basic modal logic. In D. Gabbay and F. Guenthner, editors, *Handbook of Philosophical Logic. Vol. II*, pages 1–88. Reidel, 1984.

[Bull, 1966] R. Bull. That all normal extensions of S4.3 have the finite model property. *Zeitschrift für mathematische Logik und Grundlagen der Mathematik*, 12:341–344, 1966.

[Chellas, 1980] B. Chellas. *Modal Logic.* Cambridge University Press, 1980.

[Clarke and Emerson, 1981] E. Clarke and E. Emerson. Design and synthesis of synchronization skeletons using branching time temporal logic. volume 131 of *Lecture Notes in Computer Science*, pages 52–71. Springer Verlag, 1981.

[Clarke *et al.*, 1983] E. Clarke, E. Emerson, and A. Sistla. Automatic verification of finite state concurrent systems using temporal logic specifications: a practical approach. In *Proc. 10th ACM Symp. on Principles of Programming Languages*, pages 117–126, 1983.

[Cleaveland, 1990] R. Cleaveland. Tableau-based model checking in the propositional mu-calculus. *Acta Informatica*, 27:725–747, 1990.

[Courcoubetis *et al.*, 1986] C. Courcoubetis, M. Vardi, and P. Wolper. Reasoning about fair concurrent programs. In *Proc. of 18th ACM Symp. on Theory of Computing*, pages 283–294, 1986.

[De Nicola and Vaandrager, 1990] R. De Nicola and V. Vaandrager. Three logics for branching bisimulation. In *Proc. 5th IEEE Symp. on Logic in Computer Science*, pages 118–129, 1990.

[De Nicola, 1987] R. De Nicola. Extensional equivalences for transition systems. *Acta Informatica*, 24:211–237, 1987.

[Dijkstra, 1976] E. Dijkstra. *A Discipline of Programming.* Prentice-Hall, 1976.

[Emerson and Clarke, 1980] E. Emerson and E. Clarke. Characterizing correctness properties of parallel programs using fixpoints. volume 85 of *Lecture Notes in Computer Science*, pages 169–181. Springer Verlag, 1980.

[Emerson and Halpern, 1982] E. Emerson and J. Halpern. Decision procedures and expressiveness in the temporal logic of branching time. In *Proc. 14th ACM Symp. on Theory of Computing*, pages 169–180, 1982.

[Emerson and Halpern, 1986] E. Emerson and J. Halpern. "sometimes" and "not never" revisited: on branching versus linear time. *J. Assoc. Comput. Mach.*, 33:151–178, 1986.

[Emerson and Sistla, 1984] E. Emerson and A. Sistla. Deciding full branching time logic. *Information and Control*, 61:175–201, 1984.

[Emerson, 1983] E. Emerson. Alternative semantics for temporal logics. *Theoretical Computer Science*, 26:121–130, 1983.

[Fischer and Ladner, 1979] M. Fischer and R. Ladner. Propositional dynamic logic of regular programs. *J. Comput. System Sci.*, 18:194–211, 1979.

[Fitting, 1983] M. Fitting. *Proof Methods for Modal and Intuitionistic Logics.* Reidel, 1983.

[Floyd, 1967] R. Floyd. Assigning meanings to programs. In J. Schwartz, editor, *Mathematical Aspects of Computer Science*, pages 19–32. American Math. Soc., 1967.

[Gabbay *et al.*, 1980] D. Gabbay, A. Pnueli, S. Shelah, and J. Stavi. On the temporal analysis of fairness. In *Proc. 7th ACM Symp. on Principles of Programming Languages*, pages 163–173, 1980.

[Gabbay, 1976] D. Gabbay. *Investigations In Modal And Tense Logics With Applications To Problems In Philosophy And Linguistics.* Reidel, 1976.

[Gabbay, 1981] D. Gabbay. Expressive functional completeness in tense logic. In U. Monnich, editor, *Aspects of Philosophical Logic*, pages 91–117. Reidel, 1981.

[Gabbay, 1989] D. Gabbay. The declarative past and imperative future: executable temporal logic for interactive systems. volume 398 of *Lecture Notes in Computer Science*, pages 431–448. Springer Verlag, 1989.

[Goldblatt, 1976] R. Goldblatt. Metamathematics of modal logic. *Reports on Mathematical Logic*, 6/7:41–78 and 21–52, 1976.

[Gurevitch and Shelah, 1985] Y. Gurevitch and S. Shelah. The decision problem for branching time logic. *J. of Symbolic Logic*, 50:668–681, 1985.

[Hafer and Thomas, 1987] T. Hafer and W. Thomas. Computation tree logic CTL* and path quantifiers in the monadic theory of the binary tree. volume 267 of *Lecture Notes in Computer Science*, pages 269–279. Springer Verlag, 1987.

[Harel *et al.*, 1982] D. Harel, D. Kozen, and R. Parikh. Process logic: expressiveness, decidability, completeness. *J. Comput. System Sci.*, 25:144–170, 1982.

[Harel, 1984] D. Harel. Dynamic logic. In D. Gabbay and F. Guenthner, editors, *Handbook of Philosophical Logic. Vol. II*, pages 497–604. Reidel, 1984.

[Hennessy and Milner, 1980] M. Hennessy and R. Milner. On observing nondeterminism and concurrency. volume 85 of *Lecture Notes in Computer Science*, pages 295–309. Springer Verlag, 1980.

[Hennessy and Milner, 1985] M. Hennessy and R. Milner. Algebraic laws for nondeterminism and concurrency. *J. Assoc. Comput. Mach.*, 32:137–162, 1985.

[Hennessy and Stirling, 1985] M. Hennessy and C. Stirling. The power of the future perfect in program logics. *Information and Control*, 67:23–52, 1985.

[Hennessy, 1984] M. Hennessy. Axiomatizing finite delay operators. *Acta Informatica*, 21:61–88, 1984.

[Hennessy, 1988] M. Hennessy. *An Algebraic Theory of Processes.* MIT Press, 1988.

[Hintikka, 1962] J. Hintikka. *Knowledge And Belief.* Cornell University Press, 1962.

[Hoare, 1969] C. Hoare. An axiomatic basis for computer programming. *Comm. ACM*, 12:576–580, 1969.

[Hughes and Cresswell, 1973] G. Hughes and M. Cresswell. *An Introduction To Modal Logic.* Methuen, 1973.

[Hüttel, 1990] H. Hüttel. SnS can be modally characterized. *Theoretical Computer Science*, 74:239–248, 1990.

[Kamp, 1968] H. Kamp. *Tense Logic and the Theory of Linear Order.* PhD thesis, University of California, 1968.

[Kannellakis and Smolka, 1990] P. Kannellakis and S. Smolka. CCS expressions, finite state processes, and three problems of equivalence. *Information and Computation*, 86:43–68, 1990.

[Keller, 1976] R. Keller. Formal verification of parallel programs. *Comm. Assoc. Comput. Mach.*, 19:561–572, 1976.

[Koymans, 1989] R. Koymans. *Specifying Message Passing and Time-Critical Systems with Temporal Logic.* PhD thesis, Technical University of Eindhoven, 1989.

[Kozen and Parikh, 1981] D. Kozen and R. Parikh. An elementary proof of the completeness of pdl. *Theoretical Computer Science*, 14:113–118, 1981.

[Kozen, 1981] D. Kozen. On the duality of dynamic algebras and Kripke models. volume 125 of *Lecture Notes in Computer Science*, pages 1–11. Springer Verlag, 1981.

[Kozen, 1983] D. Kozen. Results on the propositional mu-calculus. *Theoretical Computer Science*, 27:333–354, 1983.

[Kripke, 1959] S. Kripke. A completeness proof in modal logic. *J. Symbolic Logic*, 24:1–14, 1959.

[Kripke, 1963] S. Kripke. Semantical analysis of modal logic I: normal propositional calculi. *Zeitschrift für mathematische Logik und Grundlagen der Mathematik*, 9:67–96, 1963.

[Lamport, 1980] L. Lamport. "Sometime" is sometimes "not never"— on the temporal logic of programs. In *Proc. 7th Annual ACM Symp. on Principles of Programming Languages*, pages 174–185, 1980.

[Lamport, 1983] L. Lamport. What good is temporal logic? In *Proc. IFIP Congress*, pages 657–668. North-Holland, 1983.

[Larsen, 1988] K. Larsen. Proof systems for Hennessy-Milner logic with recursion. volume 299 of *Lecture Notes in Computer Science*. Springer Verlag, 1988.

[Lemmon, 1977] E. Lemmon. *An Introduction to Modal Logic*, volume 11 of *Am. Phil. Quart. Monograph*. Oxford, 1977.

[Lichtenstein and Pnueli, 1984] O. Lichtenstein and A. Pnueli. Checking that finite state concurrent programs satisfy their linear specification. In *Proc. 10th ACM Symp. Principles of Programming Languages*, pages 97–107, 1984.

[Manna and Pnueli, 1981] Z. Manna and A. Pnueli. Verification of concurrent programs: the temporal framework. In R. Boyer and J. Moore, editors, *The Correctness Problem in Computer Science*, pages 215–273. Academic Press, 1981.

[Manna and Pnueli, 1989] Z. Manna and A. Pnueli. The anchored version of the temporal framework. volume 354 of *Lecture Notes in Computer Science*, pages 201–284. Springer Verlag, 1989.

[Manna and Wolper, 1984] Z. Manna and P. Wolper. Synthesis of communicating processes from temporal logic specifications. *ACM Trans. Prog. Lang. and Syst.*, 6:68–93, 1984.

[Milner, 1989] R. Milner. *Communication and Concurrency.* Prentice Hall, 1989.

[Moszkowski, 1986] B. Moszkowski. *Executing Temporal Logic Programs.* Cambridge University Press, 1986.

[Park, 1981] D. Park. Concurrency and automata on infinite sequences. volume 154 of *Lecture Notes in Computer Science*, pages 561–572. Springer Verlag, 1981.

[Pnueli, 1977] A. Pnueli. The temporal logic of programs. In *Proc. 18th Annual Symp. Foundations Computer Science*, pages 46–57, 1977.

[Pratt, 1976] V. Pratt. Semantical considerations on Floyd-Hoare logic. In *Proc. 17th IEEE Symp. on Foundations of Computer Science*, pages 109–121, 1976.

[Pratt, 1979] V. Pratt. Process logic. In *Proc. 6th ACM Symp. on Principles of Programming Languages*, pages 93–100, 1979.

[Pratt, 1980a] V. Pratt. Dynamic algebras and the nature of induction. In *Proc. 12th ACM Symp. Theory of Computing*, pages 22–28, 1980.

[Pratt, 1980b] V. Pratt. A near optimal method for reasoning about action. *J. Comput. System Sci.*, 20:231–254, 1980.

[Pratt, 1982] V. Pratt. A decidable mu-calculus. In *22nd IEEE Symp. on Foundations of Comp. Sci.*, pages 421–427, 1982.

[Prior, 1957] A. Prior. *Time and Modality.* Oxford University Press, 1957.

[Prior, 1967] A. Prior. *Past, Present, and Future.* Oxford University Press, 1967.

[Quielle and Sifakis, 1981] J. Quielle and J. Sifakis. Specification and verification of concurrent systems in CESAR. volume 137 of *Lecture Notes in Computer Science*, pages 337–350. Springer Verlag, 1981.

[Rabin, 1969] M. Rabin. Decidability of second-order theories and automata on infinite trees. *Trans. Amer. Math. Soc.*, 141:1–35, 1969.

[Rescher and Urquhart, 1971] N. Rescher and A. Urquhart. *Temporal Logic.* Springer-Verlag, 1971.

[Salwicki, 1977] A. Salwicki. Algorithmic logic: a tool for investigations of programs. In Butts and Hintikka, editors, *Logic, Foundations of Mathematics, and Computability Theory*, pages 281–295. Reidel, 1977.

[Sambin and Vaccaro, 1988] G. Sambin and V. Vaccaro. Topology and duality in modal logic. *Annals of Pure and Applied Logic*, 37:249–296, 1988.

[Schlingloff, 1990] B.-H. Schlingloff. Expressive completeness of temporal logic over trees, 1990. To appear in *Journal of Applied Non Classical Logics.*

[Sistla and Clarke, 1985] A. Sistla and E. Clarke. The complexity of propositional linear temporal logic. *J. Assoc. Comput. Mach.*, 32:733–749, 1985.

[Sistla *et al.*, 1987] A. Sistla, M. Vardi, and P. Wolper. The complementation problem for Büchi automata with applications to temporal logic. *Theoretical Computer Science*, 49:217–237, 1987.

[Sistla, 1985] A. Sistla. On characterisation of safety and liveness properties in temporal logic. In *Proc. 4th ACM Symp. Princ. of Dist. Comp.*, pages 39–48, 1985.

[Stirling and Walker, 1989] C. Stirling and D. Walker. Local model checking in the propositional mu-calculus. volume 351 of *Lecture Notes in Computer Science*, pages 369–383. Springer Verlag, 1989.

[Stirling, 1987] C. Stirling. Modal logics for communicating systems. *Theoretical Computer Science*, 49:311–347, 1987.

[Stirling, 1989] C. Stirling. Comparing linear and branching time temporal logics. volume 398 of *Lecture Notes in Computer Science*, pages 1–20. Springer Verlag, 1989.

[Streett and Emerson, 1989] R. Streett and E. Emerson. An automata theoretic decision procedure for the propositional mu-calculus. *Information and Computation*, 81:249–264, 1989.

[Streett, 1982] R. Streett. Propositional dynamic logic of looping and converse is elementarily decidable. *Information and Control*, 54:121–141, 1982.

[Thomas, 1987] W. Thomas. On chain logic, path logic, and first-order logic over infinite trees. In *Proc. 2nd IEEE Symp. on Logic in Computer Science*, pages 245–256, 1987.

[Thomas, 1989] W. Thomas. Automata on infinite objects. In J. van Leeuwen, editor, *Handbook of Theoretical Computer Science*. North-Holland, 1989. Published 1990.

[Thomason, 1984] S. Thomason. Combinations of tense and modality. In D Gabbay and F Guenthner, editors, *Handbook of Philosophical Logic. Vol. II*, pages 135–165. Reidel, 1984.

[van Benthem, 1983] J. van Benthem. *Modal Logic and Classical Logic.* Bibliopolis, 1983.

[van Benthem, 1984] J. van Benthem. Correspondence theory. In D. Gabbay and F. Guenthner, editors, *Handbook of Philosophical Logic. Vol. II.* Reidel, 1984.

[van Benthem, 1989] J. van Benthem. Modal logic as a theory of information. Report LP-89-05, Institute for Language, Logic and Information, University of Amsterdam, 1989.

[van Benthem, 1990] J. van Benthem. Temporal logic, 1990. Draft chapter for *Handbook of Logic in Artificial Intelligence and Logic Programming*, D. Gabbay, C. Hogger and J. Robinson, editors, Oxford University Press. To appear.

[Vardi and Wolper, 1986] M. Vardi and P. Wolper. Automata-theoretic techniques for modal logic of programs. *J. Comput. System Sci.*, 32:183–221, 1986.

[Winskel, 1985] G. Winskel. A complete proof system for SCCS with modal assertions. volume 206 of *Lecture Notes in Computer Science*, pages 392–410. Springer Verlag, 1985.

[Winskel, 1989] G. Winskel. Model checking the modal nu-calculus. volume 372 of *Lecture Notes in Computer Science*. Springer Verlag, 1989.

[Wolper *et al.*, 1983] P. Wolper, M. Vardi, and A. Sistla. Reasoning about infinite computation paths. In *Proc. 24th Annual Symp. on Foundations of Computer Science*, pages 185–194, 1983.

[Wolper, 1983] P. Wolper. Temporal logic can be more expressive. *Information and Control*, 56:72–99, 1983.

[Zanardo, 1991] A. Zanardo. A complete deductive-system for since-until branching-time logic. *Journal of Philosophical Logic*, 20:131–148, 1991.

Author index

Index